Iceland

Fran Parnell
Etain O'Carroll

Denmark
Strait

ÍSAFJÖRÐUR (p177)
Take in Iceland's most isolated
town among a spectacular setting
in the rugged Westfjords

Bolungarvík
Suðureyri
Ísafjörður

Drangajökull

Norðurfjörður

JÖKULSÁ-AUSTARI (p203)
Discover whitewater rafting
on glacial rivers and some
of Iceland's best horse riding

Skagafjörður

76

Húnaflói

Drangey

745

Þingeyri

Skagaströnd

Sauðárkrókur

74

Bíldudalur

Hólmavík

Blönduós

75

Patreksfjörður

711

Brjánslækur

Flatey

Breiðafjörður

Hvammstangi

Höp

SNÆFELLSNES (p158)
Marvel at the Snæfellsjökull peak and
glacier, the setting for *Journey
to the Centre of the Earth*

Stykkishólmur

Búðardalur

1

35

Hellissandur-Rif
Ólafsvík
Grundarfjörður

Snæfellsnes

GEYSIR & GULLFOSS (p120)
Don't miss Iceland's 'big two', a
regularly exploding geyser and the
majestic waterfall of Gullfoss

Eiríksjökull
(1675m)
▲

Langjökull

54

Borgarnes

Faxaflói

ÞINGVELLIR
NATIONAL
PARK

REYKJAVÍK (p65)
Enjoy manic nightlife, great
restaurants, museums and
culture in this intimate capital

Akranes

Geysir

Gullfoss

REYKJAVÍK
✪

Þingvallavatn

Keflavík
Hafnarfjörður
Kópavogur

30

Landmannalaugar

Njarðvík

1

Hveragerði

425

Selfoss

BLUE LAGOON (p111)
Bathe in the steaming blue
waters of this famous thermal pool

Grindavík

Þorlákshöfn

Hella

Selvogsgrunn

Myrdalsjökull

Eyrarbakkabugur

Hvolsvöllur

LANDMANNALAUGAR (p277)
Relax among hot springs, lavas
and colourful rhyolite hills

Eyjafjallajökull

(1450m
▲

N O R T H

A T L A N T I C

O C E A N

Heimaey
Heimaey

Skógar

Vík

VESTMANNAEYJAR

Surtsey

VESTMANNAEYJAR (p142)
Watch thousands of puffin chicks
take flight from these spectacular
islands every August

Arctic Circle

Grímsey

SIGLUFJÖRÐUR (p208)
Detour to this remote
former herring capital – still
a beautiful fishing village

HÚSAVÍK (p241)
Spot whales on a trip in a
traditional fishing boat

**JÖKULSÁRGLJÚFUR
NATIONAL PARK (p242)**
Hike in the canyon and explore
Europe's most powerful waterfall
at this national park

Raufarhöfn

Pistilfjörður

Öxarfjörður

Þórshöfn

Bakkaflói

Flatey

iglufjörður

Ólafsfjörður

Dalvík

Húsavík

JÖKULSÁRGLJÚFUR
NATIONAL
PARK

Bakkafjörður

Vopnafjörður

SEYÐISFJÖRÐUR (p263)
Go sea kayaking from
this bohemian, friendly
Eastfjords town

Akureyri

Reykjahlíð

Mývatn

MÝVATN (p227)
Embrace this stunning lake
with prolific bird life, hot springs,
lava flows and an active volcano

AKUREYRI (p210)
Soak up the 'capital of the north',
with parks, gardens, midnight
golf and a fine fjord setting

Egilsstaðir

Seyðisfjörður

Neskaupstaður

Eskifjörður

Reyðarfjörður

Fáskrúðsfjörður

Stöðvarfjörður

Breiðdalsvík

ASKJA CALDERA (p307)
Take a day trip into the interior
via this massive crater lake

ofsjökull

Djúpivogur

**KVERKFJÖLL ICE
CAVES (p309)**
Explore fire and ice at these
hot spring–filled ice caves

Kverkfjöll
(1860m)

Vatnajökull

Stafafell

Grímsvötn
(1719m)

SKAFTAFELL
NATIONAL
PARK

Höfn

Hvannadalshnúkur
(2119m)

Skaftafell

JÖKULSÁRLÓN (p291)
Photograph this classic postcard
scene: a lagoon filled with
icebergs from Vatnajökull

Kirkjubæjarklaustur

**SKAFTAFELL NATIONAL
PARK (p285)**
Get up close and personal with a
glacier, then hike through this
beautiful national park

LEGEND
Primary Road
Secondary Road
Tertiary Road
Unsealed Road

0 ——— 40 km
0 ——— 20 miles

ITINERARIES

Iceland is an island of contrast – isolated yet cutting edge, desolate yet romantic, ultra modern yet mystical. This unpopulated wilderness, shaped by sheer force of nature, is a magical epic land. If you're keen to explore, there's plenty to see and do: plunge into a geothermal pool, play with puffins, and if you're lucky catch the aurora borealis skip across the midnight sky. They may have the longest nights but Icelanders are the sunniest people on Earth.

'Watch the skies for flickering comets and pulsing curtains of light...'

Seasonal Activities

Iceland makes a fantastic adventure playground. You can try out so many different activities here, always surrounded by scenery of exceptional beauty. Although some pursuits are limited to the light, warm days of summer, don't despair if you're here out of season – there's always something fun to do.

❶ Snowmobiling
You might think that snowmobiling is only possible in winter, but Iceland's permanent icecaps Mýrdalsjökull (p140) and Vatnajökull (p294) make bouncing over the snow on a souped-up Skidoo a year-round activity.

❷ Geothermal Swimming Pools
Nothing beats lazing in hot water under a cool sky. Every two-bit town has a swimming pool, warmed by geothermal heat. Laugardalslaug (p71) is Reykjavík's finest pool, and of course there's the Blue Lagoon (p111).

❸ Caving
The lava fields around Reykjavík hide several long tunnels, full of weird-coloured minerals, stalactites and (in winter) icicles. They're impossible to find without guidance, but tours (p80) run year-round.

❹ Highland Hiking
You can do many shorter walks in any season, but the trully great wilderness treks in Iceland: Landmannalaugar–Þórsmörk (p280), Snæfell–Lónsöræfi (p259) and Hornstrandir (p194), are only do-able from July to early September.

❺ Waterworlds
From June to early September hire kayaks in Breiðafjörður (p161), Seyðisfjörður (p264), Neskaupstaður (p269) and Stokkseyri (p130); or go whitewater rafting on glacial rivers around Varmahlíð (p203) and Drumboddsstaðir (p121).

❻ Skiing & Skating
Many towns – Siglufjörður (p209), Ísafjörður (p180), Seyðisfjörður (p264) – have ski slopes. The biggest ski area, Bláfjöll (p76), is just outside Reykjavík; and you can skate on the city's lake, Tjörnin (p76).

❼ Icelandic Horse Riding
With their peaceful temperaments and smooth running gait (the famous *tölt*), floppy-fringed Icelandic horses are ideal for all levels of rider. You can go horse riding in all parts of the country (p53).

❽ Northern Lights (Aurora Borealis)
The heavenly light show of the aurora borealis can be seen in Iceland on icy-clear winter nights from September to March – watch the skies for flickering comets and pulsing curtains of light (p46).

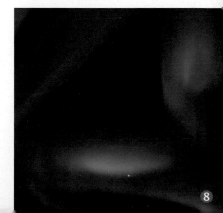

'Get abducted by singing Vikings at the kitsch Fjörukráin restaurant.'

In Search of the Vikings

The sagas conjure up vivid pictures of Viking heroes, and many of the stories' sites can be visited today. Although there's often no more to see than an abandoned farm or a grassed-over grave, these atmospheric places are drenched in history – sit down a while and let it seep into your bones.

① Viking Remains in Reykjavík
Immerse yourself in Viking history at the National Museum (p75); Reykjavík 871 +\-2 (p75), based on a recently discovered long-house; the fun Saga Museum (p75); and the Culture House (p76), which contains original saga manuscripts.

② Before & After – A 12th-Century Farm
Hekla's volcanic tantrums covered a farm at Stöng (p123) with ash in 1104. Visit the crumpled ruins, then see how it would have looked at the reconstructed Þjóðveldisbær (p124).

③ Traders, Guv, not Raiders
Right from settlement times, Gásir (p220) was one of the most important ports and market-places in Iceland. The ruins are scant, but it's a shiver-inducing spot wreathed in history.

④ Grettir's Saga
The tragic hero Grettir the Strong was slain on atmospheric Drangey (p206) in northwest Iceland; in summer you can visit this sheer-sided island, alive with sea birds and evil spirits.

⑤ Egil's Saga
The murderous, poetry-composing, vomiting Viking Egill has a great exhibition dedicated to him at Borgarnes (p155). Snorri Sturluson, author of *Egil's Saga*, lived at Reykholt (p156), where you can still see his medieval hot tub.

⑥ America Ahoy!
The first Viking to spot America was Bjarní Herjólfsson, born at tiny Eyrarbakki (p129). However, Leifur Eiríksson ended up with all the glory – visit his family's reconstructed farm at Eiríksstaðir (p168).

⑦ Hrafnkell's Saga
In east Iceland stretch your legs on a 10km walk, setting off from Hrafnkell's farm and burial mound at Aðalból (p259) and following a marked saga trail through other important story sites (p260).

⑧ Njál's Saga
This epic (p136) is set around Hvolsvöllur. Visit the remains of Njál's farm at Bergþórshvoll (p135), the turf-roofed farm at Keldur (p134), or the Markarfljót river (p135), where Skarphéðinn slid to safety over the ice.

⑨ Eat Like a Viking
Get abducted by singing Vikings at the kitsch Fjörukráin restaurant (p104); or visit Iceland in midwinter for the traditional Þorrablót feast (p58), and dine on smoked lamb, *brennivín* and boiled sheep's head.

'Geysers gush into the quiet night air, even if you are their only audience.'

Sleepless in Reykjavík

Put down that mug of cocoa! Desist with the lullabies! Why even try to sleep in a land that never goes dark? Instead, take advantage of Iceland's 'light nights' from mid-May to July, and spend 24 hours awake in the city and its surrounds.

1 See the Sights
In the morning, get top views of the city from the lofty spire of Hallgrímskirkja (p71). Make time for the capital's museums (p75) and galleries (p76). Or watch whales roll slowly out of the waves (p75).

2 Café Culture
Every one of Reykjavík's eccentric little cafés is a perfect place to watch Icelandic life go by (p89). Spend the afternoon filling yourself with coffee for your 24-hour marathon.

3 Evening Entertainment
Goggle at past eruptions at the cinematic Volcano Show (p75), pick up the latest gossip in the geothermal swimming pool (p71), or join the city's spooks on an entertaining Ghost Walk (p80).

4 Runtur Pub Crawl
At the weekend you'll be wakeful in good company. From midnight until 5am, cool young Icelanders swirl round Reykjavík's tiny, vibrant bars and clubs, drinking, dancing, laughing and gossiping, only slowing down for hot dogs (p93).

5 Midnight at the Golden Circle
If a night of drinking's not your thing, plan a late-night hire-car excursion instead. Þingvellir's fissures yawn, the waterfall Gullfoss thunders, and geysers gush up into the quiet night air, even if you are their only audience (p115).

6 Menningarnott (Culture Night)
Driven near insane by months of light, the city explodes with giddy excitement during its biggest festival in mid-August. There's fashion, art and music on every street corner, and a tremendous fireworks display rounds the night off p81).

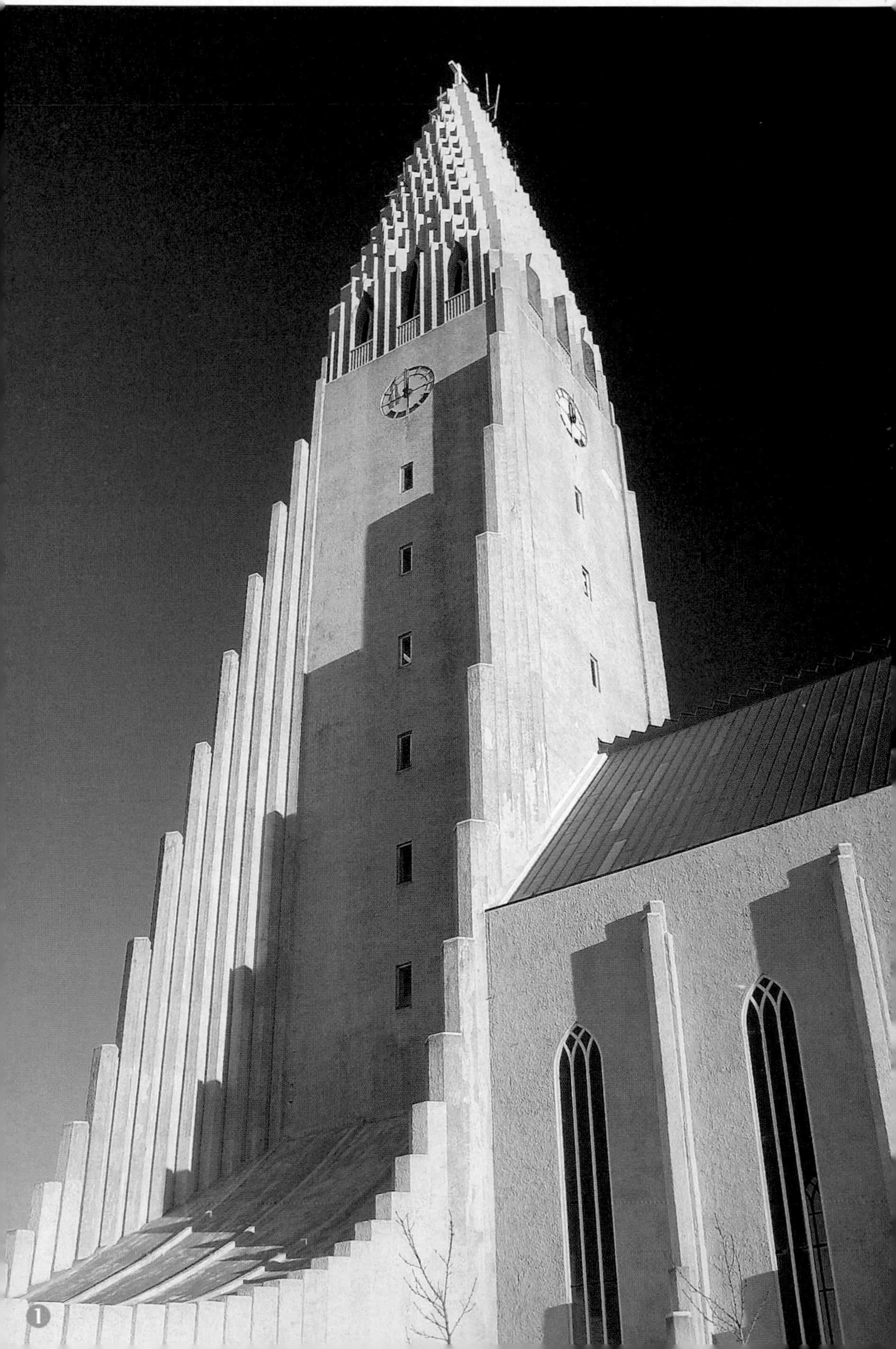

Contents

Regional Map Contents

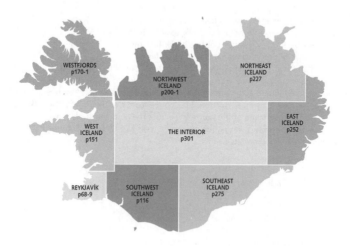

The Authors

FRAN PARNELL

Coordinating Author, Highlights, Destination Iceland, Snapshot, The Culture, Food & Drink, Reykjavík, Southwest Iceland, East Iceland, Southeast Iceland, The Interior

Fran's passion for Scandinavia began while studying for a masters degree in Anglo-Saxon, Norse and Celtic. Initial brushes with Old Norse left her swearing at the grammar book, but a strange slide show featuring sublime Icelandic mountains and a matter-of-fact man who'd literally dug his own grave awakened a fascination with Iceland that has just kept on growing. Since then, Fran has returned to the country as often as her finances have allowed and, when not in Iceland, can read, think and dream of little else. Fran has also worked on Lonely Planet's guides to Scandinavian Europe, Sweden and Reykjavík.

My Favourite Trip

Iceland is so gobsmacking that it's a difficult choice; however, for sheer diversity the stretch of coast between Skógar and Skaftafell is an easy but awe-inspiring drive. First I'd visit **Skógafoss** (p138), a dizzying column of water that topples into a mist of rainbows, before wandering around the fantastic **Skógar Folk Museum** (p138), crossing my fingers that I shan't be forced to sing! Next stop is **Dyrhólaey** (p140), a beautiful coastal rock arch and nature reserve, and its neighbour **Vík** (p140). Both have thousands of puffins, evil skuas, pebbly black beaches and spectacular views of the Vestmannaeyjar. If I had time I'd

probably head inland and stay overnight at the secluded camp site at **Þakgil** (p142), hidden among mountains that change appearance with every passing cloud. I'd spend the day walking in the area, before returning to the Ring Rd and civilisation at **Kirkjubæjarklaustur** (p279), a tiny green village where they sell the funniest beanbag nuns. Bolstered by coffee from the friendly **Systra kaffi** (p282), I'd turn with trepidation to the next stage of the journey – across the soul-shakingly bleak sandar (glacial sand plains). After driving through this wasteland, the green oasis of **Skaftafell National Park** (p285), flanked by glaciers, comes as a welcome relief.

LONELY PLANET AUTHORS

Why is our travel information the best in the world? It's simple: our authors are independent, dedicated travellers. They don't research using just the internet or phone, and they don't take freebies in exchange for positive coverage. They travel widely, to all the popular spots and off the beaten track. They personally visit thousands of hotels, restaurants, cafés, bars, galleries, palaces, museums and more – and they take pride in getting all the details right, and telling it how it is. For more, see the authors section on www.lonelyplanet.com.

ETAIN O'CARROLL   Getting Started, History, Environment, Activities, West Iceland, The Westfjords, Northwest Iceland, Northeast Iceland, Gateway to Greenland & the Faeroes, Directory, Transport

Etain's love affair with cold climates began after leaving college when a spur-of-the-moment decision and a stroke of incredible luck took her to Arctic Canada to work for an NGO. The three-month placement became a three-year sojourn on the tundra and resulted in an enduring fascination with the extremes of weather, terrible beauty and wonderful people of the far north. Since then, she has written about, photographed and travelled through the white outs, endless days and perpetual nights of the European and North American Arctic, both for work and for the sheer pleasure of waking up to pure blue skies and temperatures low enough to numb the mind. Etain is also the coordinating author of Lonely Planet's *Greenland & the Arctic*.

My Favourite Trip

Despite the painfully slow driving on the long, windy and potholed roads of the Westfjords, some of my favourite Icelandic territory is on these lush, sweeping green fjords that cover the coastline. Few tourists make it here, which makes it all the more rewarding. For wildlife experiences the comic antics of the puffins on the cliffs near **Látrabjarg** (p172) really can't be rivalled – bumping into each other, crash landing and huddling round to watch a fight, they're incredibly entertaining birds. Driving on between the little sleepy villages from **Patreksfjörður** (p173) to **Bíldudalur** (p174) and past the thundering falls at **Dynjandi** (p175) is really spectacular. The road snakes along the coast, over some incredible passes and through otherworldly lunar landscapes. At the end of the long drive you're rewarded with the sights, sounds and tastes of the very cosmopolitan **Ísafjörður** (p177), a real treat after days off the beaten track. If there's time, hiking in **Hornstrandir** (p194) offers some fantastic scenery, towering bird cliffs, a massive icecap and plenty of challenging trails. Alternatively, the drive up the Strandir coast to **Djúpavík** (p193) is magnificently peaceful and all but deserted by other travellers. Lined with rugged mountains and wild, craggy cliffs, it really feels like the end of the world.

Destination Iceland

Few visitors can travel around Iceland without their hearts leaping into their mouths at the sheer beauty of it all; or leave the country without a pang and a fervent vow to return. It's that sort of place.

Although it sits bashfully on the edge of the Arctic, this wonderful little island contains some of the most impressive natural wonders in Europe (it just doesn't like to boast!). Here the continent's biggest waterfalls thunder down with such force that the ground trembles under your feet, the bleak and barren highlands form Europe's largest and loneliest desert, and the awesome icecap Vatnajökull is the biggest outside the poles. Other spectacular natural phenomena include smouldering volcanoes, slow-flowing glaciers, black nightmares of lava, gushing geysers, bubbling mudpots, soothing thermal pools and, in the darkness of winter, the magical Northern Lights.

About 20 years ago a trickle of tourists came to Iceland for nature and isolation, challenging hiking, adventurous travel, and eerily remote wilderness. That's still the case today, but now Iceland is one of Europe's hottest travel destinations. As well as awe-inspiring nature, it also boasts its cute, compact capital Reykjavík, which has a buzzing cultural scene. It's particularly renowned for its high-energy nightlife and kaleidoscopic music scene – an ever-changing line-up of fresh, feisty bands.

Icelanders are a tough, independent bunch, but they're also very warm and welcoming and keen to share their island with tourists. It's relatively easy to get around by public transport (in summer at least), and it's actually a pleasure to drive around the Ring Rd. Although it's the country's major highway, you frequently have to wait for sheep to amble out of the way or herds of horses to gallop across the tarmac.

There are activities to suit all ages, many of which can be organised from Reykjavík. They include horse riding, fishing, golf, elf hunting, whitewater rafting, glacier walks, canyoning, caving and sea kayaking in calm fjords. One of the big attractions is whale watching – in summer this is probably the best place in Europe to see minkes and humpbacks, as well as dolphins and seals. The sea cliffs around the country are a paradise for bird-watchers, but even if you're not a twitcher you'll be blown away by the sight of 20,000 puffins nesting on a cliff top.

OK, so it does tend to rain a lot, the country's beauty is apparent only when the mist clears and it's one of the world's most expensive destinations. But don't let those things put you off. If you come prepared for all weather conditions, appreciate every moment in the sun and do a little forward planning to keep the costs down, you will never, ever regret your visit. Geologically, Iceland is one of the world's hot spots. As a travel destination, it could hardly get any hotter. Either way, there's nowhere else quite like it.

Getting Started

Nothing quite prepares you for a trip to Iceland. Most visitors expect wild nightlife, pristine scenery and frighteningly expensive credit-card bills; to some extent that's all true, but Iceland offers so much more than this and if you're travelling on a budget there are a few very simple ways to keep costs down. A little planning is the best way to ensure you find the remote but stunningly beautiful fjords, waterfalls and geysers, dig out the best pubs and clubs, and find the country's hidden gems – from luxurious spas to ends-of-the-earth–style wilderness camping – all on whatever budget you can afford.

Iceland is a very seasonal destination, though, and planning ahead will mean you won't spend hours driving to see a puffin colony that migrated out to sea months previously, or get stuck waiting for a bus that will never come. Although the short summer season (June to August) offers the widest choice of activities and destinations, an off-season visit can be magical and gives you the benefit of having the top tourist attractions entirely to yourself.

WHEN TO GO

Iceland has two very distinct tourist seasons. Peak season runs from June to mid-August and during this time you'll have the best weather, incredibly long days, the pick of tours and excursions, and the best choice of accommodation. You'll also experience crowds at major attractions and swarms of irritating mosquitoes.

September and May are also good times to travel, with generally good weather and far fewer tourists. Public transport will not be on a full schedule at these times, however, and, if you're hiking, snow may not clear from high passes until well into July.

For more information, see Climate Charts, p316.

Outside peak season everything slows down. From late August rural attractions can start to close, by 1 September buses revert to a severely reduced winter schedule, and by the end of the month the days are getting noticeably shorter, tours are almost nonexistent and many museums, attractions and guesthouses outside Reykjavík and Akureyri have closed. Listings throughout the book give details of opening times, though, and despite reduced facilities it's well worth considering an off-season trip to see mighty waterfalls frozen in time, experience the aurora borealis (see p46), ski, snowmobile or ice fish, or just luxuriate in a steaming hot pool surrounded by snow. And everywhere

---

DON'T LEAVE HOME WITHOUT...

- Sleeping bag – even if you're not camping, you can save a packet by opting for a bed without linen at hostels, guesthouses and some hotels. A blow-up pillow is also handy.

- Plenty of film or a large memory card for your camera – neither are cheap to buy locally.

- Swimsuit and towel – for those glorious natural hot springs, geothermal pools and hot pots (outdoor hot tubs).

- Rain gear and thermals – if you're planning to hike, cycle or hitch, don't dream of travelling without them.

- Credit card – Icelanders wouldn't know what to do without plastic.

- A good dose of patience and a sense of humour – for those days when fog and low cloud shrouds everything in your path or you're holed up in a hut while a summer blizzard rages outside.

IF YOU DON'T LIKE THE WEATHER NOW...

Although the Icelandic summer is short, the days are long and the climate is generally mild. Daytime temperatures hover around 12°C to 15°C, with lows of about 5°C overnight. May and June are the driest months, but coastal areas, particularly in the south and west, are prone to rain at any time. Thanks to the moderating effects of the Gulf Stream, winters are surprisingly mild, and it's often warmer in Reykjavík in midwinter than in New York or Zurich. Be prepared for fierce, wind-driven rain, gales and fog, though, and shrieking winds and icy blizzards in the interior. The clearest and coldest winter weather is generally around Akureyri and Mývatn in the central north. You'll find a daily weather forecast in English at www.vedur.is/english, but if you're in any doubt just refer to the old local saying: 'If you don't like the weather now, wait five minutes – it'll probably get worse.'

---

you go you'll get an especially warm welcome from the locals. Another benefit is that accommodation costs drop substantially from about mid-September to mid-May, when you'll get up to 40% off the cost of a peak-season hotel room and a 20% to 30% reduction in the rates of guesthouses. If you're planning to travel around the country in the off season you'll need your own transport, and you should check road conditions locally as rural roads and mountain passes can be closed due to snow.

COSTS

Iceland is famed for being an expensive destination, but with a little careful planning travellers can make substantial savings, and those looking to indulge a little will find that prices aren't that much higher than elsewhere in northern Europe. Iceland is an almost cashless society – Icelanders use their credit and debit cards for almost every transaction, so you don't need to make large cash withdrawals in order to get around.

HOW MUCH?

Guesthouse accommodation Ikr2000-4000

Campsite free-Ikr800

Reykjavík-Akureyri bus Ikr6600

1L petrol Ikr132

Cup of coffee Ikr280

Pint of Egil's beer Ikr600

Loaf of bread Ikr300

Whale-watching trip Ikr3700

Icelandic knitted jumper Ikr8000-10,000

Knitted hat Ikr1700

Cuddly troll Ikr1900

The cheapest accommodation option in Iceland is camping, but if you don't fancy a night under canvas you can keep costs down by choosing sleeping-bag accommodation in guesthouses. A bed in a guesthouse or farmhouse will cost roughly Ikr1800 to Ikr2500 for sleeping-bag accommodation and Ikr4000/7000 for singles/doubles with made-up beds. A hotel room will cost about Ikr14,000/18,000 for a single/double in high season, with prices dropping by up to 40% in low season. Families or groups can get cheaper deals by finding multiple-bed rooms or, in rural areas, stay in self-contained cottages or cabins. You can stay in wonderful timber cabins (sleeping up to six) with kitchen, lounge, bathroom, barbecue deck and a couple of bedrooms for under Ikr12,000 – far better than any hotel room.

Eating out in Iceland can be expensive unless you're prepared for an overdose of fast food. Inexpensive, filling but largely unhealthy meals are available at the ubiquitous grill bars in petrol stations, where you'll get a burger or fried chicken, chips and a drink for about Ikr500. Alternatively, you can fill up in a fast-food pizza joint for under Ikr1500. To eat well you'll need to cook for yourself or be prepared to pay for the privilege. Fish and lamb are the main-course staples at most Icelandic restaurants, with fish dishes costing about Ikr1800 to Ikr2500 and lamb dishes anywhere from Ikr2200 to Ikr4000. Add dessert or the odd bottle of wine and eat out over the course of your holiday, and your credit-card bill can be criminal. One helpful tip is to eat your main meal in the middle of the day, when lunch-time buffets or tourist menus can be great value.

Although car hire in Iceland is expensive (about Ikr33,000 to Ikr40,000 per week), a car offers far greater freedom to visit out-of-the-way attractions; splitting the cost between other travellers can keep costs down and begin to

---

OUR FAVOURITE FESTIVALS & EVENTS

Icelanders love to party, and whatever time of year you visit you'll find celebrations of music, culture, history or even the changing of the seasons happening around the country. The following are our top 10 favourites; for a more comprehensive list of festivals and events, see p318.

- Þorrablót (Viking Midwinter feast; nationwide) February (p318)
- Reykjavík Rite of Spring (Reykjavík) May (p81)
- Sjómannadagurinn (Sailors' Day; coastal towns) First week in June (p319)
- Akureyri Arts Festival (Akureyri) June to mid-August (p215)
- Icelandic Independence Day (nationwide) 17 June (p319)
- Midsummer (nationwide) Around 24 June (p319)
- Þjóðhátíð Vestmannaeyjar (People's Festival; Heimaey Island, Vestmannaeyjar) First weekend in August (p147)
- Verslunarmannahelgi (nationwide) First weekend in August (p319)
- Herring festival (Siglufjörður) Early August (p209)
- Airwaves Music Festival (Reykjavík) Mid-October (p81)

---

rival the cost of bus passes. It's also worth noting that air travel in Iceland is not much more expensive than bus travel. For more information, see p328.

For a true idea of how much a trip to Iceland will cost, you'll also need to factor in things such as nightlife (in Reykjavík and Akureyri at least), museum admission (usually Ik300 to Ikr800) and activities such as horse riding (Ikr2500 an hour), whale watching (Ikr3700) or a snowmobile tour (Ikr9000). Budget travellers who camp regularly, self-cater and take the bus or share a vehicle could get by on as little as Ikr2500 a day. Add in a few nights of sleeping-bag or guesthouse accommodation, the odd meal out, a few tours and a shared hire car, and you're looking at about Ikr6000 to Ikr9000 a day. Anyone looking for some comfort either in made-up beds in guesthouses or hotel accommodation, their own car, some decent restaurant meals and the option of taking guided tours or activities should budget Ikr15,000 per day and sometimes more.

Our top tips for budget travellers:

- Bring a tent or use sleeping-bag accommodation in guesthouses.
- Look for places where you can use a kitchen and cook for yourself.
- Become a member of Hostelling International before leaving home.
- Buy a bus pass if you're planning a round-Iceland trip.
- Use public swimming pools rather than touristy nature baths.
- Choose a smaller area of the country to explore and plan to do plenty of walking.
- Travel outside peak season.

ESSENTIAL VIEWING

Watch the black comedy *101 Reykjavík* before leaving home to understand Reykjavík's late-night hedonistic spirit. For a glimpse of teen angst in rural Iceland try the quirky *Nói Albínói* instead, a touching coming-of-age movie with plenty of dark humour. Or go for Academy Award nominee, *Children of Nature*, which follows the daring escape from a retirement home of an old couple intent on getting one more look at the fjords of their youth.

For more information on Icelandic films, see p42.

ESSENTIAL READING

For a gritty glimpse of the Icelandic soul, Halldór Laxness's humorous, heart-breaking, deep-minded work *Independent People* is an absolute must. Follow it up with the dark humour and turbulent times of Einar Kárason's *Devil's Island*, a look at life in Reykjavík in the 1950s and 1960s, and some puzzling crime mysteries such as *Tainted Blood* (also known as *Jar City*) by Arnaldur Indriðason, one of Iceland's most popular authors.

For more information on Icelandic literature, see p37.

For an irreverent look at the country from a traveller's point of view, try *Letters from Iceland* by WH Auden and Louis MacNeice, an amusing and unconventional travelogue written by the two poets in 1936. In contrast, Alan Boucher's *The Iceland Traveller – A Hundred Years of Adventure* is full of 18th- and 19th-century romance, history and drama. For a warts-and-all view of contemporary Icelandic travel, Tim Moore's *Frost on My Moustache* lays bare the realities of overambitious cycle trips and hot dogs for every meal.

INTERNET RESOURCES

Icelanders have embraced the internet wholeheartedly and you'll find a wealth of information online to help plan your trip. The following are some of our favourite sites:

Affordable Iceland (www.affordable.is) Tips and listings for affordable travel around the country.

BSI (www.bsi.is) Information on bus travel around Iceland from the bus companies' consortium.

Discover Iceland (www.discovericeland.is) Background information and tips on tours, transport, accommodation and dining.

East Iceland Tourist Board (www.east.is) Everything you need to know from the East Iceland Tourist Board.

Explore Iceland (www.exploreiceland.is) Travel information, features on local culture, and booking centre.

Gisting (www.accommodation.is) Comprehensive list of accommodation options in Iceland laid out on relevant street maps.

Go Iceland (www.goiceland.org) Iceland's North American Tourist Board site.

Iceland Review (www.icelandreview.com) Excellent daily news digest from Iceland with current affairs, entertainment, culture and more.

Icelandic Tourist Board (www.icetourist.is, www.visiticeland.com) The official sites of the Icelandic Tourist Board, with plenty of travel information in several languages.

Lonely Planet (www.lonelyplanet.com) Information on travel in Iceland and plenty of traveller tips on the Thorn Tree forum.

Ministry of Foreign Affairs (www.iceland.is/travel-and-leisure) Lots of useful links from the Icelandic Ministry of Foreign Affairs.

Nordic Adventure Travel (www.nat.is) Practical information and planning tips, plus the lowdown on lots of rural towns.

North Iceland Tourist Information (www.northiceland.is) The official North Iceland tourist information site.

South Iceland Tourist Information (www.south.is) All you need to know about travel in South Iceland.

Tourist Association of Northwest Iceland (www.northwest.is) The official site of the Northwest Iceland Tourist Board.

Visit Reykjavík (www.visitreykjavik.is) Top tips on the capital city.

West Iceland Tourist Information (www.west.is) Official site of the West Iceland Tourist Board.

Westfjords Tourist Information (www.westfjords.is) The official Westfjords tourist site

What's On (www.whatson.is) A comprehensive look at what's happening in the country from the Iceland Review team.

Snapshot

Plenty of hard-hitting political issues have engrossed Iceland lately. One of the biggest is the Icelandic government's recent decision to resume commercial whaling, despite bafflement and anger from the rest of the world. In mid-October 2006 the government granted 39 hunting licences and, within a week, three endangered fin whales had been killed. Several foreign governments registered formal protests, and environmentalists were calling on visitors to boycott the country – many people in the Icelandic tourist industry were already noticing a fall in bookings for 2007. Nobody could quite understand the decision. It seems like financial suicide, especially as commercial whaling is likely to generate only a fifth of the income provided by whale-watching tours. See the boxed text, p152, for more information.

The highly controversial Kárahnjúkar hydroelectric project (which will dam two glacial rivers in the Eastern Highlands, flood a 57-sq-km area of wilderness and create a huge aluminium smelter in the Eastfjords) is well on the way to completion. At first, the project seemed to create little opposition – in fact, it was welcomed in the east of the country as a boost to employment and the local economy. However, as time went on, and Icelanders realised how much of their patrimony they were about to lose, the opposition became louder. Several high-profile protestors, such as newsreader Ómar Ragnarsson and the band Sigur Rós, and a last-ditch anti-dam demonstration by over 15,000 Icelanders, failed to halt the works, and the reservoir began filling in September 2006. See p49 and the boxed text, p250, for more information.

Most of the labourers working on the dam project are from Eastern Europe and Italy. This raises other contentious issues: immigration and foreign workers taking local jobs. Many citizens of the newer EU countries didn't have full rights in Iceland until 1 May 2006; since then there's been a large jump in the immigration figures – around 14,000 foreigners moved to Iceland in 2006, mostly from Poland. Although racism is not an obvious problem in Iceland, there has been a great deal of discussion and a few negative letters in the newspapers.

Another ongoing debate focuses on whether or not Iceland should join the EU. It could be argued that Iceland's strong independent streak is enough to keep it out of the EU, but the main issue is one of fishing rights – opponents fear Iceland could lose some of its territorial waters to other member countries at a time when fish stocks are already down. Iceland spent many years during the Cod Wars fighting for its 320km exclusion zone, and it doesn't want to lose it now. Still, Icelanders support EU membership, believing that it's vital for future trade and economic stability.

But, as ever, in the bars and the coffee houses there's much more light-hearted chatter. There were plenty of packed-out screenings at the recent Reykjavík International Film Festival – the unanimous favourite was Þetta er ekkert mál (2006) a biography of one of Iceland's tragic heroes, Jón Pál Sigmarsson, who won the World's Strongest Man competition four times and died at the age of 32. Talk of films was only surpassed by tales of drunkenness, debauchery and who was and wasn't hot at Reykjavík's massive music festival, Airwaves.

FAST FACTS

Population: 304,334

Number of foreign passengers passing through Keflavík International Airport (2005): 356,152

Oldest person: Sólveig Pálsdóttir, 109 years

Icelanders who use the internet: 66% (the world's highest proportion)

Most popular girl's name: Guðrún

Most popular boy's name: Jón

Total fish catch (2005): 1,668,927 tonnes

Icelanders who are students: 30%

Icelanders who check the weather forecast daily: 70%

History

Geologically young, staunchly independent and frequently rocked by natural disaster, Iceland has a turbulent and absorbing history of Norse settlement, literary genius, bitter feuding and foreign oppression. Life in this harsh and unforgiving landscape was never going to be easy, but the challenges and hardships of everyday life cultivated a modern Icelandic spirit that's highly aware of its stormy past yet remarkably resilient, fiercely individualistic, quietly innovative and justifiably proud.

EARLY TRAVELLERS & IRISH MONKS

A veritable baby in geological terms, Iceland was created just 17 million years ago. It was only in about 330 BC, however, when the Greek explorer Pytheas discovered the island of Ultima Thule, six days' sailing north of Britain, that the Europe became aware of a landmass beyond the confines of their maps, lurking in a sea 'congealed into a viscous jelly'. Although Pytheas was almost certainly referring to Iceland, it is unlikely he actually visited the island.

History of Iceland, by Jon R Hjalmarsson, is a lively and absorbing account of the nation from settlement to the present day, looking at Iceland's people, places, history and issues.

For many years rumour, myth and fantastic tales of fierce storms, howling winds, enigmatic lands and barbaric dog-headed people kept explorers away from the great northern ocean, *oceanus innavigabilis*. It was possibly St Brendan, an Irish monk, who was the first to venture north again. In the 6th century AD St Brendan sailed for the New World in a skin boat, stopping en route in Iceland and possibly making it as far as Newfoundland. At this time Irish monks regularly sailed to the Faeroes looking for solitude and seclusion, and voyages further afield may well have brought them to Iceland.

The first written evidence of this comes from the Irish monk Dicuil, who wrote in 825 of a land where there was no daylight in winter, but on summer nights 'whatever task a man wishes to perform, even picking lice from his shirt, he can manage as well as in clear daylight'. This almost certainly describes Iceland and its midnight sun.

It's thought that the first monks settled in Iceland around the year 700, but, being uninhabited, the island existed as a hermitage and not a mission. When the Norse began to arrive in the early 9th century, the Irish *papar* (fathers) fled, wishing to avoid confrontation and maintain their contemplative life.

THE VIKINGS ARE COMING!

After the Irish monks, Iceland's first permanent settlers came from Norway. The Age of Settlement is traditionally defined as the period between 870 and 930, when political strife on the Scandinavian mainland caused many to flee. Although much Icelandic national pride is derived from notions that they're 'children of the Vikings', most North Atlantic Norse settlers were ordinary Scandinavian citizens: farmers, herders and merchants forced to flee by Nordic despotism. They settled right across western Europe, marrying Britons, Westmen (Irish) and Scots, before being forced to flee once again when the violent and barbaric raids of the Viking Age (800–1066) caused an exodus into the North Atlantic.

www.mnh.si.edu/vikings /voyage/subset/iceland /history.html – Irish and Viking Discovery of Iceland, a Smithsonian Institute–related site, covers the early settlement of Iceland.

It's likely that the Norse accidentally discovered Iceland after being blown off course en route to the Faeroes. The first arrival, the Swede Naddoddur,

AD 600–700	850–930
Irish monks voyage to uninhabited Iceland, becoming the first (temporary) settlers.	Norse settlers from Norway and Sweden arrive, call the island Snæland (Snow Land), and set up scattered farms.

landed on the east coast around 850 and named the place Snæland (Snow Land) before backtracking to his original destination.

Iceland's second visitor, Garðar Svavarsson, came in search of Naddod-dur's reported discovery. He circumnavigated the island and then settled in for the winter at Húsavík on the north coast. When he left in the spring some of his crew remained, or were left behind, thereby becoming the island's first residents.

Around 860 the Norwegian Flóki Vilgerðarson uprooted his farm and family and headed for Snæland. He navigated with ravens, which, after some trial and error, led him to his destination. This odd practice provided his nickname, Hrafna-Flóki or Ravens' Flóki.

Hrafna-Flóki sailed to Vatnsfjörður on the west coast but quickly became disenchanted with the place. Upon seeing icebergs floating in the fjord, he renamed it Ísland (Ice Land), which he perhaps considered even less flattering than Snæland, and returned to Norway. It was a number of years before he returned to Iceland, settling in the Skagafjörður district on the north coast.

Credit for the first intentional settlement, according to the *Íslendingabók* (see p27), goes to a Norwegian called Ingólfur Arnarson, who landed at Ingólf-shöfði (southeast Iceland) in 871, then continued around the coast and set up house at a place he called Reykjavík (Smoky Bay), after the steam from thermal springs there. Ingólfur was a true Viking who'd had his day in the British Isles; he and his blood brother Hjörleifur were forced to flee Norway after they encountered some social difficulties there. Hjörleifur settled near the present town of Vík but was murdered by his slaves shortly thereafter.

As for Ingólfur, the site of his homestead was determined by the custom of the day, which required well-born intending settlers to toss their high-seat pillars, a symbol of authority and part of a Norse chieftain's pagan paraphernalia, into the sea as they approached land. Tradition and prudence dictated that they build their homes at the place where the gods chose to bring the pillars ashore. At times, settlement necessitated years of searching the coastline for stray pillars, and it's likely that Ingólfur was disappointed with the barren, rocky bay he was forced to settle on.

While Ingólfur Arnarson and his descendants came to control the whole of the southwestern part of Iceland, other settlers were arriving from the Norwegian mainland. By the time Ingólfur's son Þorsteinn reached adult-hood the island was scattered with farms, and people began to feel the need for some sort of government.

Iceland's 1100 Years: The History of a Marginal Society, by Gunnar Karlsson, provides an insightful, contemporary history of Iceland from settlement to the present.

ASSEMBLING THE ALÞING

Now firmly settled, Iceland's landowners soon became chieftains, and local disputes were normally settled at regional assemblies. As trade and commerce increased it became necessary to create a more formal form of government, however, and it was decided to set up a general assembly of the nation where the country's most powerful men could meet to discuss rulings and dispense justice. Such a structure had never proved itself before, but Icelanders reasoned that it could only be better than the fearful and oppressive system they had experienced under the Nordic monarchy.

In the early 10th century Þorsteinn Ingólfsson held Iceland's first large-scale district assembly near Reykjavík, and in the 920s the self-styled lawyer Úlfljótur was sent to Norway to prepare a code of law for Iceland.

www.viking.no is an educational site of the Viking Network Web covering the history and lifestyle of the Vikings.

871	930
Norwegian Viking Ingólfur Arnarson sails to the west coast and establishes the first major settlement at Reykjavík.	Icelandic parliament, the Alþing (National Assembly), is founded at Þingvellir.

THE VIKINGS

Scandinavia's greatest impact on world history probably occurred during the Viking Age, when the prospect of prosperity through trade, political stresses and an increasing population density inspired many Norwegians to seek out greener pastures abroad. The word Viking is derived from *vik*, which means bay or cove in old Norse and probably referred to Viking anchorages during raids.

It's suspected that the main catalyst for the Viking movement was overpopulation in western Norway, where polygamy led to an excess of male heirs and too little land to go around. In the 8th century Nordic shipbuilders developed a relatively fast and manoeuvrable sailing vessel sturdy enough for ocean crossings. While Norwegian farmers had peacefully settled in Orkney and the Shetlands as early as the 780s, it's generally accepted that the Viking Age didn't begin until 793, with the Northmen plundering St Cuthbert's monastery on the island of Lindisfarne off Britain's Northumberland coast.

The Vikings apparently had no reservations about sacking religious communities and, indeed, many Vikings believed that the Christian monasteries they encountered were a threat to their pantheistic traditions. But the Vikings also realised that monasteries were places of wealth, where a relatively quick and easy victory could result in a handsome booty. They destroyed Christian communities and slaughtered the monks of Britain and Ireland, who could only wonder what sin they had committed to invite the heathen hordes. Despite this apparent predilection for warfare, their considerable barbarism was probably no greater than the standard of the day – it was the success and extent of the raids that led to their fearsome reputation. The Vikings had no fear of death – only dishonour.

In the following years the Viking raiders returned with great fleets, terrorising, murdering, enslaving, assimilating or displacing the local population, and capturing many coastal and inland regions of Britain, Ireland, France and Russia. The Vikings travelled as far as Moorish Spain (Seville was raided in 844) and the Middle East (they even reached Baghdad). Constantinople was attacked six times but never yielded, and ultimately Vikings served as mercenaries with the forces of the Holy Roman Empire.

Between the 10th and 14th centuries the Scandinavian Norsemen also explored and settled land throughout the North Atlantic – including the Faroe Islands, Iceland, Greenland and parts of North America.

A major stepping stone across the North Atlantic was Iceland, which, unlike Greenland, remained uninhabited. Icelandic tradition officially credits the Norse settlement of Iceland to a single mainland phenomenon. From the mid- to late 9th century the tyrannical Harald Haarfager (Harald Finehair, or Fairhair), the king of Vestfold district of southeastern Norway, was taken with expansionist aspirations. In 890 he won a significant naval victory at Hafrsfjord (Stavanger), and the deposed chieftains and landowners chose to flee rather than submit. Many wound up in Iceland and the Faeroes.

While Viking raids continued in Europe, Eiríkur Rauðe (Erik the Red), having been exiled from Iceland, headed west with around 500 others to found the first permanent European colony in Greenland in 987. Eiríkur's son, Leif the Lucky, went on to visit Helluland (literally 'land of flat stones', probably Baffin Island), Markland (literally 'land of woods', most likely Newfoundland or Labrador) and Vinland (literally 'land of wine', probably somewhere between Newfoundland and New Jersey). He had set foot in the New World as early as the year 1000 – but permanent European settlement was thwarted by the *skrælings* (Native Americans), who were anything but welcoming.

The last Viking raids occurred in the 11th century, after King Harald Harðráðl died in battle in England. Almost 300 years of terrorising the seas were coming to an end.

1000	1100–1200
Iceland officially converts to Christianity under pressure from the Norwegian king, though pagan beliefs and rituals remain.	The great literary age of the sagas.

At the same time Grímur Geitskör was commissioned to find a suitable location for an Alþing (National Assembly). Bláskógar, near the eastern boundary of Ingólfur's estate, with its beautiful lake and wooded plain, seemed ideal. Along one side of the plain was a long cliff with an elevated base (the Mid-Atlantic Rift) from where speakers and representatives could preside over people gathered below.

In 930 Bláskógar was renamed Þingvellir (Assembly Plains). Þorsteinn Ingólfsson was given the honorary title *allsherjargoði* (supreme chieftain) and Úlfljótur was designated the first *lögsögumaður* (law-speaker), who was required to memorise and annually recite the entire law of the land. It was he, along with the 48 *goðar* (chieftains), who held the actual legislative power.

A remarkably peaceful system of government evolved and, although squabbles arose over the choice of leaders and allegiances were continually questioned, the new parliamentary system was deemed a success. At the annual convention of the year 1000, the assembled crowd was bitterly divided between pagans and Christians, but eventually a decree was agreed and Iceland accepted the new religion and converted to Christianity. This decision gave the formerly divided groups a semblance of national unity, and soon the first bishoprics were set up at Skálholt in the southwest and Hólar in the north.

Over the following years the two-week national assembly at Þingvellir became the social event of the year. All free men could attend. Single people came looking for partners, marriages were contracted and solemnised, business deals were finalised, duels and executions were held, and the Appeals Court handed down judgments on matters that couldn't be resolved in lower courts.

During its first century, the Alþing was stained by corruption as the *goðar* demanded bribes in exchange for favours. But by this time Icelandic society and the agrarian economy were well established and the government held. Schools were founded at the two bishoprics and elsewhere, and the resulting educational awareness prepared the way for the great literary era to come.

The Althing at Thingvellir, by Helmut Lugmayr, explains the role and history of the oldest parliament in the world and includes a section on Þingvellir's unique geology.

The Alþing, established in 930, is the oldest continuous parliamentary democracy in the world.

ANARCHY & THE STURLUNG AGE

The late 12th century kicked off the Saga Age, when epic tales of early settlement, family struggles, romance and tragic characters were recorded by historians and writers. Much of our knowledge of this time comes from two weighty tomes, the *Íslendingabók*, a historical narrative from the settlement era written by 12th-century scholar Ari Þorgilsson (Ari the Learned), and the detailed *Landnámabók*, a comprehensive account of the settlement.

Despite the advances in such cultural pursuits, Iceland was already beginning to suffer. By the early 13th century the enlightened period of peace that had lasted 200 years began to wane, and the ineffectual government and constant power struggles between rival chieftains led to violent feuds and a flourishing of Viking-like private armies who raided farms across the country. This dark hour in Iceland's history was known as the Sturlung Age, its tragic events and brutal history graphically recounted in the three-volume *Sturlunga Saga*.

As Iceland descended into chaos, the Norwegian king Hákon Hákonarson perched on the counbtry's boundaries pressuring chieftains, priests and the new breed of wealthy aristocrats to accept his authority and relinquish control of the ailing Alþing. The Icelanders, who saw no alternative, dissolved all

Iceland Saga, by Magnús Magnússon, offers an entertaining introduction to Icelandic history and literature, and explains numerous saga events and settings.

1200 — Iceland descends into anarchy during the so-called Sturlung Age. The government dissolves and, in 1291, Iceland is absorbed by Norway.

1300, 1341 & 1389 — The volcano Hekla violently erupts, causing death and widespread destruction.

but a superficial shell of their government and swore their allegiance to the king. An agreement of confederacy was made in 1262. In 1281 a new code of law, the Jónsbók, was introduced by the king and Iceland was absorbed into Norwegian rule.

Norway immediately set about appointing Norwegian bishops to Hólar and Skálholt and imposed excessive taxes. Contention flared as former chieftains quibbled over high offices, particularly that of *járl* (earl), an honour that fell to the ruthless scoundrel Gissur Þorvaldsson, who in 1241 murdered Snorri Sturluson, Iceland's best-known historian and writer (see the boxed text, p158).

Meanwhile, the volcano Hekla erupted three times, covering a third of the country in ash; a mini–ice age followed, and severe winters wiped out livestock and crops. The Black Death soon arrived, killing half the population, and the once indomitable spirit of the people seemed broken.

ENTER THE DANES

Iceland's fate was now in the hands of the highest Norwegian bidder, who could lease the governorship of the country on a three-year basis. In 1397 the Kalmar Union of Norway, Sweden and Denmark brought Iceland, still a province of Norway, under Danish rule. After disputes between church and state, the Danish government seized church property and imposed Lutheranism in the Reformation of 1550. When the stubborn Catholic bishop of Hólar, Jón Arason, resisted and gained a following, he and his two sons were taken to Skálholt and beheaded.

In 1602 the Danish king imposed a crippling trade monopoly whereby Swedish and Danish firms were given exclusive trading rights in Iceland for 12-year periods. This resulted in large-scale extortion, importation of spoilt or inferior goods and yet more suffering that would last another 250 years.

RETURN TO INDEPENDENCE

Fed up with five centuries of oppressive foreign rule and conscious of a growing sense of liberalisation across Europe, Icelandic nationalism began to flourish in the 19th century. By 1855 Jón Sigurðsson, an Icelandic scholar, had successfully lobbied for restoration of free trade, and by 1874 Iceland had drafted a constitution and regained control of its domestic affairs.

Iceland's first political parties were formed during this period, and the country began to change as the focus moved from rural to urban development and new technologies boosted agricultural and fishing production. By 1918 Iceland had signed the Act of Union, which effectively released the country from Danish rule, making it an independent state within the Kingdom of Denmark.

Iceland prospered during WWI as wool, meat and fish exports gained high prices. When WWII loomed, however, Iceland declared neutrality in the hope of maintaining their important trade links with both Britain and Germany.

On 9 April 1940 Denmark was occupied by Germany, prompting the Alþing to take control of Iceland's foreign affairs once more. A year later, on 17 May 1941, the Icelanders requested complete independence. The formal establishment of the Republic of Iceland finally took place at Þingvellir on 17 June 1944 – now celebrated as Independence Day.

The Complete Sagas of Icelanders, edited by Viður Hreinsson, is a must for saga fiends. It's a summary translation of 50 saga tales, featuring all the main yarns, along with a few shorter fantasy tales.

1397	1602
Iceland comes under Danish rule.	Denmark imposes a crippling trade monopoly, giving Danish and Swedish firms exclusive trading rights in Iceland.

WWII & THE USA MOVES IN

Iceland's total lack of any military force worried the Allied powers and so in May 1940 Britain, most vulnerable to a German-controlled Iceland, sent in forces to occupy the island. Iceland had little choice but to grudgingly accept the situation, but the country profited from British construction projects and spending that bolstered the economy.

When the British troops withdrew in 1941 the government allowed American troops to move in, on the understanding that they would move out at the end of the war. Although the US military left in 1946, it retained the right to reestablish a base at Keflavík should war threaten. After the war, and back under their own control, Icelanders were reluctant to submit to any foreign power. When the government was pressured into becoming a founding member of NATO in 1949, riots broke out in Reykjavík. The government only agreed to the proposition on the conditions that Iceland would never take part in offensive action and that no foreign military troops would be based in the country during peacetime.

War with Korea broke out in 1950 and at the request of NATO the Icelandic government agreed that the US could again take responsibility for the island's defence. By 1951 the US military had completely taken over Keflavík International Airport with no obvious intention of budging. It justified its actions by indicating that Iceland required US protection from the Soviet troops that had invaded North Korea, and indeed Iceland served as an important North Atlantic base for monitoring the Soviet Union during the Cold War.

When the Icelanders realised what was happening they were predictably unhappy, but they were powerless to evict the Americans, whose numbers and military technology at Keflavík continued to increase over the next four decades. The controversial US military presence in Iceland only ended in September 2006 when the base at Keflavík finally closed.

Daughter of Fire – a Portrait of Iceland, by Katherin Scherman, is a beautifully written and evocative historical overview of Iceland, covering the land, the people and the sagas.

MODERN ICELAND

Following the Cold War period and the demise of the herring fishing industry, Iceland went through a period of growth, rebuilding and modernisation. The Ring Rd was finally completed in 1974 – opening up transport across the remote southeast – and projects such as the Krafla power station in the northeast and the Svartsengi power plant near Reykjavík were developed.

In 1992–93, however, Iceland's fishing quotas were reduced by 22.5% to allow overfished stocks to regenerate. The fishing industry went into recession and by October 1992 unemployment had reached 3%, a previously unheard-of level in Iceland. The króna was also devalued by 6% to relieve pressure caused by turmoil in international currency markets.

The country slowly began a period of economic regeneration as the fishing industry stabilised. Iceland also secured restrictions on fishing in its waters as part of a 1993 European Economic Area agreement between the EU and the European Free Trade Association.

In the mid-1990s the Reykjavík stock market, Verðbrefaþing Íslands, commenced operations, and in 2003 Iceland resumed whaling as part of a 'scientific research programme', despite a global moratorium on hunts (see p152). In 2006 Iceland resumed whale exports to the Faeroes and announced its plans to recommence commercial whaling, in spite of condemnation from around the globe.

1855–74	1918
Iceland moves towards independence with the restoration of free trade and a draft constitution.	The Act of Union makes Iceland an independent state within the Kingdom of Denmark.

COD WARS

Protected by its isolation and often forgotten by mainland Europe, Iceland has managed to maintain a pretty low-key existence, avoiding international disputes and keeping good working relationships with most countries – that is, until something as precious as its fishing rights are disputed.

Fishing is Iceland's main source of livelihood and protection of its fishing rights are a top priority. Problems first arose in 1901 when Britain and Denmark reduced the extent of the country's offshore fishing rights to fewer than four miles (6.5km). Unhappy with this restriction, Iceland increased the limit to four miles offshore in 1952, and to 12 miles (19.3km) in 1958. The resulting skirmishes with British vessels eventually brought warships onto the scene and led to what became known as the first Cod War. By the late 1960s the lucrative herring industry had collapsed as a result of overfishing by both Icelanders and Norwegians, and the Icelanders were again thinking about increasing their fishing zone.

In 1971 Iceland expanded its exclusive fishing rights to 50 miles (80.5km), and then 200 miles (321.9km) in 1975. The subsequent net cutting and ramming of vessels soon escalated into clashes between Icelandic gun ships and British warships until finally a stopgap agreement was made in 1976. Since then British fishing boats have respected the 200-mile limit, and no new violence has erupted.

Interestingly, Iceland claims the tiny islet of Kolbeinsey, 100km north of the mainland in the Arctic Ocean, as part of the country. Although it's little more than a speck (about 40 sq m) it adds 9400 sq km to Iceland's territorial fishing waters, making it the most important piece of offshore rock in the North Atlantic. Kolbeinsey is being eroded at an alarming rate, however, and even conservative estimates state that the island is likely to completely disappear by 2020.

Politically, Iceland is a stable democratic republic with a tradition of coalition government. Legislative powers rest with the Alþing and a president is elected to a four-year term by majority vote. The prime minister is the country's head of government and is selected by the president.

In May 2006 Geir Haarde, leader of the Independence Party, became Prime Minister of Iceland after Halldor Asgrimsson stepped down following a poor performance by his Progressive Party in local elections. The return to office of Iceland's largest political party is likely to signal a move towards tighter fiscal policy. Iceland was dogged by record inflation rates and spiralling prices in 2006, with a slide in the value of the króna further adding to the country's economic woes. With the economy reliant on the fishing industry and highly dependent on imported goods, prices remain high and the economy vulnerable. Inflation rates were expected to reach 11% by late 2006, far above the government target of 2.5%.

> Iceland has the highest density of mobile phone use in the world – there are more mobiles in use than there are people.

Despite this, Iceland is one of Europe's most developed countries with extremely high literacy levels, consistently high standards of living, one of the highest levels of computer and mobile phone use in Europe, and an increasingly wealthy elite. State education and health-care facilities are so good that there is no demand for private facilities, crime levels are extremely low, life expectancy is high, and Icelanders consistently rate as one of the happiest nationalities on earth. For most Icelanders the most pressing questions today are the possibility of EU membership and the environmental issues surrounding new hydroelectric power plants and aluminium smelters in east Iceland (see p49).

1940–41	2006
British troops occupy Iceland; a US base is later established at Keflavík.	The controversial US base at Keflavík closes down after 45 years in service; the government also approves resumption of whaling.

The Culture

THE NATIONAL PSYCHE

Centuries of isolation and hardship, and a small, homogenous population have instilled particular character traits in Icelanders. This is a tightknit nation of only 300,000 souls, where everyone seems to know each other or to be distantly related: family ties are overridingly important.

Naturally enough for people living on a remote island in a harsh environment, Icelanders are self-reliant individualists who don't like being told what to do. The current whaling debacle is a prime example. Although most Icelanders wouldn't dream of eating whale meat, a majority are in support of hunting – a silent sticking-up of two fingers at the disapproving outside world.

Icelanders have a reputation as tough, hardy, elemental types, and it's true that rural communities are mainly involved in the fishing or farming industries. But these aren't badly educated bumpkins. Iceland has always had a rich cultural heritage and an impossibly high literacy rate, and its people have a passion for all things artistic. This is true of the whole country, but it's particularly noticeable in downtown Reykjavík. Although people adopt an attitude of cool fatalism, get them talking about something they enjoy and the pessimism falls away. Most young Icelanders play in a band, dabble in art, or write poetry or prose – they're positively bursting with creative impulses, and there's an underlying sense that it's possible to achieve anything.

However, this buoyant, confident, have-a-go attitude is, paradoxically, tinged with insecurity. Icelanders know that it's easy to be a big fish in a small pond, but how might they fare outside their cosy nation? Will the rest of the world…*think they're any good*? Icelanders who achieve international success (singer Björk, the band Sigur Rós, novelist Halldór Laxness, footballer Eiður Gudjohnsson), winning honour and prestige for their homeland, become heroes.

Many young Reykjavík-dwellers bitch that there's nothing for them in Iceland: the country's too small, they've tried everything there is to try, the

Xenophobe's Guide to the Icelanders, by Richard Sale, is a compact, humorous look at the Icelandic character and foibles – everything from customs and driving habits to obsession with material possessions.

WHAT'S IN A NAME?

Icelanders' names are constructed from a combination of their first name and their father's (or, more rarely, mother's) first name. Girls add the suffix *dóttir* (daughter) to the patronymic and boys add *son*. Therefore, Jón, the son of Einar, would be Jón Einarsson. Guðrun, the daughter of Einar, would be Guðrun Einarsdóttir.

Because Icelandic surnames only tell people what your dad's called, Icelanders don't bother with 'Mr Einarsson' or 'Mrs Einarsdóttir'. Instead they use first names, even when addressing strangers. It makes for a wonderfully democratic society when you're expected to address your president or top police commissioner as Oliver or Harold!

About 10% of Icelanders have family names (most dating back to early settlement times), but they're rarely used. In an attempt to homogenise the system, government legislation forbids anyone to take on a new family name or adopt the family name of their spouse.

There's also an official list of names that Icelanders are permitted to call their children. Any additions to this list have to be approved by the Icelandic Naming Committee before you can apply them to your child – so there are no Moon Units, Lourdeses or Apples running round here! Interestingly, there's a lingering superstition around naming newborns: the baby's name isn't usually revealed until the christening, which can take place several months after the child is born.

Until recently, foreign immigrants had to give themselves Icelandic names before they could become citizens, but the naming committee has relaxed this rather stringent requirement!

only option is to emigrate. Don't be fooled – their feet may be itchy, but their hearts are full of righteous pride for this lovely land. It's no coincidence that Icelandair wishes a heartfelt 'Welcome home!' to its passengers when the plane touches down at Keflavík.

Town layouts, the former US military base, the popularity of TV programmes such as *Desperate Housewives* and *Lost*, and the prevalence of hot dogs and Coca-Cola point to a heavy US influence, but a 2006 survey showed that 69% of Icelanders see their relationship with the rest of Scandinavia as the most important.

www.statice.is – the Statistics Iceland site has thousands of fascinating facts and figures about Iceland.

Indeed, they have much in common, although Icelanders are not as aloof as their Scandinavian counterparts in Sweden, Norway and Finland. They're curious about visitors and eager to know what outsiders think of them. 'How do you like Iceland?' is invariably an early question. While most Icelanders speak English very well, they're extremely proud of their language, and to greet them with a little carefully pronounced Icelandic will result in a look of mild surprise (bordering on shock) followed by a broad smile.

While Icelanders are generally quite reserved and stoical, an incredible transformation comes over them when they party. On a Friday or Saturday night inhibitions are let down, and conversations flow as fast as the alcohol!

LIFESTYLE

In the last century the Icelandic lifestyle has shifted from isolated family communities living on scattered farms and in coastal villages to a more urban-based society with the majority of people living in the southwestern corner around Reykjavík. Despite this more outward-looking change, family

SUPERNATURAL ICELAND: GHOSTS, TROLLS & HIDDEN PEOPLE

Once you've seen some of the lava fields, eerie natural formations and isolated farms that characterise much of the Icelandic landscape, it will come as no surprise that many Icelanders believe their country is populated by *huldufólk* (hidden people) and ghosts.

In the lava are *jarðvergar* (gnomes), *álfar* (elves), *ljósálfar* (fairies), *dvergar* (dwarves), *ljúflingar* (lovelings), *tívar* (mountain spirits), and *englar* (angels). Stories about them have been handed down through generations, and many modern Icelanders claim to have seen them…or to at least know someone who has.

As in Ireland, there are stories about projects going wrong when workers try to build roads through *huldufólk* homes: the weather turns bad, machinery breaks down, labourers fall ill – until the construction company decides to build around the fey folk's rock or hill and all goes smoothly once more. In fact, the town council at Hafnarfjörður contains three people who can mediate with elves during building projects.

As for Icelandic ghosts, they're not like the wafting shadows found elsewhere in Europe but are strangely substantial beings. Írafell-Móri (*móri* and *skotta* are used for male and female ghosts respectively) needed to eat supper every night, and one of the country's most famous spooks, Sel-Móri, got seasick when he stowed away in a boat. Even more strangely, two ghosts haunting the same area often join forces to double their trouble. And Icelandic ghosts can even age – one rather sad *skotta* claimed she was becoming so decrepit that she had to haul herself about on her knees.

Many folk stories explain away rock stacks and weird lava formations by saying that they're trolls, caught out at sunrise and turned forever to stone. But we don't know anyone who claims to have seen a troll – they're more the stuff of children's stories.

A quick word of warning – you might not be surprised to hear that many Icelanders get sick of visitors asking them whether they believe in supernatural beings. Their pride bristles at the 'Those cute Icelanders! They all believe in pixies!' attitude…and even if they don't entirely disbelieve, they're unlikely to admit it to a stranger!

SWIMMING-POOL SENSE

Icelanders are a relaxed bunch with a live-and-let-live attitude, but there is a sure-fire way of unwittingly causing offence. The one time we've seen Icelanders get visibly angry, disgusted and upset is when talking about tourists abusing their swimming pools. It's vital to conform to Icelandic etiquette by washing thoroughly without a swimsuit before hopping into the water. (It makes good hygiene sense, as Icelandic swimming pools don't contain chemical cleaners.)

---

connections are still very strong in Iceland, but young people growing up in rural Iceland are more likely to move to Reykjavík to study and work.

Icelanders work hard – the retirement age is 70 – and enjoy a very high standard of living. But keeping up with the Jónssons and Jónsdóttirs comes at a price. It's not unusual for young Icelanders out of school to borrow money to buy a house or 4WD and spend the rest of their days paying off loans and living on credit. And you'll often come across Icelanders who are supposedly on their summer holiday leading treks, running tours and generally spending their 'free time' immersed in a second job!

This addiction to grafting explains several strange features of Icelandic recreation: Icelanders work hard, and they have a fairly excessive idea of play too. The bingeing in Reykjavík on Friday and Saturday nights is relaxation gone mad. So too are the hundreds of summer houses you'll see when you're driving round the Golden Circle, and the exceptional number of swimming pools, which form the social hub of Icelandic life.

The social care system is so good here that young Icelandic women have few worries about the financial implications of raising their child alone. And since there's no stigma attached to unmarried mothers, you'll see lots of pushchairs with contented-looking young mums behind them (rather than the haggard, harried faces you see on some of their counterparts elsewhere in the world!).

Although there were apparently two carjackings last year (shock! horror!), crime is noteable for its absence. We can't think of a safer city than the country's capital.

According to a 2005 report by Transparency International, Iceland is the least corrupt country in the world (the UK was 11th and the US came 17th).

POPULATION

The population reached the nice round number of 300,000 at 7.20am on 10 January 2006. (At the time of writing, it had crept up to a less pleasing 304,334.) A whopping 38% of all Icelanders live in Reykjavík, and the number is growing steadily as more people migrate from the country to the city – around 4000 people drift into town every year.

The Icelandic birth rate has been very high over the last few years, and the population is increasing by around 2.2% annually – that's around one baby popping out every hour. And the little nippers can expect to live long in a pleasantly empty land: Iceland has one of the world's highest life expectancies – 78.9 years for men and 82.8 years for women – and the lowest population density in Europe, with only 2.9 people per sq km.

SOCIAL ETIQUETTE

Although Icelanders don't often stand on ceremony, there are a few simple rules to follow that will pave the way for a smooth trip. It's important to take your shoes off as soon as you enter a house, and if you've been lucky enough to be invited for dinner it's a good idea to bring a gift for your host – a bottle of foreign wine is usually welcomed. To make a toast you should say 'Skál!', and at the end of the meal, 'Takk fyrir mig' shows your appreciation to your host.

Icelanders discovered only fairly recently that much of their genetic make-up is Celtic, suggesting that far more of the Viking settlers had children by their slaves than originally thought. Even though they speak the nearest thing to Viking in existence, Iceland is actually the least purely Scandinavian of all the Nordic countries.

Iceland's population has tripled in the last 100 years.

MULTICULTURALISM

Immigration used to be very strictly controlled, but a shortage of Icelandic workers to do more menial work and the opening up of Europe have prompted a massive surge in immigration.

In the mid '80s only about 600 foreigners per year settled here. In 2006 around 5000 immigrants arrived to work temporarily in the country, and a further 6000 were granted Icelandic citizenship. The number of foreign workers in the country is now thought to be around 6% of the total population, with Polish people forming the largest group of immigrants, followed by Danes.

MEDIA
Newspapers & Magazines

Homer Simpson's friend and nuclear-plant colleague Carl Carlson was born in Iceland!

Iceland's main daily newspapers are published only in Icelandic. The biggest-selling, *Morgunblaðið*, is moderately right wing, but Icelanders generally don't take journalists much more seriously than they do their politicians.

For snippets of Icelandic news, the *Iceland Review* website (www.icelandreview.com) has a free daily news digest (which you can have delivered to your email inbox), and its glossy quarterly magazine has some entertaining, light articles about Icelandic people, culture, history and nature.

An excellent read for Icelandic news, views, reviews and what's hot in Reykjavík is the new *Grapevine* magazine, a fortnightly newsprint magazine distributed free in summer. The editors are not afraid to write at length about big issues in Iceland, but it's done with humour and a deft writing style. It's available at the tourist office, hotels and bars in Reykjavík.

ICELANDIC ANCESTRY & GENETIC RESEARCH

Thanks to Ári the Learned's painstaking 12th-century works, Icelanders can trace their family trees right back to the 9th century through two books – the *Landnámabók* and the *Íslendingabók*, which is all very interesting for history buffs. But add this well-documented genealogical material to Iceland's unusually homogenous population and you end up with something potentially quite sinister – a unique country-sized genetic laboratory.

Controversially, in 1998 the Icelandic government voted to allow the creation of a single database containing all Icelanders' genealogical, genetic and medical records. Even more controversially, in 2000 the government then allowed American biotech company deCODE access to it all.

The decision sparked public outrage in Iceland and arguments across the globe about its implications for human rights and medical ethics. The chief questions it raised were: should a government be able to sell off its citizens' medical records? And is it acceptable for a private corporation to use such records for profit? The company claimed that its encryption methods meant that individuals could not be identified by researchers (but read *Tainted Blood* by Arnaldur Indriðason for a cynical take on this statement).

The biotech company set to work, using the database to trace inheritable diseases and pinpoint the genes that cause them. The database was declared unconstitutional in 2004, and deCODE had to change its procedure, but it has still succeeded in isolating 15 genes linked to heart attacks, strokes and asthma. This information will be used to develop new drugs to combat the diseases. As a kind of payoff to the guinea pigs, deCODE have promised that any drugs created through its research will be free to Icelanders.

BUILDING BRIDGES – THE A-HÚS INTERCULTURAL CENTRE

What is the A-Hús Intercultural Centre?
The intercultural centre serves immigrants by giving them information about their rights and obligations, and we teach Icelanders about immigration issues, do antiracism training, and run courses on how to have a more multiculturally friendly company.

Where do immigrants come from?
It's very much talked about, how many people have come from Eastern Europe recently. When Europe opened up, Iceland used its adjustment time and a lot of the newer countries didn't get complete rights here until 1 May 2006. The incomers are mostly in blue-collar labour: construction, fisheries, maintenance and so on.

How well do foreigners settle in?
One of the issues that we're concentrating on is getting people to integrate. Blue-collar workers spend 12 hours a day in gruelling labour, and they just don't have a lot of spare time [for mixing with Icelanders]. They're dead tired. And as the foreign community gets bigger, they have their own support network – Polish people can work, live and hang out with other Polish people. Our teachers go into companies where there are lots of foreigners and teach occupation-related language classes. We're trying to break down that barrier – where Polish people are sitting at one table in the lunch room and Icelanders are at another.

Are Icelanders generally welcoming?
Well, there is naturally some racism; there's no escaping it, unfortunately. There are people that occasionally write in to the papers and say negative things. But, overall, I think things are pretty positive. A recent Gallup survey found that the majority of Icelanders were positive about having a multicultural society or said they didn't care where people came from.

Tell us about Café Cultura.
It's the face of the intercultural centre. It's a popular café with foreigners and Icelanders as well. There'll be all sorts of people here: actors, politicians, media people, theatre students – a bohemian crowd. You can hear all sorts of different languages being spoken, and there're always different things going on. Last weekend was a Russian weekend, with a Russian DJ playing Russian house music, and Russian vodkas to sample!

Thanks to Barbara Kristvinsson, A-Hús Intercultural Centre

TV & Radio

Until 1988 Iceland had only one state-run TV station – which went off air on Thursdays so that citizens could do something healthier instead. (It's said that most children born before 1988 were conceived on a Thursday...) Today, there are three stations and they broadcast on a Thursday. So, now you have a choice.

TV and radio are more for entertainment than enlightenment, although the Ríkisútvarpið (RÚV; Icelandic National Broadcasting Service) evening news is the country's second-most-watched programme. If you're near a TV on Saturday night, check out Iceland's favourite show – the unfathomable current-affairs satire *Spaugstofan*, which is watched by over half the country. Much of the programming, particularly in the evenings, comes from the USA and the UK – in English, with Icelandic subtitles.

An Icelandic TV show that you might already have seen, particularly if you have children, is the violently colourful *Latibær* (Lazy Town), starring Sportacus, Stephanie, Robbie Rotten and some shudderingly ugly puppets. It was recently nominated for the American Emmy and British Bafta awards.

RELIGION

Norse

The original religion in Iceland at the time of the Settlement was Ásatrú, which means 'faith in the Aesir (the old Norse gods)'. It was the ancient religion of most Germanic peoples and also appears as far away as India. The medieval Icelandic text, the *Galdrabók*, reveals that people were calling upon the Aesir long after Christianity was adopted across Northern Europe.

There were many gods in the pantheon, but Þór (Thor), Óðinn and Freyr were the major trinity worshipped across Scandinavia. The religion is also closely linked to a reverence for the natural world.

Óðinn, the god of war and poetry, was the highest-ranking deity, chief of the gods, and a brooding and intimidating presence. He influenced the sway of battle and handed out literary talent to those deemed worthy.

Free from warfare, in Iceland most people were devoted to Þór (and there are still plenty of Icelandic people with names such as Þórir, Þórdís and Þóra). This giant, rowdy god of the common people controlled thunder, wind, storm and natural disaster, so he was a vital deity for farmers and fishermen to have on their side. He was depicted as a burly, red-haired, red-bearded dolt, who rumbled through the heavens in a goat-drawn chariot.

Freyr and his twin sister Freyja, the children of the sea god Njörður, served as the god and goddess of fertility and sexuality. Freyr was the one who brought springtime, with its romantic implications, to both the human and the animal world and was in charge of the perpetuation of all species.

Icelanders peacefully converted to Christianity more than 1000 years ago, but the old gods are being revived by followers of the modern Ásatrú religion (see the boxed text, opposite). The modern religion evolved in the 1970s, almost simultaneously in Iceland, the US and the UK. Farmer-poet and high priest Sveinbjörn Beinteinsson managed to get the **Íslenska Ásatrúarfélagið** (www.asatru.is) recognised by the Icelandic government as early as 1973.

The two main rituals of Ásatrú are *blót* (the sacrifice) and *sumbel* (the toast). Nowadays 'sacrifices', which take place on the winter and summer solstices, on the first day of winter and summer, and at Þorrablót (see p58), are usually libations made with mead, beer or cider. The *sumbel* is a ritualised three-part toast: the first is made to the god Óðinn (it's also wise to pour a few drops for Loki, the trickster, to ward off nasty surprises); the second round is to the ancestors and honourable dead; and the third round is to whomever one wishes to honour.

Whereas membership of other religions in Iceland has remained fairly constant, Ásatrúarfélagið is growing quickly and now has around 1000 registered members and eight priests (five of whom can perform marriage ceremonies). At the time of writing, the society was building its first temple in Reykjavík, due for completion in 2008 or 2009.

Christianity

Traditionally, the date of the decree that officially converted Iceland to Christianity has been given as 1000, but research has determined that it probably occurred in 999. What is known is that the changeover of religions was a political decision. In the Icelandic Alþing (National Assembly), Christians and pagans had been polarising into two radically opposite factions, threatening to divide the country. Þorgeir, the *lögsögumaður* (law-speaker), appealed for moderation on both sides, and eventually it was agreed that Christianity would officially become the new religion, although pagans were still allowed to practise in private.

Today, as in mainland Scandinavia, most Icelanders (around 84%) belong to the Protestant Lutheran Church.

Thursday is named after Thor (Thor's Day); but you knew that already, right?

RETURN OF THE GODS

Can you tell us about your religious beliefs?
The short answer is that we follow the sun. Our celebrations are in June, September, December and March, on the solstices and the equinoxes. The Norse gods are our gods…Þór, Óðinn. We are a nature-based religion, although we're not environmentalists in the modern sense. We don't kill for fun, but we don't mind killing an animal if the purpose is eating it. We're not prudes. Our main sacred place is Þingvellir…you've been there? So you have seen the beauty of it?

Do you see Ásatrú as an unbroken tradition?
Yes, we do. It did have some hard times over the last centuries, but it never completely disappeared. We lack some information about the tradition 1000 years ago, but it's not that bad. We know what it's all about, anyway.

It seems to us that although many Icelanders are outwardly Lutheran, inside they have an interest in nature and the old ways.
Yes, you're right. Our existence is accepted by the population, but the head of the church doesn't like us at all. This is fine, because every time the bishop says something negative about us, we get more members. So he is in a way, although not deliberately, something of a friend of ours!

Your membership is growing, and now we hear you're building your first temple.
It'll be in Öskjuhlíð, on the slopes of that hill. The place is not especially significant, but the temple will be. We want to have quality. We don't want it to be…what's the word? Kitsch. It will be modern but also based on old traditions. We want it to be of such quality that it will be a landmark in Reykjavík in future times.

Will it be open to the public?
It will absolutely be open to everyone. Everyone is always welcome to our gatherings.

Thanks to Óttar Ottósson, Ásatrú follower

ARTS
Literature
Bloody, black and powerful, the late 12th- and 13th-century sagas are without doubt Iceland's greatest cultural achievement. Written in terse Old Norse, these epics continue to entertain Icelanders and provide them with a rich sense of heritage.

But Icelanders are never ones to rest on their literary laurels, and today the country produces the most writers and literary translations per capita of any country in the world.

THE SAGAS
Iceland's medieval family sagas have often been called the world's first novels. They're certainly some of the most imaginative and enduring works of early literature – epic and brutal tales that suddenly flower with words of wisdom, elegy or love.

Written down during the late 12th to late 13th centuries, they generally look to earlier times – they're tales of bloodthirsty disputes, doomed romances and the larger-than-life characters who lived during the Settlement Era. Most were written anonymously, though *Egil's Saga* has been attributed to Snorri Sturluson (see the boxed text, p158).

The sagas provided not just entertainment but a strong sense of cultural heritage, as they were written, over the long desperate centuries of Norwegian and Danish subjugation, when Icelanders had very little else. On winter nights, people would gather in farmhouses for the *kvöldvaka* (evening vigil),

Betra er berfættum en bókarlausum að vera.
(It's better to be barefoot than bookless.)

a time of socialising and storytelling. While the men twisted horsehair ropes and women spun wool or knitted, a family member would read the sagas and recite *rímur* (later verse reworkings of the sagas).

And the sagas are very much alive today. Because modern Icelandic has scarcely changed since Viking times, Icelanders of all ages can (and do) read the sagas in Old Norse, the language in which they were written 800 years ago. Most people can quote chunks from them, know the farms where the characters lived and died, and flock to cinemas to see the latest film versions of these eternal tales.

One of the best known, *Egil's Saga,* revolves around the complex, devious Egill Skallagrímsson. A renowned poet and skilled lawyer, he was also the grandson of a werewolf and a murderous drunk. Other favourite works include *Grettir's Saga*, about a superhuman but doomed outlaw, Grettir the Strong; *Laxdæla Saga*, the tragic account of a family in Northwest Iceland; and *Njál's Saga* (see p136), another tragedy about two warring families, whose heroic characters make it one of the most popular sagas of all.

You can admire the original saga manuscripts in Reykjavík's Þjóðmenningarhús (p76).

EDDIC & SKALDIC POETRY

The themes of Icelandic poetry were probably dreamt up in mainland Scandinavia, but they weren't actually written down until the 12th-century Saga Age.

Eddic poems are subdivided into three classes – the Mythical, the Gnomic and the Heroic – and were composed in free variable metres with a structure very similar to that of early Germanic poetry. Mythical poetry was based on the antics of the Norse gods and was probably promoted as an intended affront to growing Christian sentiments in Norway. Gnomic poetry consists of one major work, the *Hávamál*, which extols the virtues of the common life. The Heroic Eddic poems are similar in form, subject matter and even characters to early Germanic works such as the *Nibelungenlied*.

Skaldic poetry was developed and composed by Norwegian court poets, or *skalds*, in veneration of heroic deeds by the Scandinavian kings, but other themes were introduced as the genre grew in popularity. The most renowned *skald* was Egill Skallagrímsson – he of *Egil's Saga* – who amid his other exploits ran afoul of Eirík Blood-Axe, king of Jorvík (modern-day York), in 948. After being captured and sentenced to death, on the night before his execution Egill composed an ode to Eirík. The flattered monarch released Egill unharmed, and the poem is now known as the *Höfuðlausn* (Head Ransom).

Skaldic poems are mainly praise-poems, with lots of description packed into tightly structured lines. As well as having fiercely rigid alliteration, syllable counts and stresses, they're made more complex by *kennings*, a kind of compact word-riddle. Blood, for instance, is 'wound dew'; an arm might be described as a 'hawk's perch'; and battle is often referred to as 'the Valkyries' glorious song'.

20TH-CENTURY LITERATURE

Nobel Prize–winner Halldór Laxness is Iceland's undoubted literary genius. His work is magnificent – for more details, see the boxed text, opposite.

Other authors you may come across are the early-20th-century children's writer Reverend Jón Sveinsson (nicknamed Nonni), who grew up in Akureyri. Although he mostly wrote in German, his old-fashioned tales of derring-do have a rich Icelandic flavour, and they were translated into 40 languages. *At Skipalón* is the only one readily available in English. Just after him, Jóhann

Iceland publishes the greatest number of books per capita in the world, and the literacy rate is a perfect 100%.

You might think *Icelandic Folktales*, translated by Alan Boucher, is just a collection of children's tales, but these light-hearted little gems encompass Icelandic history, humour and belief; they're the stories the country has been telling itself for hundreds of years.

HALLDÓR LAXNESS – ICELAND'S FINEST AUTHOR

It's frightening how we miss out on literary masterpieces from other countries, simply because no-one bothers to translate them. Halldór Laxness (1902–98) is Iceland's most celebrated author of the 20th century, and his genius was recognised when he won the Nobel Prize for Literature in 1955. However, his greatest work took years to appear in English, and only a portion of his 51 novels and countless short stories, articles, plays and poems are currently available in translation.

The author was born as Halldór Guðjónsson, but he took the name of his family's farm Laxnes (with an extra 's') as his *nom de plume*. Laxness, a restless, inquisitive, prolific soul, had work published from the age of 14 and began travelling at the age of 17, wandering and writing around Scandinavia. Three years later he joined a monastery in Luxembourg and converted to Catholicism, studying Latin, praying fervently and writing his first proper novel, *Undir Helgahnúk (Under the Holy Mountain)*. However, he soon became disillusioned with monastic life. After briefly returning to Iceland he went to Italy, where he wrote of his disaffection with the church and his increasingly leftist leanings in *Vefarinn Mikli frá Kasmír (The Great Weaver from Kashmir)*. Laxness then set off for America to try his luck in the fledgling Hollywood film industry. There he wrote one of his best-known works, *Salka Valka*, as a screenplay. It was during this stay in America during the Great Depression of the 1930s that he became a communist sympathiser. Quickly finding himself facing deportation from the USA, he bought a ticket to Germany.

Laxness became so absorbed with the Communist Party that he attended the 1937 purge trials in Moscow and deliberately misrepresented them in his writings (by his own later admission) lest he in any way defame the system in which he had placed all hope and trust. Most of Laxness' work during his communist days reflects everyday life in Iceland, often with thinly disguised autobiographical details. *Independent People* describes the harsh conditions under which the average Icelander lived in the early 20th century, focusing on the heartbreakingly bloody-minded farmer Bjartur of Summerhouses, one of the most perfectly drawn characters in world literature.

His other major novels include *Iceland's Bell* and *The Atom Station*. The former is a three-part work, a sagalike portrait of extreme poverty and skewed justice. Set in an Iceland subjugated by Danish rule, it revolves around the interweaving fates of destitute farmer and possible murderer Jón Hreggviðsson, and the stoical beauty Snæfríður, sister-in-law of the bishop of Skálholt. The second book, written prophetically in 1948, is a slim, droll volume about the American military presence in Iceland, nuclear proliferation and the socialist struggle for state welfare provision. His other works currently available in translation are *World Light*, *The Fish Can Sing*, *Paradise Reclaimed* and *Under the Glacier*.

All of Laxness's works are masterpieces of irony; his characters, however misguided, are drawn with sympathy; and seams of the blackest humour run through them all. Whatever you think of his works, it's impossible not to be affected by them. At the time of writing, they were very controversial – quite a few Icelanders disputed his observations, although their complaints were often motivated by national pride and reluctance to publicise Iceland's relative backwardness. However, when Laxness won the Nobel Prize for Literature in 1955, in true Icelandic style he became a hero of the people.

By 1962 Laxness had settled in Reykjavík for good (his home at Laxnes, near the suburb of Mosfellsbær, has now been turned into a museum – see p104). Apparently mellowed by his experiences with extremism at both ends of the spectrum, he wrote *A Poet's Time*, which recanted everything he'd ever written in praise of the Communist Party.

Sigurjónsson wrote *Eyvind of the Hills*, a biography of the 18th-century outlaw Fjalla-Eyvindur, which was later made into a film. Two other masters of Icelandic literature are Gunnar Gunnarsson (1889–1975) and Þórbergur Þórðarson (1888–1974), who was beaten to the Nobel Prize by Laxness. You'll have to look out for their work in second-hand bookshops.

For more up-to-date and easily available fare, try Einar Kárason's outstanding *Devil's Island*, about Reykjavík life in the 1950s; it's the first of a trilogy,

If you read nothing else, at least read Halldór Laxness's dark, funny, painful masterpiece *Independent People* – it's fantastic, and you'll marvel all the more at Iceland's progress in the last 70 years.

but unfortunately the other two haven't been translated into English. *101 Reykjavík*, by Hallgrímur Helgason, is the book on which the cult film was based. It's a dark comedy following the torpid life and fertile imagination of out-of-work Hlynur, who lives in downtown Reykjavík with his mother. Even more black, with flashes of humour, is the strange *Angels of the Universe*, by Einar Már Gudmundsson, about a schizophrenic man's spells in a psychiatric hospital.

Currently surfing a tidal wave of success is Arnaldur Indriðason, whose Reykjavík-based crime fiction regularly tops the bestsellers list. Works available in English include *Voices*, the award-winning *Silence of the Grave*, and our favourite, *Tainted Blood* (also published as *Jar City*).

Music
POP

Internationally famous Icelandic musicians include (of course) Björk. In Reykjavík, look out for the bestselling *Gling Gló*, a collection of Björk-sung jazz standards and traditional Icelandic songs that's quite difficult to find outside the country. Sigur Rós are following Björk to stardom; their last album *Takk* (2005) garnered rave reviews around the world. You may also be familiar with Emiliana Torrini, the Icelandic-Italian singer who sang the spooky *Gollum's Song* in the Lord of the Rings film *The Two Towers*.

Back home, Reykjavík's music scene continues to flourish – at times it seems the whole city acts as a dizzying music-producing machine, with everyone under 30 playing an instrument or singing in a band. (Something to do on those long, dark nights?) A swirling maelstrom of musicians play gigs, record albums, go solo and re-form, creating a constantly changing line-up of new bands and sounds.

It's hard to pin them all down. Currently popular are Leaves (called 'the new Radiohead' by NME); Trabant (who describe themselves as 'Monty Python meets Thomas Dolby'), Mugison (introspective but tuneful songs from one man and his guitar), Múm (weird electronica mixed with real instruments), Mínus (whose thrashy guitars have supported Foo Fighters and Metallica), *My Summer as a Salvation Soldier* (poignant acoustic songs from singer Þórir), Hafdís Huld (spiky female popstress critically acclaimed in the UK), Cynic Guru (perky pop encompassing lots of different styles), Benny Hemm Hemm (highly rated guitar strumming with blasts of brass), and Tilraunaeldhúsið (Kitchen Motors; experimental 'sound sculpturists' whose ages range from 20-something to 70-something).

MOOD MUSIC FOR ICELAND

Download these Icelandic tunes to get into the quirky Reykjavík spirit. If you can't find them on conventional music-download sites, go to www.musik.is and search for individual bands' websites and MySpace pages there.

■ The Sugarcubes – *'Birthday'*

■ Jakobínarína – *'His Lyrics Are Disastrous'*

■ Emiliana Torrini – *'Sunny Road'*

■ Leaves – *'Whatever'*

■ Sigur Rós – *'Sé Lest'*

■ Mammút – *'Thorkell'*

■ Hafdís Huld – *'Ice Cream Is Nice'*

■ Cynic Guru – *'Digging the Holes'*

TOP MUSIC FROM 12 TÓNAR

Best Icelandic band at Airwaves 2006?
Mammút – they were great. And Jakobínarína – very good, too.

Current bestselling CD?
Fjölskyldualbúm Tilraunaeldhússins (Kitchen Motors Family Album) – it's been our bestseller ever since it came out. It's a compilation album; they've worked with lots of artists and have done some exclusive stuff with Sigur Rós.

Best venue for seeing live bands?
At the moment? NASA (p94).

Band of the future?
Hmm…looking into my crystal ball…Rökkurró (www.myspace.com/rokkurro). They're going to be big.

Thanks to Helgi Hauksson and Einar Kristjánsson, 12 Tónar (independent music shop)

Several of these bands were brought to a wider audience by the music documentary *Screaming Masterpiece* (2005), which contains moments of toe-curling pretentiousness but is worth watching to grasp the sheer diversity of Icelandic music.

At the time of writing, Reykjavík's two oldest and best music venues had closed, to the shock and outrage of all. It wasn't quite clear which bars might take over staging bands, although Café Amsterdam (p95) was looking likely. Check the free paper *Grapevine* for current news. As computer-mad internet fiends, a lot of Icelanders spread their music via sites such as MySpace. The best music festival in Iceland is Airwaves (held in Reykjavík in October), which showcases the cream of Iceland's talent along with international acts.

TRADITIONAL MUSIC

Until rock and roll arrived in the 20th century, Iceland was a land practically devoid of musical instruments. The Vikings brought the *fiðla* and the *langspil* with them from Scandinavia – both a kind of two-stringed box that rested on the player's knee and was played with a bow. They were never solo instruments but merely served to accompany singers, as did the few church organs that appeared in the 19th century.

It's not really surprising, in a country permanently on the verge of starvation, that instruments were an unheard-of luxury, and that singing was the sole music. The most famous song styles are the *rímur*, poetry or stories from the sagas performed in a low, eerie chant (Sigur Rós have dabbled with the form), and *fimmundasöngur*, sung by two people in harmony. Cut off from other influences, the Icelandic singing style barely changed from the 14th century to the 20th; it also managed to retain harmonies that were banned by the church across the rest of Europe for being the work of the devil!

Iceland also has hundreds of traditional ditties that most Icelanders learn before school age and are still singing with relish in their old age. They're dredged up whenever an occasion brings the generations together: family parties, outings, camping. The two favourites (which you'll hear exhaustively) are *Á Sprengisandi*, a cowboy song about sheep herders and outlaws in the desert interior, and a tear-jerking lullaby based on a legend about outlaw Fjalla-Eyvindur's wife, who threw her starving baby into a waterfall. Several collections of traditional Icelandic music are available from Reykjavík music shops and souvenir shops around the country.

www.musik.is – this useful website contains links to the websites and MySpace pages of most of the underground bands currently rocking Reykjavík.

CONVERSATION ABOUT AN OLD ICELANDIC INSTRUMENT

Author: I'd love to hear how a *langspil* sounds – do you know where I could listen to one?
Museum curator: No, sorry, I don't.
A: Do any folk groups use them in their music?
MC: No, I can't think of any.
A: So not many people play them these days?
MC: No, not many.
A: Why's that, then?
MC: Well...they sound awful.

Cinema

Iceland's film industry is young – regular production started only around the early 1980s – but it's developing at a cracking pace. Icelandic short films in particular have received all kinds of international awards. Full-length features are rarer, but they often contain the same quirky, dark subject matter and superb cinematography, using Iceland's powerful landscape as a backdrop.

In 1992 the film world first took notice of Iceland when *Children of Nature* was nominated for an Academy Award for Best Foreign Film. In the film, an elderly couple forced into a retirement home in Reykjavík make a break for the countryside where they belong. The film's director, Friðrik Þór Friðriksson, is something of a legend in Icelandic cinema circles, although some of his films are definitely better than others. *Cold Fever* (1994), *Angels of the Universe* (2000) and the English-language *Niceland* (2004) are three that are worth watching.

Massive acclaim at home doesn't necessarily translate into international fame. Certain films have been storming successes in Iceland, but aren't well known outside the country. These include *Íslenski Draumurinn* (The Icelandic Dream; 2000), a comic drama about a man whose life revolves around soccer, juggling current and former girlfriends, and peddling imported cigarettes; *Mávahlátur* (Seagull's Laughter; 2001), following the lives of a group of women in a 1950s fishing village; and *Þetta er ekkert mál* (2006), a biography of Jón Pál Sigmarsson.

If one film *has* put Iceland, and especially Reykjavík, on the cinematic stage, it's *101 Reykjavík* (2000), directed by Baltasar Kormákur and based on the novel by Hallgrímur Helgason. This dark comedy explores sex, drugs and the life of a loafer in downtown Reykjavík. Kormákur's most recent release, though, *A Little Trip to Heaven* (2005), has received rather mixed reviews.

Some other films that have gone some way to emulating *101 Reykjavík's* success include *Nói Albinói* (2003), directed by Dagur Kári, about a restless adolescent in a snowed-in northern fjord town, and *Kaldaljós* (*Cold Light*; 2004), a slow-moving, poignant film about life in another isolated fjord, with a stunning performance from the little boy on whom it centres. And perhaps forthcoming Icelandic films such as Árni Ólafur Ásgeirsson's *Blóðbönd* (*Thicker than Water*), Björn Björsson's *Cold Trail* and Kormákur's *Jar City* will become hits.

Iceland's immense beauty and the government's 12% discount (or bribe) for filmmakers have encouraged Hollywood directors to make movies here. Try to spot the Icelandic scenery in blockbusters such as *The Fifth Element* (1997), *Tomb Raider* (2001), *Die Another Day* (2002), *Batman Begins* (2005), *Flags of Our Fathers* (2006), and the forthcoming Robert de Niro fairy tale *Stardust*.

www.icelandicfilmcentre.is – catch up on the latest in the Iceland film industry.

Architecture

People who come to Iceland expecting to see Viking longhouses will be disappointed, as the turf-and-wood buildings haven't stood up to the ravages of time. At best you'll see grassed-over foundations. These materials, however, were used right up until the 19th century, and several later turf-roofed buildings around the country have been preserved as folk museums – there are good examples at Keldur (p134) and Skógar (p138) in southwest Iceland, and Glaumbær (p204) in north Iceland.

For information on architecture in Reykjavík, see the boxed text, p78.

Painting & Sculpture

Iceland's most successful artists have traditionally studied abroad (in Copenhagen, London, Oslo or elsewhere in Europe), before returning home to wrestle with Iceland's enigmatic soul. The result is a European-influenced style but with Icelandic landscapes and saga-related scenes as key subjects.

The first great Icelandic landscape painter was the prolific Ásgrímur Jónsson (1876–1958), who was attracted to impressionism while studying in Italy. He produced a startling number of oils and watercolours depicting Icelandic landscapes and folk tales. You can see his work at Reykjavík's National Gallery (p77).

One of Ásgrímur's students was Johannes Kjarval (1885–1972), Iceland's most enduringly popular artist, who lived in the remote east Iceland village of Borgarfjörður Eystri as a child. His first commissioned works were, rather poignantly, drawings of farms for people who were emigrating, but he's most famous for his early charcoal sketches of people from the village and for his surreal landscapes.

A Guide to Icelandic Architecture (Association of Icelandic Architects) looks at 250 Icelandic buildings and designs.

Contemporary artists to look out for include pop-art icon Erró (Guðmundur Guðmundsson), who has donated his entire collection to Reykjavík Art Museum's Hafnarhúsið (p77); mural and glass artist Sjofn Har; and Tryggvi Ólafsson (p268), whose strikingly colourful abstracts depicting Icelandic scenes hang in national galleries in Reykjavík, Sweden and Denmark.

Sculpture is very well represented in Iceland, with works dotting parks, gardens and galleries across the country, and its most famous sculptors all have museums dedicated to them in Reykjavík. Notable exponents include Einar Jónsson (1874–1954; p76), whose mystical works dwell on death and resurrection; Ásmundur Sveinsson (1893–1982; p77), whose tactile work is very wide ranging but tends to celebrate Iceland, its stories and its people; and Sigurjón Ólafsson (1908–92; p77), who specialised in busts but also dabbled in abstract forms.

Reykjavík heaves with modern-art showrooms full of love-'em-or-hate-'em installations – ask the tourist office for a full list of galleries, and see also p76.

Environment

It's difficult to remain unmoved by the amazing diversity of the Icelandic landscape. Contrary to popular opinion, it's not an island completely covered in ice, nor is it a barren lunar landscape of congealed lava flows and wind-swept tundra. Both of these habitats exist, but so too do steep-sided fjords sweeping down to the sea, lush farmland, rolling hills, glacier-carved valleys, steaming fields, bubbling mudpots and vast, desertlike wasteland. It is this rich mix of scenery and the possibility of experiencing such extremes, so close together, that attract, surprise and enthral anyone who has been lucky enough to visit the country.

THE LAND

Plonked firmly on the Mid-Atlantic Ridge, a massive 18,000km-long rift between two of the earth's major tectonic plates, Iceland is a shifting, steaming lesson in school-room geography. Suddenly you'll be racking your brains to remember long-forgotten homework on how volcanoes work, how glacial moraines are formed, and why lava and magma aren't quite the same thing. With 22 active volcanoes, 250 geothermal areas, 780 hot springs and the world's third-largest icecap (after Antarctica and Greenland), it's a vast reserve of information for scientists and a stunning playground for the rest of us.

Iceland is roughly equal in size to England, but with only 300,000 people (as opposed to England's 49 million), scattered around its coast. Beyond the sliver of habitable land along its shores, half the country is covered by the inhospitable desert and another 15% is taken up by icecaps. Add on some lava fields and a few sandar (glacial sand plains), sprinkle generously with geysers, fumaroles and hot springs, and you've pretty much covered the island.

Iceland isn't truly an arctic country, though – the northernmost point of the mainland falls short of the Arctic Circle by a few kilometres. To cross that imaginary boundary you'll need to travel to the island of Grímsey (p223), Iceland's only true piece of arctic territory.

NATURE'S FURY

Iceland's unique position on a simmering fault line brings it plenty of low-cost energy, hot water and incredible landscapes, but the highly active rift has also caused frequent natural disasters.

In the 14th century a series of violent eruptions caused widespread death and destruction among Iceland's Norse settlers, and towards the end of the 16th century severe winters and widespread crop failure meant that 9000 Icelanders starved to death. The following two centuries were not much better. Continuous eruptions from Hekla, Krafla and Öræfi characterised the 17th century, and in 1783 Lakagígar (Laki) erupted, resulting in a poisonous haze that destroyed pastures and crops. Nearly 75% of Iceland's livestock and 20% of the human population died. A series of earthquakes and another spell of severe winters followed, pushing the already suffering Icelandic population close to despair.

Natural disasters continue to occur, but better communications, advance warning and the urban population have reduced their impact considerably. In 1963 an underwater eruption created the new island of Surtsey just southwest of Vestmannaeyjar. Ten years later Heimaey experienced a terrible eruption that created a new mountain and buried most of the town, and in 1996 Grímsvötn went off and released the largest jökulhlaup (flooding caused by volcanic eruption beneath an icecap) of the 20th century. Hekla erupted in February 2000, and a series of powerful earthquakes shook the country four months later. Earthquakes and subsurface volcanic rumblings continue – stay tuned for the next 'big one'.

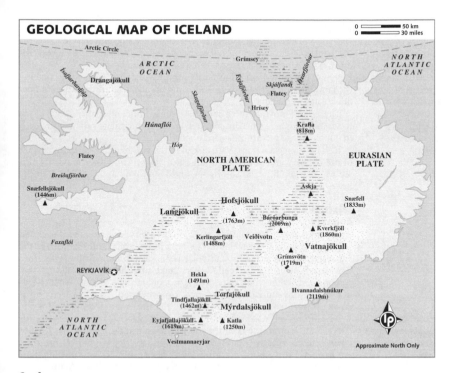

Geology

A mere baby in geological terms, Iceland is the youngest country in Europe, formed by underwater volcanic eruptions along the joint of the North American and Eurasian plates 17 to 20 million years ago. These two massive tectonic plates create a fault line across the centre of Iceland and right down the Atlantic Ocean.

The earth's crust in Iceland is only a third of its normal thickness, and magma (molten rock) continues to rise from deep within, forcing the two plates apart. The result is clearly visible at Þingvellir (p115), where the great rift Almannagjá broadens by about 1mm per year, and at Námafjall and Dalfjall (p235), where a series of steaming vents mark the ridge.

Along with the dramatic steaming vents, bubbling mudpots, weird rock formations and lava fields that draw in valuable tourist currency, Iceland's unique position on top of a highly active fault line brings other benefits. Turn on any Icelandic shower and you'll have piping hot water instantly (but try to brush your teeth and you'll have to wait several minutes for the cold water to filter through). Iceland has a surplus of superheated steam and hot water that is used to produce cheap electricity, heat buildings and swimming pools, and even keep the pavements of Reykjavík clear of snow in winter.

Iceland's use of geothermal power is one of the most creative in the world, and the country's energy experts are now advising both Chinese and Indian industries on possible ways to harness geothermal sources. Iceland is also hoping to reduce its dependency on imported fossil fuels, and it has begun to invest in hydrogen fuel research with the aim of phasing out petrol- and diesel-powered cars by midcentury.

Iceland is one of the world's most active hot spots – one-third of all the lava to surface on earth in the last 1000 years is of Icelandic origin.

Glaciers & Icecaps

Geology of Iceland: Rocks and Landscape, by Þorleifur Einarsson, is a comprehensive guide to the country's geology, discussing volcanic and geothermal activity, rock formation, and plate tectonics.

Glaciers and icecaps cover about 15% of Iceland, many of which are remnants of a cool period that began 2500 years ago. Icecaps are formed as snow piles up over millennia in an area where it's never warm enough to melt. The weight of the snow causes it to slowly compress into ice, eventually crushing the land beneath the icecap and allowing the ice around the edges to flow downward in glaciers.

These slow-moving rivers of ice have carved out and shaped much of the Icelandic landscape since its creation, creating the glacial valleys and fjords that make those picture-postcard photos today.

Iceland's largest icecap, Vatnajökull in the southeast, covers almost 13% of the country and is the third-largest in the world. Other major icecaps are Mýrdalsjökull in the southwest, and Langjökull and Hofsjökull in the interior.

WILDLIFE
Animals

Apart from sheep, cows and horses, you'll be very lucky to have any casual sightings of animals in Iceland. The only indigenous land mammal is the elusive arctic fox, and although polar bears occasionally drift across from Greenland on ice floes, armed farmers make sure they don't last long.

Your best bet for wildlife spotting is probably in east Iceland, where herds of reindeer can sometimes be spotted from the road. The deer were introduced from Norway in the 18th century and now roam the mountains.

Plants and Animals of Iceland, by Benny Génsböl and Jon Feilberg, is an illustrated guide to all of Iceland's flora and fauna, including birds, marine mammals and 220 species of plants.

Bird life, however, is prolific, at least from May to August. On coastal cliffs and islands around the country you can see a mind-boggling array of sea birds, often in massive colonies. Most impressive for their sheer numbers are gannets, guillemots, razorbills, kittiwakes, fulmars and puffins. Less numerous birds include wood sandpipers, arctic terns, skuas, Manx shearwaters, golden plovers, storm petrels and Leach's petrels. In addition, there are many species of ducks, ptarmigans, whooping swans, redwings, divers and gyrfalcons, and two species of owl. For more information on where to see the birds, turn to p51.

Another drawcard is the rich marine life, particularly whales. On whale-watching tours from Hafnarfjörður, Keflavík and Ólafsvík in western Iceland, and Húsavík in northern Iceland (among other places), you'll have an excellent chance of seeing minke, humpback, sperm, fin, sei, pilot and blue whales. Orcas (killer whales), dolphins, porpoises and seals can also be spotted. Seals

---

AURORA BOREALIS

The Inuit thought they were the souls of the dead, and their shamans called upon them to cure the sick; Scandinavian folklore described them as the final resting place for the spirits of unmarried women; and the Japanese believed that a child conceived under the dancing rays of the aurora borealis would be fortunate in life. Modern science, however, has reduced these romantic notions to a more prosaic explanation.

The magical natural phenomenon that creates the curtains of colour that streak across the northern night sky can be explained as the result of solar wind – a stream of particles from the sun that collides with oxygen and hydrogen atoms in the upper atmosphere. The collisions produce the greens and magentas of the aurora as the earth's magnetic field draws the solar wind particles towards the polar regions.

The best time to see the aurora in Iceland is between late September and early May, but everything depends on solar activity and, of course, cloud cover. For information on the best times and places to view the aurora, and tips on photographing it, visit www.northern-lights.no.

LITTLE NORTHERN BROTHERS

Cute, clumsy and endearingly comic, the puffin *(Fratercula arctica)* is one of Iceland's best-loved birds. Known for its goofy antics in the air, crash landings and frantic fluttering, this bird is also incredibly graceful underwater and was once thought to be a bird-fish hybrid.

The puffin is a member of the auk family and spends most of its year at sea. For four or five months it comes to land to breed, generally keeping the same mate and burrow from year to year. Sixty percent of the world's population of puffins breed in Iceland, and from late May to August you'll see them in huge numbers around Lundey (p240), the Vestmannaeyjar (p142) and Látrabjarg (p172).

Despite extended trips out to sea, the puffin is far from graceful in the air, flapping its wings up to 400 times per minute just to stay afloat. Neither is landing a puffin's forte – it often tumbles onto the grass, knocking over other birds in its way, or resorts to a crash landing on water. Puffins are also very curious and often gather in large numbers to watch others fighting.

In recent years there has been a decline in the number of puffins in many areas, and in 2006 baby birds were weighing in at around 200g, instead of their normal 300g. Similar problems in other countries have been blamed on overfishing: as the adult birds fly farther to find food, chicks starve before they return. Many others drown in fishing nets set in the water. With a normal life expectancy of about 20 years, a life cut short could severely affect numbers seen in Iceland in coming years.

---

can be seen in waterways around the Eastfjords, on the Vatnsnes peninsula in northwest Iceland, in the Mýrar region on the southeast coast (including at Jökulsárlón), in Breiðafjörður in the west, and in the Westfjords. For more information on whale watching, see p56.

Plants

Although ostensibly pretty barren in places, the vegetation in Iceland is surprisingly varied – you just need to get close to see it. Most vegetation is low growing, staying close to the ground and spreading as much as possible to get a better grip on the easily eroded soil. Even the trees, where there are any, are stunted. As the old joke goes, if you're lost in an Icelandic forest, just stand up.

For more information on Icelandic fauna, try www .fauna.is.

If you're visiting in summer, you'll be treated to incredible displays of wild flowers blooming right across the country. Most of Iceland's 440 flowering plants are introduced species. You'll see the bright-pink flowers of the tall arctic fireweed around riverbeds; the distinctive, graceful bell shape of the purple arctic harebell; and several varieties of colourful saxifrage and daisies lining every trail. In grassy lowlands look out for the pale and dainty northern green orchid, and in upland areas the white heads of arctic cotton, the soft yellow petals of the upright primrose and the small, pretty flowers of the mountain heath. Coastal areas are generally characterised by low grasses, bogs and marshlands, while at higher elevations hard or soft tundra covers the ground.

Another common sight when walking just about anywhere in Iceland is the profusion of fungi. There are about 1500 types of fungi growing in Iceland, and you'll see everything from pale white mushrooms to bright orange flat caps as you walk along trails, by roadsides or through fields. In southern and eastern Iceland new lava flows are first colonised by mosses, which create a velvety green cloak across the rough rocks. Older lava flows in the east and those at higher elevations are generally first colonised by lichens.

Colonies of puffins can only be seen around Iceland's coast during nesting season, from around May to mid-August. After that they take off en masse to breed out at sea.

NATIONAL PARKS & RESERVES

Although Iceland has only four national parks, they protect some of the country's most pristine wilderness and most significant historical areas. In addition to the parks, over 80 nature reserves, natural monuments, country

---

REDUCING YOUR ENVIRONMENTAL IMPACT

As Iceland becomes more accessible and more popular, the number of travellers visiting the country increases, and with each arrival comes a potential negative impact on the environment. The magnificent wilderness that attracts visitors is one of the most fragile on earth, and a footprint, tyre track or fire ring can scar the landscape for many years; the slow-growing vegetation or barren lava fields are unable to cover the damage.

To minimise your impact and help protect the fragile environment, follow these rules:

■ always keep to established paths and trails

■ camp in designated camp sites whenever possible, and carry out all rubbish

■ question tour companies about their environmental policies and impact

■ consider arriving in Iceland by ferry rather than by plane

■ use public transport

■ buy locally produced souvenirs and food

■ speak out against careless exploitation and industry in Iceland

■ if hiring a 4WD vehicle, stick to marked trails; offroad driving is illegal as it causes irreparable damage to the delicate landscape

---

parks and wildlife reserves are scattered around the country. The parks (other than Þingvellir) are managed by **Umhverfisstofnun** (Environment & Food Agency; http://english.ust.is). The website contains a comprehensive section on each national park including maps and information on hiking, flora and fauna, and nature conservation.

Þingvellir (www.thingvellir.is; see p115), Iceland's oldest national park, is as famous for its scenic 84-sq-km lake and the geologically significant Almannagjá rift as for its historical significance as the site of the original Alþing (National Assembly). The park is administered directly by the prime minister's office and is a Unesco World Heritage site.

Icelandic Geographic is a glossy annual magazine featuring the most interesting and unique aspects of the Icelandic landscape; check it out online at www.icelandic geographic.is.

Skaftafell (http://english.ust.is/Skaftafellnationalpark; p285) in southeast Iceland is a classic wilderness park with superb hiking trails and glacier views. The park was enlarged in 2004 and now covers about two-thirds of Vatnajökull, as well as a volcanic fissure, a crater area and an outwash plain.

Jökulsárgljúfur (http://english.ust.is/Jokulsargljufurnationalpark; p242) in northeast Iceland protects 120 sq km of rugged land, including a canyon carved out by a glacial river, some bizarre rock formations and the awesome Dettifoss waterfall.

Snæfellsjökull (http://english.ust.is/Snaefellsjokullnationalpark; p163) in west Iceland is the country's newest national park, established in June 2001. The park protects the Snæfellsjökull glacier and the surrounding lava fields and coast.

Many of Iceland's other spectacular natural features are protected by nature reserves, such as the hiking areas of Fjallabak, Lónsöræfi and the Kverkfjöll mountains, islands such as Hrísey, Surtsey and Flatey, and waterfalls such as Gullfoss. Mývatn is classed as a 'special conservation area'.

ENVIRONMENTAL ISSUES

Iceland's small population, pristine wilderness, lack of heavy industry and high use of geothermal and hydroelectric power give it an enviable environmental reputation. Recycling programmes are expanding, and many guesthouse and farmhouse owners are signing up to the Green Globe initiative (www.greenglobe.org), a worldwide certification programme for businesses committed to protecting the environment. However, pressing environmental concerns have forced a realisation among Icelanders that the continued existence of their pristine backyard is not an absolute birthright.

One of Iceland's most enduring environmental issues is soil erosion caused by high winds and overgrazing of sheep. Iceland was possibly deforested by overgrazing shortly after settlement, and today the sheep continue to chew vegetation down to the roots and expose the underlying soil to the forces of water and the fierce winds. In parts of the country, particularly around Mývatn lake, results are dramatic, reducing formerly vegetated land to barren wastes.

One measure used to tackle the problem was the introduction of the nootka lupine plant in 1945 to help anchor and add nitrogen to the soil. The project has been a victim of its own success, however, revegetating vast tracts of land but now also affecting Iceland's biodiversity. The lupine's bitter taste means that grazing sheep will not feed on it, so it continues to spread its relatively tall foliage, blocking light for indigenous mosses, lichens and shrubs.

A Guide to the Flowering Plants and Ferns of Iceland, by Hörður Kristinsson, is the best all-round field guide to Icelandic flowers.

Whaling is also a pressing issue in Iceland. In 2003 the country resumed whaling as part of a 'scientific research programme', despite a global moratorium on whale hunting, and in 2006 Iceland announced plans to resume commercial whaling, much to the consternation of environmentalists around the globe. For more information on the whaling debate, see the boxed text, p152.

As elsewhere around the world, global warming is a serious concern for Iceland. Warming sea temperatures could force the cod and herring stocks, so vital to the Icelandic economy, to migrate to cooler waters, and receding glaciers could affect Iceland's ability to produce energy from meltwater. Vatnajökull, Iceland's largest icecap, is already receding at a furious rate of about 1m per year. At this pace it could completely disappear in 300 years. More worrying, however, is the disruption of ocean currents, and consequently global climate systems, which could be caused by increased fresh water flowing out to sea.

The global push for cleaner, cheaper energy has also affected Iceland in other ways. Thanks to an abundance of so-called green energy and a special allowance under the Kyoto protocol, Iceland attracts multinationals in search of cheap energy, and the Icelandic government seems keen to help out. If its current plans for increased energy production to service heavy industry go ahead, then all of Iceland's glacial rivers would need to be harnessed. Environmental campaigners foresee catastrophic environmental damage, while politicians and multinational big shots peddle promises of untold economic benefits and jobs for all.

The most controversial scheme is the Kárahnjúkar hydroelectric project in the Eastfjords. The project involves construction of a network of dams, a vast reservoir, tunnels, a power station and high-tension lines to power an Alcoa aluminium smelter. It's the biggest construction project in Iceland's history and threatens to devastate the starkly beautiful landscape of the area.

Marimo balls (golf-ball-sized spheres of algae) are found naturally in only two places in the world: Lake Akan in Japan and Iceland's Mývatn lake.

Although it's claimed that the project will create about 1000 jobs, most of these are monotonous, low-paid positions unlikely to tempt young locals to stay in rural areas. So far over 80% of the workforce on the project is foreign.

As more information emerges about the project, even formerly uninterested Icelanders are beginning to protest. The Icelandic High Court has ruled that a proper environmental impact assessment was never carried out, gagging orders have been placed on critics, and concerns about the seismic instability of the area on which the dam is built have been sidelined. Additionally, many Icelanders are furious that taxpayers' money has funded the construction of the dam.

Despite claims by Alcoa that the plant will be one of the 'most environmentally friendly in the world', severe habitat destruction, dust storms, toxic fumes and pollution of the ground water are very real threats. For more information on the project, see the boxed text, p258.

TRAVEL WIDELY, TREAD LIGHTLY, GIVE SUSTAINABLY – THE LONELY PLANET FOUNDATION

The Lonely Planet Foundation proudly supports nimble nonprofit institutions working for change in the world. Each year the foundation donates 5% of Lonely Planet company profits to projects selected by staff and authors. Our partners range from Kabissa, which provides small nonprofits across Africa with access to technology, to the Foundation for Developing Cambodian Orphans, which supports girls at risk of falling victim to sex traffickers.

Our nonprofit partners are linked by a grass-roots approach to the areas of health, education or sustainable tourism. Many – such as Louis Sarno who works with BaAka (Pygmy) children in the forested areas of Central African Republic – choose to focus on women and children as one of the most effective ways to support the whole community. Louis is determined to give options to children who are discriminated against by the majority Bantu population.

Sometimes foundation assistance is as simple as restoring a local ruin like the Minaret of Jam in Afghanistan; this incredible monument now draws intrepid tourists to the area and its restoration has greatly improved options for local people.

Just as travel is often about learning to see with new eyes, so many of the groups we work with aim to change the way people see themselves and the future for their children and communities.

While the Kárahnjúkar project steals most of the current headlines, many other areas of Iceland are under threat from proposed dam projects, aluminium plants and smelters. In east Iceland, Eyjabakkar, the country's second-largest highland wetlands, is under threat from massive dams; Langisjór, at the western edge of Vatnajökull, is targeted for destruction; Kerlingarfjöll, southwest of Hofsjökull, is to be harnessed for its geothermal energy; north Iceland's Skálfandafljót, with its magnificent waterfalls Aldeyjarfoss and Goðafoss, is under threat; and the glacial rivers of Skagafjörður and Jökulsá á fjöllum are potential power sources.

Environmental experts predict that the area around Reykjavík will soon become one of the most heavily polluted in Europe.

Another aluminium plant is planned for Bakki near Húsavík, with test drilling for the site already begun near Krafla; existing smelters in southwest Iceland are to be expanded; a new smelter is planned for close to Keflavík; and permission has been given for an anode-rod plant at Katanes in Hvalfjörður.

Despite the severity and intensity of the work facing campaigners, there is some cause for hope. In south Iceland the Þjorsarver wetlands were recently given a lucky reprieve when plans for a hydroelectric scheme on the protected nature reserve were finally shelved. The wetlands are home to many nesting birds and are the world's largest breeding ground for pink-footed geese.

Some useful websites:

Iceland Nature Conservation Association (www.inca.is) Independent conservation organisation looking at environmental issues affecting Iceland.

Kárahnjúkar Hydroelectric Project (www.karahnjukar.is) Official site of Iceland's largest and most controversial energy project.

Nature Watch (www.natturuvaktin.com/english.htm) Action group fighting for the preservation of Iceland's highlands.

Saving Iceland (www.savingiceland.org) Campaign group calling for action on Iceland's most pressing environmental issues.

WWF (www.panda.org/arctic) A look at issues affecting arctic regions and what can be done about them.

Activities

Iceland's dramatic scenery, pristine wilderness and abundance of tour operators mean that it's easy to get into the great outdoors and enjoy the country at its best. Whether you're a weather-beaten adrenalin junkie looking for the next high or an armchair adventurer content with some leisurely walking and great photo opportunities, Iceland has something for you. This chapter will give you an overview of what's on offer; you'll find information on local trails, operators and activities listed in the destination chapters.

OUTDOOR ACTIVITIES
Bird-Watching
On coastal cliffs right around the country you can see huge numbers of sea birds, often in massive colonies. The best time for bird-watching is between June and mid-August, when gannets, guillemots, razorbills, kittiwakes, fulmars and puffins can be seen. Some of the best spots for bird-watching include the Látrabjarg peninsula (p172) and Grímsey (p193) in the Westfjords; Hrísey (p221), Drangey and Málmey Islands (p206) in northwest Iceland; Mývatn (p227), Lundey (p240) and the Langanes peninsula (p249) in northeast Iceland; and Breiðamerkursandur (p290) in southeast Iceland.

For more comprehensive information on the bird species in Iceland, see p46.

Caving
Caving and potholing are relatively new sports in Iceland and only a couple of operators run tours. Lava caves dating back more than 10,000 years are the most common types of cave and can be toured with minimum caving gear and experience. Organised tours are operated by **Ultima Thula** (www.ute .is), **Iceland Excursions** (www.icelandexcursions.is) and **Iceland Total** (www.icelandtotal.com). Experienced cavers in search of something more challenging should contact the **Icelandic Speleological Society** (www.speleo.is) for assistance in organising a caving expedition and advice on which caves to visit. Iceland's spectacular ice caves are extremely challenging and require professional equipment and knowledge.

Iceland's ice caves were formed by geothermal runoff water.

Cycling
Iceland is a great place for cycling independently or as part of a group. For more information on bike touring, see the boxed text, below; for general advice see p328.

Diving
Little known but incredibly rewarding, diving in Iceland is becoming increasingly popular. The clear water and great wildlife, and some spectacular lava ravines, wrecks and thermal chimneys make it a dive destination like no other.

MOUNTAIN-BIKE CLUB

To learn about cycling in Iceland from locals who 'fear only a flat planet', contact the **Icelandic Mountain Bike Club** (☎ 562 0099; www.mmedia.is/ifhk/tourist.htm; Brekkustígur 2, IS-125 Reykjavík). Between late May and early September the club organises cycling trips around the country, and visitors are welcome to join in. For up-to-date information and advice on cycling in Iceland, visit the website or try **Icebike** (www.icebike.net).

The best dive sites are conveniently placed around the Reykjanes peninsula and Þingvellir, with other less-frequented sites on the Vatnsnes peninsula and in Seyðisfjörður and Vestmannaeyjar. There are only two local operators, but between them they offer day and multiday tours as well as training. For more information, contact **Diveiceland** (☎ 421 7100; www.dive.is; Keflavík) or **Dive Iceland** (☎ 699 3000; www.diveiceland.com; Hafnarfjörður). **Iceland Excursions** (www.icelandexcursions.is) can also organise day trips. Divers need to have a recognised scuba qualification and dry suit experience or a minimum of 10 logged dives.

Dogsledding

Dogsledding, where you're pulled along behind Greenlandic huskies, is another typically arctic experience organised for tourists. A one-hour tour costs around Ikr8500. Longer expeditions can be arranged with sufficient numbers.

Try the following operators:

Activity Group (☎ 580 9900; www.activity.is)
Dog Steam Tours (☎ 487 7747; www.dogsledding.is)
Eskimos (☎ 414 1500; www.eskimos.is)

Fishing

Iceland's salmon fly-fishing is world renowned, but try it on the most popular lakes and rivers and it could be some of the most expensive fishing you ever do. One-day licences can cost up to Ikr250,000 on the Laxá river (p234), and that's before you pay for gear hire, a guide or transport. The good news is that with all the celebrity fishers in the one place, you can safely avoid them by heading for some of the country's cheaper rivers, where day licences cost a more reasonable Ikr20,000 per day (book in advance). The salmon-fishing season runs from early June to mid-September.

From April to mid-September you can also fish for rainbow trout, sea trout and arctic char on a more reasonably priced voucher system. Ice fishing is also possible in some areas in winter.

For further information, contact the **National Angling Association** (☎ 553 1510; www.angling.is).

Hiking

The opportunities for hiking in Iceland are virtually endless, from leisurely half-day walks to multiday wilderness treks. However, the unpredictable weather is always a consideration, and rain, fog and mist can turn an uplifting hike into a miserable trudge. Come prepared with good rain gear and strong boots, and if you're planning anything other than a short hike carry good maps, as many trails are unmarked. You'll also need to ford rivers on many trails (see p306), and look out for fissures, which can be hundreds of metres deep.

In the highlands the best months for walking are July and August, since late or early snow is a real possibility; in some places it never melts. May to September is a good time throughout the rest of the country, and popular trekking routes may be less crowded late or early in the season. Weather conditions can change in minutes at any time of year, so always be prepared.

For more information on hiking and mountaineering, contact the Iceland Touring Association **Ferðafélag Íslands** (☎ 568 2533; www.fi.is; Mörkin 6, IS-108 Reykjavík), or **Íslenski Alpaklúbburinn** (☎ 581 1700; www.isalp.is/english; Pósthólf 1054, 121 Reykjavík).

These are our top hikes:

■ Landmannalaugar–Þórsmörk trek (p280)
■ Fjallabak Nature Reserve (p276)
■ Skaftafell National Park (p285)

Visit www.outdoors.is for good information on hiking in Iceland.

SAFE AND RESPONSIBLE HIKING IN ICELAND

Before embarking on a walking trip, consider the following points to ensure a safe and enjoyable experience that minimises your impact on the environment:

- Obtain reliable local information about conditions along your intended route.
- Be aware of local regulations about wildlife and the environment.
- Walk only in regions, and on trails, within your realm of experience.
- Check weather forecasts before setting out, and be prepared for dramatic changes in temperature and outlook. Icelandic weather is very fickle and conditions can deteriorate quickly.
- Stick to existing trails and avoid short cuts. Hill sides and mountain slopes, especially at high altitudes, are prone to erosion; walk through, rather than around, muddy patches so as not to increase the size of the patch. Avoid removing the plant life that keeps topsoils in place.
- Do not light camp fires. Bring a stove for cooking.
- Carry out all your rubbish. This includes orange peel, cigarette butts, plastic wrappers, tampons, condoms and toilet paper.
- Never bury your rubbish: digging disturbs soil and ground cover and encourages erosion. Buried rubbish will likely be dug up by animals, who may be injured or poisoned by it. It may also take years to decompose.
- Minimise waste by taking minimal packaging, and make an effort to carry out rubbish left by others.
- Keep it clean: contamination of water sources by human faeces can lead to the transmission of all sorts of nasties. Where there is a toilet, use it. Where there is none, bury your waste in a hole 15cm (6in) deep and at least 100m (320ft) from any watercourse. Cover the waste with soil and a rock. In snow, dig down to the soil.
- Use biodegradable soaps, detergents or toothpastes and wash at least 50m (160ft) away from any watercourse. Disperse the waste water widely to allow the soil to filter it fully. Wash cooking utensils 50m (160ft) from watercourses using a scourer, sand or snow instead of detergent.
- Discourage the presence of wildlife by not leaving food scraps behind you. Place gear out of reach and tie packs to rafters or trees.
- Do not feed the wildlife as this can lead to animals becoming dependent on hand-outs, and to unbalanced populations and diseases.

- Dettifoss–Asbýrgi Canyon (p247)
- Lónsöræfi (p296)
- Snæfell–Lónsöræfi trek (p259)
- Hverfell & Dimmuborgir Trail (p232)
- Kjölurvegur trek (p302)
- Hornstrandir peninsula (p194)
- Seyðisfjörður–Vestdalur (p265)

Horse Riding

Horses are an integral part of Icelandic life and you'll see them all over the country. Riding is a popular activity and the naturally gentle breed is ideal for even inexperienced riders.

You can hire horses and take riding tours in every part of the country, often which often take you into wild and otherwise inaccessible corners of the landscape (check the destination chapters for details of operators). Expect to pay about Ikr200/10,000 per hour/day trip. Longer tours, including tent or hut

---

THE ICELANDIC HORSE

Pure bred, sturdy and short, the Icelandic horse *(Equus scandinavicus)*, is a mild-mannered breed widely used on farms and recreationally. Horses first arrived in Iceland with the early Norse settlers, and since no other horses have been imported recently, the breeding stock remains pure.

Standing about 1.3m high, the Icelandic horse is a photogenic creature but a tough breed perfectly suited to the rough Icelandic conditions. Like some Mongolian breeds, they have five gaits: *fet* (walk), *brokk* (trot), *stökk* (gallop), *skeið* (pace) and the famous *tölt* (running walk), which is so smooth and steady that the rider scarcely notices any motion.

Today the horses are mostly used during the autumn sheep roundup, but in the early days horse fights were organised as entertainment and the meat was consumed as a staple and used in pagan rituals.

---

accommodation, guides and meals, cost about Ikr14,000 per day. In September you can also volunteer for the *réttir* (sheep roundup): contact local tourist offices to make arrangements.

Horse fanatics might be interested in the **Landsmót** (National Horse Festival; www .landsmot.is/english), which takes place every two years in Skagafjörður in the north of Iceland.

Note that foreign riding clothing or equipment (saddles, bridles etc) must be disinfected upon entry into the country.

Ice Climbing

For information on ice climbing and mountaineering, visit the Icelandic Alpine Club at www.isalp.is /english.php.

Iceland offers some excellent opportunities for ice climbing, with plenty of unclimbed routes and lots of ice virtually free of other climbers. Most routes are close to main roads and can be climbed between November and mid-April. Possibly the best time to visit is in February, when the Icelandic Alpine Club holds their annual ice-climbing festival.

Some of the most popular ice climbing areas are in the west of the country. They include Múlafjall on the southern side of Hvalfjörður, and Glymsgil on Iceland's highest waterfall Glymur – these routes are best from December to February; Haukadalur on Rte 586 near Eiríksstaðir; Kaldakinn in Skjálfanda near Björg on Rte 851 northeast of Akureyri; and Öræfasveit, one of the most varied but inaccessible ice-climbing areas of the country, about an hour from Höfn. For more information, contact local mountaineering clubs (see below).

Mountaineering & Ice Trekking

Mountaineering in Iceland, by Ari Trausti Guðmundsson, has basic information on ascents of peaks as well as rock- and ice-climbing locations.

Unfortunately for rock climbers, Iceland's young and crumbly rock formations don't lend themselves well to technical rock climbing, but experienced mountaineers will find lots of scope for adventure. Anywhere on the ice, however, dangerous crevasses may lurk beneath snow bridges, and even innocent-looking snowfields may overlie rock and ice fissures, so technical expertise and equipment are essential. Crampons, ropes and ice axes are needed for any walk on glacial ice, and clothing must be able to withstand extreme conditions, especially on alpine climbs.

Unless you're proficient, experienced and well prepared, the best way to get involved in mountaineering is with a local, organised expedition. Contact the **Iceland Touring Association** (☎ 568 2533; www.fi.is) or the commercial outfit **Mountain Guides** (☎ 587 9999; www.mountainguide.is). For more information on routes and conditions, visit www.outdoors.is/mountaineering.

If you're just after a quick look at the glaciers, several operators including **Explore Adventures** (www.explore.is) run tours. For more details, see the destination chapters.

Sea Kayaking

Kayaking is gaining popularity, particularly in the calm, accessible waters of the Eastfjords and the rugged Westfjords. You can go out on guided kayaking trips in Seyðisfjörður (p263) and Neskaupstaður (p268) and in the lagoons of Stokkseyri (p130); it's also possible to rent kayaks in some places, such as Mývatn (p227). A number of Reykjavík-based adventure-tour operators include kayaking in their programmes; try www.seakayakiceland.com for more information.

Skiing

Iceland has some enjoyable, little-known slopes offering pleasant, no-frills skiing. In winter cross-country skiing is possible throughout the country, and in the highland areas it continues until early July. The main drawback is the limited winter transport and the bitter winds.

Reykjavík and Akureyri both have downhill resorts with ski rental and instructors, though Bláfjöll and Skálafell (p76), the two closest to Reykjavík, get very busy. Hlíðarfjall (p215), near Akureyri, is quieter. Expect to pay about Ikr1400 for combination day and evening lift tickets.

There are also more basic resorts at Ísafjörður (p180), Siglufjörður (p209), Ólafsfjörður (p223) and Dalvík (p222), Húsavík (p240) and Eskifjörður (p268).

In the summer of 2003, Shawna Franklin and Leon Sómme completed an unsupported circumnavigation of Iceland in sea kayaks in less than three months. In the same year Briton John Burleigh did the same trip solo in 77 days.

Snowboarding & Snowkiting

Snowboarding is slowly becoming more popular, and dedicated trails and terrain parks can be found at Bláfjöll near Reykjavík and in Akureyri. For four weeks of the year the **Nikita Iceland Park Project** (www.icelandparkproject.com) runs a snowboarding camp on the Snæfellsnes peninsula, near the Snæfellsjökull glacier.

Snowkiting (high-adrenaline snowboarding with a kite) is also taking off in Iceland, with good conditions and plans to host a snowkite cup competition on Langjökull. For more information or to organise a trip, contact **Vindsport** (snowkiter.co.uk).

Snowmobiling

Tearing around an icecap on a snowmobile can be exhilarating, but for most travellers an hour or two is more then enough. For glacier tours the best places are Mýrdalsjökull, Vatnajökull and Langjökull, and the cost is about Ikr8000 to Ikr10,000 per hour, including transport and gear.

While high-altitude glacier tours run rom April to August, during the January to May there are possibilities for snowmobiling in other parts of Iceland. Adventure-tour operators in Reykjavík and Akureyri can organise trips. The northern coastal highlands, such as Ólafsfjörður, provide excellent opportunities. See the destination chapters for details.

Swimming

Thanks to Iceland's abundance of geothermal heat, swimming is a national institution, and nearly every town has at least one *sundlaug* (public swimming pool). Most pools also offer hot pots (small outdoor heated pools), saunas and Jacuzzis. Admission is usually around Ikr280/130 per adult/child.

Icelandic swimming pools have a strict hygiene regimen, which involves a thorough shower without swimsuit *before* you enter the swimming area. Watch what Icelanders do and observe signs and instructions. There are also plenty of glorious natural hot springs; see the destination chapters for details. If swimming in natural springs, remove all jewellery before entering the water as the minerals can quickly discolour the metal.

Whale Watching

Visit www.icewhale.is for lots of info on whales, whale watching and whaling in Iceland.

Iceland is one of the best places in the world to see whales and dolphins, and tours on quiet oak-hulled boats minimise disruption so you can get astonishingly close. The most common sightings are of minke whales, but you can also spot humpback, fin, sei and blue whales. The best places for whale watching are Keflavík (p108), Ólafsvík (p164) and Húsavík (p241). A three-hour trip costs around Ikr3700, and there are sailings from mid-May to late August.

Whitewater Rafting

With glacial rivers flowing off icecaps and thundering towards the coast, whitewater rafting can be an exhilarating Icelandic experience. Some of the best rafting rivers and most established operators are in north Iceland. **Activity Tours** (☎ 453 8383; www.rafting.is) in Varmahlíð offers day trips or multiday safaris of the east and west glacial rivers, while **Arctic Rafting** (☎ 562 7000; www.arcticrafting.is) has trips on the Hvítá, Þjórsá, Markarfljót and Hólmsá rivers.

Rafting trips include guides, equipment and refreshments, and overnight trips usually include transport, accommodation (tents or huts) and food. Expect to pay Ikr6000 to Ikr10,000 for a day trip.

SPORT

Football (soccer) is a national passion for both spectators and players. Although Iceland doesn't win a lot of international games, several Icelandic players have made it on to top European or English premier-league teams. The biggest national venue is the 14,000-seat Laugardalsvöllur stadium in Reykjavík, and matches are keenly followed.

Check out www.ksi.is – the official site of the Football Association of Iceland.

The next most popular team sport is handball, a game played by two teams of seven. Internationally, Iceland has had increasing success with the game, finishing seventh in the 2003 world championships and the 2006 European championships. You can see handball matches at sports halls around the country – Reykjavík, Hafnarfjörður and Akureyri are good places.

Iceland's most traditional sport is *glíma* (Icelandic wrestling), a unique national sport with a history dating back to Viking settlement in the 9th century. Icelanders still practise the sport, but it's not common on a competitive level and you're most likely to see it as a demonstration at a traditional festival.

Food & Drink

For much of its history Iceland was a poverty-stricken hinterland where food was solely about survival. Its traditional dishes reflect a 'waste not, want not' frugality and are viewed by foreigners less as sustenance and more as body parts from a slasher movie (see p58).

Icelandic farmer-fishermen had a hard time: sparse soil and long, harsh winters meant crop-growing was limited, and those who lived by the coast wrested a dangerous living from the sea and shore. Sheep, fish and sea birds and their eggs were common foods, and every part of every creature was eaten – fresh, or preserved by drying, salting, smoking, pickling in whey or even burying underground, in the case of shark meat.

In terms of the staples little has changed over the centuries – fish, seafood, lamb, bread and simple vegetables such as potatoes form the basis of a typical Icelandic diet. However, the way in which these ingredients are prepared has changed drastically over the last 10 or 20 years. Now it's a source of national pride to serve up traditional food as tastily and imaginatively as possible, using methods borrowed from fashionable culinary traditions from around the world. You can see examples of innovative fusion food absolutely everywhere, for example reindeer ravioli at La Primavera (p87), *svartfugl* (literally 'blackbird', but in fact guillemot) marinaded in far Eastern spices at Indian Mango (p87), 'jungle satay' monkfish at Sjávarkjallarinn (p89) and puffin tapas at Tapas Barinn (p88).

There's no denying that dining out in Iceland is expensive, but it's worth spending a little extra and trying some of Reykjavík's top restaurants. If you're being determinedly frugal, you'll almost certainly be eating French fries, hot dogs, hamburgers and pizzas – cheaper eats in Iceland are heavily influenced by the USA.

Icelandic Food and Cookery, by Nanna Rögnvaldardóttir, is an excellent book full of foodie history, festivals, customs and interesting recipes.

STAPLES & SPECIALITIES
Fish & Seafood

Fish has always been the mainstay of the Icelandic diet. Fish served in restaurants or on sale in markets is always fresh, and when cooked it usually comes boiled, pan-fried, baked or grilled.

In the past, Icelanders merely kept the cheeks and tongues of *þorskur* (cod) – something of a delicacy – and exported the rest; but today you'll commonly find cod fillets on the menu, along with *ýsa* (haddock), *bleikja* (arctic char) and popular meaty-textured *skötuselur* (monkfish). Other fish include *lúða* (halibut), *steinbítur* (catfish), *sandhverfa* (turbot), *síld* (herring), *skarkoli* (plaice) and *skata* (skate). During the summer you can sometimes get *silungur* (freshwater trout) and *lax* (salmon). Wild salmon is called *villtur* and farmed salmon is *eldislax*.

Harðfiskur, a popular snack eaten with butter, is found in supermarkets and at market stalls. To make it, haddock is cleaned and dried in the open air until it has become dehydrated and brittle, then it's torn into strips.

Saltfish (wind-dried, salted fillets of cod) was so important to the Icelanders that it once appeared in the centre of the country's flag.

WHALE MEAT

Although some older Icelanders love whale meat it's not particularly popular with younger generations, which makes the recent resumption of commercial whaling even harder to understand. Many readers have written to us about their distress on discovering whale meat on menus. We've tried to indicate where this is the case by using '[Whale meat served]' in restaurant reviews.

ONE-OFF ICELANDIC WONDERS

Eyeball a plate of old-fashioned Icelandic food, and chances are it will eyeball you back. In the past nothing was wasted, and some traditional specialities remind sensitive 21st-century souls more of horror-film props than food. However, you won't be faced with these dishes on many menus – they're generally only eaten at the Þorrablót winter feast.

Þorrablót specials:

- *Svið* – singed sheep's head (complete with eyes) sawn in two, boiled and eaten fresh or pickled
- *Sviðasulta* (head cheese) – made from bits of *svið* pressed into gelatinous loaves and pickled in whey
- *Slátur* – a mishmash of sheep leftovers tied up in a sheep's stomach and cooked
- *Blóðmör* – sheep's blood and suet sewn up in a sheep's diaphragm
- *Súrsaðir hrútspungar* – rams' testicles pickled in whey and pressed into a cake
- *Hákarl* – Iceland's most famous stomach churner. *Hákarl* is Greenland shark, an animal so inedible that it has to rot away underground for six months before humans can even digest it. Most foreigners find the stench (a cross between ammonia and week-old roadkill) too much to bear, but it actually tastes better than it smells… It's the aftertaste that really hurts. A shot of *brennivín* (schnapps) is traditionally administered as an antidote.

Other Icelandic snacks are more palatable:

- *Brennivín* – sledgehammer schnapps made from potatoes and flavoured with caraway
- *Hverabrauð* – a rich, dark rye bread baked underground using geothermal heat; try it at Mývatn
- *Lundi* (puffin) – this cute little sea bird looks and tastes like calf liver
- *Skyr* – delicious concoction made of pasteurised skimmed milk and a bacteria culture similar to yogurt, sweetened with sugar and berries
- *Hangikjöt* – hung meat, usually smoked lamb, served in thin slices
- *Harðfiskur* – brittle pieces of wind-dried haddock, usually eaten with butter

---

Shrimp, oysters and mussels are caught in Icelandic waters, and *leturhumar* are a real treat. These are what the Icelanders call 'lobster', although the rest of the world know them as langoustine. Höfn, in southeast Iceland, is particularly well known for them and even has an annual lobster festival (see p295).

Meat

New Icelandic Cookbook, by Atli Vagnsson, is an impressive 144-page volume featuring traditional and modern Icelandic recipes and plenty of photographs from around the country. It's available in English, Swedish and German.

Icelandic lamb is hard to beat. During summer sheep roam free to munch on chemical-free grasses and herbs in the highlands and valleys, before being rounded up in the September *rettir* and corralled for the winter. The result of this relative life of luxury is very tender lamb with a slightly gamey flavour. You'll find lamb fillets, pan-fried lamb or smoked lamb on most restaurant menus.

Beef steaks are also excellent but are not as widely available and are consequently more expensive. Horse is still eaten in Iceland, although it's regarded as something of a delicacy – so if you see 'foal fillets' on the menu, you're not imagining things.

In eastern Iceland wild reindeer roam the highlands, and reindeer steaks are a feature of local menus.

Birds have always been part of the Icelandic diet. You'll often come across *lundi* (puffin), that sociable little sea bird, which appears smoked or broiled in liver-like lumps on many dinner plates. Another sea bird is *svartfugl*, commonly translated as blackbird on English-language menus, but what you'll actually get is guillemot *(langvía)*. High-class restaurants favouring seasonal ingredients often have succulent roasted *heiðagæs* (pink-footed goose) in autumn. Later in the year *rjúpa* (ptarmigan), a plump but tough bird related to the grouse, plays the same part in the Icelandic Christmas dinner as the turkey does in the British. The bird is officially protected, but *rjúpa* hunting is still a popular pastime.

Sweets & Desserts

Don't miss out on *skyr*, a delicious yogurtlike concoction made from pasteurised skimmed milk. Despite its rich and decadent flavour, it's actually low in fat and is often mixed with sugar, fruit flavours (such as blueberry) and cream to give it a wonderful flavour and texture. *Skyr* can be found in any supermarket (it's a great snack for kids) and as a dessert in restaurants.

'They taste great...but you have to eat a family of the little guys to feel full.'

Icelandic *pönnukökur* (pancakes) are thin, sweet and cinnamon flavoured. Icelandic *kleinur* (doughnuts) are a chewy treat, along with their offspring *ástar pungur* (love balls), deep-fried, spiced balls of dough. You'll find these desserts in bakeries, along with an amazing array of fantastic pastries and cakes – one of the few sweet legacies of the Danish occupation.

DRINKS
Nonalcoholic

Life without *kaffi* (coffee) is unthinkable. Every café and petrol station will usually have an urn full of filter coffee by the counter, and some shops offer complimentary cups to customers. A coffee costs anywhere from Ikr200 to Ikr290, but you'll normally get at least one free refill. European-style cafés where you can get espresso, latte, cappuccino, mocha and imported coffee are becoming popular in Reykjavík. Tea is available but clearly doesn't offer the caffeine fix Icelanders need.

www.vinbud.is – check here for the opening times of the government alcohol shops Vín Búð.

And they really are caffeine addicts. Besides all that coffee, Icelanders drink more Coca-Cola per capita than any other country (about 25 gallons each per year). Another very popular soft drink is the home-grown Egils Malt Extrakt, which tastes like sugar-saturated beer. At Christmas time, Malt Extrakt (or sometimes alcoholic beer) is mixed with orangeade to form *jólaöl* (Christmas brew), which has a taste generously described as Guinness seasoned with Marmite.

Bottled water is widely available, but tap water is delicious and free.

Alcoholic

Icelanders generally don't drink alcohol to savour the taste – getting trollied is the aim of the game. Particularly in Reykjavík, it's the done thing to go out at the weekend and drink till you drop (see p93). However, you might be surprised to learn that drinking during the week hasn't been culturally acceptable in the past. It's becoming more common but, if you order a midweek pint in the countryside, people may assume you have an alcohol problem! In Reykjavík many of the cafés become bars at night, staying open

---

WOULD YOU BELIEVE

...that beer was illegal in Iceland until just 18 years ago? In an attempt to circumvent the law, several Reykjavík pubs began serving nonalcoholic beer mixed with vodka, until this too was banned in 1985. The nation gathered in protest, held mock funerals and sang dirges for the swill that had become a national staple. Suddenly, in 1988 a vote was taken to legalise real beer, and on 1 March 1989 the amber fluid began to flow. Reykjavíkurs have never looked back!

until 1am from Sunday to Thursday, and until between 3am and 6am on Friday and Saturday.

You must be at least 20 years old to buy beer, wine or spirits, and alcohol is only available from licensed bars, restaurants and the government-run Vín Búð liquor stores. There are 39 shops around the country; most towns of any size have one, and Reykjavík has five. Opening hours vary but are usually from 11am to 6pm Monday to Thursday, 11am to 7pm on Friday, and 11am to 2pm on Saturday (closed Sunday), although in some places they only open for a couple of hours a day. Expect queues around 5pm on a Friday. You can pick up a bottle of imported wine for around Ikr1000 (and up), and beer is about a third of what you'll pay in a bar.

www.tekstotaal.com /cbrenvin.html – this comical page tells you how to make your own approximation of *brennivín* (Icelandic schnapps).

Petrol stations and supermarkets sell the weak and watery 2.2% brew known as Pilsner, but most Icelanders would sooner not drink it at all.

There are three brands of Icelandic beer: Egil's, Thule and Viking, all fairly standard lager or Pils brews; you can also get imported beers such as Carlsberg and (in Irish bars) Guinness. A pint of beer in a pub costs about Ikr700; a glass of house wine or a shot of spirits in a restaurant costs Ikr600 to Ikr800.

The traditional Icelandic alcoholic brew is *brennivín* (literally 'burnt wine'), a potent schnapps made from potatoes and caraway seeds, with the foreboding nickname *svarti dauði* (black death).

WHERE TO EAT & DRINK
Restaurants

Iceland's best restaurants are in Reykjavík (p87), although you'll come across the odd gem on your travels outside the capital. Bear in mind that the price difference between an exceptional restaurant and an average one is often small, so it can be well worth going upmarket. However, much of the time in rural Iceland, you may not have a choice – the town's only eating place will probably be the restaurant in the local hotel (or the grill in the petrol station – see opposite).

WHAT'S HAPPENING AT REYKJAVÍK'S TOP RESTAURANT?

Tell us about Sjávarkjallarinn (p89)
Sjávarkjallarinn is the most popular restaurant in Iceland! We make very good fusion food – Icelandic ingredients, mixed up with Asian. We alter the menu very regularly, just whenever we feel, 'Ahhh, we want a change'. We'll make three new main courses, and the next week we'll make three new starters.

Which one would you recommend?
We have one dish that's been on the menu from the start, and that's lobster served in a special way. It's called 'pick-me-up' because you have to pick the lobster up out of the jar. It's very good, although I change my own favourite dish very often. At the moment it's our Icelandic cod, salted overnight with many types of spices.

Does anybody really eat traditional Icelandic food any more?
Icelanders always eat traditional food once a year. At Þorrablót everybody eats the old food. Most Icelandic people don't eat it for the taste. It's just for the fun – like being a Viking! I really like sheep's head, and we eat the eyes and the tongue also.

Why Is modern Icelandic cuisine such a success?
I think Icelandic food is so good because we are always trying different things. We follow worldwide food fashion; and then we are always doing something new and fresh as well.

Thanks to Hrefna, Head Chef, Sjávarkjallarinn

ICELANDIC PÝLSUR

Along with copious amounts of coffee, the *pýlsur* (hot dog) is the fuel of modern Iceland. Hot dogs are for sale (around Ikr230) in every petrol station and fast-food kiosk. You can choose between toppings of raw onion, crunchy deep-fried onion, ketchup, mustard and tangy rémoulade, or just ask for *'ein með öllu'* (one with everything).

Locals in Reykjavík reckon the world's greatest hot dogs come from Bæjarins Beztu (p91), a busy hot-dog stand opposite the Kolaportið flea market. Rumour insists that they're so delicious because they're cooked in beer. We think that must be an Icelandic joke.

Main courses at eateries usually cost between Ikr1600 and Ikr5000, depending on where you are and what you choose to eat. Á la carte menus usually offer at least one fish dish, one veggie (invariably pasta) choice and several meat mains, and lots of restaurants also have a menu of lighter, cheaper meals such as hamburgers, sandwiches and pizzas. In Reykjavík, and to a lesser extent Akureyri, there are an increasing number of ethnic restaurants, including Thai, Vietnamese, Italian, Mexican, Indian and Chinese.

Restaurants usually open from 6pm to 10pm, and some also open for lunch from noon to 2pm.

Cafés & Pubs

Downtown Reykjavík has a great range of smoky bohemian café-bars where you can happily while away the hours sipping coffee, eating good-value meals, gossiping, tinkering with your laptop, and people watching. Typically creative menus range from simple soups, bagels and gourmet burgers to fish dishes, and café-bars offer some of the best bargain meals in Iceland (from about Ikr800).

Most of Reykjavík's cafés metamorphose into wild drinking dens on Friday and Saturday nights. Suddenly DJs appear, beer swills, and merry people dance, screech and stagger around until somewhere between 3am and 6am.

Some other towns around the country have café-bars created along similar lines, for example Karolína Café (p218) in Akureyri.

In rural Iceland the local bar is usually in a restaurant or hotel.

Quick Eats

KIOSKS

Icelanders love fast food, and you'll soon discover that a cheap way to stave off hunger until dinner is to have a *pýlsur* (hot dog). Most towns have a kiosk serving hot dogs, burgers and chips.

PETROL-STATION GRILLS

Outside Reykjavík, many large petrol stations have good, cheap grills and cafeterias attached to them – often the busiest eating place in town. They generally serve sandwiches and fast food from around 11am to 9pm or 10pm. Some also offer hearty set meals at lunch time, such as Icelandic meatballs, fish of the day or plates of lamb.

BAKERIES

We can't praise the wonderful Icelandic *bakari* (bakeries) enough. Every town has one, usually open from 7am or 8am until 5pm on weekdays (sometimes also Saturday). They sell all sorts of inexpensive fresh bread, buns, cakes, sandwiches and coffee, and provide chairs and tables where you can sit to eat and drink.

Self-Catering

Every town and village has at least one small supermarket. The most expensive are 10-11 and 11-11, and Bónus (easily recognised by its garish yellow-and-pink pig sign) is the country's budget supermarket chain. Others include Nóatún, Krónan, Kasko, Samkaup-Strax and Samkaup-Úrval. Opening times vary greatly; in Reykjavík most are open from 9am to 11pm daily, but outside the capital hours are generally shorter.

Iceland imports most of its groceries, so prices are exorbitant – roughly three times what you'd pay in North America, Australia or Europe. Tinned fish and dairy products represent the best value. Some fruit and vegetables are grown locally, and these tend to be fresh and tasty, but imported vegetables usually look tragic by the time they hit the supermarket shelves. Fruit and veg prices were fluctuating wildly at the time of writing, so if you're on a very tight budget it's probably worth shopping around.

VEGETARIANS & VEGANS

You'll have no problem in Reykjavík – there are three excellent meat-free, organic café-restaurants in the city, and many more eateries offer vegetarians plenty of choice. Outside the capital most restaurants have one veggie item on the menu – although as this is invariably cheese-and-tomato pasta or cheese-and-pepper-and-onion pizza, you could get very bored. Vegans will have to self-cater.

It's unlikely that you'll ever have to explain yourself in Icelandic but, just in case, *'Ég er grænmetisæta'* means 'I'm a vegetarian' and *'Ég borða ekki kjöt'* means 'I don't eat meat.'

Geothermal greenhouses are used to grow Iceland's fruit and vegetables.

HABITS & CUSTOMS

Icelandic eating habits are similar to elsewhere in northern Europe and Scandinavia. Breakfast is usually light (often just coffee), as is lunch (soup and bread or a snack). Dinner is the main meal of the day.

Three strange little foodie festivals follow the bloody Þorrablót feast in February (see p58). First off is Bolludagur (Bun Day; 23 February), when Icelanders gorge themselves sick on puff-pastry cream buns. Kids get up early to 'beat' the buns out of their parents with a *bolluvöndur* (literally 'bun wand'). The following day is Sprengidagur (Bursting Day; 24 February), when the aim is to stuff yourself with *saltkjöt og baunir* (salted meat and split peas) until you burst. Both are Lenten traditions.

Continuing the excess, Beer Day (1 March) is a less traditional celebration. It dates back to the glorious day in 1989 when beer was legalised in Iceland. As you'd expect, Reykjavík's clubs and bars get particularly wild.

On Christmas Day *hangikjöt* (hung meat) – which is normally smoked lamb – is served, as well as *flatkökur* (unleavened bread, or pancakes, charred on a grill or griddle without fat).

EAT YOUR WORDS

See p338 for pronunciation guidelines.

Food Glossary
STAPLES & CONDIMENTS

brauð	bread
(soðið) egg	(boiled) egg
flatkökur	rye pancakes
hrísgrjón	rice
hunang	honey
krydd	seasoning

marmelaði	marmalade
morgunkorn	cereal
ostur	cheese
pipar	pepper
salt	salt
sinnep	mustard
smjör	butter
sulta	jam
sykur	sugar
tómatsósa	ketchup (tomato sauce)

FISH

bleikja	arctic char
fiskur	fish
harðfiskur	dried haddock
humar	lobster
lax	salmon
lúða	halibut
rækja	shrimp
reyktur	smoked salmon
sandhverfu	turbot
sild	herring
silungur	freshwater trout
skata	skate
skötuselur	monkfish
steinbítur	catfish
villtur	wild salmon
ýsa	haddock
þorskur	cod

www.isholf.is/gullis /jo – Jo's Icelandic Recipes is a great independent website full of recipes and customs, written by an Icelander with a passion for food.

MEAT

bjúgu	smoked minced-meat sausage
hangikjöt	smoked lamb
hreindýrakjöt	reindeer
kjöt	meat
kjötsúpa	lamb, rice and vegetable soup
kjúklingur	chicken
lambakjöt	lamb
lundi	puffin
nautakjöt	beef
pýlsa	hot dog, sausage
saltkjöt	salted lamb or mutton
skinka	ham
svínakjöt	pork

VEGETABLES

blómkál	cauliflower
græn paprika	green pepper
grænar baunir	green peas
grænmeti	vegetables
gulrætur	carrots
gúrka	cucumber
hvítkál	cabbage
hvítlaukur	garlic
kartöflur	potatoes

laukur	onion
salat	lettuce
sveppir	mushrooms

FRUIT

ananas	pineapple
appelsínur	oranges
apríkósur	apricots
ávextir	fruit
bananar	bananas
bláber	blueberries
epli	apples
ferskjur	peaches
jarðarber	strawberries
krækiber	crowberries
perur	pears
sítróna	lemon
vínber	grapes

SWEETS & DESSERTS

ávaxtagrautur	stewed fruit
búðingur	pudding
ís/rjómaís	ice cream
kaka	cake
kleinur	Icelandic doughnuts
pönnukökur	thin, sweet, cinnamon-dusted pancakes
skyr	thick yogurtlike concoction made from skimmed milk and bacteria culture
smákökur/kex	biscuits
súkkulaði	chocolate

DRINKS

appelsínsafi	orange juice
ávaxtasafi	fruit juice
bjór	beer
brennivín	literally 'burnt wine'; Icelandic caraway-flavoured schnapps
drykkir	drinks
G-mjólk	longlife milk
gosdrykkir	soft drinks
jógúrt	yogurt
kaffi (með mjólk/svart)	coffee (white/black)
mjólk	milk
rauðvín/hvítvín	red/white wine
súrmjólk	sour milk
te	tea
vatn	water
whisky	whisky

MEALS

hádegismatur	lunch
kvöldmatur	dinner
morgunmatur	breakfast

In the depths of winter the sun doesn't rise above Iceland's most steep-sided fjords. When it does eventually reappear, villagers gather to drink caraway-flavoured *sólarkaffi* (sun coffee) and celebrate their first glimpse of sunlight in months.

Reykjavík

The world's most northerly capital combines colourful buildings, quirky people, a wild night-life and a capricious soul to devastating effect. Most visitors fall helplessly in love, returning home already saving to come back.

The city's charm lies in its many peculiar contrasts, which, like tectonic plates clashing against one another, create an earthquake of energy. Reykjavík offers a bewitching combination of village innocence and big-city zeal. It's populated by darkly cynical citizens who are nevertheless filled with unstoppable creativity and enthusiasm. In summer the streets are washed by 22 hours of daylight; in winter they're scoured by blizzards and doused in never-ending night. Reykjavík is a city that treasures its Viking past but wants the future – the very best of it – NOW!

You'll find all the cultural trappings of a large 21st-century European city here: cosy cafés, world-class restaurants, fine museums and galleries, and state-of-the-art geothermal pools. Reykjavík has also become infamous for its kicking music scene and its excessive Friday-night *runtur*, a wild pub crawl round the small, superstylish clubs and bars.

Add to this a backdrop of snow-topped mountains, an ocean that wets the very toes of the town, air as cold and clean as frozen diamonds, and incredible volcanic surroundings, and you'll agree that there's no better city in the world.

TOP FIVE

- Swig coffee in a quirky **café** (p89), or treat yourself to some top-quality **Icelandic seafood** (p88), in Reykjavík
- Join the **runtur** (p93), a wild pub crawl through Reykjavík's tiny but oh-so-cool bars and clubs
- Enjoy the geothermal pools at **Laugardalslaug** (p71), **Nauthólsvík Beach** (p71) and of course the **Blue Lagoon** (p111)
- Hear spooky stories on a **ghost walk** (p80) round the city's haunted places
- Immerse yourself in Icelandic culture at the **National Museum** (p75), the brand-new exhibition **Reykjavík 871 +\-2** (p75) or the family-friendly **Saga Museum** (p75)

- POPULATION: 180,000

HISTORY

Ingólfur Arnarson, a Norwegian fugitive, became the first official Icelander in AD 871. Myth has it that he tossed his *öndvegissúlur* (high-seat pillars) overboard, settling where the gods washed them ashore. This was at Reykjavík (Smoky Bay), which he named after steam rising from geothermal vents. According to 12th-century sources, Ingólfur built his farm on Aðalstræti, and excavations have unearthed a Viking longhouse there – see p75.

Reykjavík remained just a simple collection of farm buildings for centuries to follow. In 1225 an important Augustinian monastery was founded on the offshore island of Viðey (p100), although this was destroyed during the 16th century Reformation.

In the early 17th century the Danish king imposed a crippling trade monopoly on Iceland, leaving the country starving and destitute. In a bid to bypass the embargo, local sheriff Skúli Magnússon, the 'Father of Reykjavík', created weaving, tanning and wool-dyeing factories – the foundations of the city – in the 1750s.

Reykjavík really boomed during WWII, when it serviced British and US troops stationed at Keflavík. Since the 1950s Reykjavík has become unstoppable, throwing itself passionately into the 21st century. In a neat bit of historical irony, the Vikings' 'Smoky Bay' is now known as the 'smokeless city' due to its complete adoption of geothermal energy.

ORIENTATION

The city is spread out along a small peninsula, with Reykjavík Domestic Airport and the long-distance bus terminal BSÍ in the southern half, and the picturesque city centre and harbour occupying the northern half. The international airport is 48km away at Keflavík (a special airport bus provides connections to the centre of Reykjavík). The camp site and hostel are around 2km east of the centre, in the Laugadalur valley.

The city centre is very compact, and contains most of Reykjavík's attractions. The main street is Laugavegur. At its very furthest eastern end is Hlemmur bus terminal, one of the two main city bus stations. Moving westwards, this narrow, one-way lane blossoms with Reykjavík's flashiest clothes shops, bars and eateries. It changes its name to Bankastræti, then Austurstræti as it runs across the centre. Running uphill off Banka-

stræti at a jaunty diagonal, the artists' street Skólavörðustígur ends at the spectacular modernist church Hallgrímskirkja.

Two-laned Lækjargata cuts straight across Bankastræti/Austurstræti. To its west are the old town squares Austurvöllur and Ingólfstorg. At the northern end is Lækjartorg bus terminal, the other important city bus stand. To the northwest lies Reykjavík's working harbour. Tjörnin lake is to the south.

Maps

The tourist information centres are on the ball, and will provide you with a free city plan with your route marked on it probably while you're still pondering where you want to go. Most plans contain city bus maps, but you can also pick up the excellent Strætó bus-route map from Lækjartorg and Hlemmur bus stations.

The largest selection of road maps and trekking maps is in the bookshops listed in the following section.

INFORMATION
Bookshops

Reykjavík's two big bookshops have a superb choice of English-language books, newspapers, magazines and maps.

Eymundsson (Map p72; ☎ 511 1130; Austurstræti 18; ☼ 9am-10pm Mon-Fri, 10am-10pm Sat, 1-10pm Sun)

Mál og Menning (Map p72; ☎ 515 2500; shopping@edda.is; Laugavegur 18; ☼ 9am-10pm Mon-Fri, 10am-10pm Sat & Sun)

Also try:

Bókin ehf (Map p72; ☎ 552 1710; Klapparstígur 25-27; ☼ 11am-6pm Mon-Fri, noon-5pm Sat) Great second-hand bookshop run by exactly the right kind of eccentric!

Bóksala Stúdenta (Map pp68-9; ☎ 570 0777; www .boksala.is; Hringbraut) University bookshop.

Iða (Map p72; ☎ 511 5001; Lækjargata 2a; ☼ 9am-10pm) Tourist shop and bookshop combined.

Cultural Centres

A-Hús Intercultural Centre (Alþjóðahús; Map p72; ☎ 530 9300; www.ahus.is; Hverfisgata 18) Advice bureau for immigrants, with occasional events held downstairs in Café Cultura (see p90).

Alliance Française (Map pp68-9; ☎ 552 3870; www.af .is; 2nd fl, Tryggvagata 8) Book and video library, and regular programme of films, lectures etc.

Norræna Húsið (Nordic House; Map pp68-9; ☎ 551 7030; www.nordice.is; Sturlugata 5; ☼ 8am-5pm Mon-Fri, noon-5pm Sat & Sun) Scandinavian cultural centre.

GAY REYKJAVÍK

Reykjavík is a very tolerant place; its bar and club scene is so integrated that segregated gay bars disappear almost before they've opened.

The gay and lesbian organisation **Samtökin '78** (Map p72; ☎ 552 7878; office@samtokin78.is; 4th fl, Laugavegur 3; ☺ office 1-5pm Mon-Fri) provides information during office hours and doubles as an informal gay community centre with a drop-in **café** (☺ 8pm-11pm Mon & Thu year-round, sometimes also Sat late Jul-Aug). Created especially for gay, lesbian and bisexual visitors to Iceland, www. gayice.is is an English-language website with great information and upcoming events.

The only gay café-bar in Reykjavík is **Café Cozy** (Map p72; ☎ 511 1033; Austurstráeti 3; snacks from Ikr300; ☺ 10am-1am Mon-Fri, 8am-5.30am Sat & Sun), near Ingólfstorg. The only specifically gay club in Reykjavík is a men-only leather bar, **MSC Iceland** (Map p72; ☎ 562 1280; Bankastræti 11; ☺ from 11pm Sat).

There are several good gay-friendly guesthouses close to the centre – see Tower Guesthouse (p84) and Room with a View (p84). Reykjavík has a lively Gay Pride celebration – see p81 for more information.

Discount Cards

The **Reykjavík Tourist Card** (24/48/72hr Ikr1200/1700/2200) is available at various outlets including the tourist offices. The card gives you free admission to Reykjavík's swimming pools, galleries and museums (Árbæjarsafn, ASÍ Art Museum, Ásmundarsafn, Culture House, Hafnarhús, Kjarvalsstaðir, National Gallery of Iceland, National Museum, Reykjavík 871 +/-2, Reykjavík Zoo, Sigurjón Ólafsson Museum, and museums in Hafnarfjörður). It's worth it if you make use of the buses and swimming pools but might not be good value if you're just visiting museums and galleries, since many of them are free one day per week anyway.

Emergency

For an ambulance, the fire brigade or the police, dial ☎ 112.

Landspítali University Hospital (Map pp68-9; ☎ 543 2000; Fossvogur) It has a 24-hour casualty department.

Internet Access

The cheapest internet places are Reykjavík's libraries (see right). Many hotels and guesthouses have free internet access; the youth hostel and several private tourist offices have rather overpriced services. If you've brought your laptop with you, many cafés have free wi-fi access where you can tap away for the price of a coffee.

Ground Zero (Map p72; ☎ 562 7776; per 15/35/60min Ikr200/300/500; Vallarstræti 4; 11am-1am Mon-Fri, noon-1am Sat & Sun) Reykjavík's only dedicated internet café, full of game-playing teenagers.

Internet Resources

Some good websites for information on Reykjavík:

Culture in Iceland (www.culture.is) Cultural events in Reykjavík.

Grapevine (www.grapevine.is) English-language newspaper's website, with lively news and reviews.

Reykjavik.com (www.reykjavik.com) Straight-down-the-line English-language magazine website containing current events and reviews.

Visit Reykjavík (www.visitreykjavik.is) Official tourist-office website.

Laundry

Most people rely on their hostel, hotel or guesthouse for laundry.

Úðafoss (Map p72; ☎ 551 2301; Vitastígur 13; ☺ 8am-6pm Mon-Thu, to 6.30pm Fri) This central dry-cleaner also does laundry (Ikr1375/1925 for 1kg/5kg).

Left Luggage

Most hotels have left-luggage facilities, as do the camp site and youth hostel.

BSÍ bus terminal (Map pp68-9; ☎ 591 1000; Vatnsmýrarvegur 10; ☺ 7.30am-10pm) Luggage storage Ikr150/700 per day/week.

Libraries

The following offer books, novels and periodicals in English, French and other languages, and internet access for Ikr200 per hour.

Aðalbókasafn (Map p72; ☎ 563 1717; www .borgarbokasafn.is; Tryggvagata 15; ☺ 10am-9pm Mon, to 7pm Tue-Thu, 11am-7pm Fri, 1-5pm Sat & Sun) Excellent main library, in the heart of Reykjavík.

Kringlusafn (Map pp68-9; ☎ 580 6200; www .borgarbokasafn.is; cnr Borgarleikhús & Listabraut;

REYKJAVÍK

REYKJAVÍK

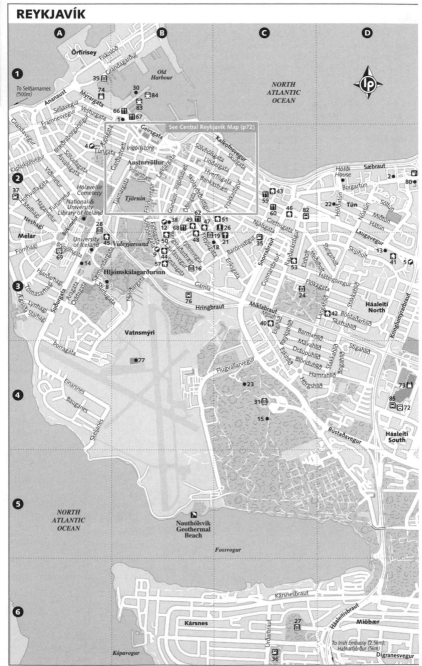

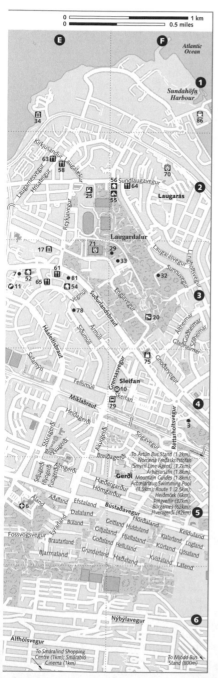

10am-7pm Mon-Wed, to 9pm Thu, 11am-7pm Fri, 1-5pm Sat & Sun) Branch by the Kringlan shopping centre.

Medical Services

For a dentist, call ☎ 575 0505.

Health Centre (Map p72; ☎ 585 2600; Vesturgata 7) A doctor's appointment costs Ikr700 (under 16s pay 25%).

Læknavaktin (☎ 1770) Nonemergency telephone medical advice between 5pm and 11.30pm.

Lyfja (Map p72; ☎ 552 4045; Laugavegur 16; ✆ 10am-6.30pm Mon-Fri, 11am-4pm Sat) Central pharmacy.

Lyfja Apótek (Map pp68-9; ☎ 533 2300; Lágmúli 5; ✆ 8am-midnight) Late-night pharmacy, near Hótel Nordica. Buses S2, 15, 17 and 19.

Money

Beware of changing currency at hotels or private exchange offices in the city; commissions can reach 8.75% and exchange rates may be poor. There are central branches, with ATMS, of all three major Icelandic banks.

Landsbanki Íslands (Map p72; ☎ 410 4000; www.landsbanki.is; Austurstræti 11)

Glitnir (Map p72; ☎ 440 4000; www.glitnir.is; Lækjargata 12)

KB Banki (Map p72; ☎ 525 6000; www.kaupthing.net; Austurstræti 5)

Post

Some Nóatún supermarkets have post-office desks that remain open until 9pm.

Main post office (Map p72; ☎ 580 1000; Pósthússtræti 5; ✆ 9am-4.30pm Mon-Fri, plus 11am-2pm Sat Jun-Aug) With an efficient parcel service, philatelic desk (www.stamps.is), and poste restante service.

Post office branch (Map pp68-9; Grensásvegur 9; ✆ 9am-8pm Mon-Fri, 10am-2pm Sat) Opens til late.

Telephone

Public phones are becoming elusive in mobile-crazy Reykjavík. Try the tourist office, the post office, by the southwestern corner of Austurvöllur, on Lækjargata, or at Kringlan shopping centre.

At the city hostel you can make cheap international calls using an Atlas telephone card.

Tourist Information

Reykjavík has a very good main tourist office and several smaller private centres. Besides providing information, they can make accommodation, bus-tour and entertainment bookings.

Pick up the free booklets *Reykjavík This Month* and *What's On in Reykjavík* for events

REYKJAVÍK

in the capital. The excellent English-language newspaper *Grapevine*, widely distributed, has the lowdown on what's new in town.

Main Tourist Office (Upplýsingamiðstöð Ferðamanna; Map p72; ☎ 590 1550; www.visitreykjavik.is; Aðalstræti 2; ☼ 8.30am-7pm daily Jun-Aug, 9am-6pm Mon-Fri, 9am-2pm Sat & Sun Sep-May) Staff are friendly, and there are mountains of free brochures and leaflets, plus some maps for sale. Internet access costs Ikr350/500 per 30/60 minutes.

BSÍ bus terminal desk (Map pp68-9; Vatnsmýrarvegur 10) Information leaflets.

Raðhús Tourist Information Desk (Map p72; ☎ 411 1000; Tjarnargata 11; ☼ 8.20am-4.30pm Mon-Fri, noon-4pm Sat & Sun mid-May–mid-Sep, closed Sun mid-Sep–mid-May) Small tourist desk inside the city hall.

Iceland Visitor (Map p72; ☎ 511 2442; www.iceland visitor.com; Lækjargata 2; ☼ 9am-10pm Jun-Aug, 10am-6pm Mon-Sat Sep-May) Private office.

Kleif Travel Market (Map p72; ☎ 510 5700; www .kleif.is; Bankastræti 2; ☼ 8am-10pm May-Aug, 9am-6pm Sep-Apr) Private office.

Travel Agencies

Numerous travel agents and tour companies in Reykjavík specialise in trips around Iceland by bus or plane. A few agents can also arrange international travel. Also see p333.

Exit: Stúdentaferðir (Map pp68-9; ☎ 562 2362; www .exit.is; Borgartún 29) Student travel agency specialising in international travel.

Ferðaþjónusta Bænda (Icelandic Farm Holidays; Map pp68-9; ☎ 570 2700; www.farmholidays.is) Arranges farm holidays and self-drive tours around Iceland.

IcelandTotal (Map pp68-9; ☎ 585 4300; www.iceland total.com; Lágmúli 4) Can organise coach tours, car hire and complete holiday packages.

Norræna Ferðaskrifstofan (☎ 570 8600; info@smyril-line.is; Stangarhyl 1) The local agent for Smyril Line, which runs ferries to the Faeroes, Norway and Denmark, and Scotland (the latter in summer only).

Úrval Útsýn (Map pp68-9; ☎ 585 4000; www.urvalut syn.is; Lágmúli 4) Mainstream travel agency specialising in international travel.

Útivist (Map pp68-9; ☎ 562 1000; www.utivist.is; Laugavegur 178) Owns several mountain huts, including some at Þórsmörk and Landmannalaugar, and runs guided treks.

DANGERS & ANNOYANCES

If you find a safer city, let us know! Accidental injury at the hands of drunken revellers is a possibility, although considering how many beers are sunk at the weekend, it's surprising there isn't more trouble.

SIGHTS & ACTIVITIES

Hallgrímskirkja

Reykjavík's most attention-seeking building is the immense concrete church **Hallgríms-kirkja** (Map pp68-9; ☎ 510 1000; www.hallgrimskirkja .is; Skólavörðuholt; ☉ 9am-5pm), star of a thousand postcards and visible from 20km away. For an unmissable view of the city, make sure you take an elevator trip up the 75m-high **tower** (adult/child Ikr350/50).

In contrast to the high drama outside, the church's interior is puritanically plain. The most startling feature is the vast 5275-pipe **organ**, which has a strangely weapon-like appearance. Between mid-June and mid-August you can hear this mighty beast in action three times per week at lunchtime/evening **concerts** (admission Ikr1000/1500).

The church's radical design caused huge controversy, and its architect, Guðjón Samúelsson, never lived to see its completion – it took a painstaking 34 years (1940–74) to build. Those sweeping columns on either side of the tower represent volcanic basalt – a favourite motif of Icelandic nationalists. Hallgrímskirkja was named after the poet Reverend Hallgrímur Pétursson, who wrote Iceland's most popular hymn book.

Gazing proudly into the distance outside is a **statue** of the Viking Leifur Eiríksson, the first European to stumble across America. It was a present from the USA on the 1000th anniversary of the Alþing (p78).

Geothermal Pools & Spas

Reykjavík's heavenly pools (and beach) are the heart of the city's social life: children play,

teenagers flirt, business deals are made, and everyone catches up on the latest gossip. Volcanic water keeps the temperature at a mellow 29°C, and most of the baths have *heitir pottar* (hot pots), Jacuzzi-like pools kept at a toasting 37°C to 42°C. Admission usually costs Ikr280/120 for adults/children aged 6 to 15, and towels and swimming costumes can be rented for Ikr300 each. For further information, see www.spacity.is.

Reykjavíkurs get very upset by dirty tourists in their nice, clean pools (for good reason – the city's pools are free of chemicals). To avoid causing huge offence, visitors *must* wash thoroughly without a swimsuit before hopping in.

The dinky **Nauthólsvík Geothermal Beach** (Ýl-ströndin; Map pp68-9; ☎ 511 6630; ☉ 10am-8pm mid-May–mid-Sep) on the edge of the Atlantic should by rights be visited only by seals and seagulls. However, it's packed with happy bathers in summer, thanks to golden sand imported all the way from Morocco and an artificial hot spring that keeps the water at a pleasant 18°C to 20°C. There are sociable hot pots on shore and in the sea, a snack bar, changing rooms (Ikr200), and canoes and rowing boats for hire on Thursday. Get there on bus 16.

Laugardalslaug (Map pp68-9; ☎ 553 4039; Sundlaugavegur 30a; ☉ 6.30am-10.30pm Mon-Fri year-round, plus 8am-10pm Sat & Sun Apr-Sep, 8am-8pm Sat & Sun Oct-Mar) is the largest pool in Iceland, with the best facilities: an Olympic-size indoor pool, an outdoor pool, four hot pots and a whirlpool, a steam bath, and a curling 86m water slide. Take bus 14.

The new five-star **Laugar spa** (Map pp68-9; ☎ 553 0000; www.laugarspa.is; spa admission Ikr3600; ☉ spa 6.30am-10.30pm Mon-Fri year-round, plus 8am-10pm Sat & Sun Apr-Sep, 8am-8pm Sat & Sun Oct-Mar, beauty salon 9am-7pm Mon-Fri, 11am-6pm Sat, massage salon 9am-9pm Mon-Fri, 11am-6pm Sat) is attached to Laugardalslaug (see above), and offers delicious ways to pamper yourself. There are six themed saunas and steam rooms, a vast and well-equipped gym, and beauty and massage clinics with soothing treatments (detox wraps, facials and hot-stone therapies).

It's a step out of town, but the slickly designed **Árbæjarlaug** (☎ 567 3933; Fylkisvegur, Elliðaárdalur; ☉ 6.30am-10pm Mon-Fri year-round, plus 8am-10pm Sat & Sun Apr-Sep, 8am-8pm Sat & Sun Oct-Mar; ☍) is well known as the best family pool: it's half inside and half outside, and there are lots of watery amusements (slides, waterfalls and massage jets) to keep the kids entertained. Take bus 19.

CENTRAL REYKJAVÍK

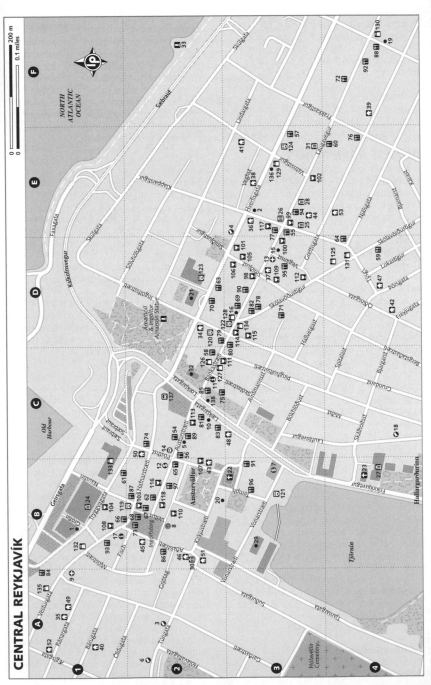

Other central pools include the following two:

Sundhöllin (Map pp68-9; ☎ 551 4059; Barónsstígur 16; ⏱ 6.30am-9.30pm Mon-Fri, 8am-7pm Sat & Sun) Reykjavík's oldest swimming pool (with a definite 'municipal baths' feel to it) is close to the Hlemmur bus station and is the only indoor pool within the city.

Vesturbæjarlaug (Map pp68-9; ☎ 551 5004; Hofsvallagata; ⏱ 6.30am-10pm Mon-Fri, 8am-8pm Sat & Sun) Also within walking distance of the centre (or take bus 15), Vesturbæjarlaug has a basic 25m pool and three hot pots.

REYKJAVÍK IN...TWO DAYS

Day One

Early risers should visit the bustling **working harbour** to watch the fishing boats come in. It's backed by stunning views of the peak **Esja**, across the fjord in southwest Iceland. Afterwards, head for breakfast at **Grái Kötturinn** (p91), a tiny eccentric café serving bacon, eggs and hunks of fresh bread.

Next meander up arty **Skólavörðustígur**, poking your nose into its crafty little galleries. At the top of the hill is the immense concrete church **Hallgrimskirkja** (p71), Reykjavík's most dramatic building. For a perfect view of the city, take an elevator trip up the tower.

Once you've plumped back down to earth, pop across the road to the **Einar Jónsson Museum** (p76). You'll get a free glimpse of this gloomy sculptor's weird works in the garden round the back; if you like what you see, there's plenty more fantastical sculptures inside.

For further research into the Icelandic mind, head to the **National Gallery of Iceland** (p77). Here, paintings by the country's most treasured artists include hallucinogenic landscapes and eerie depictions of folk-tale monsters.

Pop into cosy **Café Paris** (p90) for a light lunch – it's a prime people-watching spot. Then, if you're here at the weekend, make **Kolaportið** (p79) your next stop – rummaging through foreign flea markets is always enlightening! You can also buy cubes of infamous *hákarl* (rotten shark meat) from the fish market – it might look innocuous, but find a quiet bin to stand by...

Next, catch bus 18 from Lækjartorg bus station to **Perlan** (opposite). There are two excitements here: first is the superb **Saga Museum**, which brings Iceland's early history to life with fantastically realistic models and a soundtrack of horrible screams – we think the Vikings would approve. Second is the hexagonal **viewing deck and café**, where you'll get tremendous views.

If you're cunning, last week you'll have booked a table at **Sjávarkjallarinn** (p89), a town-centre restaurant currently far ahead of the game. Once the bill's been settled, head back to your hotel for a kip and a brush-up: you're going to need some energy to get you through the **runtur** (p93), Reykjavík's notorious Bacchanalian pub crawl, which starts around midnight and carries on till 5am. Rather than cosying down in one venue, it's the done thing to cruise from bar to bar. To get you started, our top tips are: **Sirkus** (p92), **Kaffibarinn** (p92), **Kaffi Sólon** (p91) and **Thorvaldsen** (p92).

Day Two

After the night you've just had, start the recovery slowly with brunch at **Café Oliver** (p92).

At 12.30pm we recommend taking the 'express' version of the **Golden Circle tour**. OK, so it's a bit of a rush – maybe next time you'll book more than two days in lovely Iceland! At least you get to see some of the Icelandic countryside and marvel over two of its natural wonders – the tumbling waterfall **Gullfoss** (p120) and the spouting hot springs at **Geysir** (p120).

Tired but happy, you'll get back to Reykjavík in the early evening just in time for tea. For a dash of spice, why not try an Indian meal made with Icelandic ingredients? Go for succulent tandoori salmon at **Austur Indía Félagið** (p87), or try the unique guillemot dish at **Indian Mango** (p87). Round off the evening at the **Volcano Show** (opposite), an explosive introduction to Iceland's violent geography.

'What about the **Blue Lagoon** (p111)?' we hear you ask. Well, here's the clever part – you can visit Iceland's number one attraction on your way back to the airport tomorrow. Wallowing in its warm, sapphire-blue waters is certainly a fantastic last memory to take home.

Whale Watching

Iceland is a fantastic place for whale watching – its waters hold over 20 species of cetacean. In Faxaflói bay you'll most commonly come across white-beaked dolphins, harbour porpoises and minkes; humpbacks were also spotted from time to time in 2006.

Between April and October two companies run three-hour trips from Reykjavík's old harbour, at 9am and 1pm (1pm only in October; also at 5pm June to August): **Elding** (Map pp68-9; ☎ 555 3565; www.elding.is; adult/6-15yr Ikr3900/1600; 👤) and **Hvalstöðin Whale-Watching Centre** (Map pp68-9; ☎ 533 2660; www.whalewatching.is; adult/7-15yr Ikr3800/1500; 👤). Hvalstöðin also has a floating nature centre, with whale models and films. In breeding season (mid-May to mid-August), both companies visit around Akurey island, offshore from Reykjavík, to look at the **puffins**.

The rusting **old whaling ships** (Map pp68–9) *Hvalur 6, 7, 8* and *9* are moored directly opposite the whale-watching companies. Ladders and gangplanks enable visitors to climb aboard for a closer look.

Puffin Watching

Around 50,000 of these wonderful little birds (see the boxed text, p47) nest on Lundey and Akurey, two islands just offshore from Reykjavík. Between mid-May and mid-August you can visit them on the one-hour **Puffin Express boat trips** (Map pp68-9; ☎ 581 1010; www.ferja.is; adult/under 12yr Ikr2500/1000), which sail from Reykjavík harbour at 10.30am and 4.30pm daily.

Also see Whale Watching, above.

Volcano Show

Eccentric eruption-chaser Villi Knudsen is the photographer, owner and presenter of the fascinating **Volcano Show** (Map pp68-9; ☎ 845 9548; vknudsen2000@yahoo.com; Red Rock Cinema, Hellusund 6a; adult/child/student 1hr show Ikr900/250/750, 2hr show Ikr1150/300/950; in English 11am, 3pm & 8pm daily, in German 6pm daily, in French 1pm Sat Jul & Aug, in English 3pm & 8pm daily Sep & Apr-Jun, 8pm Oct-Mar), a film show that captures 50 years of Icelandic volcanoes. Although some of the footage is a bit old and wobbly, you're still left reeling by images of the town Heimaey being crushed by molten lava, or the island Surtsey boiling its way out of the sea.

Perlan & the Saga Museum

Looking like half of Barbarella's bra, **Perlan** (Map pp68-9; ☎ 562 0200; www.perlan.is; 👤 10am-10pm) is a complex based around the huge hot-water tanks on Öskjuhlíð hill. It's about 2km from the city centre (take bus 18 from Hlemmur).

The main attraction is the endearing bloodthirsty **Saga Museum** (Map pp68-9; ☎ 511 1517; www.sagamuseum.is; adult/child/concession Ikr900/450/700; 👤 10am-6pm Apr-Sep, noon-5pm Oct-Mar), where Icelandic history is brought to life by eerie silicon models and a soundtrack of thudding axes and hair-raising screams. Don't be surprised if you see some of the characters wandering around town, as moulds were taken from Reykjavík residents (the museum's owner is Ingólfur Arnarson, and his daughters are the Irish princess and the little slave gnawing a fish!).

The hexagonal **viewing deck** offers a tremendous 360-degree panorama of Reykjavík and the mountains: multilingual recordings explain the scenery. There's a busy **café** (👤 10am-9pm) on the same level, so if it's brass-monkey weather, you can admire the same beautiful views over coffee and crepes. The mirrored dome on top of the tanks contains one of the city's finer restaurants, Perlan (see p87).

Two **artificial geysers** will keep small children absolutely enthralled: the one inside blasts off every few minutes, while the outside geyser comes on in the afternoon. There are numerous **walking and cycling trails** on the hillside, including a path to Nauthólsvík hot beach (see p71).

Museums

Displays at the **National Museum** (Þjóðminjasafn; Map pp68-9; ☎ 530 2200; www.natmus.is; Suðurgata 41; adult/under 18yr/concession Ikr600/free/300, free Wed; 👤 10am-5pm daily May–mid-Sep, 11am-5pm Tue-Sun mid-Sep–Apr) are well thought out and give an excellent overview of Iceland's history and culture. The strongest section delves into the Settlement Era, with swords, silver hoards and a great little bronze **model of Thor** on display. However, the most treasured artefact in the museum is a beautiful 13th-century **church door**, carved with the touching story of a knight and his faithful lion! Upstairs, you really get a sense of the country's poverty over the following 600 years. Simple, homy artefacts utilise every scrap: check out the **gaming pieces** made from cod ear bones, and the **wooden doll** that doubled as a kitchen utensil.

The city's newest exhibition **Reykjavík 871 +/-2** (Settlement Exhibition; Map p72; ☎ 411 6370; www.reykjavik871.is; Aðalstræti 16; adult/12-18yr Ikr600/300; 👤 10am-5pm; 👤) is based around a single 10th-century Viking house but shows what miracles can be achieved when technology, archaeology

REYKJAVÍK

REYKJAVÍK IN WINTER

It's bitterly cold and the sun barely rises, but there are *some* advantages to wintery Iceland. The major joy, of course, is watching the unearthly glory of the **Northern Lights** (see p46).

The **Reykjavík Skating Hall** (Map pp68-9; ☎ 588 9705; www.skautaholl.is; Múlavegur 1, Laugardalur; adult/child Ikr500/400, skate hire Ikr300; ☒ noon-3pm Mon & Tue, noon-3pm & 5-7.30pm Wed & Thu, 1-8pm Fri, 1-6pm Sat & Sun Sep-Apr) throws open its doors in winter. Some people also skate on **Tjörnin** (p78) when it freezes.

The **skiing** season runs from November to April, depending on snowfall. The three ski areas close to Reykjavík (Bláfjöll, Hengill and Skálafell) are managed by the organisation **Skíðasvæði** (☎ 510 6600; www.skidasvaedi.is; Frikirkjuvegur 11, IS-101 Reykjavík). Iceland's premier ski slopes are at 84-sq-km **Bláfjöll** (☎ 561 8400; ☒ 2-9pm Mon-Fri, 10am-6pm Sat & Sun), which has downhill, cross-country and snowboarding facilities – and gets swamped by eager city dwellers when the snow begins to fall. Passes cost Ikr1700/500 per adult/child 6 to 16, and you can hire skis, poles, boots and other gear at reasonable rates. The resort is located about 25km southeast of Reykjavík on Rte 417, just off Rte 1. Buses leave from the Mjódd bus stand southeast of town.

More **bus tours** (p80) operate in winter than you might imagine, offering a startling vision of familiar places: a white and frozen Gullfoss, caves full of icicles, and snow-covered mountains.

---

and imagination meet. Through 21st-century wizardry, a fire leaps from the hearth, while around the walls ghostly settlers materialise to tend crops, hunt, launch a boat, and bury their dead. Go and marvel while it's all pristine!

Creeping into the darkened rooms of the **Culture House** (Þjóðmenningarhúsið; Map p72; ☎ 545 1400; www.thjodmenning.is; Hverfisgata 15; adult/under 16yr/concession Ikr300/free/200, free Wed; ☒ 11am-5pm; ☒) is a true thrill for saga lovers. A permanent exhibition covers saga history: from a Who's Who of Norse gods to a fascinating account of Árni Magnússon, who devoted his life to saving Icelandic manuscripts, and died of a broken heart when his Copenhagen library went up in flames. Two hushed display rooms contain the original vellums; if you're interested in seeing more, contact the **Árni Magnússon Institute** (Map pp68-9; ☎ 525 4010; www.am.hi.is; Suðurgata).

Quaint old buildings have been uprooted from their original sites and rebuilt at the open-air **Árbæjarsafn** (☎ 411 6300; www.arbaejarsafn.is; Kistuhylur 4; adult/under 18yr Ikr600/free; ☒ 10am-5pm daily Jun-Aug, by tour only 1pm Mon, Wed & Fri Sep-May), a kind of zoo for houses, 4km from the city centre. Alongside the 19th-century homes are a turf-roofed church, and various stables, smithies, barns and boathouses – all very picturesque. There are summer arts-and-crafts demonstrations, and it's a great place for kids to let off steam. Take bus 12.

Despite its grand name, the **Reykjavík Museum of Photography** (Ljósmyndasafn Reykjavíkur; Map p72; ☎ 563 1790; www.photomuseum.is; 6th fl, Grófarhús, Tryggvagata 15; admission free; ☒ 1-7pm Mon-Fri, to 5pm Sat & Sun) is really just an exhibi-

tion room above Reykjavík City Library. It's definitely worth dropping in, though – its quintessentially Scandinavian exhibitions are free and usually thought-provoking. If you take the lift up, walk down the stairs, which are lined with funny old black-and-white photos.

Based appropriately in a former freezing plant for fish, the small new **Víkin Maritime Museum** (Víkin Sjóminjasafnið; Map p72; ☎ 517 9400; www.sjominjasafn.is; Grandagarður 8; adult/under 18yr/concession Ikr500/free/300; ☒ 11am-5pm Tue-Sun Jun-Sep, Sat & Sun Oct-May) celebrates the country's seafaring heritage, focusing on the trawlers that transformed Iceland's economy. Much of the information is in Icelandic only, but silent film footage of trawler crews in action is worth a look.

Reykjavík has several specialist museums dealing with natural history, medicine, banknotes and coins, and hydroelectricity; contact the tourist office for details.

Galleries

Einar Jónsson (1874–1954) is Iceland's foremost sculptor, famous for his intense symbolist works. Chiselled allegories of Hope, Earth, Spring and Death burst from basalt cliffs, weep over naked women, sprout wings and slay dragons. For a taster, the **sculpture garden** (admission free) behind the museum contains 26 bronze casts; they're particularly effective at dusk. If these appeal to your inner Goth, you'll find gleaming white-marble sculptures on similar themes inside the fascinating **Einar Jónsson Museum** (Map pp68-9; ☎ 551 3797; www.skulptur.is; Njarðargata; adult/under 16yr/concession Ikr400/free/200; ☒ 2-5pm

Tue-Sun Jun–mid-Sep, 2-5pm Sat & Sun mid-Sep–Nov & Feb-May). The building itself was designed by the artist and contains his austere penthouse flat, with unusual views over the city.

The **Reykjavík Art Museum** (Listasafn Reykjavíkur; www.listasafnreykjavikur.is; adult/under 18yr Ikr500/free, free Mon) is split over three sites – one ticket admits you to all if you visit on the same day.

There's something immensely tactile about Ásmundur Sveinsson's monumental concrete creations – see for yourself in the **garden** (admission free) outside the rounded, white **Ásmundar-safn** (Ásmundur Sveinsson Museum; Map pp68-9; ☎ 553 2155; Sigtún; 10am-4pm May-Sep, 1-4pm Oct-Apr). Duck inside the museum for smaller, spikier works in wood, clay and metals, exploring themes as diverse as folklore and physics. Ásmundur (1893–1982) designed the building himself; getting into the spirit of things, the council later added an igloo-shaped bus stop in front. Buses 14, 15, 17, 19 and S2 pass close by.

Hafnarhúsið (Map p72; ☎ 590 1200; Tryggvagata 17; 10am-5pm; &) is a former warehouse now converted into a severe steel-and-concrete exhibition space. Pride of place is usually given to the distinctive, disturbing comic-book paintings of Erró (Guðmundur Guðmundsson; 1932–), a political artist who has donated several thousand works to the gallery. The rest of the industrial interior holds temporary installations: fluorescent paintings of moss, a kaleidoscopic coffin and children's toys made from fish bones were recent offerings. The café has great harbour views.

Jóhannes Kjarval (1885–1972) was a fisherman until his crew paid for him to study at the Academy of Fine Arts in Copenhagen. He's one of Iceland's most popular artists, and his unearthly landscapes can be seen inside the angular glass-and-wood **Kjarvalsstaðir** (Map pp68-9; ☎ 552 6131; Flókagata; 10am-5pm; &), alongside changing installations.

Surreal mud-purple landscapes are intermingled with visions of trolls, giants and dead men walking at the **National Gallery of Iceland** (Listasafn Íslands; Map p72; ☎ 515 9600; www.listasafn.is; Fríkirkjuvegur 7; admission free; 11am-5pm Tue-Sun; &). Iceland's main art gallery, overlooking Tjörnin, certainly gives an interesting glimpse into the nation's psyche. As well as a huge collection of 19th- and 20th-century paintings by Iceland's favourite sons and daughters (including Ásgrímur Jónsson, Jóhannes Kjarval and Nína Sæmundsson), there are works by Picasso and Munch. If you want to see more of Jónsson's

work, the National Gallery also owns the **Ásgrímur Jónsson Museum** (Map pp68-9; Bergstaðastræti 74), open by appointment only.

The **Sigurjón Ólafsson Museum** (Map pp68-9; ☎ 553 2906; www.lso.is; Laugarnestangi 70; adult/under 18yr Ikr300/free; 2-5pm Tue-Sun Jun-Aug, 2-5pm Sat & Sun Sep-Nov & Feb-May) is a peaceful little place showcasing the varied works – portrait busts, driftwood totem poles and abstract football players – of sculptor Sigurjón Ólafsson (1908–82). A salty ocean breeze blows through the wooden rooms, which also contain Reykjavík's only shoreside café. On Tuesday from mid-July to August there are classical concerts at 8.30pm. Buses 12 and 16 pass close by.

Close to Reykjavík University, **Norræna Húsið** (Nordic House; Map pp68-9; ☎ 551 7030; www.nordice.is; Sturlugata 5; 8am-5pm Mon-Fri, noon-5pm Sat & Sun) is a Scandinavian cultural centre with a **gallery** (adult/under 15yr/concession Ikr300/free/150; noon-5pm Tue-Sun), a library of Scandinavian literature, a pleasant café, and regular Nordic-themed concerts, lectures and films.

Reykjavík has many small contemporary art galleries. **SAFN Gallery** (Map p72; ☎ 561 8777; www.safn.is; Laugavegur 37; admission free; 2-6pm Wed-Fri, to 5pm Sat & Sun) is one of the best: this tall wooden building contains three floors of conceptual art – beer cans in perspex and floating teacups – created by home-grown and international artists. **ASÍ Art Museum** (Map pp68-9; ☎ 511 5353; Freyjugata 41; admission free; 2-6pm Tue-Sun) often has interesting installations; and there are similar exhibitions at **Kling & Bang** (Map p72; ☎ 696 2209; http://this.is /klingogbang; Laugavegur 23; 2-6pm Thu-Sun), **i8** (Map p72; ☎ 551 3666; www.i8.is; Klapparstígur 33; 11am-5pm Tue-Fri, 1-5pm Sat) and **Nýlistasafnið** (Map p72; ☎ 551 4350; www.nylo.is; Laugavegur 26; 1-5pm Wed-Sun).

Parks & Gardens

Reykjavík Botanic Gardens (Map pp68-9; ☎ 553 8870; botgard@rvk.is; Skúlatún 2; admission free; greenhouse 10am-10pm Apr-Sep, to 5pm Oct-Mar) contains over 5000 varieties of subarctic plant species, colourful seasonal flowers, a summer café serving coffee and waffles, and lots of bird life (particularly grey geese and their fluffy little goslings).

Laugardalur (Map pp68–9) was once the main source of Reykjavík's hot water supply – the name translates as 'Hot-Springs Valley'. Just north of the botanic garden you'll find the **old wash house** (Map pp68–9) – sadly, rather graffitied – where washerwomen once scrubbed the city's dirty laundry in sulphurous pools. A small open-air exhibition of old photos brings the past to life.

Reykjavík's Family Fun Park & Zoo (see opposite) is also based in the valley, along with most of the city's sport and recreational facilities. Buses 14, 15, 17, 19 and S2 pass within a few hundred metres of Laugardalur.

At the heart of the city, grassy **Austurvöllur** (Map p72) was once part of first settler Ingólfur Arnarson's hay fields. Today it's a favourite spot for lunchtime picnics and summer sunbathing, and is sometimes used for open-air concerts and political demonstrations. The statue in the centre is of Jón Sigurðsson, who led the campaign for Icelandic independence.

The parks around the lake Tjörnin (see below) are great for strolling.

Buildings & Monuments

Tjörnin (Pond; Map p72) is the placid lake at the centre of the city. It echoes with the honks, squawks and screeches of over 40 species of visiting birds, including swans, geese and artic terns; feeding the ducks is a popular pastime for the under fives. Pretty sculpture-dotted parks line the southern shores, and their lacing paths are much used by cyclists and joggers. In winter, hardy souls strap on ice skates and turn the lake into an outdoor rink. For a self-guided art tour round Tjörnin, buy the brochure 'The City Statues' (Ikr200) from the tourist office.

Reykjavík's waterside **Ráðhús** (City Hall; Map p72; ☎ 563 2005; Vonarstræti; admission free; ☯ 8am-7pm Mon-Fri, noon-6pm Sat & Sun) is a postmodern construction that divides all who see it into 'hate-its' or 'love-its'. Concrete stilts, tinted windows and mossy walls make it look like a half-bird, half-building rising from Tjörnin. Inside there's a fabulous 3D map of Iceland – all mountains and volcanoes, with flecks of nothing-towns disappearing between the peaks. There's also a pleasant café, with free internet access for customers and an intimate view of the ducks.

Compared to the sky-scraping hulk of Hallgrímskirkja (p71), Iceland's main cathedral, **Dómkirkja** (Map p72; ☎ 520 9700; www.domkirkjan .is; Lækjargata 14a; admission free; ☯ 10am-5pm Mon-Fri) is a modest affair, but it played a vital role in the country's conversion to Lutheranism. The current building (from 1848) is small but perfectly proportioned, its plain wooden interior animated by glints of gold.

Iceland's first parliament, the Alþingi, was created at Þingvellir in AD 930. After losing its independence in the 13th century, the country gradually won back its autonomy, and the modern **Alþingi** (Map p72; ☎ 563 0500; www.althingi.is; Túngata) moved into the current basalt building in 1881; a stylish glass-and-stone annexe was completed in 2002. You're welcome to attend **sessions** (☯ 3pm Mon, 1.30pm Tue & Wed, 10.30am Thu Oct-May) when parliament is sitting.

Popular with skateboarders, the stone square **Ingólfstorg** is notable for its billowing **steam vent**, where pent-up geothermal energy finds a release.

REYKJAVÍK'S ARCHITECTURE

The old town's mid-18th-century houses demonstrate the Icelandic talent for adaptation. In a country devoid of many building materials, most are made from driftwood (which floated from Siberia and South America) and covered in sheets of corrugated tin to protect them from the elements. Even churches, such as the **Fríkirkjan í Reykjavík** (1899; Map p72), were made the same way. By happy chance, this light construction method also makes the buildings pretty earthquake-proof.

Building houses from scraps didn't mean that artistic impulses were squashed – check out **A-Hús** (Map p72), from 1906, one of the city's finest examples of wood-and-tin architecture. Its tall turrets are topped by swirling arabesques, and the wooden struts supporting the balconies are carved with whales.

As the country rallied from almost 700 years of deprivation, a new pride worked its way into Iceland's public architecture. Basalt became a nationalist symbol – the country's parliament building, the **Alþingi** (above), is built from blocks of the stuff, and **Hallgrímskirkja** (p71) flaunts its basalt columns with unquenchable pride.

Today, the city is snowballing. Much of the current growth is an ugly suburban sprawl, but there are some genuinely startling constructions going up, such as the new avant-garde harbourside concert hall, due for completion in 2010.

Some of the city's oldest houses line the square. **Fálkahús** (Map p72; Hafnarstræti 1) has a particularly interesting history – it's where Icelandic falcons were kept before being shipped off to Europe's noblemen.

Reykjavík is littered with fascinating statues and abstract monuments, but it's Jón Gunnar Árnason's shiplike **Sun-Craft** (Map p72) sculpture that seems to catch visitors' imaginations. Its situation – facing the sea and snow-capped Esja – may have something to do with it.

Horse Riding

Trotting through lava fields under the midnight sun is an unforgettable experience. Horse farms around Reykjavík offer tours for all ages and experiences, and can collect you from your hotel. Most operate at least some of their trips year-round.

Two long-established companies offer everything from 1½- to two-hour outings (Ikr3000 to Ikr5000), to nine-day tours into the wilderness, including riding and rafting/whale-watching/Blue Lagoon combinations (Ikr7500 to Ikr10,000):

Eldhestar (☎ 480 4800; www.eldhestar.is; Vellir) Near Hveragerði.

Íshestar (☎ 555 7000; www.ishestar.is; Sörlaskeiði 26, Hafnarfjörður)

There are also two farms, based near the eastern suburb of Mosfellsbær, that offer rides in the area round Halldór Laxness' former home:

Ferðahestar (☎ 517 7000; www.travelhorse.is; Viðigrund, Mosfellsbær)

Laxnes (☎ 566 6179; www.laxnes.is; Mosfellsbær)

Cycling

See p97 for information.

REYKJAVÍK FOR CHILDREN

Icelanders love their kids, but they're treated as small adults rather than as a separate species; consequently, there are only a handful of entertainments aimed specifically at children. However, kids get discount rates at the theatre and cinema, and can travel free or at discount rates on many excursions.

The **Family Fun Park & Zoo** (Fjölskyldu-og húsdýragarðsins; Map pp68-9; ☎ 575 7800; www.mu.is; Laugardalur; adult/5-12yr Ikr500/450, 1-/10-/20-ride tickets Ikr170/1500/2800; 🕙 10am-6pm mid-May–mid-Aug, to 5pm mid-Aug–mid-May; ♿) is the city's only attraction especially for (youngish) children. Don't expect lions and tigers; think seals, foxes

and farm animals with slightly dismal enclosures. The family park section is jolly, with a mini-racetrack, child-size bulldozers, a giant trampoline, boats and kids' fairground rides. Future plans include an Imax cinema and an aquarium, but at the time of writing building work hadn't started.

Water babies will go mad for Reykjavík's wonderful geothermal **swimming pools** (p71), particularly Laugardalslaug and Árbæjarlaug. **Icelandic horse-riding** (left) is a great confidence-booster for novice riders – the horses have calm temperaments…and aren't too high off the ground. The 18-lane bowling-hall **Keiluhöllin** (Map pp68-9; ☎ 511 5300; www.keiluhollin.is; Öskjuhlíð; disco bowling 1/2/3 games Ikr720/1270/1820, other evening & weekend times 1/2/3 games Ikr600/1150/1490, cheaper weekdays; 🕙 11am-midnight Sun-Thu, to 2am Fri & Sat) has arcade games and pool tables; its weekend **disco-bowling sessions** (🕙 11am-3pm Sat & Sun) may appeal to teenyboppers. In winter, **skating** (p76) is a popular family activity.

The best museums for children are the open-air **Árbæjarsafn** (p76), where they can zoom around in a safe green space; and the **Saga Museum** (p75), which will appeal to Viking fans. The **National Museum** (p75) has dressing-up clothes, and puzzles and games relating to the museum's collections.

Over in Hafnarfjörður, take younger children hunting for elves on a **Hidden Worlds tour** (p103).

QUIRKY REYKJAVÍK

Held in a huge industrial building by the harbour, the weekend **Kolaportið Flea Market** (Map p72; Geirsgata; 🕙 11am-5pm Sat & Sun) is a Reykjavík institution and definitely worth a visit. Browse through piles of second-hand clothes, music, antiques and children's toys, or pick up Icelandic fish delicacies including cubes of *hákarl*.

For an Icelandic joke, at the beginning of Bankastræti look north towards the detached building **Stórnarráðið** (Map p72), which contains the prime minister's offices. The statues outside are of Hannes Hafstein, leader of the first home-rule government, and King Christian IX presenting Iceland with its constitution. If you get the right perspective, you can recreate a shot from the cult movie *101 Reykjavík* – the king stuffing the constitution up Hafstein's rear.

Voodoo is generally associated with the steamy Mississippi delta, but **Nornabúðin** (The Witch Shop; Map p72; ☎ 552 3540; Vesturgata 12; 🕙 2-6pm

Mon-Sat) sells Icelandic voodoo dolls – perfect for wreaking havoc on your enemies, although you may need a dictionary to work out what damage you're doing.

On the same street is **Kirsuberjatréð** (Cherry Tree; Map p72; ☎ 562 8990; www.kirs.is; Vesturgata 4; ⊙ 10am-6pm Mon-Fri, 11am-3pm Sat), a collective of women artists selling weird and wonderful designs – fish-skin handbags, woven music boxes and (our favourite) beautiful coloured bowls made from radish slices!

TOURS
Walking Tours
Reykjavík is perfect for exploring under your own steam, but if you'd like a little guidance, the tourist office sells themed brochures (Ikr200). They're easy to follow; the 'City Centre Walk' is probably the most interesting, followed by 'The City Parks' and 'The City Statues'.

The 1½- to two-hour **Original Haunted Walk of Reykjavík** (Map p72; ☎ 696 7474; www.hauntediceland .is; adult/under-12yr Ikr1500/free; ⊙ 8pm Jun–mid-Sep), which leaves from outside the main tourist office, is a new and extremely successful attraction. The walks are quite long, but the enthusiasm of Jónas the guide makes them very enjoyable. He manages to combine the ghost stories – gruesome, sad or just plain strange – with Viking history, environmentalism and visits to homes of the hidden people. The tour finishes, as all ghost walks should, in a twilight graveyard…

Menningarfylgd Birnu (☎ 862 8031; www.birna.is; per person Ikr4000, minimum 2 people; ⊙ by arrangement) aims to show visitors around Reykjavík 'the cat's way'! But rather than go yowling on a dustbin, Birna leads people on 1½-hour cultural tours, dropping in on artists' studios, local characters and places of culinary interest, as well as the mainstream sights.

Bus Tours
Some associate coach tours with over-60s trips to the seaside, but a day-long bus tour from Reykjavík is one of the best ways to see some of the country's spectacular natural wonders. They're also good if you want to combine sightseeing with snowmobiling, horse riding, kayaking, rafting and other exhilarating activities.

SUGGESTED TOURS FROM REYKJAVÍK

Destination/Activity	Price	Season
Diving/snorkelling at Þingvallavatn	Ikr24,500/12,500	year-round
Geysir & Gullfoss, plus horse riding	Ikr9400-9800	year-round
Golden Circle (Þingvellir, Geysir, Gullfoss)	Ikr6200-7000	year-round
Hekla volcano	Ikr22,700	Jul-Sep
Landmannalaugar geothermal area	Ikr9500-11,000	Jul & Aug
Exploring a lava tunnel	Ikr6200-13,300	year-round
Northern Lights spotting	Ikr3500-6000	Oct-Mar
Rafting on the Hvítá river	Ikr13,300	May–mid-Sep
Reykjanes peninsula & Blue Lagoon	Ikr5800-6200	year-round
Snæfellsnes coast	Ikr11,900	mid-May–mid-Sep
Snæfellsnes coast & boat ride or whale watching	Ikr13,500- 13,900	Jun-Aug
Snowmobiling	Ikr15,500-16,500	year-round
South coast	Ikr9500-9900	year-round
Þórsmörk nature reserve	Ikr9500	Jun–mid-Sep
Quad biking	Ikr15,000	year-round

Tours need to be booked in advance (either at the tourist office, at your hotel or hostel, or directly with the company) and they may be cancelled if there are insufficient numbers or if the weather turns rancid. Young children generally can travel free or at discounted rates.

Three of the biggest and best tour operators:

Iceland Excursions (Allrahanda; Map pp68-9; ☎ 540 1313; www.icelandexcursions.is; Höfðatún 12) The cheapest bus-tour operator, with comprehensive day trips plus horse riding, whale watching, underground explorations, diving, and self-drive holidays.

IcelandTotal (Map pp68-9; ☎ 585 4300; www.iceland total.com; Lágmúli 4) IcelandTotal is part of the Icelandair group, and can organise a huge range of winter and summer bus trips, activities and special-interest tours, such as sagas, bird-watching, fishing and cycling.

Reykjavík Excursions (Kynnisferðir; Map pp68-9; ☎ 562 1011; www.re.is; BSÍ bus terminal, Vatnsmýrarvegur 10) The most popular bus-tour operator has summer and winter programmes. Extras include horse riding, snowmobiling, and themed tours tying in with festivals.

The boxed text opposite shows examples of places to visit and things to try, with approximate prices and seasonal availability. We recommend bringing a bag of cash and giving them all a whirl! See p51 for a rundown on major activities available in Iceland.

Super-Jeep & Supertruck Tours

If you fancy bigger wheels and a little more exclusivity, you can go sightseeing by super-Jeep or supertruck instead of by bus. Most of the places and activities listed in the previous section are on offer (prices are at least double).

Activity Group (☎ 580 9900; www.activity.is) Super-Jeep and supertruck activity and sightseeing tours.

Atours (☎ 517 4455; www.amazingtours.is) Super-Jeep trips to the Golden Circle, Landmannalaugar, Þórsmörk and the south coast, plus the option of adding on outdoor activities.

FESTIVALS & EVENTS

Also see the list of national festivals (p318), most of which are celebrated with gleeful enthusiasm in Reykjavík. For forthcoming live music, see www.musik.is.

February

Winter Lights In mid- or late February Reykjavík celebrates the end of winter with cultural events, a mini food festival, and lots of illuminated buildings.

May

Listahátíð í Reykjavík (Reykjavík Arts Festival; www .artfest.is) Held from mid-May every year, this popular three-week event features films, dance, theatre, concerts and art exhibitions from Iceland and around the world.

Rite of Spring (www.riteofspring.is) A new world-music festival featuring everything from jazz to folk and blues.

August

Gay Pride (www.gaypride.is) This is Iceland's second-biggest festival – thousands of people parade carnival-style through the streets of Reykjavík on the third weekend of the month, with open-air concerts in the city centre.

Reykjavík Marathon (www.marathon.is) Held on a Saturday in mid-August, with shorter distances and fun runs for those who like to grit their teeth less.

Menningarnott (Culture Night; www.menningarnott.is) Iceland's biggest festival is this evening of cultural events that follows the marathon – over a third of Iceland attends. It includes musicians on every street corner, citywide cultural and artistic performances, much drunkenness, and a massive fireworks display.

Tango on ICEland (www.tango.is) Tango has really gripped the Icelandic soul. This three-day annual event at the end of August is composed of dance workshops and performances.

September

Jazzhátíð Reykjavíkur (www.jazz.is) The five-day Reykjavík Jazz Festival at the end of September attracts a range of local and international talent.

Reykjavík International Film Festival (www.filmfest .is) Also at the end of the month, this is a 10-day celebration of art-house films, with screenings across the city and talks by Icelandic and international directors – for example, this year's guests include Atom Egoyan, Yoko Ono and Aleksandr Sokurov, director of *Russian Ark*.

October

Iceland Airwaves (www.icelandairwaves.com) This four-day event in mid-October is one of the world's coolest music festivals. Homegrown talent and international DJs and bands play their souls out in various intimate venues around the city; past acts have included Sigur Rós, Fat Boy Slim, the Flaming Lips and Hot Chip.

SLEEPING

Reykjavík has loads of accommodation choices, with midrange guesthouses and business-class hotels predominating. In July and August accommodation fills up quickly; reservations are strongly advised. Most places open year-round apart from Christmas (we've noted where accommodation is summer only), and offer 20% to 45% discounts from October to April.

Budget

Reykjavík camp site (Map pp68–9; ☎ 568 6944; www
.reykjavikcampsite.is; Sundlaugavegur 34; sites per person
Ikr800; ☺ mid-May–mid-Sep) The only camping
option in the city (right next door to the city
hostel) gets very busy in summer, but with
space for 650 people in its three fields, you're
likely to find a place. Facilities include free
showers, bike hire, a kitchen and barbecue
area, and a reception desk selling gas bottles
and postcards; you can share the hostel's internet access and laundry room, but emphati-
cally *not* its kitchens. From June to August
a direct bus runs to the BSÍ bus terminal at
7.30am every morning.

ourpick Reykjavík City Hostel (Map pp68–9; ☎ 553
8110; www.hostel.is; Sundlaugavegur 34; sb 6-bed dm Ikr1800,
sb 4- or 6-bed dm with bathroom Ikr2600, sb bed in 2-bed
room with bathroom Ikr3700) Reykjavík's eco-friendly
youth hostel sleeps 170 people and has excellent facilities. There are three guest kitchens,
a library, four internet-linked computers, free
wi-fi, a laundry room (Ikr300 per washer/
dryer) and bike hire, as well as regular film
shows, pancake nights and pub crawls. Its
lovely staff can book trips and the airport bus.
The downsides are that it's a good 2km out of
town; and screaming, door-slamming school
kids may drive you to murderous despair. In
summer and at weekends, make early reservations or bring a tent.

The bus from the airport should drop you
off here directly. Bus 14 (Ikr250, every 20 to
30 minutes) runs to Hlemmur and Lækjartorg
in the city centre.

NIGHT-NIGHT, SLEEP TIGHT...

Restless sleepers may struggle in Iceland.
Despite the 'light nights', a surprising
number of hostels, guesthouses and hotels have transparent curtains, flimsy blinds
or nothing at all across the windows. You
might look a fool, but an eye mask will cut
out that satanic 24-hour sunshine.

If you're staying in a city-centre hotel,
something to consider is weekend noise –
drunken partygoers falling out of bars and
clubs can be irritating if you're desperate for
sleep before that 7am excursion. Wear ear
plugs, choose a room that doesn't overlook
bar-lined streets or public squares, or decide
that 'if you can't beat them, join them' and
head for the nearest pub!

Central Guesthouse (Map pp68–9; ☎ 552 2822; www
.central-guesthouse.com; Bólstaðarhlíð 8; sb/s/d/tr Ikr2500/
4700/6100/8700; ☐) This welcoming place is
about 10 minutes' walk from the BSÍ bus terminal and Perlan. Rooms are light, trim and
uncomplicated; the attic room, with sloping
ceilings and private balcony, has the most
character. Breakfast isn't included, but there's
a guest kitchen.

Litli Ljóti Andarunginn (Map p72; ☎ 552 2410; www
.andarunginn.is; Lækjargata 6b; s/d without bathroom
Ikr6900/7900) 'The Ugly Duckling' restaurant has
a few simple rooms overhead. They're not a
bad price for such a convenient central location but are in need of some tender DIY! One
has a private bathroom (Ikr8900); the others
have washbasins. Noise from the restaurant-
bar below may disturb light sleepers.

Salvation Army Guesthouse (Gistiheimili Hjálpræði-
shersins; Map p72; ☎ 561 3203; www.guesthouse.is; Kirkju-
stræti 2; sb Ikr2500, s/d/tr Ikr5500/8000/10,500) The rooms
at this pleasant Christian guesthouse are small,
functional and frill-free, but dorms are more
spacious. Although it doesn't have the whizzy
extras offered by the city hostel, its superb
location makes it a attractive alternative – step
outside and the whole of Reykjavík is at your
feet. There's a backpackery atmosphere and
a guest kitchen, and it's extra-cheap (private
room prices include breakfast).

Midrange

GUESTHOUSES

Reykjavík is packed with *gistiheimili* (guesthouses) and there are new places opening
every year. Most are in converted houses, so
rooms often have shared bathrooms, kitchens and TV lounges. Some offer sleeping-bag
accommodation.

Guesthouse Butterfly (Map p72; ☎ 894 1864; www
.kvasir.is/butterfly; Ránargata 8a; s/d/apt from Ikr6900/
8900/13,900; ☺ Jun–Aug; ☐) On a quiet residential street within fluttering distance of the
centre, Butterfly has neat, simply furnished
rooms. There's a guest kitchen and wi-fi access, and the friendly Icelandic-Norwegian
owners make you feel right at home. The top
floor has two self-contained apartments with
kitchen and balcony.

Álfhóll Guesthouse (Map p72; ☎ 898 1838; www
.islandia.is/alf; Ránargata 8; s/d/tr Ikr6800/9000/11,000, 2-
to 6-person apt Ikr12,000–18,000; ☺ Jun–Aug) Almost
identical in feel and facilities to Butterfly is
this neighbouring guesthouse, run by a family
of elf enthusiasts.

Galtafell Guesthouse (Map pp68-9; ☎ 699 2525; www
.galtafell.com; Laufásvegur 46; s/d/apt Jun-Sep from Ikr7900/
8900/16,900, Oct-May from Ikr6000/6900/12,000; ✗) Recommended by readers, this new guesthouse
has a great location – in a quiet, well-to-do
suburb within easy walking distance of town.
The four spruce apartments each contain a
fully equipped kitchen, a cosy seating area and
a separate bedroom, and there are also three
doubles with access to a guest kitchen. The
only drawback is that they're basement rooms,
so no views of anything but the pavement!

Guesthouse Andrea (Map pp68-9; ☎ 552 5515; www
.aurorahouse.is; Njarðargata 43; sb/s/d Ikr2900/7000/9000;
☑ mid-May–mid-Sep; ▣) Friendly Siggi runs this
hidden place, tucked down a side street in a
tranquil residential area. Its five private rooms
have smart wooden floors and are ideal for
self-caterers; each has a sink, a cooker, a fridge
and a tiny two-seater table.

Gistiheimilið Aurora (Map pp68-9; Freyjugata 24; ☑ mid-
May–mid-Sep; ▣) Just around the corner from the
Andrea, this place is also run by Siggi. Room
33, with a balcony and sea view, is the best
(the sleeping-bag accommodation is a little
cramped). The non-sleeping-bag prices include breakfast, and there's an internet computer plus wifi access.

Gistiheimilið 101 (Map pp68-9; ☎ 562 6101; www
.iceland101.com; Laugavegur 101; s/tw/tr/q Ikr7300/9600/
11,900/13,900) Slightly cheaper than the 4th
Floor Hotel on the floor above (especially as
a breakfast buffet is included), these rooms in
a converted office building are good value for
such a central location. White is the dominant
colour, with startling splashes of red here and
there. All rooms have washbasins.

Guesthouse Baldursbrá (Map pp68-9; ☎ 552 6646;
baldursbra@centrum.is; Laufásvegur 41; s/d Ikr6700/9700;
▣) This great little guesthouse, on a quiet
street close to Tjörnin and the BSÍ bus station, has helpful owners and decent-sized,
comfy rooms, all with washbasins. Additional
facilities are admirable – a sociable sitting
room–TV lounge, wi-fi, and a private garden
with a fab hot pot, sauna and barbecue. Rates
include breakfast.

Guesthouse Óðinn (Map p72; ☎ 861 3400; www
.odinnreykjavik.com; Óðinnsgata 9; s/d/tr from Ikr7600/
9800/12,200; ▣) New owners took over this
guesthouse in April 2005, bringing extra
touches (like the handsome breakfast room
with sea views) to this long-standing favourite. You'll find simple white rooms here with
dashes of colourful artwork, and an excellent

buffet breakfast is included in the rates. Some
en-suite rooms are available.

Gistiheimilið Ísafold (Map p72; ☎ 561 2294; isafold@
itn.is; Bárugata 11; s/d from Ikr7300/9800) This recommended, rambling old house (a former rehab
centre/bakery/bookshop) lies in peaceful old
Reykjavík. Sun-filled bedrooms contain washbasins and rustic beds; there are tea-making
facilities in the lounge; and solemn Icelandic
dolls keep an eye on diners in the attic breakfast
room. At the nearby annexe (Bárugata 20), all
accommodation comes with private bathrooms
(around Ikr1000 extra).

our pick **4th Floor Hotel** (Map pp68-9; ☎ 511
3030; www.4thfloorhotel.is; Laugavegur 101; s/d/tr without bathroom Ikr7900/9900/11,900, d/tr/ste with bathroom Ikr11,900/13,900/15,900, d with balcony Ikr11,900;
▣) Close to Hlemmur bus station, the 17
squeaky-clean rooms here (most with shared
bathrooms) have great accoutrements – desk,
fridge, kettle, TV, washbasin, wifi access…and
duvets printed with zebra stripes! Four have
sea views, and two have balconies. The owners
are very helpful, there's a guest sitting room,
and breakfast (Ikr950) may be available.

Bolholt Guesthouse (Map pp68-9; ☎ 517 4050; www
.bolholt.is; Bolholt 6; d/f Ikr10,500/13,900; ▣) This new
guesthouse tries to tempt you 1.5km out of
the city centre by offering large 'studio' rooms
with great kitchenettes, satellite TV, and free
laundry and internet access. It's all very smart,
clean and modern, and the family rooms are
especially good value. The big, busy road outside calms down at night.

our pick **Gistiheimilið Sunna** (Map pp68-9; ☎ 511
5570; www.sunna.is; Þórsgata 26; s/d from Ikr8400/10,700;
P ✗ ▣) Rooms at this guesthouse are sim-
ple and sunny with honey-coloured parquet
floors, and several at the front have good views
of Hallgrímskirkja. You can choose to pay
extra for a private bathroom. Families are welcomed; there's a handful of brand-new studio
apartments for one to four people (Ikr13,300
to Ikr22,500). Breakfast – with home-baked
bread – is included.

Garður Inn (Map pp68-9; ☎ 562 4000, 551 5900; www
.inns-of-iceland.com; Hringbraut; sb dm/s/tw Ikr2400/4400/3400,
s/d Ikr8300/10,900; ☑ Jun-late Aug; P) In summer
once the students have left, the university
campus offers visitors utilitarian rooms with
shared bathrooms. The cheapest sleeping-bag
accommodation is in 16-person dorms. Single/
double rates include breakfast.

Domus Guesthouse (Map p72; ☎ 561 1200; www
.domusguesthouse.is; Hverfisgata 45; sb/s/d Ikr2900/9500/

11,300) Once the Norwegian embassy, Domus's rooms have stately old proportions but vaunt modern touches such as radio alarms and TVs. The 1st-floor rooms are best, with hardwood floors, leather sofas and artwork on the walls (none has a private bathroom). Breakfast is included in accommodation above sleeping-bag level, and there's a kitchen.

Alba Guesthouse (Map pp68-9; ☎ 552 9800; www.alba .is; Eskihlíð 3; s/d/tr Ikr9000/11,500/14,500; P ☒ ☐) In a quiet residential area fairly close to Perlan, Alba is a peaceful choice. It's relatively new, with fresh, modern, attractive rooms (shared bathrooms) and pleasant staff; even in the short time it's been open plenty of guests have returned. There's free wi-fi and a garden, and breakfast is included.

Travel-Inn Guesthouse (Map pp68-9; ☎ 561 3553; www .dalfoss.is; Sóleyjargata 31; s/d Ikr10,500/12,300; ☒ ☐) A short walk from the BSÍ bus terminal, this guesthouse was recommended by a reader largely due to its dynamic host Einar! Besides the exuberant service, rooms are basic but large and bright, and breakfast is included in the rates. Extras include a sauna in the basement, free wireless internet access, and bike hire.

our pick **Tower Guesthouse** (Map p72; ☎ 896 6694; www.tower.is; Grettisgata 6; d Ikr9900-13,900, 1-4–person apt Ikr18,900-32,900) This castlelike place has a sweeping spiral staircase and elegant apartments, and you can stargaze from the rooftop Jacuzzi. The guesthouse is popular with gay travellers, and there's the odd phallus-shaped plant pot around, but everyone is welcome. Breakfast isn't provided, but there are kitchen facilities.

Gistihúsið Hvíti Svanurinn (Map p72; ☎ 533 4101; www.whitesvanur.com; Vatnsstígur 11; s/d/tr/q incl breakfast Ikr12,100/18,500/21,200/28,800; ☺ May-Sep; ☐) The brand-new White Swan Guesthouse, tucked down a quiet side street near the city centre, may not look much from outside, but it's a damn decent choice. Its 23 fresh-looking rooms all come with TVs, internet connection points and space-age coffee machines, and are decorated in inoffensive Scandinavian style (pale-wood floors, blond furnishings…oh, and fluorescent-green bedside lamps!). They're remarkable for their size – these must be the largest guesthouse rooms in Reykjavík.

APARTMENTS

Apartments in Reykjavík are often very good value.

Forsæla Guesthouse (Map p72; ☎ 551 6046; www .apartmenthouse.is; Grettisgata 33b; s/d Ikr8000/11,000, 2-/3-/4-person apt Ikr14,000/17,000/20,000, house Ikr40,000; ☒) This is a really lovely option in Reykjavík's conservation area. Star of the show is the 100-year-old wood-and-tin house, for four to eight people, which comes with all the old beams and tasteful mod-cons you could want. Three apartments have small but cosy bedrooms and sitting rooms, fully equipped kitchens, and washing machines. There's a minimum three-night stay, and the friendly owners prefer prebookings; B&B may be possible.

our pick **Three Sisters** (Þrjár Systur; Map p72; ☎ 565 2181; www.threesisters.is; Ránargata 16; 1-/2-person apt €98/148, family apt €210; ☺ Jun-Aug; ☒ ☐) A twinkly eyed former fisherman runs the Three Sisters, a scrumptious townhouse in old Reykjavík, now divided into eight studio apartments. Comfy counterpart beds are flanked by old-fashioned easy chairs and state-of-the-art flatscreen TVs. Each room comes with a cute fully equipped kitchen. A second building has sleeping-bag accommodation in six-bed dorms (around Ikr2600).

Room with a View (Map p72; ☎ 552 7262; www .roomwithaview.is; Laugavegur 18; 1-/2-/3-/4-bedroom apt around Ikr12,900/25,900/29,900/39,900) This ridiculously central apartment hotel offers one- to four-bedroom apartments, decorated in Scandinavian style and with private bathrooms, kitchenettes, CD players, TVs and washing machines. Half have those eponymous sea and city views, and most have access to a Jacuzzi. They're very varied – check the website for a wealth of details.

HOTELS

Many of Reykjavík's midrange hotels are places built for and favoured by business travellers, and the places can be pretty bland. Rooms have private bathrooms unless mentioned otherwise.

Hótel Frón (Map p72; ☎ 511 4666; www.hotelfron.is; Laugavegur 22a; s/d/studio/2-bed apt Ikr11,900/13,900/14,900/ 21,900) If you can overlook the city's moodiest receptionists, this bright blue hotel has lots in its favour – particularly its excellent location overlooking Laugavegur, and stylish apartments in the new wing. They come with TV, safe, hardwood floors, modern bathrooms and well-equipped kitchenettes (cooker, fridge and microwave) – try to bag one with a balcony. Older rooms are less inspiring. Breakfast costs Ikr800, and there's wireless internet access.

Metropolitan Hotel (Map p72; ☎ 511 1155; www .metropolitan.is; Ránargata 4a; s/tw/tr Ikr11,600/15,600/18,800;

🖳) In the peaceful old town, within a few blocks of the city's core, the Metropolitan received a top-to-toe makeover in 2004. This couldn't alter the small size of its 31 rooms, but they certainly look much better! Facilities stretch to TVs, mini-fridges and wireless internet access (for a fee), and there's a decent buffet breakfast. Essentially, this is a fairly basic three-star hotel, given a shine by its good location and friendly staff.

Hótel Leifur Eiríksson (Map pp8-9; ☎ 562 0800; www .hotelleifur.is; Skólavörðustígur 45; s/d/tr Ikr14,200/17,400/20,500) This hotel glories in one of the best locations in Reykjavík: it's slap on the end of arty Skólavörðustígur, and half its 47 rooms have inspiring views of Hallgrímskirkja. They're fairly small and plain (with blue carpeting, narrow beds, TVs and phones), but you're paying for the hotel's coordinates rather than its interior design. There's no lift, but there is free coffee downstairs.

Hótel Plaza (Map p72; ☎ 590 1400; www.plaza.is; Aðalstræti 4; s/d Ikr15,600/19,500; P 🖳 ⑤) The 104-room Plaza has the feel of a smaller, family-run affair. Rooms have all mod-cons (digital TVs, kettles, bathrobes and free broadband connections) and come in two styles. Half are modern and businesslike, with navy furnishings and clean-lined wooden furniture – most look onto bustling Ingólfstorg. Those in the new extension feature antique beams and a softer beige décor, although some are a little dark. The superior double (Ikr25,700) on the 6th floor has superb views of the square, sea and mountains from its glassed-in balcony. Buffet breakfast is included.

Fosshótel Barón (Map pp8-9; ☎ 562 3204; www .fosshotel.is; Barónsstígur 2-4; standard s/d Ikr16,200/20,900, 1-/2-bed apt Ikr23,900/27,900; P 🖳) The corporate chain-hotel Barón is fairly central, and its 4th and 5th floors have marvellous views of the sea and Esja. There are 14 apartments with cooking facilities. Laptop users have free wi-fi coverage, or there's internet access in the lobby.

Park Inn Ísland (Map pp8-9; ☎ 595 7000; www.reykjavik .rezidorparkinn.com; Ármúli 9; 🖳 ⑤) Standard-issue rooms have good facilities, and some even manage to break free of the chain-hotel mould. Go for ones with kitchenettes, or stunning panoramic views of Reykjavík and the mountains. All have TV, telephone, minibar and tea-making kit. There's wi-fi throughout, guests (rather sweetly) get free admission to the city's swimming pools, and there's a filling hot-and-cold breakfast buffet.

our pick **CenterHotel Klöpp** (Map p72; ☎ 595 8520; www.centerhotels.is; Klapparstígur 26; s/d from 14,900/19,900; ⊗ closed 18-27 Dec; P 🖳) This is a very mellow place with a boutique-hotel spirit. The foyer–breakfast area sets the tone, with gleaming hardwood floors, genial staff and lots of light pouring in. Rooms are modest in size with minimal furnishings, but warm woody tones, textured mauve textiles and stylish slate-floored bathrooms give them a modern yet cosy feel. All contain TV, fridge, radio, kettle and internet connection point, and you can just about see the sea and mountains from the 5th-floor rooms.

CenterHotel Skjaldbreið (Map p72; ☎ 595 8510; www.centerhotels.is; Laugavegur 16; s/d from 14,900/19,900; ⊗ closed 18-27 Dec; 🖳) Once a dental surgery, this old townhouse has large rooms decorated with grandma-style orange-and-green chintz. If you can ignore the décor, it's ideally situated – right in the thick of things, with most rooms overlooking Laugavegur (the curved corner rooms are best). Rates include breakfast in a light and modern rooftop room. There are internet connections in the rooms, and a computer for guest use.

Top End
All rooms in this category have bathroom, TV, phone and minibar; rates rarely include breakfast!

Hótel Reykjavík (Map pp8-9; ☎ 514 7000; www.hotel reykjavik.is; Rauðarárstígur 37; s/d from Ikr17,200/22,500; P 🖳 ⑤) In a commercial area close to the Hlemmur bus station, the Hótel Reykjavík is a no-nonsense business hotel that offers decent rates. Many of its respectably sized rooms have been Ikea-ified recently, with hardwood floors and new fixtures – TVs, mini-fridges, phones, wireless internet access and tea-making facilities. A good buffet breakfast is included, and there's a cosy, classy steak restaurant.

our pick **Hótel Óðinsvé** (Map p72; ☎ 511 6200; www.hotelodinsve.is; Þórsgata 1; s/d from Ikr16,900/22,900; 🖳) A boutique hotel with bags of personality, Óðinsvé contains 43 sun-drenched rooms with wooden floors, original artwork and classic furnishings. They're all very different – some are split-level, some have balconies and many have bathtubs – but only room 117 has a resident ghost! The restaurant is run by Siggi Hall, Iceland's most famous TV chef, with Icelandic-Mediterranean fusion dishes taking precedence.

Hótel Reykjavík Centrum (Map p72; ☎ 514 6000; www.hotelcentrum.is; Aðalstræti 16; s/d from Ikr20,700/25,900; ⓖ) This central hotel has striking architecture – mezzanines and a glass roof unite two buildings, giving the whole place a spry, light feel. Its 89 neatly proportioned rooms come in two styles – 'traditional', with patterned wallpaper and white-painted furniture, and 'deluxe', with leather seats and a more contemporary feel. Both have safes, minibars, pay TVs (with films to order), tea-making facilities and wi-fi internet access.

Radisson SAS 1919 Hotel (Map p72; ☎ 599 1000; www.1919.reykjavik.radissonsas.com; Pósthússtræti 2; standard/ deluxe d Ikr20,900/27,600; ⌨ ⓖ) Although this is part of a large chain, the catchily named Radisson SAS 1919 Hotel is a boutique place with plenty of style. Attractive rooms sport wooden floors, large beds, flatscreen TVs and wireless access. Keep walking up the carved iron stairwells to the 4th floor and you reach the large, comfy suites (rooms 414 and 412). Other bonuses include a fantastic location, a gym, a restaurant and the cool Salt Lounge Bar.

Hótel Nordica (Map pp68-9; ☎ 444 5000; www.icehotel .is; Suðurlandsbraut 2; s/d from Ikr25,100/27,900; ⓟ ⌨) Bring your autograph book to the Nordica, Icelandair's huge flagship hotel – it's where visiting pop stars often stay. Cool Scandinavian chic oozes from every part, with amenities such as 24-hour room service, gym, spa (Ikr2500), and the gourmet restaurant Vox (see p88). Rooms are decorated in restful shades of cream and mocha; those on the upper floors have super sea views. Rates exclude breakfast (an extra Ikr1500). The hotel's about 2km from the city centre, but it runs a free city-centre shuttle service.

ourpick **Hótel Borg** (Map p72; ☎ 551 1440; www.hotel borg.is; Pósthússtræti 9-11; s/d/ste Ikr23,500/29,500/45,000; ⌨) This striking 1930s Art Deco palace is the most characterful of Iceland's hotels – it's like stepping back in time. A copper-and-wood elevator rattles up to individually designed rooms, decorated with antique furniture but complete with all mod cons, and bathrooms containing enormous showerheads. It's located in prime position on Austurvöllur square, and its newly renovated restaurant, Silfur, is run by the same people as the city's favourite Sjávarkjallarinn (p89). The buffet breakfast costs an extra Ikr1300.

101 Hotel (Map p72; ☎ 580 0101; www.101hotel .is; Hverfisgata 10; s/d/ste from Ikr27,900/29,900/37,900; ⌨ ⓖ) Reykjavík's newest boutique hotel is

devilishly divine. Its sensuous rooms – with yielding downy beds, iPod sound docks and Bose speakers, rich wooden floors, and glass-walled showers – may mean you skip the bars and opt for a night in instead. A spa with masseurs, a small gym and a glitterati restaurant-bar add to the opulence. Some people have been underwhelmed by the service, but all in all this is one of the city's sexiest places to stay.

EATING

Reykjavík's eateries vary from hot-dog stands to world-class restaurants. Two things are consistent: high quality, and high prices. For the types of eatery and opening hours, see p60. Reykjavík's dining places are found mainly along Laugavegur, Hverfisgata and also Austurstræti.

Restaurants
ASIAN

Nuðluhúsið (Map p72; ☎ 552 2400; Vitastígur 10; mains from Ikr900; ☷ 11.30am-9pm Mon-Fri, 5-9pm Sat & Sun) City workers flock to this good-value Thai place for spicy lunchtime hits of spring rolls, curry and a huge selection of noodle dishes. There are a few basic tables, plus a handy takeaway.

Ning's (Map pp68-9; ☎ 588 9899; Suðurlandsbraut 6; mains Ikr1000-1700; ☷ 11.30am-10pm) A mouthwatering smell of frying pork greets you at this Chinese fast-food restaurant, handy for the City Hostel. There's a good, cheap menu of noodles and stir-fries, and the cooking is MSG-free. The set lunch is very popular at lunchtime, or there's a takeaway counter.

Krua Thai (Map p72; ☎ 561 0039; www.kruathai .is; Tryggvagata 14; mains Ikr990-1900; ☷ noon-9.30pm Mon-Sat, 6-9.30pm Sun) Look beyond the simple interior to the tasty food: here you'll find genuine recipes, popular with Thai residents of Reykjavík. The glossy photo-menu shows soups, spicy salads, curries and stir-fries; you order at the counter, and generous, freshly-cooked dishes appear looking just like they do in the snaps.

Maru (Map p72; ☎ 511 4440; www.maru.is; Aðalstræti 12; Ikr1800-3000; ☷ 5.30-10pm Sun-Thu, to 11pm Fri & Sat) Sushi is the focus of this stylish restaurant, which uses fresh Icelandic fish to create dainty Japanese dishes. It also serves up all manner of miso soups, rice-noodle dishes and *yakitori* (Japanese kebabs), and there's a pleasant amount of choice for vegetarians. Eat in with moonlike lampshades glowing overhead, or make use of the takeaway service.

INDIAN

our pick **Austur Indía Félagið** (Map p72; ☎ 552 1630; Hverfisgata 56; mains Ikr2200-3700; ☺ 6-10pm Sun-Thu, to 11pm Fri & Sat) The northernmost Indian restaurant in the world is an upmarket experience, with a minimalist interior and a select choice of sublime dishes (a favourite is the tandoori salmon). One of its finest features, though, is its lack of pretension – the atmosphere is relaxed and the service warm. Apparently Harrison Ford likes it – and who dares argue with Indy?

Indian Mango (Map p72; ☎ 551 7722; www.indian mango.is; cnr Frakkastígur & Grettisgata; mains Ikr1900-3000; ☺ 11am-10pm Mon-Sat) This new restaurant specialises in Goan food, serving beef, duck, fish and some veggie mains. Its chef – poached from a five-star restaurant – makes up light, spicy, delicious dishes. Its bestselling creation is an Icelandic-Indian hybrid completely unique to this restaurant – *svartfugl* (guillemot) marinaded in Indian spices (Ikr2000). The only downside is the furniture, crammed in higgledy-piggledy and creating a rather chaotic atmosphere.

ITALIAN

Hornið (Map p72; ☎ 551 3340; Hafnarstræti 15; pizzas Ikr1200-2000, mains Ikr1700-3000; ☺ 11.30am-11pm) There's an easy-going air at this bright Art Deco café-restaurant, with its warm terracotta tiles, weeping-fig plants and decently spaced tables. Pizzas are freshly made before your eyes, the prettily presented pasta meals will set you up for the day, and you can sample traditional Icelandic fish dishes.

Ristorante Ítalía (Map p72; ☎ 562 4630; www.italia .is; Laugavegur 11; dishes Ikr1700-3500; ☺ 11.30am-11.30pm) One of the better Italian options, this family-run place has a proper wood-fired pizza oven, and good pasta and *secondi piatti* (mains). It's a romantic option for a candle-lit dinner.

our pick **La Primavera** (Map p72; ☎ 561 8555; www .laprimavera.is; Austurstræti 9; mains Ikr1600-3650; ☺ noon-2.30pm & 6-10.30pm Mon-Fri, 6-10.30pm Sat & Sun) Pizza Hut it ain't. This is a cultivated eatery serving contemporary Italian dishes – the pastas, gnocchi and polenta are all homemade. The menu is select, with some imaginative combinations – for example, pan-fried scallops with pomegranate and lime.

STEAKHOUSES

Hereford Steakhouse (Map p72; ☎ 511 3350; www .hereford.is; Laugavegur 53b; mains Ikr2500-4000; ☺ 6-10pm) This modern 1st-floor steakhouse grills up top-class steaks (of beef, lamb, turkey, veal and whale), priced by weight and cut. You can pick from fillets, T-bones, rib eyes and entrecôtes, and watch as they're cooked at the grilling station in the centre of the dining room. There's a good red-wine list. [Whale meat served.]

Café Ópera (Map p72; ☎ 552 9499; www.cafeopera.is; Lækjargata 2; mains Ikr3000-5000; ☺ 5-10.30pm Mon-Thu, to 11.30pm Fri-Sun) Soothing Café Opera, based upstairs in an old merchant's house, occasionally has a piano player tickling the ivories. The house speciality is the entertaining 'Hot Rock Fantasy' – sizzling meat or fish steaks that you get to 'cook' yourself on slabs of mountain granite.

Argentína (Map p72; ☎ 551 9555; www.argentina.is; Barónsstígur 11a; mains Ikr3000-5000; ☺ 6-10.30pm Sun-Thu, to 11.30pm Fri & Sat) This dark, fiery steakhouse rightly prides itself on its succulent locally raised beef – the best red meat you'll eat in Reykjavík. It also serves tender char-grilled salmon, reindeer, lamb, pork and chicken, with a wine list to complement whatever choice you make.

GOURMET/ICELANDIC

Most upmarket restaurants (including those in the city's top hotels) take great national pride in presenting Icelandic ingredients in their finest possible glory. Gourmet menus generally feature *bacalao* (salt cod), smoked lamb and seafood, and more unusual dishes such as guillemot, puffin and reindeer. Also see Seafood, p88.

Lækjarbrekka (Map p72; ☎ 551 4430; www.laek jarbrekka.is; Bankastræti 2; mains Ikr2000-5000; ☺ 11am-11.30pm) This top-notch restaurant has built up its reputation over 20 years, cooking traditional Icelandic dishes (game, lobster, juicy pepper steak and mountain lamb) with half an eye on the tourist dollar. From June to August it puts on a high-quality fish buffet every evening from 6pm.

Perlan (Map pp68-9; ☎ 562 0200; www.perlan.is; Öskjuhlíð; mains Ikr3000-5000; ☺ from 6.30pm) Perched on top of the city's water tanks is the revolving restaurant Perlan, which spins at one sedate revolution every two hours. The views are superb, and, if you can tear your eyes away from the city-and-mountain vista, the grub (reindeer, lamb, flounder, guillemot) isn't bad either. [Whale meat served.]

our pick **Einar Ben** (Map p72; ☎ 511 5090; www .einarben.is; Ingólfstorg; mains Ikr2600-4500; ☺ 6-10pm Mon-Thu, to 11pm Fri-Sun) One of the city's finest restaurants, Einar Ben is frequented by diplomats and is renowned for its top-class service and gastronomical marvels. Dishes are Icelandic with a continental twist – think puffin terrine, and lamb Dijon with blueberries and thyme.

our pick **Vox** (Map pp68-9; ☎ 444 5050; www.vox restaurant.com; Suðurlandsbraut 2; mains Ikr3500-5500; ☺ 6-10pm) The head chef at the Hótel Nordica's five-star restaurant serves up superb seasonal dishes – think pink-footed goose with caramelised apples – and there's usually a veggie option. The waiters sometimes bring out extra little treats for you to try – for example their amazing 'invisible gazpacho'! The daytime bistro puts on a recommended Sunday-brunch hot buffet (Ikr2300/1150 for adults/children six to 12) – gorge on fruit, bread, shrimps, bacon, eggs, sausage and pancakes until you burst.

Skólabrú (Map p72; ☎ 562 4455; Skólabrú 1; mains Ikr2500-6000, 4-course gourmet menu Ikr8900; ☺ noon-2pm & 6-10pm Tue-Fri, 6-10pm Sat) The wonderfully cosy and romantic Skólabrú is in an old wood-and-tin house just off Austurvöllur. It specialises in Icelandic fare presented with a nouvelle cuisine–style perfection – langoustines on puff pastry, glazed breast of duck with vanilla sauce, and various lamb and fish creations. If you just can't choose, go for the 'surprise' menu (Ikr6900).

INTERNATIONAL

Café Victor (Map p72; ☎ 561 9555; www.cafévictor .is; Ingólfstorg; light meals Ikr790-1500, mains Ikr1300-3000; ☺ 11.30am-10pm) The Victor is a scruffy bar-bistro with a beery smell, reminiscent of an English pub (there's even an old red phone box and premiership footy matches). British families gravitate here for lunch or early-evening meals – English breakfast, burgers, nachos and pizza, or more substantial spare ribs and seafood. At weekends its large spaces fill with drinkers and it turns into a big, loud club.

Enrico's (Map p72; ☎ 552 0077; www.enricos.is; Laugavegur 3; lunch specials Ikr850-1300, evening mains Ikr1500-2700; ☺ 11.30am-11pm Sun-Thu, to 11.30pm Fri & Sat) Low-slung coffee tables and leather sofas line the windows, with a more classical set-up at the back for evening dining. Prices are lower than you might expect from the décor, and the wide-ranging world menu contains some stomach-pleasing items. Lunchtime soups, salads, noodles and sandwiches are particularly good value.

Askur Brasserie (Map pp68-9; ☎ 553 9700; www.askur .is; Suðurlandsbraut 4; mains Ikr2000-3500; ☺ 11.30am-10pm)

Close to the big hotels on Suðurlandsbraut, this relaxed family restaurant is popular with tourists and locals alike. Despite its noncentral location, it's wise to book on Friday and Saturday. There's a long menu of burgers, steaks, pasta, lamb, fish and sizzling fajitas, many of which come with soup and a free visit to the salad bar (loosen your belts). The weekday lunchtime buffet is good value at Ikr1590.

Apótek (Map p72; ☎ 575 7900; www.veitingar.is; Austurstræti 16; mains Ikr2300-4500; ☺ 11.30am-1pm Mon-Thu, to 11.30pm Fri & Sat, 3pm-midnight Sun) Apótek's cheerful café presents Asian food along with workaday staples such as ham sandwiches. The restaurant proper is all hard modern lines, softened slightly by velvet drapes and delicate Chinese-silk light shades. It's a little clinical, but the sophisticated Asian-Icelandic fusion dishes (such as grilled tuna with wasabi) are full of clean, sharp flavours.

our pick **Tapas Barinn** (Map p72; ☎ 551 2344; www .tapas.is; Vesturgata 3b; tapas plates from Ikr450; ☺ 5-11pm Sun-Thu, to 1am Fri & Sat) Indecisive types will have a tough time at this outstanding tapas bar, with over 50 different dishes on the menu – a thousand possible combinations! Alongside familiar Spanish nibbles such as mixed olives and *patatas bravas*, you'll find Icelandic ingredients turned into tasty titbits – puffin with blueberries, saltfish, and pan-fried lobster tails. Expect to spend around Ikr3500 per person for a full meal.

SEAFOOD

our pick **Sægreifinn** (Map pp68-9; ☎ 553 1500; Verbúð 8, small-boat harbour; mains Ikr900-2000; ☺ 11am-10pm) Eccentric Sægreifinn serves up fresh seafood in what looks almost like a 1950s English chip shop…except for the stuffed seal. The owner is a sprightly old gent who buys and cooks all the fish himself – lobster soup (Ikr650) and fish kebabs (Ikr600) are specialities. He only speaks Icelandic, so make sure you know what you're asking for! [Whale meat served.]

Litli Ljóti Andarunginn (Map p72; ☎ 552 2410; www .andarunginn.is; Lækjargata 6b; mains Ikr1500-2500; ☺ noon-midnight Sun-Thu, to 3am Fri & Sat) Descend into this old wooden bar-restaurant to sample home-style cooking in cosy candle-lit surroundings. This relaxed bar-restaurant serves hearty Icelandic food at reasonable prices. Between May and October its nightly all-you-can-eat fish buffet (Ikr2500, with salad and soup) is good value.

Lauga-Ás (Map pp68-9; ☎ 553 1620; www.laugaas.is; Laugarásvegur; mains Ikr2000-3500; ☺ 11am-9pm Mon-Fri,

3-9pm Sat & Sun) For about 30 years this small, friendly restaurant, close to the City Hostel, has been quietly cooking up some great-tasting grub. It's particularly well known for its seafood soup and lobster but it also serves deceptively large portions of pasta, steaks and lighter meals. Book ahead on Friday and Saturday night.

Vín og Skel (Map p72; ☎ 534 4700; www.vinogskel .is; Laugavegur 55b; mains Ikr2000-4000) Tucked inside a courtyard off Laugavegur, this simple restaurant (which feels like a French seaside eatery) devotes itself wholeheartedly to perfect seafood. Bouillabaisse soup, scallops, langoustines, cod and mussels all feature on its menu, chalked up on a big Gallic-looking blackboard. [Whale meat served.]

our pick Við Tjörnina (Map p72; ☎ 551 8666; www .vidtjornina.is; Templarasund 3; Ikr2000-4000; ☺ from 6pm) People return again and again to this famed seafood establishment, tucked away near Tjörnin. It serves up beautifully presented Icelandic feasts such as guillemot with port, garlic langoustine, or the house speciality marinated cod chins (far more delicious than they sound!). The restaurant itself is wonderfully distinctive – it feels like a quirky upperclass 1950s drawing room.

Þrír Frakkar (Map pp68-9; ☎ 552 3939; www.3frakkar .com; Baldursgata 14; mains Ikr2700-4000; ☺ noon-2.30pm & 6-10pm Mon-Fri, 6-11pm Sat & Sun) Owner-chef Úlfar Eysteinsson has built up an excellent reputation at this snug little restaurant – apparently a favourite of Jamie Oliver's. Specialities include salt cod, anglerfish and *plokkfiskur* (fish stew) with black bread. You can also sample nonfish items, such as seal, puffin…and lovingly prepared whale steaks. [Whale meat served.]

Siggihall (Map p72; ☎ 511 6677; www.siggihall.is; Hótel Óðinsvé, Þórsgata 1; mains Ikr3500-4500; ☺ from 6pm Tue-Sun) Run by Iceland's most famous TV chef, this upmarket seafood restaurant is regarded as one of the finest in Reykjavík. The menu features many fishy favourites, with Icelandic-Mediterranean fusion dishes taking precedence. Siggihall is best known for its *bacalao*, served in different styles.

Tveir Fiskar (Map pp68-9; ☎ 511 3474; www.restaurant .is; Geirsgata 9; mains Ikr3000-5000; ☺ from 5pm) Right on the harbour, with a great view of the boats, this is one of Reykjavík's most famous fish restaurants. It's an upmarket place serving everything from langoustine and caviar to *bacalao* (salt cod). Its chef has won prizes for his delectable seafood, as fresh as it comes and highly

recommended. The speciality here is bouillabaisse. [Dolphin and whale meat served.]

Humarhúsið (Map p72; www.humarhusid.is; ☎ 561 3303; Amtmannsstígur 1; mains Ikr3100-5000) Understated and utterly elegant, the Lobster House is justly celebrated for its succulent shellfish, langoustine and lobster. Although crustaceans feature in most dishes, you can also sample game, fish, lamb and beef; plus there's a vegetarian option for that awkward critter in your dining party.

our pick Sjávarkjallarinn (Map p72; ☎ 511 1212; www.sjavarkjallarinn.is; Aðalstræti 2; dishes Ikr3000-5800; ☺ 11.30am-2pm & from 6pm) Currently *the best* dining experience to be had in Reykjavík, this atmospheric subterranean restaurant serves up exotic dishes. Shimmering fish and succulent crustaceans are combined with the unexpected – pomegranate, coconut, litchi and chilli – and presented like miniature works of art. It's at the top end of the price scale but worth every króna – go on, treat yourselves.

VEGETARIAN

Grænn Kostur (Map p72; ☎ 552 2028; www.graennkostur .is; Skólavörðustígur 8; daily special Ikr1100; ☺ 11.30am-9pm Mon-Sat, 1-9pm Sun) Tucked away in a small shopping arcade off Skólavörðustígur, this friendly little café serves great-tasting veggie set meals, with a daily-changing menu. There are also lighter snacks such as pizza, pies and salads. The high round tables and bar stools aren't particularly relaxing, but it's worth sitting up straight for good food.

our pick Á Næstu Grösum (First Vegetarian; Map p72; www.anaestugrosum.is; ☎ 552 8410; Laugavegur 20b; daily special Ikr1350; ☺ 11.30am-10pm Mon-Sat, 5-10pm Sun) This first-rate veggie restaurant, in a cheerful orange room overlooking Laugavegur, offers several daily specials. It uses seasonal organic veg, and inventive dressings guaranteed to give even lettuce new appeal. Things get extra spicy on Indian nights (Friday and Saturday), and organic wine and beer are available.

Cafés

Reykjavík's cool and cosy cafés are one of the city's best features. Lingering is encouraged – many offer magazines and free wi-fi access. They're the best places to go for morning coffee and light, tasty lunches. As the evening wears on, most undergo a Jekyll-and-Hyde transformation – coffee becomes beer, DJs materialise in dark corners, and suddenly you're not in a café but a kick-ass bar! Magic. Because the dividing line is so blurred, also see p92.

Babalú (Map p72; ☎ 552 2278; Skólavörðustígur 22a) More inviting than your own living room, this new café is übercute (if smoky). It only sells tea, coffee, hot chocolate and the odd crepe, but once you've settled into one of its snug corners you won't want to move. In summer there's occasional live music.

Ömmu Kaffi (Map p72; ☎ 552 9680; Austurstræti 20; snacks Ikr250-500; ☺ closed Sun; ✗) Friendly faces greet you at this nonsmoking coffee shop. A short list of edibles includes soup, lasagne, cakes and Icelandic doughnuts, and there are some unusual coffees on offer. Grab a paper or zone out to the mellifluous sound of live jazz (Thursday).

Kaffi Mokka (Map p72; ☎ 552 1174; Skólavörðustígur 3a; ☺ 9.30am-11.30pm Mon-Sat, noon-11.30pm Sun) Reykjavík's oldest coffee shop is an acquired taste. Its décor hasn't changed since the 1950s, and its original mosaic pillars and copper lights either look retro-cool or dead tatty, depending on your mood! It has a very mixed clientele – from older folk to tourists to trendy young artists – and a selection of sandwiches, cakes and giant waffles.

Kofi Tómasar Frænda (Koffin; Map p72; ☎ 551 1855; Laugavegur 2; snacks around Ikr600; ☺ 10am-1am Mon-Thu, to 5.30am Fri & Sat, 11am-1am Sun) Subterranean Koffin has a studenty feel. Relax with magazines and a snack (nachos, lasagne, sandwiches, cakes or chocolate-coated marzipan) and watch disconnected feet scurry along Laugavegur. At night the place turns into a candle-lit bar with DJs. It's a wireless hot spot.

Café Paris (Map p72; ☎ 551 1020; Austurstræti 14; snacks Ikr450-870; ☺ 8am-1am Mon-Thu, to 3am Fri, 9am-3am Sat, 9am-1am Sun) This old favourite has undergone a recent refit and is now better than ever – leather-upholstered chairs provide a level of bum-comfort previously missing. Although there's a selection of light meals – sandwiches, crepes, tacos – people come here for coffee and cakes, and to check out the crowds.

Café Konditori Copenhagen (Map pp68-9; ☎ 588 1550; www.konditori.is; Suðurlandsbraut 4a; ☺ 8am-6pm Mon-Fri, to 5pm Sat, 9am-5pm Sun) For pure cake porn, head to this café near the city hostel – Danish-influenced delicacies flaunt glazed strawberries, curls of chocolate and dribbled cream. It also does more prosaic sandwiches and good coffee, which you can consume from supercomfy leather seats. There's a branch at the Kringlan shopping centre.

Café Garðurinn (Map p72; ☎ 561 2345; Klapparstígur 37; soup/main/both Ikr650/1050/1500; ☺ 11am-6.30pm Mon-Fri, noon-5pm Sat, closed Aug) This tiny but tasteful veggie café is based round seven tables and the hum of civilised conversation. Choice is limited, but the daily soup and main are always delicious and unusual (we can vouch for the weird-sounding Catalonian tofu balls!). Half portions are available.

Té og Kaffi (Map p72; ☎ 562 2322; www.teogkaffi .is; Laugavegur 24; snacks Ikr600-1100; ☺ 7.30am-7pm Mon-Fri, 10am-7pm Sat, 11am-6pm Sun) A Starbucks-style café, complete with barristas and a huge coffee menu (including Baileys and Swiss chocolate flavours). There are plenty of yummy cakes, quiches, salads and soups too. It's popular with families, footsore Saturday shoppers and LP readers.

Kaffitár (Map p72; ☎ 511 4540; www.kaffitar.is; Bankastræti 8; ☺ 7.30am-6pm Mon-Sat, 10am-5pm Sun; ✗) Another of the modern breed of coffee shops, Kaffitár has opted for barristas, flavoured syrups, merchandised mugs and Italian biscuits by the till. The service is personal, and there's even a small play area for toddlers. It's a wireless hotspot, and there's a branch at the Kringlan shopping centre.

Kaffi Hljómalind (Map p72; ☎ 517 1980; Laugavegur 21; www.kaffihljomalind.org; snacks Ikr650-1100; ☺ 9am-11pm Mon-Fri, 11am-11pm Sat & Sun; ✗) This commendable organic and Fair Trade café is run on a not-for-profit basis. It looks like a 1950s home with 1970s flourishes (prayer flags, patterned chairs, hand-painted cups and saucers), and is a meeting-place for Reykjavík's radicals. Wireless hot spot.

ourpick Café Cultura (Map p72; ☎ 530 9314; www .cultura.is; Hverfisgata 18; snacks/light meals Ikr800-1400; ☺ 11.30am-1am Mon-Thu, to 4am Fri & Sat, 1pm-1am Sun) Cosmopolitan Cultura has scratched-up wooden floors, mosaic tables, and well-priced Asian, Mediterranean- and Arabic-influenced nosh – stir-fries, felafel, spicy meatballs and couscous cuisine. There's a tolerant attitude to kids. Free tango lessons start at 8pm on Wednesday, and it becomes a funky bar at weekends.

Svarta Kaffið (Map p72; ☎ 551 2999; Laugavegur 54; snacks/light meals Ikr800-1450; ☺ 11am-1am Sun-Thu, to 3am Fri & Sat; ✗) Order the thick homemade soup (one meat and one veg option daily for Ikr1090) at this quirky cavelike café – it's served piping hot in fantastic bread bowls. Other light lunches include nachos, burritos, toasted sarnies and lasagne. It's also a whimsical nightspot, with African masks and dim lighting adding a certain frisson.

Vegamót (Map p72; ☎ 511 3040; www.vegamot.is; Vegamótastígur 4; snacks/light meals Ikr800-2190) A long-running café-bar-club, but still a voguish place to eat, drink, see and be seen. There's a startling choice on the 'global' menu, including Mexican salad, seafood *quesadilla*, sesame-fried monkfish, and blackened chicken. The attached takeaway charges 10% less.

Kaffi Sólon (Map p72; ☎ 562 3232; www.solon.is; Bankastræti 7a; snacks/light meals Ikr900-2000; ☻ 11am-1am Mon-Thu, to 5am Fri & Sat, noon-midnight Sun) Decked out with white-leather seats and oversized artwork, this ultracool bistro (and nightspot) offers tasty international dishes at reasonable prices. There's a separate 'health' menu with calorie-lite meals, and veggies should head here for the best quiche in town. Wireless hot spot.

our pick b5 (Map p72; ☎ 552 9600; www.b5.is; Bankastræti 5; light lunch Ikr800-1200, evening mains Ikr1500-3000; ☻ 11am-midnight Sun-Wed, to 1am Thu, to 2am Fri & Sat) With its barely there name (short for Bankastræti 5), supersleek interior, and sketchpads in case you're seized by artistic inspiration, you may suspect this new bistro-bar of great pretentiousness. Thankfully, you'd be wrong: customers loll on the huge leather sofa wolfing down light Scandinavian-style bistro meals without the slightest hint of snobbery. On Friday and Saturday night it becomes a laid-back bar playing ambient tunes. Wireless hot spot.

Grái Kötturinn (Map p72; ☎ 551 1544; Hverfisgata 16a) This tiny six-table café looks like a cross between an eccentric bookshop and a lop-sided art gallery – quite charming! Opening hours are odd, but it serves breakfast from 7am weekdays and 8am weekends – toast, bagels, American pancakes, or bacon and eggs served on thick, buttery slabs of freshly baked bread.

Quick Eats
HOT DOGS, KEBABS & PIZZAS
Icelanders are utterly addicted to hot dogs, and they swear the best come from **Bæjarins Beztu** (Map p72; Tryggvagata; ☻ 10am-1am Sun-Thu, 11am-4am Fri & Sat), a van near the harbour patronised by Bill Clinton! Use the vital sentence *Eina með öllu* ('One with everything') for mustard, ketchup, rémoulade and crunchy onions. The kiosks of **Hlölla Bátar** (Map p72; ☻ 11am-2am Sun-Thu, 10am-7am Fri & Sat) and **Emmessís & Pylsur** (Map p72; ☻ 10am-11pm) on Ingólfstorg sell ice cream and hot dogs (Ikr330 to Ikr790).

Nonnabiti (Map p72; ☎ 551 2312; Hafnarstræti 18; snacks Ikr280-690; ☻ to 2am) serves burgers and hot dogs; when you've overdone the fried meat, **Kebabhúsið** (Map p72; ☎ 561 3070; Lækjargata 2; ☻ to 11pm Sun-Thu, to 7am Fri & Sat) offers falafel and fish and chips (around Ikr800).

Reykjavík residents are devoted to the pizzeria **Eldsmiðjan** (Map pp68-9; ☎ 562 3838; www.eldsmidjan.is; Bragagata 38a; pizzas around Ikr1100; ☻ 11.30am-11.30pm), tucked away on a quiet residential street. Its fiercely busy takeaway serves the best pizzas in the city, baked in a brick oven fired by Icelandic birch, or you can sit down to devour.

There is a **food court** (Map pp68-9; Miklabraut; ☻ 11am-7pm Mon-Wed, to 9pm Thu, to 8pm Fri, 10am-6.30pm Sat, noon-5.30pm Sun) upstairs in the Kringlan shopping centre.

WORKERS' CANTEENS
Several workers' canteens around town serve cheap, filling traditional grub.

Fljótt og Gott (Map pp68-9; ☎ 552 1288; Vatnsmýrarvegur 10; mains Ikr1100-1700; ☻ 7am-11.30pm) Inside the BSÍ bus terminal, this cafeteria serves burgers, sandwiches and 'food like Mum makes it': big roast dinners and Icelandic delicacies such as *svið* (singed sheep's head), *plokkfiskur* (creamy haddock and potato mash) and salt cod.

Múlakaffi (Map pp68-9; ☎ 533 7737; www.mulakaffi.is; Hallarmúli; canteen meals Ikr1100-1600; ☻ 7.30am-8pm Mon-Fri, to 2pm Sat, 11am-8pm Sun) Múlakaffi has recently been renovated, but the shining-white walls and brand-new tables can't disguise its old-fashioned soul, and the clientele is still 100% working men. Hearty local meals such as meatballs, salt cod, roast pork and rye bread are dished up from the hotplate.

Self-Catering
ALCOHOL
Alcohol is prohibitively pricey in all bars and restaurants. The only shop licensed to sell alcohol is the government-owned liquor store Vín Búð, which has six branches across Reykjavík. The most central branch is on **Austurstræti** (Map p72; ☎ 562 6511; Austurstræti 10a). There are also branches in **Kringlan shopping centre** (Map pp68-9; ☎ 568 9060) and **Smáralind shopping centre** (☎ 544 2112). All open 11am-6pm Monday to Thursday and Saturday, and 11am to 7pm Friday.

BAKERIES
Iceland has fantastic bakeries with good coffee, sandwiches, soup and drool-inducing cakes, and many have tables for eating them.

Korniô (Map pp68-9; ☎ 564 1828; Hrísateigur 47; ⏰ 7am-6pm Mon-Fri, 7.30am-4pm Sat, 8.30am-4pm Sun) Handy for the City Hostel and camp site.
Korniô (Map p72; ☎ 552 1803; Lækjargata 4; ⏰ 7am-6pm Mon-Fri, 8am-5pm Sat, 9am-5pm Sun) Central bakery, open till 10pm in summer.
Bakarí Sandholt (Map p72; ☎ 551 3524; www .sandholt.is; Laugavegur 36; ⏰ 7.30am-6.15pm Mon-Fri, to 5.30pm Sat, 8.30am-5pm Sun) An old favourite on Laugavegur.

SUPERMARKETS
Bónus (⏰ 11am-6.30pm Mon-Thu, 10am-7.30pm Fri, 10am-6pm Sat, Kringlan also noon-6pm Sun) The cheapest supermarket, at Laugavegur 59 (Map p72) and Kringlan shopping centre (Map pp68–9).
10-11 (⏰ 8am or 9am-11pm or midnight) Has many branches in the city, at Austurstræti (Map p72), Hverfisgata (Map pp68–9) and Laugalækur (Map pp68-9).

DRINKING
See the boxed text, opposite, for all the low-down on Reykjavík's infamous pub crawl.

Bars
ourpick Café Oliver (Map p72; ☎ 552 2300; www.caféoliver .is; Laugavegur 20a) One of Reykjavík's newest café-bars, Oliver is the most in-vogue place for brunch, and for partying late in superstyle. DJs pump out the tunes on Thursday, Friday and Saturday, with long queues snaking back from the doors.
ourpick Sirkus (Map p72; ☎ 511 8022; Klapparstígur 31) Our personal favourite, this kooky bar has dinky fairy lights, bus seats in the attic, an annual Tom Selleck Moustache Competition, and a loyal local following. DJs and bands play regularly, and there's a summer garden where you can snatch gulps of fresh air.
Kaffibarinn (Map p72; ☎ 551 1588; Bergstaðastræti 1) This old house, with the London Underground symbol over the door, contains one of Reykjavík's coolest bars; it even had a starring role in cult movie *101 Reykjavík*. At weekends you'll need a famous face or a battering ram to get in. At other times it's a place for artistic types to chill with their Macs. Wireless hot spot.
Vegamót (Map p72; ☎ 511 3040; www.vegamot.is; Vegamótsstígur 4) Vegamót is another smart café-by-day, club-by-night – wear your best togs if you want to fit in. The buzzy balcony is a fine place to watch the fashion-conscious flocks. There are usually top DJs and a thronging dance floor. The minimum age here is 22.

Thorvaldsen Bar (Map p72; ☎ 511 1413; www .thorvaldsen.is; Austurstræti 8-10) This understated modernist bar is ultraposh, from the fusion-style food to the clientele. There are DJs from Thursday to Saturday – dress up well or you won't get in, and after midnight be prepared to queue…and queue. There's a tiny dance floor, and 'theme nights' on Caribbean Wednesday, Mojito Thursday and Sushi Sunday.
ourpick Salt Lounge Bar (Map p72; ☎ 599 1000; Pósthússtræti 2) A lustrous bar-restaurant attached to the Radisson SAS 1919 Hotel, Salt is gloriously upmarket. It's all clean Scandinavian lines, low luxurious seats and soft purple-toned lighting – and they even bring the cocktails to your table. It's not a place to get raddled in, but maybe one for early-evening drinkies.
101 Hotel Bar (Map p72; ☎ 580 0101; www.101hotel .is; Hverfisgata 10) Frankly, we fear being ejected as riffraff from this beautiful granite-and-white-leather cocktail bar. Based inside the ultracool 101 Hotel, this long, thin, sleek, chic space is favoured by local glamourpusses and celebrities. Although it gets rammed to the rafters at weekends, it also closes early (at 1am) – dress to the hilt, and get on down there.
Q Bar (Map p72; ☎ 551 9660; Ingólfsstræti 3) This is one of the smallest bars in Reykjavík. It's smart, stylish and minimalist, with tables outside in summer – perfect for a mellow early-evening pint. There's live jazz/blues on Thursday.
Hressingarskálinn (Map p72; ☎ 561 2240; www .hresso.is; Austurstræti 20) 'Hressó' to its friends, this spacious L-shaped café-bar serves a diverse menu til 10pm daily (everything from porridge to *plokkfiskur*; mains Ikr980 to Ikr1180). At weekends it loses its civilised veneer and concentrates on beer, bar and dancing till 5.30am; a garden out the back provides fresh air. There's also usually a DJ or live music on Thursday night. Wireless hot spot.
Barinn (Map p72; ☎ 578 7800; Laugavegur 22) At the time of writing the jury was still out on Barinn. Its previous incarnation was a laid-back bluesy-grungy kind of place, but it's since been revamped and has yet to find its crowd. It's all much whiter and brighter, with chalkboard menus, bistro food and weekend DJs. Drop by to see how it's shaping up.
Kaffi Reykjavík (Map p72; ☎ 552 3030; www .kaffireykjavik.is; Vesturgata 2) Kaffi Reykjavík is more restaurant than hot nightspot, but it's mentioned here because of its USP – a small ice bar carved from chunks of a glacier. Pop in

if you're restless for novelty – ponchos and mittens are provided.

Pubs

The following are our picks for a more relaxed night on the town.

our pick Kaffi Brennslan (Map p72; ☎ 561 3600; www.brennslan.is; Pósthússtræti 9) All kinds of folk frequent Brennslan, an unpretentious Art Deco café-bar – conventional types mix with the avant-garde. It entices a 20s and 30s crowd with beers from 20 countries, but it never gets so packed that you can't move.

Bar 11 (Map p72; ☎ 511 1180; Laugavegur 11) This bar has calmed down over the last couple of years: it's now more of a place for groups of younger blokes to have a matey beer. It has a great jukebox (a rare thing in DJ-obsessed Reykjavík) and there's table football upstairs.

Ölstofan (Map p72; ☎ 552 4687; Vegamótastígur 4) Locals come to this no-nonsense bar specifically to avoid all that dancing rubbish. You turn up to drink beer and relax. It's one of the few drinking holes in the capital without music.

Prikið (Map p72; ☎ 551 2866; Bankastræti 12) Atmospheric Prikið draws in a youngish crowd, particularly towards the end of the night – it's one of the later-closing bars (5.30am). Dancers grind away cheek to cheek on the jammed dance floor. If you survive the night you can come back at noon the next day for a 'hangover sandwich'.

Nelly's (Map p72; ☎ 551 2477; Þinghóltstræti 2) By serving the cheapest beer in town (Ikr900 for 1.5L), publike Nelly's naturally pulls in a young, studenty crowd. There's a cheerful atmosphere, DJs and live bands play regularly, it opens until 6am at weekends, and there are daily offers on alcohol.

our pick Dillon (Map p72; ☎ 511 2400; Laugavegur 30) Beer, beards and the odd flying bottle…after changing hands the other year, atmospheric Dillon has turned into more of a RRRRROCK pub. There are occasional live concerts, and an unusual DJ in white-haired white-wine-and-rum-swilling 'rokkmamman' Andrea Jonsdóttir, a kind of female Icelandic John Peel.

Grand Rokk (Map p72; ☎ 551 5522; www.grandrokk.is; Smiðjustígur 6) This down-to-earth pub was once a great live-music venue, but in a recent shock-horror statement the owners announced that they're going to install large-screen TVs upstairs and turn it into a sports bar.

If Víking beer isn't doing it for you, head for a pint of Guinness at one of Reykjavík's two Irish pubs – **Celtic Cross** (Map p72; ☎ 511 3240; Hverfisgata 26), done up like a funeral parlour and with bands in the basement at weekends, and **Dubliner** (Map p72; ☎ 511 3233; Hafnarstræti 4), with live music every night from 10.30pm.

Clubs

The clubs below tend to shut between 5am and 6am at the weekend. Some charge admission.

Pravda (Map p72; ☎ 552 9222; Austurstræti 22) Based in an old police lock-up, Pravda is full of cutting-edge design, and has four bars and one of the city's largest dance floors. It hosts the longest-running club night held in Reykjavík – a drum-and-bass *(bumba & bassi)* night on the first Thursday of the month – and thrives on a 20s-30s clientele. Admission is Ikr500 after midnight.

** our pick** **Kaffi Sólon** (Map p72; ☎ 562 3232; www.solon.is; Bankastræti 7a) This great bistro becomes a swish club (admission free) for a beautiful, martini-drinking set by night. There are long queues, in-demand DJs, moody lighting and a dance floor containing around 17 people per sq m. There are usually DJs or live music on Thursday.

Glaumbar (Map p72; ☎ 552 6868; Tryggvagata 20) This American-style sports bar is young, brash and boisterous, with a huge video screen showing matches, deafening music, and weekend DJs. It's where very drunk people tend to end up at dawn, thanks to its late opening hours (to 6am).

Hverfisbarinn (Map p72; ☎ 511 6700; www.hverfisbarinn.is; Hverfisgata 20) Although it's been around for years now, Hverfisbarinn is still a strong runner for the title of Reykjavík's most popular club. Attracting a stylish, studenty crowd, it has long queues at weekends. It's decorated in cool Scandinavian style, there's cheap Carlsberg and live music on Thursday from 9.30pm, and DJs do their stuff till late on Friday and Saturday.

NASA (Map p72; ☎ 511 1313; nasa@nasa.is; Austurvöllur) The biggest nightclub in Reykjavík, NASA is a stripped-pine affair filled with Prada-clad crowds. It plays chart music and club anthems, and is also a venue for live bands – email for upcoming music. Admission is Ikr1000.

Rex (Map p72; ☎ 552 5599; www.rex.is; Austurstræti 9) Rex caters to an older, richer and more beautiful crowd than your average club. It's a place where business deals are made over perfect cocktails, and where visiting celebs can party in peace. Its three floors glow with rich red wallpaper, soft velvet seats and chandeliers.

ENTERTAINMENT
Cinemas

Cinemas in Reykjavík are usually American-style multiplexes showing American block-busters. Movies are screened in their original language with Icelandic subtitles. All cinemas charge Ikr800/450 per adult/child under six, and films are usually shown at 6pm, 8pm and 10pm. The free newspaper *Morgunblaðið* lists shows and times, or click on the 'Í Bíó' tab at www.kvikmyndir.is.

Háskólabíó (Map pp68-9; ☎ 525 5400; Hagatorg) At the university; sometimes shows arts films.

Laugarásbíó (Map pp68-9; ☎ 553 2075; Laugarás) Near the City Hostel.

Regnboginn (Map p72; ☎ 551 9000; Hverfisgata 54) Central cinema, sometimes shows arts films.

Sambíóin (Map pp68-9; ☎ 588 0800; Kringlunni 4-6) In Kringlan shopping centre.

Smárabíó (☎ 564 0000; Kópavogur) Iceland's biggest cinema, in Smáralind shopping centre.

Cultural Activities

Reykjavík has several theatre groups, an opera house and a symphony orchestra. Information on current events can be found in *What's On in Reykjavík*, *Grapevine* or the daily papers.

Íslenska Óperan (Map p72; ☎ box office 511 4200; www.opera.is; Ingólfstræti) The Icelandic Opera has a busy programme of international operas. Lunchtime concerts cost Ikr1000 and evening shows Ikr2900 to Ikr4800.

Iceland Symphony Orchestra (Map pp68-9; ☎ 545 2500; www.sinfonia.is; Háskólabíó, Hagatorg; tickets Ikr2500-3800) The orchestra will move to flashy new harbourside premises in 2009, but for now it's based at the Reykjavík University cinema. There are around 60 classical performances per season, normally on Thursday at 7.30pm.

National Theatre (Map p72; ☎ 585 1200; www.leikhusid.is; Lindargata 7; tickets adult/under 16yr Ikr3000/2300; ⊙ box office 12.30-6pm Mon & Tue, to 8pm Wed-Sun, theatre closed Jul & Aug) The most important of several venues in the city, the National Theatre has three separate stages and puts on around 12 plays, musicals and operas per year, from modern Icelandic works to Shakespeare.

Reykjavík City Theatre (Map pp68-9; ☎ 568 8000; www .borgarleikhus.is; Kringlan, Listabraut 3; adult/concession/ under 12s from Ikr2900/2200/free) The other important theatre in Reykjavík, this venue is behind Kringlan shopping centre. It stages at least six plays and musicals per year, showing at around 8pm from Thursday to Sunday. The **Icelandic Dance Company** (☎ 588 0900; www.id.is) is in residence there.

Iðnó Theatre (Map p72; ☎ 551 9181; Baldursgata 37; tickets adult/7-12yr Ikr2500/1800; ☽ 8.30pm) In July and August there are tourist performances at this lakeside venue. 'The Best of Light Nights', a mixed bag of Icelandic history, dance, folk tales, ghost stories and a slide show, usually runs on Monday and Tuesday. 'How Do You Like Iceland?', a two-actor romp through history, is shown on Wednesday.

Live Music

At the time of writing, Reykjavík was reeling with shock as one of the city's oldest venues went bankrupt and a second pronounced that it no longer wanted to stage live bands! But the Reykjavík scene is robust and strangely organic, and other venues are already beginning to emerge. **Café Amsterdam** (Map p72; ☎ 551 3800; Hafnarstræti 5) has been around for aeons, but it now seems to be evolving as *the* new place to catch up-and-coming bands, and there are frequent live performances at various bars, pubs and clubs, including **Nelly's** (p93), **Sirkus** (p92) and **NASA** (opposite).

To catch up with the current state of Icelandic music, consult the free English-language paper *Grapevine* (widely available), or pop into one of the city's two independent music shops (see p96), where you might even catch a live performance.

Sport

The country's passion for football (soccer) is huge. However, the Icelandic league is on a tiny scale and matches are generally played at suburban sports grounds. One of Reykjavík's biggest teams is **KR** (www.kr.is), who play in Newcastle United strip! Their home ground is KR-völlur. Cup and international matches are played at the **national stadium** (Laugardalsvöllur; Map pp68-9; ☎ 510 2914) in Laugardalur; see the sports sections of Reykjavík's newspapers for fixtures, and buy tickets directly from the venue.

The Reykjavík Marathon (see p81), held annually in August, is tremendously popular. Contact your local running club for information on how to participate, or turn up to cheer the runners on.

SHOPPING

Spending sprees in Reykjavík are an expensive business – most items are cheaper back home. However, there are some tantalising shops selling unusual presents. Look out for well-made Icelandic sweaters, cutting-edge T-shirts and jewellery, CDs of the latest bands, bags of dried fish, chocolate-covered liquorice, and bottles of the Icelandic schnapps *brennivín* (your friends may not thank you!).

Austurstræti and Hafnarstræti contain tourist stores selling puffin mugs and troll trinkets; Skólavörðustígur sells arty-crafty one-offs; and Laugavegur is the main shopping street.

For information about tax-free shopping, see p317.

Antiques & Bric-a-Brac

There are several 'antique' shops about, but they're basically overpriced junk shops. For details of the Kolaportið Flea Market, see p79.

Friða Frænka (Map p72; ☎ 551 4730; Vesturgata 3; ☽ noon-6pm Mon-Fri, 10am-2pm Sat) This place is a two-storey treasure trove of everything from antique furniture to '60s plastic kitsch. Items are piled precariously in tiny side rooms – the art-installation effect adds to the experience.

Clothes

Reykjavíkurs are style crazy, and new clothing boutiques are always opening up. For international brand-name clothing, try the two big shopping centres (see p96).

66° North (Map p72; ☎ 517 6020; www.66north.is; Bankastræti 5; ☽ 10am-6pm Mon-Fri, to 4pm Sat) Iceland's outdoor-clothing company began by making all-weather wear for Arctic fishermen. This metamorphosed into weatherproof but fashionable streetwear – coats, fleeces, hats and gloves. The branch at Kringlan shopping centre also opens on Sunday.

ELM (Map p72; ☎ 511 0991; www.elm.is; Laugavegur 1; ☽ 11am-6pm Mon-Fri, to 4pm Sat) Black-and-cream women's fashion is on sale here – the designs are unmistakeably Icelandic, with sharp, eccentric but very flattering cuts.

Handknitting Association of Iceland (Map p72; ☎ 552 1890; www.handknit.is; Skólavörðustígur 19; ☽ 9am-6pm Mon-Fri, to 4pm Sat, 11am-4pm Sun) Traditional handmade hats, socks and sweaters are sold at this knitting collective, or you can buy yarn and knitting patterns and do it yourself! There's a smaller branch at Laugavegur 64 (☎ 562 1890; shorter hours, closed Sunday).

Naked Ape (Map p72; ☎ 551 1415; www.dontbenaked
.com; Bankastræti 14; ☻ 11am-6pm Mon-Fri, to 4pm or
5pm Sat) This 2nd-floor boutique-gallery has just celebrated
its first birthday. Drop in for ultracool T-shirts and hoodies,
mostly in bright graffiti-like colours, designed by a bunch of
artist-friends.

Liborius (Map pp68-9; ☎ 551 6811; nonni@dead.is;
Mýrargata; ☻ 11am-6pm Mon-Sat) The complete opposite of Naked Ape's jolly technicolour designs are clothes
designed by artist Jón Auðarson, whose 'Dead' range was
popular with celebs from Metallica to Scarlett Johansson.
This is his new shop; stop by to see what he's getting up
to next.

Jewellery
Various shops along Laugavegur specialise in
Icelandic jewellery.

Aurum (Map p72; ☎ 551 2770; Bankastræti 4;
☻ 10am-6pm Mon-Fri, 11am-4pm Sat) Guðbjörg at
Aurum is one of the more interesting designers; her
whisper-thin gold and silver jewellery is sophisticated stuff,
its shapes often inspired by leaves and flowers.

Guðbrandur Jósef Jezorski (Map p72; ☎ 552 3485;
Laugavegur 48; 10am-6pm Mon-Fri, to 1pm Sat) Tasteful
silver and gold jewellery incorporating little lumps of lava
and Icelandic stones.

Music
Skífan Kringlan shopping centre (Map pp68-9; ☎ 591
5320; ☻ 10am-6.30pm Mon-Wed, to 9pm Thu, to
7pm Fri, to 6pm Sat, 1-5pm Sun); Laugavegur (Map p72;
☎ 525 5040; Laugavegur 26; ☻ 10am-10pm Mon-Sat,
noon-10pm Sun); Smáralind shopping centre (☎ 591
5330; ☻ 11am-7pm Mon-Fri, to 6pm Sat, 1-6pm Sun)
Reykjavík's biggest, slickest music chain store has lots of
choice, bargain-bin offers, and listening headsets so you
can try CDs before you buy.

Smekkleysa Plötubúð (Map p72; ☎ 534 3730; www
.smekkleysa.net; Klapparstígur 25; ☻ noon-6pm Mon-
Thu, to 7pm Fri, to 5pm Sat) Bad Taste records is the label
that launched The Sugarcubes, and they're still producing
new music – if you're lucky, you might catch the next big
thing playing live in the shop.

12 Tónar (Map p72; ☎ 511 5656; www.12tonar.is;
Skolavörðustígur 15; ☻ 10am-6pm Mon-Fri, to 2pm or
4pm Sat) Another very cool place to hang out is 12 Tónar,
responsible for launching some of Iceland's favourite new
bands. In the three-floor shop, you can listen to CDs, drink
coffee and maybe catch a live performance or two.

Outdoor Equipment
Útilíf (Map pp68-9; ☎ 545 1500; www.utilif.is) Climbing, camping, cycling and fishing equipment and repairs
are available from Útilíf, in Kringlan and Smáralind shopping centres and the small Glæsibær arcade.

Shopping Centres
Mallrats can choose between two large shopping centres. Both contain big-name clothing chains, home-furnishing outlets, a Vín
Búð alcohol shop, banks, a food court and
a cinema.

Kringlan (Map pp68-9; ☎ 588 788; www.kringlan.is;
☻ 10am-6.30pm Mon-Wed, to 9pm Thu, to 7pm Fri, to
6pm Sat, 1-5pm Sun) Reykjavík's biggest shopping centre,
1km from town, has more than 130 shops. Take bus S1-6,
13 or 14.

Smáralind (☎ 528 8000; www.smaralind.is; Hagasmári
1; ☻ 11am-7pm Mon-Wed & Fri, to 9pm Thu, to 6pm Sat,
1-6pm Sun) A smaller centre 6km away in the suburb of
Kópavogur. Take bus S2.

Souvenir Shops
Rammagerðin (Map p72; ☎ 551 1122; www.iceland
giftstore.com; Hafnarstræti 19) This 60-year-old tourist
shop is the oldest and biggest. Besides the usual trinkets
(coffee-table books, souvenir mugs and plastic Viking
helmets), it has a large range of knitwear and a handmade
glass and ceramics section.

GETTING THERE & AWAY
Air
Reykjavík's **domestic airport** (Innanlandsflug;
Map pp68–9) is based just south of Tjörnin.
Morning till evening, planes fly between
Reykjavík and Akureyri (Ikr8300 one way),
Egilsstaðir (Ikr9400) and Ísafjörður (Ikr8300);
as well as to Greenland and the Faeroes. Internal flight operator **Flugfélag Íslands** (Air Iceland;
☎ 570 3030; www.flugfelag.is) has a desk at the airport, but you can usually save money if you
book over the internet (a computer terminal
is provided near the check-in desks).

International flights operate through **Keflavík
Airport** (www.keflavikairport.com), 48km west of Reyk-
javík. The easiest way to get there is on the
Reykjavík Excursions Flybus – see opposite.
For international airlines, see p326.

Bus
Almost all long-distance buses use the **BSÍ bus
terminal** (Map pp68-9; ☎ 562 1011; www.bsi.is; Vatnsmýrarvegur 10), near the domestic airport – the
company name is pronounced *bee ess ee*. The
desk here can book you onto bus services
around Iceland. You can pick up summer
(June to August or mid-September) or winter
(mid-September to May) bus timetables, and
there's also a rack of tourist information available. There's a good cafeteria (see p91) with
internet access.

In summer regular direct services include those listed in the table below (there's reduced or no service the rest of the year).

For other destinations on the northern and eastern sides of the island (eg Egilsstaðir, Mývatn and Húsavík), you'll need to change buses in Höfn or Akureyri, which may involve an overnight stop.

Buses to Reykjanes, Snæfellsnes and the main towns on Rte 1 run year-round, with the exception of the section from Akureyri to Höfn. Services are less frequent on all routes between September and May.

Buses to the Westfjords (see p170) only run from June to August, and routes across the interior also close down for winter.

Ferry

For information on the Viðey ferry service, see p101.

GETTING AROUND
To/From the Airport

From Keflavík International Airport it's easy: the **Flybus** (☎ 562 1011; www.re.is) meets all international flights. Tickets cost Ikr1100/550 per adult/child 12 to 15 (credit cards are accepted) and the journey to Reykjavík takes around 50 minutes. On the return journey the bus leaves the BSÍ bus terminal two hours before international departures. Reykjavík City Hostel and the main hotels can arrange free transfers to the bus station. The Flybus will also drop off and pick up in Garðabær and Hafnarfjörður, just south of Reykjavík, if you book in advance. Taxis to/from the airport cost at least Ikr8000 one way.

From the domestic airport terminal it's a 1km walk into town or there's a taxi rank outside. Bus 15 runs from here to Hlemmur bus station.

Bicycle

Reykjavík has a steadily improving network of well-lit cycle lanes – ask the tourist office for a map, or see www.rvk.is/paths. At times, though, you will probably end up on busy roads. Be cautious, as drivers show little consideration for cyclists. Refreshingly, you are actually allowed to cycle on pavements as long as you act sensibly and don't cause pedestrians any problems.

Bicycles are available for hire from **Borgarhjól SF** (Map p72; ☎ 551 5653; www.borgarhjol .net; Hverfisgata 50; 10hr/24hr/week Ikr1500/2000/10,500; ⊙ 8am-6pm Mon-Fri, 10am-2pm Sat), and available from Reykjavík City Hostel (p82) and the camp site (p82).

BUS SERVICES FROM REYKJAVÍK

Destination	Duration	Frequency	Price	Year-round
Akranes	50min	several daily	Ikr250	Yes
Akureyri	6hr	daily	Ikr6600	Yes (reduced winter)
Blue Lagoon	45min	several daily	Ikr3800 (incl lagoon admission)	Yes
Borgarnes	1¼hr	several daily	Ikr1600	Yes
Geysir/Gullfoss	2½hr	daily	return Ikr4400	Jun-Aug
Höfn	8hr	daily	Ikr7400	Yes (reduced)
Hveragerði	40min	many daily	Ikr950	Yes
Keflavík	40min	several daily	Ikr900	Yes
Kirkjubæjarklaustur	5hr	daily	Ikr4400	Yes (reduced)
Landmannalaugar	4½hr	daily	Ikr4800	early Jun-early Sep
Ólafsvík	3hr	several daily	Ikr4200	Yes
Þorlákshöfn (for the Vestmannaeyjar ferry)	1hr	daily	Ikr1000	Yes
Þórsmörk	3½hr	1 or 2 daily	Ikr3700	Jun–mid-Sep
Reykholt	2hr	Fri & Sun	Ikr2200	May-Aug
Selfoss	1hr	many daily	Ikr1200	Yes
Skaftafell	6hr	daily	Ikr5400 (stops at Freysnes winter)	Jun–mid-Sep
Vík í Mýrdal	3½hr	3 daily	Ikr3800	Yes (reduced)

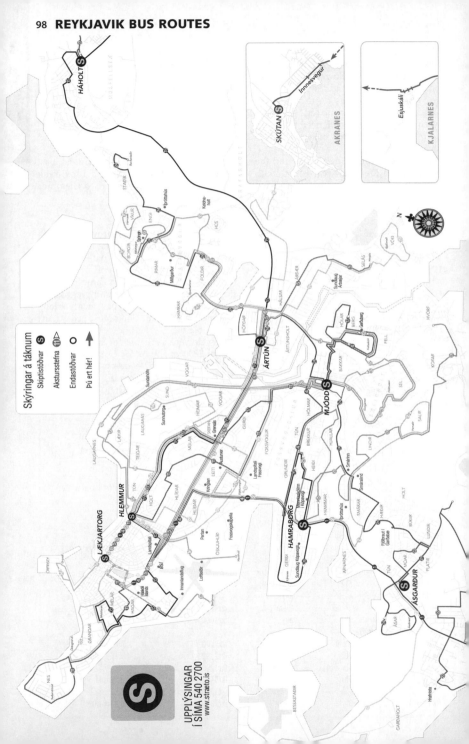

Bus

Reykjavík's excellent **Strætó city bus system** (☎ 540 2700; www.bus.is/english) offers regular and easy transport around central Reykjavík and out to the suburbs of Seltjarnarnes, Kópavogur, Garðabær, Hafnarfjörður and Mosfellsbær.

Strætó loves to fiddle with its bus routes and numbers. For the most up-to-date information, pick up a copy of the clear and useful *Reykjavík Bus Map* from tourist offices or bus stations.

Buses run from 7am until 11pm or midnight daily (from 10am on Sunday). Services depart at 20-minute or 30-minute intervals. A limited night-bus service (just the buses S1 to S6) runs until 2am on Friday and Saturday. Buses only stop at designated bus stops, marked with a big, yellow letter 'S'.

TICKETS & FARES

The fare is Ikr250/75 per adult/child six to 12 (no change is given). You can also buy books of 10 tickets for the price of eight (Ikr2000). If you need to take two buses to reach your destination, *skiptimiði* (transfer tickets) are available from the driver – you have a limited time (30 to 45 minutes) to use them.

The Reykjavík Tourist Card (see p67) includes a free Strætó bus pass.

BUS STATIONS

The two central terminals are **Hlemmur** (Map pp68–9), at the far end of the main shopping street Laugavegur; and **Lækjartorg** (Map p72), right in the centre of town. Check your route carefully, as not all buses stop at both.

Big suburban bus stands include Grensás (Map pp68–9), Hamraborg in Kópavogur, Fjörður in Hafnarfjörður (Map p102), Háholt in Mosfellsbær, Ártún in the suburb of Höfðar and Mjódd in the suburb of Breiðholt.

Useful routes:

S1 Hlemmur bus station, Lækjartorg bus station, National Museum, BSÍ bus terminal, hospital, Hamraborg bus station (Kópavogur), Fjörður bus station (Hafnarfjörður).

14 Lækjartorg bus station, National Museum, BSÍ bus terminal, hospital, Hlemmur bus station, Laugardalur (for swimming pool, and City Hostel and camp site).

15 Domestic airport terminal, BSÍ bus terminal, hospital, Hlemmur bus station, Laugardalur, Háholt bus station (Mosfellsbær).

Car & Motorcycle

A car is fairly unnecessary in the city, because it's so easy to travel round on foot and by bus. However, if you want to get into the country-side and don't fancy the bus tours (see p80), it's worth hiring a car.

The capital's drivers can be inconsiderate: beware of people yattering into mobile phones (illegal, in case you're wondering), drifting across lanes or cutting corners at junctions.

PARKING

The youth hostel, camp site and top-end hotels have private parking for guests; at other guesthouses and hotels, you'll have to scrum for spaces. In central Reykjavík metred street parking and municipal car parks are divided into zones – P1 is the most expensive, then P2 and P3. An hour's city-centre parking costs about Ikr150; parking is free on Sunday and in the evening.

GETTING OUT OF TOWN

Getting out of town is easy – follow the signs for Rte 1. Getting back into Reykjavík can be a more confusing, as there are dozens of exits from the highway and road signs are marked with abbreviations rather than full street names. To help you, the main road into Reykjavík is Vesturlandsvegur, which turns into Miklabraut and then Hringbraut. Exit by the Kringlan shopping centre for the Laugardalur area; at Snorrabraut for the Hallgrímskirkja area; and at Suðurgata for the town centre.

Taxi

Taxi prices are high – flagfall starts at Ikr520. Tipping is not required but expect to pay at least Ikr1000 to cross town.

There are usually taxis outside the bus stations, domestic airport, youth hostel, and pubs and bars on weekend nights (there are huu-uuge queues for the latter). Alternatively, call **Borgarbílastöðin** (☎ 552 2440), **BSH** (☎ 555 0888), **BSR** (☎ 561 0000) or **Hreyfill-Bæjarleiðir** (☎ 588 5522).

Walking

Reykjavík's compact layout means that it's very easily walkable. Most restaurants, bars, hotels and attractions are clustered within a 1.5-sq-km area.

AROUND REYKJAVÍK

One of the fantastic things about Reykjavík is the sea that practically surrounds it. Get closer to the ocean by visiting the island Viðey, a nugget of nature just a few minutes offshore, or the stony beaches at Seltjarnarnes, on the western tip of the Reykjavík peninsula.

Several nearby towns have been sucked into Reykjavík's sprawl and are now part of its suburbs. Kópavogur, Garðabær, Hafnarfjörður and Mosfellsbær, which are of varying degrees of interest to visitors, can all be easily reached by city bus.

VIÐEY

If the weather's fine, the tiny uninhabited island of Viðey makes a wonderful day trip. It's just 1km north of Reykjavík's Sundahöfn Harbour, but it feels like another world. Strange modern artworks, an abandoned village and shipwreck sites add to its melancholy spell. Here, life slows right down – the only sounds are the wind, the waves, and golden bumblebees buzzing among the tufted vetch and hawkweed.

History

Viðey had an explosive beginning – it's actually the tip of a long-extinct volcano. Despite its tiny size, the island has played a prominent part in Iceland's history. Its main roles were as a pilgrimage place and religious battleground.

In 1225 a wealthy Augustinian monastery was founded here; it kept the coffers full by imposing a cheese tax on a massive area of land round about. During the 16th-century Reformation, the monastery was sacked by Danish Lutherans and all its riches taken. Incensed by this cultural and religious outrage, Iceland's last Catholic bishop, Jón Arason, made a stand. He seized the island in 1550 and built the fort Virkið (no longer visible) to protect it, but he was captured and then beheaded in November that year.

Skúli Magnússon, the founder of the modern city of Reykjavík, built the fine mansion Viðeyarstofa here in 1751–55. It's now Iceland's oldest stone building. The island existed quietly for the next few centuries before it was donated to the city of Reykjavík in 1986, on the 200th anniversary of its municipal charter.

Sights

Just above the harbour, you'll find Viðeyarstofa, an 18th-century wooden **church**, and a small **monument** to Skúli Magnússon. Excavations of the old **monastery foundations** turned up some 15th-century wax tablets and a runic love letter, now in the National Museum; less precious finds can be seen in the basement of Viðeyarstofa. Higher above the harbour is

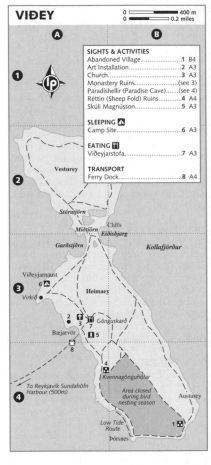

VIÐEY

0 — 400 m
0 — 0.2 miles

SIGHTS & ACTIVITIES
Abandoned Village.......................1 B4
Art Installation............................2 A3
Church..3 A3
Monastery Ruins.......................(see 3)
Paradíshellir (Paradise Cave)......(see 4)
Réttin (Sheep Fold) Ruins............4 A4
Skúli Magnússon.........................5 A3

SLEEPING
Camp Site....................................6 A3

EATING
Viðeyjarstofa...............................7 A3

TRANSPORT
Ferry Dock....................................8 A4

Ólafur Eliasson's interesting **art installation** *The Blind Pavilion* (2003).

The whole island is crisscrossed with **walking paths**. Some are cycleable if you bring a bike with you; others are more precarious. A good map at the harbour shows which paths are which. The whole island is great for **birds** (30 species breed here) and budding botanists (over one-third of all Icelandic **plants** grow on the island). In August, some Reykjavík inhabitants come here to pick **wild caraway**, originally planted by Skúli Magnússon.

From the harbour, trails to the southeast lead you past the natural sheep fold **Réttin**, the tiny grotto **Paradíshellir** (Paradise Cave), and then to the old **abandoned fishing village** at Sundbakki. Most of the south coast is a protected area for birds and is closed to visitors from May to June.

Trails leading to the northwest take you past low ponds, monuments to several shipwrecks, the low cliffs of Eiðisbjarg and **basalt columns** at Vesturey at the northern tip of the island. Richard Serra's **artwork**, made from huge pairs of basalt pillars, rings this part of the island.

Sleeping & Eating

Viðeyjarstofa (☎ 6607886; ⊙ 1-5pm Jun-Aug) is a lovely restored mansion where coffee and waffles are served. It's possible to camp at Viðeyjarnaust – ask permission at the café.

Getting There & Away

The summer-only **Viðey ferry** (☎ 892 0099) takes a mere seven minutes to skip across to the island from Reykjavík. It operates from Sundahofn (Map pp68–9) from early May to early September, leaving at 1pm, 2pm, 3pm, 4pm, 5pm and 7pm, returning 15 minutes later. There's also a boat from Reykjavík harbour from June to early September, leaving at noon and returning at 3.15pm. The return fare is Ikr750/330 per adult/child under 12.

SELTJARNARNES
pop 4660

Visiting the coast at Seltjarnarnes is a strange feeling. Head 1.5km west from the bustle of Lækjartorg, and you reach a red-and-white **lighthouse** and a strip of **lava-strewn beach**. Waves rush in, the air has that salt-sea tang, fish-drying racks sit by the shore, and arctic terns scream overhead – it all feels a million miles away from Reykjavík. It's a haven for **bird-watching** – 106 visiting species have been recorded here. The offshore island **Grótta**, where the lighthouse stands, is accessible at low tide but closed from May to July due to nesting birds. Across the water of the fjord there are super **views of Esja** (909m), and on clear days you can even see the glacier Snæfellsjökull.

Lots of people visit Seltjarnarnes specifically to drink in the glass-domed square **Rauða Ljónið** (☎ 551 6600; Eiðistorg 15), which is alleged to be the largest pub in the world – it's more like a covered market square with beer vendors.

One of the nicest ways to get to Seltjarnarnes is by walking or cycling along the good coastal path. You can also take bus 11 from Hlemmur or Lækjartorg bus station.

KÓPAVOGUR
pop 26,510

Kópavogur, the first suburb south of Reykjavík, is just a short bus ride away – but it feels far from the tourist trail. There are a few culture-vulture attractions in the complex next door to the distinctive arched church.

Sights

The cultural complex **Menningarmiðstoð Kópavogs** (Map pp68–9) contains Kópavogur's **Natural History Museum** (Náttúrufræðistofa Kópavogs; ☎ 570 0430; www.natkop.is; Hamraborg 6a; admission free; ⊙ 10am-8pm Mon-Thu, 11am-5pm Fri, 1-5pm Sat & Sun), which explores Iceland's unique geology and wildlife. There's an orca skeleton, a good collection of stuffed animals and geological specimens, and a fish tank housing some of Mývatn lake's weird *marimo* balls.

You'll also find Iceland's first specially designed concert hall there, built entirely from Icelandic materials (driftwood, spruce and crushed stone). **Salurinn** (☎ 570 0400; www.salurinn.is; Hamraborg 6) has fantastic acoustics – see the website for details of its (mostly classical) concert programme. Tickets cost from Ikr1500 to Ikr3000 depending on the concert.

Next door, there are changing modern-art exhibitions in the beautifully designed **Gerðarsafn Art Museum** (Map pp68-9; ☎ 554 4501; www.gerdarsafn.is; Hamraborg 4; adult/under 14yr Ikr400/free, free Friday; ⊙ 11am-5pm Tue-Sun). Its small café has mountain views.

If you're testing out the city's geothermal pools, try the Olympic-sized **Sundlaug Kópavogs** (Map pp68-9; ☎ 570 0470; Borgarholtsbraut 17; adult/child Ikr280/120; ⊙ 6.30am-10pm Mon-Fri, plus 8am-7pm Sat & Sun Apr-Sep & 8am-6pm Sat & Sun Oct-Mar), popular with families, with children's pool, slide, sauna and hot pots.

Getting There & Away

Buses S1 and S2 leave every few minutes from Hlemmur or Lækjartorg in central Reykjavík, stopping at the Hamraborg stop in Kópavogur (look out for the church). The journey takes about 10 minutes.

HAFNARFJÖRÐUR
pop 22,500

The 'Town in the Lava' rests on a 7000-year-old flow and hides a parallel elfin universe, according to locals. Its old tin-clad houses and numerous lava caves are overshadowed by heavy marketing of the hidden people and

REYKJAVÍK

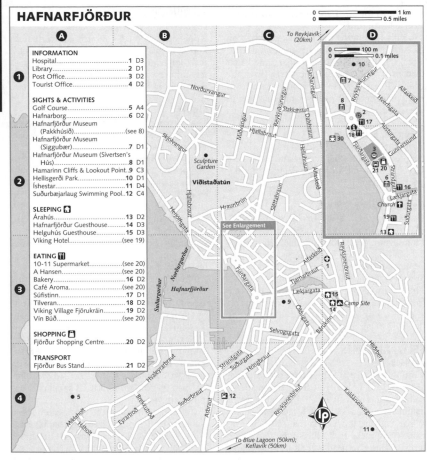

HAFNARFJÖRÐUR

INFORMATION	
Hospital.....................................1	D3
Library.....................................2	D1
Post Office...............................3	D2
Tourist Office...........................4	D2

SIGHTS & ACTIVITIES	
Golf Course..............................5	A4
Hafnarborg...............................6	D2
Hafnarfjörður Museum	
(Pakkhúsið)....................(see 8)	
Hafnarfjörður Museum	
(Siggubær)...........................7	D1
Hafnarfjörður Museum (Sivertsen's	
Hús)...................................8	D1
Hamarinn Cliffs & Lookout Point..9	C3
Hellisgerði Park......................10	D1
Íshestar.................................11	D4
Suðurbæjarlaug Swimming Pool..12	C4

SLEEPING	
Árahús...................................13	D2
Hafnarfjörður Guesthouse.........14	D3
Helguhús Guesthouse...............15	D3
Viking Hotel....................(see 19)	

EATING	
10-11 Supermarket...........(see 20)	
A Hansen........................(see 20)	
Bakery..................................16	D2
Café Aroma.....................(see 20)	
Súfistinn...............................17	D1
Tilveran................................18	D2
Viking Village Fjörukráin..........19	D2
Vín Búð..........................(see 20)	

SHOPPING	
Fjörður Shopping Centre...........20	D2

TRANSPORT	
Fjörður Bus Stand....................21	D2

Vikings – 10 out of 10 to the tourist office for effort! It's worth a visit on a sunny summer's day, but in winter, unless the Christmas market is on, tumbleweeds roll.

Hafnarfjörður was once a major trading centre, monopolised by the British in the early 15th century, the Germans in the 16th, and the Danes in the 17th. Many of the finest houses in town once belonged to rich merchants. Today the town is spreading like spilt milk, but the endless new-building estates east of the harbour hold nothing of interest for visitors.

Information

The friendly **tourist office** (☎ 565 0661; www .hafnarfjordur.is; Strandgata 6; 8am-5pm Mon-Fri, 10am-3pm Sat & Sun Jun-Aug, 8am-5pm Mon-Fri Sep-May) is in the town hall (Raðhús).

Internet access is available at the **library** (☎ 585 5690; Strandgata 1; 10am-7pm Mon-Wed, 9am-9pm Thu, 11am-7pm Fri year-round, plus 11am-3pm Sat Oct-May) for Ikr200 per hour.

There are banks with foreign-exchange desks and ATMs at the Fjórður shopping centre, right by the bus station.

Sights

The **Hafnarfjörður Museum** (Byggðasafn Hafnarfjarðar; ☎ 585 5780; adult/under 16yr Ikr300/free) is divided over three buildings. **Pakkhúsið** (Vesturgata 8; 1-5pm daily Jun-Aug, 11am-5pm Sat & Sun Sep-May) is the main section, with three storeys of exhibits. The ground floor may interest English visitors. It deals with the British invasion of (neutral) Iceland in WWII – how many of us were taught that in history lessons?! Upstairs, there are displays on the history of Hafnarfjörður, and a small toy museum in the attic.

Next door, **Sívertsen's Hús** (Vesturgata 6; 11am-5pm Jun-Aug) is a beautiful 19th-century home belonging to merchant Bjarni Sívertsen, once the most important man in Hafnarfjörður. It's decked out with period pieces – a piano, rich drapes, woven wallpaper, mahogany furniture, delicate crockery and silver spoons.

To take on board the huge contrast between Bjarni's lifestyle and the typical impoverished Icelander's, you can visit another home from the same period – the tiny restored fishing hut **Siggubær** (Sigga's House; Kirkjuvegur 10; 11am-5pm Sat & Sun Jun-Aug), next to the park at Hellisgerði.

The upbeat modern-art gallery **Hafnarborg** (555 0080; www.hafnarborg.is; Strandgata 34; adult/under 12yr/concession Ikr400/free/300; 11am-5pm Wed-Mon, free Fri) has two floors of regularly changing exhibitions, and occasional musical concerts.

The tourist office publishes a **sculpture trail** map; the highlight is **Hellisgerði** (Reykjavíkurvegur), a peaceful park filled with lava grottoes and apparently one of the favourite places of the hidden people. As well as tiny residents, the park exhibits tiny trees in the world's most northerly **bonsai collection** (admission free; 3-10pm Mon-Fri, 1-6pm Sat & Sun Jun-Sep). Another pleasant stroll is to the home of elfish royalty, **Hamarinn Cliffs**, where there's a lookout and view disc.

Activities & Tours

Find out if you have second sight on a 1½-hour **Hidden Worlds tour** (694 2785; www.alfar.is; per person Ikr2500; 2.30pm Tue & Fri year-round). Your guide, Sibba, leads you around the homes of the hidden people, telling folktales and stories about elf spottings. Various locals in costume put in an appearance and the tours are great fun for kids. A copy of the (otherwise rather overpriced) *Hidden Worlds* map is included, which marks the Hafnarfjörður homes of elves, fairies, hermits and dwarves.

Inland there are loads of **walking trails** in the tree plantations around lake Hvaleyrarvatn and on the slopes of the mountain Helgafell (338m) – shown on the free map *Ratleikur*, available from the tourist office.

There are two good swimming pools in town – the better (outdoor) pool is **Suðurbæjarlaug** (565 3080; Hringbraut 77; adult/child Ikr220/100; 6.30am-9.30pm Mon-Fri, 8am-6.30pm Sat, 8am-5.30pm Sun), to the south of the centre. There's also a **golf course** (565 3360) surrounded by lava at Hvaleyrarvöllur.

If you fancy a trot, the horse farm Íshestar (see p79) is based in Hafnarfjörður.

Festivals

In mid-June the peace is shattered as Viking hordes invade town for the **Viking festival**. Its staged fights and traditional craft demonstrations are centred on the Fjörukráin hotel.

Sleeping

Hafnarfjörður Guesthouse (565 0900, 863 4155; www .hafnarfjordurguesthouse.is; Hjallabraut 51; tw without/with linen & breakfast Ikr2500/3500; May-Aug;) This place, overlooking the strange sculptures of the Víðistaðatún recreation grounds, once offered hostel-style accommodation in a stylish decking, glass and concrete building. It's now under new management and being revamped, but its good facilities (guest kitchen, laundry and internet access) are to be retained. Campers using

---

HIDDEN WORLDS

Many Icelanders believe that their country is populated by hidden races of little folk – *jarðvergar* (gnomes), *álfar* (elves), *ljósálfar* (fairies), *dvergar* (dwarves), *ljúflingar* (lovelings), *tívar* (mountain spirits), *englar* (angels) and *huldufólk* (hidden people).

Although most Icelanders are embarrassed to say they believe, around 90% of them refuse to say hand-on-heart that they *don't* believe. Most Icelandic gardens feature small wooden cut-outs of *álfhól* (elf houses) to house the little people in case the myths are true.

Hafnarfjörður is believed to lie at the confluence of several strong ley lines (mystical lines of energy) and seems to be particularly rife with these twilight creatures. In fact, construction of roads and homes in Hafnarfjörður is only permitted if the site in question is free from little folk. A local seer, Erla Stefánsdóttir, has drawn a map, available from Reykjavík and Hafnarfjörður tourist offices for Ikr1000, showing the best spots to catch a glimpse of these hidden worlds. There are also tours in Hafnarfjörður to find them – see above.

the camp site (Ikr1000 per person, open June to September) can also make use of them.

Árahús (☎ 555 1770; Strandgata 21; s/d Ikr5500/7500; ☻ Jun-Aug) A very central option on the pedestrian main street, Árahús has just been redecorated and looks very fresh and pleasant. It has a homy feel, with bookshelves, paintings, leather settees in the sitting room, and two good guest kitchens. Prices include breakfast. It becomes a student house from September, but there may still be room for guests – call to check.

Helguhús Guesthouse (☎ 555 2842; www.helguhus .is; Lækjarkinn 8; s/d/tr May-Sep Ikr5100/7900/9900, Oct-Apr Ikr3500/4500/5500; ☻ year-round) Close to a small lake a 10-minute walk out of town, Helguhús is a well-turned-out townhouse with cosy, cream-coloured rooms (all with shared bathrooms). Breakfast is included.

Viking Hotel (☎ 565 1213; www.fjorukrain.is; Strandgata 55; s/d Ikr11,300/14,500 Apr-Sep, Ikr6300/8600 Oct-May; ▣) The over-the-top Viking Village complex Fjörukráin also offers 42 hotel rooms. Rather than being stuffed full of swords and battle-axes, they're surprisingly smart modern rooms, with TV, tea-making kit, phone and bathroom. There's also a hot tub for guests. Breakfast is included.

Eating

our pick **Súfistinn** (☎ 565 3740; Strandgata 9; ☻ 8.15am-11.30pm Mon-Thu, to midnight Fri, 10am-midnight Sat, noon-11.30pm Sun) This great café-bar is the most cheerful place to eat in town – ladies lunch, readers read, kids play chess, and half of Hafnarfjörður gathers to gossip about the other half. There's a satisfying selection of salads, sarnies, pies, quiches and coffee.

Café Aroma (☎ 555 6996; www.aroma.is; Fjörður, Fjarðargata; ☻ 10am-midnight Mon-Wed, to 1am Thu, to 3am Fri & Sat, 1pm-midnight Sun) This café inside the shopping centre has less character, but it makes up for it with huge windows and stunning sea views. There's also a very popular salad bar (Ikr990). It becomes a bar later on.

Tilveran (☎ 565 5250; Linnetstígur 1; mains Ikr1800-3300; ☻ noon-11pm) On the main pedestrian street, this dim little restaurant serves burgers and pizza, as well as more upmarket meals such as baked mushrooms stuffed with blue cheese, and tagliatelle with lobster.

Viking Village Fjörukráin (☎ 565 1213; www .vikingvillage.is; Strandgata 50a & 55; mains Ikr2000-3500; ☻ from 6pm) The tacky but strangely endearing restaurant Fjörukráin is housed in a to-

tally outrageous reconstruction of a Viking longhouse, complete with carved pillars and dragons on the roof. It offers Viking feasts (*hákarl*, dried fish, braised lamb, fish soup and *skyr*), served up by singing Vikings. If you're going to be a spoil sport, you can order Icelandic specialities from the Viking-free Fjaran restaurant in the same complex.

A Hansen (☎ 565 1130; www.ahansen.is; Vesturgata 4; mains Ikr2300-4000) This is the pick of the town's restaurants for a civilised meal. Housed in an old house built in 1880, A Hansen specialises in fine Icelandic food (fish, lobster, lamb) and has a nice old-world atmosphere. There's a bar upstairs, with a happy hour (8pm to 10pm Sunday to Thursday).

For self-caterers, there's a tiny **bakery** (☻ 8am-6pm Mon-Fri, 9am-4pm Sat & Sun) on the main street; or the Fjörður shopping centre has a 10-11 supermarket, a bakery and a Vín Búð liquor store.

Getting There & Around

It's an easy 30-minute bus ride from Reykjavík to the Fjörður bus stand at Hafnarfjörður. From Reykjavík, bus S1 (Ikr250) leaves every 10 minutes from Hlemmur or Lækjartorg.

If you book ahead, the **Flybus** (☎ 562 1011) to Keflavík airport will stop in Hafnarfjörður; confirm the exact location of the bus stop on booking.

Hafnarfjörður is small and easy to get around on foot. For a taxi, phone **BSH** (☎ 555 0888).

MOSFELLSBÆR
pop 6960
Fast-growing Mosfellsbær (www.mosfellsbaer .is) has more or less become another of Reykjavík's suburbs, although it's 15km from the city centre. There's some good **walking** in the surrounding hills, including long day treks to Þingvellir (p115) and the geothermal field at Nesjavellir (p118) – see the pamphlet *Útivist í Mosfellsbæ*, available from the town library.

The home of Nobel Prize–winning author Halldór Laxness is now open to visitors. The **Gljúfrasteinn Laxness Museum** (☎ 586 8066; www .gljufrasteinn.is; Mosfellsbær; adult/under 16yr Ikr500/250; ☻ 9am-5pm daily Jun-Aug, 10am-5pm Tue-Sun Sep-May), just outside the suburban centre on the road to Þingvellir, is a superb example of an upperclass 1950s house, complete with original furniture and Laxness' fine-art collection. A guided audio-tour leads you round; highlights include the study where Laxness wrote his defining works, and his beloved Jaguar parked outside.

Near to the museum are several **horse-riding farms** (see p79). If you're in need of retail therapy, the factory outlet shop **Álafoss** (☎ 566 6303; Álafossvegur 23; ⏰ 9am-6pm Mon-Fri, to 4pm Sat) sells woollen goods that are slightly cheaper than at the city's tourist shops.

The town **camp site** (☎ 566 6754; sites per person Ikr600; ⏰ Jun-Aug) is next to the river Varmá and has toilets, sinks and showers, and free admission to Mosfellsbær geothermal pool. **Fitjar** (☎ 565 6474; www.fitjarguesthouse.com; s/d without bathroom Ikr5000/7500, with bathroom Ikr6000/8500, self-catering apt from Ikr8000), 4km north of Mosfellsbær off Rte 1, is a stylish modern house. Some rooms (three en suite, three with shared bathroom) have views towards Reykjavík, and the house is surrounded by wonderful countryside. There's a guest kitchen and a laundry.

REYKJANES PENINSULA

From the air, or when you're sitting on the bus between Keflavík airport and Reykjavík, the Reykjanes Peninsula can look like the flattest, bleakest, most disheartening place on earth. Cast off your misery! Dispel the gloom! For isn't the Blue Lagoon somewhere amongst those lava fields?

Besides Iceland's most famous attraction, there are plenty of other marvels hidden in this forbidding landscape. Give it time, and the grey waves, smoking earth and mournful beauty of the black lava will mesmerise you.

Most towns – Keflavík, Njarðvík, Vogar – are squeezed into Miðnes, a small spur on the northern coast of the peninsula; the rest is wilderness. Northwest of the international airport are the wave-lashed fishing villages of Garður and Sandgerði, lost places where you can watch migrating birds while the wind blows all your thoughts away. A back road runs south from Keflavík along the rugged coast to Reykjanestá, a wonderful spot full of battered cliffs and strange lava formations.

The only town on the south coast is Grindavík, home to the Saltfish Museum. Northeast lies the Reykjanesfólkvangur wilderness reserve, full of wild lava landscapes and geothermal springs.

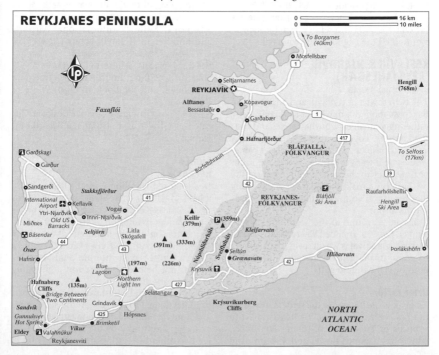

REYKJAVÍK

GOODBYE TO THE MILITARY BASE

Keflavík owes a great deal of its prosperity to the former American military base, which closed down in September 2006.

In 1951 a fear of Reds under the bed led the US to establish a military presence in Iceland, which was a handy submarine fuelling stop between America and Russia. Over the years various passionate protests were made demanding that the troops leave, but all came to nothing. It was only as submarines became more advanced and the Cold War ended that US operations in Iceland were scaled back.

America eventually made tentative noises about a complete closure. Contrarily, this time many Icelanders demanded that the soldiers stay – the jobs that the base provided and the money it brought into the economy were too valuable to lose; and how could Iceland defend itself without an army of its own?

But the units drifted home and the base powered down, until on 30 September 2006 a simple ceremony took place – the US flag was lowered, and the Icelandic flag was raised in its place, ending 55 years of occupation.

There are no plans yet for the enormous military zone on Reykjanes. The Lego-like barracks, the shooting ranges, the miles of razor wire – all lie abandoned. It's estimated that it will cost the Icelandic government Ikr5 billion to clean up toxic areas and demolish unwanted buildings. It will be interesting to see how these scarred, ugly sites are used in the future.

Public transport to Keflavík, Grindavík and the Blue Lagoon is fast and frequent, but you'll need private transport to reach more remote parts of the peninsula. Buses within Reykjanes are provided by **SBK** (☎ 420 6000; www .sbk.is). There's also a new bus company, **Blue Line** (☎ 421 1515), who run a service from Reykjanesbær to the Blue Lagoon and Grindavík.

KEFLAVÍK & NJARÐVÍK (REYKJANESBÆR)

combined pop 11,240

The twin towns of Keflavík and Njarðvík, on the coast about 50km west of Reykjavík, are a rather ugly mush of suburban boxes and fast-food outlets. Together they're known simply as 'Reykjanesbær'. Although they aren't somewhere you'd want to spend a massive amount of time, they're the largest settlement on the peninsula and make a good base for exploring the area. If you've an early flight they're handy for the airport.

If you're around at the beginning of September, the well-attended **Night of Lights** (Ljósanótt í Reykjanesbæ) festival is worth seeing, particularly its grand finale, when waterfalls of fireworks pour over the Bergið cliffs.

Orientation

Keflavík is the biggest of the settlements, with the best visitor facilities. To its east are the suburbs of Ytri-Njarðvík (Outer Njarðvík), which has a youth hostel and a swimming pool, and forlorn little Innri-Njarðvík (Inner Njarðvík).

Information

There's a small **tourist information desk** (☎ 425 0330; www.reykjanes.is; ⏰ 6am-8pm Mon-Fri, noon-5pm Sat & Sun) at Keflavík International Airport, and another in Keflavík **library** (☎ 421 5155, 421 6777; www.reykjanes.is; Hafnargata 57; ⏰ 10am-7pm Mon-Fri, to 4pm Sat), where net access is available for Ikr250 per hour. Ask for a free map of Keflavík and the booklet 'Enjoy More of Reykjanes'.

ATMs and foreign-exchange desks are located at Glitnir and also at Landsbanki on Hafnargata.

Sights
KEFLAVÍK

In a long red warehouse by the harbour, **Duushús** (☎ 421 6700; Grófin; adult/under 18yr Ikr450/free; ⏰ 1-5.30pm) is Keflavík's culture house. There's a permanent exhibition of around 60 of Grímur Karlsson's many hundreds of miniature ships, made compulsively over a lifetime; a gallery where seven international art exhibitions are held each year; and a changing local-history display.

The area around Duushús is the prettiest part of Keflavík; just to the east on the seashore is an impressive **Ásmundur Sveinsson sculpture**, used as a climbing frame by the local kids. There are two other interesting artworks in front of

KEFLAVÍK & NJARÐVÍK

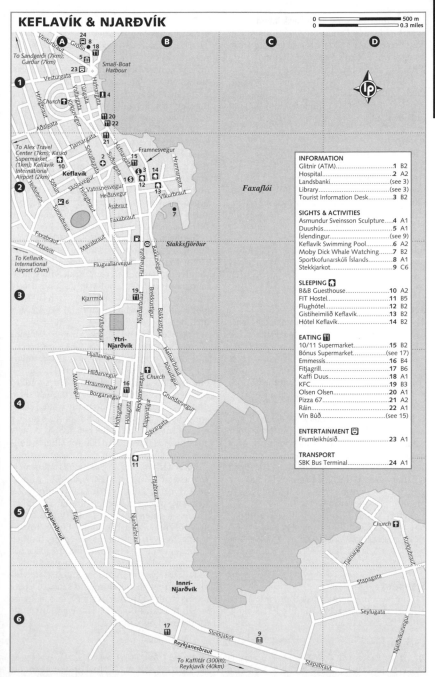

0 — 500 m
0 — 0.3 miles

INFORMATION
Glitnir (ATM)...............................1 B2
Hospital..2 A2
Landsbanki............................(see 3)
Library.....................................(see 3)
Tourist Information Desk............3 B2

SIGHTS & ACTIVITIES
Asmundur Sveinsson Sculpture....4 A1
Duushús...5 A1
Íslendingur................................(see 9)
Keflavík Swimming Pool..............6 A2
Moby Dick Whale Watching.......7 B2
Sportkofunarskóli Íslands.............8 A1
Stekkjarkot...................................9 C6

SLEEPING
B&B Guesthouse........................10 A2
FIT Hostel....................................11 B5
Flughótel....................................12 B2
Gistiheimilið Keflavík..................13 B2
Hótel Keflavík............................14 B2

EATING
10/11 Supermarket....................15 B2
Bónus Supermarket................(see 17)
Emmessís....................................16 B4
Fitjagrill.......................................17 B6
Kaffi Duus..................................18 A1
KFC...19 B3
Olsen Olsen...............................20 A1
Pizza 67......................................21 A2
Ráin..22 A1
Vín Búð..................................(see 15)

ENTERTAINMENT
Frumleikhúsið.............................23 A1

TRANSPORT
SBK Bus Terminal........................24 A1

the terminal building at **Keflavík International Airport** – Magnús Tómasson's *Þotuhreiður* (Jet Nest) resembles a Concorde emerging from an egg, while Rúrí's *Regnbogi* (Rainbow) is a glittering arch of steel and coloured glass.

Keflavík has started its own Hollywood Blvd – Clint Eastwood, fresh from filming *Flags of Our Fathers* (2006), gamely left his **hand print** outside the theatre on the main street!

NJARÐVÍK

Close to the Bónus supermarket at Ytri-Njarðvík is a reconstructed turf farmhouse **Stekkjarkot** (☎ 421 3155; admission free; ⏱ 1-4pm Thu-Sun summer) containing a small folk museum. Outside is the **Íslendingur**, a curvaceous reconstruction of the Viking Age *Gokstad* longship. It was built in 2000 by a direct descendent of Leifur Eiríksson, who then sailed it successfully from Iceland to America, proving it was possible using Viking technology. It's a lovely piece of engineering, and a ladder has been left so you can climb aboard.

Activities

The scuba-diving outfit **Sportköfunarskóli Íslands** (☎ 421 7100; www.dive.is; dives per person with 2 people or more Ikr14,000-19,000, with 1 person Ikr17,000-23,000, equipment hire Ikr5000) arranges dry-suit dives in the breathtaking rift between the North American and European plates at the bottom of Þingvellir lake, or off the coast at Keflavík. Also see p51.

Moby Dick Whale Watching (☎ 421 7777; www.dolphin.is; adult/6-12yr Ikr3400/1700) runs three-hour whale- and dolphin-spotting trips from May to October, usually at 9am (and at 1pm July and August). It may be possible to get dropped off afterwards at the Blue Lagoon (Ikr700) – a great way of cramming in the sights if you're on a short stopover in Iceland.

Keflavík and Njarðvík both have pools, but the 25m outdoor **swimming pool** (☎ 421 1500; Sunnubraut; adult/child Ikr220/110; ⏱ 6.45am-9pm Mon-Fri, 8am-5pm Sat, 9am-4pm Sun) in Keflavík is the better one.

Sleeping

All the sleeping options listed provide a free airport transfer, except for the FIT hostel, where it costs extra.

KEFLAVÍK

Alex Travel Center (☎ 421 2800; www.alex.is; Aðalgata 60; sites per person Ikr750, sb in dm Ikr1750, tw Ikr8900, hut Ikr10,900; 🖳) A mere two-minute drive from the airport, Alex offers all things to all visitors. There's a small camp site for campers; 14-person dormitory accommodation for hostellers; simple bedrooms for guesthousers; and small wooden chalets for Swiss yodellers. Extras include a guest lounge and kitchen, free luggage storage, and bike and car rental. It's 1.5km from the town centre.

B&B Guesthouse (☎ 421 8989, 867 4434; Hringbraut 92; s/d/tr Ikr5500/7500/8200; 🖳) This green-and-yellow guesthouse above a fresh-fish shop is neat as a pin inside. Rooms are all parqueted and non-idiosyncratic, but there are some quirky touches in the common areas – like the peacock tapestry over the stairs and the cosy curvy settee in the TV room. Prices include free internet and breakfast.

Gistiheimilið Keflavík (☎ 420 7000; www.hotelkeflavik.is; Vatnsnesvegur 9; s/d Ikr7800/9800) Run by Hótel Keflavík, this is a pricey option with slightly old-fashioned rooms (all with shared bathroom and TV), but you do have use of the hotel's four-star facilities. There's also a guest kitchen, and a continental breakfast is included in the price.

Flughótel (☎ 421 5222; www.icehotel.is; Hafnargata 57; s/d/tr Ikr15,600/19,500/21,500; 🖳) The green-and-cream rooms at this typical Icelandair property are clean, comfortable and modern – but brrr! it's a chilly welcome. The standard rooms are just as comfortable as the deluxe, so don't pay extra unless you really want a kettle and a bathrobe. There's a hot pot, a sauna, a restaurant and free internet access. A new guesthouse (Ikr8000/10,000 for singles/doubles) was due to open at the time of writing.

Hótel Keflavík (☎ 420 7000; www.hotelkeflavik.is; Vatnsnesvegur 12-14; s/d Ikr19,800/22,800; 🖳) Almost next door to Flughótel is family-run Hótel Keflavík, where the people are far friendlier. There's a smell of clean laundry and coffee as you enter, and the lobby fairly thrums with activity. Its 70 rooms are comfy if much chintzier than the Flughótel, but the place has equally good facilities – there's a glass-walled restaurant, free internet access, and a large fitness centre with solarium and sauna. Deluxe rooms (with CD player, large TV and bath) are worth the extra Ikr2000. There are discounts for internet bookings.

NJARÐVÍK

FIT Hostel (☎ 421 8889; www.fithostel.is; Fitjabraut 6a; sb/s/d Ikr1750/3250/5500; 🖳) In a gruesome industrial estate off busy Rte 41, this hostel has an unfortunate location but quite decent facilities – good, clean rooms (holding up to seven people), left luggage (Ikr250), internet access (Ikr500 per hour), laundry (Ikr400) and a hot tub. You can catch buses to Reykjavík and Keflavík in front of the hostel, but a car or a love of walking through concrete suburbs would be helpful here.

Eating
KEFLAVÍK
There are enough drive-through snack bars and greasy grills in Keflavík to give you an instant burger-induced coronary. For more civilised fare, there are several places along the main street; plus the two hotels (see opposite) have high-quality restaurants.

Olsen Olsen (☎ 421 4457; Hafnargata 17; snacks Ikr600-900; ◷ 11am-10pm) In the 1950s, thanks to rock and roll, Keflavík was the coolest place in Iceland. This American-style diner transports locals back to the glory days, with shiny silver tables, red plastic seats and pictures of Elvis on the walls. There's a gigantic range of hoagies, as well as sandwiches, burgers, and a kids' meal.

Pizza 67 (☎ 421 4067; Hafnargata 30; meals Ikr1500-2200) Popular with families and young couples, this chain restaurant sells pizzas named after 1960s songs. There's a takeaway service, with free delivery anywhere in Keflavík or Njarðvík.

Kaffi Duus (☎ 421 7080; Duusgata 10; mains Ikr700-2800; ◷ kitchen noon-10pm, bar to 1am Fri & 2am Sat) This friendly nautical-themed café-restaurant-bar, decorated with whale vertebrae and giant crabs, overlooks the small-boat harbour and cliffs. The menu is fish, fish, fish, fresh out of the sea, with a few pasta dishes, salads and burgers thrown in. It's a popular evening hangout with occasional live bands.

Ráin (☎ 421 4601; www.rain.is; Hafnargata 19a; mains Ikr2400-4000; ◷ 11am-3pm & 6-10pm) If you visit on a day like we did, Ráin's renowned panoramic views of sea, mountains and distant Reykjavík will be nothing but mist! Keflavík's finest restaurant is large but friendly and serves a familiar menu of Icelandic fish, lobster, lamb and beef.

Self-caterers have plenty of supermarkets to choose from, including the **10-11** (Hafnargata 53-55), next door to the tourist office, and a Kaskó close to the Alex Travel Center. There's also a **Vín Búð** (☎ 421 5699; Hafnargata 51-55; ◷ 11am-6pm Mon-Thu, to 7pm Fri, to 4pm Sat).

NJARÐVÍK
You're damned for food in Njarðvík unless you love drive-thrus and supermarkets. Choose from the car-friendly **Emmessís, KFC** or **Fitjagrill**; or the **Bónus supermarket** (Fitjum; ◷ noon-6.30pm Mon-Thu, 10am-7.30pm Fri, 10am-6pm Sat, noon-6pm Sun) and giant **Kaffitár** (☎ 420 2710; www.kaffitar.is; Stapabraut 7; ◷ 8am-6pm Mon-Fri, 10am-6pm Sat, 1-5pm Sun) on Rte 41.

Getting There & Around
TO/FROM THE AIRPORT
Most of Reykjanesbær's accommodation options offers free airport transfers for guests. A taxi will cost about Ikr2000 – call **Aðalbílar Nýung** (☎ 421 1515; www.airporttaxi.is) or **Hreyfill-Bæjarleiðir** (☎ 588 5522; www.hreyfill.is). For information on the Flybus between the airport and Reykjavík, see p97.

AIR
Apart from flights to Greenland and the Faeroes, all of Iceland's international flights use Keflavík International Airport. For more information, see p326.

BUS
SBK (☎ 420 6000; www.sbk.is) runs five daily buses between Reykjanesbær and Reykjavík from Monday to Friday, and three on Saturday. The fare is Ikr1000/5000 per adult/child four to 11. A couple of buses run on weekdays from Keflavík to Sandgerði and Garður – see p110 for details.

Local Strætó buses run between Keflavík and Njarðvík – there are services every 30 minutes or so between 7am and 7pm, and hourly between 8pm and 11pm.

A new company, **Blue Line** (Bláa Línan; ☎ 421 1515), has just begun a service that runs around seven buses per day between Keflavík airport, Reykjanesbær (Alex Travel Center/Flughótel/Hótel Keflavík/Njarðvík bus stop) and the Blue Lagoon; three buses continue to Grindavík. The airport–Reykjanesbær leg is free, from the airport to the Blue Lagoon is Ikr500, and from the Blue Lagoon to Grindavík is Ikr500.

CAR
Car-rental representatives at the international airport include **Avis/Europcar** (☎ 421 1690; www.avis.is), **Bílaleiga Akureyrar/National** (☎ 425 0300; www.nationalcar.is) and **Hertz** (☎ 425 0221; www.hertz.is); prices are around Ikr13,000 for a day's hire in summer.

NORTHWESTERN REYKJANES

The western edge of the Reykjanes Peninsula is rugged and exposed – perfect if you love wild rain-lashed cliffs and beaches! There are several fishing villages and some quirky sights to be seen in among the lava fields.

Garðskagi

From Keflavík, if you follow Rte 41 for 9km, on through the village of Garður, you'll reach the beautiful wind-battered Garðskagi **headland** (www.sv-gardur.is), one of the best places in Iceland for bird spotting – it's a big breeding ground for sea birds, and it's often the place where migratory species first touch down. It's also possible to see seals, and maybe whales, from here.

Two splendid **lighthouses**, one old and one new, add drama – you can get near-360-degree sea views from the old lighthouse. There's also a small **folk museum** (☎ 422 7220; admission Ikr200; ♥ 1-5pm Apr-Oct), filled with a pleasing mishmash of fishing boats, birds' eggs and sewing machines. It contains the balconied **Flösin Cafeteria** (☎ 422 7214; ♥ 1-5pm daily Apr-Dec, 1-5pm Fri, Sat & Sun Jan-Mar, sometimes later), with superb views over the ocean to Snæfellsjökull.

There's a tranquil, free camping area by the lighthouse, with toilets and fresh water.

Sandgerði

Five kilometres south of Garður, it's worth stopping at this industrious fishing village to see the classroom-like but interesting **Fræðasetrið nature centre** (☎ 423 7551; Gerðavegur 1; adult/child Ikr400/300; ♥ 9am-noon & 1-5pm Mon-Fri, 1-5pm Sat & Sun year-round), where there are stuffed Icelandic creatures (including a monstrous moth-eaten walrus), jars of pickled things (look out for the freaky Gorgonocephalus), and a small aquarium with sea squirts, crabs and anemones.

There are some quite nice **beaches** on the coast south of Sandgerði, and the surrounding marshes are frequented by more than 170 species of **birds**. About 7km south, you can walk to the ruins of the fishing village **Básendar**, which was destroyed by a giant tidal wave in 1799.

Getting There & Away

On weekdays, **SBK** (☎ 420 6000; www.sbk.is) has two buses (Ikr300/200 per adult/child four to 11) from Keflavík to Sandgerði (10 minutes) and Garður (15 minutes). Heading back to Keflavík, you should book with SBK.

SOUTHWESTERN REYKJANES

The vast lava flows at Reykjanesviti were spewed out by a series of small shield volcanoes. The area is crisscrossed by walking tracks that are marked on the *Enjoy More of Reykjanes* map, available from most tourist offices, including those in Keflavík and at the international airport. However, the terrain is tough and not all the paths are clearly marked.

Keflavík to Reykjanesviti

If you turn off Rte 41 onto Rte 44 just outside Keflavík, you'll first pass the deserted barracks, barbed-wire fences and tank ranges of the **old US military base** (see p106).

After several kilometres the road zooms past the fading fishing village of **Hafnir**. There's nothing much to see here – just humps and bumps in a field, thought to be a 9th-century longhouse belonging to Ingólfur Arnarson's foster brother, and the anchor of the 'ghost ship' *Jamestown*, which drifted ashore mysteriously in 1870 with a full cargo of timber but no crew.

About 8km south, a 30-minute walk from the road will take you to the sea cliffs of **Hafnaberg**, an important bird-nesting area and a good lookout point for whales.

A little further south, just off the main road, is the so-called **Bridge Between Two Continents**. It's basically a photo stop – a bridge spanning a sand-filled gulf between the North American and European plates.

In the far southwest of the peninsula the landscape breaks down into wild volcanic crags and sea cliffs. Several bizarre-looking **factories** here exploit geothermal heat to produce salt from sea water. The black beaches near Sandvíkur also stood in for Iwo Jima in Clint Eastwood's WWII epic *Flags of Our Fathers* (2006).

One of the most wild and wonderful spots is **Valahnúkur**, where a dirt track leads off the main road through 13th-century lava fields down to the most desolate cliffs imaginable. You can clamber up to the ruins of the oldest lighthouse (1878) in Iceland, destroyed by a devastating earthquake, and contemplate the fragility of life and the futility of everything. From here you can see the flat-topped rocky crag of **Eldey**, 14km out to sea, which is home to the world's largest gannet colony. Some claim the last great auk was killed and eaten here, though this is disputed by Faeroe islanders, who insist that the event occurred at Stóra Dímun. Today Eldey is a protected bird reserve.

Back towards the main road is a steaming multicoloured **geothermal area**. This includes the hot spring **Gunnuhver**, named after the witch Gunna, who was trapped by magic and dragged into the boiling water to her death.

Pick a bleak and blasted day to appreciate the last natural wonder before reaching Grindavík. About 7km east of Gunnuhver, slabs of cracked black lava are battered by grey breakers and waves spray up inside the churning, cauldron-shaped hole **Brimketil**.

Getting There & Away

There are no public bus routes in this area. If you're driving, you'll need enough petrol to last you from Keflavík to Grindavík.

BLUE LAGOON

As the Eiffel Tower is to Paris, as Disney World is to Florida, so the **Blue Lagoon** (Bláa Lónið; ☎ 420 8800; www.bluelagoon.com; adult/12-15yr Ikr1400/700, towel/swimsuit/robe hire Ikr300/350/700; ☷ 9am-9pm mid-May–Aug, 10am-8pm Sep–mid-May; ☒) is to Iceland…with all the positive and negative connotations that implies. Those who say it's too expensive, too clinical, too crowded are kind of right, but you'll be missing something special if you don't go.

Set in a tortured black lava field, just off the road between Keflavík and Grindavík, the milky-blue spa is fed by water (at a perfect 38°C) from the futuristic Svartsengi geothermal plant. The silver towers of the plant provide an off-the-planet scene setter for your swim; add roiling clouds of steam and people daubed in blue-white silica mud, and you're in another world.

The lagoon has been imaginatively landscaped with hot pots, wooden decks and a piping-hot waterfall that delivers a powerful hydraulic massage – it's like being pummelled by a troll. There are also two steam rooms and a sauna. At the time of writing the lagoon was being doubled in size; building work should be finished by 2007.

The superheated sea water is rich in blue-green algae, mineral salts and fine silica mud, which condition and exfoliate the skin – sounds like advertising-speak, but you really do come out as soft as a baby's bum. The water is always hottest near the vents where it emerges, and the surface is several degrees warmer than the bottom.

If lounging in this warm, salty, soothing water isn't relaxing enough, you can lie on a floating lilo and have a masseuse knead out your knots (Ikr1300/2500/5800 per 10/20/50 minutes); be aware, though – you need to book spa treatments sometimes days in advance. The complex also includes a snack bar, a restaurant with good food but fairly poor service, and a shop selling Blue Lagoon products.

Three warnings: the Blue Lagoon requires the same thorough naked prepool showering that applies in all Icelandic swimming pools. The water can corrode silver and gold, so leave watches and jewellery in your locker. You'll also need bucketfuls of conditioner afterwards – all that briney water plays havoc with your hair.

Sleeping & Eating

There's nowhere to stay in the actual Blue Lagoon complex, but the Northern Light Inn is just across the lava.

our pick **Northern Light Inn** (☎ 426 8650; www .northernlightinn.is; s/d/tr Ikr12,000/16,500/25,000; ☐ ☒) This large bungalow-style hotel has 21 spacious en-suite rooms with fridge, phone and TV. Free transfers are provided to the lagoon and international airport.

Kristjana's Kitchen (mains Ikr1700-3000; ☷ 11.30am-1.30pm & 5.30-9pm) The Northern Light Inn's fab panoramic restaurant serves 'hearty Nordic soul food' – this means herring platters, fish dumplings, smoked lamb and other Icelandic favourites; plus there's a choice of veggie dishes. Wireless hot spot.

Getting There & Away

The lagoon is 50km southwest of Reykjavík, but there are plenty of bus services that run there year-round. You'll need to book in advance.

The best and cheapest is **Þingvallaleið Bus Service** (☎ 511 2600; www.bustravel.is), which leaves every few hours from 9.30am to 6pm from the BSÍ bus terminal in Reykjavík, or the company picks up from hotels. You can return to the city, or three services continue to the international airport. The return journey (or journey there and then onward to the airport) is a bargainous Ikr3000, including lagoon admission.

Alternatively, **Reykjavík Excursions** (☎ 562 1011; www.re.is) runs a trip costing Ikr3400, including lagoon admission. And if you just can't wait, you can make it your first stop in Iceland. **Iceland Excursions** (☎ 540 1313; www.icelandexcursions .is) has two departures from the airport at 3pm and 4.30pm daily (Ikr3700).

GRINDAVÍK

pop 2610

Grindavík (www.grindavik.is), the only settlement on the south coast of Reykjanes, is one of Iceland's most important fishing centres. If this were an English seaside town, its waterfront would be full of B&Bs, pubs and shops selling sticks of rock; here, all flimflam is rejected in favour of working jetties, cranes and warehouses. The busy harbour and tourist-free town are actually quite refreshing.

Sights & Activities

The main attraction here is **Saltfisksetur Íslands** (Saltfish Museum; ☎ 420 1190; www.saltfisksetur.is; Hafnargata 12a; adult/under 8yr/8-16yr Ikr500/free/250; ◷ 11am-6pm), a pretty well done museum dedicated to explaining the fish-salting industry. An audioguide (English, German or French) leads you over wooden piers to tableaus showing various stages of the process. It's probably not for everyone, but if you're interested in Icelandic history, an understanding of the saltfish industry is vital – after all, it was so important that the country's coat-of-arms was a filleted cod until 1904. The museum contains a small **tourist information desk** (☎ 426 9700; www.grindavik.is), open the same hours.

There's a good modern **swimming pool** (☎ 426 7555; Austurvegur 1; adult/child Ikr300/150; ◷ 7am-9pm Mon-Fri, 10am-3pm or 6pm Sat & Sun), with a rather littery, graffitied reconstruction of a **Viking temple** outside.

Sleeping & Eating

In summer, you can camp for free at the Austurvegur **camp site** (☎ 420 1190), near the swimming pool, with toilets, sinks and showers.

[our pick] **Heimagisting Borg** (☎ 895 8686; bjorksv@hive.is; Borgarhraun 2; s/d Ikr5700/7700; ▯) This wonderfully clean and congenial guesthouse is one of the best-value places to stay in Reykjanes. Mellow creamy-pink rooms have big squishy beds, there's a TV lounge with English satellite channels, internet computer, washing machine and kitchen, and prices include a great little serve-yourself breakfast. This is definitely a place you'd come back to.

Besides the usual petrol-station grills and snack bars, Grindavík actually has some very nice eating options.

[our pick] **Lukku Láki** (☎ 426 9999; Hafnargata 6; dishes Ikr750-2000; ◷ 6pm-1am Mon-Thu, to 3am Fri, 3pm-3am Sat, 3pm-1am Sun) The Lucky Luke sports bar–bistro is a crazy mixed-up place – African masks, big-screen football, a bar made from old five-aurar pieces, fairy lights, and blues on the stereo all compete for your attention. But the confusion somehow makes for a great atmosphere. Add free internet access, beer, and huge portions of well-priced bar meals (fish and chips, burgers, chicken nuggets) and you're on to a winner.

Veitingahúsið Brim (☎ 426 8570; www.brim-veitingar .is; Hafnargata 9; mains Ikr1800-2900) This restaurant, just opposite the museum, offers a taste of saltfish – with spinach and tomatoes in white-wine sauce – so you can see what the fuss is about. Alongside other superfresh fish dishes, you can sample lamb, beef and chicken mains, or go for a lighter burger (including one for veggies), soup or sandwich snack.

Salthúsið (☎ 426 9700; www.salthusid.is; Stamphólsvegur 2; dishes Ikr2000-4000; ◷ 5-9pm Tue-Fri, 11.30am-9pm Sat & Sun) The classy wooden Salthúsið is the first dedicated saltfish restaurant in Iceland. The *baccalao* is prepared in different ways (with ginger, chilli, olives and garlic; au gratin; as nibbly nuggets; or with mushrooms, red onion and capers), so there's plenty of variety. If the idea of saltfish doesn't grab you, fall back on perfectly prepared lobster, chicken or lamb.

Getting There & Away

Five daily buses travel between Reykjavík and Grindavík (Ikr1000, one hour), past the Blue Lagoon.

REYKJANESFÓLKVANGUR

For a taste of Iceland's weird and empty countryside, you could visit this 300-sq-km wilderness reserve, a mere 40km from Reykjavík. Its three showpieces are Kleifarvatn, a deep grey lake with submerged hot springs and black-sand beaches; the spitting, bubbling geothermal zone at Seltún; and the southwest's largest bird cliffs, the epic Krýsuvíkurberg.

The reserve was established in 1975 to protect the elaborate lava formations created by the Reykjanes ridge volcanoes. The whole area is crossed by dozens of **walking trails**, which mostly follow old paths between abandoned farms. They're detailed in the good pamphlet map *Walking & Hiking in Krýsuvík* (in English) available from the tourist offices at Keflavík or Hafnarfjörður. There are parking places at the beginnings of most of the popular walks, including the loop around Kleifarvatn, and the tracks along the craggy Sveifluháls and Núpshlíðarháls ridges.

Kleifarvatn

This huge, creepy 1km-deep lake sits in a volcanic fissure, surrounded by wind-warped lava cliffs and black-sand beaches. Legend has it that a worm-like monster the size of a whale lurks somewhere in its depths. At the southern end of the lake steam billows from dozens of hot springs. A walking trail runs right around the lake, offering dramatic views and the eerie crunch of volcanic cinders underfoot.

Krýsuvík & Seltún

The volatile **geothermal field** Austurengjar, about 2km south of Kleifarvatn, is often called Krýsuvík after the nearby abandoned village. Even by Icelandic standards, this area is prone to geological tantrums. The temperature below the surface is 200°C and the water is boiling as it emerges from the ground. A borehole was sunk here to provide energy for Hafnarfjörður during the 1990s, but it exploded without warning in 1999 and the project was abandoned.

At Seltún, boardwalks meander round a cluster of **hot springs**. The steaming vents, mud pots and solfataras (volcanic vents) shimmer with rainbow colours from the strange minerals in the earth, and the provocative eggy stench will make a lasting impression.

Nearby is the lake **Grænavatn**, an old explosion crater filled with weirdly green water – caused by a combination of minerals and warmth-loving algae.

Krýsuvíkurberg

South of Seltún, about half a kilometre past Krýsuvík church, a dirt track leads down to the coast at **Krýsuvíkurberg**. These bleak black cliffs stretch for 4km and are packed with puffins, guillemots and other sea birds in summer. A walking path runs along their length.

Getting There & Away

There's no public transport to the park, but you could get here on an organised bus trip. Reykjavík Excursions and other tour agents offer six-hour tours through the Reykjanes Peninsula (see p80).

Otherwise, you'll need a bike or hire car. Follow unsurfaced Rte 42 from Hafnarfjörður, which continues eastwards through lava fields to Þorlákshöfn, passing more dramatic volcanic scenery. Rte 427 from Grindavík will also get you to the reserve.

Southwest Iceland

SOUTHWEST ICELAND

Geysers spout, waterfalls topple, black beaches stretch into the distance, and brooding volcanoes and glittering icecaps line the horizon. The beautiful southwest contains many of Iceland's most famous natural wonders – and is consequently a relatively crowded corner of the country. But get off the Ring Rd (Rte 1) and there are plenty of quiet valleys and splashing streams you can have all to yourself.

Almost everyone who comes to Iceland visits the Golden Circle, east of Reykjavík. Here you'll find the gorgeous national park Þingvellir, a Unesco World Heritage site; the bubbling springs and spouting geysers at Geysir; and one of the country's most dazzling rainbow-tinged waterfalls, Gullfoss.

On the coast, you can visit the entertaining little fishing villages Eyrarbakki and Stokkseyri, or walk the black beaches at drop-dead beautiful Vík. Just offshore, the charming Vestmannaeyjar are filled with fearless puffins and friendly people. Inland you'll find one of Iceland's best museums at Skógar; important saga-age ruins in the Þjórsárdalur valley; or wonderful walking at Þórsmörk. And, if you want more of an adrenaline rush, try snowmobiling or dogsledding on the Mýrdalsjökull glacier.

TOP FIVE

- Wait for water to shoot skywards at **Geysir** (p120), or watch it tumbling down at **Gullfoss** (p120)

- Go dogsledding or snowmobiling on **Mýrdalsjökull icecap** (p140)

- Scream like a girl at the **Stokkseyri Ghost Centre** (p130), or enjoy a dose of culture at the brilliant **Skógar Folk Museum** (p138)

- Fall in love with puffins, volcanoes and teetering cliffs on the wonderful **Vestmannaeyjar** (p142)

- Stroll black-sand beaches at **Vík** (p140) and **Reynisfjara** (p140), and watch otherworldly ocean sunsets from nearby **Dyrhólaey** (p140)

GETTING THERE & AROUND

For information on bus routes and schedules in the southwest, contact the **BSÍ bus station** (☎ 562 1011; www.bsi.is), or bus companies **Austurleið Kynnisferðir** (☎ 562 1011; www.austurleid.is) or **Þingvallaleið** (☎ 511 2600; www.bustravel.is).

Frequent organised tours visit this area (see p80 for ideas). Hiring a car can work out cheaper; most southwestern roads are suitable for 2WDs.

THE GOLDEN CIRCLE

Gullfoss, Geysir and Þingvellir are unique sites commonly referred to as the Golden Circle. These sites make up Iceland's major tourist destinations, offering visitors the opportunity to see a wild, roaring waterfall, spouting hot springs and the country's most important historical area in one condensed, doable-in-a-day tour. Although they're mobbed by coach parties year-round, they're still worth visiting for their undeniable natural beauty.

Hiring a car will mean you'll be able to enjoy other nearby highlights. Nesjavellir is great for its surreal other-planet landscape; on clear days, the active volcano Hekla is a sublime sight; and there are interesting Viking ruins in the scenic Þjórsárdalur valley.

ÞINGVELLIR

This **national park**, 23km east of Reykjavík, is Iceland's most important historical site and a place of lonely beauty. The country's first national park, it was finally made a Unesco World Heritage site in 2004.

The Vikings established the world's first democratic parliament, the Alþing, here in AD 930. As with many saga sites, there aren't many Viking remains to be seen, but the park has a superb natural setting, inside an immense rift valley caused by the separating North American and Eurasian tectonic plates. Its undulating mossy lava flows are scarred by streams and rocky fissures. It's particularly awesome in autumn, when the dwarf birch forests glow with brilliant red, orange and yellow hues.

History

Many of Iceland's first settlers had run-ins with royalty back in mainland Scandinavia. These chancers and outlaws decided that they could live happily without kings in the new country, instead creating district *þings* (assemblies) where justice could be served.

Eventually, a nationwide *þing* became necessary. One man was dispatched to Norway to study law, while his foster brother travelled the country looking for a suitable site. Bláskógur – now Þingvellir (Parliament Fields) – lay at a crossroads by a huge fish-filled lake. It had plenty of firewood and a setting that would make even the most tedious orator dramatic, so it fitted the bill perfectly. Every important decision affecting Iceland was argued out on this plain – new laws were passed, marriage contracts were made, and even the country's religion was decided here. The annual parliament was also a great social occasion, thronging with traders and entertainers.

Over the following centuries, escalating violence between Iceland's most powerful men led to the breakdown of law and order. Governance was surrendered to the Norwegian crown and the Alþing was stripped of its legislative powers in 1271. It functioned solely as a courtroom until 1798, before being dissolved entirely. When it regained its powers in 1843, members voted to move the meeting place to Reykjavík.

Information

On Rte 36, the **Park Service Centre** (Þjónustumiðstöð; ☎ 482 2660; www.thingvellir.is; ☉ 8.30am-8pm daily Jun, Jul & Aug, 9am-5pm daily May & Sep, 9am-5pm weekends Oct-Apr) contains a café and a seasonal tourist desk, with books and maps for sale.

Above the park, on top of the Almannagjá rift, is an interesting **multimedia centre** (admission free; ☉ 9am-7pm daily Jun-Aug, 9am-5pm daily Apr, May, Sep & Oct, 9am-5pm weekends Nov-Mar) exploring the area's nature and history.

Sights & Activities
THE ALÞING

The Alþing used to convene annually at the **Lögberg** (Law Rock), between the Flosagjá and Nikulásargjá fissures. This was where the *lögsögumaður* (law-speaker) recited the law to the assembled parliament each year. After Iceland's conversion to Christianity, the site shifted to the foot of Almannagjá cliffs, which acted as a natural amplifier, broadcasting the voices of the speakers across the assembled crowds. The site is marked by a flagpole, and a path leads down to it from the multimedia centre at the top of Almannagjá.

SOUTHWEST ICELAND

SOUTHWEST ICELAND

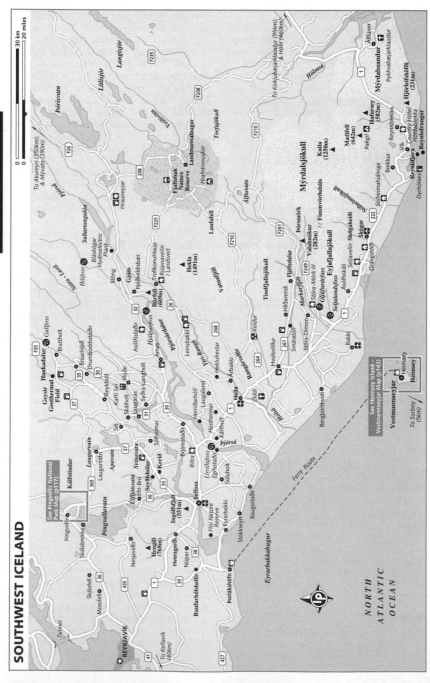

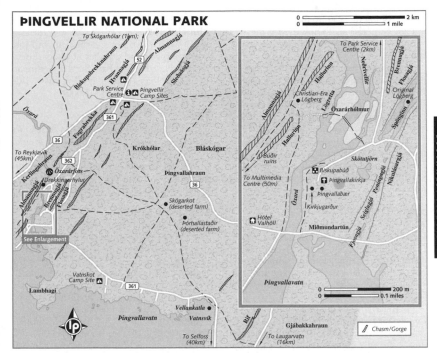

PINGVELLIR NATIONAL PARK

Decisions were reached by the Lögrétta (Law Council), made up of 146 men (48 voting members, 96 advisers and two bishops) who are thought to have assembled in front of the cliffs. **Neðrivellir** (Low Fields), the flat area in front of the cliffs.

FISSURES & WATERFALLS
The Þingvellir plain is precariously situated on a tectonic plate boundary – here, North America and Europe are tearing away from each other at a rate of 2mm per year. As a result, the plain is scarred by a series of dramatic fissures, including the great rift **Almannagjá**. A broad track follows the fault from the multimedia centre on top of the cliffs to the plain below.

The river Öxará cuts across the rift, tumbling towards the lake in a series of pretty cascades. The most impressive is **Öxarárfoss**, hidden away behind the eastern lip of the fault. The pool **Drekkingarhylur** was used to drown women found guilty of infanticide, adultery or other serious crimes.

There are other smaller fissures on the eastern edge of the plain. During the 17th century nine men accused of witchcraft were burnt at the stake in **Brennugjá** (Burning Chasm). Nearby are the fissures of **Flosagjá** (named after a slave who jumped his way to freedom) and **Nikulásargjá** (after a drunken sheriff discovered dead in the water). The southern end of Nikulásargjá is known as **Peningagjá** (Chasm of Coins) for the thousands of coins tossed into it by visitors.

BÚÐIR
On the left of the path as you walk down Almannagjá are the ruins of various *búðir* (booths). These small stone-and-turf shelters were where parliament-goers camped; and they also acted like stalls at today's music festivals, selling beer, food and vellum to the assembled crowds. Most of the remains date from the 17th and 18th centuries; the largest, and one of the oldest, is **Biskupabúð**, which belonged to the bishops of Iceland and is located north of the church.

ÞINGVALLABÆR & ÞINGVALLAKIRKJA
The little **farmhouse** in the bottom of the rift is Þingvallabær, built for the 1000th anniversary

of the Alþing in 1930 by the state architect Guðjón Samúelsson. It's now used as the park warden's office and prime minister's summer house.

Behind the farmhouse is a **church** (9am-7pm mid-May–Aug), Þingvallakirkja, one of Iceland's first. The original church was consecrated in the 11th century, but the current wooden building only dates from 1859. Inside are several bells from earlier churches, a 17th-century wooden pulpit, and a painted altarpiece from 1834. The Independence-era poets Jónas Hallgrímsson and Einar Benediktsson are interred in the small cemetery behind the church.

ÞINGVALLAVATN

At a whopping 84 sq km, Þingvallavatn is Iceland's largest **lake** . Pure glacial water from Langjökull glacier filters through bedrock for 40km before emerging here. It's joined by the hot spring Vellankatla, which spouts from beneath the lava field on the northeastern shore.

Þingvallavatn is an important refuelling stop for **migrating birds** (including the great northern diver, barrow's golden-eye and harlequin duck). Weirdly, its waters are full of bleikja (arctic char) that have been isolated for so long that they've evolved into four subspecies.

An unforgettable way of exploring the lake is by **scuba diving** (see p51). The visibility is stunning, and there are several dive sites, although the most popular is the fissure Silfra.

WALKS AROUND ÞINGVELLIR

The brochure *Þingvellir Þjóðgarður*, available from the Park Service Centre, contains a small foldout map showing an overview of Þingvellir and its walking trails.

Serious walkers should bring the Landmælingar Íslands sheets *Þingvellir* 1:25,000 and *Hengill* 1:100,000. Most trails converge on the abandoned farm at Skógarkot. Southeast lie the ruins of another farm, Þórhallastaðir, where ale was brewed and served to 13th-century Alþing participants. The 5km walk from Þingvellir to the western rim of the continental rift takes a few hours.

Walking trails at the southern end of Lake Þingvallavatn cut south across the slopes of the volcano Hengill (768m) to Hveragerði and the Hengill ski area, just off Rte 1. See p126 for more information.

HORSE TREKKING

Íslenskir Ferðahestar (894 7200; www.centrum.is /travelhorse) has two horse farms, one in Mosfellsbær (p79) and another at Skógarhólar, just 2km north of the Park Service Centre on Rte 52. It offers a three-day all-inclusive ride around Þingvallavatn (Ikr53,000).

Tours

Various companies offer Golden Circle tours to Þingvellir, Geysir and Gullfoss from around Ikr6500 (see p80).

Within the park, there are free one-hour **guided tours** (departures- 10am & 3pm Mon-Fri Jun-Aug) in summer, setting off from the church.

Sleeping & Eating

Þingvellir camp sites (482 2660; sites per person Ikr600) The Park Service Centre oversees five camping grounds at Þingvellir. The best are the two at Leirar, near the café – Syðri-Leirar is the biggest and Nyrðri-Leirar has laundry facilities. Fagrabrekka and Hvannabrekka are for campers only (no cars). The fifth camp site, Vatnskot, is down by the lake side.

Hótel Valhöll (480 7100; www.hotelvalholl.is; s/d Jun-Aug Ikr15,000/21,000, Sep-May Ikr10,000/17,000; P) Valhöll is a large farmhouse in Þingvellir National Park, down at the base of the rift. Some of the rooms are on the small side, but they've all been renovated recently; other positives include peaceful surroundings, a very good restaurant, and the prime minister for your neighbour!

Getting There & Away

The easiest way to get here is on a Golden Circle tour (p80) or in a hire car.

From June to August the new daily **Austurleið** (562 1011; www.austurleid.is) bus service 6/6A will run at 8.30am from Reykjavík to Þingvellir, stopping for 45 minutes at the Park Service Centre before continuing to Geysir, Gullfoss and back to Reykjavík (return trip Ikr5100).

There's no public transport to the southern end of Þingvallavatn.

AROUND ÞINGVELLIR
Nesjavellir

Whenever you step into that pongy shower in Reykjavík, think of the weird shining **Nesjavellir geothermal plant**, southwest of Þingvallavatn. It's here that boreholes plunge 2km into the earth, bringing up water heated to 380°C by toasting-hot bedrock. It drives a series of huge turbines that produce the city's electricity. Hot water is also channelled off to Reykjavík, 23km away. The whole system is explained at the **visitor centre** (☎ 480 2408; ⏰ 9am-5pm Mon-Sat, 1-6pm Sun Jun-Aug), where you can admire the immaculate-looking machinery; and there are **hot rivers** and **steaming vents** all around (stick to paths).

The large bungalow guesthouse, **Fosshótel Nesbúð** (☎ 482 3415; www.nesbud.is; sb from Ikr3200, s/d Ikr7500/9900, s/d with bathroom Ikr10,900/13,900) , just off Rte 360, is within sight of the gleaming geothermal plant and the volcano Hengill, with views over the whole steaming, eggy-smelling zone. It offers comfortable rooms and a good restaurant – and hot pots, of course! – and prices include breakfast. Hiking tours can be arranged.

In summer the **Iceland Excursions** (☎ 540 1313; www.icelandexcursions.is) Golden Circle Classic day tour (Ikr6200) visits Nesjavellir, Þingvellir, Gullfoss, Geysir and Hveragerði.

You can also walk to Nesjavellir from Hveragerði via the volcano Hengill (see p126).

Laugarvatn
pop 150

Laugarvatn (Hot Springs Lake) wasn't named this way for nothing – this agreeable body of water is fed not only by streams running from the misty fells behind it but by the hot spring Vígðalaug, famous since medieval times. A village, also called Laugarvatn, sits on the lake's western shore, and it is one of the best places to base yourself in the Golden Circle area. Naturally, there's a swimming pool here.

SIGHTS & ACTIVITIES
Down by the shore is **Vígðalaug**, used for early Christian baptisms. Rather more gruesomely, the bodies of Jón Arason (Iceland's last Catholic bishop) and his sons were dug up a year after they were executed in 1550, and brought here to be washed and blessed: the bier stones **Líkasteinar** are where they were laid.

Near Vígðalaug, **boat and windsurfer hire** (☎ 486 1235; ⏰ Jun-Aug) is available, or visit the natural **geothermal steam bath** (Gufubað; ☎ 486 1235; Lindarbraut 1; adult/under 12yr Ikr350/200; ⏰ noon-9pm Jun-Aug, 2-6pm Sat & Sun Sep-May), which also has two hot pots.

Many short hikes are possible from Laugarvatn, including one up to the viewpoint Hringsjá, north of the village.

SLEEPING & EATING
Laugarvatn camp site (☎ 486 1155; tjaldmidstodin@ simnet.is; sites per person Ikr600; ⏰ May-Sep) By the highway just outside the village, this is a major Icelandic party venue on summer weekends. If you want quiet, stay elsewhere! Good facilities include showers (Ikr150) and a washing machine (Ikr400).

Laugarvatn Youth Hostel (☎ 486 1215; laugarvatn@ hostel.is; sb dm/s/d/tr/q Ikr1900/3100/5000/6400/8300; 🖳) This large year-round hostel is a great place to stay. The owners have recently added a whole new floor, giving guests an extra kitchen (with great lake views while you're washing up). Its neat rooms are indistinguishable from those of the average Icelandic guesthouse, particularly as you can pay extra for a private bathroom. There's a hot tub, an internet connection (Ikr200 per 30 minutes), and the possibility of breakfast (Ikr900) if you desire it.

Edda hotels (☎ 444 4000; www.hoteledda.is; sb from Ikr1700, s/d Ikr5800/7200, s/d with bathroom Ikr9000/11,300; ⏰ mid-Jun–mid-Aug) Laugarvatn's two big schools become hotels in summer, both with the usual serviceable rooms and good restaurants.

our pick **Lindin** (☎ 486 1262; Lindarbraut 2; mains Ikr2500-5100; ⏰ noon-11.30pm Mon-Thu, noon-1am Fri-Sun mid-May–Aug) Lindin is the best restaurant for miles. Its menu uses local and seasonal ingredients – fresh char from the lake, reindeer, goose and guillemot – and quiet jazz and candlelight create a relaxing atmosphere. Its Belgian dark chocolate mousse, with raspberry purée and watermelon pieces, is allegedly the best in the world – and, having tasted it, we won't argue!

GETTING THERE & AWAY
There's a year-round bus service to Laugarvatn. From June to August the bus leaves at 8.30am daily from Reykjavík, calling at Laugarvatn (Ikr2000, two hours) and continuing on to Gullfoss, Geysir and then returns to Reykjavík. From September to May the bus leaves at 8.30am on weekdays and at 5pm at weekends but does not stop at Gullfoss and Geysir.

In summer a dirt road called Gjábakkavegur (Rte 365) provides a shortcut between Laugarvatn and Þingvellir. It's impassable in winter – you'll have to drive south almost to Selfoss, before heading north on Rte 36 to Þingvellir. In the other direction, Rte 37 heads east to Gullfoss and Geysir.

SOUTHWEST ICELAND

GEYSIR

One of Iceland's most famous tourist attractions, Geysir (pronounced GAY-zeer) is the original blasting **hot-water spout** after which all other geysers around the world are named. The Great Geysir used to gush water up to 80m into the air but, sadly, it became clogged in the 1950s when tourists threw rocks into the spring in an attempt to set it off. Large earthquakes in 2000 seem to have shifted some of the blockage – it has begun erupting two or three times daily, although not to its former height.

Luckily for visitors, the world's most reliable geyser, **Strokkur**, is right next door. You rarely have to wait more than six minutes for the water to swirl and vanish down what looks like an enormous plughole, before bursting upwards in an impressive 15m to 30m plume. Don't stand downwind.

Geysers are formed when geothermally heated water becomes trapped in narrow fissures. The water at the surface cools, whereas the water below the ground becomes superheated, eventually turning into steam and blasting out the cooler water above it.

Geysir and Strokkur are surrounded by smaller colourful springs, bubbling milky pools and steam vents, where water emerges from the ground at 100°C. The geothermal area is free (it was only ever a paying venue when an Englishman owned it in 1894).

Sights & Activities

GEYSIR CENTER

Across the road from the geysers you'll find this **tourist complex** (☎ 480 6800; www.geysircenter .com; ☽ 9am-7pm). It contains a petrol station, a café, a huge souvenir shop and **Geysisstofa** (☎ 480 6800; www.geysircenter.com; adult/6-12yr Ikr500/ 200; ☽ 10am-7pm Jun-Aug, noon-5pm Sep-May), an audiovisual exhibition on geysers and volcanoes, with an earthquake simulator and some folk-museum pieces upstairs. It might provide 20 minutes' distraction, but really the geysers themselves are far more fun.

HAUKADALUR

A pleasant 2km stroll north of the steaming springs is Haukadalur, a major centre of learning in Viking times. As with many saga sites, there isn't a lot to see now, but it's a picturesque walk. The Icelandic Forestry Commission (yes, there really is one!) has planted thousands of trees in the area.

HORSE RIDING

It's possible to rent horses from Hótel Geysir. Rates start at Ikr3000 for a one-hour horse trek. Experienced riders can do a day trip to Gullfoss (Ikr10,800).

Sleeping & Eating

Geysir camp site (sites per person Ikr600; ☽ May-Sep) Stay at this camp site and you'll get to marvel at the spouting springs before the coach parties arrive. Pay at Hótel Geysir, where you can use the hot tub and pool for free.

Hótel Geysir (☎ 480 6800; www.geysircenter.com; s/d/ d from Ikr3000/9200/11,200; P ☒) Accommodation is in spick, span and tasteful alpine-style cabins; there's a geothermal pool (open mid-April to August) and two hot pots, and the hotel can arrange horse rides (see above). There are plans to build new rooms overlooking the geyser field for 2007–08 – what a sight to wake up to! The hotel restaurant (mains Ikr2200 to Ikr3700) already has a prime view of the geysers, and serves good meaty dishes like reindeer steak with truffle gravy.

There's a reasonable **café** (snacks Ikr250-990; ☽ 9am-7pm) inside the Geysir Centre.

Getting There & Away

From June to August, scheduled Þingvallaleið (☎ 511 2600; www.bustravel.is) bus 2/2a does an 8½-hour circuit from the BSÍ bus station in Reykjavík to Geysir and Gullfoss (8.30am and 12.30pm). This bus works a bit like a tour, stopping for at least half an hour at each site. On Saturday an extra bus leaves Reykjavík at 5pm and goes as far as Geysir, returning at 7pm.

Also from June to August, the new **Austurleið** (☎ 562 1011; www.austurleid.is) daily bus 6/6a (return Ikr5100, 8.30am) stops at Þingvellir, Geysir and Gullfoss for at least 45 minutes each, before returning to Reykjavík.

Very popular Golden Circle tours run year-round from Reykjavík (see p80).

GULLFOSS

Iceland's most famous waterfall, Gullfoss is a spectacular double cascade. It drops 32m, kicking up a sheer wall of spray before thundering away down a narrow ravine. Whether or not you're suitably impressed can depend on the weather: on sunny days the spray creates shimmering rainbows, and it's also magical in winter when the falls glitter with ice. On grey, drizzly days, mist can envelop the second drop, making Gullfoss slightly underwhelming.

The falls came within a hair's breadth of destruction during the 1920s, when a team of foreign investors wanted to dam the river Hvitá for a hydroelectric project. The landowner, Tómas Tómasson, refused to sell, but the developers went behind his back and obtained permission directly from the government. Tómasson's daughter, Sigríður, walked to Reykjavík to protest, even threatening to throw herself into the waterfall if the development went ahead. Thankfully, the investors failed to pay the lease, the agreement was nullified and the falls escaped. Gullfoss was donated to the nation in 1975 and has been preserved as a nature reserve ever since.

Above Gullfoss is a small visitor centre and a good **café** (☎ 486 8683; snacks Ikr500-980; 9am-9pm Jun-Aug, to 6pm Mon-Fri, to 7pm Sat & Sun Sep-May), whose speciality is lamb soup. A tarmac path suitable for wheelchairs leads to a lookout over the falls, and a set of steps continues to the water.

With a 4WD it's possible to continue from Gullfoss to the glacier at Langjökull and other parts of the interior via mountain road F35.

Sleeping

Hótel Gullfoss (☎ 486 8979; www.hotelgullfoss.is; s/d/tr Ikr9000/13,500/16,500; mid-May–Sep, bookings necessary Oct–mid-May) There's accommodation a few kilometres before the falls at this large, modern bungalow hotel. Its en-suite rooms, overlooking the moors, are modest-sized and businesslike, and there's a hot pot and a restaurant. Breakfast is included.

Getting There & Away

See opposite for bus information.

GULLFOSS TO SELFOSS

From Gullfoss there are several possible routes back to the Ring Rd, passing through an agricultural region dotted with farms, hamlets…and countless summer houses. There isn't too much to see in this area, but there are plenty of possible bases for exploring the Golden Circle.

Most people follow surfaced Rte 35, which passes the turn-off to the Arctic Rafting HQ (see the boxed text, below), continues through Reykholt, then meets the Ring Rd about 2km west of Selfoss. You can detour off Rte 35 to Skálholt, once Iceland's religious powerhouse.

Alternatively, you could follow Rte 30, which is intermittently surfaced and passes through Flúðir, meeting Rte 1 about 15km east of Selfoss. An interesting detour from this road is through the scenic Þjórsárdalur valley, along Rte 32. From here you can follow Rte 26 past the foothills of the Hekla volcano, emerging on Rte 1 about 6km west of Hella.

Reykholt
pop 180

The rural township of Reykholt – one of several Reykholts around the country – is centred on the hot spring Reykjahver. Several local farms have greenhouses heated by the springs, and there's the inevitable **swimming pool** (☎ 486 8807; adult/7-12 yr Ikr250/120; 2-6pm Mon, Wed, Sat & Sun, 2-10pm Tue & Thu, closed Fri). Services include a petrol station and grill, a shop, a post office and a bank.

SLEEPING & EATING
Húsið (☎ 486 8680; husid@best.is; Bjarkarbraut 26; sb Ikr2700, made-up bed Ikr4000) This friendly place

---

RAFTING IN SOUTHWEST ICELAND

The great glacial rivers of southwest Iceland provide some wonderful opportunities for whitewater rafting. **Arctic Rafting** (☎ 562 7000; www.arcticrafting.is; Jun-early Sep) offers something to suit everyone, from an easy 3½-hour River Fun trip (Ikr5990, with pick-up Ikr8990) to the experienced-rafters-only adrenaline rush down the Hólmsá (Ikr7990, with pick-up Ikr10,990). You have to be at least 12 years old for most of the trips. It's best to book ahead; and bring a swimsuit.

Arctic Rafting do other exciting action trips – kayaking, glacier walks, ice climbing, and (if you ever wanted to be Lara Croft) canyoning, which involves climbing waterfalls, hurling yourself off cliffs and swimming in watery caves!

The company can pick you up from Reykjavík and hotels on the southwest coast, but if you want to save on the pick-up cost you can drive there yourself. The Arctic Rafting HQ is at Drumboddsstaðir; head 7km north from Reykholt on Rte 358, then take the signposted right turn – it's about 2.5km further along on a bone-shaking dirt track.

has B&B and sleeping-bag accommodation in a quiet cul-de-sac; there's a hot tub and a barbecue. Camping (☎ 486 9816) is also available.

Gilbrún (☎ 486 8925; Dalbraut 1) This farmhouse, just off the main road, has B&B and sleeping-bag accommodation.

Kaffi Klettur (☎ 486 1310; mains Ikr990-2500; 🕒 noon-9pm Jun-Aug) Decorated in mock-old-fashioned style, with tapestries, old coffee mills and horse bridles, this place has a wide selection of pizzas, burgers, crepes, pasta, and traditional fish and meat mains. It's housed in a wooden lodge in a large garden with children's swings.

There's also the **petrol-station grill** (🕒 9am-6pm Mon-Fri, 11am-6pm Sat & Sun).

GETTING THERE & AWAY
See right for details.

Skálholt & Laugarás

The name of Skálholt (population 184) resounds through Iceland's history. This hugely important religious centre was one of two bishoprics (the other was Hólar in the north) that ruled Iceland's souls from the 11th to the 18th centuries.

Skálholt rose to prominence under Gissur the White, the driving force behind the Christianisation of Iceland. The Catholic bishopric lasted until the Reformation in 1550, when Bishop Jón Arason and his two sons were executed by order of the Danish king. Skalhólt continued as a Lutheran centre until 1797, when the bishopric shifted to Reykjavík.

Unfortunately, the great cathedral that once stood here was destroyed by a major earthquake in the 18th century. Today there's just a modern theological centre and a church with a tiny basement **museum** (admission Ikr100; 🕒 9am-7pm except during services or concerts). Its most interesting item is the stone sarcophagus of Bishop Páll Jónsson (bishop from 1196 to 1211). According to *Páls Saga*, the earth was wracked by storms and earthquakes when he died; and, spookily, a huge storm broke at the exact moment that his coffin was reopened in 1956.

Given that Skálholt played such a major role in Iceland's history, the modern settlement is rather a letdown. If you want a clearer picture of its former wealth and power, read the brilliant *Iceland's Bell* by Halldór Laxness, which contains a vivid picture of Skálholt in the 17th century.

Just 1.5km from Skálholt is the village Laugarás (population 120), mainly known for its greenhouses. If you've got young children, you could pop into the little family park, **Slakki Dýragarður** (☎ 868 7626; www.slakki.is; adult/2-16yr Ikr550/400; 🕒 10am-6pm Jun–mid-Sep). Its beguilements include minigolf, farm animals, parrots and ice cream.

There's an important free classical-music festival, **Sumartónleikar í Skálholtskirkju** (☎ 562 1028; www.sumartonleikar.is), at Skálholt for five weeks from July to early August, featuring composers and musicians from all over Iceland and Europe.

SLEEPING & EATING
Hótel Hvítá (☎ 486 8600; hotelhvita@simnet.is; sites per person Ikr500, sb from Ikr2000, s/d/tr Ikr8500/11,000/13,500; 🕒 May-Sep; 🖳) In a great location beside the suspension bridge in Laugarás, this hotel caters for different budgets, with a camping area, sleeping-bag bunk beds and simple parquet-floored guesthouse rooms. The new owners are currently building a wing of brand-new rooms. There's also a grill-style restaurant, with a splendid view over the Hvítá river.

You may be able to stay at the theological centre **Skálholtsskóli** (☎ 486 8870; skoli@skalholt .is) – contact them for information.

GETTING THERE & AWAY
From June to August, scheduled **Þingvallaleið** (☎ 511 2600; www.bustravel.is) bus 2/2a does an 8½-hour circuit from Reykjavík to Geysir and Gullfoss, calling at Reykholt and Laugarás/Skálholt. The bus leaves the city at 8.30am and 12.30pm, with an extra service on Saturday at 5pm.

In winter buses run directly from Reykjavík to Laugarás/Skálholt (Ikr2100, 1¾ hours) and Reykholt (Ikr2100, 2¼ hours) at 8.30am weekdays and at 5pm weekends.

To drive to Skálholt, take Rte 35 from Selfoss. After around 30km, turn right onto Rte 31; the settlement is a couple of kilometres further along.

Kerið & Seyðishólar

Around 10km further southwest of Skálholt and Laugarás, Rte 35 passes Kerið, a 3000-year-old explosion crater containing a spooky-looking green lake. Björk once performed a concert from a floating raft in the middle; and it's said that some joker has introduced fish to the water.

About 3km northeast across the road is the bright-red Seyðishólar crater group, which produced most of the surrounding lava field.

FLÚÐIR
pop 340

Flúðir's mainly known for its mushrooms, grown in geothermal greenhouses, and for its many summer houses where hardworking Reykjavíkurs come to throw off big-city cares. This peaceful green settlement is the largest in this area; it has all necessary services and makes an alternative base for exploring the Golden Circle (it's around 25km south of Gullfoss and Geysir).

There's a **swimming pool** (☎ 486 6790; adult/child Ikr250/100; ⏱ 4-9pm Mon-Fri, 10am-6pm Sat, 1-6pm Sun), a small folk museum at the farm **Gróf** (☎ 486 6634), a bank with ATM and a post office. **Horse riding** is available at Syðra-Langholt – see below.

Sleeping & Eating
Syðra-Langholt (☎ 486 6574, 861 6652; sydralangholt@ emax.is; sites per person Ikr600, sb/s/d/tr Ikr2500/5000/8000/ 10,300) Ten kilometres southwest of Flúðir on Rte 340 is this big white farmhouse. The owners are a lively bunch and the house has all mod cons, including a hot pot. Room prices include breakfast. Horse riding is available for Ikr2500/3500 per hour/two hours.

Hótel Flúðir (☎ 486 6630; Vesturbrún 1; s/d Ikr13,000/ 16,200; ⏱ early Jan-late Dec) Icelandair own this stylish chaletlike bungalow, which has much more warmth than other hotels in the chain. Comfortable rooms have parquet floors, brown leafy bed covers, and soothing prints of fruit and flowers. They all have bathroom, TV, phone and minibar, and there's a good restaurant that opens for dinner daily.

Ferðamiðstoðin (☎ 486 6535; snacks Ikr500-900; ⏱ Easter-Aug) This cafeteria in Flúðir has a sheltered camp site (sites per tent Ikr1000) behind it.

Kaffi Sel (☎ 486 6454; Efra-Sel; pizzas Ikr1000, snacks Ikr800-1400; ⏱ 8am-9pm Mon-Thu, 8am-10pm Fri-Sun May–mid-Sep) We recommend this comical option, 3km northwest of Flúðir – the local golf clubhouse! It's strange but satisfying to sit among golf trophies while you eat your lunch, watching people thwack balls around on the green. There's a good menu of homemade soup, burgers, pizzas and Mexican dishes, and sociable staff.

Flúðir has a **Samkaup-Strax supermarket** (⏱ 9am-7pm Mon-Fri, 10am-7pm Sat, 10am-5pm Sun), and

a pizzeria, **Útlaginn** (☎ 486 6425; www.utlaginn.is; pizzas Ikr900-2000).

Getting There & Away
The bus service from Reykjavík to Flúðir (Ikr2200, two hours) runs at 5pm daily, returning at 8.30am and 7.15pm, from June to August; from September to May it runs at 8.30am on weekdays and at 7pm at weekends. Most Flúðir buses run via Árnes (Ikr2100, one hour 40 minutes), and pass 5km from Syðra-Langholt.

ÞJÓRSÁRDALUR
The Þjórsá is Iceland's longest river at 230km, a fast-flowing, churning mass of milky glacial water that runs from Vatnajökull and Hofsjökull to the Atlantic. With its tributaries, it accounts for almost one third of Iceland's hydroelectric power.

You can follow it upstream awhile via Rte 32, along a valley of Saga Age farms, past the hydroelectric plants Búrfell and Bláskógar, and through the lava fields of Hekla. Rte 32 eventually meets up with mountain road F26, which continues across the interior; if you don't have a 4WD you can turn back towards the coast here along Rte 26.

Árnes
The tiny settlement of Árnes, near the junction of Rtes 30 and 32, is a possible base for exploring Þjórsárdalur. **Árnes HI Hostel** (☎ 486 6048; arnes@hostel.is; sites per tent Ikr1000, sb Ikr2500) isn't the cosiest place on earth, but its twin rooms and dorm are adequate, plus there's a guest kitchen, a licensed **restaurant** (⏱ Jun-Aug) and small octagonal **pool** (⏱ 5-10pm Jun-Aug, 7-10pm Mon, 5-10pm Wed & 1-5pm Sat Mar-May & Sep-Nov, closed Dec-Feb).

Most buses between Reykjavík and Flúðir go via Árnes – see above.

Stöng & Þjóðveldisbær
Heading along Rte 32 from Árnes towards Stöng and Þjóðveldisbær, take a short (2km) detour along a signposted track to the delightful waterfall **Hjálparfoss**, which tumbles in two chutes over a scarp formed from twisted basalt columns.

The **ancient farm** at Stöng was buried by white volcanic ash in 1104, during one of Hekla's eruptions. It once belonged to Gaukur Trandilsson, a 10th-century Viking with a tempestuous life. Unfortunately, the centuries have

SOUTHWEST ICELAND

destroyed all traces of his saga; brief mentions in some 12th-century graffiti in Orkney, in *Njál's Saga* and in a scurrilous medieval rhyme hint that he had a fling with the housewife at the nearby farm Steinastöðum and was killed over the affair in an axe duel.

Stöng was excavated in 1939 – Iceland's first proper archaeological dig – and is an important site, used to help date Viking houses elsewhere. The farm ruins are covered over by a large wooden shelter at the end of a bad, bumpy dirt road that branches off Rte 32 about 20km beyond Árnes. You can still see stone-lined fire pits and door lintels, made from octagonal basalt columns, and the surrounding lava landscape is impressively desolate. A **walking path** behind the farm takes you a couple of kilometres to a strange and lovely little valley, full of twisting lava and waterfalls.

We happen to think it's an atmospheric spot, but the **reconstructed Viking-era farm** (☎ 488 7713; www.thjodveldisbaer.is; adult/under 13yr Ikr500/free; 😊 10am-noon & 1-6pm Jun-Aug) in Þjóðveldisbær is more photogenic. The farm was built using traditional methods, and it exactly reproduces the layout of Stöng and its neighbouring church. The two farms are like a cosmetic surgeon's 'before' and 'after' photos.

South of the reconstructed farm is the **Búrfell hydroelectricity plant**. It's a strange place for a sculpture, but one of Sigurjón Ólafsson's larger works adorns this hydro station.

From Stöng you can walk 10km northeast along a 4WD track to Iceland's second-highest waterfall, **Háifoss**, which plunges 122m off the edge of a flat plateau. You can also get most of the way there by 4WD.

SLEEPING

From May to September you can camp in a plantation of fir trees at **Sandártunga** (☎ 893 8889; sites per person Ikr600), about 7km before Búrfell. Alternatively, you could stay at the nearby farm **Ásólfsstaðir** (☎ 486 6063; asolfsstadir@ simnet.is; 😊 Jun-Aug), which has sleeping-bag accommodation.

GETTING THERE & AWAY

Reykjavík Excursions (☎ 562 1011; www.re.is) runs a 12-hour tour (Ikr10,300) from Reykjavík to Landmannalaugar that stops at Þjórsárdalur. The tour runs at 8am on Tuesday, Thursday and Sunday from July to September. **Iceland Total** (☎ 585 4300; www.icelandtotal.com) has a similar tour.

THE SOUTHWEST COAST

Coming from Reykjavík, this is one of the most exciting bits of the southern coast, simply because of the suspense. Rte 1 trundles through a flat, wide coastal plain, full of horse farms and greenhouses, before the landscape suddenly begins to spasm and grow jagged. Mountains thrust upwards on the inland side of the road and the first of the awesome glaciers appears.

Public transport isn't bad along the Ring Rd, which is studded with interesting settlements: Hveragerði is famous for its geothermal fields and hot springs; Hvolsvöllur is the leaping-off point for Þórsmörk, one of Iceland's most popular hiking destinations; further east, Skógar is home to one of Iceland's best folk museums; and Vík, surrounded by glaciers, vertiginous cliffs and black beaches, will leave you giddy with love.

Treats lying off the Ring Rd include the tiny fishing villages of Stokkseyri and Eyrarbakki; brooding volcano Hekla (a possible gateway to hell!); the Mýrdalsjökull icecap, where you can go dogsledding or snowmobiling; and farms and valleys rich with saga heritage.

HVERAGERÐI

pop 2080

At first glance, you might write Hveragerði off as a dull grid of boxy buildings. However, spend longer than half an hour here and your ominous muttering should fade away. This friendly town has soul, and lots of small, strange things to see and do.

Hveragerði sits on top of a highly active geothermal field, which provides heat for hundreds of greenhouses. Locally, the town is famous for its horticultural college and naturopathic clinic. There are also some fantastic hikes in the area, so it makes a good walking base.

Information

Hveragerði contains the regional tourist office for the whole south coast, **Upplýsingamiðstöð Suðurlands** (☎ 483 4601; www.southiceland.is; Sunnumörk 2-4; 😊 9am-5pm Mon-Fri, noon-4pm Sat & Sun summer, 9am-5pm Mon-Fri winter), which shares its premises with the post office, inside the shopping centre. It can book accommodation for an Ikr300 fee.

A tiny room with three internet computers (Ikr150 per half-hour) can be accessed from both the tourist office and the friendliest **library**

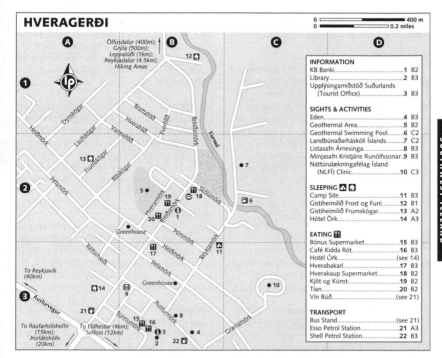

(☎ 483 4531; Sunnumörk 2; ⌚ 2-7pm Mon & Wed-Fri, to 9pm Tue, 11am-2pm Sat) in Iceland. While you're here (yes, inside the building!), look down by your feet at the rift, discovered during the construction of the shopping centre.

There's a KB Banki on Breiðamörk and an ATM in the shopping centre entrance.

Sights
GEOTHERMAL FIELDS
There's a small **geothermal area** (☎ 483 5062; Hveramörk; admission Ikr200; ⌚ 9-11am & 5-8pm Mon-Thu, 9-11am & 2-4pm Fri, 2-4pm Sat & Sun Jun-Aug) in the centre of town, with baked earth, small mudpots and several hot springs and pools. They're a little tame, but the information sheet contains some great stories – read all about the hot-spring spider *Pirata piraticus*, the burping Garbage Spring, and the murderous mudpot. In summer there's a small café where you can buy eggs (Ikr150) to boil in the water. Out of season, ask the tourist office to unlock the gates.

For something a little more explosive, head up Breiðamörk and on out of town. This valley is **Ölfusdalur**, site of several mudpots, steaming vents and the geyser **Grýla** (on the left), which

erupts 12m several times daily. There's also an artificial borehole, **Leppalúði**, on the right by the bridge near the golf-course road, which erupts continually. If you keep going a further 1.5km, you'll reach a car park; from here, it's a 3km walk to unmissable **Reykjadalur**, a delightful geothermal valley where there's a bathable **hot river** – bring your swimsuit.

EDEN & OTHER GREENHOUSES
If you take many bus tours east from Reykjavík, you could end up quite sick of the greenhouse **Eden** (☎ 483 4900; www.eden.smart.is; Austurmörk 25; admission free; ⌚ 9am-11pm summer, 9am-7pm winter) – it's Iceland's nearest thing to a tourist trap, and all passing tour groups are shepherded through its doors. Having said that, there are worse places designed to separate fools and money. Bananas and papayas add a touch of the tropics, there's an enormous postcard selection; and it sells Hveragerði's famous Kjörís ice cream, made just round the corner.

The greenhouses around town are great at night, when they glow radioactive orange, and several are open to the public. It's also fine to amble into the **Landbúnaðarháskóli Íslands**

(Agricultural University of Iceland; ☎ 433 5000; www.lbhi.is; Reykir; ☺ 9am-5pm) to look at the plants.

NLFÍ CLINIC

Iceland's most famous clinic, **Náttúrulækningafélag Ísland** (NLFÍ; ☎ 483 0300; www.hnlfi.is; Grænmörk 10; adult/concession/under 12yr Ikr600/300/300; ☺ bath house 7.30-11am, 1-6pm & 7-9.30pm Mon-Fri, 10am-6pm Sat & Sun), has mainly treated prescription-only patients in the past. However, it's keen to throw open its doors to visitors seeking relaxing massages (Ikr4100 to Ikr8300) and deep-heat mud baths (Ikr3600). NLFÍ has excellent new facilities, including indoor and outdoor pools, hot pots, a sauna, a steam bath, and a relaxation room. Treatments are available year-round, mainly on weekdays – book ahead.

GALLERIES & MUSEUMS

Close to Eden, the large, modern art gallery **Listasafn Árnesinga** (☎ 483 1727; www.listasafnarnesinga.is; Austurmörk 21) has some great temporary exhibitions, although opening times are hazy (ring to check).

Minjasafn Kristjáns Runólfssonar (☎ 483 1997; Austurmörk 2; adult/under 12yr Ikr500/free; ☺ 2-6pm daily) This two-room private collection belongs to Kristján, who has been collecting old folk items since he was a kid. Most are labelled in Icelandic, but Kristján is happy to explain what things are and who they belonged to.

Activities
HIKING

There are loads of interesting walks around Hveragerði. Bring the Landmælingar Íslands sheet *Hengill* 1:100,000, or ask the tourist office for the map *Hiking Trails in the Hengill Area* (Ikr600).

Most trails begin from the small car park in Ölfusdalur (follow Breiðamörk out of town, and don't turn right into Gufudalur and the golf course). From here it's a 3.5km walk up through beautiful Reykjadalur (see p125) to the Dalsel survival hut.

From Dalsel, several trails cut across the hills to the shores of the great lake Þingvallavatn (p118). The shortest routes run northeast to Úlfljótsvatn (13km) or due north to Ölfusvatn (13.5km). A longer route will take you over the summit of Hengill (768m; 11.7km from Dalsel) to Nesjavellir (p118), 18.7km from Dalsel.

If you just want to climb Hengill, you can drive as far as the Hengill ski area (off Rte 1,

16km west of Hveragerði), from where it's 7km to the summit along the ridge to the west, or 6km via the Hengladalir valley. All routes to the top of Hengill are black walking trails – officially 'tough, and should not be walked alone'.

SWIMMING

Hveragerði's open-air **geothermal swimming pool** (☎ 483 4113; Laugaskarði; adult/child Ikr270/100; ☺ 7am-8.30pm Mon-Fri, 10am-5.30pm Sat & Sun), beside the Varmá river just north of town, is among Iceland's favourites. Goodies include a massaging hot pot and a steam room built directly over a natural hot spring.

HORSE RIDING

A few kilometres east of Hveragerði, the recommended horse farm **Eldhestar** (☎ 480 4800; www.eldhestar.is; Vellir) has all kinds of riding tours, from one-hour trots (around Ikr3000) in the surrounding area to multiday tours into the interior (contact Eldhestar for prices).

Sleeping

Camp site (☎ 483 4601; Reykjamörk 1; sites per person Ikr500) This excellent modern camp site is just east of the centre, and has toilets, showers, a cooking area and a laundry.

Gistiheimilið Frumskógar (☎ 896 2780; www.frumskogar.is; Frumskógar 3; s/d/apt Ikr4000/5500/9000) Clean, good-value rooms are offered at this cosy suburban guesthouse. They all come with comfy beds, thick duvets, TVs, washbasins and dressing gowns. A yummy breakfast (Ikr850) can be ordered, and there's a hot pot in the garden. Self-catering apartments at the back have TV, bathroom and kitchen.

Gistiheimilið Frost og Funi (Frost & Fire Guesthouse; ☎ 483 4959; www.frostandfire.is; Hverhamar; s/d Ikr9500/14,900) This quite a romantic spot, with access to a private pool, an idyllic riverbank hot pot and a natural steam sauna. Eight of the 14 rooms are brand spanking new; they're simple but tasteful, with large beds, TVs, en-suite bathrooms and modern Icelandic artwork on the walls. Breakfast is included.

Hótel Eldhestar (☎ 480 4800; www.eldhestar.is; sb/s/d Ikr2400/10,900/16,400; 🖳 ♿) About 3km east of Hveragerði, the popular riding school Eldhestar offers large comfy rooms, all named after the farm's horses, in a purpose-built modern building. There's a great lounge with an open fire, and an outdoor hot pot – both perfect for relaxing after a day in the saddle. The sleeping-bag accommodation is in little huts in the garden.

Hótel Örk (☎ 483 4700; www.hotel-ork.is; Breiðamörk 1; s/tw/tr Ikr13,900/16,900/18,900; 🖳 🖭) Although the rooms in this big custom-built building are staid and slightly old-fashioned, unusually for Iceland they all have bathtubs. The hotel itself has excellent facilities, particularly for families – saunas, tennis courts, a nine-hole golf course, a ping-pong table, and an excellent swimming pool with slide, hot tubs and children's pool. Breakfast is included.

Eating

Hverabakarí (☎ 483 4879; Breiðamörk 10; 🕙 7am-6pm Mon-Fri, 9am-6pm Sat & Sun) An unusual cake maker works at this little bakery – look out for the marzipan chessboard and buns pulling horrible faces. There are plenty of tables, and good coffee and snacks.

Kjöt og Kúnst (☎ 483 5010; Breiðamörk 21; 🕙 10am-8pm Mon-Fri) This deli serves delicious nibbly things for picnics – mouthwatering salads, cakes, roast chicken, slices of meat and fish. You can also eat in – choose from various different hotplate courses, then take your plate to be weighed. Dishes are cooked using steam from nearby hot springs.

Café Kidda Rót (☎ 552 8002; Sunnumörk 2; mains Ikr990-2000; 🕙 11am-10pm Sun-Thu, to 11.30pm Fri & Sat) In the shopping centre, the town's most popular café-bar sells good coffee, and a diverse menu of pizzas, burgers, Chinese meals and

cheap (although not hugely flavoursome) wild trout. It also doubles as a kind of art gallery; and old men come in to watch the news on a giant-screen TV.

Hótel Örk (☎ 483 4700; Breiðamörk 1; mains Ikr2600-3400) The restaurant at Hótel Örk is the poshest place in town, and it serves a small menu of Icelandic specialities such as *hangikjöt* (smoked lamb) and *bacalao* (salt cod), plus burgers, beef steaks and seafood kebabs.

There are several fast-food places in town, including **Tían** (☎ 483 4727; Breiðamörk 19) and the grills at the petrol stations.

Self-caterers should head for the **Hverakaup** (☎ 483 4655; Breiðamörk 27; 🕙 9am-9pm Mon-Sat, 10am-9pm Sun) or cheaper **Bónus** (☎ 482 1818; Sunnumörk 2; 🕙 noon-6.30pm Mon-Thu, 10am-7.30pm Fri, 10am-6pm Sat, noon-6pm Sun) supermarkets. There's a **Vín Búð** (☎ 483 4242; Breiðamörk 1; 🕙 2-6pm Mon-Thu, 2-7pm Fri, 11am-4pm Sat) at the Esso garage.

Getting There & Away

The bus stop is at the Esso petrol station on the main road into town. All buses from Reykjavík to Selfoss and places further east stop in Hveragerði (Ikr950, 40 minutes).

AROUND HVERAGERÐI

Rte 38 runs south from Hveragerði to Þorlákshöfn (20km), the departure point for the ferry to Vestmannaeyjar .

Raufarhólshellir

This 11th-century lava tube is over 1km long, and contains some wonderful (protected) lava columns. You'll need a torch and sturdy boots to explore; the going underfoot can be quite treacherous from earlier cave-ins. In winter cold air is funnelled down and trapped inside, producing amazing ice formations. You'll find the tube southwest of Hveragerði, just off the Reykjavík–Þorlákshöfn route (Rte 39), which passes right over the tunnel.

Þorlákshöfn
pop 1420
Most people come to this fast-growing fishing town, 20km south of Hveragerði, to catch the ferry to the Vestmannaeyjar. There's a **camp site** (☎ 483 3807; sites per person/tent Ikr200/200) next to the swimming pool if you need to stay over.

GETTING THERE & AWAY
The bus service from Reykjavík to Þorlákshöfn connects with the ferry – see p149.

THE CHRISTMAS LADS

The natural and artificial geysers at Hveragerði are named for Grýla and Leppalúði, a child-devouring troll woman and her henpecked husband. This gruesome pair are said to be the parents of the 13 *jólasveinar* (Christmas lads). One of these horrible hooligans turns up every day between 12 and 24 December, trying to steal his favourite food or cause some other mischief.

Although they're little imps, Ladle-Licker, Sausage-Snatcher, Window-Peeper and the rest of the brothers also leave a small gift in good children's shoes when they arrive (naughty kids get a raw potato). From Christmas Day onwards, the Christmas lads leave one by one, with the last, Candle-Beggar, heading back to the mountains on Twelfth Night.

Just outside Þorlákshöfn, Rte 38 runs to Hveragerði, Rte 39 runs to Reykjavík, and unsurfaced Rte 427 runs west along the bottom of the Reykjanes Peninsula to Krýsuvík.

SELFOSS
pop 5700

Selfoss is the largest town in southern Iceland, an important trade and industry centre, and witlessly ugly. Iceland's Ring Rd is its main shopping street – as a pedestrian, you're in constant danger of ending up as road jam.

The main reason to come here is for a big grocery shop before heading off into the interior; to establish a base to explore the Flói nature reserve (p130) or the wonderful fishing villages of Eyrarbakki (opposite) and Stokkseyri (p130); or if you're desperate to go to the cinema. The nicest part is the winding river Ölfusá.

Information

The **tourist information desk** (☎ 480 2422; www .arborg.is/tourinfo; Austurvegur 2; ☺ 10am-7pm Mon-Fri, 11am-2pm Sat Jun-Aug) inside the town library, close to the roundabout on the main road, is staffed

in summer; at other times, leaflets are available. Pick up the free pamphlet *Árborg*, which is full of tourist information about the Selfoss-Eyrarbakki-Stokkseyri district. The library offers internet access for Ikr200 per hour.

Landsbanki Íslands, KB Banki and Glitnir all have branches with ATMs on Austurvegur.

Activities

Selfoss has a fine **geothermal swimming pool** (☎ 480 1960; Bankavegur; adult/child 6-16yr Ikr310/150; ☺ 6.45am-9.15pm Mon-Fri, 10am-8pm Sat & Sun Apr–mid-Sep, 6.45am-9.15pm Mon-Fri, 10am-6pm Sat & Sun mid-Sep–Apr), with hot pots, water slides and a kids' play pool.

Mountain Cruiser (☎ 892 4030; www.simnet.is/kiddib) offers various 4WD tours, including trips to Þórsmörk and Landmannalaugar – contact it for details.

Sleeping

Gesthús (☎ 482 3585; www.gesthus.is; Engjavegur; sites per person Ikr500, sb/s/d/tr cabin Ikr2500/6900/8900/10,200; ☺ sites mid-May–mid-Sep, cabins year-round; ♿) For a choice of accommodation – sleeping-bag/ camping/made-up beds in wooden cabins –

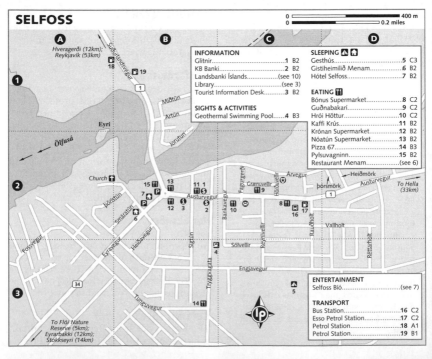

SELFOSS

0 — 400 m
0 — 0.2 miles

INFORMATION
Glitnir.................................1 B2
KB Banki.............................2 B2
Landsbanki Íslands.........(see 10)
Library...............................(see 3)
Tourist Information Desk..........3 B2

SIGHTS & ACTIVITIES
Geothermal Swimming Pool......4 B3

SLEEPING 🏠 🏨
Gesthús................................5 C3
Gistiheimilið Menam...............6 B2
Hótel Selfoss........................7 B2

EATING 🍴
Bónus Supermarket................8 C2
Guðnabakarí.........................9 C2
Hrói Höttur..........................10 C2
Kaffi Krús............................11 B2
Krónan Supermarket.............12 B2
Nóatún Supermarket.............13 B2
Pizza 67...............................14 B3
Pylsuvagninn........................15 B2
Restaurant Menam...............(see 6)

ENTERTAINMENT
Selfoss Bíó..........................(see 7)

TRANSPORT
Bus Station..........................16 C2
Esso Petrol Station................17 C2
Petrol Station.......................18 A1
Petrol Station.......................19 B1

try this friendly place by the park. There's a sociable kitchen hut and a laundry for campers, and the two- to four-bed cabins are nicely equipped with desks, kitchenettes and TVs. There are two hot pots for guests.

Gistiheimiliõ Menam (☎ 482 4099; www.menam .is; Eyravegur 8; s/d/tr Ikr5900/8200/9300) This is a small guesthouse above the Thai restaurant in the town centre. Although the sitting room is dowdy and smells of tobacco, the rooms themselves are pleasantly furnished and cosy, with proper venetian blinds to keep out the midnight sun. Bathrooms are shared.

Hótel Selfoss (☎ 480 2500; www.hotelselfoss.is; Eyravegur 2; s/d May-Sep from Ikr14,300/17,900, Oct-Apr Ikr10,600/13,200; 🖥 ᵹ) This is a 99-room behemoth near the bridge, with four-star business-style hotel rooms and great facilities. Make sure you get a room overlooking the broad and lovely river Ölfusá, rather than the car park. There's a good restaurant, and at the time of research a spa and fitness centre was set to open in 2007.

Selfoss has a couple of modest guesthouses in addition to Menam; ask at the tourist office for details.

Eating

Guðnabakarí (☎ 482 1755; Austurvegur 31b; snacks Ikr580-680; 🕓 8am-5.30pm Mon-Fri, to 4pm Sat, 9.30am-4pm Sun) The sweet people in this busy bakery-café have a small menu of crêpes, soup and pasta, as well as buns and sandwiches.

Hrói Höttur (☎ 482 2899; Austurvegur 22; pizzas Ikr800-1400) This pizzeria and takeaway fairly heaves with families and gangs of teens on a Friday and Saturday night.

Pizza 67 (☎ 482 2267; Tryggvagata 40) Another pizzeria, similar to Hrói Höttur.

Restaurant Menam (☎ 482 4099; Eyravegur 8; mains around Ikr1790; 🕓 11.30am-2pm & 5-10pm) For a break from grills and fish and chips, head for this authentic Thai place on the road to Stokkseyri. There's a big choice of beef, lamb, chicken and pork dishes, as well as a small international menu, although there's not much of interest for veggies.

Kaffi Krús (☎ 482 1672; www.kaffikrus.is; Austurvegur 7; snacks Ikr350-1200, mains Ikr1500-2200; 🕓 10am-midnight Sun-Thu, to 2am Fri & Sat; ✗) Krús is a café-bar based in a fantastic old house, with beams and creaking floorboards. There's a varied menu of coffees and light meals – salads, sandwiches, burgers, nachos, felafel and more substantial fish-of-the-day mains.

Self-caterers have a choice between the **Bónus** (☎ 481 3710; Austurvegur 42; 🕓 noon-6.30pm Mon-Thu, 10am-7.30pm Fri, 10am-6pm Sat, noon-6pm Sun), **Krónan** (☎ 482 3910; Tryggvatorg; 🕓 11am-7pm Mon-Thu, to 8pm Fri, to 7pm Sat, noon-7pm Sun) and **Nóatún** (☎ 482 1000; Austurvegur 3-5; 🕓 til 9pm) supermarkets on the main road. For fast food, try the drive-through hot-dog stand **Pylsuvagninn** (☎ 482 1782; hot dogs Ikr300-800) in the hotel car park.

Entertainment

There aren't many cinemas on the south coast – catch up with Hollywood at **Selfoss Bíó** (☎ 482 3007; www.selfoss.bio), a shiny cinema inside Hótel Selfoss.

Getting There & Away

All buses between Reykjavík and Höfn, Skaftafell, Fjallabak, Þórsmörk, Flúðir, Gullfoss, Langarvatn and Vík pass through Selfoss; there are numerous options daily. The hour-long journey from Reykjavík costs Ikr1200.

EYRARBAKKI
pop 580

It's hard to believe, but tiny Eyrarbakki was Iceland's main port and a thriving trading town well into the 20th century. Farmers from all over the south once rode here to barter for supplies at the general store – the crowds were so huge it could take three days to get served!

Eyrarbakki is as bleak as you like in winter, when you'll slither down its only street without seeing a soul, but there are some interesting summer sights.

Sights

One of Iceland's oldest houses, **Húsið**, was built by Danish traders in 1765. Today it contains the darling **Árnessýsla Folk Museum** (☎ 483 1504; www.husid.com; Hafnarbrú 3; admission to both museums Ikr500; 🕓 11am-5pm Jun-Aug, 2-5pm Sat & Sun Apr, May, Sep & Oct), which has glass display cabinets explaining the town's history, rooms restored with original furniture, a bird's-egg collection, and even a gallery of naïve artwork. Look out for Ólöf Sveinsdóttir's shawl, hat and cuffs, knitted from her own hair.

Just behind Húsið is a small maritime museum, **Sjóminjasafnið á Eyrarbakka** (☎ 483 1082; Túngata 59; admission Ikr500 to both museums; 🕓 11am-5pm Jun-Aug, 2-5pm Sat & Sun Apr, May, Sep & Oct), with displays on the local fishing community. Its main exhibit is the beautiful, tar-smelling, 12-oared fishing boat, *Farsæll*.

The wild, sandy coastline is a fine place to observe migrating **birds**, and you'll often see **seals** loafing about on the rocks.

Another of Eyrarbakki's claims to fame is that it's the **birthplace of Bjarní Herjólfsson**, who made a great sea voyage in AD 985 and was probably the first European to see America. Unfortunately, Bjarní turned back and sold his boat to Leifur Eiríksson, who went on to discover Vinland and ended up with all the glory.

The large fenced building to the east of the village is Iceland's largest **prison**, Litla-Hraun.

Sleeping & Eating

There's a rudimentary free **camping area** on a patch of scrub at the western end of the village, with toilets and tap water.

For cheap eats, there's the grill at the Olís petrol station.

Rauða Húsið (☎ 483 3330; www.raudahusid.is; Búðarstíg 4; mains Ikr2900-4200; ☽ 11.30am-9pm Sun-Thu, to 10pm Fri & Sat, closed Mon) Arch-rival of the lobster restaurant in Stokkseyri, this restaurant operates in an old red house, with cheery staff and great fresh seafood. *Bacalao* and grilled lobster are specialities, and there are unusual choices such as chicken in lime. It gets the prize for best dessert name – 'Þjórsá lava', a cracked chocolate muffin.

Getting There & Away

Buses on the Reykjavík–Þorlákshöfn–Eyrarbakki–Stokkseyri–Selfoss–Reykjavík route run once daily throughout the year. They leave Reykjavík at 11am, arrive in Eyrarbakki (Ikr1250) at 12.15pm and Stokkseyri (Ikr1250) at 12.25pm, and are back in Reykjavík by 1.55pm. In the other direction, a bus leaves Selfoss at 10.15am daily, getting to Stokkseyri at 10.30am and Eyrarbakki at 10.40am.

On weekdays only, another service departs at 3pm from Reykjavík, calling at Selfoss, Stokkseyri and Eyrarbakki.

FLÓI NATURE RESERVE

Bird-watchers should head for the estuarine **Flói Nature Reserve** (☽ summer only), an important marshland on the eastern bank of the Ölfusá. It's visited by many wetland birds – common species include red-throated divers and various kinds of ducks and geese – with the biggest numbers appearing during the nesting season (May to July). There's a 2km circular hiking trail through the marshes. For more

information, contact the **Icelandic Society for the Protection of Birds** (☎ 562 0477; www.fuglavernd.is).

The reserve is 3km northwest of Eyrarbakki – you'll need your own transport.

STOKKSEYRI

pop 470

Eyrarbakki's twin lies east along the shore. It's another small fishing village, with a tourist emphasis less on museums and more on family fun. Again, winter is not the time to visit, but come in summer and you could easily spend a day enjoying the two villages' attractions.

Sights & Activities

For spooky (if pricey) fun, the first port of call should be **Draugasetrið** (Ghost Centre; ☎ 483 1202; www.draugasetrid.is; Hafnargata 9; adult/under 12/12-16yr Ikr1400/500/900; ☽ 2-9pm summer, 1-9pm Sat & Sun winter), on the top floor of a huge warehouse in the village centre. A 40-minute CD-guide (in English, French or German) tells you blood-curdling ghost stories in each of the 24 dark, dry-ice-filled rooms. The ghost centre recommends itself to over-12s; it certainly scared our pants off.

Tots will love the supercute family park **Töfragarðurinn Stokkseyri** (☎ 897 3801, 483 3800; v/ Stjörnusteina; adult/2-12yr Ikr550/400; ☽ 10am-6pm May-Aug), signposted from the centre. Sweet baby animals – Arctic foxes, puppies, piglets, rabbits, lambs and goats – frolic in ridiculously green enclosures. There's also a big climbing frame, a bouncy castle and a café. It's only titchy but infinitely nicer than Reykjavík's zoo (see p79).

Kajakferðir Stokkseyri (☎ 896 5716; www.kajak.is; Heiðarbrún 24; ☽ Apr-Oct) does guided kayaking on the nearby lagoon (Ikr2900/3900 per one/two hours), or on the sea (two hours Ikr4900). You can also wander off on a 'Robinson Crusoe' – guideless but with a 'treasure map' to follow (adult/child six to 14 Ikr2900/500). Prices include admission to Stokkseyri's swimming pool, where Kajakferðir is based.

If you fancy exploring the lovely coastline in 1960s style, the Shell petrol station has 50cc **mopeds** (☎ 483 1485; 1hr/2hr/3hr/day Ikr2500/4000/6000/8000) for hire.

If you're passing, you could stick your head into the tiny, dark **Þuríðarbúð** (☎ 483 1267; admission free), behind the Shell station. This turf-roofed fishing hut is a reconstruction of one that belonged to local lass Þuríður Einarsdóttir (1777–1863), one of the very few female boat captains in Iceland.

About 6km east of Stokkseyri is **Rjómabúið á Baugsstöðum** (Baugsstaðir Creamery; ☎ 486 3369; adult/child Ikr300/free; ⊗ 1-6pm Sat & Sun Jul & Aug, 2-5pm Apr, May, Sep & Oct), an old dairy cooperative (1905–52) that still has its original machinery. Interestingly, most of its produce was sold to England – so some readers' grandparents may have eaten butter from here!

Sleeping & Eating

Við Fjöruborðið (☎ 483 1550; www.fjorubordid.is; Eyrabraut 3a; mains Ikr1500-3500; ⊗ noon-10pm daily Jun-Aug, 5-9pm daily May & Sep, 5-9pm Wed-Fri, noon-9pm Sat & Sun Oct-Apr) This upmarket seafood restaurant on the shore has a reputation for serving the best lobster in Iceland. The legendary lobster soup costs Ikr1690 and is worth every penny. The décor's quite distinctive – old flagstones, fishermen's glass floats, black tablecloths – although the service is a bit sniffy.

There's a little grassy camp site off Dvergasteinar, with toilet and running water. For cheap meals, there's a grill at the Shell petrol station.

Getting There & Away

For details on bus services to Stokkseyri, see opposite.

AUSTUR-FLÓI

The low-lying agricultural region east of Selfoss, reaching as far as the beautiful glacial river Þjórsá (Iceland's longest river at 230km), is called Austur-Flói. Watch out for the violent ghost, Kampholtsmóri, who haunts the area.

Sights & Activities

URRIÐAFOSS

This waterfall doesn't have the slender height of many south-coast falls: its drop is a mere 6m. However, it manages to pack in the power, and it's worth a quick detour from the Ring Rd (on Rte 302) just to see what 360 cu metres of water per second looks like (pretty impressive).

HORSE RIDING

At an old ferry crossing just south of Urriðafoss, the horse farm **Egilsstaðir 1** (☎ /fax 567 6268; www.egilsstadir1.com; rides from Ikr2500 per hr) offers guided rides in the rolling farmland roundabout. The B&B is open year-round.

Sleeping & Eating

Bitra (☎ 482 1081; www.bitra.is; sb/s/d from Ikr2000/4800/8000) This modern black-and-white farmhouse

on a hillock just off Rte 1 (about 15km east of Selfoss) has the same owners as Gesthús in Selfoss. It offers tidy parquet-floored rooms, some with private bathrooms, and homemade evening meals on request. Room prices include breakfast.

HELLA

pop 670

This small agricultural community sits on the banks of the pretty Ytri-Rangá river in an important horse-breeding area. It's also the nearest village to the hulking, shadow-wreathed volcano Hekla (p132), 35km north up Rtes 264 then 268.

The Olís petrol station has tourist information leaflets, and the desk is staffed occasionally in summer. Pick up the free guide map *Power and Purity*, which covers the region from Hella to Skógar.

Sights & Activities

HORSE RIDING

With its many horse farms, dramatic volcanic backdrop and proximity to the highlands, Hella is a good place for hacks into the wilderness. Most places offer trips for more experienced riders – unguided horse hire and longer tours into the interior. Some local horse farms:

Hekluhestar (☎ 487 6598; www.islandia.is/hekluhestar; Austvaðsholt) Rtes 271 then 272, 9km northeast of Hella. Six- to eight-day tours to Landmannalaugar/Fjallabak.

Herríðarhóll (☎ 487 5252; www.herridarholl.is) Off Rte 284, 15km northwest of Hella. Week-long tours in July and August.

Hestheimar (☎ 487 6666; www.hestheimar.is) Near Rte 281, 7km northwest of Hella. Horse rental.

Kálfholt (☎ 487 5176; www.kalfholt.is; Ásahreppi) Rte 288, 17km west of Hella (eastern bank of the Þjórsá). Two- and three-day rides in July.

Leirubakki (☎ 487 8700; www.leirubakki.is) Rte 26, 30km northeast of Hella (near Hekla). Horse rental.

OTHER SIGHTS & ACTIVITIES

Of course, Hella has a good **geothermal swimming pool** (☎ 487 5334; ⊗ 7am-9pm Mon-Fri, 10am-7pm Sat & Sun Jun–mid-Aug, 4-9pm Mon-Fri, 1-6pm Sat & Sun mid-Aug–May), with hot pots and sauna.

Oddi (about 8km south of town on unsurfaced Rte 266) was once the site of an important Saga Age monastery – see the boxed text, p132. There's nothing much to see here today, though; you'll get a better sense of Viking history from reading the Eddas themselves.

SOUTHWEST ICELAND

THE EDDAS

The medieval monastery at Oddi was the source of the Norse Eddas, the most important surviving books of Viking poetry. The *Prose Edda* was written by the poet and historian Snorri Sturluson around 1222. It was intended to be a textbook for poets, with detailed descriptions of the language and metres used by the Norse *skalds* (court poets). It also includes the epic poem *Gylfaginning*, which describes the visit of Gylfi, the king of Sweden, to Ásgard, the citadel of the gods. In the process, the poem reveals Norse creation myths, stories about the gods, and the fate in store for men at Ragnarök, when this world ends.

The *Poetic Edda* was written later in the 13th century by Sæmundur Sigfússon. It's a compilation of works by unknown Viking poets, some predating the settlement of Iceland. The first poem, *Voluspá (Sibyl's Prophecy)*, is like a Norse version of the Book of Genesis: it covers the beginning and end of the world. Later poems deal with the story of how Óðinn discovered the power of runes, and the legend of Siegfried and the Nibelungs, recounted in Wagner's *Ring Cycle*. The most popular poem is probably *Þrymskviða*, about the giant Thrym, who stole Þór's hammer and demanded the goddess Freyja in marriage in exchange for its return. To get his hammer back, Þór disguised himself as the bride-to-be and went to the wedding in her place. Much of the poem is devoted to his appalling table manners at the wedding feast, during which he consumes an entire ox, eight salmon and three skins of mead.

Sleeping & Eating

Árhús (☎ 487 5577; www.arhus.is; Rangárbakkar; sites per person Ikr600, sb Ikr2000, self-catering cabins Ikr5500-12,000) Right on the riverbank south of Rte 1, Arhús offers a well-equipped camp site and 28 wooden cabins that sleep three to four people, all with bathroom and kitchenette. There's also a café (light meals from Ikr500 to Ikr1800) – it's worth stopping just to enjoy the lovely river views from the outside balcony. Breakfast is Ikr950.

Gistiheimilið Brenna (☎ 487 5532; www.mmedia.is /toppbrenna; Þrúðvangur 37; sb Ikr1900, made-up beds Ikr2300) Down by the river north of Rte 1, this pink guesthouse has the most beautiful window boxes, and offers hostel-style accommodation. There are three family and three double rooms, plus a cute little kitchen and a guest sitting room. Walls are quite thin, so you'll have to tiptoe on those laminated floors.

Fosshótel Mosfell (☎ 487 5828; bokun@fosshotel.is; Þrúðvangur 6; s/d with washbasin Ikr7500/9900, with bathroom Ikr14,700/19,000; 🖳) Contrary to most Fosshótels, the staff here are really charming! Most of the 53 rooms are en suite, with neat if unremarkable green décor; however, upstairs rooms are half-price because they're tiny and bathroomless. The hotel has plenty of big communal spaces, plus there's internet access in the lobby.

Hótel Rangá (☎ 487 5700; www.icehotels.is; Suður-landsvegur; s/d from Ikr16,900/21,100; 🗶 🖳 🔥) Midway between Hella and Hvolsvöllur, Icelandair have created what is essentially a luxurious log cabin. It has cosy wood-panelled rooms (all with verandas, bathtubs and the extras you'd expect from a top hotel), outdoor hot pots and a superior restaurant. Activity tours can be arranged, and there's a decent annexe 8km northeast. Prices include breakfast.

The cheapest place to eat is the grill at the Olís petrol station. Alternatively, there's **Kanslarinn** (☎ 487 5100; Dynskálum 10c; meals Ikr800-2700) on the main road or the bar-restaurant **Kristján X** (☎ 487 5484; Þrúðvangur 34; meals Ikr400-2500). Both serve the usual burgers, fish, grills and pizzas.

There's also an **11-11 supermarket** (☎ 585 7585; Suðurlandsvegur 1).

Getting There & Away

Daily buses between Reykjavík and Þórsmörk, Vík and Höfn make a brief stop at Hella. In winter the schedule is reduced and there are no buses on Saturday. The fare from Reykjavík is Ikr2000.

HEKLA

The name of Iceland's most famous and highly active volcano means Hooded One, as its 1491m-high summit is almost always shrouded in ominous-looking cloud. Hekla has vented its fury numerous times throughout history, and was once believed to be the gateway to hell.

The volcano is due to blow its top again round 2010. Several walking trails lead up to the summit, but many people are happy just to see Hekla at a distance.

History

Viking era settlers built farms on the rich volcanic soils around Hekla, only to be wiped out by the eruption of 1104, which buried everything within a radius of 50km. Since then there have been 15 major eruptions – the 1300 eruption covered more than 83,000 sq km in ash.

By the 16th century, Europe had decided that Hekla was the entrance to hell. Contemporary literature reported that the black skies overhead were filled with vultures and ravens, and that you could hear the howling of the damned.

In 1947, after more than 100 years of inactivity, Hekla belched a mushroom cloud of ash more than 27km into the air. This was followed by another huge eruption in 1970. Since then Hekla has gone off at roughly 10-year intervals, with short but powerful outbursts in 1980, 1991 and 2000. The main danger comes from the ash, whose high fluorine content has poisoned thousands of sheep; although, unexpectedly, the 2000 eruption produced a small pyroclastic flow (a high-speed and highly destructive torrent of rock particles and gas, which typically travels at over 130km per hour and can reach temperatures of 800°C).

Sights & Activities

HEKLA EXHIBITION CENTRE

At the time of writing, a small **exhibition centre** (☎ 487 8700; adult/under 12yr Ikr600/free; ☯ 9am-11pm) devoted to Hekla was due to open in 2007 at the Leirubakki farm (see right). There'll be eruption footage, samples of ash and lava, an earthquake simulator and other exhibits.

CLIMBING HEKLA

You can climb Hekla, but remember that it's still an active volcano. There's never much warning before eruptions, which are usually indicated by multiple small earthquakes a mere hour or two before it blows!

Stick to days when the summit is free from heavy cloud, and carry plenty of water. There's a small car park where mountain road F225 branches off Rte 26 (about 18km northeast of Leirubakki, or 45km northeast of Hella). With a 4WD you can continue along F225 to the foot of the volcano. From here, a well-marked walking track climbs steadily up to the ridge on the northeastern flank of the mountain and then southwest to the summit crater, the scene of the 2000 eruption. Although the peak is often covered in snow, the floor of the crater

is still hot. From the Rte 26-F225 junction, the return trip takes at least eight hours; from near the bottom of the volcano, the return trip takes about four hours. Former access routes on the western side were damaged during the 1991 eruption and are not recommended.

In winter you can take snowmobile tours to the summit of Hekla with **Toppferðir** (☎ 487 5530; www.mmedia.is/toppbrenna) – call for prices.

Sleeping

Rjúpnavellir í Landsveit (☎ 892 0409; www.simnet .is/rjupnavellir; sb Ikr1900) The closest accommodation to the Rte 26-F225 junction are these two large wooden cabins, with sleeping-bag space for 44 people and cooking facilities. There's also a five-person hut for hire.

Hótel Leirubakki (☎ 487 6591; www.leirubakki.is; sites per person Ikr750, guesthouse sb/s/d/tr Ikr2800/8400/12,900/ 15,300, hotel s/d Ikr13,800/16,800) This exceptionally appealing historical farm (18km from the Rte 26-F225 junction) has accommodation for everyone. There's a quiet camp site by the old churchyard; an 11-room guesthouse with shared bathrooms and guest kitchen; and a brand-new hotel with bright parquet-floored rooms, half with volcano views. Super facilities include five hot tubs; an information and exhibition centre; horse hire (Ikr3500 per hour); petrol station (open 8am to 10pm daily); and a first-class restaurant (scheduled to open in 2007) that will serve trout and lamb prepared in the farm's own smokehouse.

Getting There & Away

From 9 June to 10 September **Austurleið** (☎ 562 1011; www.austurleid.is) has a daily bus at 8.30am from Reykjavík to Landmannalaugar, which passes Leirubakki (Ikr2900, 2¼ hours) at 10.45am. The return trip passes Leirubakki at 4.15pm.

From July to September you can go on tours from Reykjavík. **Mountain Taxi** (☎ 544 5252; www.mountain-taxi.com; per person Ikr21,000) and **Iceland Total** (☎ 585 4300; www.icelandtotal.com; per person Ikr22,000) both run a 4WD trip to Hekla and Landmannalaugar at 8am daily.

HVOLSVÖLLUR

pop 760

The countryside surrounding Hvolsvöllur is soaked with history. Its farms were the setting for the bloody events of *Njál's Saga* (see the boxed text, p136), one of Iceland's favourites; today, though, the saga sites exist mainly as place names, peaceful grassed-over ruins or modern agricultural buildings.

Hvolsvöllur itself is a small village dominated by a huge petrol station at either end. It's a jumping-off point for Þórsmörk, and the last place where you can stock up on supplies.

There's a seasonal **tourist office** (☎ 487 8043; www.hvolsvollur.is; ⏱ 9am-6pm Mon-Fri, 10am-6pm Sat & Sun May-Sep) inside Sögusetrið – see below.

Sights & Activities

As you might expect, **Sögusetrið** (Saga Centre; ☎ 487 8781; Hliðarvegur; njala@njala.is; adult/under 12yr Ikr500/free; ⏱ 9am-6pm Mon-Fri, 10am-6pm Sat & Sun May-Sep) is devoted to the events of *Njál's Saga*, which took place in the surrounding hills. A roomful of written boards explains the most dramatic parts of the story (in Icelandic, English and German). It's OK if you just want a potted version of the saga, but you're probably better off reading the real thing (books are on sale in the attached souvenir shop).

The town has a good outdoor **swimming pool** (☎ 487 8607; Vallarbraut 16; adult/6-14yr Ikr250/150; ⏱ 7am-9pm Mon-Fri, 10am-5pm Sat & Sun) with a baby pool and a hot pot.

Ask the tourist office about local **horse riding**.

Sleeping & Eating

Camp site (☎ 487 8043; sites per person Ikr500) There's a site opposite the Shell station on Austurvegur; pay for your pitch at the tourist office.

Hvolsvöllur Youth Hostel (☎ 487 5750; hvolsvollur@ hostel.is; sb/s/d Ikr2100/3500/6600) Formerly known as Ásgarður (and still signposted as such at the time of writing), this quiet hostel is most unhostel-like – accommodation is in trim one- or two-bed rooms inside small wooden cabins in a peaceful garden. There's a kitchen and a lounge in the postcard-perfect main house. The hostel is 500m off the Ring Rd, signposted up Rte 261; the owner also runs the Esso garage, so ask there if you're lost.

Vestri-Garðsauki (☎ 487 8078; www.gardsauki.is; s/d/tr Ikr3500/6000/8500; ⏱ Jun-Aug) This summer guesthouse just off Rte 1 is run by a friendly Icelandic-German farming family. The four neat, plain rooms are all in the basement but are surprisingly bright; they share two bathrooms. There's also a kitchen for guest use. Breakfast can be ordered for Ikr500.

Hótel Hvolsvöllur (☎ 487 8050; www.hotelhvolsvollur .is; Hliðarvegur 7; s/d with shared bathroom Ikr6200/8500, with en suite Ikr11,500/15,300; ▢ ♿) This large business-class hotel is under new management, and

LOCAL ADVICE ON CLIMBING HEKLA

'Yes, of course you can walk up there! I've done it many times. Just don't blame me if the volcano erupts.'

Anders, local horse breeder, Leirubakki

there are big changes planned. By 2007, 50 of the 63 comfortable, green-shaded rooms will be en suite; the fish restaurant (open 11.30am to 10pm) is to be improved; and a fitness centre will join the existing rooftop hot tub in 2008. It's already a decent hotel, but these alterations should bump it up a level.

Gallerí Pizza (☎ 487 8440; Hvolsvegur 29; Ikr900-1900) The town pizzeria, one street back from the main road, is a busy, beery place with a cheery atmosphere. It also sells burgers, sandwiches and grills.

Café Eldstó (☎ 482 1011; Austurvegur 2; soup, bread & salad Ikr1200; ⏱ noon-7pm Tue-Sun May-Sep) This posh little café serves light meals (soup, salad and sandwiches) from its own handmade crockery. Opera plays in the background, the scent of coffee wafts…nice, but portions are on the small side.

There are **grills** (⏱ to 9pm) at both the Esso and Shell petrol stations; the Esso garage also has a **Vín Búð** (☎ 487 7797; ⏱ 11am-6pm Mon-Thu, to 7pm Fri, to 4pm Sat Jun-Aug, shorter hr Sep-May). If you're heading to Þórsmörk you can pick up supplies at the 10-11 supermarket, opposite the Esso garage.

Getting There & Away

Buses stop at the Esso station on the main road. Public transport to Hvolsvöllur is identical to that going to Selfoss or Hella; the fare from Reykjavík is Ikr2220.

From June to mid-September, buses to Þórsmörk (Ikr1900, 1¼ hours) leave Hvolsvöllur at 10.30am daily, returning at 3.30pm. On weekdays from 15 June to 31 August, a second service leaves Hvolsvöllur at 7pm. In the reverse direction, it leaves Þórsmörk at 8.30am.

Charter flights to Heimaey (see p143) leave from the airstrip at Bakki, about 27km south of Hvolsvöllur.

AROUND HVOLSVÖLLUR
Keldur

About 5km west of Hvolsvöllur, unsurfaced Rte 264 winds north along the Rangárvellir valley to the **medieval turf-roofed farm** (☎ 487 8452) at Keldur. This historic settlement once belonged to Ingjaldur Höskuldsson, a character in *Njál's Saga*. The interior was closed to visitors in 2000 after earthquake damage, but it's still worth visiting to see these Saga Age buildings. There's no public transport along Rte 264, but the 12km walk to Keldur is pleasant enough.

About 2km before Keldur, good en-suite rooms are available at **Hótel Rangársel** (As Hótel Rangá), an annexe of Icelandair's Hótel Rangá.

Bergþórshvoll

Down by the coast, Bergþórshvoll was Njál's farm (although there's not too much to see today). *Njál's Saga* relates that this is where he and his wife and grandchild were burnt to death in their bed in 1011; interestingly, an archaeological excavation in 1951 did find traces of a burnt-out building here. About 4km east of Hvolsvöllur, Rte 255 and then 252 will take you there (21km).

Hvolsvöllur to Fljótsdalur

At the edge of Hvolsvöllur, Rte 261 turns east off the Ring Rd. It follows the edge of the Fljótshlíð hills, offering great views over the flood plain of the Markarfljót river and the Eyjafjallajökull glacier. There are several B&Bs along the surfaced section of the road, which ends near the farm and church at **Hlíðarendi**, once the home of Gunnar Hámundarson from *Njál's Saga*. Although it seems tantalisingly close, Þórsmörk can be reached only by 4WD via mountain road F249, on the far side of the Markarfljót bridge on Rte 1.

About 8km after the tarmac ends, Rte 261 passes the turf-roofed youth hostel at **Fljótsdalur**. This is a very popular place to stay, and there are great walks in the surrounding countryside, including the 10km trek northeast to the icecap at **Tindfjallajökull** (1462m). With a 4WD you can continue along mountain road F261 towards Landmannalaugar or up to the glacier Mýrdalsjökull.

SLEEPING & EATING

Kaffi Langbrók (☎ 487 8333; Kirkjulækur III; sites per person Ikr600; ☺ May-Aug; ☑) This wooden ranch-style building 10km from Hvolsvöllur has a peaceful camp site on its grounds. There's also a café with internet access.

ourpick Fljótsdalur Youth Hostel (☎ 487 8498; www.hostel.is; Fljótshlíð; sb adult/child 6-11yr Ikr1400/700; ☺ May-Sep) If you're looking for a simple but peaceful base for highland walks, with knowledgeable staff, a beautiful garden, a homey kitchen, a cosy sitting room, an excellent library, and mountain views that make your knees tremble, then you'll find it at Fljótsdalur. Advance booking is a must – its one seven-mattress and two four-bed rooms are often booked out by Dick Phillips' walking groups (see p333). The nearest shop is 27km away at Hvolsvöllur, so bring in all supplies.

Breiðabólstaður (☎ 487 8010; breidabolstadur@simnet .is; sb Ikr2000, linen hire Ikr800; ☺ Jun-Sep) Owned by the minister of the church next door, this friendly farm 4km from Hvolsvöllur has a bright and comfortable wooden bunkhouse with kitchen, TV lounge and indoor barbecue area.

Smárátun (☎ 487 8471; www.smaratun.is; sb Ikr2800, made-up bed Ikr5400-7400, summerhouse from Ikr12,800) This attractive white farm with a blue tin roof has horses, a hot tub, sleeping-bag spaces, B&B rooms and four- to six-person summerhouses. It's about 13km from Hvolsvöllur.

Hvolsvöllur to Þórsmörk

The road to Þórsmörk (Rte 249/F249) begins just east of the Markarfljót river on Rte 1. Although it quickly turns into a 4WD-only road, there are some interesting sights at the start of the road that can be reached by car.

From the highway you can see the beautiful high falls at **Seljalandsfoss**, which tumble over a rocky scarp into a deep, green pool. It's perfect for romantics who dream of walking behind waterfalls – a (slippery) path runs round the back. Buses on the Höfn–Reykjavík route often wait here for the Þórsmörk bus, giving passengers time for a few quick photos.

A few hundred metres further down the Þórsmörk road, in the grounds of the farm Hamragarðar, is the spooky waterfall **Gljúfurárfoss**, which gushes into a hidden canyon. To see the falls, you have to wade into the stream beside the farm.

SLEEPING

Hamragarðar (☎ 488 4200; arni@hvolsvollur.is; sites per person Ikr600; ☺ Jun-Aug) You can camp at this farm, right next to the hidden waterfall at Gljúfurárfoss.

Stóra-Mörk III (☎ 487 8903; storamork@isl.is; sb Ikr1500, made-up bed Ikr2300) About 5km closer to Þórsmörk (still on Rte 249), this historical farmhouse (mentioned, of course, in *Njál's Saga*) offers rooms with or without bathroom, a guest kitchen, and a good breakfast spread.

SOUTHWEST ICELAND

NJÁL'S SAGA

One of Iceland's best-loved sagas deals with two friends, Gunnar Hámundarson and Njál Þorgeirsson, destined by fate to become bitter enemies. A petty squabble between their wives kicks off a bloodthirsty feud, which escalates until practically everyone in the saga is dead. Written in the 13th century, it recounts 11th-century events that took place in the hills around Hvolsvöllur.

The saga's doomed hero is Gunnar of Hlíðarendi (near Fljótsdalur), who falls for and marries the beautiful, hot-tempered Hallgerður, who has long legs but – ominously – a 'thief's eyes'. Hallgerður has a falling-out with Bergþóra, wife of Njál of Bergþórshvoll (near Hvolsvöllur). Things become increasingly strained between Gunnar and Njál as Hallgerður and Bergþóra begin murdering each other's servants.

In one important episode, Hallgerður sends an accomplice to burgle food from a man named Otkell, who has unwisely refused to trade with her. When Gunnar comes home and sees Hallgerður's stolen feast, his temper snaps. 'It's bad news indeed if I've become a thief's accomplice', he says, and slaps his wife – an act that later comes back to haunt him.

Through more unfortunate circumstances, Gunnar ends up killing Otkell and is eventually outlawed and sentenced to exile. As he rides away from home, his horse stumbles. Fatally, he takes one last glance back at his beloved farm Hlíðarendi and is unable to leave the valley.

His enemies gather their forces and lay siege to the farm, but Gunnar manages to hold off the attackers until his bowstring breaks. When he asks Hallgerður for a lock of her hair to repair it, she refuses, reminding him of the slap she received years earlier – and Gunnar is killed.

The feud continues as Gunnar and Njál's clan members try to avenge their slaughtered kin. (Another famous episode sees Njál's son Skarphéðinn axe another man to death before sliding away to safety across the frozen river Markarfljót.) Njál himself acts as a peace broker, forming treaties between the two families, but in the end it all comes to nothing. Njál and his wife are besieged in their farm; although they're given the option to leave, they wearily refuse. Tucking themselves up in bed with their little grandson between them, the couple allow themselves to be burnt alive.

The only survivor of the fire is Njál's son-in-law Kári, who launches a legal case against the arsonists, commits a bit of extrajudicial killing himself and is finally reconciled with his archenemy, Flosi, who ordered the burning of the Njál family. The story is incredibly convoluted and it can be hard to keep track of who is murdering whom, but it's certainly epic.

ÞÓRSMÖRK

One of the most beautiful places in Iceland is Þórsmörk, a stunning valley full of weird rock formations, twisting gorges, a singing cave, mountain flowers and icy streams. Three glaciers (Tindfjallajökull, Eyjafjallajökull and Mýrdalsjökull) shelter it from harsher weather and provide a stunning backdrop. Way back in 1921, the loveliness of Þórsmörk was officially recognised when it was given national reserve status.

Be warned, though: Þórsmörk's ravishing appearance and proximity to Reykjavík (130km) make it an extremely popular spot in summer. It gets particularly crowded in July, when students from around Iceland descend to party. But if you like your countryside boom box free, you don't have to go too far to escape the crowds.

The main accommodation area is at Húsadalur (Map p278), where the Austurleið

bus from Reykjavík terminates. The large, artificial hot pool **Þórslaug** is a welcome new feature here – perfect for easing tired muscles after a long walk. On the hill behind the hut is the cave **Sönghellir** (one of several singing caves in Iceland), from where a maze of walking trails leads through scrubby dwarf birch forests to the Þórsmörk hut, about 3km further up the valley. The summit of **Valahnúkur** (458m), immediately west of Þórsmörk hut, has a view disc that identifies all the surrounding mountains. Allow about an hour to get there from either Húsadalur or Þórsmörk.

The higher reaches of the valley are known as **Goðaland** (Land of the Gods) and are full of bizarre hoodoo formations. There's a mountain hut at Básar (Map p278), on the far bank of the Krossá river, which marks the start of the popular trek over Fimmvörðuháls Pass to Skógar. The trail passes right between Eyjafjallajökull and Mýrdalsjökull, and the pass itself makes an easy day trek from either Þórsmörk or Básar. To get to Básar from further down the valley, you must cross the pedestrian bridge over the Krossá, just downstream from the Þórsmörk hut. It's one of Iceland's more dangerous rivers for 4WDs – only attempt to cross, in a high-clearance 4WD vehicle, if you know what you're doing.

Þórsmörk is accessible from June to early September, when plenty of scheduled buses and tours run to the area.

Trekking

Myriad treks are possible in the mountains around Þórsmörk, and most can be undertaken independently. The relevant topographic sheet is the Landmælingar Íslands *Þórsmörk/Landmannalaugar* 1:100,000. As well as local hikes, you can continue inland to Landmannalaugar (see p277). Alternatively, you could head down to the coast at Skógar via Fimmvörðuháls Pass – see below.

SHORT TREKS

From Rte F249, you can easily hike up to **Steinholtsjökull**, a tongue of ice extending off the north side of Eyjafjallajökull. The ice has carved a sheer-sided, 100m-deep gorge, and the short river Stakksholtsá flows out from under it and winds down to Markarfljót. Further west the larger glacier **Gígjökull** descends into a small lagoon right beside Rte F249, filling it with carved icebergs. To explore the main icecaps at Eyjafjallajökull and Mýrdalsjökull you'll need special equipment – including ropes, crampons and ice axes – and ideally a GPS device.

ÞÓRSMÖRK TO SKÓGAR TREK

The dramatic and popular trek from Þórsmörk to Skógar passes right between the glaciers of Eyjafjallajökull and Mýrdalsjökull. The trek can be done in a long day, but it's more enjoyable to break the journey at Fimmvörðuháls Pass (1093m), which has a mountain hut run by Útivist (see following). Although the glaciers seem close enough to touch, this walk is fairly easy and you won't need any special gear. It's best attempted from mid-July to early September, but always keep an eye on the weather – it can change rapidly up here.

The trek starts about 1.5km east of the Básar hut at Goðaland and then climbs steadily to **Mornisheiði**, which has dramatic views over Mýrdalsjökull, and Eyjafjallajökull. From here,

you face a steep ascent to the ridge at **Heljarkambur**. The next stage takes you across tundra and snowfields to **Fimmvörðuháls Pass** itself, with Mýrdalsjökull on the left and Eyjafjallajökull on the right. The Fimmvörðuskáli mountain hut is a short walk off the main track, near a small lake.

The following day, you can begin the trek down to Skógar. The main trail is clear and well trodden, but an interesting alternative is to leave the track at the footbridge and follow the stream down to the waterfall **Skógafoss**, about 1km west of Skógar village. Both routes are marked on the Landmælingar Íslands map *Landmannalaugar-Þórsmörk*.

From Reykjavík, between June and August only, **Iceland Total** (www.icelandtotal.com) offers a package with bus transfers and accommodation in the mountain huts at Fimmvörðuháls Pass and Húsadalur for Ikr16,000. You're dropped off at Skógar, and picked up again at Húsadalur.

Útivist (☎ 562 1000; www.utivist.is) and **Ferðafélag Íslands** (☎ 568 2533; www.fi.is) both run guided treks from Skógar over Fimmvörðuháls to Þórsmörk for around Ikr10,000; contact them for details.

Sleeping

There are three huts in the Þórsmörk area – at Þórsmörk, Básar and Húsadalur – and another at the top of the Fimmvörðuháls Pass. All have cooking facilities, showers and running water, but they tend to get packed out, particularly at weekends. Bring your own food and sleeping bag; a stove is also a good idea, to avoid waiting for the crowded facilities.

Wild camping is prohibited, but the three Þórsmörk huts have tent sites around them; the hut at Fimmvörðuháls Pass doesn't, as the ground is too rocky.

To book spaces at the huts (strongly advised), contact the organisations listed below.

HÚSADALUR

The eight **Húsadalur huts** (sites per person Ikr600, sb Ikr2000-2900, 5-person cottages Ikr7500), along with the café and new hot pool, almost form a tourist village. Book through **Reykjavík Excursions** (☎ 580 5400; www.thorsmork.is, www.re.is; Vatnsmýrarvegur 10, IS-101 Reykjavík).

ÞÓRSMÖRK HUT

The Þórsmörk hut **Skagfjörðsskáli** (☎ 854 1191 mid-May-Sep; sites per person Ikr700, sb Ikr2000) can sleep

75. Book through **Ferðafélag Íslands** (☎ 568 2533; www.fi.is; Mörkin 6, IS-108 Reykjavík). This organisation can also take bookings for huts along the Landmannalaugar–Þórsmörk track.

BÁSAR HUT & FIMMVÖRÐUHÁLS PASS

There's space for 80 people in the hut at **Básar** (sites per person Ikr700, sb Ikr1800), booked through **Útivist** (☎ 562 1000; www.utivist.is; Laugavegur 178, IS-101 Reykjavík).

The comfortable 23-bed hut at **Fimmvörðuskáli** (sb Ikr1800), on the pass between Eyjafjallajökull and Mýrdalsjökull, is also Útivist's. It lies 600m west of the main trail and is easy to miss in poor weather (GPS ref N 63°37.320', W 19°27.093'). Útivist tour groups have priority here, so it's often booked out. There's no camp site.

Getting There & Away

BUS

Austurleið-Kynnisferðir (☎ 562 1011; www.austurleid.is) run scheduled services. From 1 June to 9 September, buses leave Reykjavík for Þórsmörk (Ikr3700, 3½ hours) at 8.30am daily, reaching Húsadalur around noon and returning at 3.30pm (there's also an extra bus from the city at 5pm on Fridays).

From 15 June to 31 August, an extra service leaves Reykjavík at 5pm Saturday to Thursday; in the reverse direction, the extra bus leaves Þórsmörk at 8.30am.

From 1 June to 9 September, there's a 'sightseeing' bus that runs at 1pm from Húsadalur to Básar, returning at 1.40pm.

Several companies run day trips from Reykjavík in summer for around Ikr9500 – see p80.

CAR & BICYCLE

Even though Þórsmörk seems almost touchable from the Ring Rd (only 30km along F249), you *cannot* drive there without a 4WD with decent clearance. The gravel road surface eventually turns into boulders, and even a 4WD car probably won't make it over the bumps.

Plenty of cyclists fight their way up to Þórsmörk, but it's a hard slog. You can shave off a few kilometres by leaving Rte 1 near the farm Vorsabær and taking the old bridge over the Markarfljót, which is now closed to cars.

HIKING

You can walk to Þórsmörk from Landmannalaugar (three or four days), Skógar (one or two days) or along Rtes 249 and F249 from

Seljaland (one long day). The Skógar trek is covered in more detail on p137, and the Landmannalaugar to Þórsmörk trek is covered in the boxed text, p280.

SKÓGAR & AROUND

pop 23

You begin to enter the south coast's realm of ice at Skógar, which nestles under the Eyjafjallajökull icecap about 1km off Rte 1. This tiny settlement offers two corking attractions. At its western edge, the dizzyingly high Skógafoss waterfall tumbles down a mossy cliff. On the eastern side you'll find the fantastic folk museum, open year-round for your delectation.

The village is also the start – or the end – of the trek over the Fimmvörðuháls Pass to Þórsmörk (see p137).

Folk Museum

The highlight of Skógar – indeed of this whole stretch of coast – is the wonderful **Skógar Folk Museum** (☎ 487 8845; www.skogasafn.is; adult/under 16yr Ikr700/free; ☉ museum 9am-6.30pm Jun-Aug, 10am-5pm May & Sep, 11am-4pm Oct-May, café 10am-5pm Jun-Aug, 11am-4pm May & Sep), which covers all aspects of Icelandic life. The vast collection was put together by 85-year-old Þórður Tómasson, who has been amassing items for 71 years. You might be lucky enough to meet Þórður in person – he often comes in to play traditional songs for visitors on an old church organ (be prepared to *SING!*). There are also various restored buildings (church, turf-roofed farmhouse, cowsheds etc) in the grounds, and a hangar-like building at the back houses an interesting transport museum, plus a café and souvenir shop.

Skógafoss

The 62m **waterfall** of Skógafoss topples over a rocky cliff at the western edge of Skógar in dramatic style. Climb the steep staircase alongside for giddying views downwards; or walk to the foot of the falls, shrouded in sheets of mist and rainbows. Legend has it that a settler named Þrasi hid a chest of gold behind Skógafoss; sometimes you can almost see it glittering…

Activities

The most popular walk in the area is the two-day trek (see p137) over Fimmvörðuháls Pass to Þórsmörk. However, you can also take a morning trek up to the pass and return to Skógar the same day. The trail starts on the 4WD track to Skógarheiði behind the village. The return trip should take about seven hours.

Horse riding can be arranged through the farm **Skálakot** (☎ 487 8953; www.skalacot.com; sb Ikr1800), 6km west of Skógar. Short rides cost Ikr2500 per hour; you can wander up by the glacier on four-hour trips (Ikr6000) or plan an all-inclusive riding holiday (around Ikr15,000 per day). Skálakot also has rather strange sleeping-bag accommodation, in a dorm that looks straight into the stables!

Sleeping & Eating
SKÓGAR

Skógar camp site (☎ 893 8726, 845 8724; sites per person Ikr600) This place has a great location, right by Skógafoss; the sound of falling water makes a soothing lullaby. There's a small toilet block with fresh water.

Skógar Youth Hostel (☎ 487 8801; skogar@hostel .is; sb/d/tr Ikr1800/4900/5550; ☷ 10 May-10 Sep) In an old school, this 30-bed hostel is very close to the waterfall…but, unfortunately, you can't quite see it from the building! Never mind – a minute's walk and you're there. There's a guest kitchen and a laundry.

Edda Hotel (☎ 444 4000; www.hoteledda.is; sb/d Ikr1700/5800/7200; ☷ mid-Jun–mid-Aug; ✗) This modern and comfortable summer hotel close to the museum is split over two buildings. Sleeping-bag spaces are in the gym, or choose simple rooms with shared bathrooms. The Edda Hotel has a licensed restaurant and a hot pot.

Hótel Skógar (☎ 487 8988; www.hotelskogar.is; s/d from 12,000/15,000; ☷ daily May-Sep, weekends only Oct-Apr; ☐) Breaking the Ikea mould, this architecturally interesting hotel has unusual but quite romantic rooms, all en suite with embroidered curtains and bedspreads, and wooden animals dotted about. There's a decent restaurant, a hot tub and sauna in the garden, a computer for internet access, and a bad bird-eating cat.

WEST OF SKÓGAR

There are several places to stay at Ásólfsskáli, around 14km west of Skógar; and at Raufarfell, about 6km west of Skógar.

Seljavellir (☎ 487 8810; Raufarfell; sites per person Ikr600; ☷ Jun-Aug) This farm, 3km along Rte 242, has a lovely camp site with running water, toilet and showers, a geothermal pool and hot pots.

Hótel Edinborg (☎ 487 8011; www.islandia.is/thorn; Raufarfell; sb/s/d Ikr2500/9000/12,000) Near Drangshlíð I is this tall tin-clad house with inviting wooden en-suite rooms. Non-sleeping-bag prices include breakfast.

Drangshlíð I (☎ 487 8868; drangshlid@simnet.is; Raufarfell; s/d Ikr6800/13,900) At the foot of a green cliff full of nesting birds, this modern white farmhouse has large guest rooms, all with private bathroom, and a big, bright dining room for meals. Look out for the barns built into caves in the surrounding fields. Prices include breakfast. The friendly folk there were considering providing sleeping-bag accommodation – contact them for details.

our pick Country Hotel Anna (☎ 487 8950; www .hotelanna.is; Ásólfsskáli; s/d summer Ikr11,100/15,200, winter Ikr6500/9500; ☐) Ooh, this place is nice! Its five en-suite rooms are furnished with antiques, embroidered bedspreads settle over big, comfy beds, and facilities include minifridges, kettles and satellite TV. The hotel has a Green Globe award for environmental goodness. Prices include breakfast, and evening meals are possible if prebooked. There's also a white-washed café (open 2pm to 8.30pm mid-June to August).

Getting There & Away
All buses from Reykjavík to Höfn or Vík stop at the Edda Hotel in Skógar (Ikr3200, three hours).

SKÓGAR TO VÍK Í MÝRDAL
Sólheimajökull
One of the easiest glacial tongues to reach is Sólheimajökull, which unfurls from the main Mýrdalsjökull icecap. A 5km bumpy dirt track (Rte 221) leads off the Ring Rd to a small car park; from there, the ice is approximately 800m away. You can scramble up onto the glacier, but keep an eye out for fissures and crevasses. The sand and gravel deposited by the rivulets running out of the end of the glacier are a definite no-go area because of quicksand.

Much better than slithering in normal shoes, you can strap on crampons and go for a proper walk up Sólheimajökull with the **Icelandic Mountain Guides** (☎ 587 9999; www .mountainguide.is). Their Blue Ice Adventure (Ikr3500 per person, 1½ hours, trips at 9am and 4pm; minimum age eight) or longer Sólheimajökull Exploration (Ikr6900 per person, 3½ hours, 11.30am; minimum age 12) leave from the car park between June and August. The guides also do trips on Svínafellsjökull in Skaftafell National Park – see p289.

Mýrdalsjökull

The gorgeous glacier Mýrdalsjökull is Iceland's fourth-largest icecap, covering 700 sq km and reaching a thickness of almost 750m in places. The volcano Katla snoozes beneath, periodically blasting up through the ice to drown the coastal plain in a deluge of meltwater, sand and tephra (rock and other material blasted out from a volcano). Scientists predict that another eruption is due some time during the noughties.

ACTIVITIES

With the right equipment, treks are possible on the main icecap and on the fingerlike projection Sólheimajökull, close to Skógar (see p139). You can also walk to the icecap from the lovely Þakgil camp site (p142).

For Jeep, snowmobile and dogsled tours, turn off the Ring Rd and head 10km up Rte 222 to the mountain hut Sólheimaskli. Here you'll find **Arcanum** (☎ 487 1500; www.snow.is), who can take you bouncing over the glacier on one-hour snowmobiling trips (Ikr13,500/19,000 with one person/two people aboard), or on a super-Jeep tour over the ice. If you don't have a vehicle, they can pick you up from Vík (Ikr12,500), Skógar (Ikr7000) or just off Rte 1 (Ikr5000).

Although they have similar frostproof ears and thick furry coats, the dogs that pull the sleds at **Dogsledding.is** (☎ 487 7747, 863 8864; www .dogsledding.is) are Greenland dogs, not huskies! At the time of writing, the business was changing hands – contact the new owners for prices. Rides generally run between December and August.

TOURS

Various tour companies (see p80) offer trips from Reykjavík to Mýrdalsjökull.

SLEEPING & EATING

Sólheimahjáleiga (☎ 487 1320; www.solfarm.sveit.is; sb/d Ikr2000/8100) This peaceful farmhouse, about 1km along Rte 222, is the closest accommodation to the glacier. It has eight smart double rooms, and there's a lovely garden. Breakfast costs Ikr900, and other meals can be requested.

Dyrhólaey

One of the south coast's most recognisable natural formations is the rocky plateau and huge stone sea arch at Dyrhólaey (10km west of Vík), which rise dramatically from the surrounding plain. The promontory is a nature reserve and is particularly rich in bird life; however, it's closed to visitors during the nesting season. At other times you can visit its crashing black beaches and get the most awesome views from the top of the archway (best seen in its entirety from Reynisfjara – see below).

You can take a tour through the arch in an amphibious vehicle with **Dyrhólaeyjarferðir** (☎ 487 8500; www.dyrholaey.com; tours adult/under 14s Ikr3500/2500).

According to *Njál's Saga*, Kári – the only survivor of the fire that wiped out Njál's clan – had his farm here. Another Viking Age connection is the cave **Loftsalahellir**, reached by a track just before the causeway to Dyrhólaey, which was used for council meetings in saga times.

SLEEPING

Camping is prohibited on Dyrhólaey.

Hótel Dyrhólaey (☎ 487 1333; dyrholaey@islandia.is; s/d/tr Ikr9500/12,900/17,900) About 9km west of Vík at the farm Brekkur I, this large green guesthouse has the usual big rooms that you find in all modern bungalow hotels in Iceland; some have great views of the coast. There's also a restaurant.

Reynisfjara

On the west side of Reynisfjall, the high ridge above Vík, a dirt road leads down to the black volcanic beach at Reynisfjara, which is backed by an incredible stack of **basalt columns**, which look like a giant church organ. The surrounding cliffs are full of caves formed from twisted and tortured basalt, and puffin chicks belly-flop off the cliffs here every summer. Immediately offshore are the sea stacks of **Reynisdrangur**. There are fabulous views west along the beach to the rock arch at Dyrhólaey.

VÍK Í MÝRDAL
pop 290

One of our favourite places in Iceland, Vík is a tiny strip of green wedged between the looming glacier Mýrdalsjökull and a battered beach of black sand and pebbles. It's a welcoming little community surrounded by natural wonders. The village started life as a fishing outpost, but a cooperative society was formed here in 1906 and is still Vík's biggest employer.

VILLI KNUDSEN'S HOTTEST VOLCANO

Personally, I've been waiting for the Katla volcano, underneath the Mýrdalsjökull glacier, to erupt for more than 30 years. Sometimes we thought the eruption might be beginning – like in 1982–83, we had earthquakes every single day for a year, and I had a camera there for months and months and months and months and months. But nothing happened.

But two years ago scientists saw signs of movement. And the earthquakes, which are normally on the eastern side, underneath the glacier, have been moving towards the west. This indicates that the water this time could come out of the glacier in more places.

After what happened in Asia [on 26 December 2004], people are getting more interested in tsunamis. Some eruptions of Katla in the past have created tidal waves which have boomeranged off Vestmannaeyjar and gone back to the town of Vík. Recent studies of the shore show that the water went much further inland than people previously thought.

The eruption is going to start with a big explosion, and there will be ashfall for many days – we don't expect any lava. The likelihood is there will be three floodings in the south and one to the west. Down by the town of Vík, the water will rise 100m to 150m. A lot of people will be stranded – rescue work will be very difficult. There's nowhere the people can go except to the next highest hill.

It's going to be a complicated eruption to film – and expensive! Because it's close to the sea, the air is very turbulent. I've had some nervous moments in planes there. The national TV station RÚV have a webcam by the side of Vík, so maybe you can see the flood happen [www.ruv.is/katla].

Thanks to Villi Knudsen, volcano chaser and film-maker, The Volcano Show, Reykjavík

---

Information

The **tourist office** (☎ 487 1395; www.vik.is; Víkurbraut 28; ☑ 10.30am-1.30pm & 2.30-5pm Jun-Aug) is housed in the historic trading house Brydebúð. KB Banki has an ATM and foreign-exchange desk. The post office has internet access (Ikr600 per hour).

Sights & Activities

Vík's most famous sight is the cluster of sea stacks at **Reynisdrangur**, which rise from the ocean at the western end of the **black-sand beach** like sinister rocky fingers. The highest stack is 66m tall. The nearby cliffs are good for puffin watching. A highly recommended **walk** (upwards from the western end of Vík) takes you to the top of the ridge **Reynisfjall** (340m), which offers superb views along the coast.

The tin-clad house **Brydebúð** was built in Vestmannaeyjar in 1831 and moved to Vík in 1895. Today it houses the tourist office, the Halldórskaffi restaurant and a small **museum** (adult/under 16yr Ikr500/free; ☑ 10.30am-1.30pm & 2.30-5pm Jun-Aug), with displays on fishing, what it's like to live under the volcano Katla, and locally made church vestments.

Vík's **church** has some unusual red-and-white stained-glass windows in spiky geometrical shapes. The big souvenir shop **Víkurprjón** (☎ 487 1250; www.vikwool.is; Rte 1) is a coach-tour hit – you can watch woolly jumpers being made here.

Vík has a small open-air **swimming pool** (☎ 487 1174; Mánabraut 3; adult/child Ikr300/150; ☑ 7.10am-9pm Mon-Fri, 10am-7pm Sat & Sun Jun-Aug, shorter hr winter).

Sleeping & Eating

Vík camp site (☎ 487 1466, 899 2406; sites per person Ikr600, cottages Ikr5000) The camp site sits under a grassy ridge at the eastern end of the village, just beyond the Edda Hótel. There's an octagonal building with cooking facilities, washing machine, toilets and free showers. Six-person farmhouse-style cottages are also available.

Norður-Vík Youth Hostel (☎ 487 1106; www.hostel.is; Suðurvíkurvegur; sb dm/sb d Ikr1800/3000; ☑ Apr-Oct) Vík's friendly hostel is this old beige house on the hill behind the village. Good facilities include guest lounge, kitchen, breakfast (Ikr800) and bike hire (per half-day/day Ikr1000/1500). It's usually booked out in summer.

Gistihús Ársalir (☎ 487 1400; simon@ismennt.is; Austurvegur 7; sb/s/d Ikr1900/4500/6000) There are spacious rooms with shared bathrooms (some with balconies) at this white house on the outskirts of the village, plus a kitchen and mountain-bike hire.

Guesthouse Puffin (Víkurbraut 24a; sb Ikr2600) This place has very thin bedroom walls but a great old guest kitchen (check out the diagonally open-ing drawers) and a possibly haunted lounge. The guesthouse is attached to Hótel Lundi (following).

Hótel Lundi (☎ 487 1212; www.hotelpuffin.is; Víkur-braut 24-26; s/d with bathroom Ikr9850/14,300) This small old-fashioned family-run hotel has rooms with telephones and bathrooms, and a respectable restaurant; prices include breakfast.

Edda Hótel Vík í Mýrdal (☎ 444 4000; www.hoteledda .is; s/d Ikr10,300/12,900; ☼ May–mid-Sep; ☐) One of the three-star Edda Plus hotels, this service-able modern place has good, clean rooms with phone, TV and en-suite bathroom. There's a restaurant with ocean views, and free internet in the dining room.

Halldórskaffi (☎ 487 1202; Austurvegur 18; mains Ikr400-1800; ☼ 11am-11pm Sun-Fri, to 2am Sat Jun-Aug, 6-11pm Fri, to 2am Sat Sep-May) In the same build-ing as the tourist office, this recommended place serves pizzas, burgers, sandwiches, fish mains and beer in an old-world wooden din-ing room.

Apart from Halldórskaffi, diners have the choice of the restaurants at the Edda Hótel and Hótel Lundi. For cheap eats with a view of Reynisdrangur, head to the restaurant-grill **Víkurskáli** (☎ 487 1230; snacks Ikr790-1800; ☼ to 9pm) at the Esso petrol station, which also has a **Vín Búð** (☼ 5-6pm Mon-Thu, 4-7pm Fri). Self-caterers can make use of the large **Kjarval supermarket** (☎ 487 1250; Víkurbraut 4) near Brydebúð.

Getting There & Away

Vík lies on the main bus route between Höfn and Reykjavík, and buses stop at the Esso petrol station. From June to mid-Septem-ber, the bus from Reykjavík leaves at 8.30am, stopping at places of interest, and returns from Vík at 12.30pm (one-way Ikr3800, five hours). In winter, the bus runs from Reykjavík at 12.30pm on Tuesday, Friday and Sunday only, returning at 4pm; this direct journey is a shorter 3¼ hours.

EAST OF VÍK
Mælifell

On the edge of the glacier, this 642m-high **ridge** and the countryside around it are just spectacular. The simple but idyllic camp site at **Þakgil** (☎ 853 4889; www.thakgil.is; sites per person Ikr600; ☼ Jun & Jul), a green bowl among stark mountains, makes a convenient base from which to explore. You can walk up Mælifell, or even get up onto the glacier – a path leads

to the nunatak (hill or mountain completely surrounded by a glacier), Huldufjöll. You can drive to Þakgil, 14km along a rough dirt road (Rte 214), which branches off Rte 1 about 5km east of Vík, or there are two walking paths from Vík.

Country Hótel Höfðabrekka (☎ 487 1208; www .hofdabrekka.is; s/d Ikr11,100/15,300; ☐) At the start of Rte 214, this is a large and reputedly haunted hotel! It offers tasteful wood-panelled rooms with en suite, four hot tubs, a guest kitchen and a good restaurant (open from 6pm to 10pm; bookings necessary in winter). Internet access costs Ikr300 per 20 minutes.

Mýrdalssandur

The vast black lava sand flats of Mýrdalssan-dur, just east of Vík, are formed from mater-ial washed out from underneath the glacier Mýrdalsjökull. This 700-sq-km area of sand is bleak and desolate, and apparently lifeless, but arctic foxes (which have a black coat in summer) and sea birds are common sights here. To the south of Rte 1, the small peak of **Hjörleifshöfði** (231m) rises above the sands and offers good views towards Vestmannaeyjar. On the other side of Rte 1, the green hill of **Hafursey** (582m) is another possible destina-tion for walks from Vík. As you head east towards Höfn, look out for stone cairns con-structed by early travellers to mark safe routes across the sands.

VESTMANNAEYJAR

Black and brooding, Vestmannaeyjar forms 15 eye-catching silhouettes off the southern shore. The islands were formed by submarine volcanoes around 11,000 years ago, except for sulky-looking Surtsey, the archipelago's newest addition, which rose from the waves in 1963.

Several islands are scattered with summer huts, used by bird hunters and egg collectors, but Heimaey is the only inhabited one. Its little town and sheltered harbour lie between dramatic *klettur* (escarpments) and two omi-nous volcanoes – conical Helgafell and blood-red Eldfell. The latter has only been around for 34 years – it was created during the huge five-month eruption that buried parts of the town under 30 million tonnes of lava. Hei-maey is famous for its puffins – around 10 million birds come here to breed – and for

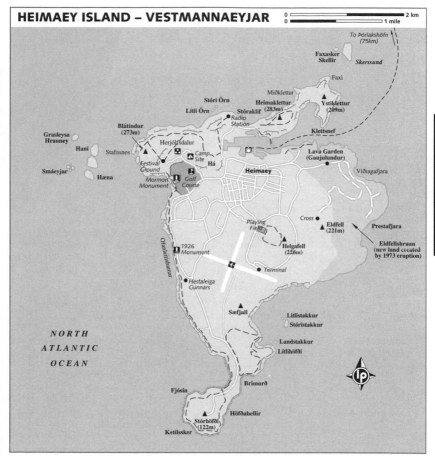

HEIMAEY ISLAND – VESTMANNAEYJAR

SOUTHWEST ICELAND

Þjóðhátíð, Iceland's biggest outdoor festival, held in August.

Maybe it's the relative isolation or maybe it's because everyone lives on top of a temperamental volcano – whatever the reason, Heimaey is one of the friendliest places you'll find. It's also a self-sufficient working town – the islands supply around 15% of Iceland's fish catch.

The ferry *Herjólfur* provides daily connections to Þorlákshöfn on the mainland. It carries cars, but Heimaey is small enough to explore on foot. There are also flights here from Reykjavík and Bakki (near Hvolsvöllur). An undersea tunnel was discussed recently, but the 100-billion-krónur price tag looks a little high.

HEIMAEY
pop 4170

Heimaey enjoys a spectacular setting, squeezed between dramatic cliffs to the west, and the two looming volcanic cones to the east. It has better tourist facilities than many towns on the mainland.

History

The island has had a turbulent and bloody history. The *Landnámabók* recounts that Ingólfur Arnarson originally came to Iceland with his blood-brother Hjörleifur, who was murdered by his Irish slaves (Westmen) shortly after landing. The slaves then fled to Heimaey, but Ingólfur hunted them down and killed them all.

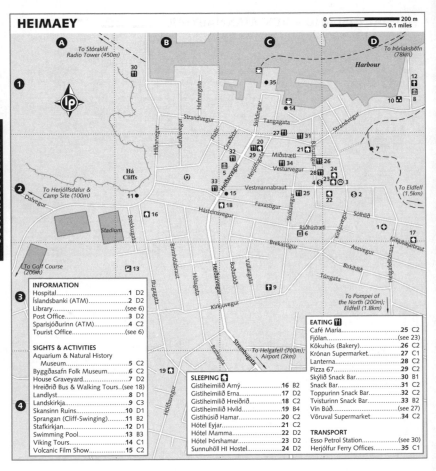

HEIMAEY

INFORMATION	
Hospital..1	D2
Íslandsbanki (ATM).....................2	D2
Library...(see 6)	
Post Office......................................3	D2
Sparisjóðurinn (ATM)................4	C2
Tourist Office.................................(see 6)	

SIGHTS & ACTIVITIES	
Aquarium & Natural History	
Museum..5	C2
Byggðasafn Folk Museum..........6	C2
House Graveyard...........................7	D2
Hreiðrið Bus & Walking Tours..(see 18)	
Landlyst..8	D1
Landskirkja..9	C3
Skansinn Ruins............................10	D1
Sprangan (Cliff-Swinging).......11	B2
Stafkirkjan.....................................12	D1
Swimming Pool............................13	B3
Viking Tours..................................14	C1
Volcanic Film Show....................15	C2

SLEEPING	
Gistiheimilið Arný......................16	B2
Gistiheimilið Erna......................17	D2
Gistiheimilið Hreiðrið..............18	C2
Gistiheimilið Hvild.....................19	B4
Gistihúsið Hamar.......................20	C2
Hótel Eyjar.....................................21	C2
Hótel Mamma.............................22	D2
Hótel Þórshamar.......................23	D2
Sunnuhöll HI Hostel.................24	D2

EATING	
Café María......................................25	C2
Fjólan..(see 23)	
Kökuhús (Bakery)......................26	C2
Krónan Supermarket.................27	C1
Lanterna...28	C2
Pizza 67...29	C2
Skyllið Snack Bar........................30	B1
Snack Bar.......................................31	C2
Toppurinn Snack Bar................32	C2
Tvisturinn Snack Bar.................33	B2
Vín Búð...(see 27)	
Völuval Supermarket................34	C2

TRANSPORT	
Esso Petrol Station......................(see 30)	
Herjólfur Ferry Offices.............35	C1

Over the centuries the island was a marauders' favourite. The English raided Heimaey throughout the 15th century, building Iceland's stone fort Skansinn as their HQ. In 1627 Heimaey suffered the most awful attack by Algerian pirates, who went on a killing spree around the island, murdering 36 islanders and kidnapping 242 more (almost three-quarters of the population). The rest managed to escape by abseiling down cliffs or hiding in caves along the west coast. Those who were kidnapped were taken as slaves to north Africa; years later, 27 islanders had their freedom bought for them…and had a long walk home.

The volcanoes that formed Heimaey have come close to destroying the island on several occasions. The most famous eruption in modern times began unexpectedly at 1.45am on 23 January 1973, when a vast fissure burst open, gradually mutating into the volcano Eldfell, and prompting the island's evacuation.

Information

The summer **tourist office** (☎ 481 3555; www .vestmannaeyjar.is; Raðhústræti; ⏰ 9am-5pm Mon-Fri, 11am-4pm Sat & Sun May-Aug) is in the same building as the library and folk museum, and is well signposted from the harbour. The good brochure *Hiking High in Vestmannaeyjar* shows the main walking paths on Heimaey island.

There are **Sparisjóðurinn** (☎ 488 2100; Bárustigur 15) and **Íslandsbanki** (☎ 440 3000; Kirkjuvegur 23) banks with ATMs near the post office.

THE 1973 ERUPTION

Without warning, at 1.45am on 23 January 1973 a mighty explosion blasted through the winter's night as a 1.5km-long volcanic fissure split the eastern side of the island. The eruption area gradually became concentrated into a growing crater cone, which fountained lava and ash into the sky.

Normally the island's fishing boats would have been out at sea, but a force-12 gale had prevented them from sailing the previous afternoon. Now calm weather and a harbourful of boats allowed the island's 5200 inhabitants to be evacuated to the mainland. Incredibly, there was just a single fatality: an alleged drug addict who attempted to loot the town pharmacy and died of smoke and gas inhalation.

Over the next five months more than 30 million tonnes of lava poured over Heimaey, destroying 360 houses and creating a brand-new mountain, the red cinder cone Eldfell. One third of the town was buried beneath the lava flow, and the island increased in size by 2.5 sq km.

As the eruption continued, advancing lava threatened to close the harbour and make the evacuation permanent – without a fishing industry, there would have been no point in returning. In an attempt to slow down the inexorable flow of molten rock, firefighters hosed the lava with over six million tonnes of cold sea water. The lava halted just 175m short of the harbour mouth – actually improving the harbour by creating extra shelter!

The islanders were billeted with friends and family on the mainland, watching the fireworks and waiting to see if they could ever go home. Finally, the eruption finished five months later at the end of June. Two-thirds of the islanders returned to face the mighty clean-up operation.

Internet access is available for Ikr200 per hour at the **library** (☎ 481 1184; Ráðhústræti; 🕒 10am-6pm Mon-Thu, to 5pm Fri year-round, plus 1-4pm Sat mid-Sep–mid-May).

Sights

FISKA-OG NÁTTÚRUGRIPASAFN

The **Aquarium & Natural History Museum** (☎ 481 1997; Heiðarvegur 12; adult/6-12yr Ikr400/200; 🕒 11am-5pm mid-May–mid-Sep, 3-5pm Sun mid-Sep–mid-May) has an interesting collection of stuffed birds and animals, plus fishtanks of hideous Icelandic fish and a live video link to a puffin colony. The museum acts as a hospital for puffin chicks.

BYGGÐASAFN

Housed in Heimaey library, this **folk museum** (Byggðasafn; ☎ 481 1194; Raðhústræti; adult/6-12yr Ikr400/200; 🕒 11am-5pm mid-May–mid-Sep, by arrangement at other times) has loads of local-history displays, including fascinating photos of Heimaey's 1973 evacuation. Note the cabinet of Nazi regalia, from Vestmannaeyjar's short-lived branch of the Nazi Party. The items on display were deposited anonymously at the museum in the middle of the night!

VOLCANIC FILM SHOW

The explosive hour-long **show** (☎ 481 1045; Heiðarvegur; admission Ikr600; 🕒 11am, 2pm, 3.30pm & 9pm mid-Jun–mid-Aug, by request rest of yr) plays at the local cinema, and includes footage of Surtsey, the 1973 eruption and puffin rappelling. The film quality is naturally rather old and snowy, but it's fascinating stuff.

In the foyer there's some useful information about walking trails.

SKANSINN

This lovely green area by the sea has several unique historical sights. The oldest structure on the island was **Skansinn**, a 15th-century fort built to defend the harbour (not too successfully – when Algerian pirates arrived in 1627, they simply landed on the other side of the island). Its walls were swallowed up by the 1973 lava, but some have been rebuilt. Above them, you can see the remains of the town's **old water tanks**, also crushed by molten rock.

A shocking 80% of Heimaey's babies once died at birth, until in the 1840s an island woman, Sólveig, was sent abroad to be trained as a midwife. The tiny wooden house **Landlyst** (adult/child Ikr400/200; 🕒 11am-5pm Jun-Aug, by arrangement other times) was Sólveig's maternity hospital, and today contains a small display of her blood-letting equipment and other 19th-century medical paraphernalia.

Also here is the bitumen-coated **Stafkirkjan** (admission free; 🕒 11am-5pm Jun-Aug), a reconstruction of a medieval wooden stave church. It was presented to Heimaey by the Norwegian government in 2000 to celebrate 1000 years of Christianity. You can deafen yourself by ringing the bell on the way out.

HOUSE GRAVEYARD & POMPEI OF THE NORTH

Four hundred buildings lie buried under the 1973 lava. On the edge of the flow is an eerie **graveyard** where beloved homes rest in peace. **'Pompei of the North'** (www.pompeinordursins.is) is a modern 'archaeological' excavation in which 10 houses are being dug up. So far, the crumpled concrete remains of No 25 Suðurvegur have been unearthed.

STÓRAKLIF

The top of the craggy precipice **Stóraklif** is a treacherous 30-minute climb from behind the Esso petrol station at the harbour. The trail starts on the obvious 4WD track; as it gets steeper you're 'assisted' by ropes and chains (don't trust them completely), but it's worth the terror for the outstanding views. Up there are a weather station and radio tower.

ELDFELL & HELGAFELL

The 221m-high **volcanic cone** Eldfell appeared from nowhere in the early hours of 23 January 1973 (see the boxed text, p145). Once the fireworks finished, heat from the volcano provided Heimaey with geothermal energy from 1976 to 1985. Today the ground is still hot enough in places to bake bread or char wood. Eldfell is an easy climb from town, up the collapsed northern wall of the crater; stick to the path, as the islanders are trying to save their latest volcano from erosion.

Neighbouring **volcano** Helgafell (226m) erupted 5000 years ago. Its cinders are grassed over today, and you can scramble up here without much difficulty from the football pitch on the road to the airport.

ELDFELLSHRAUN

Known as Eldfellshraun, the new land created by the 1973 lava flow is now crisscrossed with a maze of hiking tracks that run down to the fort at Skansinn and the 'house graveyard', and all around the bulge of the raw, red eastern coast. Here you'll find small black-stone beaches, a lava garden (Gaujulundur) and a lighthouse.

HERJÓLFSDALUR & THE WEST COAST

Sheltered by an extinct volcano, green and grassy Herjólfsdalur was the **home of Vestman-naeyjar's first settler,** Herjólfur Barðursson. Excavations have revealed remains of a Norse house (not the bizarre construction in the bowl of the volcano, but a more unassuming site near the golf course). The island's camp site is also here.

On the cliffs west of the golf course, there's a little **monument** to the 200 people who converted to Mormonism and departed for Utah in the 19th century.

Several perilous tracks climb the almost sheer slopes around Herjólfsdalur and run along the top of Norðklettur to **Stafsnes**. The ascent is exhilarating, but there are some sheer drops. A gentler walk runs south along the western coast of the island, passing above numerous lava caves where local people hid from the pirates in 1627. At **Ofanleitishamar** hundreds of puffins nest in the cliffs, and you can often get within metres for close-up photos.

STÓRHÖFÐI

A windy meteorological station has been built on Stórhöfði, the rocky **peninsula** at the southern end of Heimaey. It's linked to the main island by a narrow isthmus (created by lava from Helgafell's eruption 5000 years ago), and there are good views from the summit. It's possible to scramble down to the boulder beach at **Brimurð** and continue along the cliffs on the east coast, returning by the main road just before the airport. From June to August the sea cliffs at **Lítlihöfði** are a good place to watch puffins.

LANDSKIRKJA

The lava stopped just short of the Landskirkja **church** in the middle of town. The church's carved wooden doors feature scenes from Vestmannaeyjar's history.

Activities

Heimaey's large indoor saltwater **swimming pool** (adult/child Ik300/150; ⊙ 7am-9pm Mon-Fri, 9am-5pm Sat & Sun) has outdoor hot pots and a gym.

Golfers can hire clubs at the 18-hole **golf course** (☎ 481 2363; www.eyjar.is/golf) in the Herjólfsdalur valley; green fees are Ikr3000.

Horse riding is available through **Hestaleiga Gunnars** (☎ 481 1478, 861 1476) at the farm Lukka, near the airport.

In summer you can see locals practising the ancient art of **sprangan** (cliff-swinging) – an essential skill for egg-collectors and puffin-hunters – on the cliffs between the harbour and Herjólfsdalur.

PUFFIN FOR TEA?

These tiny, colourful birds have been an important source of food in the Vestmannaeyjar since Viking times. Puffins are still hunted here in the traditional way: either by climbing the cliffs or by fishing them out of the air with a long net called a *hafur*. They end up on the menu in most Heimaey restaurants, either roasted or smoked. Apparently they're very tasty, although some people might be traumatised by the idea of digesting these sociable little characters.

Of course, not all the locals regard puffins as free lunch. Every August, Heimaey is bombarded by puffin chicks attempting to fly for the first time. They're supposed to be heading out to sea, but some get confused by the lights and end up round the harbour. Many locals gather up the chicks and release them by hand at the water's edge.

For more on puffins, see the boxed text, p47.

Tours

From May to August, **Viking Tours** (☎ 488 4884; www.vikingtours.is; small boat harbour, off Ægisgata; adult/9-14yr Ikr2900/1900) run daily two-hour **boat tours**, leaving at 10.30am and 3.30pm. They bounce right around the island, slowing for the big bird-nesting sites on the south coast, and sailing into the sea-cave Klettshellir, where the boat driver gets to show off his saxophone skills! His wife, Unnur, runs recommended two-hour bus tours at 8am and 1pm in summer (possible out of season if prebooked). Viking are also planning four-hour boat trips around Surtsey – contact them for details.

The friendly folk at Hreiðrið guesthouse run **walking tours** (per person Ikr800, Ikr5000 minimum) when there's a group, and two-hour **bus tours** (Ikr2200) of the island on Tuesday and Wednesday from June to August: you'll get to sample bread cooked in the still-smoking ash of Eldfell.

Festivals & Events

The country's biggest outdoor festival is the three-day **Þjóðhátíð** (People's Festival; admission Ikr9900), held at the festival ground at Herjólfsdalur over the first weekend in August. It involves music, dancing, fireworks, a big bonfire, gallons of alcohol and, as the night progresses, lots of drunken sex (it's something of a teen rite of passage). Icelanders seem to have mixed feelings about the festival, particularly as they get older, but that doesn't stop upwards of 11,000 people attending. Extra flights are laid on from Reykjavík, but you should book transport and accommodation far in advance.

Historically, the festival was first celebrated when bad weather prevented Vestmannaeyjar people from joining the mainland celebrations of Iceland's first constitution (1 July 1874). The islanders held their own festival a month later, and it's been an annual tradition ever since.

Sleeping

Heimaey has a camp site, several hotels and loads of guesthouses, but they fill up fast after the ferry arrives. Most places drop their rates by around 20% in winter.

CAMPING & HOSTEL

Camp site (☎ 692 6952; sites per person Ikr700; ☯ Jun-Aug) Cupped in the bowl of an extinct volcano, this dandelion-dotted camping ground has hot showers, a laundry room and cooking facilities. The wind can get strong.

our pick Sunnuhöll HI Hostel (☎ 481 2900; www.hotelvestmannaeyjar.is; Vestmannabraut 28b; sb from Ikr2200, s/d Ikr4200/6200) Sunnuhöll hostel looks and feels just like a little guesthouse! Its plain, neat single and double rooms (no dorms) have TVs, and there's a guest kitchen and sitting room. You can also use the laundry in Hótel Mamma across the road. Hótel Þórshamar acts as the reception.

GUESTHOUSES

Gistiheimilið Erna (☎ 481 2112; www.simnet.is/gisting; Kirkjubæjarbraut 15; sb/made-up bed/apt Ikr1800/3000/12,000) On the edge of the 1973 lava flow, Erna is a great budget choice. It's a friendly family home with cooking facilities, laundry, a Jacuzzi, bikes to borrow, and a TV in every room. The apartment fits eight people.

Gistiheimilið Hreiðrið (☎ 481 1045; http://tourist .eyjar.is; Faxastígur 33; sb/s/d Ikr1800/3500/5800) Run by the helpful volcano-show people, Ruth and Sigurgeir, this winning guesthouse has a family feel. Features include wall-to-wall puffins, a well-stocked kitchen, a cosy TV lounge and bike hire. Breakfast (Ikr800) is available year-round. They also run walking and bus tours in summer, and can run you to the far end of the island for Ikr500.

Gistiheimilið Hvíld (☎ 481 1230; www.simnet.is /hvild; Höfðavegur 16; sb Ikr2000, s/d/tr Ikr3500/6000/8000)

A friendly family owns this large green house, which has smallish guest rooms with shared bathroom, a TV lounge, and a peaceful garden. There's no breakfast, but there is a guest kitchen where you can prepare your own.

Gistiheimilið Árný (☎ /fax 481 2082; Illugagata 7; sb/s/d Ikr2800/4200/6900) A charming couple runs this neat suburban house, which also offers guests a kitchen and washing machine, and packed lunches by arrangement. Upstairs rooms have epic views, and the owner prays for a sound sleep for all her guests!

Hótel Mamma (☎ 481 2900; www.hotelvestmannaeyjar.is; Vestmannabraut 25; s/d/tr Ikr5550/7900/10,500) This is a cheery, peaceful Hótel Þórshamar–owned guesthouse with spacious rooms, all with TV and shared bathroom. There are two guest kitchens and a laundry in the basement. The attic steps are extremely small and steep – avoid if you're at all clumsy.

Gistihúsið Hamar (☎ 481 2900; www.hotelvestmannaeyjar.is; Herjólfsgata 4; s/d/tr Ikr7460/9990/12,990; 🖳) Also owned by Þórshamar, this place has large, modern en-suite rooms and wireless internet access. Reception for both Hamar and Hótel Mamma is at Þórshamar.

HOTELS

Hótel Eyjar (☎ 481 3636; www.hoteleyjar.eyjar.is; Bárustígur 2; s/d Ikr6200/9400) This hotel, on the corner of Strandvegur, offers huge and comfortable apartment-style rooms with bathrooms, kitchens and lounges – basically they're suites at room prices! The hotel bar is quite a popular spot for watching big-screen football matches.

Hótel Þórshamar (☎ 481 2900; www.hotelvestmannaeyjar.is; Vestmannabraut 28; s/d/ste Ikr10,290/15,050/20,210; 🖳) Iceland's first cinema is now a hotel, with pale, pleasant rooms and facilities including a sauna, hot tubs and a snooker room. Of the older rooms, 209 is best, tucked in the corner with its own balcony; otherwise, go for the three stylish new suites. Breakfast included.

Eating

Kökuhús (Bárustígur 7; ☾ 7.30am-5.30pm Mon-Fri, 8.30am-4pm Sat, 10am-4pm Sun) This is a great sit-down café-bakery, with a constant flow of people through the doors. It sells hot soup, buns and sandwiches (which can be made to order).

Pizza 67 (☎ 481 1567; Heiðarvegur 5; pizzas Ikr950-2000) Feathered friends are firmly off the menu: chomp pizzas and crunchy garlic bread instead in a relaxed, publike atmosphere.

'Oh my God! I woke up on the mainland, in a skip. I don't know how I got there. Or where my shoes had gone.'

Icelander Einar reminisces about
Þjóðhátíð

Café Maria (☎ 481 3160; Skólavegur 1; mains Ikr1400-3500; ☾ 11.30am-11.30pm Sun-Thu, 11.30am-1am Fri & Sat) A stuffed gannet surveys proceedings at this pleasant café-restaurant, which is quiet during the day but busy at night. Pizzas, burgers, savoury crepes, and fresh-fish and meat mains are served here – plus, yes, fresh puffin.

Lanterna (☎ 481 3393; Bárustígur 11; mains Ikr1500-3500; ☾ 11am-2pm & 6-10.30pm) This cosy wood-panelled place, decorated with local black-and-white photos, specialises in Vestmannaeyjar delicacies and, em, Wiener schnitzel. The brave can try puffin in a sweet sauce; catch of the day costs Ikr1500.

ourpick Fjólan (☎ 481 3663; Vestmannabraut 28; mains from Ikr2000; ☾ 7am-11pm) This upmarket restaurant lacks atmosphere (although we like the glitzy gold columns!), but it comes up trumps on the food. It serves the best fish in Heimaey, along with other traditional homemade dishes. There's also a buffet breakfast on offer.

Heimaey has several cheap petrol-station snack bars where you can get French fries, hot dogs and burgers for between Ikr300 and Ikr1000. For self-catering, there's the igloo-like **Vöruval supermarket** (☎ 481 3184; Vesturvegur 18; ☾ 9am-7pm daily), and two streets away is **Krónan supermarket** (Strandvegur; ☾ 11am-7pm). The local **Vín Búð** (☎ 481 1301; ☾ 12.30-6pm Mon-Thu, 11am-7pm Fri, 11am-2pm Sat) is also on Strandvegur.

Getting There & Away

AIR

The Vestmannaeyjar airport is about 3km from Heimaey – a taxi (☎ 698 2038) will cost about Ikr1000, or you could walk it in 20 minutes. Scheduled flights to Heimaey are offered by **Landsflug** (☎ 481 3300; www.airiceland.is), which flies two or three times daily from Reykjavík's domestic airport. The flight lasts 25 minutes, and the fare is Ik7200 for a full-price one-way ticket.

Flugfélag Vestmannaeyja (☎ 481 3255; www.eyjaflug.is) runs charter flights from the small airstrips at Bakki, Selfoss, Skógar and Hella. Most flights require a minimum of five persons.

FERRY

The ferry **Herjólfur** (☎ 481 2800; www.herjolfur.is) sails from Þorlákshöfn (on the mainland) at noon and 7.30pm, and returns from Heimaey at 8.15am and 4pm daily throughout the year. The boat can carry cars, but Heimaey is so small it's scarcely worth bringing one. The crossing takes 2¾ hours. The one-way fare per adult/child 12 to 15 years is Ikr1800/900. Motorbikes/cars cost an additional Ikr1200/1800.

If the sea looks rough, a Vestmannaeyjar tip is to book a cabin, dose yourself with seasickness tablets, and try to sleep your way through the trip.

The bus service between Reykjavík and Þorlákshöfn (Ikr1050, one hour) is run to connect with the *Herjólfur*. It leaves the city at 11am and 5.50pm daily, and it leaves Þorlákshöfn at 11.10am and 7pm.

Getting Around

The whole island can be comfortably explored on foot. If you need a taxi, call ☎ 698 2038.

SURTSEY

In November 1963 the fishing boat *Ísleifi II* noticed something odd – the sea south of Heimaey appeared to be on fire. Rather than flee, the boat drew up for a closer look – and its crew were the first to set eyes on the world's newest island.

The incredible subsea eruption lasted for 4½ years, throwing up cinders and ash to form a 2.7-sq-km piece of real estate (since eroded to 1.4 sq km). What else could it be called but Surtsey (Surtur's Island), after the Norse fire giant who will burn the world to ashes at Ragnarök.

It was decided that the sterile island would make a perfect laboratory, giving a unique insight into how plants and animals colonise new territory. Surtsey is therefore totally off limits to visitors (unless you're a scientist specialising in biocolonisation). Just so you know, though, in the race for the new land, the blue-green algae *Anabaena variabilis* got there first.

You can get a vicarious view of Surtsey's thunderous birth by visiting the Volcano Show (p75) in Reykjavík, or the Volcanic Film Show (p145) on Heimaey. You can also charter a flight over the islands with Flugfélag Vestmannaeyja (see opposite), while Viking Tours (p147) may be running boat trips around it in 2007.

And here's a little conundrum for you: what are fossils doing on this newly minted island?

SOUTHWEST ICELAND

West Iceland

Little visited, under appreciated and yet spectacularly scenic, west Iceland is in many ways a microcosm of what is on offer elsewhere in the country. Add the fact that it's easily accessible from Reykjavík and it becomes an ideal destination for shorter trips. You can avoid the long days on the road that awaits those screaming around the Ring Rd and still get to see glaciers, fjords, wild volcanic landscapes and some excellent museums. Thanks to the region's low-key presence on the tourist radar, you'll get most of these sights entirely to yourself.

Along the coast the glacial landscape is particularly striking with alternating fjords and peninsulas scattered with isolated fishing villages. Inland, dramatic lava fields are dotted with impressive waterfalls and incredible lava caves. West Iceland's most memorable feature, though, is the Snæfellsnes peninsula, a rugged and mountainous finger of land boasting jagged peaks, beautiful beaches, steaming geothermal fields, excellent bird-watching and its very own icecap, Snæfellsjökull.

Historical links are strong, with the *Laxdæla* and *Egil's* sagas sprouting from this area and the remnants of Viking farms still visible. The Settlement Centre in Borgarnes offers a fascinating insight into this period, and the medieval study centre in Reykholt gives a glimpse of the life and times of one of Iceland's most beloved historians, Snorri Sturluson.

Whether you're in search of the inspiration behind Iceland's sagas, wild and otherworldly scenery, a glimpse of the biggest mammals on earth or adrenaline-pumping activities, west Iceland offers an incredibly diverse range of highlights within a manageable distance.

WEST ICELAND

TOP FIVE

- Explore Iceland's subterranean world in the lava caves of **Viðgelmir**, **Surtshellir** and **Stefánshellir** (p157)
- Breathe deep as you take in the incongruous golden sands and turquoise water of **Skarðsvík beach** (p165)
- Get out on foot to explore the wild volcanic landscapes and dramatic ice floes at the western end of **Snæfellsnes** (p158)
- Drive through the remote and alien landscape of the **Kaldidalur valley** (p158)
- Step back in time and experience utter tranquillity with a visit to the traditional island of **Flatey** (p161)

Flatey Island ★

Skarðsvík ★
★ Snæfellsnes

Viðgelmir, Surtshellir ★ & Stefánshellir

Kaldidalur ★

Getting There & Around

If driving take Rte 1 west out of Reykjavík to reach west Iceland. Most roads in the area are paved and driving conditions are good. West Iceland also has good public-transport connections, with regular services from Reykjavík to Akranes, Borgarnes, Reykholt and Búðardalur, as well as daily buses to Stykkishólmur, Grundarfjörður and in summer to Ólafsvík and Hellissandur-Rif.

HVALFJÖRÐUR

If you've got plenty of time it's worth taking the 80km scenic route around Hvalfjörður rather than the 5.7km-long tunnel that runs beneath its waters. The fjord offers good hiking and fishing and is home to Iceland's highest waterfall. In summer there's also a good chance of spotting whales from the shore.

Sights

Dramatic **Esja** (914m), on the southern side of the fjord, is a great spot for wilderness hiking. The trail to the summit begins from the old farm Esjuberg, site of Iceland's first church, and ascends via the 850m spur Krehólakambur

and 830m Kistufell. To get here, turn off Rte 1 just north of Mosfellsbær.

For a more leisurely walk, a 5km trail runs up the Botnsdalur valley at the head of the fjord to **Glymur**, Iceland's highest waterfall (198m). Set in a deep, short canyon, the waterfall is at its most dramatic after heavy rain or snow-melt – in a dry period it can be a little underwhelming.

As you join the north shore of the fjord you'll pass the Miðsandur NATO Fuel Depot, once the site of Iceland's main **whaling station**. In 1989 protesters sank two of Iceland's whaling boats and sabotaged the plant, forcing Iceland to finally submit to the international moratorium on whaling. Although there's little to see today, grisly pictures of whale processing in operation are on display at the Olís petrol station at Fertikkiskáli, 4km further west. With increasing support for the pro-whaling lobby internationally (see p152), it's feared that the station may some day come back into operation.

Just past the petrol station at **Saurbær**, the local church is worth a look for its beautiful stained-glass work. Built in memory of

WEST ICELAND

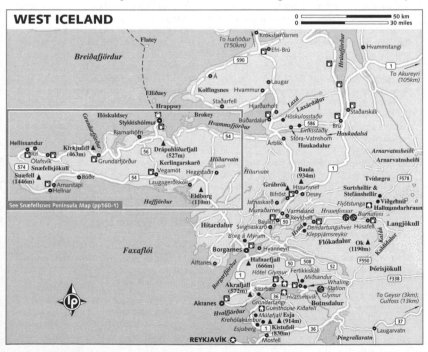

WEST ICELAND

0 ⟩⟩⟩⟩⟩⟩ 50 km
0 ⟩⟩⟩⟩⟩⟩ 30 miles

TO WHALE OR NOT TO WHALE?

In 1986 the International Whaling Commission (IWC) introduced a worldwide ban on commercial whaling; Iceland, however, decided to continue hunting. Under the auspices of a 'scientific research programme' the country's trawlers headed out to sea and killed 90 cetaceans in the following three years. Quite where the scientific research came in was never fully explained, as the whale meat was sold to restaurants in Iceland and Japan, and the carcasses were made into pet food, vitamins and lubricating oil – all of which had cheaper and more environmentally sound substitutes.

International pressure and direct action by conservationists finally forced Iceland to call a halt to its whaling activities in 1989. Iceland quit the IWC in protest. By 2002 whaling was back on the Icelandic agenda and they slinked back into the organisation and attempted to push through a proposal to slaughter 100 minke whales, 100 fin whales and 50 sei whales as part of a so-called 'feasibility study' to research the effect of whales on the marine environment.

With support from pro-whaling Norway and Japan, Iceland passed the motion by one vote in August 2003. Conservationists the world over were stunned and the IWC itself issued a formal protest, backed by members of the international scientific community and Iceland's tourism industry. Iceland's new image as a sanctuary for the magnificent creatures had created a whale-watching industry drawing 82,000 visitors to the country annually and generating US$27 million for the Icelandic economy – far more than commercial whaling ever did.

Despite this, the hunt resumed and conservationists from all over the world flocked to Iceland to protest. To appease the situation the Icelandic government promised that all whales would be caught outside whale-watching areas – that was until the first kill occurred in September, right in the main whale-watching area south of Reykjavík.

In spite of international condemnation, Iceland and Japan continued to hunt whales under the auspices of scientific research and Norway ignored the ban altogether. In the hope of eventually taking control of the IWC, these pro-whaling nations spent the following years encouraging small and developing nations to join the IWC and investing in their fisheries industries. By June 2006 they had garnered enough extra support for their policies to push through a resolution supporting a return to commercial whaling. Although the 33-32 vote left the pro-whaling members far from the 75% majority needed to overturn the 1986 ban, their campaign gained serious momentum and the anti-whaling lobby was dealt a serious blow.

Three months later Iceland decided to resume whale-meat exports banned by the UN's Convention on International Trade in Endangered Species (CITES) agreement. Iceland (along with Norway and Japan) has conveniently exempted itself from the CITES restrictions and has begun exporting to the Faeroes, an area not covered by CITES. It seemed only a matter of time before the country decided to flout the international ban altogether.

The swiftness of Iceland's decision surprised many, however. By mid-October the Icelandic government announced its plans to resume commercial whaling, granting 39 licences to commercial hunters – 30 for minke whales and nine for the endangered fin whale. Within a week of the announcement three fin whales had been killed. While pro-whalers cite cultural traditions, creation of jobs and adverse affects on the cod stock as reasons to resume the hunt, there seems to be little evidence to support their claims. Recent opinion polls show that there is little or no market for whale meat, and there is a dearth of scientific evidence to show that whales significantly contribute to the depletion of fish stocks. Most bewildering of all, economic predictions suggest that commercial whaling would be likely to generate only a fifth of the income currently provided by whale-watching tours.

Few understand why the Icelandic government has given in to such a small interest group in the face of such compelling evidence against the resumption of the hunt. Regardless, it looks as though the battle to save the whale is right back on the agenda.

For the latest on this controversial issue, visit the following websites:

Greenpeace http://whales.greenpeace.org
International Whaling Commission www.iwcoffice.org
Ocean Alliance www.oceanalliance.org
Whale & Dolphin Conservation Society www.wdcs.org

Hallgrímur Pétursson, who composed Iceland's most widely known religious work, *50 Passion Hymns*, the church is only slightly more modest than Reykjavík's Hallgrímskirkja, also named after the composer.

Sleeping & Eating

Hvammsvík (☎ 566 7023; www.hvammsvik.is; sites per tent Ikr500; ☺ Jun-Aug) On the southern side of the fjord you can stay at this beautifully situated recreation centre set right on the water at the foot of a sweeping slope. It's a dramatic place offering a nine-hole golf course (Ikr1000 per day) and kayaking (three-hour tours Ikr4500).

Guesthouse Kiðafell (☎ 566 6096; www.dagfinnur.is /kidafell; sb/s/d May-Sep Ikr2500/4200/7900, Oct-Apr Ikr2000/3500/6500) For more comfort, try this farmhouse offering pleasant accommodation in wood-panelled rooms. Breakfast (Ikr900), evening meals (Ikr2000) and horse riding (one hour Ikr2300) are also available.

Hótel Glymur (☎ 430 3100; www.hotelglymur.is; s/d/tr May-Oct Ikr16,900/23,900/30,400, Nov-Apr Ikr14,900/ 18,900/25,400) On the northern side of the fjord, this sleek hotel offers luxurious, contemporary-styled minisuites. Giant windows with great views, abstract art and swish bathrooms are on offer, as well as a huge open-plan restaurant, a library and lounge and two outdoor hot pots looking out over the fjord.

Getting There & Away

There is no public transport around Hvalfjörður, so you'll need your own vehicle to get here. Coming from Reykjavík, take Rte 47 just before the tunnel under the fjord. If you take the tunnel on Rte 1 the toll is currently Ikr1000/400 per car/motorcycle. Cyclists aren't permitted to use the tunnel.

AKRANES

pop 5900

Set under the imposing concave plateau Akrafjall (572m), the pleasant town of Akranes lies at the tip of the peninsula separating Hvalfjörður from Borgarfjörður. According to the Icelandic history text the *Landnámabók*, the town was settled in around 880 by a group of Irish hermits, but today fish processing and cement production are the main industries. Home to an excellent museum, a decent beach and some lovely old wooden buildings, the town is worth a brief detour on the trip west.

Information

The friendly **tourist office** (☎ 431 5566; www.visit akranes.is; ☺ 10am-5pm mid-May–mid-Sep, 1-5pm mid-Sep–mid-May) is based at the museum centre. You'll find the post office and several banks with ATMs on Kirkjubraut, the main street.

Sights & Activities
AKRANES MUSEUM CENTRE

The town's main attraction is the engaging **Museum Centre** (☎ 431 5566; www.museum.is; adult/ under 16yr Ikr500/free; ☺ 10am-5pm mid-May–mid-Sep, 1-5pm mid-Sep–mid-May), which is full of nautical relics, crystals, fossils, tales of sporting heroes and local lore. Outside, you can explore a restored boathouse, a drying shed, a church and several historic houses, and take a look at a collection of fishing boats, including the cutter *Sigurfari*. The museum is about 1km east of the centre, just off Graðagrund.

OTHER ATTRACTIONS

Akranes old town is well worth a wander for a look at the lovely old wooden buildings still in use. The most interesting section runs between the cinema and the pretty little church on Skólabraut. Also worth a visit is the 1km-long sandy beach at **Langisandur**, good for gentle walks or swimming on a warm day. On windy or wet days the town's **geothermal swimming pool** (☎ 433 1100; adult/under 14yr Ikr200/free; ☺ 6.15am-9pm Mon-Fri, 9am-6pm Sat & Sun) is a better option, as the beach can feel quite exposed. For some more serious walking, the 572m peak **Akrafjall** can be easily climbed in a day via the Berjadalur valley, which splits the plateau in two.

Sleeping & Eating

Camp site (☎ 864 5510; sites per tent/person Ikr400/300; ☺ mid-May–mid-Sep) The well-maintained town camp site is close to the shore and has sweeping views over the fjord to Snæfellsjökull on clear days. There are good washing facilities and a free washing machine and tumble dryer.

Heimagisting Ólínu (☎ 431 1408; olina@mailbox.is; Háholt 11; s/d Ikr3000/5000) Right in the centre of town on a quiet street, this pleasant B&B offers made-up beds in cosy rooms. Breakfast costs Ikr700.

Móar (☎ 431 1389; sollajoh@simnet.is; sb/made-up bed Ikr2500/3500; ☺ Jun-Aug) Although 4km from town, this friendly, modern farmhouse is well worth seeking out for its comfortable rooms and excellent service. Summerhouses sleeping up to five people can also be rented for

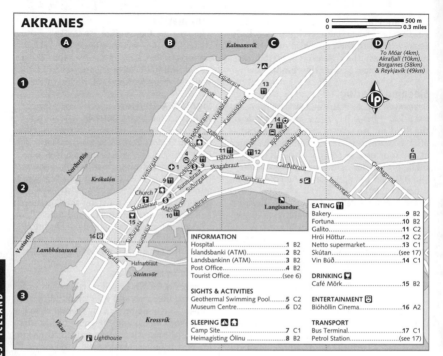

AKRANES

To Móar (4km),
Akrafjall (10km),
Borgarnes (38km)
& Reykjavík (49km)

Kalmansvík

Langisandur

Lambhúsasund

Steinsvör

Krossvík

Lighthouse

INFORMATION
Hospital...1 B2
Íslandsbanki (ATM)....................2 B2
Landsbankinn (ATM)..................3 B2
Post Office.....................................4 B2
Tourist Office............................(see 6)

SIGHTS & ACTIVITIES
Geothermal Swimming Pool.......5 C2
Museum Centre............................6 D2

SLEEPING
Camp Site.......................................7 C1
Heimagisting Ólinu 8 B2

EATING
Bakery..9 B2
Fortuna...10 B2
Galito...11 C2
Hrói Höttur..................................12 C2
Netto supermarket....................13 C1
Skútan......................................(see 17)
Vin Búð..14 C1

DRINKING
Café Mörk....................................15 B2

ENTERTAINMENT
Bíóhöllin Cinema.......................16 A2

TRANSPORT
Bus Terminal...............................17 C1
Petrol Station.........................(see 17)

Ikr10,000 per night. Móar is just off Rte 1 near Akranesvegamót, 4km east of Akranes.

Galito (☎ 430 6767; Stillholt 16-18; mains Ikr800-2100; ⏰ 11.30am-9pm Mon-Thu, to 10pm Fri-Sun) This modern but nondescript place is a good bet for a reasonably priced meal that's a step up from the usual fast food. It serves a decent selection of reliable favourites including pizza, panini and burgers.

Fortuna (☎ 431 3737; Mánabraut 20; mains Ikr1000-2500; ⏰ 11.30am-2.30pm Mon-Fri) Akranes' best bet for lunch is this popular eatery in the basement of a building close to the harbour. The menu offers a good selection of fish, steak and vegetables as well as exotic fare such as burritos.

For fast food, try the **Hrói Höttur** (☎ 431 1200; Stillholti 23; pizzas Ikr1100-2250) pizzeria or the bus-station grill **Skútan** (☎ 431 2061; Þjóðbraut 9). There are also several supermarkets near the town centre, a **bakery** (Kirkjubraut) and a branch of **Vin Búð** (Þjóðbraut 13).

Drinking & Entertainment
Your best bet for entertainment is to go back in time with a visit to the wonderfully old-fashioned cinema **Bíóhöllin** (☎ 431 1100; Vesturgata

27), which shows films several times weekly, and follow the movie with a drink at nearby **Café Mörk** (☎ 431 5030; Skólabraut 14).

Getting There & Away
Akranes is part of the Reykjavik city transport area; bus 27 runs every two hours to Mosfellsbær, from where bus 15 runs to the city centre. The entire journey takes about 80 minutes and costs Ikr250.

BORGARNES
pop 1800
Looking out over the brooding waters of Borgarfjörður and the steep slopes of Hafnarfjall, Borgarnes has a pretty spectacular setting. It's an unassuming town, deprived of any serious fishing potential by strong tidal currents in the fjord, but a bustling service point for travellers and home to one of Iceland's newest and most fascinating museums. To get a real sense of what the town is like, leave behind the cluster of petrol stations, cafeterias and supermarkets on the main road and venture into the old town, where rambling streets and quaint buildings portray a very different character.

Information

The main tourist office for west Iceland, **Vesturland** (☎ 437 2214; www.west.is; ☻ 9am-6pm Mon-Fri, 10am-3pm Sat & Sun May-Aug, 10am-4pm Mon-Fri Sep-Apr), is in the Hyrnan complex by the Esso petrol station. Internet access is available for Ikr100 per 10 minutes. There's a Sparisjóðurinn bank with ATM and a post office on Brákarbraut.

Sights

Housed in a wonderful restored warehouse by the harbour, the new **Borgarnes Settlement Centre** (☎ 437 1600; www.landnam.is; Brákarbraut 13-15; adult/under 14yr for one exhibition Ikr800/600, for both Ikr1400/1000; ☻ 10am-7pm mid-May–mid-Sep, 11am-5pm Wed-Mon mid-Sep–mid-May) offers a fascinating insight into the history of Icelandic settlement and the saga era. The museum is divided into two exhibitions, one covering the discovery and settlement of the island and the other recounting the adventures and tales of the man behind *Egil's Saga* (see p156). Although it's expensive, the museum is a wealth of information and gives a wonderful insight into Iceland's history and a firm context in which to place your Icelandic visit.

As part of the museum's efforts, stone cairns have been erected at the most important *Egil's Saga* sites around the region. A free leaflet includes a map and guide to the route. One such site is the town park **Skallagrímsgarður** (Skallagrímsgata) where the burial mound of the father and son of saga hero Egill Skallagrímsson can be seen, along with Viking weapons and equipment.

For more history, head for the **Borgarfjörður Museum** (☎ 430 7200; Bjarnarbraut 4-6; admission free; ☻ 1-6pm daily year-round, plus to 8pm Tue & Thu Jun-Aug), where the very traditional exhibits include local art, stuffed birds and farmhouse equipment.

Also worth a visit is the wonderful outdoor and indoor **swimming pool** (☎ 437 1444; Þorsteinsgata; adult/under 14yr Ikr310/155; ☻ 7am-10pm Mon-Fri, 9am-6pm Sat & Sun), which has water slides, a sauna and hot pots. Golf fanatics can take in a game at the 18-hole **Golfklúbbur Borgarnes** (☎ 437 1663; www.gbborgarnes.net; green fees Ikr4000) north of the centre on Rte 1.

Sleeping

Hostel Hamar (☎ 437 2000; www.gbborgarnes.net; sb/s/d members Ikr1950/2950/4900) Set in a large restored farmhouse above a golf club, this hostel is a cosy, well-equipped place with a basic kitchen, a café and a TV lounge. The rooms are small and functional, but they're the cheapest sleep around. The hostel is about 3km north of town on Rte 1. Nonmembers must pay a small supplement to stay.

Bjarg (☎ 437 1925; bjarg@simnet.is; sb/s/d Ikr2000/4400/8800) One of the nicest places to stay in town, this attractive farmhouse set overlooking the fjord has warm, cosy rooms with tasteful wood panelling, crisp white linens and lots of little extras such as TV, radio and personal lamps over the beds. There's a shared guest kitchen, spotless bathrooms and an additional self-catering apartment sleeping four. Bjarg is about 1km north of the centre, just off Rte 1.

Mótel Venus (☎ 437 2345; motel@centrum.is; 311 Borgarnes; sites per tent Ikr500, sb Ikr2500, s/d without bathroom Ikr5300/6800, d with bathroom Ikr9300) Like something out of the American Midwest, this rather forlorn-looking motel on the far side of the bridge across the fjord has functional, modest rooms and a decent restaurant and pizza bar (mains Ikr1400 to Ikr1600). Room rates drop about 30% in winter.

Hótel Borgarnes (☎ 437 1119; www.hotelborgarnes .is; Egilsgata 14; s/d Ikr10,900/12,900) Big, bright but tired rooms with typical business-style décor are available at this large and rather characterless hotel in the centre of town. The restaurant offers two-course traditional meals for Ikr2900, and in winter the room rates drop by about 40%.

Hotel Hamar (☎ 433 6600; www.icehotels.is; 310 Borgarnes; s/d Jun-Sep Ikr13,600/17,000, Oct-May Ikr8200/10,200; ☐) Sleek, stylish and by far the best spot to sleep in town, this new hotel has a series of contemporary-styled rooms with large windows and great views, private terraces and wi-fi access. The restaurant (mains Ikr2800 to Ikr5500) serves an excellent choice of fish, lamb and veal, and there are three outdoor hot pots for relaxing.

Eating

Matstofan (☎ 437 2017; Brákarbraut 3; mains Ikr550-1350) Serving an unusual combination of Icelandic, Filipino and fast food, this basic place on the way to the harbour is popular with locals. Although stylistically challenged (think gingham tablecloths teamed with plastic placemats), the steaming plates of *adobo* (Filipino curry) go down well.

Búðarklettur (☎ 437 1600; Brákarbraut 13; mains Ikr1400-2900; ☻ 10am-9pm daily mid-May–mid-Sep, 11am-5pm Wed-Mon mid-Sep–mid-May) Borgarnes' best bet for food is this bright and airy restaurant at the Settlement Centre. The large windows, stripped wood floors and modern furniture give it a wonderfully contemporary style, while the menu features a tempting range of lamb, fish and pasta dishes as well as lighter snacks and cakes.

For the usual array of burgers, fried chicken and doughy pizza, you could also try the grill bars at the Esso and Shell petrol stations. Self-caterers should head for the **Bónus supermarket** (Borgarbraut 57). There's a branch of Vín Búð in the Hyrnu Torg centre on the main road.

Getting There & Away
All buses between Reykjavík and Akureyri, the Westfjords and Snæfellsnes stop near the Esso and Shell petrol stations at the Hyrnan complex. The one-hour trip to Reykjavík costs Ikr1600. In winter high winds rolling in off the Atlantic can frequently close the southern approach to Borgarnes.

AROUND BORGARNES
Borg á Mýrum
Iceland's most famous farm, Borg á Mýrum (Rock in the Marshes), lies just north of Borgarnes on Rte 54. Although there's little to see here except the large rock *(borg)* that gave the farm its name, the site holds great significance for Icelanders as the core location in *Egil's Saga*. The saga recounts the tale of Kveldúlfur, grandfather of the warrior-poet Egill Skallagrímsson, who fled to Iceland during the 9th century after falling out with the king of Norway. Kveldúlfur grew gravely ill on the journey however, and instructed his son, Skallagrímur Kveldúlfsson, to throw his coffin overboard after he died and build the family farm wherever it washed ashore – this just happened to be at Borg. Skallagrímur's son, Egill Skallagrímsson, grew up to be a bloodthirsty individual who killed his first adversary at the age of seven and went on to carry out numerous raids on the coast of England. The complex tale of the family's adventures is believed to have been written by the historian Snorri Sturluson, who married into the family in 1197. Snorri (see p158) lived briefly at Borg, but the marriage broke down and he moved inland to Reykholt. As well as the large stone marker, you can see a wooden church and a modernist sculpture by Ásmundur Sveinsson. In case you were wondering, the Icelandic beer Egil's is named after Egill Skallagrímsson.

UPPER BORGARFJÖRÐUR
Bifröst
Heading north along Rte 1 you'll pass through a large lava field belched out by the 3000-year-old cinder cones of Grábrók and Grábrókarfell, which rise dramatically from the flat surroundings just beyond the village and college complex at Bifröst. There are plenty of walking trails crisscrossing the area, and a well-worn track leads up through the moss, lichen and dwarf birch to the lip of **Grábrók** (173m), which offers great views over the surrounding lava flow but can be extremely windy. Nearby, **Grábrókarfell** has been rather disfigured by gravel extraction.

Bifröst lies on the main bus route between Reykjavík and Akureyri; the fare from Reykjavík is Ikr2400.

Reykholt
Laid-back, postcard pretty and incredibly unassuming, Reykholt is a sleepy kind of place that on first glance offers few clues to its bustling past as one of the most important medieval settlements in Iceland.

To get some insight into the significance of the area, visit the fascinating medieval study centre **Snorrstofa** (☎ 435 1491; www.reykholt.is; admission Ikr500; ☼ 10am-6pm Jun-Sep), devoted to the celebrated medieval historian Snorri Sturluson. The displays here explain the laws, literature, society and way of life in medieval Iceland, the country's golden age. Iceland's oldest document, the 12th-century deeds to the original church, are also here, and a new exhibition looks at the role of women in 13th-century society.

The centre is also home to one of Iceland's newest churches. Built in 1996, the simple but harmonious structure contains some beautiful contemporary stained glass woven with lines from early Christian poetry. The church also features an early Lutheran baptismal font and a 600-year-old organ that was originally installed in Reykjavík cathedral. If you're visiting in late July, look out for information on the annual classical-music festival.

Behind the centre, a pretty 19th-century church stands out brightly against the surrounding hills, and beyond it a grassy field covers the site of a recent archaeological dig. At the time of writing it was planned that medieval finds from the dig would be displayed by the National Museum in Reykholt from 2007. Further on, you'll come to **Snorralaug** (Snorri's

Pool), a circular, stone-lined pool fed by a hot spring. The stones at the base of the pool are original, and it is believed that this is where Snorri came to bathe. Behind the pool is a passage believed to lead to the cellar where Snorri Sturluson was murdered.

SLEEPING & EATING

Camp site (☎ 435 1182; sites per person Ikr500) The nearest camping ground is set beside the tiny geothermal centre of Kleppjárnsreykir on Rte 50 about 6km west of Reykholt.

Brennistaðir (☎ 435 1193; brennist@islandia.is; sb/made-up bed/summerhouse Ikr1800/3600/7200) This bright and cheery farmhouse is 11km down the valley on Rte 50.

Fosshótel Reykholt (☎ 435 1260; www.fosshotel.is; s/d Jun-Aug Ikr10,700/17,900, Sep-May Ikr9300/13,700) Housed in a modern block behind the old church, this well-equipped hotel has comfortable, businesslike rooms and a Norse mythology theme. Exhibits on each floor delve into Icelandic mythology, runes and sagas. The hotel has a decent restaurant (mains Ikr2000 to Ikr3000) and a wellness centre offering massage, aromatherapy and a Jacuzzi steam bath and sauna. Cheaper rooms with shared bathrooms are also available.

GETTING THERE & AWAY

Reykholt is 40km northeast of Borgarnes on Rte 518. Public buses from Reykjavík leave at 5pm on Friday and Sunday (Ikr2200, two hours). In the opposite direction the bus leaves Reykholt at 7.15pm.

Around Reykholt
DEILDARTUNGUHVER

Europe's biggest **hot spring**, Deildartunguhver spews up billowing clouds of steam as 180L of boiling water bubbles from the ground every second. The incredibly powerful hot spring provides the region with its boiling-hot water, while a 64km-long pipeline takes a supply to Borgarnes and Akranes. Any excess goes to heating the greenhouses that dot the surrounding area.

Deildartunguhver is close to Rte 50, just north of Kleppjárnsreykir, close to the turn-off for Reykholt.

Húsafell

Tucked between the river Kaldá and the edge of the desolate lava fields at Hallmundarhraun, Húsafell is a popular outdoor retreat for Reykjavík residents. The leisure complex **Ferðaþjónustan Húsafelli** (☎ 435 1550; www.husafell.is; sites per person Ikr750, sb Ikr1400, s/d with shared bathroom Ikr8500/9500) is a one-stop shop, with a camp site, cabin and farmhouse accommodation, a guest kitchen, a laundry and a restaurant (mains Ikr1200 to Ikr2200). There's also a lovely outdoor geothermal swimming pool (Ikr400/250 for adult/child under 14, open 10am to 10pm daily June to September, shorter hours other months), a children's playground, a nine-hole golf course and a petrol station.

There's no public transport to Húsafell, but twice a week you can get as far as Reykholt by bus (see p157). Several companies also offer day trips to Kaldidalur (p158) that pass through Húsafell.

Around Húsafell
HRAUNFOSSAR & BARNAFOSS

Four kilometres west of Húsafell is Hraunfossar, a series of trickling **cascades** that emerge as if by magic from beneath an ancient lava flow. From here a short trail leads upstream to Barnafoss (Children's Waterfall), where the river Hvítá roars through a cauldronlike gorge. There used to be a rock arch here, but two children were swept off it to their deaths – hence the waterfall's name – and the arch was destroyed.

HALLMUNDARHRAUN

East of Húsafell the vast, barren lava flows of Hallmundarhraun make up an eerie landscape dotted with gigantic lava tubes. These long tunnel-like caves are formed by flows of molten lava beneath a solid lava crust, and they look as though they've been burrowed out by some hellish giant worm.

Closest to Húsafell, further along Rte 518, is the 1.5km-long lava tube **Víðgelmir**. The cave is preserved and can only by visited on guided tours arranged through local guesthouse **Fljótstunga** (☎ 435 1198; www.fljotstunga.is; 1-/3-hr tours per person Ikr1200/3500, minimum 4 people over 8yr). The roof of the cave close to the entrance has collapsed, creating a dramatic rock arch and two forbidding black chasms descending into the earth. Inside you'll see weird rock formations, and on the longer tour you'll descend to the bottom of the cave. Accommodation in the cosy, wood-panelled rooms at Fljótstunga costs Ikr2000/2700/4000 for sleeping bags/singles/doubles.

Even more dramatic are the tubes of **Surtshellir** and **Stefánshellir**, further to the east. Here

---

SNORRI STURLUSON

The chieftain and historian Snorri Sturluson is one of the most important figures in medieval Norse history – partly because he wrote a lot of it down himself. Snorri was born at Hvammur near Búðardalur (further north), but he was raised and educated at the theological centre of Oddi near Hella and later married the heir to the farm Borg near Borgarnes. For reasons not fully revealed, he abandoned his family at Borg and retreated to the wealthy church estate at Reykholt. At the time Reykholt was home to 60,000 to 80,000 people and was an important trade centre at the crossroads of major routes across the country. Snorri composed many of his most famous works at Reykholt, including *Prose Edda* (a textbook to medieval Norse poetry) and *Heimskringla* (a history of the kings of Norway). Snorri is also widely believed to be the hand behind *Egil's Saga*, a family history of Viking *skald* (court poet) Egill Skallagrímsson (see p156).

At the age of 36 Snorri was appointed *lögsögumaður* (lawspeaker) of the Alþing (Icelandic parliament), but he endured heavy pressure from the Norwegian king to promote the king's private interests at the parliament. Instead Snorri busied himself with his writing and the unhappy Norwegian king Hakon issued a warrant for his capture – dead or alive. Snorri's political rival and former son-in-law Gissur Þorvaldsson saw his chance to impress the king and possibly snag the position of governor of Iceland in return. He arrived in Reykholt with 70 armed men on the night of 23 September 1241 and hacked the historian to death in the basement of his home.

---

the tube roof has collapsed in three places, and you can enter at the far end and scramble back toward the road along the tube floor, exiting via a cairn of stones in the first chasm. The floor of the tube is covered in slippery boulders so don't attempt this without a torch. To get to the caves, turn onto mountain road F578, midway between Fljótstunga and Húsafell, and continue for about 8km.

If you've got a 4WD it's possible to continue along Rte F578 to the lakes of **Arnarvatnsheiði** and on to Hvammstangi.

KALDIDALUR & LANGJÖKULL
Southeast of Húsafell, the Kaldidalur valley skirts the edge of a series of glaciers and offers incredible views of the Langjökull icecap and on fine days the snows of Eiríksjökull, Okjökull and Þórisjökull. Although there's no public transport along unsurfaced Rte 550, you can drive south in a private vehicle to Þingvellir.

Many tour companies including **TREX** (www.hopferd.is/engl/tours/daytours.htm), **Activity Group** (www.activity.is), **Mountain Taxi** (www.mountaintaxi.is) and **Eskimos** (www.eskimos.is) offer tours of the region looping from Reykjavík through some or all of the following: Borgarnes, Reykholt, Húsafell, Surtshellir, Kaldidalur and Þingvellir. Tours take between eight and 10 hours and cost from Ikr9000 to Ikr20,900. More expensive tours include an hour's snowmobiling.

Activity Group also offers whitewater rafting on the river Hvítá (Ikr5900) and dogsledding on Langjökull (Ikr6900).

SNÆFELLSNES

Lush fjords, volcanic peaks, dramatic sea cliffs, sweeping golden beaches, a glistening icecap and Iceland's newest national park make up the diverse and fascinating landscape of the 100km-long Snæfellsnes peninsula. The area is dominated by the icecap Snæfellsjökull, immortalised in Jules Verne's fantasy tale *Journey to the Centre of the Earth*, but today it's a lot more accessible. Good roads and regular buses mean that it's an easy trip from Reykjavík and ideal for a short break, offering a cross section of the best Iceland has to offer in a very compact region.

Most of Snæfellsnes' inhabitants live on the rugged and mountainous north coast, with the national park protecting the western end of the peninsula. The area can get a bit of a hammering from the weather, so be prepared and bring your rain gear if you're planning any outdoor activities.

Snæfellsnes is a **Green Globe** (www.greenglobe.org) community, dedicated to sustainable development for travel and tourism and committed to environmental protection.

STYKKISHÓLMUR
pop 1240
The charming town of Stykkishólmur, the largest on the Snæfellsnes peninsula, is built up around a natural harbour protected by a dramatic basalt island. It's a picturesque place with

a friendly, laid-back attitude and lots of brightly coloured wooden buildings, in use since the town's heyday in the late 19th and early 20th centuries. With a good choice of accommodation and restaurants, good public transport, and a ferry to Flatey and the Westfjords, it's an excellent base for exploring the area.

Information

Tourist information is available at the **Sæferðir Information Centre** (Seatours Information Centre; ☎ 438 1450; Smiðjustíg 3; ⏲ 8am-8pm Jun-Aug, to 5pm Sep-May), which also has internet access (Ikr100 for 15 minutes). Internet access is also available at the **library** (☎ 438 1281; Bókhlöðustígur; 30 min Ikr200; ⏲ 3-7pm Mon & Thu). The KB Banki and post office are on Aðalgata.

Sights & Activities

Much of Stykkishólmur's charm comes from the cluster of wooden warehouses, stores and homes around the town's harbour. Most date back about 150 years and many are still in use. Pick up a copy of the free 'Old Stykkishólmur' brochure at the tourist office for information on the buildings.

One of the most interesting is the **Norska Húsið** (Norwegian House; ☎ 438 1640; norkshus@simnet.is; Hafnargata 5; adult/6-16yr & senior Ikr400/200; ⏲ 11am-5pm Jun-Aug), now the municipal museum. Built by trader Árni Þorlacius in 1832, the house has been skilfully restored and displays a wonderfully eclectic selection of farm equipment, butter churns, sewing machines, saddles, wooden skis and other salvaged items of local history. On the 2nd floor you can see the typical layout of an upper-class home in 19th-century Iceland.

Looking decidedly out of place in the surrounding landscape, Stykkishólmur's futuristic **Stykkishólmskirkja** is a striking white church with a sweeping bell tower and what looks like a giant ship's vent to the rear. The interior is known for its hundreds of suspended lights and huge modern painting of the Virgin Mary and Jesus floating in the night sky.

Also worth exploring is the basalt island of **Súgandisey**, which protects the town harbour and offers grand views across Breiðafjörður. You can get to the island by walking across the stone causeway from the harbour.

There's excellent swimming at the town's **geothermal swimming pool** (☎ 438 1372; adult/under 14yr Ikr280/120; ⏲ 7am-10pm Mon-Fri, 10am-7pm Sat & Sun), which has water slides and hot pots.

For information on fishing, kayaking, cycling and other activities, see Tours, below.

Tours

Sæferðir (Seatours; ☎ 438 1450; www.seatours.is; Smiðjustígur 3; ⏲ 9am-8pm daily Jun-Aug, 8am-4pm Mon-Fri Sep-May) runs a variety of boat tours, including popular nature-watching cruises to the islands of Breiðafjörður, where you can see seals, puffins and eagles (Ikr4400, 2¼ hours); sea-angling trips (Ikr4150, 2¼ hours) and whale-watching tours from Ólafsvík (see p164). Most activities run June to August only, but some are year-round. You can also hire bikes (Ikr1500 per day). Kayaking tours around the islands of Breiðafjörður (see p161) can be arranged through **Seakayak Iceland** (☎ 690 3877; http://seakayakiceland.com; 2-4hr Ikr5500). If you'd like the lowdown on the history of the town and its lovely buildings, Dadda Dagbjöst offers **guided tours** (☎ 438 1121; Sjavalborg, Hafnargata 4; 1hr per person Ikr600) of the town for five to six people.

Sleeping

Camp site (☎ 438 1750; sites per person Ikr600) Near the pool, the site has toilets and sinks.

Sjónarhóll HI Hostel (☎ 438 1417; www.hostel .is; Höfðagata 1; sb members/nonmembers Ikr1650/2000, d 5000; ⏲ May-Sep) Set in one of the town's oldest buildings, this renovated hostel has clean, simple rooms and a decent kitchen. Dorms sleep two to four people, and there are also some private rooms.

Heimagisting María Bæringsdóttir (☎ 438 1258; fax 438 1245; Höfðagata 11; s/d Ikr3800/6500) Set back from the waterfront in a residential street, this homey guesthouse has a selection of cosy rooms and a wonderfully warm welcome. There's a garden and veranda overlooking the bay, and a sumptuous breakfast is included in the price. Book in advance.

Hótel Breiðafjörður (☎ 433 2200; www.prinsvali ant.is; Aðalgata 8; s/d Jun-Aug Ikr8900/11,000, Sep-May Ikr7100/9200; ⬚) Right in the centre of town, this small hotel offers bright, spacious rooms with modern furniture and good views from the balconies. The décor is simple and neutral, and all the fittings are new.

Hótel Stykkishólmur (☎ 430 2100; www.hotel stykkisholmur.is; Borgarbraut 6; s/d Apr-May & Sep-Nov Ikr8900/10,900, Jun-Aug Ikr11,900/13,900; P ⬚) Slightly out of the centre and set on a hill, this hotel was once the top spot in town but is now looking pretty dated. The business-style rooms are simple enough, with plenty of

WEST ICELAND

SNÆFELLSNES PENINSULA

space and good views, and there's a time-warp restaurant (mains Ikr1750 to Ikr3800) serving traditional Icelandic food.

Eating

Bakery (Nesvegur 1; ⏰ 8.30am-6pm Mon-Fri, 8am-4pm Sat) On the main road out of town, with plenty of seating, this bakery is a good choice for breakfast or lunch. It serves good sandwiches and cakes as well as *ástar-pungur* (literally 'love balls'; fried balls of dough and raisins).

Fimm Fiskar (☎ 436 1600; Frúarstígur 1; mains Ikr800-2800) Across the road from and not quite so charming as Narfeyrarstofa (following), this place has a good range of the more predictable pizzas, grills and seafood dishes.

our pick **Narfeyrarstofa** (☎ 438 1119; Aðalgata 3; mains Ikr1500-3700) Stykkishólmur's top spot for food is this atmospheric place serving up a bumper selection of excellent dishes. There's plenty of fish with heavenly sauces, succulent burgers, and such delicacies as black guillemot for the more adventurous. During the day it's a welcoming café with a good selection of cakes.

A cheap grill can be found at the petrol station, and there's a Bónus supermarket near the swimming pool. The local Vín Búð is at the hardware store Skípavík HF, behind the Norska Húsið.

Getting There & Away

BUS

Buses run to/from Reykjavík (Ikr3300, 2½ hours) once daily (twice on Friday and Sunday), with a change to a connecting bus in Vatnaleið. You'll also need to change in Vatnaleið for the service to Grundarfjörður, Ólafsvík and Hellissandur-Rif. In summer, buses also run around the tip of the peninsula to Hellnar once daily. Services from Vatnaleið are limited and don't always link well with the *Baldur* ferry to and from the Westfjords. In Stykkishólmur, buses stop at the petrol station on the main road.

FERRY

The car ferry **Baldur** (☎ 438 1450; www.seatours.is) operates between Stykkishólmur and Brjánslækur in the Westfjords (2¼ hours), via Flatey. From June to August there are daily departures from Stykkishólmur at 9am and 3pm, returning from Brjánslækur at noon and 6pm. On

Monday, Wednesday and Friday from June to August buses connect from Ísafjörður, leaving at 9.30am to connect with the ferry and pick up ferry passengers to go to Patreksfjörður and Látrabjarg. The afternoon ferry connects with Westfjord buses to Ísafjörður, while the morning ferry connects with buses to the bird cliffs at Látrabjarg. Buses from Ísafjörður also connect with the morning ferry.

Adult fares to Brjánslækur and Flatey are Ikr2190 and Ikr1530 respectively (Ikr1250/ 1095/free for seniors/child 12 to 15/child under 12). Vehicles up to 5m long cost Ikr2190 and motorcycles cost Ikr825.

AROUND STYKKISHÓLMUR
Helgafell
About 5km south of Stykkishólmur is the **holy mountain** Helgafell (73m) that was once venerated by worshippers of the god Þór. The first Icelandic *þing*, or assembly, met here in the 9th century, but it was later moved to the flat promontory Þingvellir after assembly members defiled the sacred mountain with their toilet ablutions – this triggered several bloody battles in saga times. A Christian church was

built here in the late 10th century by Snorri Goði, a Þór worshipper who converted to Christianity, and the nearby farm at Helgafell was where the conniving Guðrún Ósvífursdóttir of the *Laxdæla Saga* spent her lonely old age. You can still see the ruins of the church on the hill top, from where you'll also get great views over the islands of Breiðafjörður.

Breiðafjörður
Created by trolls from the Westfjords – so legend has it – and now home to a rich selection of bird life, the thousands of tiny islands that block the waterway between Hvammsfjörður and Breiðafjörður create an idyllic tapestry of greens and blues across the water. The only inhabited island is Flatey; the other low, rocky islets are home only to kittiwakes, fulmars, gulls, guillemots, puffins, cormorants and eagles. Seals are also commonly seen on low-lying skerries. A free brochure available in the tourist office in Stykkishólmur gives details on the fjord and the birds that can be seen here.

FLATEY
For a glimpse of Icelandic island life it's well worth taking the trip to the low-lying island of Flatey. Here, life runs at an even slower pace and the brightly coloured wooden houses seem little changed in centuries. The island was the site of a literary monastery in the 11th century, and today it is full of historical buildings and has a church with paintings by Spanish-Icelandic artist Baltasar. More recently, Flatey was used as the location of the film *Nonni & Manni*.

You can take a day trip to Flatey with Sæferðir (see opposite). You can camp at **Ferðiþjónustan Grænigarður** (☎ 438 1451; sites per person Ikr600; ☾ mid-Jun–mid-Sep), 300m from the ferry dock. In summer accommodation is also available at **Gisting Jónsdóttir** (☎ 438 1476; sb Ikr2200), in summerhouses with shared kitchens, and at pleasant **Hotel Flatey** (☎ 422 7610; www.hotelflatey.is; s/d Ikr13,900/16,900; ☾ mid-Jun–mid-Sep), which has comfy rooms and great views over the fjord.

Berserkjahraun
The sweeping lava field Berserkjahraun (Berserks Lava), stretches inland from Rte 54 about 15km west of the intersection with the Stykkishólmur road. This lunar landscape backed by sweeping mountain sides is named after a tale from the *Eyrbyggja Saga* – see p163.

WEST ICELAND

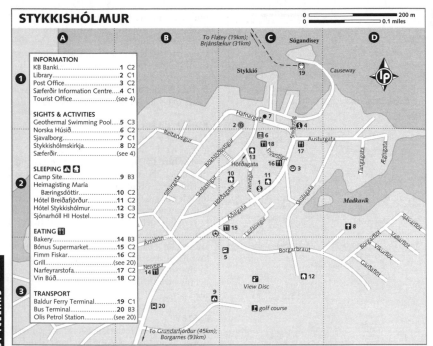

STYKKISHÓLMUR

INFORMATION
KB Banki..................................1 C2
Library.....................................2 C1
Post Office..............................3 C2
Sæferðir Information Centre....4 C1
Tourist Office......................(see 4)

SIGHTS & ACTIVITIES
Geothermal Swimming Pool.....5 C3
Norska Húsið............................6 C2
Sjavalborg................................7 C1
Stykkishólmskirkja..................8 D2
Sæferðir.............................(see 4)

SLEEPING
Camp Site................................9 B3
Heimagisting María
    Bæringsdóttir....................10 C2
Hótel Breiðafjörður.............11 C2
Hótel Stykkishólmur...........12 C3
Sjónarhóll HI Hostel.............13 C2

EATING
Bakery....................................14 B3
Bónus Supermarket..............15 C2
Fimm Fiskar...........................16 C2
Grill..................................(see 20)
Narfeyrarstofa......................17 C2
Vin Búð..................................18 C2

TRANSPORT
Baldur Ferry Terminal...........19 C1
Bus Terminal..........................20 B3
Olis Petrol Station.............(see 20)

If you're feeling peckish after a walk around the area you can detour to the farm **Bjarnarhöfn** (☎ 438 1581) to see the Icelandic delicacy *hákarl* (putrid shark meat) being produced. The farm is at the end of a dirt track, signposted off Rte 54 – call ahead to make sure someone is in.

Kerlingarskarð

About 25km south of Stykkishólmur, **Kerling-arskarð** (Witch Pass) was named after a female witch or troll who was turned into the stone pillar at the northwestern foot of Kerlingar-fjall, the mountain east of the pass. Nearby lake **Baulárvallavatn** is reputed to be the home of a Nessie-style lake monster. Buses between Reykjavík and Stykkishólmur pass the lake, but the pass itself is reached via a long track that branches off Rte 54 just east of the junction with Rte 56.

GRUNDARFJÖRÐUR

pop 980

Spectacularly set on a dramatic bay, the friendly little town of Grundarfjörður is backed by the steep slopes of the forbidding Helgrindur (986m) and protected from the sea by the strik-ing peak of Kirkjufell (463m). The town itself is a typical prefab Icelandic fishing community, but the facilities are good and the surrounding landscape is just aching to be discovered.

The incredibly friendly **Eyrbyggja Heritage Centre** (☎ 438 1881; Grundargata 35; ⏰ 10am-6pm) acts as tourist office, café, internet point (access Ikr200 for 10 minutes) and local museum (admission Ikr400). Displays centre on rural life in Iceland from 1900 to 1950, and there are screenings of Icelandic films each day in summer.

The local **swimming pool** (adult/under 14yr Ikr200/100; ⏰ 8.15am-9pm Mon-Fri, noon-5pm Sat & Sun) is a great place on a wet day and has two hot pots to relax in after your breathtaking descent.

Sleeping

Grundarfjörður Hostel (☎ 562 6533; Hlíðarvegur; sb member/nonmember May-Sep Ikr1600/1950, Oct-Apr Ikr1750/1400, tw/s Ikr2550/3150; 🖵) Friendly, central and well equipped, the local hostel has a range of simple rooms and good kitchen facilities. Spearheading the local campaign for environmental responsibility, the hostel runs on green principles and encourages sustainable devel-

WEST ICELAND

opment in town. It can organise a variety of local tours, has bike hire (Ikr1200 per day) and offers unlimited internet access for Ikr300 per day.

Hótel Framnes (☎ 438 6893; www.hotel-framnes.is; Nesvegur 8-10; sb/s/d Jun-Aug Ikr4000/9000/11,5000, Sep-May Ikr3500/5100/7500) Comfy but fairly predictable, this hotel by the docks has decent but characterless rooms in a modern building. The restaurant offers a set two-course dinner (Ikr2800 to Ikr3500), and the hotel can organise various local tours including town walks and horse riding. At the time of writing, the hotel was set to change management.

Other accommodation options:

Kverná (☎ 438 6813; www.simnet.is/kverna; s/d Ikr4000/7000) Cosy farm just outside town offering cottage accommodation, horse riding and walking tours.

Suður-Bár (☎ 438 6815; www.sudurbar.sveit.is; s/d with bathroom Ikr6500/9200, without bathroom Ikr7900/11,200) Friendly guesthouse 7km east of town with pleasant rooms and horse riding (Ikr2500 per hour).

Eating

Kaffi 59 (☎ 438 6446; Grundargata 59; mains Ikr700-950; ⊙ 9am-11pm Mon-Thu, to 1am Fri & Sat, to 10pm Sun) Less formal and more predictable than Krákan (following), this is the place for pizza, burgers, sandwiches and beer, served up in a diner-style modern building by the main road through town.

Krákan (☎ 438 6999; Sæbol 13; mains Ikr1000-1600) This cosy restaurant hidden down a residential street towards the western end of the village serves up a good selection of fresh fish and lamb dishes as well as delicious lighter snacks such as lobster soup.

There's the ubiquitous grill at the Esso station and a **supermarket** (⊙ 9am-7pm) just down the road towards the docks.

Getting There & Away

There are daily bus serices to and from Reykjavík (Ikr3800, 2¾ hours), and there's a summer service around the head of the peninsula (see p167).

SNÆFELLSJÖKULL NATIONAL PARK

In June 2001 the tip of Snæfellsnes peninsula, including the mighty glacier, became Iceland's newest national park. The icecap is famous around the world, courtesy of Jules Verne, who used it as the setting for his famous *Journey to the Centre of the Earth*. In the book a German geologist and his nephew embark on an epic journey into the crater of Snæfells, guided by a 16th-century Icelandic text with the following advice:

Descend into the crater of Yocul of Sneffels, Which the shade of Scartaris caresses, Before the kalends of July, audacious traveller, And you will reach the centre of the earth. I did it.

Arne Saknussemm

It's easy to see why Jules Verne selected Snæfell – the dramatic peak was torn apart when the volcano beneath the icecap exploded and the volcano subsequently collapsed into its own magma chamber, forming a huge

WEST ICELAND

GONE BERSERK

The wild lava flows southwest of Stykkishólmur were named after an unusual tale from the *Eyrbyggja Saga*. Apparently, the farmer of Hraun was frustrated with having to walk around these ragged flows to visit his brother at the farm Bjarnarhöfn. Returning from a voyage to Norway, he brought back two berserkers – insanely violent fighters who were employed as hired thugs in Viking times – but to his dismay one of the berserkers took a liking to his daughter. He turned to the local chieftain, Snorri Goði, for advice, but Snorri had his eye on the farmer's daughter himself and he recommended setting the berserker an impossible task. The farmer decided to promise the amorous berserker his daughter's hand in marriage if he was able to clear a passage through the troublesome lava field – surely impossible for a normal man.

To the horror of both Snorri and the farmer, the two berserkers set to work and soon managed to rip a passage straight through the lava flow. Rather than honouring the promise, the farmer trapped the berserkers in a sauna and then murdered them, later agreeing to give Snorri his daughter's hand in marriage. The passage through the lava between Hraun and Bjarnarhöfn can still be seen, and a grave discovered there in recent digs was found to contain the remains of two large men.

caldera. Among certain New Age groups, Snæfellsjökull is considered one of the world's great 'power centres', and it definitely has a brooding presence.

Today the crater is filled in with ice and makes a popular hiking destination in summer. There are several routes to the summit. The shortest start on mountain road Rte F570, which cuts across the peninsula from Arnarstapi to Ólafsvík. A longer and more interesting route climbs the western slope along the Móðulækur river, passing the red scoria craters of Rauðhólar and the waterfall Klukkufoss.

On any of these routes you should be prepared for harsh weather and carry food and water as well as a map and compass. If you want to reach the summit you'll need crampons and ice axes. With a 4WD you can drive some of the way along all of these routes. From either Ólafsvík or Arnarstapi allow at least five hours for the ascent and another three hours to get down. The western approach takes considerably longer and will require an overnight stay on the mountain.

For more information, contact the **park rangers** (☎ 436 6860; http://english.ust.is/Snaefellsjokull nationalpark; Klettsbud 7, Hellissandur) or pay a call to the visitor centre at Hellnar (see p166).

Tours

Snowmobile tours on the glacier are run by **Ferðaþjónustan Snjófell** (☎ 435 6783; www.snjofell.is) at Arnarstapi. In summer snowcat tours of the glacier cost Ikr4000 per person, or there's a snowmobile tour (Ikr7000 per person, minimum of six people). Midnight sun tours are also available. If you just want a lift as far as the snow line, it will cost you Ikr1300 return.

ÓLAFSVÍK
pop 1010

Quiet, unassuming and well kept, workaday Ólafsvík is primarily worth a visit for its excellent whale-watching tours. Although it's the oldest trading town in the country (it was granted a trading licence in 1687), Ólafsvík is a modern place, and few of its original buildings survive.

Sights & Activities

The old packing house **Gamla Pakkhúsið** (☎ 436 1543; Ólafsbraut; adult/under 16yr Ikr300/free; ⏰ 9am-7pm Jun-Aug) is home to the local tourist office as well as an interesting folk museum telling the story of the town's development as a trading

centre. The building was constructed in 1841 by the Clausen family, who owned Ólafsvík's leading trading firm.

Down by the harbour, the small maritime museum **Sjávarsafnið Ólafsvík** (☎ 436 6961; ⏰ 10am-6pm) has displays on local history and fishing fleets.

Ólafsvík is also a potential starting point for hikes up Snæfellsjökull; the difficult trail begins 1km east of the camp site. Allow five hours to reach the edge of the ice, and bring crampons and ice axes if you intend to go out onto the icecap.

The local **swimming pool** (☎ 436 1199; adult/under 14yr Ikr250/150) is on Ennisbraut.

Tours

Ólafsvík is one of the best locations for whale watching on the western coast. Tours are run by **Sæferðir** (Seatours; ☎ 438 1450; www.seatours.is; adult/12-15yr Ikr4900/2450) at 11am and 3pm daily from June to August. The trips take about three hours and offer good chances to see orcas, minke whales, humpback whales and occasionally blue whales; dolphins are also spotted on most trips. The best sightings are usually in late June and early July.

Sleeping & Eating

Camp site (☎ 436 1543; sites per person/tent Ikr300/300) Situated by the road 1km east of town, this basic site has hot and cold running water and showers.

Hótel Ólafsvík (☎ 436 1650; www.hotelolafsvik.is; Ólafsbraut 20; s/d from Ikr11,950/14,800; 🖥) A mighty step up from camping, this large hotel has spacious, functional rooms with tiled floors, neutral décor and very little character. The hotel also offers cheaper rooms with shared bathroom (Ik6700/8400 for singles/doubles) in an annexe next door. The hotel restaurant (mains Ikr1830 to Ikr2300) is probably the best place to eat in town and offers a range of high-quality Icelandic meals as well as pizzas and burgers.

Prinsinn (☎ 436 1362; Ólafsbraut; mains from Ikr300; ⏰ 10am-11.30pm Mon-Fri, 11.30am-11.30pm Sat & Sun) The local fast-food joint, this place is in the main shopping centre and serves the usual pizza and burgers.

There's also a grill at the petrol station, a good bakery opposite the hotel, and a large supermarket by the harbour. The Vin Búð alcohol shop is on Mýrarholt, uphill from the main street.

Getting There & Away

There are two to three services daily to/from Reykjavík to Ólafsvík, connecting through Vegamót (Ikr4200, 2¾ hours). All buses continue on to Hellissandur (Ikr250, 15 minutes). The buses drop off and pick up at the petrol station in Ólafsvík.

A summer round-glacier bus takes passengers around the tip of the peninsula; see p167 for details.

HELLISSANDUR-RIF

pop 580

Perched out on the westernmost tip of the Snæfellsnes peninsula, the tiny twin towns of Hellissandur and Rif are good bases from which to explore the national park. Hellissandur (sometimes called Sandur) is the original fishing village, while Rif is a modern cluster of buildings built up around the new town harbour. Hellissandur has a petrol station, a post office and an ATM.

The only artificial sight in the area is **Sjómannagarður** (☎ 436 6784; admission Ikr300; ⊙ 9am-6pm Thu-Tue Jun-Aug), a small maritime museum set in a turf-roofed sea shanty. There are lots of old photos here and plenty of local memorabilia, including a set of lifting stones used to test the strength of prospective fishermen. The museum is by the main road on the western edge of town.

About 2km inland from Hellissandur is the church at **Ingjaldshóll**, the first concrete church in Iceland (built in 1903). If the doors are open you can see some ancient heraldic tombstones and painted wooden altarpieces inside.

If you'd like to stay, the free **camp site** (☎ 436 1543), opposite the Edda hotel, has basic facilities including sinks and toilets but can be pretty windswept. You can get limited groceries at the petrol station.

For far more comfort, check into the **Edda Hótel** (☎ 444 4940; www.hoteledda.is; Klettsbúd; s/d Ikr10,300/12,900; ⊙ mid-May–mid-Sep; ☐), a well-run place offering bright, modern rooms with contemporary interiors and sparkling bathrooms. The hotel restaurant (mains Ikr2000 to Ikr3000) serves a good selection of Icelandic staples.

All buses from Reykjavík to Ólafsvík continue to Hellissandur, stopping at the Esso petrol station. The fare from Reykjavík is Ikr4400 and the journey takes about three hours.

SOUTHWEST SNÆFELLSNES

Continuing southwest from Hellissandur, the scenic but potholed Rte 574 skirts the rugged western slopes of Snæfellsjökull. Known as Forvaðinn, this desolate area offers eerie views of spurs of lava sticking up through the scree and, on misty days, when the clouds swirl among the peaks, you can easily see where legends about trolls came from. Beyond the glacier the road improves again and passes the villages of Arnarstapi and Hellnar, which are surrounded by interesting sea-sculpted rock formations, and continues east along the broad southern coastal plain, passing the huge sandy bays at Breiðavík and Búðavík.

Gufuskálar

About 2km west of Hellissandur, the huge radar mast of the US Loran Station is the tallest structure in Iceland. Nearby is the small ruined **Írskibrunnur** (Irish Well), which has a whale skull as a lintel and was built by Irish monks before Norse settlement. On the opposite side of Rte 574 is a vast lava field, Prestahraun – the lava studded with the ruins of hundreds of **fiskbyrgi** (stone fish-drying sheds) constructed by medieval Viking fishermen. A trail marked with red posts leads between the huts.

Öndverðarnes

At the westernmost tip of Snæfellsnes, Rte 574 cuts south, while a tiny bumpy track heads west across an ancient lava flow to the tip of the Öndverðarnes peninsula. En route you'll pass **Skarðsvík**, a perfect golden sandy beach lapped by blue waters and hidden by black lava cliffs. A Viking grave was discovered here in the 1960s and it's easy to see why this stunning spot in the middle of an otherwise desolate area would have been favoured as a final resting place.

From the parking area a marked trail leads across the lava flows to the imposing volcanic crater **Vatnsborg**, from where further trails lead to the nearby sea cliffs around the southern edge of the cape, where seals laze on the skerries and the cliffs are carved into dramatic sea arches and caves by the constant pounding of Atlantic breakers. The **lighthouse** at the tip of the cape can also be reached by continuing beyond Skarðsvík on the bumpy road. En route you'll pass the abandoned stone well **Fálkí**.

Southwest of the Öndverðarnes turn-off the road passes the start of the steep 4WD track to Snæfellsjökull and also the roadside scoria crater **Saxhóll**, which can be climbed in a few minutes for views northwest over the Neshraun lava flows.

Hólahólar

About 5km further south the volcanic craters of **Hólahólar** are clustered about 150m west of the road. A track passes through the wall of Berudalur, the largest, and into a natural amphitheatre inside the cone.

Dritvík & Djúpalón

About 4km further along Rte 574 a dirt road leads down to the wild black-sand beach at **Djúpalónssandur**. It's a dramatic place to walk, with a series of rocky stacks emerging from the ocean. You can also still see four 'lifting stones' on the beach where fishing-boat crews would test the strength of aspiring fishermen. The smallest stone is Amloði (Bungler) at 23kg, followed by Hálfdrættingur (Weak) at 54kg, Hálfsterkur (Half-Strong) at 100kg, and the largest, Fullsterker (Fully Strong), at 154kg. Hálfdrættingur marked the frontier of wimphood, and any man who couldn't heft it was deemed unsuitable for a life at sea. Mysteriously, there now appear to be five stones.

If you tramp up over the craggy headland you'll reach the similar black-sand **beach** at Dritvík, where around 60 fishing boats were stationed from the 16th to the 19th century. The black sands are covered in pieces of rusted metal from the English trawler *Eding*, which was wrecked here in 1948. Several freshwater pools and the rocky arch **Gatklettur** are close to the car park.

About 2km south of Djúpalón a track leads down to the rocket-shaped **lighthouse** at Malariff, from where you can walk along the cliffs to the rock pillars at **Lóndrangar**, which surge up into the air like a frozen splash of lava. Locals say that elves use the lava formations as a church.

Hellnar

The guardian spirit of Snæfells, Bárður, chose Hellnar, a picturesque spot overlooking a rocky bay, as his home. Today Hellnar is a tiny fishing village where the shriek of sea birds fills the air and whales are regularly sighted. Down on the shore the cave **Baðstofa** is chock-a-block with nesting birds while, between the village and main road, **Bárðarlaug** was supposedly the bathing pool of Bárður. East of here a dramatic ancient lava flow lies covered in

a velvet cloak of moss, backed by sweeping mountains and glorious views out to sea.

Hellnar is a remarkably peaceful place and an idyllic spot to while away a couple of days.

Gestastofa (☎ 436 6888; admission free; ⏰ 10am-6pm Jun-Aug), the national park visitor centre in Hellnar, has displays on the geology, history, people, customs and wildlife of the area and has an impressive collection of old black-and-white photographs of local people.

our pick **Hótel Hellnar** (☎ 435 6820; www.hellnar .is; s/d Jun-Aug Ikr9300/11,990, May & Sep Ikr8400/10,700; ⏰ May-Sep), Iceland's only eco-hotel, makes an excellent retreat. The twin-bedded rooms are clean, bright and minimalist, and the **restaurant** (mains Ikr2000-3500; ⏰ 7-9pm May-Sep) uses local organic produce. There's also a wonderful guest lounge with fantastic views of the sea, and there are quite regular sightings of whales.

For a light lunch **Fjöruhúsið** (☎ 435 6844; snacks Ikr200-1000), by the harbour, is a small but good café that serves quiche, soup and coffee.

Arnarstapi

Heading northeast from Hellnar a scenic 2.5km coastal path leads past rock arches and lava flows eroded into weird and wonderful shapes to the tiny fishing village of Arnarstapi. The legend of Bárður continues here with a strange rock sculpture in his honour.

Behind the village, 526m-high **Stapafell** is supposedly home to the little people, and you'll see miniature house gables painted onto rocks in their honour. Mountain road F570 leads around Stapafell towards the glacier and passes a collapsed crater, which has created a series of strange lava caves about 1.5km from the main road. The largest cave is **Sönghellir**, which is full of 18th-century graffiti and is rumoured to resound with the songs of dwarfs. Bring a torch and look for the smallest cave entrance along the ridge.

From Stapafell, a small track branches east off Rte 574 to **Rauðfeldsgjá**, a steep and narrow cleft that disappears mysteriously into the cliff wall beside the road. A stream runs along the bottom of the gorge, and you can scramble up between the sheer walls for quite a distance.

Overnight accommodation can be found at the turf-roofed **Ferðaþjónustan Snjófell** (☎ 435 6783; www.snjofell.is; sites per tent Ikr700, sb/made-up bed Ikr2550/3400), a simple guesthouse with cosy rooms and a decent restaurant (meals Ikr690 to Ikr2990). Snjófell also runs snowmobile and snowcat tours on the glacier – see p164.

THE ROUND-GLACIER BUS

From June to August a special round-glacier bus leaves from Ólafsvík at 11.15am daily and loops around the head of the peninsula, stopping at Arnarstapi for an hour. Passengers can disembark here and walk along the scenic cliffs to Hellnar, where the bus picks up at 1.45pm, before heading north to the Djúpalón beach and back to Hellissandur. The entire circuit costs Ikr3200 and you can get off and reboard anywhere along the route. It's a handy option if you want to stop and explore the rugged southwestern tip of the peninsula, and you can use the same ticket to get back to civilisation the next day (you'll pay Ikr1600 for the first day's travel – around a section of the route – and another Ikr1600 the following day to go the rest of the way).

Breiðavík & Búðavík

East of Hellnar and Arnarstapi, Rte 574 skirts the edges of the long sandy bays at Breiðavík and Búðavík. These windswept beaches are covered in yellow-grey sand and are wonderfully peaceful places to walk. At Búðavík the abandoned fishing village of Búðir is now home to one of Iceland's best country hotels. From the hotel a walking trail leads across the elf-infested Buðahraun lava field to the crater **Búðaklettur**. According to local legend a lava tube beneath Buðahraun, paved with gold and precious stones, leads all the way to Surtshellir. It takes about three hours to walk to the crater and back.

Gistiheimilið Hof (☎ 435 6802; www.gistihof.is; sb/s/d May-Sep Ikr2000/3500/6000, Oct-Apr Ikr1000/2200/3600) has a selection of contemporary rooms with shared kitchen, living room and bathroom. The veranda has a barbecue and great views across to the icecap. The large **Gistiheimilið Langaholt** (☎ 435 6789; www.langaholt.is; sites per tent Ikr500, sb Ikr2300, d Ikr7300-9000) has bright, modern rooms with tasteful décor and good facilities.

our pick **Hótel Búðir** (☎ 435 6700; www.budir.is; d Ikr18,600-36,700; 🖵), windswept, lonely and very romantic, is a sleek, stylish hotel with understated, quirky design and not a hint of pretension. Expect individually designed rooms with elegant furnishings, flagstone bathrooms, DVD players and wi-fi access and – if you're lucky enough to bag No 23 – a freestanding bath separated from the bedroom by a wooden screen. Open fires, plenty of books and an excellent restaurant offering a menu rich in such delicacies as veal, foie gras and truffles top off the absolute luxury of the place. If you're going to splash out at any point on your trip, this is the place to do it.

Eldborg

Immediately southeast of the Snæfellsnes peninsula, the prominent egg cup–shaped volcano Eldborg rises over 100m above the desolate Eldborgarhraun plain. It's a 4km walk from Kolbeinsstaðir, which lies on the main road from Borgarnes to Ólafsvík (Rte 54). Almost opposite the turn-off to the Hótel Eldborg a dirt road leads northeast to **Gerðuberg**, a long escarpment formed from ruler-straight basalt columns.

SLEEPING

Hótel Eldborg (☎ 435 6602; www.hoteleldborg.is; sites per person Ikr800, sb Ikr2500, s/d Ikr6900/8900; ☾ Jun-Aug; 🖳) Basic rooms with simple furnishings are available at this school complex on Rte 567, about 4km from the main road. All rooms share a bathroom, but there's a decent restaurant (three-course meals Ikr3000) and a toasty geothermal swimming pool. Horse-riding trips to the nearby beach can be arranged from the hotel (Ikr7000 for three to four hours).

Snorrastaðir (☎ 435 6628; www.snorrastadir.com; sites per tent Ikr1000, sb/6-person cabin 2200/10,000) Tucked away off the main road, this down-to-earth horse farm offers basic sleeping-bag accommodation and made-up beds in wooden cottages. Horse rides along the beach cost Ikr2200 per hour. The farm is 3km from Eldborg and it's signposted from the main road.

GETTING THERE & AWAY

There's no public transport to either Hótel Eldborg or Snorrastaðir, but buses between Reykjavík and Stykkishólmur can drop you at the junction on the main road.

LAXDÆLA SAGA COUNTRY

The area around Laxárdalur served as the setting for the *Laxdæla Saga*, the most popular of the Icelandic sagas. The story revolves around a love triangle between Guðrun Ósvífursdóttir, said to be the most beautiful woman in Iceland, and the foster brothers Kjartan Ólafsson and Bolli Þorleiksson. In a fairly typical saga

WEST ICELAND

tale, Guðrun had both men wrapped around her little finger and schemed and connived until both of them were dead – Kjartan at the hands of Bolli, and Bolli at the hands of Kjartan's brothers. Most Icelanders know the stories and characters by heart and hold the area in which the story took place in great historic esteem.

Búðardalur
pop 260

Although there's not a lot to see in Búðardalur, it's a handy base for exploring the area. Founded as a cargo depot in saga times, the town now survives on fish processing and dairy farming, and it occupies a pleasant position looking out over Hvammsfjörður, at the mouth of the Laxá river. There's a bank, a petrol station and a **tourist office** (☎ 434 1410; 10am-6pm Mon-Fri, 11am-6pm Sat & Sun Jun-Aug) here, and at the time of writing there were plans to open a local museum.

If you want to stay there's a free **camp site** (☎ 434 1132) behind the school. Alternatively, guesthouse **Bjarg** (☎ 434 1644; www.aknet.is/bjarg; Dalbraut 2; s/d Ikr4200/6900; 🖳) has simple, modern rooms and an internet café in summer. The attached **Villa Pizza restaurant** (mains Ikr1000-2500) serves grilled meat and fish as well as pizza. You can also get fast food (mains Ikr300 to Ikr990) at the Esso petrol station.

Buses run between Reykjavík and Búðardalur (Ikr3400, 2½ hours) daily except on Wednesday and Saturday. Tuesday and Sunday services continue to Reykhólar in the Westfjords.

Eiríksstaðir

The farm Eiríksstaðir, across the Haukadalsá from Stóra-Vatnshorn's church, was the home of Eiríkur Rauðe (Erik the Red), father of Leifur Eiríksson, believed to be the first European to visit America. Although only a faint outline of the original farm remains, an impressive **reconstruction of the farm** (☎ 434 1118; www.leif.is; adult/under 14yr Ikr600/free; 9am-6pm Mon-Fri, 10am-6pm Sat & Sun Jun-Sep) has been built using only the tools and materials available at the time. Enthusiastic period-dressed guides show visitors around, bake bread, brandish weapons and tell the story of Erik the Red, who went on to found the first European settlement in Greenland. In July there's a Viking festival with a traditional market and games, storytelling, and theatre.

You can stay in nearby Stóra-Vatnshorn at a friendly **farmhouse** (☎ 434 1342; www.islandia .is/storavatnshorn; sb/made-up bed/summerhouse Ikr2000/ 2800/5300), which has a selection of simple but comfortable rooms and two self-catering cottages sleeping up to five.

Saga Farms

Little remains of the original farms from saga times, and although the region is central to many of the best-loved Icelandic sagas, you will need a creative imagination to make the connection.

About 4km up the Laxá river from Búðardalur, **Höskuldsstaðir** was the birthplace of Hallgerður Longlegs, wife of Gunnar of Hlíðarendi, who starred in *Njál's Saga*. Other important descendants of the family include Bolli and his foster brother Kjartan from *Laxdæla Saga*.

Across the river from Höskuldsstaðir is **Hjarðarholt**, the one-time home of Kjartan and his father, Ólafur Peacock. Their Viking farm was said to be one of the wonders of the Norse world, with scenes from the sagas carved into the walls and a huge dining hall that could seat 1100 guests, but no trace of it remains today.

Further north, the farm at **Hvammur** produced a whole line of prominent Icelanders, including Snorri Sturluson of *Prose Edda* fame. It was settled in around 895 by Auður the Deep-Minded, the wife of the Irish king Olaf Godfraidh, who has a bit part in the *Laxdæla Saga*. By coincidence, Árni Magnússon, who rescued most of the Icelandic sagas from the 1728 fire in Copenhagen, was born at Hvammur.

About 1km north of Hvammur on Rte 1, the geothermal village of **Laugar** was the birthplace of *Laxdæla Saga* beauty Guðrun Ósvífursdóttir. A small **folk museum** (☎ 434 1328; admission Ikr400; 10am-5pm Tue-Sat, to 2pm Sun Jun-Aug) in the school complex can help put the remains of the saga farms in context. You can also overnight at the school during the summer, when it becomes an **Edda Hotel** (☎ 444 4930; www.hoteledda.is; sites per person, Ikr600, sb Ikr2200, s/d with bathroom Ikr10,300/12,900, without bathroom 5800/7200). The rooms are simple, but there's a good restaurant (mains Ikr1750 to Ikr3500) and a naturally heated outdoor pool (Ikr250/130 for adult/child under 12).

Farmhouse accommodation is also available at **Þurranesi** (☎ 434 1556; www.centrum.is/thurranes; sb/s/d Ikr1800/2800/5600), where there are cosy, country-style rooms and a guest kitchen.

The Westfjords

Flung out into the North Atlantic and almost set adrift from the rest of the country, the region known as the Westfjords is one of Iceland's most spectacular. Sparsely populated, fantastically rugged, and isolated by its remote location and limited roads, the Westfjords is an outdoor adventurer's dream destination. The landscape here is truly humbling, ranging from soaring mountains and unfathomably deep and silent fjords to a tortuous coastline dotted with tiny fishing villages clinging doggedly to a traditional way of life.

To the north lies the uninhabited wilderness region of Hornstrandir, home to the 176-sq-km Drangajökull (925m), the last surviving icecap in the region. Abandoned by the last villagers in the 1950s, Hornstrandir is now one of the country's premier hiking destinations. South of here lies the region's largest town, the cosmopolitan oasis of Ísafjörður. A friendly, happening mini-metropolis, it's the place to stock up and indulge before heading for the small villages that line the coast.

Unassuming, determined and often staunchly traditional, these smaller communities have suffered serious population decline in recent years. Many struggle to persuade their young people to stay and offer a warm welcome to the tourists who bring valuable income and energy to their quiet streets. Further south, nesting birds mob the cliffs at Látrabjarg, waves lash the golden sands at Breiðavík, and craggy inlets and precipitous peaks vie for your attention at every turn.

Give yourself plenty of time for a trip to the Westfjords. The roads around the coast weave in and out of fjords and over unpaved mountain passes pitted with giant potholes. The going is frustratingly slow at times, but the scenery is never short of breathtaking.

THE WESTFJORDS

TOP FIVE

- Get to know the locals at the small fishing village of **Suðureyri** (p176)
- Soak up the wild serenity of the Strandir Coast at **Djúpavík** (p193)
- Watch the comic antics of the puffins on the cliffs at **Látrabjarg** (p172)
- Catch the first glimpse of the coast after a strenuous hike across **Hornstrandir** (p194)
- Splash out on anything that isn't a hostel- or camp site–cooked meal in cosmopolitan and isolated **Ísafjörður** (p177)

Information

Tourist offices in the region provide invaluable free *Vestfirdir* pamphlets, which list all the tourist facilities in the area. More information about the Westfjords can be found at www .westfjords.is.

Getting There & Away

There are twice-daily flights between Reykjavík and Ísafjörður (Ikr10,500) with **Air Iceland** (☎ 570 3030; www.airiceland.is), and additional summer flights to Gjögur and Bíldudalur.

Roads in the Westfjords are mostly unsurfaced and heavily rutted, and they hug the deeply indented coastline, winding in and out of fjords and around headlands, so getting about can be very slow. Public bus services are limited and infrequent, and most only run from June to August.

Coming from Reykjavík to Ísafjörður you'll need to change in Brú (further south, in west Iceland) and Hólmavík. Buses leave Reykjavík for Brú at 8.30am and 5.30pm, but they only connect with the Brú–Hólmavík service on Tuesday, Friday and Sunday; Reykjavík–Hólmavík costs Ikr4900. The bus company **Stjörnubílar** (☎ 456 3518, 893 6356; www.stjornubilar.is) runs the Hólmavík–Ísafjörður leg (Ikr4000), at 3pm on Tuesday, Friday and Sunday.

Buses also run to the Westfjords via the ferry from Stykkishólmur. There are daily buses from Reykjavík to Stykkishólmur (see p160), but these don't link well with the ferry – you'll have a few hours to look round, or even an overnight stop. For information on buses between Brjánslækur and Ísafjörður (via Látrabjarg), see p172.

If you want to travel between Ísafjörður and Akureyri, you'll also need to change in Hólmavík and Brú.

The car ferry **Baldur** (☎ 438 1450; www.seatours .is; per car/passenger one way Ikr2190/2190) operates between Stykkishólmur and Brjánslækur (2¼ hours). From June to August there are daily departures from Stykkishólmur at 9am and 3pm, returning from Brjánslækur at noon and 6pm. From September to May it leaves Stykkishólmur at 1.30pm Sunday to Friday and at 9am on Saturday, and from Brjánslækur it leaves at 5pm Sunday to Friday and 12.30pm on Saturday.

Boat transfers to the remote Hornstrandir region can be arranged from Ísafjörður and Drangsnes from June to August.

SOUTH COAST

The sparsely populated south coast of the Westfjords is the least dramatic of the region, and it's nowhere near as wild and wonderful as the wilderness areas further north and west. However, the ferry connection to Stykkishólmur on the Snæfellsnes peninsula is a handy route to the area. Although there are no towns on the south coast, you'll find a cluster of farms and guesthouses around Brjánslækur, the landing point for the ferry, and the drive west and north from here is lined with white-sand beaches before rising into the mountain passes that take you to the western fjords.

REYKHÓLAR & BJARKALUNDUR

The little town of Reykhólar sits on the tip of the kidney-shaped Reykjanes peninsula, a minor geothermal area. There's little to do here other than take a dip in the **geothermal swimming pool** (☎ 434 7738; 10am-10pm Jun-Aug, reduced hr rest of year) or take to the surrounding hills on foot.

In summer a small **tourist office** is open (☎ 434 7830; 10am-noon & 2-6pm Jun–mid-Aug), and staff can help with route planning for hikes. The hiking map *Gönguleiðir Reykhólasveit* (Ikr300) is also useful. The tiny village of Bjarkalundur on Rte 60 near the beginning of the peninsula is the starting point for hikes to the peak of Vaðalfjöll (508m).

There's a basic **camp site** (☎ 434 7738; sites per person Ikr600) near the swimming pool, and more comfortable accommodation at **Gistiheimilið Álftaland** (☎ 434 7878; www.alftaland.is; sb/ s/d Ikr3000/6500/8200; ♿). The rooms here are simple but comfortable, and there's a sauna, hot pots and a good kitchen available for use by guests.

At Bjarkalundur you can stay at **Hótel Bjarkalundur** (☎ 434 7863; www.bjarkalundur.is; sb Ikr2000, s/d incl breakfast Ikr4900/7100; ☺ Easter-Sep, then weekends to New Year), a large farmhouse with a petrol station, a restaurant (mains Ikr900 to Ikr1750) and reasonably priced rooms.

The only other food option is the supermarket and snack bar **Árnhóll** (☎ 434 7890; snacks Ikr400-900) at the petrol station in Reykhólar.

THE WESTFJORDS

Getting There & Away

Buses run between Reykjavík and Reykhólar (Ikr4800, four hours), via Króksfjarðarnes (west Iceland) on Monday, Tuesday, Friday and Sunday. There's no bus service between Bjarkalundur and Brjánslækur.

DJÚPADALUR

Heading west, you'll come to the hot springs and steaming vents of the Djúpadalur geothermal field, 20km west of Bjarkalundur. There's an indoor **thermal swimming pool** (☎ 434 7853; adult/under 14yr Ikr250/100) here and good accommodation at the welcoming **Guesthouse Djúpadalur** (☎ 434 7853; sb/made-up bed Ikr1700/2500).

FLÓKALUNDUR

The tiny village of Flókalundur was named after the Viking explorer Hrafna-Flóki Vilgerðarson (see p25), who gave Iceland its name in AD 860. Today, the most interesting thing in the area is the **Vatnsfjörður Nature Reserve**, established to protect the area around Lake Vatnsdalsvatn, a nesting site for harlequin ducks and red-throated and great northern divers (loons). Various hiking trails run around the lake and into the hills beyond.

You can stay at **Hótel Flókalundur** (☎ 456 2011; www.flokalundur.is; sites per tent/caravan Ikr1000/1500, s/d incl breakfast Ikr8800/11,700; ⊙ Jun–mid-Sep), an aging wooden bungalow-style hotel with small, wood-panelled rooms, a decent restaurant (mains Ikr1200 to Ikr2950) and a petrol station. Down the road at Flókalaug is a **thermal swimming pool** (☎ 456 2011; adult/under 12yr Ikr200/100; ⊙ 7am-noon & 4-7pm), managed by the hotel.

BRJÁNSLÆKUR

There's nothing much at Brjánslækur except the terminal for the *Baldur* ferry to Stykkishólmur and Flatey and some turf-covered 9th-century ruins just to the south.

If you get stuck here overnight there's a basic **camp site** (☎ 456 2020; sites per tent Ikr700) opposite the ferry landing. About 8km west, opposite a lovely white-sand beach, you can stay at **Gistihúsið Rauðsdal** (☎ 456 2041; raudsdal@vortex.is; sb/made-up bed Ikr2000/2600), which has decent rooms and a guest kitchen.

At Krossholt, 14km west of Brjánslækur, you'll find **Gistiheimilið Bjarkarholt** (☎ 456 2025; torfi@vestferdir.is; sb Ikr1800, made-up bed s/d Ikr2500/5000) and **Gistiheimilið Arnarholt** (☎ 456 2080; silja@snerpa.is; sb Ikr1800) next door, which runs the geothermal pool on the shore.

Getting There & Away

Bus schedules are loosely timed to connect with the **Baldur ferry** (☎ 438 1450) to Stykkishólmur; see p171.

On Monday, Wednesday and Saturday from June to August buses run from Brjánslækur to Ísafjörður (Ikr2350, two hours). In the reverse direction the bus drops off at Brjánslækur and then continues to Patreksfjörður (Ikr600, 1¼ hours) and Látrabjarg (Ikr2500, two hours), where you'll have a 90-minute stop to admire the bird life.

SOUTHWEST PENINSULA

The beautiful, sparsely populated trident-shaped peninsula in the southwest of the Westfjords is a spectacularly scenic place and the westernmost point in Europe. Sand beaches as fine as you'll find in Iceland, shimmering blue water, towering cliffs and stunning mountains weave along and between the fjords and provide fantastic territory for hiking, walking and leisurely driving. The region's most famous destination, however, is Látrabjarg, a 12km stretch of sea cliffs that is home to thousands of nesting sea birds in summer.

The roads throughout this region are rough and driving is slow. There are several small villages on the northern side of the peninsula to break your journey but only isolated guesthouses in the far south and west.

LÁTRABJARG PENINSULA

Best known for its dramatic cliffs and abundant bird life, the Látrabjarg peninsula also has wonderful deserted beaches and plenty of opportunities for long, leisurely walks.

Joining Rte 612 from Rte 62, you'll pass the rusting hulk of the fishing boat *Garðar* near the head of the fjord before passing the empty, golden beaches around the airstrip at Sauðlauksdalur. About 10km further on it's worth stopping at the entertaining **Egill Ólafsson Folk Museum** (☎ 456 1569; adult/under 14yr Ikr500/free; ⊙ 9am-6pm Jun–mid-Sep) in the tiny village of Hnjótur. The eclectic collection includes salvaged fishing boats, old aircraft and displays on the history of the region. A circle of stones behind the museum commemorates the many fishing ships lost at sea off the tip of the peninsula.

At **Breiðavík** a stunning golden-sand beach stands framed by rocky cliffs and the turquoise waters of the bay. It's an idyllic spot, certainly one of Iceland's best beaches and usually deserted. Should you find yourself with more company that you'd hoped for, head further on to Hvallátur, where there's another gorgeous golden-sand beach and excellent opportunities for wild camping.

Soon the Bjargtangar lighthouse, Europe's westernmost point, comes into view and nearby the renowned Látrabjarg **bird cliffs**. Extending for 12km along the coast and ranging from 40m to 400m, the dramatic cliffs are mobbed by nesting sea birds in summer and it's a fascinating place even for the most reluctant of twitchers. Unbelievable numbers of puffins, razorbills, guillemots, cormorants, fulmars, gulls and kittiwakes nest here from June to August. The puffins in particular are incredibly tame, and you can often get within a few feet of the birds. On calm days, seals are often seen basking on the skerries around the lighthouse.

East of the cliffs (about a 20km walk along the coast path from the lighthouse) the stunning **Rauðisandur** beach stretches out in shades of deep pink and red sands. Pounded by the surf and backed by a huge lagoon, it is an exceptionally beautiful and serene place. To get here by road you'll have to backtrack on Rte 612 towards the head of the fjord. Take a right turn onto Rte 614 soon after the airfield at Sauðlauksdalur and follow the bumpy track for about 10km.

Sleeping & Eating

Gistiheimilið Breiðavík (☎ 456 1575; www.breidavik .net; sites per tent from Ikr1000, sb/s/d without bathroom 3500/5500/8500, s/d with bathroom Ikr4000/6000; ☯ mid-May–mid-Sep) Set on a working farm by the incredible white beach at Breiðavík, this guesthouse offers homey rooms with patchwork quilts and decent furniture. Evening meals are also served (Ikr2500 to Ikr3000).

Hótel Látrabjarg (☎ 456 1500; www.latrabjarg.com; s/d without bathroom Ikr9000/10,500, with private bathroom Ikr12,000/13,500; ☯ mid-May–Aug; ▣) This former boarding school has been converted into a comfortable hotel with plain but tasteful rooms. There's a restaurant (dinner Ikr3000), free wi-fi access, and a computer for guest use. The hotel can also organise horse riding (Ikr2000 per hour) at the nearby farm Hestaleigan Vesturfari. To get to the hotel, turn right onto Rte 615 just after the museum at Hnjótur and continue for about 3km.

Getting There & Away

Southwest of Patreksfjörður Rte 62 cuts across the ridge at Kleifaheiði to the south coast, while Rte 612 runs west to the end of the Látrabjarg peninsula.

On Monday, Wednesday and Saturday from June to August buses from Ísafjörður route through Látrabjarg on their way to/from Brjánslækur, where you can pick up the *Baldur* ferry to Stykkishólmur. The buses stop at the cliffs for 90 minutes, leaving you plenty of time to explore.

If you want to stay longer you'll have to camp overnight or hike back to the guesthouse at Breiðavík or Hótel Látrabjarg. You can also reach the cliffs by hiking 5km east from Hvallátur.

PATREKSFJÖRÐUR & AROUND
pop 770

Although it's the largest village in this part of the Westfjords, Patreksfjörður has few sights or activities for tourists. The town was named after St Patrick of Ireland, who was the spiritual guide of Örlygur Hrappson, the first settler in the area. The town was devastated by a mud slide in 1983, and its modern buildings sling across the hill and gravel spit that extend into the fjord. There are several places to stay, a lovely **swimming pool** (☎ 456 1523; Eyrargata) and a bank with an ATM.

There's a camp site behind the Esso petrol station and there are two good guesthouses on the hill rising behind the church. The friendly **Stekkaból** (☎ 864 9675; stekkabol@snerpa.is; Stekkar 19; sb/made-up beds Ikr1900/3200) has bright, simple rooms and a guest kitchen, while nearby **Gistiheimili Erlu** (☎ 456 1227; Brunnar 14; sb/

THE WESTFJORDS

s/d Ikr1800/3200/6000) also has cooking facilities and modern rooms.

The restaurant **Þorpið** (☎ 456 1295; Aðalstræti 73; mains Ikr600-1800) is your best bet for food. It serves a predictable menu of grills and meat dishes, has big windows overlooking the fjord and a nice outdoor seating area for warm days. You can get snacks and light meals at **Söluturninn Albína** (☎ 456 1667; Aðalstræti 89; mains Ikr400-1500), a café with an ATM. The Esso petrol station on the main road has a grill, and there are several supermarkets and a Vín Búð liquor store on Þórsgata.

Getting There & Away

On Monday, Wednesday and Saturday from June to August there are buses between Patreksfjörður and Brjánslækur (Ikr1200, 1¼ hours), Látrabjarg (Ikr1000, two hours) and Ísafjörður (Ikr3300, two hours).

Buses also run by request from Patreksfjörður to meet flights into Bíldudalur. Call ☎ 855 3665 or ☎ 863 0990.

TÁLKNAFJÖRÐUR
pop 340

Set amid rolling green hills, rocky peaks and a wide fjord, Tálknafjörður is another soporific village surrounded by magnificent scenery. The only real thing to see or do here is to visit the outdoor **swimming pool** (☎ 456 2639; admission adult/6-12yr Ikr300/180; ☼ 9am-9pm Mon-Fri, 9am-6pm Sat & Sun Jun-Aug), fed by the nearby geothermal field. In summer, a basic tourist office operates at the pool. There's also a bank, a post office and a supermarket.

If you want to break your journey there's a **camp site** (☎ 456 2639; sites per person Ikr800; ☼ Jun-Aug) beside the swimming pool with laundry and cooking facilities. There are several guesthouses in the centre of the village. The pick of the crop is the flower-strewn **Gistiheimilið Hamrarborg** (☎ 456 2514; fax 456 2694; Strandgötu 6), but you'll also find decent rooms at **Skrúðhamar** (☎ 456 0200; skrudhamar@visir.is; Strandgötu 20; ☐) and **Bjarmalandi** (☎ 891 8038; bjarmaland06@simnet.is; Bugatún 11). All offer sleeping-bag space for around Ikr2000 and made-up beds for Ikr3500.

The best place for food is **Pósthúsið** (☎ 456 2500; Strandgata 32; mains Ikr500-1750), a decent place serving the usual array of burgers, pizzas and grills. You can also get food at the pub **Hópið** (☎ 456 2631; Hrafnardalsvegur; mains Ikr1000-3500), which sometimes has bands playing at weekends.

The Esso station sells limited groceries and the usual grills.

Getting There & Away

Buses run from Patreksfjörður to Bíldudalur on request to meet flights. Call ☎ 855 3665 or ☎ 863 0990.

BÍLDUDALUR
pop 240

Set on a gloriously calm bay surrounded by towering peaks, the sleepy fishing village of Bíldudalur has a simply gorgeous setting. Arriving by road from either direction you're treated to some spectacular outlooks. From the east a pot hole–riddled, rutted mud-and-gravel road leads over the otherworldly mountains around Suðurfirðir, and from the south the paved mountain road gives stunning views all the way.

Bíldudalur was founded in the 16th century and today is a major supplier of shrimp. For tourists there's little in the way of formal attractions, but there's a choice of accommodation, a bank and a petrol station, and the small **Tónlistarsafn** (☎ 456 2186; admission free; Tjarnarbraut 5; ☼ 1-5pm Mon-Fri mid-Jun–Sep) museum dedicated to Icelandic music from the '40s to the '60s.

If you'd like to stay there's a free camp site beside the golf course on the outskirts of town. For more comfort, try **Gistiheimilið Kaupfélagið** (☎ 456 2100; www.lokinhamrar.is; Hafnarbraut 2; sb/s/d Ikr1800/3200/6400), a guesthouse with plain but perfectly good rooms, and an attached restaurant (mains Ikr870 to Ikr1670) serving pizza, burgers and hearty sandwiches.

You can also get meals at the grill **Vegamót** (☎ 456 2232; mains Ikr600-1730), by the petrol station, or groceries at the small village supermarket.

Getting There & Away

Íslandsflug (☎ 456 2151; www.airiceland.is) provides flights every day except Saturday to/from Reykjavík (45 minutes) from April to October, with a reduced schedule in winter. The cheapest online fare for a one-way ticket is Ikr5950. Buses run on request to/from Patreksfjörður via Tálknafjörður to connect with flights. Call ☎ 855 3665 or ☎ 863 0990.

AROUND BÍLDUDALUR

Heading east from Bíldudalur you'll come to the roaring falls and small farm at **Foss** 13km from town. This is the start of the long, dramatic 15km hike along the Fossdalur valley to Tungamúli or Krossholt on the south coast road (Rte 62). The route follows a trail used by 19th-century postmen and crosses some spectacular scenery.

About 26km northwest of Bíldudalur, at Selárdalur, is the ruined wooden **farmhouse** of eccentric Icelandic artist Samúel Jónsson (1884–1969). Standing outside are some of his weathered statues of people and horses.

CENTRAL WESTFJORDS

ÞINGEYRI

pop 340

This tiny village was the first trading station in the Westfjords, but these days the world seems to have passed Þingeyri by. Although there's little to see here, the surrounding hills offer excellent walking, including the short hike up to **Sandfell**, the 367m ridge behind the village, which begins just south of the village on Rte 60.

In summer there's a **tourist office** (☎ 456 8304; www.thingeyri.is; Hafnarstræti; 🕙 10am-6pm Mon-Fri, noon-4pm Sat & Sun Jun-Aug) on the main road. The village also has a good **swimming pool** (☎ 456 8375; adult/under 16yr Ikr300/180; 🕙 7.45am-9pm Mon-Fri, 10am-6pm Sat, 10am-5pm Sun Jun-Aug).

If you'd like to stay there's a **camp site** (☎ 456 8285; sites per person Ikr600) behind the swimming pool. Alternatively, the friendly, modern guesthouse **Við Fjörðinn** (☎ 456 8172; www.vidfjordinn .is; Aðalstræti 26; sb/s/d Ikr2000/3500/6000; 👌) has bright, cheerful rooms with simple décor and plain white linens. The sparkling new bathrooms are shared, but there's a good guest kitchen and a TV lounge. The village has a small supermarket, and there's a snack bar at the Esso station.

Local **buses** (☎ 456 4258) run twice every weekday between Þingeyri and Ísafjörður (Ikr600, 30 minutes). From June to August a daily bus runs to Brjánslækur, where you'll be able to catch the *Baldur* ferry (see p171) to Stykkishólmur.

AROUND ÞINGEYRI
Þingeyri Peninsula

The Þingeyri peninsula's dramatic northern peaks have been dubbed the 'Northwestern Alps', and the region offers some excellent remote trekking. The mountains are partly volcanic in origin, and the peaks are made up of rock and scree – a marked contrast to the

green valleys elsewhere in the Westfjords. For detailed information on hiking in the area, visit www.thingeyri.is.

A dirt road runs northwest along the eastern edge of the peninsula to the scenic valley at **Haukadalur**. If the road isn't blocked by landslides, you can continue right around the peninsula with a 4WD, passing cliffs where birds perch and the remote lighthouse at **Svalvogar**.

If you're visiting on the first weekend in July it's worth checking out the local **folk festival** (www.westvikings.com), held at a reconstructed stone circle in Haukadalur. The festival celebrates the area's Viking heritage and the saga of local man Gísli Súrsson.

Inland, the Westfjords highest peak **Kaldbakur** (998m) is a good hiking spot. The steep trail to the summit begins from the road about 2km west of Þingeyri.

Over on the southern side of the Þingeyri peninsula, **Hrafnseyri** was the birthplace of Jón Sigurðsson, the architect of Iceland's independence, which took place on 17 June 1811. The small Hrafnseyri **museum** (☎ 456 8260; www .hrafnseyri.is; adult/under 14yr Ikr300/free; 🕙 10am-8pm mid-Jun–Aug) outlines aspects of his life. There's also a wooden church here dating from 1886.

Dynjandi

Tumbling in a broad sweep over a 100m-rocky scarp at the head of Dynjandivogur bay is Dynjandi (Fjallfoss), the best known and most dramatic waterfall in the Westfjords. Coming from the car park you'll pass a series of smaller falls at the base of the main chute, but it's well worth following the path up to the base of the massive cascade that plunges over the mountain side. The thundering water and views out over the broad fjord below are spectacular.

The surrounding area is protected as a nature reserve, but there's a free (if noisy) camp site right by the falls. Dynjandi is well signposted off Rte 60. Buses between Brjánslækur and Ísafjörður take a 10-minute break here to appreciate the falls.

Beyond Dynjandi, Rte 60 cuts across the desolate moonscape of the **Gláma** moors, which are covered in coarse tundra vegetation and mirror-like pools of standing water. It's possible to hike across this bleak moorland up to the ridge at **Sjónfrið** (920m) in a long, damp day.

THE WESTFJORDS

Mýrar & Núpur

Heading north from Þingeyri on the northern shore of Dýrafjörður are a series of gorgeous broad valleys. At the head of the valleys is a lovely weatherboard church and one of Iceland's oldest botanic gardens, **Skrúður** (admission free; ☑ daylight hours). Established as a teaching garden in 1905 by the local parish priest, Rev Sigtryggur Guðlaugsson, it became a pioneering environmental education centre. Today it is a peaceful glade of trees and ornamental shrubs reached through a whale-bone arch. Benches look out across the fjord and the surrounding wilderness, which is an important eider-duck breeding ground.

You can stay at the old school building, now converted into **Hotel Núpur** (☎ 456 8235; www .hotelnupur.is; sites Ikr500, sb/s/d Ikr1500/3200/5800; ☒), a comfortable but predictable place with a decent restaurant and a large indoor swimming pool. It's the huge white building with the red roof and tall chimney just off Rte 624.

Just past the hotel, the farmhouse **Alviðra** (☎ 456 8229; alvidra@snerpa.is; sb/s/d Ikr2200/5000/8000; ☑ Jun-Aug) has simple accommodation in a variety of buildings.

There's no public transport to Núpur, but Ísafjörður–Þingeyri buses can drop you by the junction of Rte 624, 2km from the Hotel Núpur and 8km from Alviðra.

Flateyri

pop 300

Once a giant support base for Norwegian whalers, Flateyri is now a sleepy little place set on a gravel spit sticking out into broad Önundarfjörður. There are few specific sights for visitors other than the chimney and boiler from the abandoned whaling station at Hóll, near the head of the fjord. Flateyri is particularly vulnerable to avalanches, and an enormous earth chute was built on the slopes above the village to defend it after a devastating avalanche in 1995.

Two- to three-hour sea-kayaking trips can be arranged through **Ferðaþónustan Grænhöfði** (☎ 456 7762; jens@snerpa.is). Longer tours are also possible. There are lots of good hiking opportunities in the hills and valleys around the Kirkjuból HI Hostel – ask the warden for some recommendations.

There is also an indoor and outdoor **swimming pool** (☎ 456 7738; adult/under 14yr Ikr300/180; ☑ 10am-noon & 4-9pm Mon-Fri, noon-4pm Sat & Sun Jun-Aug) with sauna and Jacuzzi.

The village has a free **camp site** (☎ 456 7738) next to the avalanche defences on its edge, and summerhouse rental is available from **Ferðaþónustan Grænhöfði** (☎ 456 7762; jens@snerpa .is). Chalets sleep up to six people and cost Ikr8000/37000 per day/week.

The popular Kirkjubol youth hostel **Korpudalur Kirkjuból** (Önundarfjörður Hostel; ☎ 456 7808; korpudalur@hostel.is; sb member/nonmember Ikr1650/2000; ☑ Jun-Aug) is 12km south of Flateyri at the head of Önundarfjörður. Set in a renovated farmhouse at the bottom of the broad valley, it is a great spot for wilderness hikers, bird-watchers and anglers. Pick-ups can be arranged from Ísafjörður for a small fee.

Your best bet for food in town is the **Vagninn Restaurant** (☎ 456 7751; Hafnarstræti 19; mains Ikr700-1900), a quiet place serving the usual selection of snacks and meat dishes. Alternatively, there's a grill bar at the Esso station.

GETTING THERE & AWAY

On weekdays there are three daily buses between Ísafjörður and Flateyri (Ikr250, 30 minutes). To be picked up in Flateyri, call ahead (☎ 456 4258) – otherwise the bus might not drive into the village.

SUÐUREYRI

pop 320

Perched on the tip of 13km-long Súgandafjörður, the fishing community of Suðureyri was isolated for years by the forbidding mountains that surround the village and the bad road that led over them. Now connected with Ísafjörður by a 5km tunnel, the village has got a new lease of life and is busy turning itself into a self-sustaining community with a unique take on tourism.

In many ways the village is staunchly traditional – all fishing is done by rod and hook, and the grand tourism plans being developed are all about preserving nature and sharing rather than changing this traditional way of life.

Activities

The **Sjávarþorpið Suðureyri** (Original Fishing Village; www.sudureyri.is) project allows visitors to join in the regular life of the village in order to learn and understand how things are today for fishing families in rural Iceland. You can go out on working fishing boats (Ikr12,000 for a two-hour trip for four people or a full day trip for two people) and visit the fish factory (Ikr1000). The project offers a unique insight

SUSTAINABLE SUÐUREYRI

When the tunnel through the mountains to Suðureyri was built the village acquired a reliable source of hydroelectricity. This, combined with the naturally occurring geothermal fields in the area, means that Suðureyri now gets all its energy and hot-water supplies from sustainable sources. In addition, the villagers' prime fishing grounds lie very close to shore, so little fuel is used to power boats, and traditional fishing methods mean that the natural balance of the fish stocks is not endangered.

into life in fishing communities and is the only one of its kind in the country. You can book activities online or at VEG-Gisting (see below). On the way into town you can also visit the lagoon, where wild cod can be seen. A set of information boards nearby explain what a contemporary fisherman's life is like.

If it all sounds too exciting you could just relax in the village's **geothermal swimming pool** (☎ 456 6121; Túngata 8; adult/under 14yr Ikr350/200; ⏱ 10am-9pm Mon-Fri, to 7pm Sat & Sun Jun-Sep), sauna and hot pots.

Sleeping & Eating

Camp site (☎ 456 6666; sites per person Ikr1000) The village's brand new camp site is well equipped with hot and cold water and shower blocks.

VEG-Gisting (☎ 456 6666; www.sudureyri.is/gistiheimili; Aðalgata 14; sb Ikr2000, d without/with bathroom Ikr5600/8000; 🖳) Customer focused, thoroughly modern and really comfy, this friendly guesthouse has bright, simple rooms with crisp white linens and pine furniture. Each room has washbasin, TV, phone and hair dryer, and there's free internet access and the use of a guest kitchen. There's also free wi-fi access in the building if you've brought your laptop.

ourpick **Talisman restaurant** (mains Ikr1700-2500; ⏱ mid-May–mid-Sep) Attached to VEG-Gisting, this is a swish, contemporary-styled place with moleskin chairs, large windows, and place mats and menu covers made from fish skins. The menu features a wonderful array of locally sourced food, from seafood and fish to lamb. A flatscreen TV shows a video describing a fisherman's life.

For fast food there's a grill bar at the Esso petrol station.

Getting There & Away

From Monday to Friday there are three daily local buses between Ísafjörður and Suðureyri (Ikr250, 20 minutes).

ÍSAFJÖRÐUR

pop 3500

Hub of activity in the Westfjords and by far the area's largest town, Ísafjörður is a pleasant and prosperous place and an excellent base for travellers. The town is set on a gravel spit that extends out into Skutulsfjörður, and is hemmed in on all sides by towering peaks and the eerily dark and still waters of the fjord.

The centre of Ísafjörður is littered with old timber and tin-clad buildings, many unchanged since the 18th century, when the harbour was full of tall ships and Norwegian whaling crews. Today it is a surprisingly cosmopolitan place, and after some time spent travelling in the Westfjords, feels like a bustling metropolis with its tempting cafés, cinema, great choice of restaurants and variety of accommodation.

There's good hiking in the hills around the town, skiing in winter and regular summer boats to ferry hikers across to the remote Hornstrandir peninsula. In fact, Ísafjörður's only downside is the long journey to get here. You'll either have to wind in and out of numerous fjords on bumpy roads or take a hair-raising flight into the tiny airstrip on the opposite side of the fjord. Then again, it's the town's remote location and surprisingly urbane attitude that really give it its wonderful character.

History

The region west of Ísafjörður is geologically the oldest in the country, dating back about 20 million years. However, it was not until Norwegian and Icelandic traders arrived in the 16th century that the gravel spit in Skutulsfjörður saw human inhabitation. At first the camps were temporary, but soon German and English trading firms set up shop and a permanent post was established. The first mention of trading in the area dates back to 1569, when records show a Hanseatic League trading post here, but by 1602 the Danish Trade Monopoly had taken over business and begun developing Ísafjörður as a fishing and trading centre.

In the following centuries Ísafjörður became a logistical centre for Norwegian whaling ships, although the Icelanders only took up commercial whaling in the 1950s. In later years

ÍSAFJÖRÐUR

INFORMATION
Bókhlaðan Penninn..................1 D3
Borea Adventures....................2 C1
Efnalaugin Albert....................3 C4
Gamla Apotekið...................(see 22)
Hospital................................4 C2
Islandsbanki (ATM).................5 C3
Landsbanki Íslands..................6 C2
Library.................................7 C2
Post Office............................8 C2
Tourist Office........................9 C3

SIGHTS & ACTIVITIES
Church................................10 C2
Seamen's Monument..............11 C2
Swimming Pool......................12 D2
Vesturferðir.......................(see 9)
Westfjords Folk Museum..........13 B4
Whalebone Arch....................14 B2

SLEEPING
Camp Site...........................15 B2
Gamla Gistihúsið....................16 C2
Guesthouse Litla....................17 D3
Hotel Edda..........................18 B2
Hótel Ísafjörður.....................19 C3

EATING
Bakarans............................20 C2
Fernandos...........................21 D2
Gamla Apotekið.....................22 C2
Gamla Bakaríð.......................23 D3
Hótel Ísafjörður..................(see 19)
Kaffi Langi Mangi....................24 D3
Samkaup Supermarket.............25 C2
Thai Koon........................(see 25)
Tjöruhisíð........................(see 13)
Vin Búð.............................26 D3

ENTERTAINMENT
Ísasjarðarbíó Cinema...............27 D2
Kaffi Langi Mangi.................(see 24)
Kruisin..............................28 D2

SHOPPING
Gullauga..........................(see 1)
Hafnarbúdin.........................29 C4
Rammagerð Ísafjarðar.............30 C3

TRANSPORT
Bus Stand...........................31 C2
Bus Stop............................32 B2
Esso Petrol Station...............(see 31)
Hornstrandir Boat Departures..33 D4
Vesturferðir......................(see 9)

0 ———————————— 400 m
0 ———————————— 0.2 miles

To Hnífsdalur (4km);
Bolungarvík (15km)

To Bónus Supermarket (1km);
Kvennabrekka (2km);
Tungudalur & Seljalandsdalur (2km);
Flateyri tunnel (4km);
Airport (5km); Naustahvilft (6km);
Reykjavík (457km)

the town bore witness to some of the fierce battles between whalers and environmental campaigners that eventually led to the worldwide ban on commercial whaling in 1989.

In 1991 a tunnel was constructed to link Ísafjörður and the previously isolated communities of Suðureyri and Flateyri. The three towns and nearby Þingeyri were amalgamated into a single administrative unit called Ísafjarðarbær in 1996.

Information

The friendly Vesturfirðir **tourist office** (☎ 456 8060; www.vestfirdir.is; Aðalstræti 7; 🕑 8.15am-7pm Mon-Fri, 10am-5pm Sat & Sun Jun-Aug, 10am-5pm Mon-Fri Sep-May) is down by the harbour in the Edinborgarhús, built in 1781.

You'll find all the major banks along Hafnarstræti and the post office in the Neisti Centre at Hafnarstræti 9. Internet access is available at the town **library** (☎ 456 3296; Eyrartúni; 🕑 1-7pm Mon-Fri, 1-4pm Sat) for Ikr100 per hour. The tourist office also has a single terminal that travellers can use for free for a 10-minute session. You can also use the computers at Ísafjörður's youth centre, **Gamla Apótekið** (☎ 456 7000; Hafnarstræti 18; 🕑 8am-5pm Mon-Fri Jun-Aug, to midnight Mon-Fri Sep-May), for free. It also has a wi-fi hotspot.

The bookshop **Bókhlaðan Penninn** (☎ 456 3123; Hafnarstræti 2) is well stocked and has maps and books in English. For laundry services go to **Efnalaugin Albert** (☎ 456 4670; Sindragata 14; per wash Ikr900; 🕑 8am-6pm Mon-Fri).

THE WESTFJORDS

Sights & Activities

Housed in a cluster of ancient wooden buildings by the harbour, the **Westfjords Folk Museum** (☎ 456 3293; Neðstíkaupstaður; adult/under 16yr/senior Ikr500/free/300; ☢ 10am-5pm Mon-Fri, 1-5pm Sat & Sun Jun, 10am-5pm daily Jul & Aug) is an atmospheric place full of relics. The dimly lit main building, the **Turnhús**, dates from 1784 and was originally used as a warehouse. Inside it's like stepping back in time, with every available surface covered with fishing and nautical exhibits, tools and equipment from the whaling days, and fascinating old photos depicting life in the town over the centuries. To the right of this building is the wooden **Tjöruhús** (1781), which now operates as a very pleasant café and restaurant. Two other buildings on the site, the **Faktorhús**, built in 1765 to house the manager of the village shop, and the **Krambúd** (1757), originally a storehouse, are now private residences.

From mid-June to mid-August the museum hosts film screenings (Ikr800) on Monday and Thursday evening, a slide show and lecture on the local environment (Ikr500) on Wednesday and Sunday, and a performance based on the saga of Gísli the outlaw on Friday (Ikr1500). All evening events take place at 8.30pm.

Apart from the museum, Ísafjörður's formal attractions are pretty thin on the ground. Of minor interest is the **whalebone arch** made from a whale's jawbone in the park in the centre of town. Nearby are Ísafjörður's interesting **seamen's monument** and the modernist town **church**, which looks a lot like an old-fashioned press camera with a flash on top.

There are loads of **walking** trails around Ísafjörður, most of which are covered in the pamphlet map *Gönguleiðir Í Nágrenni Ísafjardar* (Ikr300), available from the tourist office. One of the more unusual and shorter walks is up to the truncated valley of **Naustahvilft** – about 1km above the airport – which offers fantastic views over the fjord. Several other trails start near the road bridge at the head of Skutulsfjörður, where the last wizards in Iceland were burned at the stake in 1656.

In summer, **sea-kayaking** tours of Jökulfirðir can be arranged through **Vestfirskar Ævintýraferðir** (☎ 456 3574; www.vestfirdir.is/kayak).

Although plain by Icelandic standards, the town **swimming pool** (☎ 456 3200; Austurvegur 9; adult/ under 16yr Ikr300/180; ☢ 7am-9pm Mon-Fri, 10am-4pm Sat & Sun mid-Jun–Aug) makes a good retreat on a wet day.

Tours

Housed in the same building as the tourist office, and the most popular outfit around, **Vesturferðir** (☎ 456 5111; www.vesturferdir.is; Aðalstræti 7) organises a mind-boggling array of tours in the area, including trips to Vigur island (Ikr4300, three to four hours), the abandoned village at Hesteyri (Ikr4400, four to five hours), Hornstrandir Nature Reserve (Ikr9900, 12 hours) and Hornvík (Ikr15,000, 12 hours; Ikr56,900 for four nights). The company also organises puffin-watching trips to Grímsey (Ikr3500, three to four hours), sea angling (Ikr12,500, two hours), guided bike rides around Svalvogar (Ikr5300, eight hours) and kayaking trips around the bay (Ikr5300, 2½ hours).

Borea Adventures (☎ 899 3817; www.boreaadventures .com; Hlíðarvegur 38) offers multiday trips aboard *Aurora*, a yacht built for the Clipper Round the World Race, from April to September. Tours include four-day skiing and ice-climbing trips to Jökulfirðir (€1100), six-day skiing trips (€1650), five-day wildlife and photography trips (€1650), and five-day sea-kayaking trips (€1375) – all to Jökulfirðir and Hornstrandir.

Sleeping

Camp site (☎ 444 4960; Skutulsfjarðarbraut; sites per person Ikr650; ☢ mid-Jun–mid-Aug) The centrally located town camp site is just a short walk from all you'll need in town and has good washing facilities.

Camp site (☎ 456 5081; sites per person Ikr750) Further out of town but far more scenic, this second camp site is by a pretty waterfall in Tungudalur. The last stop on the town bus will take you to within 1km of the site.

Gamla Gistihúsið (Old Guesthouse; ☎ 456 4146; www .gistihus.is; Mánagata 5; sb/s/d Ikr1800/3900/6000; ☐) Bright, cheerful and immaculately kept, this excellent guesthouse has simple but comfortable rooms with plenty of homey touches. The bathrooms are shared, but each room has telephone, washbasin and bathrobes. An annexe just down the road has a guest kitchen and more modern, functional rooms.

Guesthouse Litla (☎ 474 1455; reginasc@simnet.is; Sundstraeti 43; s/d Ikr3500/7000; ☢ Jun-Aug, by reservation rest of year) Wooden floors, crisp white linen, fluffy towels and TVs are available in the high-quality rooms of Litla, another cosy guesthouse with tasteful décor. Two rooms share each bathroom, and there's a guest kitchen.

Kvennabrekka (☎ 456 5560; www.snjor.is/gisting; Skíðaskálanum Tungudal; sb/s/d Ikr2500/5000/9000) Up

THE WESTFJORDS

WESTFJORDS IN WINTER

Visiting the remotest part of Iceland in the depths of winter might sound extreme, but the mountains around Ísafjörður are a popular destination for Icelandic skiers (see www.isafjordur .is/ski). The season runs from January to Easter, and there are daily flights from Reykjavík timed to fit in with the limited daylight hours.

For downhill skiing head to Tungudalur, where there are illuminated slopes, three ski lifts and a cosy ski chalet with a café and ski hire. Passes are available at the nearby petrol station or the chalet (Ikr1000/500 per adult/child under 16). Nearby, Seljalandsdalur has gentle slopes and some of Iceland's best cross-country skiing. There are no ski lifts, but there is a basic, heated chalet.

Snow permitting, there is a lively **ski festival** (www.skidavikan.is) here during the week after Easter. The week ends with a music festival attracting top bands. In May, cross-country skiers from around Iceland head to Ísafjörður for the 50km Fossavatn **Ski Marathon** (www.fossavatn.com), which has been running since 1935.

The mountains around Ísafjörður block a lot of light in winter and from early December to late January the sun fails to make an appearance at all. However, on 23 January the place to be is Sólgata (Sun St), where locals wait to greet the return of the sun. Although it only makes a brief appearance (at about midday), it's a sign for celebration and locals gather together for coffee, pancakes and talk of spring.

---

near the Tungudal ski slopes, the new ski chalet offers basic but comfortable accommodation in two-bed rooms with modern furniture and washbasins. Bathrooms are shared, and there's a large café and restaurant downstairs.

Hotel Edda (☎ 444 4960; www.hoteledda.is; sb/s/d with shared bathroom from Ikr2000/6100/7600, d with private bathroom Ikr11,900; ☯ mid-Jun–mid-Aug) No-frills summer accommodation is available at the town's secondary school. You can choose from basic sleeping-bag accommodation in the classrooms, private rooms with shared bathrooms and doubles with private bathrooms. All rooms are pretty functional but are bright, modern and comfortable.

Hótel Ísafjörður (☎ 456 4111; www.hotelisafjordur .is; Silfurtorg 2; s/d 13,900/16,900 Jun-Aug, Ikr10,400/12,900 Sep-May) Slap bang in the centre of the town, this business-class hotel offers spacious, international-style rooms with calm, neutral décor, good bathrooms and views over the sea or town square. All rooms have phone, TV and minibar, and the top-floor suites have a variety of added extras. Sleeping-bag accommodation (Ikr4500/6500 for singles/doubles) is available out of season.

Eating
Kaffi Langi Mangi (☎ 456 3022; Aðalstræti 22; meals Ikr400-800; ☯ 11am-11pm Mon-Wed, to 1am Thu, to 2am Fri, noon-2am Sat, 1-11pm Sun) This funky little hangout with changing artists' exhibitions is a great spot for snacks and light meals. The menu in-

cludes everything from soups and sandwiches to pancakes and a range of coffees.

Thai Koon (☎ 456 0123; Neisti Centre, Hafnarstræti 9; mains Ikr790-990; ☯ 11.30am-9pm Mon-Sat, 5-9pm Sun) After a few weeks of limited choice for meals, this small Thai canteen seems decidedly exotic. Although there's no atmosphere here whatsoever, the food is excellent and served up in giant portions, making it incredible value for money.

Fernandos (☎ 456 3367; Hafnarstræti 12; meals Ikr790-2780) The cosiest eatery in town is this Italian restaurant and bar on the main drag. Bag one of the window seats for good people-watching space, and tuck into the excellent choice of pizza, pasta, meats and luscious desserts. It also serves a range of sandwiches, panini and burgers throughout the day.

Hótel Ísafjörður (☎ 456 4111; Silfurtorg 2; mains Ikr1200-3000) More formal dining is available at the hotel, where the restaurant serves the usual selection of Icelandic lamb and fish dishes. Although the atmosphere is more international than local, the windows offer great views over the fjord. Light lunches and specials make it a better deal at midday than in the evening.

ourpick Tjöruhúsið (Tar House; ☎ 456 3293; Neðstíkaupstaður; mains Ikr1500-2500; ☯ 11am-10pm Jul & Aug) The atmospheric summer restaurant at the folk museum offers some of the best fish and seafood dishes in town at very reasonable prices. Although lunch and dinner are the big

(Continued on page 189)

THE WESTFJORDS

Natural
Wonders

MARK WILLIAMS

Þingvellir (p115) is the spectacular product of two separating tectonic plates.

MARK WILLIAMS

top five

ISLANDS

Flatey (p161) Step back into the past on this historical island)

Grímsey (p223) Stroll into the Arctic Circle and get the certificate to prove it

Heimaey (p143) Visit Iceland's friendliest people, who live on top of a volcano

Lundey (p75) See millions of puffins just off the coast of Reykjavík

Papey (p273) Be wowed by the beautiful bird sanctuary of Papey

Active volcanoes, twisting lava formations, magical waterfalls, tiny islands and windswept black beaches – Iceland's scenery is simply mind-blowing. Europe's last untouched wilderness is built on top of a mighty fault line, which lends the landscape an utterly wonderful weirdness.

VOLCANOES & GEOTHERMAL ZONES

The youngest country in Europe, Iceland is still throwing its toys out of the pram (geologically speaking). A massive fault line runs across the land, causing all kinds of volcanic mayhem. Fissures rip the ground apart, volcanoes erupt, lava spills, and steam, mud and boiling water come spurting from the earth.

Some of the most dramatic scenery you'll see is evidence of past eruptions. Take a tour to the mountain **Laki** (p284), where an immense **crater row** (p284) stretches off into the distance, or to the **Askja caldera** (p307), the site of an explosion so vast it's impossible to imagine. The ground's still smoking on **Heimaey** (p143) and at **Leirhnjúkur** (p237). And as for future eruptions…they could go off anywhere, although vulcanologists are keeping an especially watchful eye on **Hekla** (p132) and **Katla** (p141).

PUFFIN SPOTTING

Puffins seem to adorn every T-shirt, paperweight and postcard in Reykjavík's souvenir shops, and you may well think you've seen enough of them before you've even left the city. But the flintiest heart will melt on a visit to one of Iceland's large puffin colonies.

These comical little critters are rubbish at flying and even worse at landing, frequently crashing at high speed into the ground. But they're also fiercely loyal to their mates, devoted to their chicks, and return to the same 'home' burrow year after year. They're immensely sociable, will gather round to watch a puffin fight, and will raise each other's babies if the parents meet with an accident.

The most fearless colonies are at **Látrabjarg** (p172), and you can also get quite close to the birds at **Heimaey** (p146) and just off the coast of Reykjavík (p75). You can see them between June and August (they live out at sea the rest of the year), although early in the puffin season they only return home towards sundown.

Impressive high-activity geothermal areas include **Hverir** (p236), a tremendous sulphur-stinking scene of multicoloured deposits, screaming vents, boiling springs and glooping mudpots, and the geothermal field at **Stórihver** (p280), where a particularly evil-looking hole belches boiling water. In the southeast similar, if smaller, scenes await near **Krýsuvík** (p113) and **Gunnuhver** (p111). **Hveragerði** (p124) even has its own tiny geothermal zone where most towns would have a municipal park!

WATER, WATER EVERYWHERE...

If you leave Iceland without seeing a single waterfall, you've done something wrong. Water topples and thunders everywhere, tinged with rainbows in the sunshine, and turned into crystal sculptures in the icy winter. **Gullfoss** (p120) is the most famous, a double-dropped beauty, and **Dettifoss** (p245) is Europe's biggest, a mighty behemoth whose crashing falls makes the ground nearby tremble. Pretty **Skógafoss** (p138) and **Seljalandsfoss** (p135) fall in narrow streams; **Hraunfossar** (p157) appears from under a lava field as if by magic; **Svartifoss** (p287) sulks among black basalt columns; **Glymur** (p151) is the highest; and **Fagrifoss** (p284) is the most lovely.

For a break from ever-falling water, why not watch it spitting upwards instead? The most famous geyser field in the world is **Geysir** (p120), after which all spouting springs are named. For a less crowded look, head for Hveragerði, where with a bit of luck you'll see **Grýla** (p125) gush.

Curtain-like Svartifoss (p287) is flanked by distinctive black basalt columns.
GRANT DIXON

EYE TO EYE WITH OCEAN GIANTS

Coming face to face with a whale is unforgettable – and Iceland is one of the best places in Europe to have a unique encounter. From mid-May to late August thousands of whales hang out in Icelandic waters. The most common varieties are minke and humpback, but you may also see fin, sei and even blue whales.

Húsavík (p241) is the whale-watching capital: it's a rare moment when a cetacean *isn't* visible in Skjálfandi bay. Shining backs roll from the waves, blasts of air spout from blowholes, and whales surface so close to the boat that you can smell their fishy breath!

It's an intense experience. But if you can't get so far north, don't worry – there are also sailings from **Reykjavík** (p75), **Keflavík** (p108), and **Ólafsvík** (p164), with high sighting rates.

HOT SPRINGS & GLACIERS

One thing that excites all visitors to Iceland is the prospect of relaxing in a hot spring. Head for the hot pools at **Landmannalaugar** (p277) and **Þórsmörk** (p136), the warm river at **Reykjadalur** (p125), Askja's hot crater lake **Víti** (p307), or of course the milky-blue spas at **Mývatn** (p230) and the **Blue Lagoon** (p111).

At the other end of the temperature scale, giant glaciers march from the interior down to Iceland's south coast – the most easily accessible are **Mýrdalsjökull** (p140), **Sólheimajökull** (p139), **Svínafellsjökull** (p289), **Skaftafellsjökull** (p287), or the daddy of them all, **Vatnajökull** (p294). An absolute must-see on the Ring Rd is **Jökulsárlón** (p291), where huge icebergs calve into a spectacular lagoon.

And when hot water and ice combine you get amazing ice caves – such as the ones at **Kverkfjöll** (p309) or near **Hrafntinnusker** (p280) – smooth and silent apart from the creaking ice and echoing drips of water.

Iceland's highest mountain, Hvannadalshnúkur (p289), Skaftafell National Park

GRAEME CORNWALL

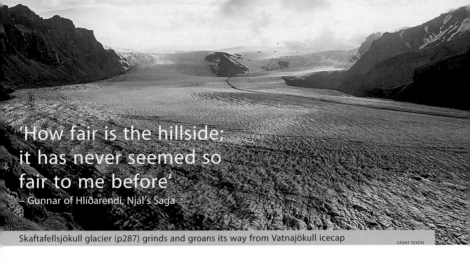

'How fair is the hillside;
it has never seemed so
fair to me before'
– Gunnar of Hlíðarendi, Njál's Saga

Skaftafellsjökull glacier (p287) grinds and groans its way from Vatnajökull icecap

GRANT DIXON

NATIONAL PARKS & NATURE RESERVES

As well as its livelier bits of landscape, Iceland has whole areas of sweeping majestic beauty – lonely mountains, hidden valleys and sinister canyons. The country's favourite national park is **Skaftafell** (p285), which encompasses glacier tongues, superb hiking trails and the world's biggest *sandar* (glacial sand plains). Also unmissable is the Unesco World Heritage site **Þingvellir** (p115), Iceland's oldest national park and one of the country's most significant historical sites.

In the north, spectacular **Jökulsárgljúfur National Park** (p242) was carved out by a huge volcanic flood. In the highlands, **Landmannalaugar** (p277) boasts the country's most colourful hills, made from beautiful many-shaded rhyolite. You can **trek** (p280) from there to **Þórsmörk** (p136), another gorgeous valley filled with sparkling streams and twisting birch forests. For more superb walking, head for the **Hornstrandir peninsula** (p194), dotted with abandoned farms and populated only by arctic foxes.

I-SPY ANIMALS – HOW MANY WILL YOU FIND?

- **Arctic fox** Try the wild Hornstrandir peninsula (p194), or (cheating) at the children's farm of Töfragarðurinn Stokkseyri (p130).
- **Raven** Please your inner Goth in Ísafjörður (p177), which seems to have a raven on every street lamp.
- **Reindeer** Look out for them across east Iceland (p259) – it doesn't count if they're on a menu.
- **Arctic tern** Beautiful to look at with their split-tailed silhouette, but go near their nests (p294) and they become demonic.
- **Seal** Seen lazing on beaches around the country – try Ósar (p201) for a colony as curious about you as you are about them.
- **Great skua** Often seen bullying other birds along the south coast (p291).
- **Oyster catcher** The dimwits of the bird world, these black-and-white, orange-beaked idiots have a suicidal attraction to tarmac.

Romantic
Iceland

Odd, comical and sociable, puffins flock in their thousands at Latrabjarg Peninsula (p173)

FRANS LEMM

A humpback whale gets up close and personable with a whale-watching boat (p56).
ANDERS BLOMQVIST

top five
ROMANTIC MOMENTS

Sitting in a **hot tub** underneath the stars

Snuggling up together to watch the **aurora borealis** (p46)

Dropping in on Café Cultura (p90) in Reykjavík for a sultry **tango lesson**

Watching the sunset from **Dyrhólaey** (p140)

Going for a windswept walk on the bird cliffs at **Látrabjarg** (p172)

Iceland's breathtaking natural beauty and rarefied air puts colour in your cheeks, a spring in your step, and passion in your soul. Take advantage by whisking your loved one away to one of the most romantic places on earth.

WILDLIFE & WESTERN SUNSETS

There's an undeniable magic in the air of the **Snæfellsnes peninsula** (p158). Begin your trip in friendly **Stykkishólmur** (p158), where bright wooden houses cluster round a sweet little harbour. The nearby fjord's thousands of tiny islands are an idyllic sight – take your loved one **kayaking** (p161), and coo over seals, puffins and eagles together. Further down the coast at Ólafsvík a **whale-watching trip** (p164) is a must. Coming eyeball to eyeball with these gentle giants will be a highlight of your holiday.

At the very western end of the peninsula, stop for a walk along **Skarðsvík** (p165), a perfect bay of golden sand, hidden by black lava cliffs. Next, pay your respects to the peninsula's guardian spirit at tiny, picturesque **Hellnar** (p166), before continuing eastwards through **lava fields** (p166) filled with 'hidden people'. Your end destination is the windswept **Hótel Búðir** (p167): elegantly furnished rooms, open fires and a luxurious restaurant make this one of the most romantic places to stay in Iceland.

A couple get warm in the geothermal pool of the Blue Lagoon (p111)

ANDERS BLOMQ

SPAS & VOLCANOES

Base yourself in Reykjahlíð, on Mývatn lake, for a few days of volcanic fun. We'd recommend the simple but pleasant **Hótel Reykjahlíð** (p232), which has the best lake views. Hire bicycles from Hlíð Camping, then spend a leisurely day **cycling** (p231) together around the lake. Stop to climb **Vindbelgjarfjall** (p235) for fabulous views of the whole area; marvel at livid-green **pseudocraters** (p233); get lost in the twisting lava formations at **Dimmuborgir** (p233); walk up the ashy crater of **Hverfell** (p233); and stop for **coffee** (p232) in a cow shed. Round off the day with a good soak in the mineral-rich **Mývatn Nature Baths** (p230), the north's answer to the Blue Lagoon.

Next day, head for more explosive sites – the wild-coloured hills at **Námafjall** (p235) and the nearby **Hverir** (p236) geothermal field, with some of the best steam vents and bubbling pools to be seen. The last and most dramatic place to visit is the huge multicoloured mudpot at **Leirhnjúkur** (p237) and the immense, still-smoking Krafla lava field. Just imagine – you're now standing on top of a giant magma chamber that could blow at any time. Life is short, people – love each other!

POPPING THE QUESTION

Paris is passé, Venice is sunk – if you want to propose to your loved one, do it at sunset in the Blue Lagoon (p111)! An astonishing 75% of visiting British women think this geothermal spa is the perfect place to get their rocks on. (We're still trying to figure out how their poor partners go down on one knee without drowning, or what happens if you drop diamonds in silica mud...).

(Continued from page 180)

events, you can also have coffee, cake and light snacks here during the day. If you're in town during one of the four summer saltfish feasts, don't miss the opportunity to sample the fish cured traditionally at the museum.

For breakfast, lunch or a midmorning sugar fix there are two extremely tempting bakeries in town. Both **Gamla Bakaríð** (☎ 456 3226; Aðalstræti; 7am-6pm Mon-Fri, to 4pm Sat) and **Bakarans** (☎ 456 4771; Hafnarstræti 14; 7.30am-6pm Mon-Sat, 9am-4.30pm Sun) have cosy seating areas and a choice of savoury and sweet snacks to obliterate any diet.

There's a Samkaup supermarket in the Neisti Centre on Hafnarstræti and a cheaper Bónus supermarket on the main road into town. The Vín Búð alcohol shop is at Aðalstræti 20.

Entertainment
The town cinema **Ísasjarðarbíó** (☎ 456 3202; Austurvegur) shows films several nights a week at 8pm.

On weekend nights Kaffi Langi Mangi becomes one of the coolest spots in town, with live bands and a chilled-out crowd. For more latenight revelry, head for the only club in town, **Krúsin** (Norðurvegur 1; 9pm-3am Fri & Sat), which plays an eclectic mix of '60s to '80s music.

Shopping
If you're heading for Hornstrandir you can buy outdoor clothing and camping equipment at **Hafnarbúdin** (☎ 456 3245; Suðurgata). **Rammagerð Ísafjarðar** (☎ 456 3041; Aðalstræti 16) sells quality glassware and other crafts, and **Gullauga** (☎ 456 3460; Hafnarstræti 4) is good for gold jewellery.

Getting There & Away
AIR
Air Iceland (☎ 456 3000; www.airiceland.is) is based at the airport and flies to/from Reykjavík two or three times daily from late March to late October, with a reduced service in winter. The cheapest online fare from Reykjavík is Ikr3970. Flights to Akureyri connect through Reykjavík.

A special bus service (Ikr500) runs to the airport about 45 minutes before departure. It starts in Bolungarvík and stops near the Hótel Ísafjörður.

BUS & BOAT
Buses stop at the Esso petrol station on Hafnarstræti. Local council buses (☎ 456 4258) run twice daily Monday to Friday from Ísafjörður to Flateyri and Þingeyri and three

times daily to Suðureyri and Bolungarvík. The fare to all these places is Ikr250.

From June to August there is a bus to Hólmavík (where you can change to buses for Reykjavík and Akureyri, see p192) on Tuesday, Friday and Sunday at 10.30am (Ikr4000, four hours) and there are daily buses to Brjánslækur (Ikr2300), where you can catch the *Baldur* ferry (see p171) to Stykkishólmur. Buses also connect to Reykjavík from Stykkishólmur (see p160). The timetables on these routes change each season and don't always allow for a through journey without an overnight stop in Stykkishólmur. For up-to-date information, visit www.bsi.is and www.stjornubilar.is.

In summer, ferries to Hornstrandir depart from the Sundahöfn docks on the eastern side of the isthmus – see p196 for more details.

Getting Around
City buses operate from 7.30am to 6.30pm on weekdays (until 10.30pm in winter) and connect the town centre with Hnífsdalur and Tungudalur (Ikr250, 10 minutes).

Vesturferðir rents out two types of mountain bike for Ikr1000/2000 for six hours or Ikr2500/3500 for 24 hours. For a taxi, call ☎ 456 3518.

AROUND ÍSAFJÖRÐUR
Tungudalur & Seljalandsdalur
These glacial valleys about 2km west of Ísafjörður, at the head of the fjord, offer some interesting hiking routes into the surrounding mountains. Tungudalur is lined with waterfalls and scrubby birch forest, and it also has a wonderful secluded camp site and a scenic **golf course** (☎ 456 5081; green fees Ikr2000, club hire Ikr1500). One pleasant walk is the 1.2km trail beside the waterfall to the viewpoint at Siggakofi.

There are also pleasant walks along the river valley Seljalandsdalur, which is lined with small lakes and leads up to the desolate moors around Breiðafell (724m). From here you can link up with the popular Hnífsdalur–Bolungarvík trek. In winter both valleys are good for skiing – see p180.

Hnífsdalur
Locally famous for producing *harðfiskur* (dried haddock) and *hákarl* (rotten shark), the village of Hnífsdalur makes an interesting side trip from Ísafjörður. Set in a deep fjord 4km north of town, Hnífsdalur has plenty of smelly fish-drying sheds and several interesting

walks in the surrounding hills. One of the best is the recommended 8km trek along the Hnífsdalur valley and over the ridge to Syðridalsvatn lake, by the Redihjallavirkjun power plant at Bolungarvík.

BOLUNGARVÍK
pop 980

Surrounded on three sides by mountains and on the fourth by the sea, the sleepy and rundown town of Bolungarvík occupies a dramatic position at the head of the fjord. Two local museums make the town worth a visit, and for hikers it's a pleasant destination at the end of the 8km trek over the ridge from Hnífsdalur (see p189).

Sights & Activities

Housed in a series of old turf-and-stone fishing shacks on the way into town, the interesting open-air **Ósvör Maritime Museum** (☎ 892 1616; adult/under 16yr Ikr400/free; ⏰ 10am-5pm May-Jun, to 6pm Jul & Aug) is well worth a visit. A guide in a typical sheepskin fisherman's outfit shows you round explaining the history of the area and the traditional methods for salting fish. The cramped fishermen's hut is full of interesting relics, and there's a fish-salting shed and drying rack full of aromatic saltfish. A traditional rowing boat and tug capstan are also on display. On a ridge across the road a **view disc** describes the surrounding landscape.

In the main shopping arcade in the middle of town, the **Natural History Museum** (☎ 456 7207; www.nave.is; Vitastíg 3; adult/under 16yr Ikr400/free; ⏰ 9am-noon & 1-5pm Mon-Fri, 1-5pm Sat & Sun Jun-Sep) has a comprehensive collection of stuffed animals and birds – including a polar bear killed by fishermen just off the Hornstrandir coast.

As well as the walk to Hnífsdalur, there are interesting **hikes** to the remote coastal valley at Skálavík, 12km from Bolungarvík along a steep mountain road.

Bolungarvík also has a **swimming pool** (☎ 456 7381; ⏰ 8-11am & 1-9pm Mon, Wed & Fri, 1-9pm Tue & Thu, 10am-6pm Sat, 10am-5pm Sun Jun-Aug). You can hire horses from the farm **Hraun** (☎ 456 7450; per hr Ikr2500).

Sleeping & Eating

Facilities for tourists in Bolungarvík are limited and you'd be better off basing yourself in Ísafjörður instead.

Camp site (☎ 456 7381; sites per person Ikr500) The basic site is by the swimming pool.

Gistiheimili Vaxon (☎ 456 7999; haukur@vagnsson.is; Aðalstæti 9; sb/s/d Ikr2000/3500/6000; 🖳) This guesthouse offers simple accommodation in modern but functional rooms in the centre of town.

Kjallarinn Krá (☎ 456 7901; Hafnargata 41) The best bet for food, this coffee shop and bar serves a selection of fairly predictable light meals.

There's also a grill bar at the Shell petrol station and a Samkaup supermarket on the main street.

Getting There & Away

A surfaced road runs around the headlands from Ísafjörður, lined with tunnels and steel nets to catch falling debris and boulders from the steep slopes above.

From June to August there are three buses (☎ 5892 1417) from Ísafjörður to Bolungarvík (Ikr250) from Monday to Friday, and two in the opposite direction.

ÍSAFJARÐARDJÚP

The largest of the fjords in the region, 75km-long Ísafjarðardjúp takes a massive swath out of the Westfjords' landmass. Circuitous Rte 61 winds in and out of a series of smaller fjords on the southern side, making the drive from Ísafjörður to Hólmavík like sliding along each tooth of a fine comb.

Súðavík
pop 170

Just east of Ísafjörður, the small fishing community of Súðavík commands an imposing view across the fjord to Hornstrandir. There's little to see or do here, but it's the last stop with any facilities if you're heading east. Two kilometres south of town at Langeyri you can see the remains of a Norwegian **whaling station** that was used until the 1900s.

If you'd like to stay there's a free camp site, with toilets and showers, near the river. The only other option is **Sumarbyggð í Súðavík** (☎ 456 4986; www.sumarbyggd.is; Nesvegi 3; sb/s/d Ikr2000/3500/600; ⏰ May-Oct), which has comfy rooms in the guesthouse as well as a selection of summerhouses.

The one-stop shop **Hjá Jóni Indíafara** (☎ 456 4981; mains Ikr600-1800; Grundarstræti 3; ⏰ 9am-6pm Mon-Fri, 11am-6pm Sat, 1-5pm Sun) serves fast food and grills, and has a petrol pump and a limited selection of groceries.

Daily from Monday to Saturday there's a private bus from Ísafjörður to Súðavík

(Ikr850, 20 minutes). The buses between Ísafjörður and Hólmavík also pass through town on Sunday, Tuesday and Friday.

Vigur

The tiny island of Vigur, at the mouth of Hestfjörður, is a haven for sea birds, including eider ducks, arctic terns, guillemots and puffins. A selection of objects from Westfjords Folk Museum (see p179) is on display in Viktoríuhus (built in 1860).

Vesturferðir (☎ 456 5111; www.vesturferdir.is) in Ísafjörður runs half-day excursions to Vigur from mid-June to August (Ikr4300).

Mjóifjörður, Vatnsfjörður & Reykjarfjörður

Detouring off the main road, winding Rte 633 leads around the three slender fjords of Mjóifjörður, Vatnsfjörður and Reykjarfjörður. This little-visited area offers good bird-watching, outdoor activities and some historic remains.

At the head of Mjóifjörður, the farm **Heydalur** (☎ 456 4824; www.heydalur.is; sites Ikr3500, sb/s/d Jun–Aug Ikr3500/5500/8000, Sep–May Ikr3000/4000/6500) offers cosy accommodation in a renovated barn and cow shed. It's a peaceful and secluded spot and a great place to go horse riding (Ikr2000 per hour) or kayaking (Ikr2000/6000 per hour/day). In winter you can go snowmobiling, cross-country skiing and ice fishing.

Heading east you'll come to the second of the fjords, Vatnsfjörður, where you'll find the ruins of turf farmhouses and fish-drying racks dating from the 9th century.

Further on, at the end of tiny Reykjarfjörður is the friendly but well-weathered **Hótel Reykjanes** (☎ 456 4844; www.rnes.is; sites Ikr1500, sb/s/d Jun–mid-Sep 2200/3800/6500, mid-Sep–May Ikr1500/2000/4000; 🖳), housed in the huge, white former district school. The rooms are compact and functional, but there's a 50m outdoor geothermal pool, a sauna, a decent restaurant (dinner buffet Ikr2800) and free wi-fi access. Campers have free access to all facilities.

Snæfjallaströnd

On the eastern shore of Ísafjarðardjúp the unsurfaced Rte 635 leads north to **Kaldalón**, a beautiful green valley running up to the receding Drangajökull icecap. It's an easy walk up to the snow line, but watch out for dangerous crevasses if you venture out onto the ice. Further north, **Snæfjallaströnd** was abandoned

in 1995, but adventurous hikers can walk from the church at Unaðsdalur along the coast to the bunkhouse at Grunnavík, from where you can catch boats to Ísafjörður and Hesteyri.

Just before the church at Unaðsdalur, **Félagsheimilið Dalbær** (☎ 456 2660; inkjar@eldhorn .is; sites per person Ikr600, sb/s/d 1800/4000/7500; 🅨 mid-Jun–mid-Aug) is a good place to get a last meal and warm night's sleep before you head off into the wilderness. It also has displays on trekking in Jökulfirðir and the local fairies, trolls and ghosts, and offers boat trips to the glacier (Ikr4700 including refreshments).

STRANDIR COAST

Sparsely populated, magnificently peaceful and all but deserted by other travellers, the eastern coast of the Westfjords is one of the most dramatic and mountainous parts of the region. Indented by a series of broad fjords and lined with a series of rugged mountains, the drive north of Hólmavík, the region's only sizeable settlement, is rough, wild and incredibly rewarding. South of here gently rolling hills stretch along the isolated coastline as far as Brú, where the sudden rush of traffic tells you that you've returned to Rte 1 and the travelling masses.

There are buses along the coast as far as Hólmavík and Drangsnes, but you'll need your own vehicle and a sense of adventure to get further.

BRÚ TO HÓLMAVÍK

The long drive north from Brú to Hólmavík is pleasantly pastoral, with rolling hills dotted with small farmhouses and churches, but fairly pedestrian if you've just come south from the dramatic fjords further north or west. There's little to stop you along this stretch but if you want to stay overnight there's accommodation at the head of Bitrufjörður at **Snartartunga** (☎ 451 3362, 853 3062; snartartunga@bigfoot.com; sb/s/d Ikr2000/4200/7200; 🅨 Jun–mid-Dec), a horse farm with pleasant guest rooms. Evening meals (Ikr1500) and horse riding (Ikr2000 per hour) are also available.

HÓLMAVÍK
pop 370

The fishing village and service centre of Hólmavík offers sweeping views over the still waters of Steingrímsfjörður and has a bizarre witchcraft museum. The town is a good place to stock up on supplies, and it has a large supermarket, a bank, a post office and a petrol station.

Information
The **tourist office** (☎ 451 3111; www.holmavik.is/info; ⌚ 9am-8pm mid-Jun–mid-Aug) is inside the modern community centre near the Esso petrol station. You can access the internet here (Ikr200 for 20 minutes) and pick up a copy of the hiking brochure *Gönguleiðir í Strandasýslu* (Ikr300), which has maps of local hikes.

Sights & Activities
Hólmavík's main tourist attraction is the popular **Exhibition of Witchcraft & Sorcery** (☎ 451 3525; www.vestfirdir.is/galdrasyning; admission Ikr500; ⌚ 10am-6pm Jun–mid-Sep), by the harbour. The museum tells the macabre but fascinating story of 17 men and women who were burnt at the stake for witchcraft in the Westfjords during the 17th century. Most of the occult practices they were accused of were simply old Viking traditions, though the necropants (see right) and *grimoires* (magic books) on display were proof enough for the local witch-hunters. In summer there's a daily bus (Ikr900, 30 minutes) to the 'sorcerer's cottage' in Bjarnarfjörður, a turf-roofed cottage said to have been home to one of the witches. The bus departs at 1.30pm and returns at 3pm.

The hills surrounding Hólmavík are good for **hiking** and the easy short walk north along the coast to the farm at Ós is a good start. From the farm the trail cuts back to town along the Stakkar ridge further inland. Another easy walk is the 4km circuit of Þiðriksvallavatn lake from the Þverárvirkjun hydroelectric plant, 2km south of Hólmavík.

If you're heading northwest it's worth stopping off at the wooden church at **Staður**, 14km from Hólmavík, to see the 18th-century pulpit there.

Sleeping & Eating
Camp site (☎ 451 3111; sites per person Ikr600) The municipal camp site, beside the community centre, has toilets, showers and a laundry.

Gistiheimilið Borgarbraut (☎ 451 3136; fax 451 3413; Borgarbraut 4; sb/made-up bed Ikr2000/2800) Set on the hill near the church, this welcoming guesthouse has old-style but well-kept rooms with great views. There's also a guest kitchen and a TV lounge.

> ### THE WRONG TROUSERS?
> One particularly gruesome display at the Hólmavík witchcraft museum is a copy of the legendary necropants – trousers made from the skin of the legs and groin of a dead man. It was believed that the necropants would spontaneously produce money when worn, as long as the donor corpse had been stolen from a graveyard at the dead of night and a magic rune and a coin stolen from a poor widow were placed in the dead man's scrotum!

Ferðaþjónstan Kópnesbraut (☎ 451 3117; solgull@islandia.is; Kópnesbraut 17; sb/s/d Ikr2200/3500/6500) Another pleasant place with just three rooms, this is a slight step up, with in-room TVs and shared kitchen and bathroom.

Kirkjubol (☎ 451 3474; www.strandir.is/kirkjubol; sb/s/d Ikr2200/3500/6000) About 8km south of Hólmavík, right by the seashore, is this big and comfortable farmhouse with cosy rooms and a warm welcome. The owners can help arrange local activities.

our pick **Café Riis** (☎ 451 3567; www.cáfériis.is; Hafnarbraut 39; mains Ikr950-2200; ⌚ 11.30am-11pm, to 3am Fri & Sat) The town pub and restaurant is an atmospheric place with stripped floors and carved magic symbols on the walls. Set in a historic wooden building that dates from 1897, this is a fine place to chill out with a beer. The menu ranges from burgers and pizzas to steak and gourmet fish dishes.

As always, cheap fast food is available at the petrol station.

Getting There & Away
From June to August buses run between Brú and Hólmavík (Ikr2600, two hours) on Tuesday, Friday and Sunday only. The same service continues from Hólmavík on to Drangsnes (Ikr800, 30 minutes) on Friday. Buses from Hólmavík to Ísafjörður (Ikr4000, four hours) are timed to connect with the service from Brú. You can connect to services to Reykjavík and Akureyri from Brú. During winter there is one bus a week (on Friday) from Reykjavík to Hólmavík via Brú (Ikr5600).

DRANGSNES
Across the fjord from Hólmavík, Drangsnes is a remote little village with views across to north Iceland and the small uninhabited

island of **Grímsey**, which is a fine place for bird-watching. The emerald-green island of Drangsnes is home to a large puffin colony, and the rocky stack **Kerling**, by the shore, is supposedly the remains of a petrified troll (see the boxed text, below). From Drangsnes several walking trails lead up to scenic lakes on the Bjarnarfjarðarháls ridge.

Drangsnes has a free **camp site** (☎ 451 3238), with a toilet block and showers, on the shore. You'll find more formal accommodation at the pleasant **Gistiþjónusta Sunnu** (☎ 451 3230; holtag10@snerpa.is; Holtagötu 10; d Ikr8000), which has a well-equipped studio apartment.

Getting There & Away

The Friday bus from Brú to Hólmavík continues on to Drangsnes (Ikr800, 30 minutes) at 1.15pm, returning at 4.15pm. No buses run north of Drangsnes, so you'll need a vehicle to reach Laugarhóll or anywhere further north.

Local fisherman **Ásbjörn Magnússon** (☎ 451 3238; sundhani@simnet.is; Kvíbala 1) runs boat trips to Grímsey at 2pm on Tuesday and Sunday and offers boat transfers up to the eastern coast of Hornstrandir – call for the current rates.

DRANGSNES TO REYKJARFJÖRÐUR

North of Drangsnes, a rough road winds around a series of gorgeous crumbling escarpments and dramatic fjords. There's no public transport and there are few services on this route, but if you've got your own vehicle the utter tranquillity, incredible views and sheer sense of isolation are truly remarkable.

The first indent along the coast is **Bjarnarfjörður**, where you'll find the **Hótel Laugarhóll** (☎ 451 3380; www.strandir.is/laugarholl; sb/s/d without bathroom Ikr2500/5300/7000, with bathroom Ikr3000/7500/10,000; 🖾), a large, modern building with spacious rooms and a lovely geothermal pool and hot tub. There's a restaurant (mains Ikr1500 to

Ikr2500) serving Icelandic staples, a small shop, and good hiking, fishing and sea angling in the surrounding area.

Near the hotel is an ancient artificial pool that was consecrated in the 16th century and is now a national monument, together with the Sorcerer's Cottage, which is part of the sorcery and witchcraft exhibition in Hólmavík. In summer there's a daily bus (Ikr900, 30 minutes) from the museum to the cottage; see opposite. Behind the hotel a marked trail leads up to the 451m peak Hólsfjall, from where you'll get good views of the surrounding area.

North of Bjarnarfjörður the scenery becomes more rugged and there are fine views across to the Skagi peninsula in north Iceland. This road often closes with the first snows in autumn and may not reopen until spring. If you're travelling late in the season ask locally for up-to-date information on conditions.

At **Kaldbaksvík** the steep sides of a broad fjord sweep down to a small fishing lake that serenely reflects the surrounding mountains. Just beyond the lake, a 4km trail runs up to the summit of craggy Lambatindur (854m). You'll notice copious amounts of driftwood piled up along the shore on this coast – most of it has arrived across the Arctic Ocean from Siberia.

REYKJARFJÖRÐUR

Tucked in beneath a looming rock wall at Reykjarfjörður, is the strangely endearing village of **Djúpavík**. Once a thriving centre for herring processing, the village was all but abandoned when the plant closed in 1950. Today it is half ghost town, half pioneering outpost. The looming bulk of the deserted factory dominates the village, but for those travellers who make it here it's one of the most memorable locations of their trip.

To the east towering cliffs plunge into the sea and behind the small cluster of houses a

THE WESTFJORDS

THE GRÍMSEY TROLLS

According to legend the island of Grímsey was created by evil trolls, now petrified into the stone stacks at Drangsnes. Intent on severing the Westfjords from the mainland, the trolls decided to dig a trench right across the peninsula one night. Unfortunately, they were so wrapped up in the job that they failed to notice the sun rising. As the first rays broke over the horizon, the two trolls working at the western end of the trench were transformed into standing stones at Kollafjörður. The female troll at the eastern end nearly escaped, but as she was turning to flee she realised that she had marooned her cow on the newly created island of Grímsey. She was turned to stone forever gazing towards her lost cow. A rock in the shape of a cow can still be seen down by the water line at Grímsey's northern end.

spectacular glittering **waterfall** tumbles over the sheer rock face. You can walk to the foot of the falls in about 30 minutes for stunning views of the fjord. The trail begins by the stream, behind the ruins of the old fishing station. Longer walks are possible at the head of the fjord, along the Reykjarfjörðardalur valley.

our pick **Hótel Djúpavík** (☎ 451 4037; www.djupavik .com; sb/s/d Ikr2000/5300/6700) This charming bolt hole set in the former factory accommodation block is the only place to stay. The small, simple rooms have brightly coloured blankets and rugs and a nostalgic air of times past. Bathrooms are shared, but there's a good restaurant (mains Ikr2000 to Ikr3500) serving tasty home-cooked food, and it's possible to go kayaking and sea angling, rent boats or take guided tours of the former factory. In winter the hotel makes an ideal base for cross-country skiers looking for a unique destination.

NORÐURFJÖRÐUR & AROUND

Heading north from Djúpavík, a scenic hiking trail runs up over the Reykjanes peninsula from Naustavík, on the northern side of Reykjarfjörður, to Árnes, where lush farmland is set against a backdrop of craggy peaks. There are two interesting wood churches at Árnes and the small museum, **Kört** (☎ 451 4025; arnes@bakkar .is; admission Ikr300; ☙ 11am-6pm), which has displays on fishing and farming, local sculpture, and a collection of traditional dolls. Just east of here, at the tip of the peninsula just beyond the airstrip at Gjögur, a 2km trail leads from a small radar station to the towering sea cliffs at **Reykjaneshyrna**.

Clinging onto life at the end of the long bumpy road up the Strandir coast is the little fishing village of Norðurfjörður. Norðurfjörður has a shop, a petrol station and a few guesthouses, and it's the last place to stock up and indulge in some home comforts before heading off to Hornstrandir. About 2km beyond Norðurfjörður, at Krossnes, there's an open-air **geothermal swimming pool** (☎ 451 4048; adult/under 14 Ikr250/100) on a wild black-pebble beach with some dramatic sea stacks.

Sleeping & Eating

Valgeirsstadir (☎ 568 2533; www.fi.is; sites per person Ikr800, sb members/nonmembers Ikr1400/2000; ☙ May-Sep) Set in a large green building at N 66°03.080', W 21°33.970', this Ferðafélag Íslands hut has accommodation for 20 in rooms sleeping up to four people. There's a fully equipped kitchen, a hot shower and a cosy atmosphere.

Gistiheimili Bergistanga (☎ 451 4003; gunnsteinn@ simnet.is; sb Ikr2000) On the hill overlooking the harbour, this friendly guesthouse has good sleeping-bag accommodation in comfortable rooms, and a guest kitchen.

Ófeigsfjörður (☎ 554 4341) Heading north along the coastal walking trail towards Hornstrandir, this free basic camp site has toilets but no kitchen facilities or showers.

Getting There & Away

No buses run to Norðurfjörður, but **Íslandsflug** (☎ 570 8090) flies twice a week between Reykjavík and the airstrip at Gjögur, 16km southeast of Norðurfjörður. Fares start at Ikr5950 one way and the trip takes 50 minutes.

Sædís (☎ 852 9367; www.freydis.is) runs scheduled trips from Norðurfjörður to Hornvík (Ikr6500) on Monday and Friday, and between Norðurfjörður and Reykjarfjörður (Ikr5000) on Wednesday between July and mid-August. Trips to other points in Hornstrandir can be arranged on request.

HORNSTRANDIR

Craggy mountains, precarious sea cliffs and plunging waterfalls ring the wonderful uninhabited Hornstrandir peninsula at the northern end of the Westfjords. This is one of Europe's last true wilderness areas and covers some of the most extreme and inhospitable parts of the country. It's a fantastic destination for wilderness hiking, with challenging terrain and excellent opportunities for spotting arctic foxes, seals, whales and teeming bird life.

A handful of hardy farmers lived in Hornstrandir until the 1950s, but since 1975 the 580 sq km of tundra, fjord, glacier and alpine upland have been protected as a national monument and nature reserve. The area has some of the strictest preservation rules in Iceland, thanks to its incredibly rich, but fragile, vegetation.

There are no services available in Hornstrandir and hikers must be fully prepared to tackle all eventualities. The passes here are steep and you'll need to carry all your gear, so hiking can be slower than you might expect. In addition, most trails are unmarked, so it's essential to carry a good map and compass and have previous navigation experience. Rivers

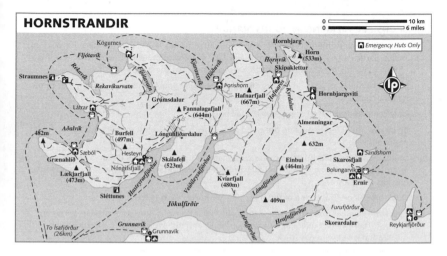

have to be forded on some trails, and others are passable at low tide only, so it's a good idea to plan ahead and seek local advice before setting out.

The best time to visit is between late June and mid-August, with the bulk of visitors arriving during the last two weeks of July. Outside these times there are few people around and the weather is very unpredictable. If travelling in the off season it is essential to plan ahead and get local advice, as vast snow drifts with near-vertical faces can develop on the mountain passes. There are emergency huts with radios and heaters at various points in the park for use in case of sudden blizzards or storms.

TREKKING AT HORNSTRANDIR

The most popular starting points for hikes are Hesteyri and Hornvík. Many of the peninsula's easiest walks are around Hesteyri, where marked trails make the going quicker and safer. From the abandoned whaling station at Hesteyri you can hike north over the ridge to the coastal village of Sæból in Aðalvík in about six hours. From here it's an easy three hours or so to the clifftop lighthouse at Straumnes. Heading east along the lagoon at Rekavík, you can follow the headland north to the pretty lake Fljótavatn (three to four hours), from where the Lönguhlíðardalur and Grúmsdalur valleys head south back to Hesteyri (seven hours). A complete circuit starting either from Hesteyri or Sæból should take about three days.

For something less challenging, hike from Hesteyri to Látrar in about four hours, or loop back on a different trail in six to seven hours. A good option for experienced hikers is the two-day hike from Hesteyri to Hornvík. From Hornvík you can take a day hike to the towering bird cliffs at Hornbjarg. Most hikers stay in the Hornvík area for two to three days exploring trails around the headland.

Over on the eastern coast, boats can drop you near the mountain huts at Reykjarfjörður or Bolungarvík, or the hot spring and abandoned church at Furufjörður, the start of the trail to Hrafnsfjörður. You can make the crossing in a day and be picked up by the Ísafjörður boat on the far side.

Outside the reserve but similarly remote is the mountainous spur at Grunnavík, bounded by the fjords Ísafjarðardjúp and Jökulfirðir. Boats run from Ísafjörður to the mountain hut here, and you can hike to dramatic sea cliffs along Snæfjallaströnd or walk up to the glacier Drangajökull along the Kaladalón valley. The best time to cross Drangajökull is in April, but hikers should be aware that it is a moving glacier with lots of craters. These can be particularly dangerous later in the summer. It is safest to join the glacier from a mountain and leave from a mountain, not from the valleys.

Hikers should bring a copy of the Landmælingar Íslands topographic sheet *Hornstrandir* 1:100,000 and tide tables for the area. Both are available at the tourist office in Ísafjörður. The tourist office in Ísafjörður can also recommend local guides.

THE WESTFJORDS

RESPONSIBLE TREKKING IN HORNSTRANDIR

The rules for responsible travel apply anywhere you're hiking in Iceland, but because of Hornstrandir's particularly sensitive ecosystem and lack of infrastructure you need to be especially careful here. Follow these simple rules to keep you safe and the park protected.

■ Leave everything as you find it. Take all rubbish out with you. Do not bury it, burn it or throw it in the toilets.

■ Only camp in designated camp sites if at all possible.

■ If you need to defecate outside the camp sites, carry a shovel, bury your waste and take toilet paper out with you.

■ Do not light fires. Fires on grass can leave a mark for up to 10 years. A fire on a beach is an international emergency signal and may prompt an unnecessary and costly search and rescue mission. Bring a stove.

■ Don't hike alone. This is one of the most difficult hiking areas in Iceland.

■ Check the weather forecast before setting out. Do not travel if north or northeast winds are forecast. These almost guarantee heavy rain, snow and fog. Visibility can be reduced very quickly and it's easy to get stuck.

TOURS

It's easy enough to organise your own transport and accommodation at Hornstrandir and then hike independently, but you need to be well prepared as the terrain is rough and the going difficult. For inexperienced hikers a tour can be a much better and safer bet.

Vesturferðir (☎ 456 5111; www.vesturferdir.is) runs a variety of organised trips from Ísafjörður, including day trips (see p179), three-day hiking and boating trips along the old postal route from Sandeyri to Grunnavík and then Hesteyri, and five-day hiking trips to Reykjarfjörður and Bolungarvík.

The Icelandic trekking organisation **Ferðafélag Íslands** (☎ 568 2533; www.fi.is; Mörkin 6, IS-108 Reykjavík) also offers a variety of guided Hornstrandir hikes several times each summer.

SLEEPING

There are various accommodation options along the coast, accessible on foot or by boat from Ísafjörður or Drangsnes. Camping in the park camp sites is free, but camping at private camp sites costs between Ikr800 and Ikr1200. Expect to pay Ikr1500 to Ikr3000 for sleeping-bag space. All the following open in summer only and have guest kitchens.

On the east coast, camping and sleeping-bag accommodation is available at **Reykjarfjörður** (☎ 456 7215, 853 1615; reykjarfjordur@simnet.is) and **Bolungarvík** (☎ 456 7192, 852 8267). You can also stay at the lighthouse at **Hornbjargsviti** (☎ 566 6762; www.ovissuferdir.net; sites Ikr800, sb Ikr2200).

On the west coast, camping and sleeping-bag accommodation is provided at **Hesteyri** (☎ 456 7183, 853 6953; sb Ikr1500) and **Grunnavík** (☎ 852 4819; www.grunnavik.is; sites Ikr1200, sb Ikr3000; ☺ mid-Jun–mid-Aug).

GETTING THERE & AWAY

Getting to Hornstrandir requires a boat trip from Ísafjörður, from where there are regular services, or from Drangsnes or Norðurfjörður, from where boats run on request.

If you'd rather make the journey on foot, you can fly from Reykjavík to Gjögur (see p194) and walk in from there. Another possible access route for trekkers is to take the Ísafjörður bus as far as the junction of Rtes 61 and 635 and then walk north along Rte 635 to the guesthouse at Dalbær (41km). From here, you can head up the Snæfjallaströnd coast to Grunnavík.

Scheduled boat services run from Ísafjörður from June to August providing there is a minimum of four passengers. Tickets can be booked directly with the boat companies or through the tour company **Vesturferðir** (☎ 456 5111; www.vesturferdir.is).

Sjóferðir (☎ 456 3879; www.sjoferdir.is) sails from Ísafjörður to Hesteyri (Ikr3800) five times a week, with two of these services continuing to Veiðileysufjörður. There are two sailings weekly to Grunnavík (Ikr3000), which continue on to Hrafnsfjörður, and two trips weekly to Hornvík (Ikr6500) and on to Sæból (Ikr4500).

Ferðaþjónustan Grunnavík (☎ 456 4664; www
.grunnavik.is) runs scheduled boat trips from
Bolungarvík (near Ísafjörður) to Grunnavík
(Ikr3000), Hesteyri (Ikr3500) and Hrafnsfjörður (Ikr4200) on Friday and Sunday from
mid-June to mid-August.

On the east coast you can charter a boat
from Drangsnes or Norðurfjörður for trips
to Reykjarfjörður, Hornvík, Bolungarvík
and a number of uninhabited coves. For details, contact **Ásbjörn Magnússon** (☎ 451 3238) in
Drangsnes or **Sædís** (☎ 852 9367; www.freydis.is) in
Norðurfjörður.

WARNING

Before disembarking on Hornstrandir, let
the boat operator know where and when
you want to be picked up. If your schedule
changes while you are walking, pass a message back to the mainland through one of
the guesthouses or through another hiker
to let them know that you won't be there
to meet the boat; otherwise, a costly and
unnecessary search-and-rescue operation
might be launched.

Northwest Iceland

Three rugged peninsulas jut out into the Arctic Ocean between the Westfjords and Eyjafjörður to make up the little-visited region of northwest Iceland. Most travellers speed along the Ring Rd to Akureyri, Iceland's second-largest city, a bustling but relaxed place with friendly locals and plenty of green spaces. Although it's an excellent base for the area, if you make a headlong rush to circumnavigate the country you'll miss out on some fantastic scenery, historic remains and rugged offshore islands.

Much of northwest Iceland has an end-of-the-world feel to it. Little fishing villages cling tenaciously to life at the end of unsealed roads, their poignant history a constant reminder of the fickle fortunes of life in the north. Remote, enchanting Siglufjörður was once a thriving herring centre, Hofsós was the departure point for thousands of Icelandic emigrants and the bishopric at Hólar was the medieval centre of the universe.

Wildlife-rich Vatnsnes, rugged Tröllaskagi and historic Skagafjörður boast impressive wildlife and rugged mountains that are perfect for hikers, while the lonely islands of the area are home to large colonies of sea birds and an impressive bunch of hardy locals. Northwest Iceland is one of the country's prime destinations for outdoor activities, with some of the best whitewater rafting and fishing rivers around, and plenty of opportunities for wilderness riding, glorious hiking and ice fishing, and skiing and snowmobiling in winter.

To appreciate this area you've got to get off Rte 1, wind your way through the bays, fjords and braided river deltas that stretch north, and discover the spectacular scenery and quirky little towns that give this region its character.

TOP FIVE

- Enjoy the cosmopolitan vibe, good food and happening bars in **Akureyri** (p210)
- Explore the incredible turf houses and then relax with tea and cakes at the atmospheric café in **Glaumbær** (p204)
- Trek cross country on horseback or experience the whitewater thrills of the **Jökulsá Austari** (p203)
- Step back in time at the former herring capital of the North Atlantic, spectacularly situated **Siglufjörður** (p208)
- Take a boat trip out to Skagafjörður's bird-rich islands of **Drangey** and **Málmey** (p206) or cross the Arctic Circle on **Grímsey** (p223)

Getting There & Away

AIR

Air Iceland (☎ 570 3030; www.airiceland.is) has up to seven daily flights between Reykjavík and Akureyri (from Ikr5060 one way, 45 minutes) and at least three weekly to Sauðárkrókur (Ikr5950, 50 minutes) and Grímsey (Ikr8135, 90 minutes).

BUS

From May to September two buses a day operate between Reykjavík and Akureyri (Ikr6600, 5¾ hours), via Brú (Ikr3500, 2¼ hours), Hvammstangi (Ikr4200, three hours), Blönduós (Ikr5000, four hours) and Varmahlíð (Ikr5900, 4½ hours). They depart Reykjavík at 8.30am and 5.30pm, arriving in Akureyri at 2.15pm and 11.15pm. From Akureyri, they depart at 8.30am and 5pm. There's a reduced service the rest of the year but still at least one bus daily. From mid-June to the end of August there is one daily service between Reykjavík and Akureyri along the interior's Kjölur route (Ikr8200, 10 hours) leaving at 8am in both directions.

Heading east, there are daily buses from Akureyri to Mývatn (Ikr2200, 1½ hours), Húsavík (Ikr2300, one hour) and Egilsstaðir (Ikr5400, four hours).

Getting Around

Away from the Ring Rd, getting around this area can be frustrating without your own transport. From May to August there are two daily buses between Varmahlíð and Sauðárkrókur, and from June to August there's a service every day except Saturday between Sauðárkrókur and Siglufjörður. There's also a weekday bus from Akureyri to Ólafsfjörður, via Dalvík.

EASTERN HÚNAFLÓI

HRÚTAFJÖRÐUR

Although sparsely populated and scattered with only a handful of tiny settlements, Húnaflói (Bear Bay – after the many Greenland bears that have come ashore there) and Hrútafjörður, the long, narrow fjord extending south from it, are rich in wildlife. The scenery of the area is far gentler than that of the Westfjords, and the low, treeless hills provide nesting sites for wild swans, ptarmigans, divers and golden plovers, while the rocky shore is favoured by seals. Add some

neatly manicured towns and a cluster of good museums, and there's plenty to keep you occupied en route to Akureyri.

Brú & Staðarskáli

No more than a busy road junction and petrol station, Brú acts as a connection point for buses between Reykjavík, Akureyri and Hólmavík. The name means 'bridge', and that fairly sums up the extent of the place.

There's no reason to stop in Brú other than to change buses, fill up with petrol or possibly for cyclists to take an overnight break. If you do want to stay, accommodation is available at **Gistihús Brú** (☎ 451 1122; s/d 2000/3500/6000), an austere-looking building with no-frills rooms and basic facilities. For more comfort, continue 5km north along the Ring Rd to **Staðarskáli** (☎ 451 1150; fax 451 1107; s/d incl breakfast Ikr7450/11,250; ⏰ Jun-Aug; 💻), where the hotel has predictable but well-equipped rooms with bathroom, TV and wi-fi. There's also a free camp site here down by the river.

Across the road there's a petrol station with a small tourist information point, an ATM and a **restaurant** (mains Ikr530-1590). Food ranges from the usual hamburgers, hot dogs and chips to meat and fish dishes and hearty curry soup.

From here you can do a two-day return hike to the Hrútafjarðarháls highlands east of Staðarskáli, where you can see Iceland's largest colony of great northern divers.

Reykir

At Reykir, an active geothermal field 12km north of Staðarskáli, you'll find the **Byggðasafu museum** (☎ 451 0040; admission Ikr500; ⏰ 10am-6pm Jun-Aug). This local folk exhibition features an array of household and agricultural implements from early Iceland, with an emphasis on the local black magic practised in early medieval times. Highlights are the well-reconstructed interior of a 19th-century homestead and the fantastic shark-fishing boat *Ófeigur*, built from driftwood in 1875 and used until 1915.

A few hundred metres from the folk museum at Reykir, the **Sæberg HI Hostel** (☎ 451 0015; saeberg@hostel.is; dm members/nonmembers Ikr1500/1900, d Ikr4600; ⏰ Jan-Nov; 💻) is a good place to break up the trip between Reykjavík and Akureyri. It's a cosy, well-equipped little hostel with a geothermally heated swimming pool and hot tubs.

NORTHWEST ICELAND

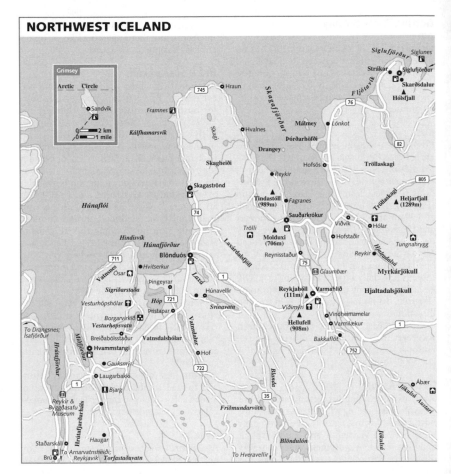

HVAMMSTANGI & AROUND
pop 590

Small, sleepy and immaculately kept, Hvammstangi is the biggest town in the region but still
a quiet place of only passing interest to travellers. A licensed trading centre since 1895, the
town survives on shrimp and mollusc fishing
today, and brightly coloured fishing boats dot
the harbour.

Hvammstangi's newest attraction is the
Icelandic Seal Centre (☎ 451 2345; www.selasetur.is;
Brekkugata 2; adult/under 14yr Ikr500/250; 🕑 9am-6pm
Jun-Aug), where you can learn about seals and
their environment, historic seal products used
in Iceland, seal conservation, and traditional
folk tales involving seals. There's also a small
tourist information point here.

If you'd like to get out and see the seals, **AKI**
(☎ 451 2394; www.aki.is) runs one- and two-hour
sightseeing tours to Hrútfjörd and Vatnsnes
(Ikr1500/3000 for one-/two-hour trips), as
well as deep-sea fishing trips (Ikr6000 for two
to three hours).

There are also some excellent opportunities for **horse riding** in the area. Eco-friendly
Gauksmýri (☎ 451 2927; www.gauksmyri.is; 1hr tours
Ikr3000), on the Ring Rd about 6km south of
Hvammstangi, offers horse hire, tuition and
longer riding holidays on demand. Accommodation (from Ikr6600/8800 for singles/
doubles) is also available here in newly renovated rooms. Rates include breakfast and drop
by about 15% in winter. Internet access is
available.

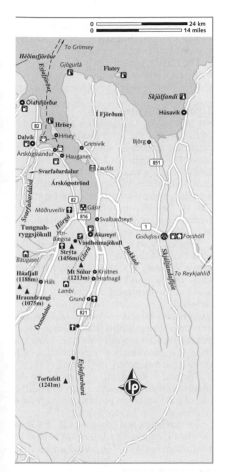

At the farm **Brekkulækur** (☎ 451 2938; www .geysir.com/brekkulaekur; d Ikr6600), 9km south of the Ring Rd, you can arrange adventurous and highly acclaimed multiday horse-riding (€1000 to €2500 for eight to 15 days) and hiking tours (€1290 to €2050 for eight to 11 days) around Arnarvatnsheiði and upper Borgarfjörður (in west Iceland). Shorter riding tours (Ikr1900 per hour) and accommodation are also available.

Sleeping & Eating

Hanna Sigga (☎ 451 2407; www.simnet.is/gistihs; Garðave-gur 26; sb/s/d Ikr3000/4650/6000) Immaculately kept and very cosy, this lovely family-run guest-house has bright, comfortable rooms, a guest kitchen and large lounge, organic breakfasts (Ikr850), and a hot tub.

Þinghús Bar & Café (☎ 451 2630; Norðurbraut 1; ❂ Fri-Sun; 🖳) This coffee shop, bar and res-taurant (mains Ikr890 to Ikr1890) does light snacks, grills and pizza as well as cakes and sandwiches throughout the day. It also offers a range of simple guest rooms (Ikr2000 for sleeping-bag space, from Ikr4400/6200 for singles/doubles). Rates include breakfast.

There's a well-stocked supermarket and Vín Búð by the harbour.

Getting There & Away

Hvammstangi is 6km off the Ring Rd. There are two daily buses from Reykjavík (Ikr4200, three hours) from May to September.

VATNSNES PENINSULA

Poking out into Húnaflói is the stubby Vatnsnes peninsula, a starkly beautiful place with a ridge of craggy hills marching down its spine, and lush, green fields along the shore. From the west coast you get wonderful views of dramatic peaks along the Strandir coast in the Westfjords, and on the east you'll find Ice-land's largest readily accessible seal colony and breeding ground at **Hindisvík**. A short walk from here, and accessible from a parking area near the road, is the bizarre 15m-high sea stack **Hvít-serkur**. Wave action has eroded the rock into a strange and whimsical formation. Legend has it that Hvítserkur was a troll caught by the sun-rise while attempting to destroy the monastery at Þingeyrar. As with all trolls caught by the sunrise, he was turned to stone.

About 10km further south is the charm-ing **Ósar Youth Hostel** (☎ 862 2778; osar@hostel.is; dm members/nonmembers Ikr1650/2000, d Ikr4500; ❂ May-Sep), one of Iceland's nicest hostels, thanks to friendly management, good views and the nearby wildlife. The hostel is on a working dairy farm, and the owner indulges his hobby of building more rooms each year. Bring your own food as there are no shops nearby.

South of the hostel is another seal colony near the partly enclosed Sigríðarstaða lagoon.

There is no public transport around the pe-ninsula, but Rte 711, a narrow gravel road that can be rough in places, weaves along the coast. If you request a pick-up in advance the hostel can arrange transport from the Viðihlíð petrol station on the Ring Rd (about Ikr2500).

ÞINGEYRAR

Originally the site of a district assembly (*þing*), and later one of Iceland's greatest literary centres, Þingeyrar is an important historic site, but as with so many in Iceland, little of its former glory remains.

Hoping to ease some of the famine and crop failure that had plagued northern Iceland in 1112, Jón Ögmundarson, the original Bishop of Hólar, vowed to build a church on the site of the Alþing. He cleared the foundations and, less than a week later, the soil regained its productivity. The bishop interpreted the miracle as a divine go-ahead for a Benedictine monastery, and by the late 12th century Þingeyrar was Iceland's greatest library, where monks wrote, compiled and copied histories and sagas.

The monastery no longer stands, but there's a wonderful stone church constructed by a Þingeyrar farmer between 1864 and 1877. The stones were dragged across Hóp on the ice. The pulpit, from the Netherlands, dates from the 17th century, and the 15th-century altarpiece was made in England and set with alabaster reliefs from the original monastery. Most impressive are the replica oak statuettes of Christ and the apostles. The originals, carved in the 16th century in Germany, stood in the church until early in the 20th century, when they were sold and later donated to the National Museum in Reykjavík.

Sitting alongside the 44-sq-km lagoon Hóp, Þingeyrar is 6km north of the Ring Rd along the unsealed dead-end Rte 721. The caretaker lives at the adjacent farm.

BLÖNDUÓS
pop 700
Although the little town of Blönduós isn't a particularly happening place, there are two interesting museums here, good food and accommodation, and a friendly welcome for tourists. It's the closest town to the northern end of the Kjölur route through the interior, and it's a great stop for hikers and cyclists.

The town is set on either side of the glacial river Blanda, and acts as a service centre for the local area and for limited shrimp- and shellfishing. It's a popular spot with visiting anglers in summer, as the nearby river Laxá offers some of Iceland's best salmon fishing. It's a game for the rich and famous, however, as a one-day licence costs from Ikr20,000 to a staggering Ikr250,000. If you'd like to fish but just can't pay those prices, smaller nearby lakes and rivers can be fished for about Ikr1500 per day.

For more information on fishing, visit the **tourist office** (☎ 452 4520; ferdamal@simnet.is; ☙ 9am-

6pm Jun & Aug, to 9pm Jul; ⌨), just off the main road east of the river. Internet access is available here for Ikr100 for 15 minutes.

The Blanda is an extremely dangerous river with fast currents and undertows. Keep all children and pets well away from the banks.

Sights & Activities
Set in a modern building on the east bank of the Blanda, the small **Textiles Museum** (Heimilisiðnaðarsafnið; ☎ 452 4067; www.simnet.is/textile; Árbraut 29; adult/under 16yr Ikr500/free; ☙ 10am-5pm Jun-Aug) displays local textiles, handicrafts and early Icelandic costumes, and hosts changing exhibitions on modern Icelandic textile artists. Part of the museum is devoted to Halldóra Bjarnadóttir, a teacher, craftswoman and advocate of women's rights.

Housed in an ancient warehouse on the west bank of the river, the **Sea Ice Exhibition Centre** (Hafíssetrið; ☎ 455 4710; www.blonduos.is/hafis; adult/under 16yr Ikr400/free; ☙ 10am-5pm late Jun-Aug) looks at the formation and types of sea ice, weather patterns, early Icelandic settlers, and ice in nearby east Greenland. One display also examines the possibility of an ice-free North Pole being used as a shipping lane. Although most of the information is in Icelandic, each display has a summary in English.

The islet of **Hrútey**, just upstream from the Blanda Bridge, is a nature reserve and the site of a reforestation project. Access is via a footbridge near the camp site.

The **swimming pool** (admission Ikr250; ☙ 8.30am-9pm Mon-Fri, 10am-5pm Sat & Sun) is just below the prominent but ugly Blönduós church.

Sleeping & Eating
Camp site (☎ 452 4520; sites per person Ikr500) Occupying a lovely setting near the river, this camp site has good washing and toilet facilities.

Glaðheimar (☎ 452 4403; www.gladheimar.is; Blöndubyggð 10; s/d Ikr6000/7500) Set in the former post-office building, this comfy guesthouse has nine simple but tasteful rooms sharing three bathrooms and two kitchens. The owners also operate a series of cabins by the camp site sleeping two to eight people (Ikr10,500 to Ikr16,000 per night). The larger cabins even have a hot tub and sauna.

Hótel Blönduós (☎ 452 4403; www.gladheimar.is; Aðalgata 6; s/d Ikr14,500/17,000; ⌨) Run by the same people as the guesthouse and summerhouses, this is the top spot in town, and is popular with visiting anglers so it's often full on summer weekends. The restaurant (mains Ikr2250 to Ikr3650, open noon to 2pm and 6pm to 10pm) has good local fish and lamb dishes, a plush dining room and a bar that's the local hang-out on weekends.

Við Árbakkann (☎ 452 4678; Húnabraut 2; mains Ikr1280-3200) This fine country-style café east of the river serves wholesome coffee, waffles, cakes, baguettes, bagels and salads as well as meat and fish specialities. Not a burger in sight! There's also a bar and a summer terrace.

Getting There & Away
Buses travelling from Reykjavík (Ikr5000, four hours) and from Akureyri (Ikr3200, two hours) stop off in Blönduós.

SKAGAFJÖRÐUR

Renowned for its horse breeding and its wild, desolate landscape, the remote Skagi penin-sula and the uninhabited islands of Dran-gey and Málmey are a little-visited region of Iceland's northwest. Hit by recession, rough weather and lonely winters, the area is littered with abandoned farms and chilling reminders of how difficult life in isolated rural Iceland can be. For visitors, however, the bleak land-scape, historic remains, abundant bird life and adrenaline-infused activities make it a rewarding destination. For more information, see www.skagafjordur.com.

SKAGASTRÖND
pop 550
One of northern Iceland's oldest trading centres, Skagaströnd was first established in the 16th century, but today its main claim to fame is as the country-music capital of Iceland. Yes, you read it right. The main rea-son to venture the 20km north of the Ring Rd is to pop into **Kántrýbær** (☎ 453 2829; www .kantry.is; Holanesvegur; ⏰ Jun-Sep), Iceland's only country-music bar. With its rustic Wild West saloon atmosphere, booth seating, checked tablecloths and constant twang of country music, this place is a unique Icelandic expe-rience. The menu (mains Ikr650 to Ikr1790) is mostly hamburgers, pizzas, nachos and pies, but the bar stays open until 3am on Fri-day and Saturday nights and it's the liveliest spot around. Upstairs is a small museum of country-music memorabilia and a working radio station.

> ### ICELANDIC COWBOY
> Hallbjön Hjartason, the 'Icelandic Cowboy', fell in love with country-and-western music while working on the American base at Keflavík in the 1960s. Even after moving back to the remote fishing community at Skagaströnd, he continued to indulge his passion for playing and recording country music. He released his first record in 1975 and organised Iceland's first country-music festival in Skagaströnd in 1984. The four-day event was held annually until 2002 and attracted fans from all over Iceland.

Apart from the bar there's a busy fish-processing plant here, a bank, a post office and a supermarket.

VARMAHLÍÐ
pop 130
Southeast of Skagaströnd, this bustling service centre with petrol station, bank, supermarket and pool is more than a road junction and yet not quite a town. Named after nearby geo-thermal sites, it's a busy place and a great base for rafting, hiking, horse riding or boating. A good short hike (about one hour) climbs to the summit of 111m **Reykjahóll**, which af-fords a broad view over the surrounding green countryside.

The **Varmahlíð tourist office** (☎ 455 6161; www .northwest.is, www.visitskagafjordur.is; ⏰ 9am-9pm Jun–mid-Aug, to 6pm mid-Aug–Sep, 10am-3pm Mon-Fri, 2-4pm Sat & Sun Oct-May; 🖥) is in the little turf-roofed cottage beside the Esso petrol station. It's a helpful place with free internet access.

Activities
WHITEWATER RAFTING
Between May and September the area around Varmahlíð offers the best whitewater rafting in northern Iceland. **Activity Tours** (☎ 453 8383; www.rafting.is) specialises in rafting trips on three local rivers. Day trips include a four- to five-hour trip on the Jökulsá Vestari (Ikr5500), with grade II to III rapids; an easy three- to four-hour paddle on the Blanda (adult/child under 14 Ikr5000/3000) with grade I to II rapids; and an exciting six- to seven-hour trip on the Jökulsá Austari (Ikr8500), where you can tackle grade III to IV+ rapids. The ultimate rafting adventure is the three-day 'River Rush' (Ikr39,000), which starts in the

interior's Sprengisandur desert and follows the Jökulsá Austari back to the coast.

South along Rte 752, in Tungusveit, the farm **Bakkaflöt** (☎ 453 8245; www.bakkaflot.com) also offers rafting on the Jökulsá Vestari and the Jökulsá Austari (Ikr4400 to Ikr7400 per person). The centre also offers comfy accommodation (Ikr2500 for sleeping-bag room, Ikr4800/7000 for singles/doubles).

HORSE RIDING

One of Iceland's most respected riding outfits, **Hestasport** (☎ 453 8383; www.riding.is), offers one-hour horse rides for Ikr2300 and full-day rides for Ikr8300. Longer trips are also available, including a nine-day journey (€1750) across the Kjölur route, a 10-day desert trip from Sprengisandur to Mývatn (€2085), and the seven-day *réttir* (round-up, €1340) in September.

The farm **Lýtingsstaðir** (☎ 453 8064; www.lythorse.com), 20km south of Varmahlíð on Rte 752, offers a similar program of tours, including one-/two-hour rides (Ikr2000/3000) and a 'stop and ride' package that includes accommodation, breakfast, dinner and a two-hour ride for Ikr7300. Longer tours are also available.

Regular horse shows are also hosted by these and other operators and include demonstrations on the five gaits of the Icelandic horse, and history on the breed. Ask at the tourist office for an up-to-date schedule of events.

Sleeping & Eating

Camp site (☎ 453 8230; sites per person Ikr500) Varmahlíð has two camp sites, one on the southern side of the Ring Rd opposite the service station and a more secluded site in the forest near the swimming pool.

Adventure Cottages (☎ 453 8383; www.rafting.is; 2-person cottages Jun-Sep Ikr15,000, Oct-May Ikr8000) Perched on the hill above Varmahlíð (follow the gravel road past Hótel Varmahlíð), this group of self-contained timber cottages has good views, comfy rooms and a very inviting stone hot pool.

Hótel Varmahlíð (☎ 453 8170; www.hotelvarmahlid.is; s/d Jun-Aug Ikr14,200/17,300, Sep-May Ikr7700/9300) This big, white hotel dominates the community and has spacious but somewhat dated rooms. Its restaurant (mains Ikr1800 to Ikr3000) is the best place for a decent meal, with good local trout and lamb dishes.

Cafeteria (mains Ikr500-1500) The busy cafeteria inside the Esso petrol station in Varmahlíð

serves lamb chops, fish dishes and hamburger meals.

There's also plenty of farmhouse accommodation in the area – the tourist office has a list. A small supermarket is attached to the petrol station.

Getting There & Away

All buses from Reykjavík (Ikr5900, 4½ hours) and from Akureyri (Ikr2200, one hour) stop at the terminal between the tourist office and the supermarket. From May to August there are daily buses to Sauðárkrókur (Ikr600, 30 minutes) and from there to Siglufjörður (daily except Saturday, Ikr2200, 1¼ hours).

AROUND VARMAHLÍÐ

A lovely **turf-covered church** (admission Ikr150; ☼ 9am-6pm Jun-Aug) dating from 1834 is set on the old chieftain's residence, **Víðimýri**, about 3km southwest of Varmahlíð. The church is still in use and houses an altarpiece that dates from 1616. Look out for a signpost just off the Ring Rd.

Glaumbær

The 18th-century **turf farm** at Glaumbær, 8km north of Varmahlíð on Rte 75, is the best museum of its type in northern Iceland and well worth the short diversion. The fascinating collection of turf houses here are some of the finest remaining examples of early Icelandic buildings you'll see.

Stuffed full of period furniture, equipment and utensils, the 18th-and 19th- century buildings are now a beautifully restored **folk museum** (☎ 453 6173; adult/under 16yr Ikr500/free, combined ticket with Minjahúsið in Sauðárkrókur Ikr600/free; ☼ 9am-6pm Jun-late Sep), that gives a real insight into the cramped living conditions of that time. Twelve buildings here are strung out along a narrow passageway, as was traditional at the time. Each room had a specific function and today is shown with the household furniture, textiles, costumes, instruments, tools and equipment of the day. The only drawback is that the tiny rooms can get pretty crowded with tourists.

Also on the site are two 19th-century timber houses, both examples of early wooden homes that replaced the turf dwellings. Áshús houses a small historical and craft exhibition, and the wonderful **Áskaffi** (☎ 453 8855; ☼ 9am-6pm Jun-Sep) is home to an impossibly quaint café with a roaring turf fire, old-world atmosphere and exceedingly good cakes. It's a perfect spot to while away some time sipping coffee and writing postcards.

The adjacent **church** dates from 1926 but has interesting Dutch pulpit paintings (1685) from a previous church on the site and an organ made entirely of pinewood: pipes, keys and all. Snorri Þorfinnsson, the first European born in North America (in 1003), is buried at Glaumbær, where he lived after his parents returned to their native Iceland.

Buses between Varmahlíð and Sauðárkrókur pass Glaumbær daily in summer.

SAUÐÁRKRÓKUR
pop 2600
The lovely little town of Sauðárkrókur is a fantastic base for travellers, with a gently happening vibe, a great museum, a clutch of beautifully restored houses and a wonderful selection of places to eat and sleep. It's also the jumping-off point for boat tours to Drangey and Málmey islands.

Economically, Sauðárkrókur is pretty well off, with fishing, tanning and trading keeping the community afloat and the population young and energetic. The community has all the services you'll need with a bank, a library, a laundry and a supermarket.

Sights & Activities
One of Sauðárkrókur's greatest pleasures just lies in wandering the streets of the old town around Aðalgata, where many of the houses have been restored and bear plaques showing when they were built. At the northern end of Aðalgata look out for **Villa Nova** (1903) a former hotel and merchant's residence.

The town museum, **Minjahúsið** (☎ 453 6870; Aðalgata 16b; adult/under 16yr Ikr500/free, combined ticket with Glaumbær Ikr600/free; ⏱ 1-6pm Jun-Aug), gives a great insight into life in the town in times past with a series of restored workshops illustrating the day-to-day living conditions for local blacksmiths, carpenters, saddlers and watchmakers. A second exhibition reveals the results of recent archaeological digs in the area, which have uncovered some of the oldest graveyards in the country with perfectly preserved human remains dating back to about 1000. There are no written records from that time, and the exhibition pieces together the history of the area. In 2009 this exhibition will focus on the rich musical history of the region.

The small blue-and-white building south of the church is the **Blacksmith's Workshop**

(☎ 453 5020; Suðurgata 5; admission free) and has been left just as it was when the last blacksmith downed tools in the mid-20th century. It can be opened on request.

A fine day hike will take you to the summit of 706m **Molduxi** for a broad view over Skagafjörður. The walk starts just past Fosshotel Áning. There's also a nine-hole **golf course**, on the hillside above town (follow Hlíðarstígur), and a winter **ski tow** (day pass Ikr800).

Sleeping
Camp site (☎ 453 8860) The free camp site beside the swimming pool has toilets, hot water and power.

Gistiheimilið Mikligarður (☎ 453 6880; www .skagafjordur.com/mikligardur; Kirkjutorgi 3; sb Ikr2500, s/d without bathroom Ikr4900/6200, with bathroom Ikr6200/9200) This welcoming place across from the church has comfortable, modern rooms with TV and tasteful décor. There's also a spacious guest kitchen and TV lounge.

Fosshotel Áning (☎ 453 6717; aning@fosshotel.is; s/d without bathroom Ikr7500/9900, with bathroom Ikr10,900/13,900; ⏱ Jun-Aug) The district boarding school becomes a basic but rather characterless hotel in summer. It's an option if everything else is full.

our pick **Hótel Tindastóll** (☎ 453 5002; www.hotel tindastoll.com; Lindargata 3; s/d Ikr11,900/16,300; 🖥) Tucked away in this understated town is one of Iceland's most charming boutique hotels, a historic place dating from 1884 and just dripping with character. The individually decorated rooms have a blend of period furniture and modern style, lots of luxuries such as minibar, bathrobe and slippers, and contemporary conveniences such as DVD players and internet connections. Legend has it that Marlene Dietrich stayed here in 1941, and it's every bit as seductive today. Outside is an irresistible stone hot tub, and in the basement there's a cosy bar to while away your evenings.

Eating
Sauðárkróks Bakari (☎ 455 5000; Hólavegi 16; ⏱ 7am-6pm) For luscious breakfasts, afternoon pick-me-ups and decent lunchtime sandwiches, this bakery and country-style café is the best place to go.

Kaffi Krókur (☎ 453 6299; Aðalgata 16; mains Ikr900-3500) This cosy café-pub looks simple enough, but the menu covers everything from burgers and fish (Ikr2290) and lamb dishes (Ikr2890) to fillet of foal (Ikr2790), and authentic pasta

(Ikr1490). The bar fires up on weekend nights, and there's a pleasant summer terrace.

Ólafshús (☎ 453 6454; www.olafshus.is, Aðalgata 15; mains Ikr2200-3300, pizzas Ikr950-2600) Almost across the road from Kaffi Krókur, this is a good restaurant for decent pizzas and Icelandic specialities such as fish and lamb. There's also some choice for vegetarians. The restaurant bar is open until 3am on Friday and Saturday.

The supermarket is on Skagfirðingabraut and the Vín Búð store is at Smáragrund 2.

Getting There & Away

In summer, two buses run daily between Varmahlíð and Sauðárkrókur (Ikr600), connecting with the Ring Rd buses to Reykjavík and Akureyri. They leave from the store opposite Hótel Tindastóll.

AROUND SKAGAFJÖRÐUR

TINDASTÓLL

North of Sauðárkrókur, Tindastóll (989m) is a prominent Skagafjörður landmark, extending for 18km along the coast. The mountain and its caves are believed to be inhabited by an array of sea monsters, trolls and giants, one of which kidnapped the daughter of an early bishop of Hólar.

The summit of Tindastóll affords a spectacular view across all of Skagafjörður. The easiest way to the top is along the marked trail that starts from the high ground along Rte 745 west of the mountain. At the mountain's northern end is a geothermal area, Reykir, which was mentioned in *Grettir's Saga*. Grettir supposedly swam ashore from the island of Drangey in Skagafjörður, and one of the hot springs at Reykir is named Grettislaug (Grettir's Bath).

From the farm Tunga, at the southwestern foot of Tindastóll, it's an 8km climb to the Trölli mountain hut at N 65°42.603', W 19°53.163'. The hut has 18 beds but no cooking facilities. To book, contact **Ferðafélags Skagafirðinga** (☎ 453 5718) in Sauðárkrókur or the tourist office in Varmahlíð.

DRANGEY & MÁLMEY ISLANDS

Guarding the mouth of Skagafjörður are the uninhabited islands of Drangey and Málmey, tranquil havens for nesting sea birds. Both are accessible on summer boat tours.

The tiny rocky islet of Drangey, in the middle of Skagafjörður, is a dramatic flat-topped mass of tuff with 170m sheer cliff sides rising abruptly from the water. The cliffs serve as nesting sites for around a million sea birds, and have been used throughout Iceland's history for egg collection and bird netting. *Grettir's Saga* recounts that both Grettir and his brother Illugi lived on the island for three years and were slain there.

The island's sheer cliff coast means that there is only one landing place, from where a steep path leads to the summit. Icelanders maintain that a prayer is necessary before ascending, since only part of the island was blessed by the early priests and the northeastern section remains an abode of evil.

Traditionally, roughly 30,000 eggs were collected here annually, but now the collection has dropped to around 5000. You'll see kittiwakes, puffins and guillemots circling above you over the sheer drops to the churning sea.

The gentler 2.5-sq-km Málmey is known mainly for its abundance of sea birds and rises to just over 150m. Legend has it that no couple could live here for more than 20 years or the wife would disappear. The island is home to Iceland's first lighthouse, which was built in a church on the island. Málmey has been uninhabited since 1951.

Several operators offer boat tours to the islands, including **Jón Eiríksson** (☎ 453 6503; fagri@ simnet.isl; tours Ikr4500-5200), who offers a five-hour trip departing from his farm, Fagranes, 7km north of Sauðárkrókur. Ask at the tourist office or your hotel for more information.

TRÖLLASKAGI

The spectacular rugged scenery on the Tröllaskagi peninsula is more reminiscent of the drama of the Westfjords than the gentle hills of northern Iceland. A maze of craggy mountains, gushing rivers and even a number of miniglaciers make it ideal hiking country and offer wonderful views for drivers making their way round Rte 76.

Tröllaskagi's best-known historical attraction is Hólar, medieval Iceland's northern bishopric, but a drive to the far north passes the peninsula's most rugged scenery en route to the picturesque fishing village and one-time herring capital of Iceland, Siglufjörður.

For information on the villages of Ólafs-fjörður and Dalvík, on the eastern side of Tröllaskagi, see p222 and p221.

HÓLAR Í HJALTADALUR

With its prominent red-stone church dwarfed by a looming mountain backdrop, this tiny **settlement** (www.holar.is) makes an interesting historical detour from the Ring Rd. The bishopric of Hólar was the ecumenical and educational capital of northern Iceland between 1106 and the Reformation, and it continued as a religious centre and the home of the northern bishops until 1798, when the bishop's seat was abolished.

Hólar then became a vicarage until 1861, when the vicarage was shifted west to Viðvík. In 1882 the present agricultural school was established, and in 1952 the vicarage returned to Hólar.

Sights

Completed in 1763, Hólar's red-sandstone **cathedral** (10am-6pm Jun-Aug), built from stone taken from looming Hólabyrða, is the oldest stone church in Iceland. The church was financed by donations from Lutheran congregations all over Scandinavia and is brimming with historical works of art, including a baptismal font carved from a piece of soapstone that washed in from Greenland on an ice floe. The extraordinary carved altarpiece was made in Germany around 1500 and was donated by the last Catholic bishop of Hólar, Jón Arason, in 1522. After he and his sons were executed at Skálholt for opposition to the Danish Reformation, his remains were brought to Hólar and entombed in the bell tower. The present church tower was built in 1950 as a memorial.

It contains a mosaic of the good reverend, a chapel and his tomb.

You can pick up a church leaflet from the information desk in the accommodation block.

An informative historical-trail brochure (available at the info desk) guides you round some of the other buildings at Hólar and is well worth picking up. **Nýibær** is a series of turf huts dating from the mid-19th century and inhabited until 1945. Although the rooms here are unfurnished, a leaflet gives a good insight into how the buildings would have looked when in use.

Also worth seeing is **Auðunarstofa**, a replica of the 14th-century bishop's residence. Built using traditional techniques and tools, Auðunarstofa houses the current bishop's office and study room, and has an exhibition of 13th-century chalices, vestments and books in the basement.

High on a hill behind the church is **Prestssæti**, a wonderful vantage point offering great views over the valley.

Ongoing archaeological digs in Hólar can be seen to the right of the road as you drive in. Finds from Iceland's first printing press and a 12th-century farmhouse here are on display in the main accommodation building.

Sleeping & Eating

Ferðaþjónustan Holum Hjaltadal (455 6333; www .holar.is; sb/s/d Ikr2300/4900/7400; Jun-Aug;) The college accommodation block operates as a summer hotel, with functional rooms and shared bathrooms. Alternatively, wooden cabins in the grounds sleep between two and 12 people and cost Ikr7800 to Ikr23,100 per night. There's also a small camp site (Ikr600 per person). The onsite restaurant specialises in local

---

THE BISHOP'S LAW

A domineering and strict moral advisor, the first bishop at Hólar, Jón Ögmundarson, ruled with an iron fist from 1106 to 1121. Church attendance and memorisation of sacred recitations were obligatory at his school, and the only books available to students were those the bishop himself judged to be edifying.

Public dances, love songs and all merriment were forbidden in the parish as evil distractions from moral values. He even changed the names of weekdays named after Norse gods (those still used in English) to the more mundane ones used in Icelandic today. In short, Bishop Jón's word was law in northern Iceland, and although his Icelandic constituency later nominated him for sainthood the canonisation was never recognised by Rome.

The first timber cathedral at Hólar, which replaced a small turf church, was constructed by Bishop Jón using Norwegian wood. Until 1135, when the Skálholt cathedral was completed, it was the world's largest wooden church.

foods (mains Ikr2850 to Ikr3200) and not-so-local pizza (Ikr1450), and there's a swimming pool (Ikr300/200 for adults/children under 12, open 7am to 9pm).

HOFSÓS

pop 170

The sleepy but attractive fishing village of Hofsós, on the eastern shore of Skagafjörður, has been a trading centre since the 1500s. Today its main attraction is the Icelandic Emigration Center, where families of Canadian and American emigrants seek their Icelandic roots. There's a bank, a post office and a petrol station here, and the Siglufjörður bus stops in town.

Sights

Housed in three lovely old buildings down by the harbour, **Vesturfarasafnið** (Icelandic Emigration Center; ☎ 453 7935; www.hofsos.is; admission all exhibits Ikr900; ☾ 11am-6pm Jun-Sep) explores the reasons behind Icelanders' emigration to the New World, their hopes for their new life and the reality of conditions when they arrived. It's a fascinating place even if you're not a descendant of Icelandic emigrants.

The main exhibition 'New Land, New Life' follows the lives of emigrating Icelanders in photographs, letters and displays, while 'Prairies Wide and Free' looks at Icelandic settlers in North Dakota. Two other exhibitions focus on the emigrant experience of Icelandic poet Stephan G Stephansson and the history of portrait photography in North America during the period of Icelandic emigration.

Also at the harbour is the historic, black-tarred **Pakkhúsið**, a log warehouse built in 1777 by the Danish Royal Greenland Company. It's one of the oldest timber buildings in Iceland.

South of town, on the shore almost directly opposite the village church, are some unusual hexagonal **basalt formations**, and near Grafarós, at the mouth of the Grafará River, are the remains of a 19th-century **trading post**.

The farm Gröf, 3km south of the river, has an old **turf-roofed church** surrounded by a circular turf wall. The church was built in the late 17th century but renovated and reconsecrated in 1953. If the key isn't in the door, ask at the farm.

Sleeping & Eating

The Emigration Center handles all accommodation queries.

Gistiheimilið Sunnuberg (☎ 453 7310; gisting@hofsos.is; Suðurbraut 8; s/d Ikr5500/7700) Opposite the petrol station and run by the Emigration Center, this place has rather old-fashioned rooms with the redeeming features of private bathrooms and plenty of space.

Sigtún (☎ 453 7393; mains Ikr900-2500) Next door to Gistiheimilið Sunnuberg, this restaurant serves coffee, burgers and tasty Icelandic meat and fish dishes. There's also a small but atmospheric bar.

Sólvík (☎ 453 7930; mains Ikr1000-1800; ☾ 10am-9pm Jun-Aug) Down at the small harbour among the museum buildings, this pleasant country-style café has a summer veranda where you can recharge with coffee, cakes and pancakes. The evening menu includes pasta, salt cod, marinated trout and other fish and lamb dishes.

Sleeping-bag space is also available for Ikr2000 at two simple cottages, Prestbakki and Kárastígur 9, in the village.

AROUND HOFSÓS

Lónkot

Battered by the wind and wonderfully blustery, this **gourmet pit stop** (☎ 453 7432; www.lonkot.is; sb/d per person Ikr2900/3900; ☾ Jun-Aug) is well worth the 11km drive from Hofsós. A traditional farmhouse with pleasant accommodation, Lónkot is also an innovative gourmet restaurant with a changing three/four-course evening menu (around Ikr3900/4500) featuring trout or perch, lamb and sometimes puffin. You can order just one or two courses, and light lunches, coffee and cakes are available all day.

Iceland's largest tent is pitched in the field nearest the road and is used for group functions and for a flea market on the last Sunday of June, July and August. There's also a sunken barbecue pit, a nine-hole golf course and a fishing pond stocked with trout, as well as a small viewing tower in a converted silo. The tower provides super sea views across to Málmey and the bizarre promontory Þórðarhöfði, which is tethered to the mainland by a delicate spit.

SIGLUFJÖRÐUR

pop 1340

The remote and isolated fishing village of Siglufjörður sits precariously at the foot of a steep slope overlooking the fjord of the same name. Once one of Iceland's boom towns, it's a quiet but endearing kind of place with a dramatic setting, plenty of historic buildings and a wonderful museum explaining the town's history as the former herring-fishing centre of Iceland.

In its heyday Siglufjörður was home to 10,000 workers, and fishing boats crammed into the small harbour to unload their catch for the waiting women to gut and salt. After the herring abruptly disappeared from Iceland's north coast in the late 1960s, Siglufjörður declined and has never fully recovered.

Today it's a sleepy kind of place with an enduring charm and it's a great base for hiking in the nearby mountains. Iceland's northernmost town, just 40km south of the Arctic Circle, it's reached along one of northern Iceland's most scenic coastal routes, a precarious but stunning paved road that winds around the northwest of Tröllaskagi.

There's a small but helpful **tourist office** (www .siglo.is) in the museum.

Sights & Activities
The big attraction in town is **Síldarminjasafnið** (Herring Era Museum; ☎ 467 1604; http://herring.siglo.is/en; Snorragata 15; adult/12-16yr Ikr800/400; ☼ 10am-6pm late Jun–mid-Aug, 1-5pm May-late Jun & mid-Aug–Sep), a fantastic recreation of Siglufjörður's boom days between 1903 and 1968. Set in an old Norwegian herring station, the museum brings the work and lives of the town's inhabitants vividly to life. In the first building, photographs, displays and 1930s film show the fishing and salting process, while the accommodation block is left much as it would have been when in use. Next door is a re-creation of the reducing plant, where the majority of herrings were separated into oil (a valuable commodity) and meal (used for fertiliser). The third and newest building is a re-creation of harbour life, with actual trawler boats and equipment based on life on the busy pier during the boom days.

If you're travelling in midsummer it's worth planning to visit on a Saturday when **herring-salting demonstrations** (admission Ikr1000; ☼ 3pm early Jul–mid-Aug) are held accompanied by lively concertina music and theatrical performances. The ticket price includes admission to the museum.

Thanks to its proximity to the bishopric in Hólar, music has always been of particular importance in Tröllaskagi, and Siglufjörður has a strong musical tradition. The **Icelandic Folk Music Centre** (☎ 467 2300; http://siglo.is/setur; adult/under 14yr Ikr600/free; ☼ 1-5pm 1-15 Jun & 15-31

Aug, 10am-6pm mid-Jun–mid-Aug) opened in 2006 and explores the history and development of Icelandic folk music. The collection is housed in the former home of Rev. Bjorn Thorsteinsson, who collected many of the instruments and recordings of traditional songs, nursery rhymes and chants on display.

Siglufjörður is a great base for hikers, with a series of interesting walks in the area. Seven of these routes are described in detail on the town website, www.siglo.is.

For a short hike you can walk north along the western shore of Siglufjörður to the abandoned herring factory, which was destroyed by an avalanche in 1919. Longer hikes will take you over the passes Hósarð and Hussarð to the wild, beautiful and uninhabited Héðinsfjörður, the next fjord to the east.

The most popular hike, however, is along the old road between Siglufjörður and Fljótavík. This allegedly haunted road was once the main route into town but was closed when an 800m-long tunnel was built. The route is prone to avalanches and only opens between early July and late August. It climbs up to the 630m Siglufjarðarskarð and then heads north along the ridge to Strákar, where there are wonderful views over the fjord and out to sea.

In winter a **ski lift** (day pass Ikr600) operates in Skarðsdalur above the head of the fjord. From there, it's a lovely day walk over Hólsfjall to the abandoned valley above Héðinsfjörður. In summer you can opt for a nine-hole round of golf at the Hóll sports centre.

Festivals & Events
Despite the utter demise of the herring industry, Siglufjörður remains nostalgic about the good old days and hosts a lively **herring festival** on the bank holiday weekend in early August. It's one of Iceland's most enjoyable local festivals with much singing, dancing, drinking, feasting and fish cleaning.

An annual Icelandic and foreign **folk-music festival** is staged over five days in mid-July, with workshops and several concerts every evening.

Sleeping
Camp site (☎ 460 5600; sites per person Ikr500; ☼ Jun-Aug) Right in the middle of town near the harbour and town square, the municipal camp site has a toilet block and a laundry.

Iþróttamiðstöðin Hóll (☎ 467 1817; sites per person Ikr500, sb 1500; ☼ Jun-Aug) The local sports hall offers basic beds in three- to six-person rooms, camping and a simple guest kitchen. To get there go past the harbour and museum to the end of Lanjeranegar.

Gistiheimilið Hvanneyri (☎ 467 1378; alla@simnet .is; Aðalgata 10; sb/s/d Ikr1800/4000/6000) Siglufjörður's top spot is this rather dated 1930s guesthouse, which now only has a glimmer of its former grandeur. The spacious, clean and comfortable rooms all have private bathroom but are past their best. There's a TV lounge, a huge dining room and a guest kitchen.

Eating

Aðalbakari (☎ 467 1720; Aðalgata 36; ☽ 7am-5pm) Ideal for breakfast or lunch, this bakery and café serves the usual selection of bread, cakes, pastries and filled rolls as well as the Icelandic speciality *ástar pungur* (love balls) – deep-fried spiced balls.

Bíobarinn (☎ 467 1111; Aðalgata 30; mains Ikr800-1800; ☽ 11.30am-9pm) This cinema-inspired diner is the only genuine restaurant in town and serves good-value burgers, pizza, and fish and lamb dishes. The small upstairs bar is open until 1am on Friday and Saturday nights and is a great place to go and meet the locals.

Pizza 67 (☎ 467 2323; Aðalgata; pizzas Ikr900-2000; ☽ noon-9pm Mon-Fri, 3-9pm Sat & Sun Jun & Jul, 5-9pm Aug–mid-Sep) Just down the road, this basic pizzeria is the only other dining choice in town.

There's a supermarket across from the harbour, and fishmonger Fiskbuð Siglufjörður is opposite Bíobarinn. The Vín Búð alcohol shop is on Tungata.

Getting There & Away

From June to August there is a bus service that runs every day except Saturday (with two services on Tuesday and Friday) between Varmahlíð and Siglufjörður with a change in Sauðárkrókur.

If you're heading east toward Akureyri in your own car, it's possible to take a short cut across Tröllaskagi on Rte 82 to Ólafsfjörður. From the turn-off to Varmahlíð (at the junction of Rtes 76 and 82, near Fljótavík) it's 37km along a narrow gravel road. Although it's a scenic route, it's usually closed in winter, so check beforehand. A planned tunnel through the mountain will cut the journey between Siglufjörður and Ólafsfjörður to only 15km, but it's not expected to be finished until 2008.

ÖXNADALUR

If you haven't the time to head north around Tröllaskagi, you'll pass instead along the Öxnadalur valley, a 30km-long narrow valley on the Ring Rd between Varmahlíð and Akureyri. The mountain pass is flanked by dramatic peaks and thin pinnacles of rock. The imposing 1075m spire of **Hraundrangi** and the surrounding peaks of **Háafjall** are probably the most dramatic in Iceland.

Early settlers considered the summit of Hraundrangi inaccessible and perpetuated legends of a hidden cache of gold that awaited the first climber to reach the top. It was finally climbed in 1956, but the treasure seemed to have already gone.

If you want to break the journey, **Halastjarna** (☎ 461 7997; www.halastjarna.com; Háls; 5-course set dinner Ikr5900; ☽ noon-10pm Jun-Aug), near the summit of the pass, does a great selection of organic and local dishes, including fish, lobster, seafood, lamb and sea birds, served alongside home-grown salads.

AKUREYRI

pop 16,580

Set at the head of a long fjord, Akureyri is a bustling, cosmopolitan town and Iceland's second-largest city. Although it falls a long way behind the capital in terms of population and facilities, its fine selection of museums, shops, cafés, bars and restaurants sets it apart from the sleepy, rural towns found elsewhere in Iceland.

Snowcapped peaks rise behind the town and across the city flower boxes, trees and well-tended gardens belie the city's location just a stone's throw from the Arctic Circle. With a lively summer festival season, some of Iceland's best winter skiing, and a relaxed and easy attitude, it's the natural base for exploring Eyjafjörður and further east to Mývatn.

HISTORY

The first permanent inhabitant of Eyjafjörður was Norse-Irish settler Helgi Magri (Helgi the Lean), who arrived in about 890. Although Helgi worshipped Þór and let the gods choose an auspicious site for him to settle by tossing his high-seat pillars overboard (they washed up 7km south of present-day Akureyri), he hedged his bets by naming his farm Kristnes (Christ's Peninsula).

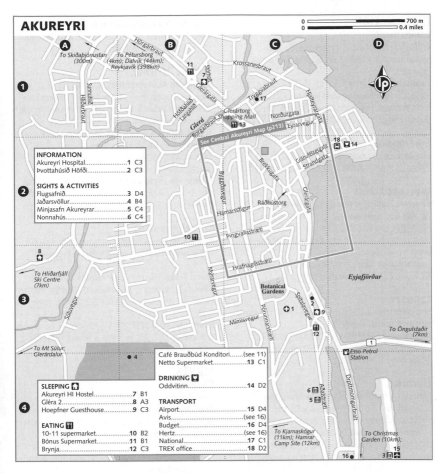

AKUREYRI

INFORMATION
Akureyri Hospital.....................1 C3
Þvottahúsið Höfði.....................2 C3

SIGHTS & ACTIVITIES
Flugsafnið.....................3 D4
Jaðarsvöllur.....................4 B4
Minjasafn Akureyrar.....................5 C4
Nonnahús.....................6 C4

SLEEPING
Akureyri HI Hostel.....................7 B1
Gléra 2.....................8 A3
Hoepfner Guesthouse.....................9 C3

EATING
10-11 supermarket.....................10 B2
Bónus Supermarket.....................11 B1
Brynja.....................12 C3

Café Brauðbúd Konditori.......(see 11)
Netto Supermarket.....................13 C1

DRINKING
Oddvitinn.....................14 D2

TRANSPORT
Airport.....................15 D4
Avis.....................(see 16)
Budget.....................16 D4
Hertz.....................(see 16)
National.....................17 C1
TREX office.....................18 D2

By 1602 a trading post had been established at present-day Akureyri. There were still no permanent dwellings, though, as all the settlers maintained rural farms and homesteads. By the late 18th century the town had accumulated a whopping 10 residents, all Danish traders, and was granted municipal status.

The town soon began to prosper and by 1900 Akureyri numbered 1370 people. The original cooperative, Gránufélagsins, had begun to decline and in 1906 it was replaced by Kaupfélagið Eyjafirdinga Akureyrar (KEA; the Akureyri Cooperative Society), whose ubiquitous insignia still graces many Akureyri businesses.

Today Akureyri is thriving. Its fishing company and shipyard are the largest in the coun-

try, and the city's university (established in 1987) gives the town a youthful exuberance.

ORIENTATION

Akureyri is small and easy to get around on foot, with a compact knot of cafés, bars, museums and shops just west of the busy commercial harbour. The town centre is concentrated around pedestrianised Hafnarstræti, with the small square Raðhústorg at its northern end. The bus station is to the south of the centre and the airport about 2km further south.

It'll take at least a day to see the museums, churches and botanical gardens in the centre of town. The bustling harbour and the oldest part of town along Hafnarstræti and Aðalstræti are also worth a visit.

INFORMATION
Bookshops
Fróði (Map p213; Kaupvangsstræti) Second-hand bookshop next to Karolína Café, full of books in several languages.

Penninn Bókval (Map p213; ☎ 461 5050; Hafnarstræti 91-93; 🕑 9am-10pm) Excellent bookshop with souvenir books in English, French and German, Icelandic titles, popular foreign-language paperbacks, DVDs, CDs and videos.

Emergency
Fire and ambulance (☎ 112, 462 2222)

Police (Map p213; ☎ 462 3222; Þórunnarstræti 138)

Internet Access
Akureyri Municipal Library & Archives (Map p213; ☎ 460 1250; Brekkugata 17; 🕑 10am-7pm Mon-Fri Jun-Aug, to 7pm Mon-Wed & Fri, to 10pm Thu, noon-5pm Sep-May; per hr Ikr200) Plenty of terminals and fast connections in a light and airy space.

Tourist Office (Map p213; ☎ 462 7733; Hafnarstræti 82; 15 min Ikr150) Three internet terminals.

Laundry
Self-service washing machines are at the camp site and youth hostel.

Þvottahúsið Höfði (Map p211; ☎ 462 2580; Hafnarstræti 34; loads up to 10kg Ikr1500; 🕑 8am-noon 3-5pm Mon-Fri) Service laundry.

Libraries
Akureyri Municipal Library & Archives (Map p213; ☎ 460 1250; www.amtsbok.is; Brekkugata 17; 🕑 10am-7pm Mon-Fri Jun-Aug, to 7pm Mon-Wed & Fri, to 10pm Thu, noon-5pm Sep-May) Has books and magazines in English (including novels) and extensive historical archives; book loan is free and available to travellers.

Medical Services
Akureyri Hospital (Map p211; ☎ 463 0100; Spítalavegur) Just south of the botanical gardens.

Heilsugæslustöðin Clinic (Map p213; ☎ 460 4600; Hafnarstræti 99) Doctors on call around the clock.

Money
All central bank branches (open 9.15am to 4pm) offer commission-free foreign exchange and have 24-hour ATMs. After hours, ask at Hótel KEA.

Íslandsbanki (Map p213; ☎ 460 7800; Skipagata 14)

KB Banki (Map p213; ☎ 444 6000; Geislagata 5)

Landsbanki Íslands (Map p213; ☎ 460 4000; Strandgata 1)

Sparisjóður Norðlendinga (Map p213; ☎ 460 2500; Skipagata 9)

Post & Communications
Main Post Office (Map p213; ☎ 460 2600; Skipagata 10; 🕑 9am-4.30pm Mon-Fri)

Tourist Offices
Ferðafélag Akureyrar (Map p213; ☎ 462 2720; www.ffa.is; Strandgata 23; 🕑 4-7pm Mon-Fri Jun-Aug) Local branch of the Icelandic Touring Association. Good for maps and hiking information.

Tourist Office (Map p213; ☎ 462 7733; www.eyjafjordur.is; www.nordurland.is; Hafnarstræti 82; 🕑 7.30am-7pm daily Jun-Aug, 7.30am-5pm Mon-Fri, 8am-5pm Sat & Sun mid-May–Jun & Sep, 10am-4pm Mon-Fri Oct-Apr) Friendly, efficient tourist office with internet access. The office may move to the new Culture House (Map p213) by the harbour in 2008.

Travel Agencies
Ferðaskristofa Akureyrar (Map p213; ☎ 460 0600; Raðhústorg 3) Domestic and international flights and ferries.

Nonni Travel (Map p213; ☎ 461 1841; www.nonnitravel.is; Brekkugata 5; 🕑 8am-6pm) Offers day trips, excursions, car rentals and flights. See p215 for details of tours.

Sporttours (Map p213; ☎ 461 2968; www.sporttours.is; Hafnarstræti 82) Agent for whale-watching, horse-riding, rafting and super-Jeep tours.

SIGHTS
Churches
Dominating the town from high on a hill, **Akureyrarkirkja** (Map p213; Eyrarlandsvegur) was designed by Guðjón Samúelsson, the architect responsible for Reykjavík's Hallgrímskirkja. The church continues his geological theme but is less blatantly 'basalt' and has a more traditional interior.

Built in 1940, Akureyrarkirkja contains a large and beautiful 3200-pipe organ and a series of rather untraditional reliefs of the life of Christ. There's also an unusual interpretation of the crucifixion and a suspended ship hanging from the ceiling. The ship reflects an old Nordic tradition of votive offerings for the protection of loved ones at sea. Perhaps the most striking feature, however, is the beautiful central window in the chancel, which originally graced Coventry Cathedral in England.

The **Catholic church** (Map p213; Eyrarlandsvegur 26) is an attractive old house built in 1912 and acquired by the church in 1952. On the nearby roundabout is Einar Jónsson's sculpture *Útlaginn* (The Outlaw).

CENTRAL AKUREYRI

0 ———— 300 m
0 ———— 0.2 miles

INFORMATION
Akureyri Municipal Library &
Archives...**1** B3
Ferðafélag Akureyrar....................**2** B2
Ferðaskristofa Akureyrar..............**3** B3
Froði...(see 37)
Heilsugæslustöðin Clinic...............**4** B3
Íslandsbanki...........................(see 41)
KB Banki.....................................**5** B3
Landsbanki Íslands........................**6** B3
Main Post Office............................**7** B3
Nonni Travel................................**8** B3

Penninn Bókval..............................**9** B3
Sparisjóður Norðlendinga............**10** B3
Sporttours.................................(see 11)
Tourist Office.............................**11** B4

SIGHTS & ACTIVITIES
Akureyrarkirkja............................**12** B4
Catholic Church...........................**13** B4
Davíðshús...................................**14** A3
Helgi the Lean Statue...................**15** A2
Listasafn.....................................**16** B3
Lystigarður Akureyrar...................**17** B4
Matthías Jochumsson Memorial Museum
(Sigurhæðir)...........................**18** B4
Sporttours.................................(see 11)
Swimming Pool............................**19** A4

SLEEPING
Akureyri Guesthouse....................**20** B3
Akurlnn......................................**21** A2

Brekkusel....................................**22** A4
Camp Site...................................**23** A4
Edda Hotel..................................**24** A4
Gistiheimilið Súlur.........................**25** A4
Gula Villan..................................**26** B3
Gula Villan II...............................**27** A4
Hotel Akureyri.............................**28** B4
Hótel Harpa............................(see 31)
Hotel Ibuðir.................................**29** B2
Hotel Ibuðir Guesthouse...............**30** B3
Hótel KEA...................................**31** B3
Hótel Norðurland.........................**32** B2
Sólgarðar................................(see 26)

EATING
Bautinn......................................**33** B3
Cafe Páris (Bláa Kannan)..............**34** B3
Friðrik V Brasserie....................(see 44)
Götu Grillið.................................**35** B3
Greifinn......................................**36** B2
Karolína Café..............................**37** B3
Karolína Restaurant..................(see 37)
Kristjáns Bakari............................**38** B3
La Vita é Bella.........................(see 33)
Nætursalan..............................(see 48)
Pengs...**39** B3
Strax Supermarket.......................**40** A4
Strikið..**41** B3
Vín Búð......................................**42** B2

DRINKING
Café Amour.................................**43** B3
Græni Hatturinn......................(see 34)
Kaffi Akureyri..............................**44** B3
Sjallinn......................................**45** B2

ENTERTAINMENT
Borgabíó Cinema.........................**46** B2
Leikfélag Akureyrar......................**47** B4
Nyja-Bíó Cinema..........................**48** B3

SHOPPING
Fold-Anna...................................**49** B3
Penninn Bókval..........................(see 9)
Viking Shop...............................(see 20)

TRANSPORT
Bus Terminal................................**50** B4
Taxi Stand...................................**51** B3

Museums

Akureyri has a large selection of museums, many of them honouring local boys made good. Although it's laudable that the town celebrates its artists, poets and authors, unless you have a particular admiration for a specific artist's work, many are of limited interest.

Minjasafnið á Akureyrar (Akureyri Folk Museum; Map p211; ☎ 462 4162; www.akmus.is; Aðalstræti 58; adult/under 16yr Ikr400/free, joint ticket with Nonni House Ikr550; ☼ 10am–5pm daily Jun–Sep, 2-4pm Sat mid-Sep–May) houses an interesting collection of art and historical items from the Settlement Era to the present. Among the displays are photographs, fish-drying racks, farming tools and re-creations of early Icelandic homes. Themed exhibitions are mounted each summer.

The **church** outside the folk museum is constructed in typical 19th-century Icelandic style. It was originally built at Svalbarðseyri on the eastern shore of Eyjafjörður and moved to its present site in 1970. The **museum garden** became the first place in Iceland to cultivate trees when a nursery was planted here in 1899.

The most interesting of the artists' homes, **Nonnahús** (Map p211; ☎ 462 3555; www.nonni.is; Aðalstræti 54; adult/under 16yr Ikr350/free, joint ticket with folk museum Ikr550; ☼ 10am–5pm Jun-Aug) was the childhood home of the renowned children's writer Reverend Jón Sveinsson (Nonni, 1857–1944). The house dates from 1850 and its cramped rooms and simple furnishings give a poignant insight into life in 19th-century Iceland.

A collection of old photographs and original books completes the display.

Listasafn (Akureyri Art Museum; Map p213; ☎ 462 2610; www.listasafn.akureyri.is; Kaupvangsstræti 12; admission lkr400; ☺ noon-5pm Tue-Sun), opposite Karolína Café, hosts changing exhibitions by local artists as well as a number of permanent works. The museum complex also houses artists' studios, commercial galleries and an art school.

Situated beside the Akureyrarkirkja stairs, the **Matthías Jochumsson Memorial Museum** (Sigurhæðir; Map p213; ☎ 466 2609; Eyrarlandsvegur 3; adult/ under 12yr lkr400/free; ☺ 3-5pm Mon-Fri 1 Jun-13 Aug) honours the former Icelandic poet laureate and dramatist Matthías Jochumsson. The ground floor of his former home is much as it would have been when he lived here and houses a collection of his works and personal property.

Northwest of the centre, **Davíðshús** (Map p213; ☎ 462 2874; Bjarkarstígur 6; admission lkr150; ☺ 1-2.30pm Mon-Fri Jun-Aug) remains much as it was on the day Icelandic poet laureate, novelist and playwright Davíð Stefánsson died in 1964.

Flugsafnið (Aviation Museum; Map p211; ☎ 863 2835; www.flugsafn.is; admission lkr400; ☺ 2-5pm Thu-Sun Jun-Aug, 2-5pm Sat Sep-May), in a hangar at Akureyri airport, charts the history of aviation in Iceland from the first flight in 1919 to the present. Photographs and memorabilia are on display, and you can visit the workshop where historic gliders and small aircraft are stored and repaired.

Botanical Gardens

A host of exotic species from as far away as New Zealand, Spain and Tanzania flourish in Akureyri's botanical gardens, **Lystigarður Akureyrar** (Map p213; ☎ 462 7487; Eyrarlandsvegur; admission free; ☺ 8am-10pm Mon-Fri, 9am-10pm Sat & Sun Jun-Oct), thanks to the region's moderate microclimate. The wealth of plant life on display is truly astonishing considering the gardens' proximity to the Arctic Circle. You'll find examples of every species native to Iceland here, as well as an extensive collection of high-latitude and high-altitude plants from around the world, all meticulously labelled with scientific names and countries of origin.

The lawns are sheltered from the wind and make a nice place to sit in the sun. Around the gardens are statues of poet Matthías Jochumsson, and Margrethe Schiöth, who voluntarily managed the gardens for 30 years, along with local contemporary art and sculptures.

Helgi the Lean

On the hill northeast of Klapparstígur, a five-minute walk from the city centre, is a **statue** (Map p213) of Helgi the Lean, the first settler in the Akureyri area. There's also a **view disc**, but the view, of shops and office buildings obscuring the fjord, isn't brilliant.

Kjarnaskógur

About 3km south of town is Iceland's most visited 'forest', the Kjarnaskógur woods. This bushland area has a 2km-long athletic course, walking tracks, picnic tables, an amusing children's playground and some novel fitness-testing devices. Check out the amusing log sundial designed by Icelandic Scouts.

ACTIVITIES
Swimming

The superb **swimming pool** (Map p213; ☎ 461 4455; Þingvallastræti 21; adult/6-15yr lkr310/150, sauna lkr500;

REVEREND JÓN SVEINSSON

The Jesuit priest Jón Sveinsson (Nonni) is one of Iceland's most famous and best-loved children's authors. His stories of derring-do were originally written in German but have a strong Icelandic flavour and have since been translated into 40 languages. Despite his great esteem in Iceland, Nonni spent only his early childhood years here. Born in 1857 at Möðruvellir, he moved south to Akureyri at the age of eight and four years later was sent to study in France.

At the age of 21 he joined the Jesuit order and eventually accepted a teaching post in Ordrup, Denmark, in 1883. He taught there for 20 years until ill health forced him to retire. It was during his retirement that Nonni began to write about his early adventures in Iceland with his brother Manni (who had died at the age of only 23). The 12 *Nonni & Manni* books are his best-known writing, and their success gave him the opportunity to travel the world lecturing on his works and his homeland, which made him something of a hero in Iceland. Many of the original copies of his books as well as numerous illustrations are now displayed in the Nonnahús museum. Nonni died in Germany in 1944.

TEEING OFF AT MIDNIGHT

For anyone who loves golf, there's something strangely appealing about playing 'midnight golf' – and there are only a handful of 18-hole courses in the world where you can do it. At a few degrees south of the Arctic Circle, Akureyri's **Jaðarsvöllur** (Map p211; ☎ 462 2974; gagolf@nett.is) basks in perpetual daylight from June to early August. In summer you can play golf here around the clock; just book ahead for a midnight tee-off. Green fees are Ikr3000 on weekdays, Ikr3800 on weekends. Club hire is Ikr2000.

The par-71 course, which boasts Jack Nicklaus as an honorary member, is home to the annual 36-hole Arctic Open, a golf tournament played overnight in late June. The most famous sportsman rumoured to come for a round here was basketballer Michael Jordan, who flew in just for the midnight-golf experience.

☯ 7am-9pm Mon-Fri, 8am-6.30pm Sat & Sun), near the camp site, is one of Iceland's finest. It has three heated pools, hot pots, water slides, saunas, pummelling water jets and a solarium – perfect for a relaxing afternoon.

Hiking & Skiing

A pleasant but demanding day hike leads up the Glerádalur valley to the summit of Mt Súlur (1144m). The trail begins on Súluvegur, a left turn off Þingvallastræti just before the Glerá bridge. Give yourself at least seven hours to complete the return journey.

With two days, you can continue up the valley to the beautifully situated Lambi mountain hut (at N 65°34.880', W 18°17.770'), which accommodates up to six people. Alternatively, from the Hlíðarfjall ski resort there's a challenging but beautiful day hike up to the small glacier Vindheimajökull and the 1456m peak Strýta.

For more information on hiking in the area, contact **Ferðafélag Akureyrar** (Map p213; ☎ 462 2720; www.ffa.is; Strandgata 23).

The **Hlíðarfjall ski centre** (☎ 462 2280; www .hlidarfjall.is; 1-day pass Ikr1200), west of town 7km up Glerárdalur, is probably Iceland's premier downhill ski slope, with green and blue pistes suitable for beginner to upper-intermediate skiers. The longest run is 2.5km, with a vertical drop of about 500m. There's also 20km of cross-country ski routes and a terrain park for snowboarders.

The ski season usually runs between mid-December and the end of April, with the best conditions in February and March. In the long hours of winter darkness, the downhill runs are floodlit. The ski lodge has a restaurant, and a ski school offers individual and group instruction and equipment hire. In season, buses connect the site with Akureyri three times daily.

TOURS

From June to September BSÍ runs sightseeing tours to Mývatn (Ikr7700, nine hours), departing at 8.15am daily from the airport and 8.30am from the bus terminal (Map p213). There's a 5% discount for bus-pass holders.

Akureyri's main tour agency, **Nonni Travel** (Map p213; ☎ 461 1841; www.nonnitravel.is; Brekkugata 5), runs a host of summer tours, including daily trips to Mývatn (Ikr7700) and whale watching at Húsavík (Ikr8000). On Monday, Wednesday and Friday self-guided trips by ferry can be arranged to Hrísey (Ikr2700) and Grímsey (Ikr5100). The Grímsey tour can also be done by combining a ferry and flight (Ikr9500). The agency also organises rafting in Varmalið (Ikr8900), horse riding (Ikr9000, four to five hours), Arctic Circle flights (Ikr14,200, 10 June to 20 August) and day trips to Greenland (Ikr39,590 to Ikr49,210).

Horse tours and hire are available from a range of outlying farms; ask at the tourist office for a full list. The best-known operator is **Pólar Hestar** (☎ 463 3179; www.polarhestar.is; one-week trips €900-1500), which offers week-long wilderness trips in the surrounding mountains and valleys – see p223. Other operators include **Hestaleigan Kátur** (☎ 862 2600), **Engimýri** (☎ 462 6838), in Öxnadalur, and **Sporttours** (Map p213; ☎ 466 1982; www.sporttours.is). Expect to pay about Ikr2500/4000/5000 for one-/two-/three-hour tours.

FESTIVALS & EVENTS

Akureyri's annual **arts festival** runs from late June to late August and attracts artists and musicians from around Iceland. There are special exhibitions, concerts, free jazz at 9.30pm on Thursday, theatre performances and everything from clay-pigeon shooting to historical walks. It all culminates in a weekend street party and parade. For details on events and exhibitions, contact the tourist office on ☎ 462 7733.

SLEEPING
Budget

Camp site (Map p213; ☎ 462 3379; hamrar@skatar.is; Þórunnarstræti; sites per person Ikr800; ☼ mid-Jun–Aug) Handy for travellers but destined to be shut down, this well-managed site across from the swimming pool has a kitchen, a toilet and shower block, and a washer and dryer. This site will close once building and roadworks are complete on the road up to the Hamrar camp site (see following). Email or ask at the tourist office for up-to-date information.

Hamrar camp site (☎ 461 2264; hamrar@hamrar.is; sites per person Ikr800; ☼ Jun–Aug; 🖳) This huge camp site, 1.5km south of town in a leafy setting, has newer facilities than the other site, and mountain views. There's a good kitchen and laundry room, ample shower rooms and internet access (Ikr200/350 for 30 minutes/ one hour).

Akureyri HI Hostel (Map p211; ☎ 462 3657; www.hostel .is; Stórholt 1; sb Ikr1800-3000, s/d/tr Ikr3900/6600/8250) This friendly, well-equipped and immaculately kept hostel is a 15-minute walk north of the city centre. There's a TV lounge, three kitchens, a barbecue deck and a laundry as well as two attractive summerhouses (Ikr14,280/49,500 for one/seven days) sleeping up to seven people. Substantial discounts are available for local restaurants, whale-watching trips (up to 35% off) and local tours, so it's a good idea to book here when you check in. Advance bookings are essential in summer.

Midrange

Akureyri has a good selection of guesthouses, but the best places get booked up fast, especially in summer. Most are open all year and offer substantial discounts in the off season.

ourpick AkurInn (Map p213; ☎ 461 2500; www .akurinn.is; Brekkugata 27a; s/d without bathroom Ikr3500/ 5000, with bathroom Ikr5200/6800) A cut above most of Akureyri's guesthouses, this heritage home has a variety of rooms with high ceilings, wood floors and period charm. Crisp white linens, pale neutral colours and simple style give the rooms a very calm atmosphere, and the large lounge and formal dining room add a touch of 1930s class.

Sólgarðar (Map p213; ☎ 461 1133; solgardar@simnet .is; Brekkugata 6; sb/s/d Ikr2900/4300/6000) Clean and well kept but quite dated, this small, friendly guesthouse has three nicely furnished rooms and an ancient kitchen. Each room has a TV, but with paper-thin walls between rooms you may need earplugs for a good night's sleep.

Hoepfner Guesthouse (Map p211; ☎ 463 3360; hoepfner@simnet.is; Hafnarstræti 20; sb/s/d/tr Ikr3600/4500/ 6500/8500; ☼ Jun-Aug; 🖳) This sparkling new guesthouse has a selection of bright, cheery rooms with plain white walls, functional but modern furniture and colourful quilt covers. There's a good kitchen and lounge for guest use and free wi-fi access.

Gula Villan (Map p213; ☎ 896 8464; www.gulavillan.is; Brekkugata 8; sb/s/d Ikr3500/5000/6600) Spotless rooms with simple but comfortable furnishings and friendly owners are available at this centrally located guesthouse. A second building (at Þingvallastræti 14, open June to August) run by the same couple offers extra space in summer. Both guesthouses have guest kitchens and breakfast served on request (Ikr950).

Brekkusel (Map p213; ☎ 462 3961, 895 1260; www .brekkusel.is; Byggðavegur 97; sb/s/d Ikr3000/4900/6800) Bright, airy and spotlessly clean, the guest rooms here have simple, modern styling, white linens and shared bathrooms. There's a large, cosy lounge and two kitchens for guest use.

Akureyri Guesthouse (Map p213; ☎ 462 5588; www .gistiheimilid.net; Hafnarstræti 104; s/d without bathroom Ikr5300/7300, with bathroom Ikr7300/9900) A cross between a budget hotel and a guesthouse, this place has plenty of rooms but none of the personal character of other accommodation options in town. Rooms are compact and simple and all have TV and sink. There's a guest kitchen and a bright top-floor dining room with a balcony overlooking the pedestrian shopping street.

Hotel Íbuðir (Map p213; ☎ 462 3727; www.hotelibudir .is; Geislagata 10; apt Ikr13,000-21,900) The good-value Íbuðir is spread over two locations, with a charming guesthouse at Brekkugata 4 (Map p213) offering spacious, contemporary rooms (Ikr8300/10,400 for singles/doubles May to September, Ikr5900/7900 for singles/doubles October to April) with decent furniture and subtle styling, and a choice of apartments sleeping two to eight in the main building on Geislagata.

Edda Hotel (Map p213; ☎ 444 4000; www.hoteledda .is; Hrafnagilsstræti; s/d without bathroom Ikr5800/7200, with bathroom Ikr10,300/12,900, ☼ mid-Jun–late Aug) Bland but comfortable rooms are available at this vast summer hotel in the local school. Most are modern and spacious and have TVs and private bathrooms, but rooms in the older wing are more dated and have shared bathrooms. There's a café and large restaurant on site.

Pétursborg (☎ 461 1811; www.petursborg.com; s/d without bathroom Ikr5300/8100, with bathroom Ikr7300/10,100) A great retreat from the city, this pleasant farmhouse on the edge of the fjord has cosy, well-furnished rooms and a wooden summerhouse (Ikr8000) sleeping six. There's an outdoor hot pot and a barbecue, a guest kitchen, and a large lounge and dining room. Pétursborg is 4km west of Akureyri, 1.5km off Rte 1.

Öngulstaðir (☎ 463 1380; www.ongulsstadir.is; s/d without bathroom Ikr5300/7000/8300, with bathroom Ikr6400/8800/10,500) This friendly farm, gallery and souvenir shop offers comfy accommodation in a range of rooms as well as an on-site restaurant if you don't want to head back into town to eat. Öngulstaðir is on Rte 829, 7km south of Akureyri (cross to the eastern side of the fjord before heading south).

Other options:

Gistiheimilið Súlur (Map p213; ☎ 461 1160; sulur@ islandia.is; Þórunnarstræti 93; sb/s/d/tr Ikr3600/5000/6800/ 8400; ✷ Jun-Aug) Bright, modern guesthouse with simple rooms and guest kitchen.

Gléra 2 (Map p211; ☎ 462 523; www.glera2.is; Gléra 2; sb/s/d Ikr2500/4000/5000) Simple, good-value rooms with TV and guest kitchen on the road to the ski resort.

Top End

Hótel Norðurland (Map p213; ☎ 462 2600; www.kea hotels.is; Geislagata 7; s/d/tr Jun-Aug Ikr11,900/15,100/ 19,600, Sep-May Ikr8900/11,300/14,700) A business hotel from the KEA chain, this place is less appealing than its sister hotels; its big, bright rooms have tired furnishings and little atmosphere. All have private bathrooms and are comfortable enough, but it's worth paying a little extra and heading to the Harpa instead.

Hotel Akureyri (Map p213; ☎ 462 5600; www.hotel akureyri.is; Hafnarstræti 67; s/d Ikr13,500/16,500) Compact rooms with simple décor, satellite TV, phone and minibar are on offer at this new hotel near the tourist office. All rooms have private bathrooms and, although comfortable, are lacking in any personal touch.

Hotel Harpa (Map p213; ☎ 460 2000; www.keahotels .is; Hafnarstræti 83-85; s/d/tr Jun-Aug Ikr12,700/16,100/20,900, Sep-May Ikr10,100/12,700/16,600) A sister property of Hótel KEA, it has smaller rooms but, thanks to a recent renovation, they're brighter, smarter and altogether better value. Contemporary styling, parquet flooring and sparkling new

bathrooms are on offer, but the reception and restaurant are shared with the KEA.

Hótel KEA (Map p213; ☎ 460 2000; www.keahotels.is; Hafnarstræti 87-89; s/d/tr Jun-Aug Ikr14,700/18,900/24,500, Sep-May Ikr11,900/14,900/19,500; ♿) The top spot in town, the KEA has spacious business-style rooms with dated design and large bathrooms. There's little local character about it, but some rooms have balconies and good views over the fjord. There's a bar, a café and a swanky but soulless restaurant.

EATING

You'll be spoilt for choice when it comes to eating out in Akureyri, with a large selection of cafés and restaurants serving everything from spicy noodles to authentic Icelandic cuisine.

Restaurants

Götu Grilið (Map p213; ☎ 462 1800; Strandgata 11; mains Ikr665-1795; ✷ noon-10pm) Simple, fresh and contemporary, this bright and airy place offers a decent range of food from seafood soup to chicken and lamb kebabs, pizza, fish, and Indian dishes. It's good value and an excellent choice for lunch.

Pengs (Map p213; ☎ 466 3800; Strandgata 13; mains Ikr1200-2000; ✷ 11.30am-2pm & 5-10pm Mon-Sat, 3-10pm Sun) Friendly service and a wide choice of dishes make Akureyri's only Chinese restaurant a good option. There's plenty of choice for vegetarians and a bumper 15-course lunch buffet available for a bargain Ikr990.

Bautinn (Map p213; ☎ 462 1818; Hafnarstræti 92; mains Ikr1300-3400) A local favourite, this friendly, relaxed place in the centre of town has an all-you-can-eat soup and salad bar (Ikr1290) and an extensive menu featuring everything from pizza, fish and lamb to such Icelandic favourites as puffin, whale and horsemeat. [Whale meat served.]

La Vita é Bella (Map p213; ☎ 462 5858; Hafnarstræti 92; mains Ikr1330-3000; ✷ lunch & dinner Jun-Aug, from 6pm Sep-May) This Italian restaurant features a good-value selection of salads, risottos and pasta, including lasagne and ravioli, a good range of pizzas and excellent Mediterranean-inspired fish and meat dishes.

Strikið (Map p213; ☎ 462 7100; www.strikid.is; Ski-pagata 14; mains lunch Ikr890-2790, dinner Ikr1590-3150) This slick, minimalist top-floor restaurant has great views over the harbour and an eclectic menu featuring everything from soup and burgers to Thai noodles, pasta, and meat and seafood dishes.

Greifinn (Map p213; ☎ 460 1600; www.greifinn.is; Glerárgata 20; mains Ikr1700-3000; ⏱ 11.30am-11.30pm) Family-friendly and always buzzing, Greifinn is one of the most popular spots in town. The menu features plenty of comfort food, from juicy burgers and nachos dripping with cheese to good pizzas, salads and devilish deserts.

Friðrik V Brasserie (Map p213; ☎ 461 5775; Strandgata 7; mains Ikr2500-4000; ⏱ 6-10pm Tue-Sun) Akureyri's gourmet hub, the Friðrik V is a formal kind of place with a hushed respect for the master chefs at work. The menu features Icelandic delicacies such as lobster tails, fresh seafood and lamb, all done in an impeccable Mediterranean style. Ideal for special night out.

our pick **Karolína Restaurant** (Map p213; ☎ 461 2755; www.karolina.is; Kaupvangsstræti 2; 2-/3-/5-course dinner Ikr4200/5400/6800; ⏱ from 6pm Tue-Sat) Hip, trendy and very slick, the upmarket Karolína is run by Iceland's Chef of the Year 2003. The menu is appropriately daring, mixing traditional Icelandic flavours with international culinary ideas (think octopus tempura and tandoori arctic char) with the emphasis on fresh and flavoursome seafood (including dolphin).

Cafés

Kristjáns Bakarí (Map p213; Hafnarstræti; ⏱ 9am-6pm Mon-Fri, 10am-2pm Sat) For a quick pit stop this small bakery and café on the main drag sells a bumper selection of fresh bread, cakes and pastries.

Café Paris (Blaá Kannan; Map p213; ☎ 461 4600; Hafnarstræti 96; lunches Ikr950; ⏱ 9am-10.30pm Mon-Sat, 10am-10.30pm Sun; ✗) This old-style café with wooden interior and chilled atmosphere is a great spot for breakfast or lunch. The huge windows and outdoor tables provide prime locations to watch the world go by and the good-value lunches (often veggie) draw the crowds.

Karolína Café (Map p213; ☎ 461 2755; Kaupvangsstræti 23; ⏱ 11.30am-1am Mon-Thu, to 3am Fri & Sat, 2pm-1am Sun) Self-consciously cool and a favoured hangout with the young and trendy, this art-strewn café is a relaxed place serving great coffee and cakes. The deep leather sofas, tasty sandwiches (Ikr700) and mellow music make it easy to while away a few hours here.

Quick Eats

Nætursalan (Map p213; Strandgata) Near the Nyja-Bíó cinema, this is the most popular fast-food place with the late-night crowd. It's open until at least 3am on Friday and Saturday night.

Brynja (Map p211; Aðalstræti 3; ⏱ 9am-11.30pm) Slightly out of the centre but well worth the effort to get to, this legendary sweet shop is known across Iceland for the best ice cream in the country.

Café Brauðbúd Konditori (Map p211; Undirhlíð) This excellent-value canteen at the Bónus supermarket, serves the usual sandwiches, cakes and soup as well as hearty pasta, pizza and meat dishes from Ikr500 to Ikr600.

On the pedestrian shopping mall are several small kiosks selling hot dogs, chips, burgers, sandwiches and soft drinks.

Self-Catering

Akureyri has a great choice of supermarkets. The biggest is the huge **Netto** (Map p211; Glerágata) in the new Glerártorg shopping mall. **Strax** (Map p213; Byggðavegur) and **10-11** (Map p211; Þingvallastræti) are both near the camp site west of the centre, and there's a cut-price **Bónus** (Map p211; Undirhlíð) right behind the youth hostel.

Vín Búð (Map p213; ☎ 462 1655; Hólabraut 16; ⏱ 11am-6pm Mon-Thu, to 7pm Fri, to 4pm Sat), the government alcohol shop, is near the Borgabíó cinema.

DRINKING

Akureyri has some lively nightlife, but compared with Reykjavík it's all pretty tame. Along with Karolína Café (left) and Café Paris (left), the hang-outs below make up the best drinking dens in town.

Café Amour (Map p213; ☎ 461 3030; Ráðhústorg 9; ⏱ 11am-1am Sun-Thu, to 4am Fri & Sat) All minimalist style and trendy sophistication, Café Amour tries hard to lure in Akureyri's bright young things with its lengthy cocktail list and New World wines. The small club upstairs is pretty garish but draws the crowds at weekends.

Kaffi Akureyri (Map p213; ☎ 461 3999; Strandgata 7; ⏱ 3pm-1am Sun-Thu, to 4am Fri & Sat) This stylish, modern café-bar is one of Akureyri's best live-music venues and gets packed on Friday and Saturday nights when bands play.

Sjallinn (Map p213; ☎ 461 2700; Geislagata 14; ⏱ to 3am Fri & Sat) Perennially popular and always jammed, this bar, club and live-music venue has DJs playing everything from chart tunes to indie rock and live bands at weekends.

Græni Hatturinn (Green Hat: Map p213; ☎ 461 4646; Hafnarstræti 96) More traditional and usually less boisterous than Sjallinn, this popular British-style pub is down a lane behind Café Paris. There's music and dancing at weekends.

Oddvitinn (Map p211; ☎ 462 6020; Strandgata 53) Down by the harbour, Oddvitinn is the sort of pub you don't often see in Iceland. It's in a historic building (with reputedly the longest bar in Iceland), is popular with a mature drinking crowd and has regular karaoke.

ENTERTAINMENT

Leikfélag Akureyrar (Map p213; ☎ 462 0200; www .leikfelag.is; Hafnarstræti 57) Akureyri's main theatre venue hosts drama, musicals, dance and opera with its main season running from September to June rather than during the summer. For information on upcoming performances, check the website or ask at the tourist office.

There are two cinemas in the town centre: **Borgabíó** (Map p213; ☎ 462 3599; Hólabraut 12), and **Nyja-Bíó** (Map p213; ☎ 461 4666; Strandgata 2), just around the corner from the town square. Both show original-version mainstream films with subtitles.

SHOPPING

Several shops on Hafnarstræti sell traditional woollen jumpers, books, knick-knacks and souvenirs under the tax-free scheme (see p317), and there are a clutch of newer, trendier boutiques along Skipagata.

Penninn Bókval (Map p213; ☎ 461 5050; Hafnarstræti 91-93; ◷ 9am-10pm) Penninn sells coffee-table books, calendars and small souvenirs.

Viking Shop (Map p213; ☎ 461 5551; Hafnarstræti 104) This place has a good selection of Icelandic knitted jumpers.

THE AKUREYRI RUNTUR

Bored, restless and keen to be seen, Akureyri's teenagers have developed their own form of *runtur* (literally 'round tour'). While the world-famous Reykjavík equivalent demands a hard stomach and good feet for the weekly pub crawl around the capital, in Akureyri you just need to be old enough to borrow a car. From about 8pm on Friday and Saturday nights you'll see a procession of cars, bumper to bumper, driving round and round in circles along Skipagata, Strandgata and Glerárgata. The speed rarely rises above 5km/h, but horns blare and teenagers scream out to each other until the small hours. Bring earplugs if you're staying in town and fancy an early night.

Fold-Anna (Map p213; ☎ 461 4120; Hafnarstræti 85; ◷ 9am-7pm Mon-Fri, 10am-2pm Sat) Marginally cheaper woollen goods can be found at this factory outlet, selling woollen jumpers, blankets, hats and gloves. Staff can generally be seen knitting behind the counter as you browse.

Christmas Garden (Jólagarðurinn; ☎ 463 1433; ◷ 10am-10pm) If you can handle the Christmas cheer out of season then the Christmas Garden, 10km south of Akureyri, has a lovely selection of locally made decorations, cards, sweets and traditional Icelandic Christmas foods.

GETTING THERE & AWAY

Air

Iceland Express (☎ in UK 0870 8500737; www.iceland express.com) flies twice a week from London Stansted (around £200, three hours).

Air Iceland (☎ 460 7000) flies up to seven times daily between Akureyri and Reykjavík (from Ikr5060, 45 minutes), and from Akureyri to Grímsey (from Ikr4865, 25 minutes), Vopnafjörður (from Ikr6125, 45 minutes) and Þórshöfn (from Ikr6125, 45 minutes). All other domestic (and international) flights are via Reykjavík. The airport (Map p211) is 2km south of town.

Bus

Akureyri is the hub for bus travel in the north. SBA is based at the tourist office and bus terminal on Hafnarstræti (Map p213), but **TREX** (Map p211; ☎ 899 4660; Kaldbaksgata) has moved to an inconvenient location in the middle of an industrial estate by the harbour. Few are happy about the move and the company is under pressure to return to the bus terminal. Check locally for up-to-date information.

Buses run between Akureyri and Reykjavík twice daily from May to September, departing at 8.30am and 5pm (Ikr6600, 5¾ hours). There is at least one service daily during the rest of the year. From mid-June to the end of August an additional service runs to Reykjavík along the interior's Kjölur route (Ikr8200, 10 hours), leaving at 8am.

Heading east, there are daily summer buses from Akureyri to Egilsstaðir (Ikr5400, four hours), calling at Reykjahlíð and Skútustaðir, at Mývatn (Ikr2200, 1½ hours). In peak season up to three additional buses run to Mývatn. From June to August there are three daily services to Húsavík (Ikr2300, one hour), from where you can connect to Ásbyrgi and Þórshöfn on weekdays. Buses to Árskógssandur and Dalvík (for the Grímsey and Hrísey ferries) and Ólafsfjörður leave up to four times a day on weekdays.

Car

Akureyri has several rental agencies, and rates here are slightly cheaper than in Reykjavík, from about Ikr6500 per day for a small car with unlimited kilometres and insurance to Ikr12,500 per day for a small 4WD. For an extra fee of around Ikr4000, most companies will let you pick up a car in Akureyri and drop it off in Reykjavík or vice versa.

Avis (Map p211; ☎ 461 2428, national reservations line 591 4000; Akureyri airport)

Budget (Map p211; ☎ 660 0629; Akureyri airport)

Hertz (Map p211; ☎ 461 1005; Akureyri airport)

National (Map p211; ☎ 461 6000; Tryggvabraut 12)

GETTING AROUND
Bicycle

Skíðaþjónustan (☎ 462 1713; Fjölnisgata 4b), located northwest of the town centre, hires out bicycles for about Ikr1500 per day. You can negotiate cheaper rates for weekends and week-long rentals.

Bus

Akureyri is easy to get around on foot, but there's a regular town bus service (fares Ikr200, running from 6.20am to 11.30pm daily). Unfortunately, it doesn't go to the airport.

Car

Akureyri introduced new parking restrictions in 2006. In the central area you must now put a parking disk (available free from all shops, guesthouses and banks) on display in your car. Spaces are marked with maximum stay allowed (from 15 minutes to two hours). Although you do not need to pay for parking, you will be slapped with a fine (Ikr500 to Ikr2000) if you exceed your allotted time.

Taxi

The BSO **taxi stand** (Map p213; ☎ 461 1010) is on the corner of Strandgata and Hofsbót. Taxis may be booked 24 hours a day.

AROUND AKUREYRI

If you have some time it's worth getting off the Ring Rd and exploring the region around Akureyri. To the north, Iceland's longest fjord,

Eyjafjörður, stretches out past the island of Hrísey to the Arctic Ocean. On the west coast you'll get fantastic views of glacial mountains and lush farms, while inland there are some excellent hiking opportunities in Tröllaskagi. On the east coast is the historic farm at Laufás, while south of Akureyri are more key historical sites and farms.

ÁRSKÓGSSTRÖND
pop 560

The rich agricultural region known as Árskógsströnd runs north along the western shore of Eyjafjörður, from where there are dramatic views across the water to the mountains opposite. The main reason to come this way, though, is to catch the ferry to Hrísey island or join whale-watching trips from Hauganes.

Once the largest port in northern Iceland, the protected ruins of the former medieval trading post of **Gásir** (www.gasir.is; admission Ikr400; ⏰ tours 1pm, 2pm & 3.30pm Mon-Fri, 11.30am, 1pm, 2pm & 3.30pm Sat Jul & Aug) make an interesting stop along this route. Jewellery, coins and implements have been unearthed, and recent evidence suggests that commercial trading here continued until the 16th century. The ruins are scant, though, so it's well worth taking the guided tour to bring the site to life. Guides explain the significance of the finds, how the trading post might have looked and what life was like while taking you around the foundations of a medieval church, a graveyard and some grass-covered outlines where port trading offices once stood. To get here, head about 7km north from Akureyri along the Ring Rd, turn east on Rte 816 (signposted), then continue another 7km along a gravel road to the site.

North of the Hörgá river is the large farm **Möðruvellir**. It was the site of a monastery founded in 1296 and the birthplace of the author Jón Sveinsson (Nonni, see p214). The present church at Möðruvellir was built in 1868 and has an attractive interior with a blue ceiling covered with stars.

Further north it's worth detouring to the village of **Hauganes** to join a whale-watching tour in the fjord. Trips aboard the former fishing boat **Niels Jonsson** (☎ 867 0000; www.niels .is; 3hr trips Ikr3700; ⏰ Jun-Aug) boast a high record spotting cetaceans and include a stop at Hrísey island. Hauganes is 2km off Rte 82 about 14km south of Dalvík.

HRÍSEY

pop 210

Iceland's second-largest offshore island (after Heimaey) is the peaceful, low-lying Hrísey, a thriving community easily reached from the mainland. Thrust out into the middle of Eyjafjörður, the island is especially noted as a breeding ground and protected area for ptarmigan, as well as being home to a flourishing population of eider duck and an enormous colony of arctic terns.

Traditionally the island was a centre for fish processing and salting, but today most of its inhabitants are employed at a quarantine station for pets and livestock being imported to Iceland.

There's a small **information office** (☎ 695 0077; ☻ 1-6pm mid-Jun–Aug) in the Pearl Gallery by the harbour. You can pick up the handy Hrísey brochure here or in Akureyri. The island also has a bank and a post office on the main street of the village.

Sights & Activities

Hrísey's bucolic charm lies in its dramatic location and its virtually traffic-free tranquillity. A leisurely half-day is enough to explore its shores, but for a more authentic glimpse of island life it's worth staying overnight.

At the island's southern end is the picturesque **village** – a cluster of houses around the harbour linked by cobbled streets frequented by incredibly tame ptarmigan. From here three marked **nature trails** loop around the southeastern part of the island and lead to some good clifftop viewpoints.

Most of the northern part of Hrísey is a private ptarmigan and eider-duck sanctuary, and visitors must obtain permission to pass through the area. The cliffs along the northeastern coast are indented by **sea caves** and the bush areas have reverted to a natural state, having been free of sheep for many years.

Guided **tractor trips** (☎ 695 0077; per person Ikr500, minimum Ikr1500) run around the island passing all the important sights. Hrísey's tiny outdoor **swimming pool** (☎ 466 3012) also has a sauna.

Sleeping & Eating

Camp site (☎ 466 1769; Skálavegur; ☻ Jun–mid-Sep; sites per person Ikr800) Camping is only permitted at this municipal site near the community centre.

Gistiheimilið Brekka (☎ 466 1751; brekkahriseyelli@ sjallinn.is; Hólabraut; s/d Ikr4900/7800) Hrísey's one-stop shop for food and accommodation, this

bright yellow restaurant and guesthouse has lovely harbour views and comfortable rooms. The restaurant (mains Ikr1100 to Ikr5000) has an extensive menu featuring everything from the usual burgers, pizza, pasta and salads to beef steaks, lamb, seafood, and even snails. Book ahead in summer.

Summer chalets (☎ 466 1079) Long-stay and overflow accommodation is available in a series of summerhouses on the island.

Eyjabud, the village store, sells organic foods and a selection of gifts and souvenirs.

Getting There & Away

The ferry **Sævar** (☎ 695 5544) runs between Árskógssandur and Hrísey (Ikr750 return, 15 minutes) every two hours from 7am to 11pm from June to August. A reduced service runs during the rest of the year. Buses from Akureyri (Ikr600) connect with the ferries three times daily from Monday to Friday.

On Tuesday and Thursday in high season the ferry **Sæfari** (☎ 458 8900) runs from Dalvík to Hrísey at 1.15pm, returning at 1.45pm.

Nonni Travel (p215) in Akureyri has six-hour tours to Hrísey by bus and ferry (Ikr2700) from Monday to Friday.

DALVÍK

pop 1800

The sleepy village of Dalvík nestles in a spectacular spot between Eyjafjörður and the hills of Svarfaðardalur. Most tourists come here to catch the ferry to Grímsey island (see p223), but if you've got some time there's good hiking, an interesting museum and a lovely swimming pool in and around town.

Much of Dalvík was destroyed by a strong earthquake in 1934, but a new harbour was built just five years later and the local fishing industry has supported the town ever since.

There's a **tourist information point** (☎ 466 3233; www.dalvik.is) at the swimming pool on Svarfaðarbraut, with 15 minutes' free internet access for visitors.

Sights & Activities

Byggðasafnið Hvoll (☎ 466 1497; www.dalvik.is /byggdasafn; Karlsbraut; adult/6-16yr Ikr400/100; ☻ 11am-6pm daily Jun-Aug, 2-5pm Sat Sep-May) This quirky local museum has an array of art and natural exhibits, including a stuffed polar bear, but there's also a room dedicated to local giant Jóhan Pétursson who, at 2.34m (almost 7ft 7in), was Iceland's tallest man. There are photos and personal effects, many from his days as a circus act. Another room is dedicated to another local, Kristjárn Eldjárn, who became president of Iceland.

Local whale-watching tours are operated by **Sjóferðir Dalvík** (☎ 466 3355; www.hvalaskodun.is; Ásvegur 6; 3hr tours Ikr3800; ☼ mid-Jun–mid-Aug). The company offers a 100% guarantee – if you don't spot any whales you'll get a second free trip instead.

The area around Dalvík is perfect for wilderness hiking or horse riding. A popular hike or riding tour from Dalvík is over **Heljardalsheiði**. This unmarked route passes through some of Iceland's best mountain scenery; you should allow at least two days for the walk. The trail begins at the end of Rte 805, 20km up Svarfaðardalur, and traverses the Tröllaskagi peninsula to Hólar. However, there's no public transport from Hólar. For hut and map information, contact Ferðafélag Akureyrar (p212) in Akureyri.

Horse riding and hire can be organised through **Tvistur** (☎ 466 1679; ebu@ismennt.is; 1-/2-/3-hr trips Ikr2000/3000/4500) a farm about 3km from town in the Svarfaðardalur valley. It's also possible to do a half-day ride along the valley, then canoe back along the Svarfaðardalsá river (around Ikr6500 per person). Canoes and bikes are available from Árgerði Guesthouse (see below).

Dalvík has a good **swimming pool** (☎ 466 3233; adult/6-16yr Ikr250/160; ☼ 6.45am-8pm Mon-Fri, 10am-7pm Sat & Sun Jun-Aug, 8am-8pm Mon-Fri, 4-7pm Sat & Sun Sep-May) with hot pots, steam bath, solarium and water slide. In winter there's a **ski tow** (☎ 878 1606; www.skidalvik.is; day pass Ikr800) on Böggvisstaðafjall, the prominent ridge above Dalvík.

Sleeping & Eating

Camp site (☎ 466 3233; ☼ Jun-Aug) There's a free camp site with only basic facilities behind the hotel.

Árgerði Guesthouse (☎ 555 4212; www.argerdi .com; s/d Ikr5000/7000) This welcoming family-run guesthouse has cosy rooms and a lovely location on the Svarfaðardalsá river. There's a summer deck with barbecue, and guests can use bicycles and canoes for a paddle on the river. Árgerði is about 1km south of town on the Akureyri road.

Hotel Sóley (☎ 466 3395; www.hotel.soley.com; Skíðabraut 18; sb Ikr2000, s Ikr4900-6900, d Ikr9800-13,800) Dalvík's only hotel was recently renovated and updated and now offers comfy accommodation in simple but tasteful rooms with private

bathroom. There's a small café and TV lounge but no restaurant for evening meals.

Bakari Axis (Hafnarbraut 5) This local bakery is a good breakfast stop, with plenty of coffee, pastries, filled rolls and fresh bread.

Kaffihúsid Sogn (☎ 466 3330; Goðabraut 3; mains Ikr700-2200; ☼ 11am-9pm Mon-Thu, to 11pm Fri, 3-11pm Sat, 3-9pm Sun) This café-bar opposite the town hall serves coffee and cakes, as well as Icelandic pancakes, tacos, tortillas, and fish and lamb dishes.

There's a supermarket in the small shopping complex opposite the harbour.

Getting There & Away

In summer **Sæfari** (☎ 458 8900; www.samskip.is) runs ferries to Grímsey at 9am on Monday, Wednesday and Friday, with bus connections from Akureyri. The return fare is Ikr4340 (Ikr5100 including a bus to/from Akureyri that leaves at 7.30am), and the one-way journey takes 3½ hours.

Buses run from Akureyri to Dalvík three times on weekdays from May to August.

ÓLAFSFJÖRÐUR

pop 1020

Beautifully situated beneath snowcapped peaks, the fishing town of Ólafsfjörður makes an ideal day trip from Akureyri. Locked in between the sheer mountain slopes and the dark waters of the fjord, the place has a real sense of rural isolation. You have to pass through a 3km tunnel just to make your way into town.

There's some excellent hiking and riding in the hills around town, lake and sea fishing, and good winter skiing and other off-season activities.

Sights & Activities

Náttúrugripsafnið (☎ 466 2651; Aðalgata; admission Ikr400; ☼ 2-5pm Tue-Sun Jun-Aug) is Ólafsfjörður's only formal sight; a small natural-history museum above the post office. There's the usual collection of stuffed seals and a polar bear and an extensive range of birds covering every species found in the region.

One of the highlights of Ólafsfjörður is **hiking** in the hills that enclose and dwarf this little fishing village. For several weeks around the end of June, the beautiful 400m-high headland **Ólafsfjarðarmúli** will allow you to see beyond the Arctic Circle and experience the real midnight sun. Unfortunately, there's no easy route up; the scree slopes are steep and rather hazardous to climb, so most people do their viewing from the high point along the rough coast road.

Ólafsfjörður receives good snow coverage in winter, when the downhill **ski slopes** (day pass Ikr500) above town lurch into action. It's also possible to arrange **snowmobile excursions** (2-3hr from Ikr6000) and **ice fishing** in winter.

Ólafsfjörður competes with Siglufjörður for the title of Iceland's northernmost **golf course**. The nine-hole course is in a lush geothermal area just north of the town.

Sleeping & Eating

Camp site (☎ 466 2363) There's a basic, free camp site with toilets beside the swimming pool.

Brimnes Hotel & Cabins (☎ 466 2400; www.brimnes .is; Bylgjubyggð 2; s/d Ikr8500/10,500, cabins Ikr12,000-14,000) All of Ólafsfjörður's accommodation options are run by the local hotel, whose bedrooms are bland but adequate. The real draw here are the cosy Scandinavian-style log cabins on the lake shore, with hot tubs built into the veranda and views over the water. The hotel restaurant (mains Ikr1520 to Ikr3000) is a bright, cheery place with good service and a decent menu of fish and lamb as well as pizza and some superb homemade Icelandic desserts. The hotel can help organise such activities as horse rental, lake and sea fishing, rowing boats, and winter snowmobile excursions.

Hólinn (☎ 466 4000; Hafnargötu 16; pizzas Ikr900-2200) Your only other option for food is this pizza place down towards the harbour. It does the usual range of pizzas to eat in or take away.

Getting There & Away

Buses run from Akureyri to Dalvík and Ólafs-fjörður three times on weekdays from May to August.

GRENIVÍK

pop 270

Tucked away at the end of the road on the eastern shore of Eyjafjörður is the tiny village of Grenivík. This sleepy place relies on fishing and fish-freezing to survive, and most visitors come here for the excellent horse tours and to visit the Laufás museum. There is no public transport to Grenivík.

Laufás

Well worth the trip from Akureyri, this 19th-century **manor farm and vicarage** (☎ 463 3196; adult/under 16yr Ikr400/free; ⏰ 10am-6pm 15 May-15 Sep) gives a wonderful insight into rural living

in times past. The gabled, turf-roofed farm-house dates from the 1850s and is set on the edge of Eyjafjörður, a particularly beautiful spot, with numerous eider-duck nesting sites nearby. The buildings were home to up to 30 people (including a team of farm hands) at any one time, and inside, the household and agricultural implements of that time are on display. The adjacent church, with a typical barrel-shaped ceiling, was built in 1865 and is dedicated to St Peter.

Attached to the farmhouse is a lovely country-style café where you can get coffee, cakes and traditional Icelandic dishes. Laufás is 11km south of Grenivík.

Tours

Pólar Hestar (☎ 463 3179; www.polarhestar.is) runs seven- to nine-day horse-riding tours from the farm Grýtubakki II, about 4km south of Grenivík. Destinations include Goðafoss, Mývatn, Gullfoss, Langjökull and the valleys and mountains of northeast Iceland. Prices range from €900 to €1500 and include ac-commodation and meals. Full-day rides are available on request.

Sleeping & Eating

Gistiheimilið Miðgarðar (☎ 463 3223; www.midgardar .com; Miðgarður 4; sb/s/d without bathroom Ikr2000/3900/7000, with bathroom Ikr5900/10600) The only guesthouse in town is this comfortable place with cosy rooms. There's a café-bar next door serving Icelandic dishes, coffee and cakes.

GRÍMSEY

pop 100

Best known as Iceland's only true piece of Arctic territory, the remote island of Grímsey is worth a visit for its dramatic sea cliffs and wonderful bird life as well as the chance to cross that all-important imaginary line – the Arctic Circle. Flung out into the Arctic Ocean, 41km from the mainland, Grímsey is roughly dissected by the Arctic Circle and basks in the midnight sun throughout the summer months.

Around the island's coast 100m-high cliffs and dramatic basalt formations plunge into the sea and make a popular home for 36 dif-ferent species of sea birds, and a playground for many others. Kittiwakes, puffins, razor-bills, fulmars, guillemots and arctic terns screech and circle above the cliffs and don't always appreciate the presence of humans. On some trails you'll need to hold a stick

NORTHWEST ICELAND

GRÍMSEY'S CHECKMATE

Although chess is no longer the sacred pastime it once was on Grímsey, the island is still known for its avid players. Historically, failure at chess was equated with failure in life on Grímsey, and the game was taken so seriously that a poor performance was often followed by a messy dive from the cliffs. This enthusiasm and dedication to the game attracted the attention of millionaire journalist and chess champion Daniel Willard Fiske in the 1870s.

Although he never visited the island, he set himself up as its protector, sending badly needed firewood, financing the island library and bequeathing part of his estate to the community. Grímsey still celebrates Fiske's birthday on 11 November, and his portrait is on display in the library at the community centre. For more on Grímsey's unconventional benefactor, read Lawrence Millman's account of a visit to the island in his book *Last Places: A Journey in the North*.

---

overhead when out walking to prevent being dive-bombed.

Historically, Grímsey provided an abundant supply of birds and fresh eggs, and its waters were some of Iceland's richest in fish. Today, fishery is still the most important income generator and the island's one settlement, Sandvík, supports a church, a swimming pool, a guesthouse and a community centre.

Tours

Nonni Travel in Akureyri (p215) runs Grímsey tours on Monday, Wednesday and Friday in summer. You can choose to fly in both directions (Ikr14,200), take a flight and ferry (Ikr9500) or travel by ferry both ways (Ikr5100). Evening Arctic Circle flights (Ikr14,200) are also available from 10 June to 20 August, giving an hour's walk on the island and a certificate to say you've crossed that all-important line. For longer stays, you can leave the tour on the island and return to Akureyri later.

Sleeping & Eating

You can camp nearly anywhere away from the village.

Gistiheimilið Gullsól (☎ 467 3190; grimsey@ismennt .is; sb/s/d Ikr1900/2400/4800) This family-run guesthouse attached to the handicrafts shop has basic rooms and a guest kitchen.

Gistiheimilið Básar (☎ 467 3103; sigrun@konica.is; sb/ s/d Ikr1800/3300/5100) Squashed between the airport and the sea, this is the island's original guesthouse, and it's still the only place to get a proper meal. Breakfast/dinner costs Ikr800/2000; snacks are available during the day.

Getting There & Away

From mid-June to late-August **Air Iceland** (☎ 467 3148; www.airiceland.is) flies every day except Saturday to/from Akureyri. From late March to

mid-June and late August to October, flights operate on Tuesday, Thursday and Saturday only. The bumpy journey takes in the full length of Eyjafjörður and is an experience in itself. The cheapest one-way fare is Ikr4865.

In summer the **Sæfari ferry** (☎ 458 8900; www .samskip.is) departs Dalvík for Grímsey at 9am on Monday, Wednesday and Friday, returning from Grímsey at 4pm. If coming from Akureyri, a bus leaves at 7.30am to connect with the ferry. The return trip costs Ikr4340 (Ikr5100 including bus to/from Akureyri), and the one-way journey takes 3½ hours. Book in advance.

UPPER EYJAFJÖRÐUR

Heading south from Akureyri, Rte 821 follows Eyjafjörður to its head, passing several sites of historical importance. If you have a vehicle and some spare time, it's worth an afternoon's excursion from Akureyri – if only to leave behind the Ring Rd traffic and get out into countryside.

About 10km south of Akureyri, **Kristnes** was the site of Helgi the Lean's original settlement. His high-seat temple pillars washed up at Pollurinn, near the head of the fjord, and Helgi decided to settle here.

A further 2km south is **Hrafnagil**, which was the historic home of Bishop Jón Arason of Hólar. Today there's accommodation at **Hótel Vin** (☎ 463 1333; www.vin.nett.is; sb Ikr1600-2900, s/d without bathroom Ikr5200/6600, with bathroom Ikr8200/10,200; 💻), with a café, a greenhouse, a summer camp site and a heated pool.

The odd little onion-domed church at **Grund**, about 5km past Hrafnagil, was built by the farmer Magnús Sigurðsson in 1905. Its neo-Romanesque style seems anomalous in Iceland, but early in the 20th century it was one of the country's most impressive churches. Ask for a key at the farmhouse.

The farm **Saurbær**, 28km south of Akureyri on Rte 821, has an interesting turf-and-stone church that dates from 1838 and is now under national protection. It was constructed on the site of a church that had existed there since the 11th century.

The eccentric **Museum of Small Exhibits** (☎ 463 1261; www.smamunasafnid.is; admission Ikr400; ☺ 1-6pm mid-May–mid-Sep) is at Sólgarður near Saurbær. It's a mind-boggling collection of watches, door knockers, bridle bits, electrical sockets and switches, kitchen equipment, tools, fishing gear and anything else you could possibly think of all meticulously mounted and displayed.

Torfufell, at the end of Rte 821, offers good hiking, including a climb up Torfufell mountain (1241m) and a walk up the Torfufellsá canyon.

GOÐAFOSS

Despite being smaller and less powerful than some of Iceland's other major waterfalls, Goðafoss (Waterfall of the Gods) is one of its most beautiful. The waterfall is formed by the cascading glacial waters of the river Skjálfandafljót, which has cut a horseshoe canyon through the 8000-year-old Bárðardalur lava field (from the Trölladyngja crater near Vatnajökull).

The falls also play an important part in Icelandic history. At the Alþing in the year 1000, the *lögsögumaður* (law-speaker), Þorgeir, was forced to make a decision on Iceland's religion. After 24 hours' meditation he declared the country a Christian nation. On his way home to Ljósavatn he passed the waterfall near his farm, Djúpá, and tossed in his pagan carvings of the Norse gods, thus bestowing the falls' present name.

Goðafoss is just off Rte 1. Although you can drive right to the falls you'll get better views and a sense of anticipation by parking at the nearby petrol station and taking the short walk (1km) up the canyon to the falls.

Right beside the falls, **Fosshóll** (☎ 464 3108; fossholl@nett.is; sites per person Ikr500, sb May-Sep only Ikr2300, s/d without bathroom Ikr6600/11,400, with bathroom Ikr7600/13,400) offers cosy rooms in its small hotel. There's also a nice café and restaurant (mains Ikr850 to Ikr2750) serving everything from soups and sandwiches to traditional meat and fish dishes.

Handknitted jumpers, jewellery, and souvenirs made from horn, bone, stone and wood are available at **Goðafossmarkaður** (☎ 464 3323; ☺ 8.30am-10pm Jun-Aug, 9.30am-6pm Sep-May), a small outlet by the petrol station. The shop is run by a women's cooperative, founded in 1992 to increase job opportunities for local people when farming was being cut back. About 90 women now produce work for the cooperative.

The adjacent petrol station has a café and information office, and sells basic groceries.

Northeast Iceland

Neatly packed into a compact area in northeast Iceland are some of the country's most popular attractions. The undisputed gem of the north, the triangle between Mývatn, Húsavík and Dettifoss boasts everything from active volcanoes to towering bird cliffs, great tracts of wilderness, Europe's best whale watching, and awe-inspiring waterfalls. The violence and turbulence of the region's volcanic setting is a constant feature on the tortured land, and it is this diversity of attractions and the short distances between them that draw the crowds to the area.

The teeming bird life, vast lava fields and gurgling mudpots of Mývatn and Krafla are an obvious highlight, while to the northeast the spectacular waterfalls, canyons and rock formations of Jökulsárgljúfur National Park offer a completely different take on the country. To the northwest the pretty fishing village of Húsavík is recognised as Iceland's whale-watching capital, and, further beyond, the remote northeastern corner of Iceland stretches to within a few kilometres of the Arctic Circle.

This remote peninsula to the northeast is a little-visited and sparsely populated area of desolate moors and wildly beautiful scenery. Bypassed by the tourist hordes who whiz around the Ring Rd to the south, and isolated from commercial development, this region feels like the ends of the earth, with a rugged and captivating character all of its own. Dotted with sleepy fishing villages and home to some of Iceland's hardiest souls, it makes a wonderful destination for wilderness hiking on the remote and uninhabited headlands that jut into the pounding seas.

TOP FIVE

- Hike, cycle and climb around the wonders of Mývatn lake before soaking your aching muscles in the **Mývatn Nature Baths** (p230)

- Experience the bizarre rock formations, vast canyons and utter tranquillity of **Jökulsárgljúfur National Park** (p242) on the Dettifoss to Ásbyrgi hike

- Spot a breaching whale and be followed by curious dolphins on a whale-watching cruise from **Húsavík** (p241)

- Walk gingerly around the lava fields, craters, turquoise lakes and bubbling mudpots at **Krafla** (p236)

- Marvel at the power of mighty **Dettifoss** (p245) as you photograph its churning waters and brilliant rainbows

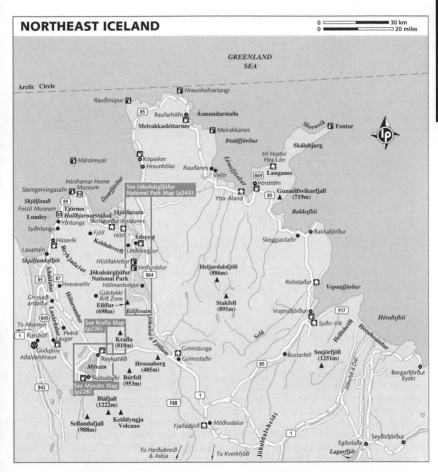

MÝVATN & KRAFLA

The undisputed gem of the region, Mývatn lake and the surrounding area are a starkly beautiful but otherworldly landscape of spluttering mudpots, weird lava formations, steaming fumaroles and volcanic craters. The Mývatn basin sits squarely on the Mid-Atlantic Ridge and the violent geological character of the area has produced colourful, diverse scenery unlike anywhere else in the country. Its abundance of dramatic features, good tourist facilities and excellent trails make it a place to savour, where you can easily settle in for a few days and experience the Iceland you've always imagined.

Thanks to its location in the rain shadow of the Vatnajökull icecap, Mývatn is statistically the driest spot in Iceland, so you can expect good weather in summer. However, the name Mývatn means 'midge lake', and unfortunately the fertile water here provides a perfect breeding ground for midge and black-fly larvae. Although the larvae can be thanked for attracting prolific bird life, they can also be the bane of travellers' lives – see p229.

History & Geology

Ten thousand years ago the Mývatn basin was covered by an icecap, which was destroyed by fierce volcanic eruptions that also obliterated the lake at its base. The explosions formed the symmetrical *móberg* peaks (flat-topped

NORTHEAST ICELAND

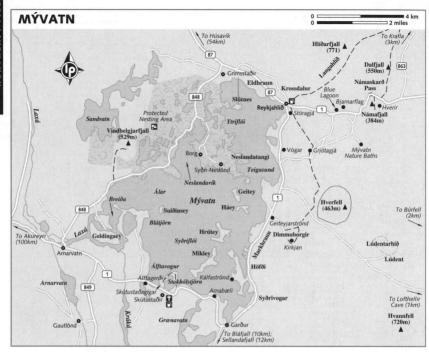

mountains formed by subglacial volcanic eruptions) south of today's lake, while volcanic activity to the east formed the Lúdent tephra (solid matter ejected into the air by an erupting volcano) complex.

Another cycle of violent activity over 6000 years later created the Ketildyngja volcano, 25km southeast of Mývatn. The lava from that crater flowed northwest along the Laxárdalur valley, and created a lava dam and a new, improved lake. After another millennium or so a volcanic explosion along the same fissure spewed out Hverfell, the classic tephra crater that dominates the modern lake landscape. Over the next 200 years activity escalated along the eastern shore and craters were thrown up across a wide region, providing a steady stream of molten material flowing toward Öxarfjörður. The lava dam formed during the end of this cycle created the present Mývatn shoreline.

Between 1724 and 1729 the Mývatnseldar eruptions began at Leirhnjúkur, close to Krafla, northeast of the lake. This dramatic and sporadically active fissure erupted spectacularly in 1984, and by the early 1990s the magma chamber had refilled, prompting experts to predict another big eruption. As yet this hasn't happened, but it's really only a matter of time.

In 1974 the area around Mývatn was set aside as the Mývatn-Laxá special conservation area, and the pseudocrater field at Skútustaðir, at the southern end of the lake, is preserved as a national natural monument.

Orientation

The lake is encircled by a 36km sealed road (Rtes 1 and 848), with the main settlement of Reykjahlíð on the northeast corner and a secondary village, Skútustaðir, on the south side. Most of the sights of interest are close to this road, or to the east and northeast. Following the Ring Rd (Rte 1) east from Reykjahlíð takes you over the Námaskarð pass to the Hverir geothermal area, then a turn-off to the north (Rte 863) leads to Krafla, 14km from Reykjahlíð.

With your own vehicle this whole area can be explored in a single day, but if you're using the bus or a bicycle allow two days. If you want to hike and explore more distant mountains and lava fields, allow at least three.

INTO THE MADDING SWARMS

Plague-like swarms of Mývatn's eponymous midges are a lasting memory for many visitors to the area in midsummer. As infuriating as they can be, these pesky intruders are a vital food source for wildlife. Their larvae are eaten by brown trout, and both the harlequin duck and Barrow's goldeneye subsist on them during the nesting season.

Unfortunately for humans, the midges are attracted to carbon dioxide, so every time you exhale, the little buggers gather around your face and invade your eyes, ears, nose and mouth. Mývatn has two types of midge, the small, skinny, mosquito-like *mýflugur* or *rikmý*, known to occasionally make kamikaze dives for your lungs, and the fatter, buzzing, hair-loving *bitmý* (blackfly).

The good news is that only one species bites, so wear a head net (which you can buy for around Ikr500 at the shop in Reykjahlíð), splash on the repellent and pray for a good wind to send the nasty little blighters diving for shelter amid the vegetation.

Getting There & Away

Daily buses run between Akureyri, Skútustaðir and Reykjahlíð (Ikr2600, 1½ hours), with four buses in either direction in summer. The Akureyri to Egilsstaðir (Ikr5400) bus also stops in Reykjahlíð daily in summer and four times a week from October to May. Buses to Húsavík (Ikr2300, 45 minutes) run daily in summer.

Two companies operate on these routes, with SBA using the car park in front of Hotel Reynihlíð as its pick-up/drop-off location, and TREX stopping at the supermarket beside the tourist office.

Getting Around

Without a car or bicycle you may find getting around Mývatn a bit frustrating. Hitchers can find the going tough, as most passing vehicles belong to tourists, many of whom are unlikely to stop for dusty and/or wet backpackers.

There are a few hiking trails, but they won't take you to all the points of interest, so you must sometimes walk along the road. Allow about three hours to walk between Reykjahlíð and Skútustaðir.

You can hire a car from **Hótel Reynihlíð** (☎ 464 4170; www.reynihlid.is; ☼ Jun-Aug). The cheapest vehicle will cost you Ikr9200 per day with 200km free, but for a small 4WD vehicle it's Ikr21,300 per day.

If you have calm weather, the best option for travellers without a car, is to hire a mountain bike. In Reykjahlíð you can rent bikes from Hótel Reynihlíð (Ikr900/1800 per half/ full day), Ferðaþjónustan Bjarg (Ikr1000/1500 for six/12 hours) and Hlíð camp site (from Ikr1200/1600 per half/full day).

The 36km ride around the lake can be easily done in a day, allowing time for sightseeing at all the major stops.

REYKJAHLÍÐ

pop 210

Reykjahlíð, on the northeastern shore of the lake, is the main village and the obvious base for trips around Mývatn. There's little to it beyond a collection of guesthouses and hotels, a supermarket, a petrol station and an information centre.

Information

The friendly **information centre** (☎ 464 4390; www .myv.is; ☼ 9am-9pm mid-Jun–mid-Aug, to 5pm Mon-Fri, to noon Sat & Sun Sep) is by the supermarket and has a display on the geology of the area as well as a large seating area perfect for waiting out bad weather. While here pick up a copy of the map *Lake Mývatn & the River Laxá* (Ikr100). The office is only open in winter if the park ranger happens to be in.

The **post office** (Helluhraun) is on the street behind the supermarket. Inside is the local Sparisjóðu Mývetninga bank with foreign exchange and a 24-hour ATM.

Internet access is available at Hotel Reynihlíð (Ikr500 for 30 minutes, free to hotel guests), Ferðaþjónustan Bjarg (Ikr400 for 30 minutes) and at Hlíð camp site (Ikr400 per 30 minutes).

Sights & Activities

During the huge Krafla eruption of 1727 the Leirhnjúkur crater, 11km northeast of Reykjahlíð, kicked off a two-year period of volcanic activity, sending streams of lava along old glacial moraines and past Reykjahlíð to the lake shore. On 27 August 1729 the flow ploughed through the village, destroying farms and buildings, but, amazingly, the well-placed wooden **church**, which sat on a low rise, was spared – some say miraculously – when the

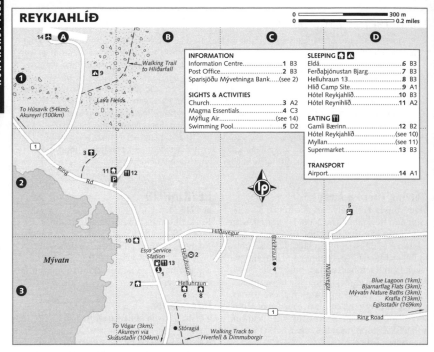

REYKJAHLÍÐ

0 ————— 300 m
0 ————— 0.2 miles

INFORMATION		SLEEPING	
Information Centre	1 B3	Eldá	6 B3
Post Office	2 B3	Ferðaþjónustan Bjarg	7 B3
Sparisjóðu Mývetninga Bank	(see 2)	Helluhraun 13	8 B3
		Hlíð Camp Site	9 A1
SIGHTS & ACTIVITIES		Hótel Reykjahlíð	10 B3
Church	3 A2	Hótel Reynihlíð	11 A2
Magma Essentials	4 C3		
Mýflug Air	(see 14)	EATING	
Swimming Pool	5 D2	Gamli Bærinn	12 B2
		Hótel Reykjahlíð	(see 10)
		Myllan	(see 11)
		Supermarket	13 B3
		TRANSPORT	
		Airport	14 A1

flow parted and missed it by only a few metres. It was rebuilt on its original foundation in 1876. You can still see remnants of the original Reykjahlíð farm, which was destroyed by the lava.

In 1962 a new church was opened close to the same site and in 1972 the original church was finally taken down. The interior of the present church is filled with carvings, paintings and batik-style art. The wooden carving on the pulpit is a representation of the church that survived the lava.

Clouds of steam rise from the turquoise blue waters at the **Mývatn Nature Baths** (Jarðbaðshólar; ☎ 464 4411; www.jardbodin.is; adult/8-16yr Ikr1100/550, towel/swimsuit hire Ikr350/350; ☼ 9am-midnight Jun-Aug, noon-10pm Sep-May), 3km east of Reykjahlíð. This is the north's answer to the Blue Lagoon, and although smaller it's a gorgeous place to relax and ease aching muscles in the mineral-rich water. There are also three natural steam baths, a hot pot and a small café.

If you fancy some pampering, **Magma Essentials** (☎ 464 3740; www.magmaessentials.com; Birkihraun 11) offers aromatherapy and Raynor massage therapy.

Alternatively, a stormy day in Reykjahlíð is well spent relaxing at the 25m outdoor **swimming pool** (adult/under 14yr Ikr280/150; ☼ 10.30am-9pm Jun-Aug, 10.30am-8pm Sep-May) and hot tub. The complex also has a sauna, solarium and gym (Ikr550).

Although there are no regular boat trips on Mývatn, you can hire rowing boats (and obtain fishing permits and gear) from Ferðaþjónustan Bjarg (opposite) for Ikr1200 per hour.

Tours

Tourism reigns supreme at Reykjahlíð and for travellers without their own transport there are numerous tours around the area. Tours can get really heavily booked during the summer months, so try to book at least a day before departure. Tours also run from the Sel-Hótel in Skútustaðir (see p234) throughout the winter.

HORSE RIDING

Horse-riding tours around the lake are available with **Hestaleiga** (☎ 464 4103; 1/2/3hr Ikr2500/4000/5500). Tours leave at 10.30am and 5pm and can be booked at Hlíð camp site (see opposite).

GEOLOGICALLY SPEAKING

Everywhere you go around Mývatn you'll be bombarded with geological jargon to describe the landscape. The terms below should help decipher the information signs and leaflets.

Basalt – the commonest type of solidified lava, this hard, dark, dense volcanic rock often solidifies into columns.
Igneous – produced under intense heat.
Moraine – a ridge of boulders, clay and sand carried and deposited by a glacier.
Obsidian – black, glassy rock formed by silica-rich magma that has reached the surface and cooled rapidly.
Rhyolite – light-coloured, fine-grained volcanic rock similar to granite in composition.
Scoria – porous volcanic gravel that has cooled rapidly while moving creating a glassy surface with iron-rich crystals that give it a glittery appearance.
Tephra – solid matter ejected into the air by an erupting volcano.

MÝVATN

SBA (http://english.sba.is) runs a 10-hour tour of the Mývatn-Krafla area from Akureyri (Ikr7700). A similar but reduced tour (Ikr7400, eight hours) continues throughout the winter.

DETTIFOSS, JÖKULSÁRGLJÚFUR & GJÁSTYKKI

Full-day tours (six to seven hours) to Krafla, Gjástykki, Hafragilsfoss, Selfoss and Dettifoss by super-Jeep depart from Hotel Reykjahlíð (Ikr9900) on request from 15 June to 30 September (minimum of four people).

LOFTHELLIR CAVE

The dramatic lava cave at Lofthellir is a stunning destination with magnificent natural ice sculptures dominating the interior. A five-hour tour to the cave by 4WD is the only way to get here, as there is no public access. Tours leave Hotel Reykjahlíð by request from 1 June to 30 September (Ikr8200, minimum of four people).

HERÐUBREIÐ & ASKJA

Mývatn Tours (☎ 464 1920; myvatntours@emax.is) runs long but rewarding day tours to Herðubreið and the Askja caldera (p304 deep in the interior). Tours (Ikr14,800, 11 to 12 hours) depart from Hotel Reynihlíð at 8am on Monday, Wednesday and Friday from 20 June to 31 August and daily from mid-July to mid-August.

AIR SIGHTSEEING

Mýflug Air (☎ 464 4400; www.myflug.is; Reykjahlíð airport) operates flight-seeing on request. The cost is from Ikr5000 per person for 20 minutes over Mývatn and Krafla; Ikr10,000 for an hour including Askja; Ikr9000 for 40 minutes over Dettifoss, Jökulsárgljúfur and Ásbyrgi; or Ikr20,000 for a supertour covering all these areas. You can also take a two-hour Arctic Circle tour to Grímsey for Ikr15,000.

Festivals & Events

Regular free summer concerts are held in the church at Reykjahlíð or Skútustaðir on Saturday night in July at 9pm. On one Saturday the concert is held in Kirkjan at Dimmuborgir.

In late June the annual **Mývatn marathon** (www.myvatn.is/marathon) follows a circuit around the lake, attracting hardy souls from across the country. The organisers also host 3km and 10km fun runs. For information, contact **Sel-Hótel Mývatn** (☎ 464 4164; www.myvatn.is).

Sleeping

Most Mývatn accommodation is in or near Reykjahlíð or at Skútustaðir (see p234).

Hlíð camp site (☎ 464 4103; hlid@isholf.is; Hraunbrún; sites per person Ikr700, sb/cabins Ikr2000/2000; 💻) This large, well-maintained camp site has showers, toilets, drying sheds and, in summer, a kitchen tent. There's also a laundry service (Ikr500 per wash and Ikr500 to dry), mountain-bike rental (Ikr1200/1600 per half/full day) and internet access (Ikr400 per 30 minutes). Sleeping bag accommodation is available across the road in no-frills rooms with a large shared kitchen. There are also six basic cabins sleeping four. The Hlíð is 300m uphill from the church.

Ferðaþjónustan Bjarg (☎ 464 4240; ferdabjarg@ simnet.is; sites per person Ikr750, sb Ikr1700-2500, d/tr Ikr8200/ 10,500; 🕐 May-Oct; 💻) This smaller site has a lovely location on the lake shore and a new shower block, a kitchen tent, a laundry service, a souvenir shop, summer boat rental (Ikr1200 for the first hour, Ikr600 per hour thereafter), bike hire (Ikr1000/1500 for six/12 hours) and internet access (Ikr400/600 per half-hour/

hour). Accommodation is also available in bright, freshly carpeted rooms in the main building. The owner sells tickets for a wide variety of tours and buses.

Eldá (☎ 464 4220; www.elda.is; Helluhraun 15; sb mid-Sep–mid-May only Ikr1900, s/d/tr Ikr7000/9900/14,000) This friendly family-run guesthouse operation owns five properties around town and offers cosy accommodation in each one. There are guest kitchens and TV lounges, and an impressive buffet breakfast is included in the rates. All guests should check in at this location.

Helluhraun 13 (☎ 464 4132; myvatn100@isl.is; d Ikr9000; ☺ May-Sep, by reservation only Oct-Apr) There are just three rooms at this small guesthouse, but they're spacious, bright and tastefully decorated with wood floors, white linens and shared bathrooms. Breakfast is included in the price.

Vógar (☎ 464 4303; www.vogarholidays.is; sites per person Ikr550, sb 4-bed r/d Ikr1800/5000, s/d/tr with bathroom Ikr12,600/14,500/19,500) This quiet farm guesthouse, on the lake road about 2.5km south of Reykjahlíð, has camping and sleeping-bag facilities in basic portacabins, and comfortable guesthouse rooms with private bathrooms. New ultra-cosy Scandinavian-style log cabins are also available.

Hótel Reykjahlíð (☎ 464 4142; www.reykjahlid.is; s/d Jun-Aug Ikr13,300/16,200, Sep-May Ikr7300/9900; ⓟ ▢) Looking out over the lake, this small hotel with a relaxed attitude has a choice of bright, spacious rooms with contemporary, neutral furnishings and handy black-out blinds. The front rooms have superb views over the lake, and there's a TV lounge, a restaurant and free internet and wi-fi access.

Hótel Reynihlíð (☎ 464 4170; www.myvatnhotel.is; s/d Jun-Aug & Christmas Ikr15,900/17,900, Sep-May Ikr8900/10,900; ⓟ ▢) Mývatn's upmarket, business-class option is a stylish place offering generous rooms with giant beds, wi-fi access, satellite TV and international style. There's a small bar and a good restaurant here. A buffet breakfast is included in the rates.

Eating & Drinking

The local food speciality is a moist, cakelike, molasses-rich rye bread known as *hverabrauð*. It's slow-baked underground in the Bjarnarflag geothermal area and served in every restaurant in town.

Vogafjós Cowshed (☎ 464 4303; Vógar; snacks Ikr500-900; ☺ 10am-10pm mid-May–mid-Sep) This bizarre but memorable café is pretty unique in that it features a glass wall between it and the dairy shed of a working farm. You can watch the cows being milked as you sip your coffee and tuck into the tasty selection of sandwiches, cakes, waffles, pancakes and smoked trout. Vógar is 2.5km south of Reykjahlíð.

Gamli Bærinn (☎ 464 4270; ☺ 11am-10pm mid-May–mid-Sep, to midnight Jul & Aug; mains Ikr1200-1990) This chilled pub-café beside Hótel Reynihlíð is the best place for a meal in town and has a menu featuring everything from traditional lamb soup (Ikr990) to smoked char with *hverabrauð* (Ikr500), pan-fried lamb (Ikr1900) and a bumper selection of desserts. In the evening it becomes the local hangout, with live music, often jazz, at weekends in high season.

Hótel Reykjahlíð (☎ 464 4142; 3 courses Ikr3200-3900; ☺ lunch & dinner Jun-Aug, dinner only May & Sep) This relaxed restaurant at the hotel has great views over the lake and serves a good selection of traditional salmon, char and lamb dishes as well as more international chicken and vegetarian specialities. Smoked trout, local rye bread and *skyr* (a yogurtlike dessert) are also featured.

Myllan (☎ 464 4170; 2-/3-course dinner Ikr3490/3990) The town's swankiest, though often quietest, spot to eat is this upmarket restaurant at Hótel Reynihlíð. There's a generous lunch buffet, and set evening meals feature traditional favourites such as arctic char, smoked and fresh lamb, hot spring-bread, and *skyr* with blueberries.

The **supermarket** (☺ 10am-8pm) at the Esso petrol station is well stocked and has a hot-dog grill.

AROUND THE LAKE

The sealed route around the lake is only 36km long, but with plenty of walks and side trips away from the road you should plan at least a day to explore the sights, and two days if you want to hike the Hverfell-Dimmuborgir trail system. Sites not to be missed along the way include **Dimmuborgir**, **Hverfell**, **Höfði**, the pseudo-craters and the view from **Vindbelgjarfjall**.

This section is organised in a clockwise direction from Reykjahlíð and includes Skútustaðir.

Hverfell & Dimmuborgir Trail

A well-marked track runs from Reykjahlíð to Hverfell (5km) and on to Dimmuborgir (a further 2.5km); it makes a good day trip in fine weather. The trail begins southeast of the intersection of the Ring Rd and the round-the-lake route.

STÓRAGJÁ & GRJÓTAGJÁ

First up along this trail (about 100m from the start) is Stóragjá a rather eerie, watery **fissure** that was once a popular bathing spot. Cooling water temperatures (currently about 28°C) and the growth of potentially harmful algae mean it's no longer safe to swim in the cave, but it's an alluring spot with clear waters and a rock roof.

Further on at Grjótagjá there's another gaping **fissure** with a water-filled cave, this time at about 45°C – too hot to soak in. It's a beautiful spot, though, particularly when the sun filters through the cracks in the roof and illuminates the interior.

HVERFELL

Dominating the lava fields on the eastern edge of Mývatn is the classic tephra ring Hverfell. This near-symmetrical crater appeared 2500 years ago in a cataclysmic eruption of the existing Lúdentarhíð complex. Rising 463m from the ground and stretching 1040m across, it is a massive and awe-inspiring landmark in Mývatn.

The crater is composed of loose gravel, but an easy track leads from the northwestern end to the summit and offers stunning views of the crater itself and the surrounding landscape. From the rim of the crater the sheer magnitude of the explosion becomes apparent – a giant gaping hole reaching out across the mountain. The trail runs along the western rim of the crater to a lookout at the southern end before descending steeply towards Dimmuborgir.

Because of damage to the formation, hikers are asked to stick to the main trail only and not to descend into the crater, which has been severely damaged by graffiti.

DIMMUBORGIR

The giant lava field at Dimmuborgir is one of the most fascinating in the country, with oddly shaped pillars, natural arches, caves and weird formations of lava formed by a succession of eruptions and lava flows across the area.

It's believed that the strange pillars and crags here were created about 2000 years ago when lava from the Þrengslaborgir and Lúdentarborgir crater rows flowed across older Hverfell lava fields. The new lava was dammed into a fiery lake in the Dimmuborgir basin and, when the surface of this lake cooled, a domed roof formed over the still-molten material below. The roof was sup-ported by pillars of older igneous material, and when the dam finally broke the molten lava drained in stages and the odd pillars of Dimmuborgir remained, marked with terraces at various levels.

A series of colour-coded walking trails run through Dimmuborgir, leading past the main formations. The most famous of these is the large lava cave known as Kirkjan, where a natural arched roof covers a gaping hole. Small and innocent-looking cracks run throughout the area, many covering deep and dangerous fissures. Stick to the marked trails and be especially watchful of children.

Höfði

One of the area's gentlest landscapes is on the forested lava headland Höfði. Wildflowers and birch and spruce trees cover the headland, and the tiny islands and crystal-clear waters attract great northern divers and other birds. Along the shore you'll see many small caves and *klasar* (lava pillars), the best known of which are at **Kálfaströnd** on the southern shore of the Höfði peninsula, where the *klasar* rise from the water in dramatic clusters. Rambling footpaths lead across the headland and can easily fill an hour.

Pseudocraters

More than 50 islands and islets are scattered across the lake, most of which were formed by gas explosions that occurred when molten lava flowed into the water. The same formations can be seen in the small hills around the southern, western and southeastern shores. Known as pseudocraters, these hills were formed as trapped subsurface water boiled and exploded in steam eruptions through the lava surface, forming small scoria cones and craters. The largest of these, which measure more than 300m across, are east of Vindbelgjarfjall on the western shore of Mývatn. The smallest ones – the islets and those south of the lake – are just a couple of metres wide and are best appreciated from the air.

SKÚTUSTAÐAGÍGAR

The most accessible pseudocrater swarm is Skútustaðagígar, near Skútustaðir on the southern lake shore. You can make a complete circuit around and over the craters on the hiking trail that starts near the camp site at Skútustaðir. The walk takes about an hour at a leisurely pace.

The nearby pond, Stakhólstjörn, and its surrounding area are havens for nesting waterfowl and were designated a national natural monument in 1973. The boggy marshland here is particularly delicate, so hikers are asked to stick to the marked trails.

Skútustaðir

The small village of Skútustaðir, on the southern shore of Mývatn, is the only settlement in the area apart from Reykjahlíð. During saga times, it was owned by the notorious Vigaskúta, who was known for his ruthlessness and was marked for assassination by his neighbours. He was clever, though, and more often than not turned the tables on those who threatened him.

The **church**, just east of the village, contains a painting of the Last Supper and makes a quiet and shady vantage point.

TOURS

To complement the summer tours run out of Reykjahlíð, Sel-Hótel Mývatn offers a program of winter tours from September to May, including snowmobiling (Ikr7500, one to two hours), 4WD tours (Ikr7900, three hours), Northern Lights tours (Ikr8500, three hours), horse riding (Ikr3900, one hour), and cross-country skiing (Ikr3300/4300/6000, one/two/three hours). Longer 4WD trips to Dettifoss (Ikr16,500, five to six hours) are also possible, as are weekend trips for gay and lesbian travellers (Ikr25,500, including four nights' accommodation).

SLEEPING & EATING

Camp site (☎ 464 4212; sites per person Ikr650) You can camp in this basic site by the roadside opposite Sel-Hótel Mývatn.

Skjölbrekka (☎ 464 4164; sb Ikr2500) For no-frills basic beds, this local community centre offers sleeping-bag space in the large communal hall, where bunk beds are packed in between the backpacks.

Skútustaðir Guest House (☎ 464 4212; www.skutustadir.com; s Ikr6000, d without/with bathroom Ikr8500/11,000) This friendly guesthouse next door to Sel-Hótel Mývatn has a selection of comfortable, homey rooms and offers sleeping-bag space (Ikr2500) in the low season.

Hótel Gígur (☎ 464 4455; www.keahotels.is; s/d/tr Ikr13,900/17,900/23,300; ☽ Jun–mid-Sep; ▯) The lovely lakeside location here compensates for the extra-compact rooms at this business-style hotel. Popular with tour groups and often full, it's a comfortable place with tasteful but simple décor, en-suite bathrooms and free internet access for guests. The restaurant (mains Ikr2190 to Ikr3590) offers one of the best lake views in the whole area, with a lovely outdoor seating area and giant glass windows inside to protect you from the swarming midges as you watch the sunset over the lake.

Sel-Hótel Mývatn (☎ 464 4164; www.myvatn.is; s/d May-Aug Ikr14,200/17,300, Sep-Apr Ikr7700/9300; ▯) Skútustaðir's top hotel is getting a little dated, but its spacious, bright rooms are still comfy. There's a hot pot, a sauna and a lounge downstairs and free internet access. The hotel cafeteria serves burgers and pizzas (Ikr650 to Ikr1450) and the restaurant (mains Ikr1390 to Ikr4900) offers traditional hot and cold meals and dinner buffets (Ikr3400).

Laxá

The clear and turbulent Laxá (Salmon River), one of the many Icelandic rivers so named, rolls across the tundra and past numerous midchannel islets from the western end of

---

MARIMO BALLS

Marimo balls (Cladophora aegagropila) are bizarre little spheres of green algae that are thought to grow naturally in only two places in the world – Mývatn and Lake Akan in Japan. The tiny balls grow slowly, to about the size of a golf ball, rising to the surface of the water in the morning to photosynthesise (when there's enough sunlight) and sinking to the bottom at night.

The balls have been honoured with a festival in Japan for some years (the name is Japanese for 'algae ball'), so Mývatn locals decided to do the same and in late September 2003 the first Marimo Festival was held at Skútustaðir. As in Japan, the festival began with a symbolic gathering of marimo balls, which were then displayed at Skútustaðir's Skjölbrekka community centre before being returned to the lake. At present the future of the festival is uncertain, with no plans for any celebrations in 2007, but ask at the information centre in Reykjahlíð or the Sel-Hotel in Skútustaðir for up-to-date information.

Mývatn towards Skjálfandi. The Laxá is one of the best – and most expensive – salmon-fishing spots in the country. More affordable brown-trout fishing is also available. For permits, call ☎ 464 4333.

Vindbelgjarfjall

The easy climb up 529m-high Vindbelgjarfjall, west of the lake, offers one of the best views across the water, the pseudocraters and the protected wetlands along the northwestern shore. The trail to the summit starts south of the peak on Rte 848. Reckon on about a half-hour climb to get to the summit.

Protected Nesting Area

The bogs, marshes, ponds and wet tundra along the northwest shore of Mývatn are a high-density waterfowl nesting zone. Off-road entry is restricted between 15 May and 20 July (when the chicks hatch), but overland travel on this soggy ground is challenging at any time.

Most species of waterfowl present in Iceland are found here in great numbers – including nearly 10,000 breeding pairs of ducks, representing 15 species – and the area is world famous among bird-watchers. Three duck species – the scoter, the gadwall and the Barrow's goldeneye – breed nowhere else in Iceland. Also present are incredible numbers of eider ducks, harlequin ducks, red-breasted mergansers, mallards, long-tailed ducks, pintail ducks, tufted ducks, wigeons, goosanders, teals, shovellers, whooper swans, horned grebes, great northern divers, red-throated divers, black-headed gulls, ptarmigans, arctic terns, great skuas, several species of geese, ravens, gyrfalcons, golden plovers, snipe, whimbrels, wheatears and lots of other species.

Mink and arctic foxes, which take advantage of the abundant avian prey, are also occasionally seen.

Eldhraun

The lava field along the northern lake shore, Eldhraun, includes the flow that nearly engulfed the Reykjahlíð church. It was belched out of Leirhnjúkur during the Mývatnseldar in 1729 and flowed down the channel Eldá. With some slow scrambling, it can be explored on foot from Reykjahlíð.

Hlíðarfjall

The prominent 771m-high rhyolite mountain Hlíðarfjall, 5km northeast of Reykjahlíð, is sometimes called Reykjahlíðarfjall. It makes a pleasant day hike from the village, affording spectacular views over the lake on one side and over the Krafla lava fields on the other.

BJARNARFLAG

Bjarnarflag, 3km east of Reykjahlíð, is an active geothermal area where the earth hisses and bubbles and steaming vents line the valley. Historically, the area has been home to a number of economic ventures attempting to harness the earth's powers. Early on, farmers tried growing potatoes here, but, unfortunately, these often emerged from the ground already boiled. In the early 1950s attempts to extract sulphur from the solfataras (fumaroles venting sulphurous gases) that dot the area proved to be uneconomical and were abandoned.

In the late 1960s, 25 test holes were bored at Bjarnarflag to ascertain the feasibility of a proposed geothermal power station. One is 2300m deep and the steam roars out of the pipe at 200°C.

Later a diatomite (microfossil) plant was set up and the skeletal remains of a type of single-cell algae were filtered and purified into filler for fertilisers, paints, toothpastes and plastics. All that remains of the processing plant today is the so-called **Blue Lagoon**, a steaming turquoise pool of bore water from the former factory.

A cinder-brick factory here continues to manufacture building materials from the volcanic ash deposits, and nearby is the underground bread oven where *hverabrauð* is packed into milk cartons and slowly baked over 22 hours. Look for the small, round glass doors that open into the ground, but don't disturb the bread.

Námafjall

Produced by a fissure eruption, the pastel-coloured Námafjall ridge lies south of the Ring Rd, 6km east of Reykjahlíð. It sits squarely on the spreading zone of the Mid-Atlantic Ridge and is dotted with steaming vents. A walking trail leads from the highway at Namaskarð pass to a view disc at the summit. This 30-minute climb provides a grand vista over the steamy surroundings. North of the pass is another ridge, Dalfjall, which sports a large and growing notch – dramatic evidence that the mountain is being torn in two by tectonic spreading.

Hverir

The ochre-coloured slopes of Hverir, the geothermal field immediately to the east of Námafjall, is a lunarlike landscape of bubbling mudpots, steaming vents, sulphur deposits, boiling springs and fumaroles, some of which are real dynamos. A heavy scent of sulphur lingers in the area and a change of wind direction can leave you shrouded by a damp, foggy cloud of pungent steam. Safe pathways through the features have been roped off, and to avoid risk of serious injury and damage to the natural features, avoid any lighter-coloured soil and respect the ropes.

KRAFLA

More steaming vents, brightly coloured craters and aquamarine lakes await at Krafla, an active volcanic region 7km north of the Ring Rd. Technically, Krafla is just an 818m-high mountain, but the name is now used for the entire area as well as a geothermal power station and the series of eruptions that created Iceland's most awesome lava field.

The heart of volcanic activity is known as the Krafla central volcano, but, rather than a cone-shaped peak, Krafla is a largely level system of north–south trending fissures underlaid by a great magma chamber. Activity is normally characterised by fissuring and gradual surface swells followed by abrupt subsidence, which triggers eruptions. At present, the ground surface is rising, indicating possible activity in the future. The **Nordic Volcanological Center** (www.norvol.hi.is) tracks the most recent developments.

As the Krafla area is still considered active, a visit will naturally involve some risk. To be safe, avoid lighter-coloured soil, which indicates a live steam vent, mudpots, sharp lava chunks and scoria slopes. Stick to marked trails, and in winter be extremely wary of hidden fissures and avoid any melting snow, which may cover a hot spot.

Kröflustöð

The idea of constructing a geothermal power station at Krafla was conceived in 1973, and preliminary work commenced with the drilling of 24 test holes to determine project feasibility. In December 1975, however, after a rest of several hundred years, the Krafla fissure burst into activity with the first in a series of nine eruptions and 20 cases of surface subsidence. This considerably lowered the site's

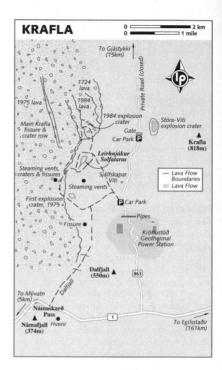

projected geothermal potential and nearly deactivated one of the primary steam sources, but the project went ahead and was completed in 1978. A second turbine unit and additional boreholes were added in 1996, and Krafla now operates at its intended capacity of 60 megawatts using on average 15 to 17 boreholes at a time. The power plant's **visitor centre** (Gestastofa; admission free; ☺ 12.30-3.30pm Mon-Fri, 1-5pm Sat & Sun Jun-Aug) explains how it all works.

Stóra-Víti

The impressive dirt-brown crater of Stóra-Víti reveals a stunning secret when you reach its rim – a glittering turquoise pool of flood water at its heart. Surrounded by steaming vents, bubbling pools and desolate land, the vibrant colour makes a lasting impression as you track around the rim of the crater on a slippery walking trail.

The 320m-wide explosion crater was created in 1724 during the destructive Mývatnseldar, and it's just one of many vents along the Krafla central volcano. Behind the crater are the 'twin lakes', boiling mud springs that spurted mud 10m into the air during the Mývatnseldar.

They're now down to a mere simmer and Víti is considered inactive.

Leirhnjúkur & Krafla Caldera

Krafla's most impressive, and potentially most dangerous, attraction is the colourful Leirhnjúkur crater, which originally appeared in August 1727. It started out as a lava fountain and spouted molten material for two years before subsiding. After a minor burp in 1746, it became the menacing sulphur-encrusted mud hole that tourists love today.

From the rim above Leirhnjúkur you can look out across the Krafla Caldera and the layers of lava that bisect it. The first of these lava flows was from the original Mývatnseldar, which was overlaid in places by lava from the 1975 eruptions, and again by 1984 lava.

The earth's crust here is extremely thin and in places the ground is ferociously hot. Steaming vents on the pastel-coloured rhyolite mountain to the west are the last vestiges of a series of explosions in 1975, when the small grass-filled crater on the western slope of the mountain south of Leirhnjúkur erupted as Kröflueldar, a continuation of Mývatnseldar.

A well-defined track leads northwest to Leirhnjúkur from the Krafla parking area; with all the volcanic activity, high temperatures, bubbling mud pots and steaming vents, you'd be well advised not to stray from the marked paths at any time.

Gjástykki

This remote rift zone at the northernmost end of the Krafla fissure swarm was the source of the first eruptions in 1724, and was activated when Leirhnjúkur went off in the 1975 eruptions. Between 1981 and 1984 the area was the main hot pot of activity in the Krafla central volcano, and the current Gjástykki lava fields date from this time. The area's best-known landmark is a red mountain that protrudes from dark fields of lava. Gjástykki is a very sensitive area and no private vehicles are allowed access. To visit you will need to join a tour; see p231.

Getting There & Away

From Reykjahlíð, a wonderful day hike leads to Hliðarfjall and Leirhnjúkur along a marked path from near the airport. Another walking route leads from Námaskarð along the Dalfjall ridge to Leirhnjúkur.

HOME-MADE HELL

The impressive crater known as Sjálfskapar Víti (Homemade Hell), near the Krafla car park, isn't like other craters in the area. When teams were drilling the Krafla boreholes, one was so powerful that when they hit the steam chamber it exploded. A huge crater was created and bits of the drilling rig were discovered up to 3km away. Miraculously, no-one was killed. Had the project been successful, this one borehole would have been sufficient to power the entire Krafla power station. Now, the same work is done by 17 boreholes.

In summer Krafla can be reached on the daily bus (Ikr900, 15 minutes), which leaves at 8am and 11.30am from Hótel Reynihlíð and returns at 11.15am and 3.15pm. The Mývatn–Dettifoss excursion bus also runs via Krafla.

SOUTHEAST OF MÝVATN

South and east of the main lake area a region of forbidding mountains, deserts and rugged geological features stretches into the interior. With plenty of time and determination, it makes challenging terrain for experienced hikers.

The **Lúdentarborgir** crater row, east of Mývatn, is part of the 8km **Þrengslaborgir** fissure. To get to Lúdent, follow the track rounding the southern base of Hverfell, then continue 5km southeastward through the Lúdentarborgir crater row to Lúdent itself.

About 13km southeast of Grænavatn, near the southern shore of Mývatn, is the 1222m-high table mountain **Bláfjall**. There are no marked routes in the area and getting there is tough going, through marshes and across ropy, chunky lava flows.

Two other table mountains visible from Mývatn are **Búrfell** (953m) and **Sellandafjall** (988m), both long and arduous hikes.

HÚSAVÍK REGION

MÝVATN TO HÚSAVÍK

The most direct route between Mývatn and Húsavík is the partially sealed Rte 87 (54km), which crosses the barren Hólarsandur before entering the gentle, grassy valleys of the Laxá and Skjálfandafljót that give few clues to the area's substantial geothermal activity. With a vehicle this whole area can be explored as a day trip from Húsavík or Mývatn.

Turning off either Rte 85 or Rte 87, the wealthy old farm **Grenjaðarstaður** served as a church and vicarage during the 19th century. In the churchyard there is a stone carved with runes dating from medieval times. The turf-roofed farmhouse, constructed in 1865, is one of only three left in the district and now houses a simple **folk museum** (☎ 464 3545; adult/ under 14yr Ikr400/150; ☺ 10am-6pm Jun-Aug) similar to Laufás near Akureyri (p223). Grenjaðarstaður is 5km from public-transport routes.

The geothermal site **Hveravellir** on Rte 87, about 26km south of Húsavík, provides some of Húsavík's hot-water supply. The farm here sells fresh vegetables from its geothermally heated greenhouses.

The alternative road from Mývatn or Akureyri to Húsavík starts on the Ring Rd before turning north on Rte 845 at **Laugar**, the main village in this area. Apart from an overnight bed there's little to detain you in Laugar. The school here was built in 1924 and now is a hotel, **Fosshótel Laugar** (☎ 464 6300; www.fosshotel.is; s/d without shower Ikr7500/9900, with shower Ikr14,700/19,000; ☺ Jun-Aug; 🖳). The rooms without bathrooms are basic, but the en-suite rooms are spacious and bright. Just past the village on Rte 1 you'll find cosy accommodation at **Narfastaðir** (☎ 464 3102; www.farmhotel.is; s/d Ikr6000/8600, s/d with bathroom Ikr8300/11,700).

HÚSAVÍK

pop 2500

Húsavík, Iceland's whale-watching capital, is a picturesque harbour town that has become a firm favourite on travellers' itineraries. With its colourful houses tumbling down to the water and the snowcapped peaks of Viknafjöll across the bay, it's the prettiest fishing town on the northeast coast. Húsavík is also home to several interesting museums: the award-winning Whale Museum, a rather bizarre but unique Phallological Museum, and a better-than-average local-history museum. The town also has a good selection of accommodation and restaurants and a lively but relaxed atmosphere, making it a perfect base to explore the area.

History

Although the honours normally go to Reykjavík and Ingólfur Arnarson, Húsavík was the real site of the first Nordic settlement in Iceland. Garðar Svavarsson, a Swedish Viking who set off around 850 for the mysterious Thule or Snæland (Snowland), was actually responsible for the island's first permanent human settlement.

After a brief stop-off at Hornafjörður in the south, Garðar arrived at Skjálfandi on the north coast and built a settlement that he called Húsavík. Modestly renaming the country Garðarshólmur (Garðar's Island), he dug in for the winter. At the advent of spring he prepared to depart, but some of his slaves were left behind. Whether by accident or design, these castaways became Iceland's first real settlers, pioneering life in a new country and yet uncredited by the history books.

Information

The **Húsavík Information Centre** (☎ 464 4300; www .husavik.is; Garðarsbraut 5; ☺ 10am-6.30pm Mon-Thu, to 7pm Fri, to 6pm Sat, noon-6pm Sun Jun-Aug) is inside the Kasko supermarket on the main street.

Húsavík has a hospital, a post office and other facilities. The **Íslandsbanki bank** (Stórigarður 1) is opposite the church and has an ATM. There's internet access at the **library** (☎ 464 6165; Stórigarður 17; per hr Ikr250; ☺ 10am-7pm Mon-Fri, to 5pm Sat).

Þórarins Stefánssonar Bookshop (☎ 464 1234; Garðarsbraut 9), beside the bank, sells a good range of souvenirs, maps, books and novels in English and German.

Sights & Activities

HÚSAVÍK WHALE MUSEUM

Best visited before you head out on a whale-watching trip, this excellent **museum** (Hvalamiðstöðin; ☎ 464 2520; www.icewhale.is; Hafnarstétt; adult/6-14yr Ikr600/250; ☺ 9am-7pm Jun-Aug, 10am-5pm May & Sep) will tell you all you ever needed to know about these gracious creatures. Housed in an old slaughterhouse at the harbour, the museum looks at the ecology and habits of whales, orcas, dolphins and other marine mammals, whale conservation, and the history of whaling in Iceland.

The 'Ocean Odyssey – Follow the Gulf Stream' exhibit has detailed information on the biology of whales, their habitats and the environmental threats they face, while the 10 enormous skeletons of humpback, minke and sperm whales (all found stranded or trapped in fishermen's nets) give you some idea of the gargantuan proportions of these mammals. There's also a 30-minute film chronicling

HÚSAVÍK

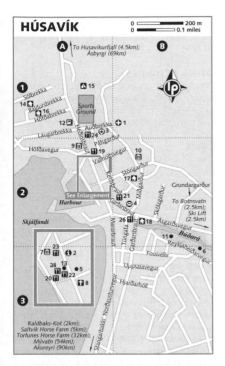

0 |=====| 200 m
0 |=====| 0.1 miles

whaling in Iceland and an exhibition devoted to Keiko, the killer whale captured off Iceland in 1979 and star of the movie *Free Willy*.

ICELANDIC PHALLOLOGICAL MUSEUM

This unique **museum** (Hid Íslanska Redasafn; ☎ 561 6663; www.phallus.is; Héðinsbraut 3a; admission Ikr500; ☺ noon-6pm late-May–mid-Sep) houses a bizarre collection of penises of all shapes and sizes. There are over 180 pickled, dried and stuffed specimens in the museum, showing off the crown jewels of everything from hamsters to a blue whale. The only missing exhibit is that of a human. But don't rush to volunteer, four donors-in-waiting have been found to add to the collection in the future.

SAFNAHÚSIÐ Á HÚSAVÍK

The **Húsavík museum** (☎ 464 1860; www.husmus.is; Stórigarður 17; adult/under 14yr Ikr400/100; ☺ 10am-6pm Jun-Aug, 9am-noon & 1-5pm Mon-Fri, 4-6pm Sun Sep-May) is one of the best local museums you'll find in Iceland. The museum occupies the 1st and 3rd floor of the building (the library is on the 2nd floor) and a nearby annexe. The natural-history display has the usual array of stuffed

animals, including arctic foxes, a frightening-looking hooded seal, and a stuffed polar bear, which was welcomed to Grímsey in 1969 with both barrels of a gun. The folk history exhibits cover everything from a re-creation of an early farmhouse, to photographic archives, paintings, traditional costumes, a healthy collection of 16th-century weapons, and historic books – including a copy of a Bible printed in 1584. There's also a carefully catalogued collection of 100,000 beer-bottle labels from around the world. Nearby, the new annexe houses an excellent maritime museum, with displays of preserved fishing boats, a pungent fish-drying shed, and lots of memorabilia and displays relating to the fishing industry.

HÚSAVÍKURKIRKJA

Húsavík's lovely and unusual **church** is quite different to anything else seen in Iceland. Constructed in 1907 from Norwegian timber, the delicately proportioned red-and-white church would look more at home in the Alps. Inside its cruciform shape becomes apparent and is dominated by a depiction of the resurrection of Lazarus on the altarpiece. The carved font is also worth seeking out, as are the 17th-century murals and candlesticks.

LUNDEY & FLATEY

The small islands of Lundey and Flatey lie anchored in Skjálfandi, near Húsavík. Lundey (Puffin Island), rises dramatically from the sea in a series of high, nest-covered cliffs and is a breeding ground for puffins, fulmars and other sea birds. Flatey (Flat Island) lives up to its name, rising only a couple of metres above sea level. It's now abandoned, but as recently as 1942 it had a population of more than 100. Tours to both islands are possible with the two whale-watching companies – see opposite.

OTHER SIGHTS

The small town park **Skrúðgardin** is a lovely place running along the southern bank of the Buðará river. It's a relaxing spot for a walk, and there are several heritage houses scattered around, including one of Húsavík's original homes, **Arholt**.

HIKING

Húsavík's lovely setting looking out over the blue-green bay to the mountains and sheer cliffs to the south makes it an appealing location for some hiking. In a couple of hours you can make it up the steep trail (4.9km) to the summit of 417m-high **Húsavíkurfjall**. The view from the top, alongside the communication antennae, is fantastic and on exceptionally clear days you can see the Vatnajökull icecap. The path starts on the main road just 1.8km north of town.

Another walk takes you to the lake **Botnsvatn**, in a hollow behind the village, where reafforestation projects are greening the landscape. It's a 5.2km walk around the lake. Campers are welcome by the lake, but there are no facilities.

HORSE RIDING

Short horse rides (one to three hours) and longer tours (five days) are available at **Saltvík horse farm** (☎ 847 9515; www.skarpur.is/saltvik), 5km south of Húsavík.

Similar services are available at **Torfunes horse farm** (☎ 464 3622; www.torfunes.com), at Ljósavatnshreppur, 32km south of Húsavík, which

offers three-hour horse rides from May to September, as well as six- to eight-day trips in July.

OTHER ACTIVITIES

Northeast of town, a **ski lift** operates during winter, and the local **swimming pool** (☎ 464 1144; Laugarbrekka 2; ☉ 7am-9pm Mon-Fri, 10am-6pm Sat) has hot pots, and water slides for children.

Tours

The SBA-Norðurleið bus picks up at Húsavík at 10am daily in summer, and does a return eight-hour excursion to Jökulsárgljúfur National Park and Dettifoss (Ikr6500), stopping at the main sights.

Highland Expedition Tours (☎ 464 3940; www.fjall asyn.is) offers super-Jeep tours year-round in the northeast region.

Sleeping

Camp site (☎ 464 1105; sites per person Ikr750; ☉ May-Sep) Next to the sports ground at the north end of town, this well-run camp site has such luxuries as heated toilets, washing machines and cooking facilities.

Kaldbaks-Kot (☎ 464 1504; www.cottages.is; 2-4 person cabins Ikr9900-12,900) Slightly out of town but great value and really cosy, these timber cottages 2km south of Húsavík have good kitchens, TVs, comfy beds and verandas with great views out to sea. There's an outdoor hot pot and horse riding for experienced riders.

Emhild Olsen (☎ 464 1618; Baldursbrekka 17; sb/s/d Ikr1800/3200/4600; ☉ Jun-Aug) Just opposite Aðalbjörg Birgisdóttir, and offering very similar facilities, is this well-priced guesthouse with comfortable rooms and friendly service.

Aðalbjörg Birgisdóttir (☎ 464 1005; onod@simnet.is; Baldursbrekka 20; sb/s/d Ikr1800/2500/5000) You'll find a few good-value, cosy rooms at this family home to the north of town. There's a guest kitchen and a warm welcome for hikers and backpackers.

Gistiheimilið Árból (☎ 464 2220; www.simnet.is /arbol; Ásgarðsvegur 2; Jun–mid-Sep s/d/tr Ikr6200/9600/ 13,400, mid-Sep–May Ikr5000/7400/9800) Friendly and well maintained but stuck in a décor time warp, this heritage house has spacious but old-fashioned rooms and bathrooms well past their best. There's an interesting collection of musical instruments, old photos and guns along the stairs.

Fosshótel Húsavík (☎ 464 1220; www.fosshotel.is; Ketilsbraut 22; s/d Jun-Aug Ikr14,700/19,000, Sep-May

WHALE WATCHING IN HÚSAVÍK

Húsavík lies on the edge of Skjálfandi, a wide, deep bay with good water circulation, natural shelter and little variation in tides – ideal conditions for whales. The area has become Iceland's premier whale-watching destination, with 12 species coming here to feed in summer. Minke whales are by far the most common species seen in the bay, with regular sightings of white-beaked dolphins, humpback whales and porpoises and less frequent appearances by orcas, fin, sei or pilot whales, and the 'big one' – blue whales.

It takes about an hour to sail to the prime feeding grounds, where crew and participants get busy looking out for telltale signs of a surfacing whale. Although whale-watching tours boast impressive success rates for sightings (95% to 98%), whales don't appear on cue. Sightings are announced using a 'clock' system, with the stern of the boat at 12 o'clock.

Different whales have different habits and identifying features. The curious minke whale surfaces two or three times in quick succession before executing a deep dive and sometimes may even approach the boat. Humpback whales breach and sometimes roll over, holding an enormous flipper in the air. Most whales arrive in Icelandic waters in spring (around May) and stay to feed until September, when they return to warmer southern waters for breeding.

Two whale-watching tours operate from Húsavík harbour. The original operator is **Norður Sigling** (North Sailing; ☎ 464 2350; www.northsailing.is; Gamli Baukur, Hafnarstétt; adult/15-16yr/under 14yr Ikr3800/1900/free), which started whale watching here in 1994. It has four boats, including the 20-tonne oak schooner *Haukur*. Trips run up to four times daily from mid-May to mid-September. The same company also runs daily combination whale- and puffin-watching tours to Lundey (Ikr4900, three to four hours) and Flatey (Ikr5300, five to six hours), as well as full day trips to Grímsey on request.

The second operator is **Gentle Giants** (Hvalferðir; ☎ 464 1500; www.gentlegiants.is; Garðarsbraut 6; adult/under 15yr Ikr3700/free), with two boats making trips up to five times daily from June to mid-September. The company also offers sea-angling trips (Ikr4900, two to three hours) and tours to Flatey (Ikr7900, five hours). You can buy tickets from the 'lighthouse' ticket booth opposite the church.

Both operators provide hot chocolate and pastries during the trip, but it's still a good idea to wrap up well before departure as it can be bitterly cold out on the boat, no matter how warm it feels in town. In early and late season both operators may have only one departure daily, so check in advance. If there are no sightings, you can usually get on another trip for free.

Ikr9300/10,700; 🖳) This large whale-themed hotel (there's even a Moby Dick bar) has compact rooms with predictable international-style décor and all the usual facilities including TV and private bathrooms.

Eating & Drinking

Restaurant Salka (☎ 464 2551; Garðarsbraut 6; mains Ikr850-2350; 🕙 11.30am-10pm Sun-Thu, to 11pm Fri & Sat) Once home to Iceland's first cooperative, this historic building now houses a popular restaurant serving everything from smoked puffin to pizza. The real speciality here, though, is seafood, with excellent lobster, shrimp and salt cod on offer.

Gamli Baukur (☎ 464 2442; Hafnarstétt; mains Ikr990-3500; 🕙 11.30am-9pm Sun-Wed, to 1am Thu, 11am-3am Fri & Sat) This rustic timber restaurant-bar down by the harbour is decorated with nautical relics and serves a good selection of fish and seafood dishes. There's a cosy little bar upstairs and a lovely terrace overlooking the harbour.

Túnberg restaurant (mains Ikr1200-3500; 🕙 noon-2pm & 6-10pm) At Fosshotel Húsavík, this rather soulless restaurant serves a standard menu of beef and lamb dishes, pasta and pizza, and the odd local speciality such as puffin.

Skuld Café (snacks Ikr350-850; 🕙 8.30am-10pm Jun-Sep) Set on the hill overlooking the waterfront, this simple, cosy summer café sells tasty baked goods, open sandwiches, light snacks, and beer and wine. It has a lovely outdoor deck area with seating for warm days.

Kofinn (🕙 8am-9pm Jun-Sep) This 'gourmet hut' aims to let visitors sample local foods such as dried haddock, marinated herring, dried reindeer and smoked trout for free, and it offers a small menu (dishes Ikr600 to Ikr1500) of traditional Icelandic foods. The outdoor terrace has great views over the harbour.

NORTHEAST ICELAND

Both the Esso and Shell petrol stations have grills selling the usual fast-food fare, while the town bakery **Heimabakarí Konditori** (☎ 464 2900; Garðarsbraut 15; ☺ 8am-5pm) sells fresh bread, sandwiches and sugary cakes. The well-stocked **Kasko supermarket** (Garðarsbraut 5; ☺ 9am-8pm) is in the centre of town, and there's a Vín Búð at Túngata 1.

Getting There & Away

There are three buses to Akureyri (Ikr2300, one hour) on weekdays (two at weekends) from June to August, and three on weekdays (one on Saturday, two on Sunday) during winter. Buses also run twice daily to Reynihlíð at Mývatn (Ikr1700, 40 minutes) and once on weekdays to Ásbyrgi (Ikr1900, 45 minutes). The bus terminal is at the Shell petrol station.

TJÖRNES

Heading north from Húsavík along Rte 85 you'll sweep along the coast of the stubby peninsula Tjörnes, which separates Skjálfandi from Öxarfjörður. There are some interesting museums and geological features along this route as well as a colony of puffins and other sea birds on the 50m-high cliffs along the eastern coast.

Ytritunga Fossils

Fossil-rich coastal cliffs flank the Hallbjarnarstaðaá river mouth 10km north of Húsavík. The cliffs are made up of alternating layers of fossil shells and lignite (a soft brown-black coal), with the oldest layers dating back about two million years. The fossils here are the shells of creatures that are now found only in waters of 12°C or warmer. The present water temperature along Iceland's Arctic Ocean coast is around 4°C, an indication that the sea here has cooled dramatically over the past two to three million years. You can get to the cliffs by turning off Rte 85 at Ytritunga farm.

To put the fossils in context and understand the process that formed the cliffs, it's worth visiting the **fossil museum** (☎ 464 1968; adult/under 14yr Ikr400/free; ☺ 10am-6pm Jun-Aug), about 2km further up Rte 85 at the farm Hallbjarnarstaðir. It displays interesting finds from the area, including plant and animal fossils from the Pleistocene era.

Þórshamar Home Museum

Set in the middle of nowhere at the tip of the peninsula is this quirky **museum** (☎ 464 1957; adult/under 14yr Ikr400/free; ☺ 9am-6pm Jun-Aug), pride and joy of a local farmer. The eclectic collection contains Viking Age jewellery and other items dating back to the Settlement Era, as well as a large variety of matchboxes and tobacco tins, old photographs, crockery, and household implements.

The museum is about 23km north of Húsavík on the farm Mánárbakki. On the headland just west of the museum is a **lighthouse** offering views out to Grímsey in clear weather.

KELDUHVERFI

Giant cracks, fissures and grabens (depressions between geological faults) up to 7m deep scar the earth at low-lying Kelduhverfi, where the Mid-Atlantic Ridge enters the Arctic Ocean. Like Þingvellir (p115), the area reveals some of the most visible evidence that Iceland is spreading from the centre. Most of the formations here were made by earthquakes and dramatic fissuring and subsidence during the Krafla eruption of 1975.

To the north of the main road a series of lakes and lagoons stretches to the ocean, offering good fishing and bird-watching.

Sleeping & Eating

Keldunes (☎ 465 2275; keldunes@isl.is; sb 2 people Ikr5000, s/d Ikr5900/7900) You'll get small but cosy rooms with sinks at this modern guesthouse near Skjálftavatn. There's a great kitchen and TV lounge, laundry, hot pot and large balconies for bird-watching. There's also a small cottage with sleeping-bag accommodation for two people. It's about 6km west of Ásbyrgi.

Hóll (☎ 465 2270; hrunda@ismennt.is; sb/made-up beds Ikr2500/3000) Even closer to the national park, this farm has four simple twin rooms in the main house and a summerhouse sleeping eight. Horse riding is available for Ikr2200 per hour.

Skúlagarður (☎ 465 2280; skulagardur@simnet.is; sb/s/d Ikr2000/5250/8000) Set in a former boarding school, this large but functional place has less personality but plenty of rooms. There's a lounge, bar and restaurant on site.

JÖKULSÁRGLJÚFUR NATIONAL PARK

One of Iceland's best-loved national parks, Jökulsárgljúfur protects the 30km gorge carved out by the formidable **Jökulsá á Fjöllum**. The river is Iceland's second longest, starting in the Vatnajökull icecap and flowing almost 200km to the Arctic Ocean at Öxarfjörður. *Jökulhlaups* (flooding from volcanic eruptions beneath the icecap), formed the canyon and have carved out a chasm that averages 100m deep and 500m wide. Minor floods occur roughly every 10 years and a major one once or twice in a century.

After the crowds at Mývatn and Krafla, the park feels incredibly remote, with limited access on rough roads and only basic facilities. A wonderful two-day hike (see p247), weaves along the canyon through and around birch forests, striking rock formations, lush valleys and commanding perpendicular cliffs, taking in all the major sights en route. If you're not so keen on hiking, the big attractions, such as the waterfalls at the southern end of the park and horseshoe-shaped Ásbyrgi canyon at the northern end, are accessible by road in a leisurely day.

History

Most of the land that is now protected within Jökulsárgljúfur historically belonged to the Ás estate, one of Iceland's largest private holdings, which extended from Dettifoss to Öxarfjörður. Until the early 19th century there was a church at Ás, near the road on the northern end, but it has now gone and only remnants of the cemetery are visible.

Ásbyrgi has long been considered prime farmland and in medieval times the living was good due to the anomalous profusion of trees – that was until *jökulhlaup* floods tore through in the 17th and 18th centuries.

The national park, which was established in 1973, initially included only the farm Svínadalur, part of Vesturdalur and a small portion of Ásheiði, but in 1974 the huge Ás estate was added. Jökulsárgljúfur now contains 120 sq km and extends 28km from north to south.

Orientation

The park's southern anchor is Dettifoss, and 8km to the north are the springs and luxuriant vegetation of Hólmatungur. Right in the heart of the park is Vesturdalur, with lots of caves and Iceland's most interesting basalt formations. Near the northern end is Ásbyrgi, a verdant, forested plain enclosed by vertical canyon walls. From Dettifoss to Ásbyrgi on Rte 864 is 25km, about 40 minutes' drive on the rough road.

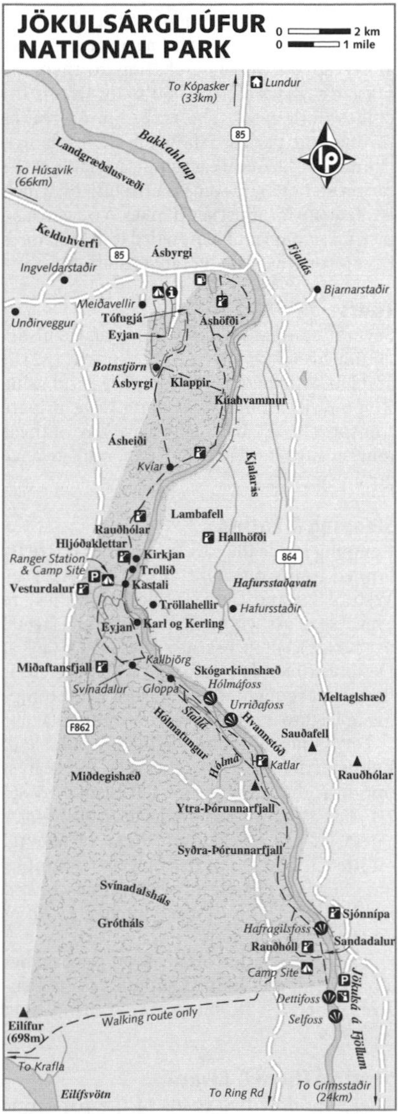

Information

Park information is available at the main ranger station in **Ásbyrgi** (☎ 465 2195; http://english.ust.is/Jokulsarglufurnationalpark; 8am-10pm Jun & Jul, shorter hr May & Sep) and at Vesturdalur. Both stations have toilets and a car park. A new visitor centre with exhibitions and information about the park is due to open at Ásbyrgi in 2007.

The best hiking map is the *Dettifoss* 1:100,000 sheet, but if you also want to hike at Mývatn it's worth purchasing the thematic *Húsavík-Mývatn* 1:100,000 map, which includes both areas. The main hiking routes through the park are shown in the park brochure (Ikr100; free if camping), available at the ranger stations and some tourist offices, which is adequate for most short hikes. You can also pick up a number of self-guided trail brochures (free) from the Ásbyrgi ranger station.

Tours

Several companies offer tours of Jökulsárgljúfur from Mývatn (p231), Akureyri (p215) and Húsavík (p240). The tours are good value if you're in a hurry and don't have private transport. You can usually leave any of these tours at any time and rejoin later, with advance arrangements.

Sleeping & Eating

Camping inside the park boundaries is strictly limited to the official camp sites at Ásbyrgi, Vesturdalur and Dettifoss. Basic facilities are available at Ásbyrgi and Vesturdalur (Ikr600 per person), but there's only a freshwater tank at Dettifoss (free). The camp site at Vesturdalur is the usual overnight stop for hikers, while camping at Dettifoss is forbidden for motorists.

Farmhouse accommodation is available in Kelduhverfi (see p242); otherwise, the nearest option is the summer hotel at **Lundur** (☎ 465 2247, 863 4311; lundur@dettifoss.is; sb/s/d Ikr2500/4500/7000; ☷ Jun–mid-Aug; ☢), 8km northeast of Ásbyrgi on Rte 85. The rooms here are pretty simple, but there's a restaurant with home-cooked meals (Ikr1500 for dinner), kitchen facilities and a swimming pool.

The petrol station on Rte 85 at Ásbyrgi has a basic grill and limited supplies of (expensive) groceries. If you're hiking bring food with you.

Getting There & Away

There are only two roads in the park, one on either side of the canyon. The western approach (Rte F862) isn't suitable for 2WD vehicles at its southern end (between Rte 1 and Hólmatungur), and its northern end is rough and slow going. On the eastern side of the canyon Rte 864, another rough gravel road, is passable by 2WD vehicles, but its rutted and potholed surface will tire even the most patient of drivers. Although the park is

open all year, snowfalls can make the roads impassable between October and May.

From late June to August, daily scheduled buses run from Akureyri (Ikr4900, 3¼ hours) and Húsavík (Ikr2800, 1¾ hours) to major sites in the park. There's also a daily Mývatn–Dettifoss (Ikr1900, 1½ hours) bus via Krafla (Ikr900, 15 minutes), leaving at 11.30am from the supermarket in Reykjahlíð and returning from Dettifoss at 2pm.

JÖKULSÁRGLJÚFUR
Ásbyrgi

Driving off Rte 85 on to the flat, grassy plain at the northern end of the park, there's little to tell you you're standing on the edge of a massive horseshoe-shaped canyon. The lush **Ásbyrgi canyon** extends 3.5km from north to south and averages 1km in width, making it difficult to discern at its widest point. Near the centre of the canyon is the prominent outcrop **Eyjan**, and towards the south the sheer, dark walls rise up to 100m in depth. The cliffs protect a birch forest from harsh winds and hungry sheep, and the trees here grow up to 8m in height.

There are two stories about the creation of Ásbyrgi. The early Norse settlers believed that Óðinn's normally airborne horse, Slættur (known in literature as Sleipnir), accidentally touched down on earth and left one hell of a hoof print to prove it. The other theory, though more scientific, is equally incredible. Geologists believe that the canyon was created by an enormous eruption of the Grímsvötn caldera beneath distant Vatnajökull. It released an immense *jökulhlaup*, which ploughed northward down the Jökulsá á Fjöllum and gouged out the canyon in a matter of days. The river then flowed through Ásbyrgi for about 100 years before shifting eastward to its present course.

HIKING

From the car park near the end of the road, several short tracks lead through the forest to viewpoints of the canyon. Heading east the track leads to a spring near the canyon wall, while the western track climbs to a good view across the valley floor. The boardwalk leading straight ahead ends at a small lake (Botnstjörn) at the head of Ásbyrgi.

You can also climb to the summit of **Eyjan** (2km, 45 minutes return) or ascend the cliffs at **Tófugjá**. From there, a loop track leads around **Áshöföi** past the gorges. Alternatively, follow the rim right around to **Klappir**, above the canyon head, from where you can head south to Kvíar (or head east to Kúahvammur) and return via the river (the route via Kvíar will take up to four hours return).

You'll find more details on hiking trails at http://english.ust.is/Jokulsarglufurnational park/Hiking.

Vesturdalur

Off the beaten track but home to diverse scenery, Vesturdalur is a favourite destination for hikers. A series of weaving trails leads from the scrub around the camp site to the cave-riddled pinnacles and rock formations of Hljóðaklettar, the Rauðhólar crater row, the ponds of Eyjan (not to be confused with the Eyjan at Ásbyrgi) and the canyon itself. Reckon on a full day, or two, to explore the area properly.

HLJÓÐAKLETTAR

The bizarre swirls, spirals, rosettes, honeycombs and columns of basalt at Hljóðaklettar (Echoing Rocks) are a highlight of any hike around Vesturdalur and a puzzling place for amateur geologists. It's difficult to imagine what sort of volcanic activity produced the twisted rock forms here. Weird concertina formations and repeat patterns occur throughout, and the normally vertical basalt columns (formed by rapidly cooling lava) show up on the horizontal here. These strange forms and patterns create an acoustic effect that makes it impossible to determine the direction of the roaring river, a curiosity that gave the area its name.

A circular walking trail (2.4km) from the parking area takes less than an hour to explore. The best formations, which are also riddled with lava caves, are found along the river, northeast of the parking area. Look out for **Trollið**, with its honeycomb pattern, **Kirkjan**, a natural cave in a grassy pit, and **Kastali**, a huge basalt outcrop.

RAUÐHÓLAR

The Rauðhólar crater row, immediately north of Vesturdalur, displays a vivid array of colours in the cinderlike gravel on the remaining cones. The craters can be explored on foot, on an interesting 5km walk from the parking area. You could also take the excursion bus from Ásbyrgi to Vesturdalur and walk back to Ásbyrgi (12.5km).

KARL OG KERLING

Two rock pillars, Karl og Kerling, believed to be petrified trolls, stand on a gravel bank west of the river, 2.5km from the Vesturdalur car park. Across the river is **Tröllahellir**, the largest cave in the gorge, but it's reached only on a 5km cross-country trek from Rte 864 on the eastern side.

EYJAN

From Karl og Kerling you can return to Vesturdalur in about three hours by walking around Eyjan, a mesalike 'island' covered with low, scrubby forests and small ponds. Follow the river south to Kallbjörg, then turn west along the track to the abandoned site of Svínadalur, where the canyon widens into a broad valley, and follow the western base of the Eyjan cliffs back to the Vesturdalur parking area.

Hólmatungur

Lush vegetation, tumbling waterfalls and an air of utter tranquillity make the Hólmatungur area one of the most beautiful in the park. Underground springs bubble up to form a series of short rivers that twist, turn and cascade their way to the canyon. The most popular walk here is the 3.5km loop from the parking area north along the Hólmá river to **Hólmáfoss**, where the harsh lines of the canyon soften and produce several pretty waterfalls. From here you head south again on the Jökulsá to its confluence with the Melbugsá river, where the river tumbles over a ledge, forming the **Urriðafoss** waterfall. To see the falls you need to walk 500m along the trail spur to Katlar. For the best overall view of Hólmatungur, walk to the hill Ytra-Þórunnarfjall, just 1km south of the car park.

Hólmatungur is accessible by car from the north or by 4WD from the south. Otherwise it's 8km on foot to either Vesturdalur or Dettifoss. Camping is prohibited at Hólmatungur, but it's a great spot for a picnic lunch on the first day of the Dettifoss to Ásbyrgi hike.

Dettifoss

The power of nature can be seen in all its glory at the mighty Dettifoss, the park's most famous attraction and Iceland's most impressive waterfall. Although Dettifoss is only 44m high, a massive 193 cu metres of water thunders over its edge every second, creating a plume of spray that can be seen 1km away. With the greatest volume of any waterfall in Europe, this truly is nature at its most spectacular. On sunny days brilliant double rainbows form above the churning milky-grey glacial waters, and you'll have to jostle with the other visitors for the best views.

The falls can be seen from either side of the canyon, with a slightly broader sweep of the water visible from the western bank. The Super Dettifoss Tour from Mývatn and the SBA bus from Ásbyrgi visit the western bank, while other tours and most independent travellers stop at the more accessible eastern bank. From the car park on the eastern bank it's a five-minute walk down to the falls. From here you can continue on another 1.5km over the boulders to **Selfoss**. It's only 11m high but it's much broader and quite a striking waterfall.

Access to the western bank of the falls from the south is by 4WD vehicle only; from the Ring Rd it's 31km to the falls on the eastern bank on a rough and badly pot-holed gravel road.

Hafragilsfoss

In one of the deepest parts of the canyon, 2km downstream from Dettifoss, the 27m-high Hafragilsfoss cuts through the Rauðhóll crater row to expose the volcanic dyke that formed it. From the eastern bank, the best view is down the canyon from the small hill just north of the Hafragilsfoss parking area. In the same area are numerous red scoria cones and craters.

The overlook on the western bank affords a marginal view of the falls, but the view down Jökulsárgljúfur is one of the best available. You can climb down to the river from the vantage point, but near the bottom you must lower yourself down a challenging vertical wall on fixed ropes.

NORTHEASTERN CIRCUIT

The wild, sparsely populated coastal route around Iceland's northeast tip is an engaging alternative to the direct road from Mývatn to Egilsstaðir. The peninsula is a largely low-lying boggy expanse, flanked by isolated beaches and beloved by summer nesting birds.

Although mostly unsealed, Rte 85 around the coast has improved dramatically in recent years and is easily tackled in a 2WD vehicle. TREX runs a scheduled bus service from Húsavík to Ásbyrgi (Ikr1900, 45 minutes), Kópasker (Ikr2200, 1¼ hours), Raufarhöfn (Ikr3300, two

hours), and Þórshöfn (Ikr4500, 3¼ hours) on weekdays all year round. There's currently no bus to or from Vopnafjörður.

KÓPASKER
pop 150

The tiny, sleepy village of Kópasker, on the eastern shore of Öxarfjörður, is the first place you pass through before disappearing into the expansive wilds of Iceland's far northeast. An international trading port since 1879, today it relies on agricultural trade and the shrimp industry.

On 13 January 1976 Kópasker suffered a severe earthquake that destroyed several buildings and cracked the harbour wall. Rock slides and fissuring were violent, and evidence of seismic activity can still be seen at Hraunhólar near Presthólar, about 5km south of the town.

About 500m before the village itself, you'll see the red-roofed **church** beside the road. Alongside the church is **Snartarstaðir**, an early district assembly site, and beside it, in what was the old school, the town **Folk Museum & Library** (☎ 465 2171; www.islandia.is/boknord; adult/under 14yr Ikr400/free; ☼ 1-5pm Tue, Thu, Sat & Sun mid-Jun–Aug). The collection includes early photos of Iceland, a horse-drawn fire engine, an elaborately carved 18th-century cabinet with sled attachments, and a series of beautiful 19th-century local textiles and costumes, including a white wedding dress (black was customary at the time).

On the main road leading into town you can't miss the elaborate **scarecrows** that a local artist has made to protect an eider-duck nesting area.

If you'd like to stay your best bet is the **HI Hostel Kópasker** (☎ 465 2314; hostel@kopasker.is; Akurgerði 7; sb members/nonmembers Ikr1700/2000, s/d Ikr2900/4600; ☼ May-Oct), a simple five-room hostel offering bright rooms with pine furniture. There's a good guest kitchen, a lounge and a washing machine.

There's also a free camp site in the village and a small supermarket by the petrol station. The bus fare from Kópasker to Raufarhöfn is Ikr1300.

MELRAKKASLÉTTARNES

The low-lying flatlands, ponds and marshes of the bleak and little-visited Melrakkasléttarnes peninsula are a haven for nesting birds. Large numbers of eider ducks, arctic terns, curlew and dunlin can be seen here on the shingle beaches and boggy surface of the tundra.

About 18km north of Kópasker you can turn off Rte 85 and head north along a rough track to the extinct 73m crater **Rauðinúpur**. Set on a wild headland with steep cliff faces, this remote finger of land feels like the end of the earth. Screeching gannets and a lonely lighthouse will be your only companions here, and as you look out to sea the power of nature and sense of dramatic isolation are immediately apparent.

Back on the main road and heading east through more fertile farmland, you approach the remote peninsula **Hraunhafnartangi**, the northernmost point of the Icelandic mainland. This desolate spot has narrowly missed being one of Iceland's biggest attractions – it's just 2.5km south of the Arctic Circle. A little further north and there could have been an interpretive centre, a tacky souvenir stall and a Christmas grotto. Instead it's a largely undiscovered headland that was a Saga Age landing site and is the burial place of saga hero Þorgeir Hávarsson, who killed 14 enemies before being struck down in battle. A marked trail leads along the gravel beach here to the brightly coloured lighthouse and the grave site.

The turn-off to the headland is not well signposted; look out for the lighthouse from the main road. Camping is possible anywhere on the headland.

RAUFARHÖFN
pop 170

Iceland's most northerly settlement of any size, Raufarhöfn (www.raufarhofn.is) is a sleepy kind of place with a picturesque harbour sheltered by the small **Ásmundarstaða Islands**, just off shore. The port has functioned since the Saga Age, but the town's economic peak came early in the 20th century during the herring boom, when it was second to Siglufjörður in volume. Today, Raufarhöfn just ticks over, its rows of dull prefab housing giving few clues to its illustrious past.

Around the town the lush, level farmland is dotted with more than 29 lakes, all teeming with bird life. There are ambitious plans afoot to draw in the crowds with a massive stone circle to be built on the hill just north of town. When completed, the **Arctic Henge** (www.arctichenge.com) will be 54m in diameter with four gates (to represent the seasons) up

---

DETTIFOSS TO ÁSBYRGI HIKE

The most popular hike in Jökulsárgljúfur National Park – and justifiably so – is the two-day trip (34km) on the western side of Dettifoss to Ásbyrgi, which takes in all of the canyon's major sights. To get to the start of the hike by public transport, take the scheduled bus (Monday to Friday) from Akureyri or Húsavík to Dettifoss, then walk north and pick up another bus in Ásbyrgi.

From Dettifoss, head north along Sandadalur until you begin seeing yellow trail markers. If you go left up the hill, it will lead you fairly easily around the rim of Hafragil. Go right and you'll descend steeply into the canyon, to re-emerge on the rim beyond Hafragilsfoss. With a heavy pack, this will be difficult as it involves some serious scrambling and climbing.

From Hafragilsfoss, the route leads north along the canyon rim to beautiful Hólmatungur. You'll cross the Hólmá on two bridges, then descend past Hólmáfoss. The trail then joins a lateral moraine beneath towering basalt cliffs and crumbled basalt columns, and follows the *yazoo* (parallel) Stallá river, which eventually must be forded. After the ford, the trail climbs back to the canyon rim for a beautiful walk over the moors.

At unassuming Kallbjörg it's a 100m detour to an overlook perched on a rock column with sheer drops on three sides. You don't realise the drama until you're right on top of it. Another short detour will take you to Gloppa, a basalt amphitheatre that ominously resembles the maw of a hellishly large shark.

The requisite first-night camp site is at the **Vesturdalur camp site** (sites per person Ikr600). The next day, the trail winds through beautiful Hljóðaklettar and Rauðhólar to the Kvíar trail junction, where you must decide whether to shoot across the moorland to the incredible view from Klappir into the Ásbyrgi canyon or continue following the main canyon rim. Both are equally worthwhile, although the former gets a bit soggy in places. There's also the Kúahvammur–Klappir trail, which takes an hour longer. The Klappir options rejoin the main canyon route at the head of Tófugjá, a challenging descent into Ásbyrgi with the aid of a fixed rope – or you can continue easily northwards to Ásbyrgi petrol station.

NORTHEAST ICELAND

to 7m in height. The plan is to use the stone henge as a finely tuned sundial to celebrate the solstices, view the midnight sun and explain the strong local beliefs in the mythological dwarves mentioned in the poem *Völuspá* (Wise Woman's Prophecy).

If you want to stay, there's a free **camp site** (☎ 465 1151; ☺ Jun-Aug) beside the swimming pool at the southern end of the village, or much more comfort at **Hótel Norðurljós** (☎ 465 1233; ebt@vortex.is; Aðalbraut 2; s/d Ikr7000/10,000), the town's only formal accommodation option. Fairly unassuming from the outside, this cosy hotel overlooking the harbour has spacious modern rooms with attached bathroom. From June to September more basic rooms with shared bathroom are available in a second building (Ikr2500/5000/7000 for sleeping-bag space/ singles/doubles). The hotel has a decent bar and a bright restaurant serving a menu of fish and meat dishes (dish of the day Ikr2000 to Ikr2200) and a set dinner (Ikr2800). There's a terrace overlooking the harbour, and kayaks are available for guest use.

The only alternatives for food are the supermarket by the main road and the usual grill at the petrol station. The bus fare from Raufarhöfn to Þórshöfn is Ikr1400.

RAUÐANES

Heading south from Raufarhöfn, there's excellent hiking at Rauðanes, where marked trails lead to bizarre rock formations, natural arches, caves and secluded beaches. The small and scenic peninsula is edged by steep cliffs full of nesting birds, caves, offshore sea stacks and an exposed rock face, **Stakkatorfa**, where a great chunk of land collapsed into the sea. Pick up a free brochure describing the walks at any of the local tourist-information points or hotels.

The turn-off to Rauðanes is about 35km south of Raufarhöfn, but the track is only suitable for 4WD vehicles. There's a parking area about 1km from Rte 85, from where it's a 4km walk to the bridge before the farm Vellir, then another 3km northeast to the cape.

ÞÓRSHÖFN

pop 410

The town of Þórshöfn (http://thorshofn.com), has served as a busy port since saga times and saw its heyday when a herring-salting station was established here in the early 20th century. Today it's a pretty modest place but makes a good base for visitors heading to the

eerily remote Langanes peninsula or on to Rauðanes.

Tourist information is available at the **swimming pool** (☎ 468 1515; ☺ 4-8pm Mon-Thu, 3-7pm Fri, 11am-2pm Sat) on the Langanes road. There's also a bank with an ATM in town. The annual **Happy Days festival** is held over a weekend in July, with markets, sporting events, dances and a bonfire.

Sleeping & Eating

Camp site (free) The municipal site has basic facilities and is just east of the centre off Hálsvegur.

Guesthouse Lyngholt (☎ 897 5064; www.lyngholt.is; Langanesvegur 12; s/b/s/d Ikr2500/4900/7900) Bright modern rooms with subtle floral-patterned duvets, contemporary furniture and friendly service are available at this lovely guesthouse near the swimming pool. There's a TV in each room, a guest kitchen and a barbecue.

Hótel Jórvík (☎ 468 1400; http://jorvik.vefur.com; Langanesvegur 31; sb/s/d Ikr2000/4900/5900) This simple place looks more like a large house than a hotel but has a series of decent, if faded, rooms, some of which have good sea views.

Ytra-Aland (☎ 468 1290; www.ytra-aland.is; sb Ikr2300, s/d without bathroom Ikr5500/9000, with bathroom Ikr6500/11,000) This lovely farm offers topnotch accommodation in simple rooms in the main house and a new accommodation block with private bathrooms. There's also a summerhouse, evening meals on request and horse-riding tours. Ytra-Aland is 18km west of Þórshöfn.

Eyrin (☎ 468 1250; Eyravegur 3; mains Ikr690-3490; ☺ 11am-11pm Sun-Thu, to 3am Fri & Sat) The local pub, café, pool hall, restaurant and hangout, this friendly place at the harbour serves up an extensive menu of pizzas, pastas, burgers, salads, and hearty meat and fish dishes.

The only alternatives for food are the small supermarket near the harbour or the grill at the Esso petrol station.

Getting There & Away

Flugfélags Íslands (☎ 468 1420; www.airiceland.is) operates flights to Þórshöfn from Reykjavík twice daily on weekdays from April to October. The cheapest one-way fare is Ikr8395 and the flight takes two hours.

TREX runs a scheduled bus service from Húsavík to Þórshöfn (Ikr4500, 3¼ hours) on weekdays all year round. There's currently no bus to or from Vopnafjörður.

LANGANES

Shaped like a goose with a very large head, the foggy Langanes peninsula is one of the loneliest corners of Iceland. The tundra plain of lakes, marshes and low hills that makes up the bulk of Langanes makes unchallenging walking country, riddled with abandoned farms, and rich in arctic and alpine flora. The southern section of the peninsula is more mountainous, with the tallest peak, **Gunnólfsvíkurfjall**, rising to 719m, while the easternmost coasts are characterised by cliffs up to 130m high. Often blanketed in a thick fog, the cliffs have long proved dangerous to passing ships.

The **lighthouse** at the cape dates from 1910, and there's a monument to the shipwrecked English sailors who died of hypothermia after ascending the ravine there. It's now called **Engelskagjá** (English Gorge). At Skoruvík, towards the end of the peninsula, there's a long bay that provides a major breeding ground for the migrant arctic tern. From the western end of Skoruvík a rough track leads across the peninsula to **Skálabjarg**, a long and formidable bird cliff on the wild southern coast of Langanes. At the turn of the century the ruined farm of Skálar, northeast of the cliff, was a prosperous fishing village.

Drinking water is plentiful in Langanes, but there are no facilities beyond Þórshöfn, so carry everything you'll need. Hikers should allow a week for the return trip from Þórshöfn to Fontur. Rte 869 ends only 17km along the 50km peninsula, and, although it's possible to continue along the track to the tip at Fontur in a 4WD vehicle, it's a pretty rough road.

If you're not camping, the best base from which to explore is the friendly **HI Hostel Ytra Lón** (☎ 468 1242; ytralon@simnet.is; sb members/nonmembers Ikr1800/2150, s/d Ikr4000/6950), 14km northeast of Þórshöfn and just off Rte 869. It's part of a working farm run by a young family, and the owners are happy for guests to take part in farm life. The rooms are basic but cosy, and there's a good kitchen, a common room and a playground. Phone in advance to arrange pick-up from the bus stop in Þórshöfn.

VOPNAFJÖRÐUR

pop 730

Tumbling down a steep hill on the side of a pretty fjord, the modern harbour town of Vopnafjörður is the largest in the region. A sleepy but thriving community, its biggest claims to fame are being home to the 1988 Miss World and the location of some of Prince Charles' angling holidays.

For visitors Vopnafjörður has all the facilities you'll need and makes a good base for hiking in the area. The **tourist office** (☎ 473 1331; www.vopnafiardarhreppur.is; ⏱ 10am-5pm Jun-Aug), in a restored warehouse, has a small exhibition on local history and environment and offers internet access (Ikr300 for 15 minutes). If you're planing to do any walking in the area ask here for advice on routes and pick up a copy of *Hiking Routes in East Iceland* (Ikr750), which has maps and descriptions of local walks.

Sights & Activities

The region's biggest attraction is the **Bustarfell folk museum** (☎ 473 1466; adult/9-13yr Ikr400/100; ⏱ 10am-6pm mid-Jun–early Sep), set in an 18th-century gabled, turf-roofed farmhouse 20km west of Vopnafjörður on Rte 85. The museum provides an interesting look at rural life two centuries ago and hosts a traditional festival on the second Sunday in July.

Vopnafjörður's **swimming pool** (☎ 473 1499) is way out of town – 12km north then 3km west of Rte 85 via a dirt road. It's a geothermally heated pool with outdoor hot pots set by the Séla river – worth a stop if you're passing by.

South of Vopnafjörður the truly spectacular mountain drive along Rte 917 takes you over Hellisheiði and down to the east coast. The road, which may be impassable in bad weather, climbs up a series of switchbacks and hairpin bends before dropping down to the striking glacial river deltas on the Héraðssandur. The views on both sides are superb.

Sleeping & Eating

Camp site (free) There's a good camp site on the outskirts of town. Follow Miðbraut north and turn left at the school.

Syðri-Vík (☎ 473 1199; budargerdi@fel.rvk.is; sb/made-up beds Ikr2000/3000; ⏱ May-Oct) Across the fjord 8km south of Vopnafjörður, this place has cosy wood-panelled rooms in the farmhouse as well as cottages sleeping six to nine guests. There's a guest kitchen, a dining room and a lounge, and horse riding and fishing are available on request.

Hótel Edda Tangi (☎ 444 4000; www.hoteledda.is; Hafnarbyggð 17; s/d Ikr8700/10,900; ⏱ May-Sep) The local hotel, restaurant and bar all rolled into one, the Hotel Tangi is the most happening place in town. The rooms here are pretty functional, but bright and modern, and the restaurant (mains

Ikr1500 to Ikr3500) serves the usual selection of pizzas and burgers, as well as local fish and meat dishes. The bar attached to the hotel is open late on Friday and Saturday night.

Guesthouse Refsstaður (☎ 473 1562; Refsstaður 2, Hófsardal; twocats@simnet.is; s/d Ikr3500/5000) This farmhouse 9km north of town has five cosy rooms with shared bathroom. There's a well-equipped kitchen for guest use, friendly owners and help in tracing genealogical roots.

The Esso petrol station, on the main road south of town, has a café, and the supermarket, by the hotel, has groceries.

Getting There & Away

Flugfélags Íslands (☎ 473 1121; www.airiceland.is) operates flights to Vopnafjörður from Reykjavík twice daily on weekdays from April to October, with a reduced service in winter. The cheapest one-way fare on this route is Ikr8395 (2½ hours).

From Vopnafjörður it is 122km to Reykjahlíð and 92km to Egilsstaðir, so check fuel levels before you leave town.

NORTHEAST INTERIOR

Heading between Mývatn and Egilsstaðir, the Ring Rd takes a drastic short cut inland across the stark and barren highlands of the northeast interior. There's little to lure travellers off the road, but the loneliness can be an attraction in itself in this eerie and otherworldly place of endless vistas.

If you won't be travelling into the interior proper (see p299), you'll catch a glimpse of it here. Ostensibly barren, and to some unimaginably dull, the bleak landscape here is dotted with low hills, small lakes caused by melting snowfields, and streams and rivers wandering aimlessly before disappearing into gravel beds. For most of the year it's a stark grey landscape, but if you're visiting in spring you'll be treated to a carpet of wild flowers that somehow gain root in the gravelly volcanic surface.

It has always been a difficult place to eke out a living, and farms here are few and far between. Near the remote farm **Grímsstaðir**,

---

---

close to the intersection of the Ring Rd and Rte 864, 3km from the Jökulsá á Fjöllum, you can see an old **ferryman's hut**, built in 1880. Before the river was bridged it was crossed by ferry, and the former ferryman is said to haunt the run-down building. The hut is on the western bank of the river, 2km downstream from the Ring Rd bridge. If you're feeling peckish, **Grímstunga** (☎ 464 4294; djupadokk@simnet.is; sb/s/d Ikr3400/7600/9600; ☾ Jun-Sep) has a small and friendly café and basic accommodation with kitchen facilities. There's also a camp site at Grímsstaðir.

Isolated **Möðrudalur**, an oasis in the barren desert amid an entanglement of streams, is the highest farm in Iceland at 470m. The bus between Egilsstaðir and Mývatn stops for half an hour at the highland café and guesthouse **Fjalladýrð** (☎ 471 1858; www.fjalladyrd.is; sites per person Ikr750, sb/s/d Ikr1950/3300/5900), where you can get hearty soups, sandwiches and cakes, and stay in cosy wood-panelled rooms. The owners can also arrange 4WD trips to Vatnajökull and other activities.

Across the road is a church (built 1949) with an interesting altarpiece.

The vast **Jökuldalsheiði** moorland, along the Ring Rd between Jökuldalur and Möðrudalur, is quite verdant and was farmed until 1875, when the cataclysmic explosion of the Askja caldera displaced its inhabitants.

East Iceland

The overeager Ring Rd charges through Egilsstaðir, completely bypassing the Eastfjords, and appearing in a terrible hurry simply to get out of the region. Many visitors follow its lead, foot to the accelerator, their eyes set on the prizes of Mývatn in the north or Skaftafell to the south. Thank them for their rabid urgency, since it leaves a largely tourist-free corner of the country for more exploratory bods to explore.

East Iceland may lack any obvious star attractions, but subtle charms unfold around the bends of its winding roads. In particular, the Eastfjords are a delight. On fine days there's nothing better than to climb a hillside, plonk yourself down in the heather, and watch as the deep water turns an unreal shade of cobalt blue, pods of dolphins break the waves, and fishing boats head home with their catch. The scenery is particularly dramatic around the northern fjord villages, backed by sheer-sided mountains covered in toppling streams and waterfalls. If the weather is fine, several days spent hiking or kayaking here may be some of your most memorable in Iceland.

Away from the coast, Iceland's longest lake, allegedly the home of a huge wormlike monster, stretches southwest from Egilsstaðir. On its eastern shore you'll find the country's largest forest – a source of great pride to tree-starved Icelanders! Head further inland still and you'll come to the forgotten farms, fells and heathlands of the empty east.

Some pretty dramatic changes are taking place in east Iceland, following the building of a controversial dam and hydroelectricity plant in the highlands, and an aluminium smelter on Reyðarfjörður. But, don't be deterred from coming to the east; it has plenty to offer.

TOP FIVE

- Arrive in the country in style: sail up a lovely 17km-long fjord to the bohemian village **Seyðisfjörður** (p263) on the Norröna ferry

- Explore the fjords at water level on a guided **midnight kayaking trip** (p264 and p269)

- Take a boat trip out to the delightful island of **Papey** (p273), inhabited only by seals and sea birds

- Sparkly…shiny…be mesmerised by Petra Sveinsdóttir's **amazing mineral collection** (p270) in Stöðvarfjörður

- Escape into isolation at the far-off youth hostel at **Húsey** (p258), end-of-the-road **Neskaupstaður** (p268) or bird-watching haven **Skálanes** (p266)

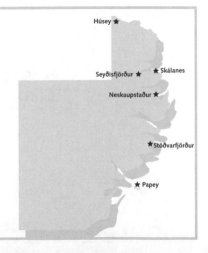

Húsey ★

Seyðisfjörður ★   ★ Skálanes

Neskaupstaður ★

★ Stöðvarfjörður

★ Papey

GETTING THERE & AROUND

AIR

In summer **Flugfélag Íslands** (Air Iceland; ☎ 471 1210; www.airiceland.is) flies about five times daily from Egilsstaðir to Reykjavík (about Ikr9400, one hour), and once or twice per day from Egilsstaðir to Akureyri (about Ikr11,700, 40 minutes).

BUS

Egilsstaðir is a major crossroads on the Ring Rd, so all buses pass through. The main bus stop is at the camp site.

From June to August there's a daily **TREX** (☎ 461 1106; www.trex.is) bus between Akureyri and Egilsstaðir, calling at Mývatn en route. It departs from Akureyri at 8am, and from Egilsstaðir at 1pm. The journey takes four hours and costs Ikr5400 one way. Between September and May a service runs on Tuesday, Wednesday, Friday and Sunday, departing at different times – see the latest schedule.

For Egilsstaðir–Höfn buses, see p296.

Ferðaþjónusta Austurlands (☎ 472 1515, 852 9250) runs a minibus–post van between Egilsstaðir and Seyðisfjörður (Ikr800, about 30 minutes). Between 1 June and 10 September it leaves Seyðisfjörður at 8.20am weekdays, with a second service at 1.30pm Wednesday and Thursday. Between 29 June and 4 August there's also a weekend service, leaving at 1.30pm Saturday and 2.15pm Sunday. The rest of the year a bus runs at 4.30pm weekdays and at 6.20pm Sunday.

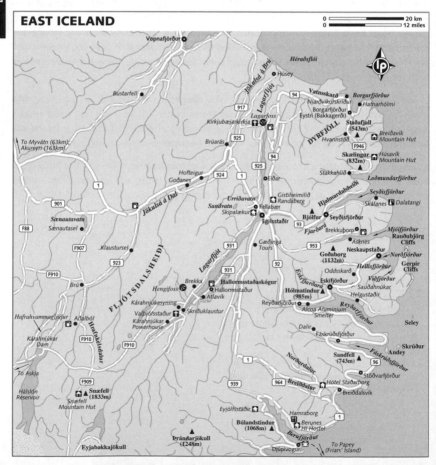

EAST ICELAND

Between 1 June and 10 September it leaves Egilsstaðir at 9.15am weekdays, with a second service at 2.20pm on Wednesday and Thursday. Between 29 June and 4 August there's also a weekend service, leaving at 2.20pm on Saturday and Sunday. The rest of the year a bus runs at 5pm Monday to Friday and at 7pm Sunday.

Austfjarðaleið (East Iceland Bus Company; ☎ 477 1713; www.austfjardaleid.is) runs buses from Egilsstaðir to villages around the fjords. The Egilsstaðir–Norðfjörður (Ikr1600, 1¼ hours) service via Reyðarfjörður (Ikr800, 30 minutes) and Eskifjörður (Ikr1100, 45 minutes) runs once or twice daily Monday to Saturday. There's also a bus that runs a 40-minute route around the Fjarðabyggð (Neskaupstaður/Eskifjörður/Reyðarfjörður) district on weekdays, at 7.40am and 5pm from Neskaupstaður, and back from Reyðarfjörður at 5.45pm. The Egilsstaðir–Breiðdalsvík (Ikr1800, 1½ hours) service via Fáskrúðsfjörður (Ikr1100, 45 minutes) and Stöðvarfjörður (Ikr1400, 1¼ hours) runs weekdays only.

INLAND

EGILSSTAÐIR

pop 1910

However much you strain to discover some underlying charm, Egilsstaðir is really not a ravishing beauty. It's the main regional transport hub, and a centre for commerce and industry. Sorry, it's about as pretty as that sounds.

Thanks to the new hydroelectricity project (see the boxed text, p258) and its influx of workers, there has been feverish house building over the last few years. In time, no doubt, the town's entertainment facilities will catch up, but at present there's little to amuse visitors. Seyðisfjörður (p263) is a more pleasant place for ferry passengers to stay.

Egilsstaðir does have one saving grace – it's built on the banks of lovely **Lagarfljót** (Lögurinn), Iceland's third-largest lake. Since the time of the sagas lake have been told of a monster, the Lagarfljótsormurinn, who lives in its depths. If you want to go and do some beastie-hunting, or to explore the forest on the eastern bank of the lake, Egilsstaðir does make a very good base. Services include an excellent regional tourist office and some decent restaurants.

Orientation & Information

North past the airport and over the lake, you'll find Egilsstaðir's twin-town. Fellabær has some pleasant accommodation options and a petrol station–bakery, but most services are in Egilsstaðir. The tourist office, petrol station, bus terminal, Landsbanki Íslands bank (with ATM), a supermarket and the camp site are all located in a single block just off the Ring Rd.

With some of the most helpful staff in Iceland, the central **tourist office** (Upplýsingamiðstöð; ☎ 471 2320; www.east.is; ☯ 8am-10pm Jun-Aug, 9am-5pm Mon-Fri, noon-4pm Sat, 2-8pm Sun Sep-May; 🖳), by the camp site and bus terminal, is a great first information stop for passengers just off the ferry. There are plenty of free brochures plus a great selection of walking maps for sale. Internet access costs Ikr200/400/500 per 15/30/60 minutes.

The post office is just up the hill on the corner of Selás and Fagradalsbraut.

The town **library** (☎ 471 1546; Laufskógar 1; ☯ 2-7pm Mon-Fri), upstairs in the same building as Minjasafn Austurlands, has internet access.

Verslunin Skógar (☎ 471 1230; Dynskógar 4), near Fosshótel Valaskjálf, is a sports store selling a range of tents, sleeping bags and other camping equipment.

Sights & Activities

Egilsstaðir's cultural museum **Minjasafn Austurlands** (East Iceland Heritage Museum; ☎ 471 1412; Laufskógar 1; adult/child Ikr400/200; ☯ 11am-5pm Jun-Aug, 1-5pm Mon-Fri Sep-May) is quite a sweet little place. Its displays focus on the history of the region, and they include a reconstructed farmhouse and 10th-century grave goods. Much of the information is in Icelandic only.

Egilsstaðir's impressive **swimming pool** (☎ 470 0777; Tjarnarbraut; adult/child Ikr300/150; ☯ 7am-9.30pm Mon-Fri, 10am-7pm Sat & Sun), with indoor and outdoor pools, saunas, hot pots and a gym, is at the top end of Tjarnarbraut, north of town.

Tours

For horse tours through the spectacular Eastfjords, **Gæðinga Tours** (☎ 471 1727; www.gaedingatours .is), 7km south of Egilsstaðir at Útnyrðingsstaðir, runs a variety of tours, including short rides and a seven-day tour of east Iceland.

LAKE CRUISES

In summertime the boat *Lagarfljótsormurinn* pootles along the pretty lake Lagarfljót. Unfortunately, although there's a terminus at

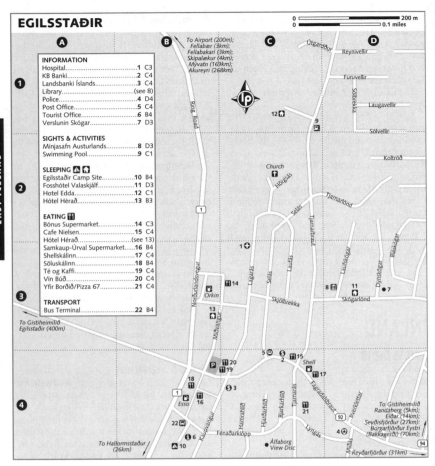

EGILSSTAÐIR

the bridge in Fellabær, you can't actually get on there; passengers must set off from the Atlavík camp site, 30km southwest of town – see p256.

Festivals & Events

If you are here in early November, stop by for the unusual 10-day **Dagar Myrkurs** (Days of Darkness), when the town perversely celebrates the failing light and the onset of winter with dark meals, dark dances, ghost stories, star walks, Northern Light spotting, and torch-lit processions! When life gives you lemons…

Around the third weekend in June, Egilsstaðir's annual jazz festival **Djasshátíð Egilsstaða** (www.jea.is) takes place at various venues in the area.

The possible existence of the lake monster Lagarfljótsormurinn is a good excuse for a week-long cultural festival, **Ormsteiti**, during late August.

Sleeping
BUDGET & MIDRANGE

Egilsstaðir camp site (☎ 471 2320; info@east.is; Kaupvangur 10; sites per person Ikr750, sb Ikr2300, 5-person hut Ikr7000; 🖳) Camping pitches are in utilitarian rows, but facilities are good – there's a kitchen, a washing machine (Ikr500), a dryer (Ikr600) and internet access in the tourist office. A dormitory building holds sleeping-bag accommodation.

ourpick Gistiheimilið Randaberg (☎ 471 1288; randaberg@simnet.is; sb d Ikr5000, made-up d Ikr6500) We really loved this place, 5km from town on the Eiðar road. Its three dinky wooden cabins have porches, flower boxes, great lake views, and tea-making equipment. Although they're fairly sparse inside – just containing a double bunk bed and a small table – there's something homey about them, and owner Vilborg is kind.

Hotel Edda (☎ 444 4000; off Tjarnarbraut; sb/s/d Ikr2200/9000/11,300; ✆ Jun–mid-Aug) Based in the school opposite the swimming pool, this is a typical Edda hotel. Rooms have private bathrooms, and there's a bar and restaurant with panoramic views.

Skipalækur (☎ 471 1324; fax 471 2413; sites per person Ikr650, May-Sep sb/made-up beds per person Ikr2100/4200, d with bathroom Ikr12,000, 4-/6-person chalet Ikr8000/11,000, discounts rest of year) In Fellabær, 4km from Egilsstaðir, this farmhouse has accommodation to suit all purses. There's a small camping area, two fairly noisy Portakabins with sleeping-bag accommodation, some rooms in a funny 1970s-decorated house, and comfortable, self-contained A-frame chalets (with bathroom, basic kitchen and lounge) overlooking the lake. All accommodation has access to showers, a kitchen, and a sitting room of some description. Short horse-riding trips (Ikr2000 per hour) are available.

ourpick **Gistiheimilið Egilsstaðir** (☎ 471 1114; www .egilsstadir.com; s/d May-Sep Ikr10,500/13,900, Oct-Apr Ikr6900/9500; P ☐) The town was named after this splendid heritage guesthouse and farm, on the banks of Lagarfljót, 300m west of crossroads. Its sensitively renovated en-suite rooms retain a real sense of character, and are decorated with antique furniture – ask for one with a lake view. Breakfast (included) is in the lake-side dining room, which also does a good Icelandic dinner buffet.

TOP END

Hótel Hérað (☎ 471 1500; herad@icehotels.is; Miðvangur 5-7; s/d Jun-Aug Ikr14,600/18,300, up to 40% discount rest of yr) This three-star Icelandair hotel is the plushest in town. It's been hugely expanded since work began on the hydroelectricity project; a whole wing contains brand-new parquet-floored rooms, with satellite TV, bathroom and buffet breakfast included. There's a small cocktail bar and a flash restaurant.

Fosshótel Valaskjálf (☎ 470 5050; www.fosshotel .is; Skógarlönd 3; s/d Jun-Aug Ikr14,700/19,000, Sep-May Ikr9300/10,700) Valaskjálf is a slightly decrepit, overpriced hotel – an option only if everything else is full.

Eating

Yfir Borðið/Pizza 67 (☎ 471 2424; Lyngás 3; pizzas Ikr900-2000; ✆ 5-10pm Sun-Thu, to 11pm Fri & Sat) This ambient bar-restaurant has a massive pizza menu (please will someone out there try the raspberry jam, green apples, almonds and camembert combo?), as well as burgers and fish mains. It's quite easy to miss – it's upstairs in what looks like an office block, opposite the Shell petrol station.

Café Nielsen (☎ 471 2626; Tjarnarbraut 1; lunch Ikr1400, dinner mains Ikr2200-3900; ✆ 11.30am-11.30pm Mon-Thu, to 2am Fri, 1pm-2am Sat, 1-11.30pm Sun) The top eating choice in town straddles the divide between smoky bar and genteel candlelit restaurant. There's plenty of variety, from veggie burgers to Icelandic favourites served with unusual flavourings – like scallops with mango and chilli. In summer there's a very pleasant leafy terrace and garden

Gistiheimilið Egilsstaðir (☎ 471 1114; www.egilsstadir .com; mains Ikr2500-4200) This lovely lakeside restaurant just 300m west of crossroads has a menu of Icelandic staples that have been given the world-cuisine treatment – salt cod with aubergines and sun-dried tomatoes, lamb with nutty Indonesian sauce. Local products include reindeer and beef from the farm, and there's always one veggie course.

Hótel Hérað (☎ 471 1500; Miðvangur 5; mains Ikr2900-3500) Hérað's stylish licensed restaurant is a good place for a splurge. It serves some interesting traditional dishes such as fresh char and lamb ribs, all livened up with modern European dressings and accompaniments. The house speciality is reindeer steak.

Té og Kaffi (☎ 471 2219; Miðvangur; ✆ til 6pm daily) Come here for great coffee, but avoid the food! It sounds really yum on paper, but in reality it's watery, claggy or tastes of onions.

Söluskálinn (☎ 470 1230), at the Esso petrol station near the tourist office, is an economical choice, with hearty daily specials of fish and meat dishes (around Ikr1800) and fast food. The **Shellskálinn** (Fagradalsbraut 13), at the Shell petrol station at the top of town, has an extremely popular set lunch.

Self-caterers have the well-stocked **Samkaup-Úrval supermarket** (✆ 9am-7pm Mon-Fri, 10am-6pm Sat, noon-6pm Sun) by the Esso garage, and the **Bónus supermarket** (☎ 471 2700; www.bonus.is; ✆ noon-6.30pm Mon-Thu, 10am-7.30pm Fri, 10am-6pm Sat, noon-6pm Sun) north of Fagradalsbraut.

The **Vín Búð** (☎ 471 2151; Miðvangi 2-4; ✆ 12.30-6pm Mon-Thu, 11am-7pm Fri, 11am-2pm Sat) alcohol shop is on the ground floor of the office building diagonally across from the Esso station.

There's a small bakery, **Fellabakarí** (☎ 471 1800), open on weekdays, at the Ólís petrol station in Fellabær.

Getting There & Away

Egilsstaðir is the transport hub of east Iceland. There's an airport (1km north of town), and all bus services pass through here (see p252).

The Ring Rd steams through Egilsstaðir, but if you want to explore the Eastfjords you need to leave it here. Rte 94 takes you north to Borgarfjörður Eystri, Rte 93 goes east to Seyðisfjörður, and Rte 92 goes south to Reyðarfjörður and the rest of the fjord towns.

Getting Around

Avis (☎ 660 0623; www.avis.is), **Hertz** (☎ 471 1210; www .hertz.is) and **Bílaleigur Akureyrar** (☎ 461 6070; www .holdur.is) all have agents at the airport.

Bus connections with the Smyril Line ferry in Seyðisfjörður can be really inconvenient. If you get stuck, a **taxi** (☎ 892 9247) between Egilsstaðir and Seyðisfjörður costs around Ikr8000.

SOUTH OF EGILSSTAÐIR
Lagarfljót

The grey-brown waters of the river-lake Lagarfljót are reputed to harbour a fearsome monster, **Lagarfljótsormurinn** (Lagarfljót Serpent), which has allegedly been spotted since Viking times. The last 'sighting' was in 1987, when it was glimpsed coiled up in an inlet at Atlavík camp site. The poor old beast must be pretty chilly – Lagarfljót starts its journey in the Vatnajökull icecap and its glacial waters flow north to the Arctic Ocean, widening into a 38km-long, 50m-deep lake, often called Lögurinn, south of Egilsstaðir.

Whether you see monsters or not, it's quite a lovely stretch of water, which can be circumnavigated by car. Rte 931, a mixture of sealed surfaces and gravel, runs all the way around the edge from Egilsstaðir-Fellabær – a distance of 56km. There's no public transport, and traffic is light on the western shore if you're planning on hitching.

The eastern shore is thick with birch and fir trees: Hallormsstaðaskógur (see right) is Iceland's biggest forest and a site of reverential pilgrimage for Icelanders. In summer you can take a pleasure cruise from the popular camp site there.

HALLORMSSTAÐASKÓGUR

The sequoia! The giant redwood! The mighty Scots pine! These are all trees that you won't see in the forest Hallormsstaðaskógur, on the eastern bank of the Lagarfljót. Although the country's coppices are comical to many foreigners ('Q. What do you do if you get lost in an Icelandic forest? A. Stand up.'), it's rude to snigger. Hallormsstaðaskógur is king of the woods and venerated by Icelanders.

There's a small petrol station near to the accommodation area in the forest, where you can pick up a free map (*gönguleiðakort*) of Hallormsstaðaskógur. It's in Icelandic-only, but shows the forest trails clearly.

Sights & Activities

Although the forest is small by most countries' standards, it's also quite cute – and a leafy reprieve after the stark, bare mountain sides to the north and south of Egilsstaðir. Common species include native dwarf birch and mountain ash, as well as 50 tree species gathered from around the world. Iceland's oldest larch colony, **Guttormslundur**, 2.5km south of Fosshótel Hallormsstaður (see opposite), was planted in 1938; some of the trees are now 20m high!

Between mid-June and August, the 110-passenger cruise ship **Lagarfljótsormurinn** (☎ 471 2900; www.ormur.is; per person Ikr2000; ❂ 8.30pm daily) runs from Atlavík camp site to Egilsstaðir and back again.

You can arrange **horse-riding tours** (☎ 847 0063; vediskl@simnet.is; ❂ 11am-7pm Jun-Aug) at the hut by Hússtjórnarskólinn summer hotel. The same people also rent out pedal boats, rowing boats and canoes from Atlavík campsite.

Sleeping

Atlavík camp site (☎ 849 1461; sites per person Ikr650) Down the hill, close to the lake shore, is this beautiful and extremely popular camp site, named after the first settler in this area, Graut-Atli. It's often the scene of raucous parties on summer weekends. The smaller, quieter Þurshofðavík camp site is just north of the petrol station.

Grái Hundurinn (☎ 471 1763; www.graihundurinn.is; Hjalli; s/d Jun-Sep Ikr6500/8700, Oct-May Ikr5400/6900) Ironically, the surrounding trees mean that the Grey Dog guesthouse's rooms are rather dark, But they all have TVs and washbasins, and a light breakfast is included. One of the doubles has its own private bathroom (Ikr12,400). The same couple runs the summer hotel Hússtjórnarskólinn next door; rooms cost the same as those in the guesthouse.

Fosshótel Hallormsstaður (☎ 471 1705; bokun@ fosshotel.is; s/d Ikr14,700/19,000; ☺ early Jun-late Aug) The en-suite, parquet-floored rooms here are small but bright and clean. Public spaces are decorated with children's drawings of the forest (this Fosshótel is a school out of season) and feel very welcoming. There's also a playground, and a swimming pool right next door. Breakfast is included.

SKRIÐUKLAUSTUR

The site of a 15th-century monastery, and the home of an Icelandic author fêted by the Third Reich, **Skriðuklaustur** (☎ 471 2990; www .skriduklaustur.is; adult/under 16yr Ikr500/free; ☺ 10am-6pm, to 10pm Wed in Jul) certainly has an interesting history. The unusual black-and-white turf-roofed building was built in 1939 by Gunnar Gunnarsson (1889–1975), and now holds a cultural centre dedicated to him. This prolific writer achieved phenomenal popularity in Denmark and Germany – at the height of his fame only Goethe outsold him! He was nominated for the Nobel Prize three times, but his books have dated badly; the most readable is *Svartfugl* (translated into English as *The Black Cliffs*), about an infamous Icelandic murder.

The house also contains an interesting exhibition about the earlier Augustinian monastery, demolished during the Reformation. Archaeological finds include bones indicating that Skriðuklaustur was used as a hospice. Its most famous artefact is a carved statue of the Virgin Mary, found hidden in an old barn wall.

Downstairs, Klausturkaffi serves a great lunch buffet (Ikr1750) made from local ingredients (wild mushrooms, reindeer meat, brambleberry puddings). For all who love gorging on sugary, creamy confections, there's an all-you-can-eat cake buffet (Ikr1250) between 2pm and 5pm at weekends.

KÁRAHNJÚKASÝNING

Just up the road from Skriðuklaustur is the **visitor centre** (☎ 861 2195; ☺ 9am-5pm Mon-Sat, 10am-5pm Sun mid-Apr–mid-Sep, 1-5pm mid-Sep–mid-Oct) for the Kárahnjúkar project (see p258).

VALÞJÓFSSTAÐUR

If you're up at this end of the Lagarfljót lake, you might as well pop into the unassuming **church** at Valþjófsstaður. One of the most amazing items in Reykjavík's National Museum, the wooden door depicting the story of the Knight of the Lion, was carved here around 1200. A replica has been fixed up at the current church.

HENGIFOSS

Hengifoss is Iceland's third-highest **waterfall**. Once you've made the climb up and into the canyon you'll be blown away by the power of the water – it sounds like a Boeing 747 taking off! The falls plummet 120m into a colourful brown-and-red-striped boulder-strewn gorge.

Getting to Hengifoss requires a return walk of about 1½ hours. From the parking area on Rte 933, about 200m south of the bridge across the lake, a well-defined path leads up the hillside – Hengifoss is soon visible in the distance. It's a steep climb in places but flattens out as you enter the gorge. Halfway up is a smaller waterfall, **Lítlanesfoss**, which is surrounded by spectacular vertical basalt columns in a honey–comb formation.

NORTH OF EGILSSTAÐIR

The region due north of Egilsstaðir is mostly water and grey sand! Few travellers visit, but if you've plenty of time, you might like to admire this landscape of dunes, basalt outcrops, marshes and river deltas (where the Lagarfljót and Jökulsá á Brú join the sea).

There's no regular public transport, but with your own vehicle you could do a loop drive along Rtes 94 and 925.

Eiðar

Eiðar, 14km north of Egilsstaðir on Rte 94, was the farm of Helgi Ásbjarnarson, grandson of Hrafnkell Freysgoði (see the boxed text, p260). The **church**, built in 1887, contains an interesting statue of Christ that washed up on the shore at Héraðssandur, north of Eiðar. Its location beside a popular trout lake, Eiðavatn, makes it especially appealing for anglers.

Hotel Edda (☎ 444 4000; www.hoteledda.is; sb Ikr1700-2200, s/d Ikr5800/7200; ☺ mid-Jun–Aug), in the local school just off the Egilsstaðir–Borgarfjörður road, is a summer hotel with lots of sleeping-bag space, rooms with washbasins, a swimming pool and a licensed restaurant.

Kirkjubæjarkirkja

One of Iceland's oldest wooden churches, Kirkjubæjarkirkja (1851) is set in a peaceful deep-grassed graveyard, 3km west of Lagarfoss.

EAST ICELAND

It's a quaint little place, with a dusty harmonium, a sky-blue ceiling, creaking stairs up to a tiny gallery and the oldest pulpit in the country – a great 16th-century piece, carved with medieval-looking saints.

Húsey

The only reason to venture out to the isolated farm at Húsey, 60km north of Egilsstaðir near the shores of Héraðsflói, is to stay at the friendly **Húsey HI Hostel** (☎ 471 3010; husey@simnet .is; sb Ikr2400, made-up bed Ikr3100). Apart from the sheer isolation and the stark but beautiful surroundings, this is a great spot for birdwatching – more than 30 species breed here. There are also lots of seals (the farmers hunt, tan and eat them). If you don't have a vehicle the wardens might pick up prebooked guests (for a fee) from Egilsstaðir. There are cooking facilities at the hostel but there's nowhere to buy food, so bring supplies. Breakfast (Ikr1000) can be ordered.

THE HIGHLANDS
Jökulsá á Dal

At the time of writing, this large, turbulent river was still flowing strong, from the Vatnajökull icecap all the way to Héraðsflói bay, 150km away. By the time you read this, it will be an ex-river as the completed Kárahnjúkar dam will block off the water after it has travelled a mere 20km from the glacier, and the river will back up to become the Hálslón reservoir.

A small stream, formed by rivulets from the hillsides, will still puddle through the old riverbed. The part alongside the Ring Rd is said to be haunted by mischievous leprechauns and bloodthirsty Norse deities.

KÁRAHNJÚKAR – OPENING THE FLOODGATES   Stuart Cooper

The Kárahnjúkar Hydroelectric Project: monstrous in scale, costly compared to the alternatives, controversial at home and attracting a storm of international protests. Just why has the state power company, Landsvirkjun, built the largest infrastructure project in Iceland's history?

The simple answer is that Alcoa, the American multinational, will use power generated by damming two rivers to smelt aluminium, and that it will be cheaper for them to do so this way than to use conventional methods. (Although it's not cheaper than recycling existing aluminium products.) There is brave talk of 1000 additional jobs and a new Golden Circle, as tourists flood in to use the new roads created by the project. The Eastfjords, traditionally one of Iceland's poorest regions, has seen an increase in visitors wanting to study the site of the project, and a steady supply of work.

However, the project's critics are numerous: the Iceland Conservation Association (INCA), the Icelandic Society for the Protection of Birds, Greenpeace and the WWF, not to mention Björk's mum, and one of the most well-known newsreaders in the country! The Halslón reservoir, to be created by the massive Kárahnjúkar dam, will alone submerge 57 sq km of wilderness, and there are concerns for the habitats of reindeer and pink-footed geese, as well as the harbour seals at Reyðarfjörður, site of the smelting works.

Icelanders themselves are deeply divided – the National Planning Authority initially refused plans for the project on environmental grounds, but was overruled by the environment minister. Protestors set up camp near the site, but lost support when they occupied the offices of a local architect; some local people question the right of outsiders to tell them what to do, and welcome the development whatever the cost, believing it will deliver them from years of isolation and relative poverty.

The dam and smelter are a dramatic illustration of the dilemma Iceland now faces: with staple industries such as fishing in decline and threatened by overexploitation, how will Icelanders earn their living in the future? Through tourism, and thriving cultural industries such as design and music-making; or by opening up vast tracts of their wilderness to industrial megaprojects?

Reykjavík is thriving – it has joined the global network of hip city destinations – and many of its inhabitants are appalled by the scale of and the devastation caused by the Kárahnjúkar project. Iceland is resonant with history, it's one of the last European wildernesses and it's a country like no other. Whether it remains so – a pristine land of lava and lichen – is now open to serious question for the first time in its history. The waters in the reservoir are rising, and power will start flowing to the smelter in 2009.

The outcrop called **Goðanes**, about 3km west of the farm Hofteigur, was the site of an ancient pagan temple where some ruins are still visible. The iron-stained spring **Blóðkelda** (Blood Spring) carries an apocryphal legend that the blood of both human and animal sacrifices once flowed into it.

Consider breaking up a long car journey with kids at **Klaustursel** (☎ 471 1085; allis@centrum .is), 6km off the Ring Rd along rough Rte 923 (the alarming little bridge you cross was once part of the American railway!). The farm has swans and geese, and you can pat the soft noses of the oh-so-pretty reindeer.

Continuing along Rte 923 leads you to the valley of **Hrafnkelsdalur** (about 100km from Egilsstaðir), full of Saga Age sites relating to *Hrafnkell's Saga* (see the boxed text, p260). The farm **Aðalból** (☎ 471 2788; www.simnet.is/samur; sites per person Ikr500, sb Ikr2200, made-up bed Ikr3300; ☯ Jun–mid-Sep) was the home of the saga's hero, Hrafnkell Freysgoði, and his burial mound is there. At the time of writing the current occupier, Sigurður, was marking a 10km-long saga trail, threading together places mentioned in the story; even if you're not a raving saga addict it's an interesting walking area, off the tourist trail.

There's simple accommodation available at Aðalból farm, and a petrol pump, but unless you preorder meals Egilsstaðir is the nearest place to buy food. The road becomes the F910 before you reach Aðalból, but it's easily driveable (if a bit skiddy) in a normal car. It's definitely 4WD only once you continue past Aðalból – an alternative route to Snæfell, or to the **Kárahnjúkar dam** (see the boxed text, opposite).

The reconstructed turf farmhouse **Sænautasel** (☎ 471 1086; ☯ daily Jul & Aug), dating from 1843, really brings the past to life…plus it sells pancakes and coffee! This is one of several old farms on Jökuldalsheiði that were originally abandoned when Askja erupted in 1875. The building is beside the lake Sænautavatn, 32km west of Hofteigur and 4km south of the Ring Rd via Rte 907. This area was a source of inspiration for Halldór Laxness' master work, *Independent People*; you may notice that many of the farm names here match those of the fictional farms in the book.

Snæfell

No-one seems to know whether 1833m-high Snæfell is an extinct volcano, or it's just hav-

'Why's the dam being built? Greed and local politics. It makes no sense. We need to remember: what we do today will affect little Vikings in 100 years' time. People need to wake up.'

Jónas, Original Haunted Walk of Reykjavík

ing a rest! Iceland's highest peak outside the Vatnajökull massif is relatively accessible, making it popular with hikers and mountaineers. Snæfell looms over the southern end of Fljótsdalsheiði, an expanse of spongy tussocks of wet tundra, boulder fields, perennial snow patches and alpine lakes, stretching westwards from Lagarfljót into the interior.

Work on the dam has improved the roads around Snæfell, with Rte F910 from Fljótsdalur being the best way up. (It's still pretty vertical, though!) Along the way, watch for wild reindeer. At the base of the peak, at 800m elevation, is Ferðafélag Íslands' **Snæfell mountain hut** (N 64°48.250′, W 15°38.600′; per person Ikr2000), accommodating up to 62 people, with a kitchen, a camping area and showers.

Although climbing the mountain itself is not difficult for experienced, well-prepared hikers, the weather can be a concern and technical equipment is required. Discussing your route first with the hut warden is a good idea.

SNÆFELL–LÓNSÖRÆFI TREK

One of Iceland's most challenging and rewarding treks takes you from Snæfell to the Lónsöræfi district (see p296) in southeast Iceland. The five-day route begins at the Snæfell hut and heads across the glacier Eyjabakkajökull (an arm of Vatnajökull) to Geldingafell, Egilssel and Múlaskáli huts before dropping down to the coast at Stafafell.

This route should not be approached lightly – it's for experienced trekkers only. You'll need good route-finding skills and, for the glacier crossing, you must be able to use a compass and have a rope, crampons and an ice axe. If you're unsure of your skills, you'd be much wiser doing the trip commercially with Ferðafélag Íslands.

Advance hut bookings are advised for July and August – contact **Ferðafélag Íslands** (☎ 568 2533; www.fi.is; Mörkin 6, IS-108 Reykjavík).

You'll need the following topo sheets for walking in this region: *Hornafjörður* 1:100,000 (1986), *Hamarsfjörður* 1:100,000 (1987) and *Snæfell* 1:100,000 (1988).

EAST ICELAND

HRAFNKELL'S SAGA

The saga of Hrafnkell is one of the most widely read Icelandic sagas, thanks to its short, succinct plot and memorable characters. The tale is particularly interesting because its premises seem to derail any modern notions of right, wrong and justice served. The only conclusions one can really draw are 'it's better to be alive than dead'; and 'it's better to have the support of powerful chieftains than rely on any kind of god'.

The main character, Hrafnkell, is a religious fanatic who builds a temple to Freyr on the farm Aðalból in Hrafnkelsdalur (see p258). Hrafnkell's prized stallion, Freyfaxi, is dedicated to the god, and Hrafnkell swears an oath to kill anyone who dares ride him without permission. As might be expected, someone does. The stallion himself tempts a young shepherd to leap onto his back and gallop off to find a herd of lost sheep. Discovering the outrage, Hrafnkell takes his axe to the errant youth.

When the boy's father, Þorbjörn, demands compensation for his son's death, Hrafnkell refuses to pay up, offering instead to look after Þorbjörn in his old age. Proudly, the man refuses, and the characters are launched into a court battle that ultimately leads to Hrafnkell being declared an outlaw. He chooses to ignore the sentence and returns home.

Before long, Þorbjörn's nephew Sámur Bjarnason arrives to uphold the family honour, stringing Hrafnkell up by the Achilles tendons until he agrees to hand over his farm and possessions. Sámur then offers him a choice: to live a life of subordination and dishonour, or to die on the spot; you might think a saga hero would go for death, but Hrafnkell chooses life.

Sámur moves into Aðalból, and makes a few home improvements. The pagan temple is destroyed, and the horse Freyfaxi weighted with stones, thrown over a cliff and drowned in the water below. Hrafnkell, by now convinced that his favourite god doesn't give two hoots about him, renounces his religious beliefs and sets up on a new farm, Hrafnkelsstaðir. He vows to change his vengeful nature and becomes a kind and simple farmer, becoming so well-liked in his new neighbourhood that he gains even more wealth and power than before.

One day, Sámur and his brother Eyvindur pass by en route to Aðalból. Hrafnkell's maid sees them and goads her employer into taking revenge for his earlier humiliation. Hrafnkell abandons the Mr Nice Guy routine, sets out in pursuit of the troublesome brothers, kills Eyvindur, and offers Sámur the same choice that he was offered before – give up Aðalból and live in shame, or be put to death. Sámur also decides not to die. Hrafnkell thus regains his former estates and lives happily ever after at Aðalból.

THE EASTFJORDS

Unlike the histrionic, wildly folding Westfjords, the Eastfjords wiggle more modestly around the coast. It's like the difference between an overtheatrical actor chewing up the scenery, and an underemoting character in some Scandinavian arthouse film.

Despite good surfaced roads and all the smelter-related activity, the Eastfjords still feel pretty remote – a feeling enhanced by immense, dramatic mountain sides and the tiny working fishing villages that nestle under them.

The fjords are a definite highlight of eastern Iceland. There are some lovely walks, you can kayak to far-off headlands, thousands of sea birds nest along the cliffs, and it's amazing how many dolphin pods you can spot if you choose a good vantage point and wait.

In a Finest Fjord competition it would be hard to pick a winner – Borgarfjörður is great for its off-the-tourist-track air, Seyðisfjörður has a cheery bohemian atmosphere, atmospheric Mjóifjörður is full of ruined buildings, and Norðfjörður feels like the Lost Valley. You'll just have to visit and choose your own favourite.

The following section is organised from north to south.

BORGARFJÖRÐUR EYSTRI (BAKKAGERÐI)
pop 100

This village, the most northerly in the Eastfjords, is in a stunning location. It's framed by a backdrop of rugged rhyolite peaks on one side and the spectacular Dyrfjöll mountains on the other. There's very little in the village itself, although weird driftwood sculptures, crying sea birds and pounding waves exude a strange charm. The main reason to come here is to hike in the surrounding hills. (If anyone happened to watch the reality TV programme *Rockstar Supernova*, this is where Magni is from!).

The Álfasteinn rock shop and Fjarðarborg community centre (see right) are the two places to go for information. Fjarðarborg sells a good booklet of walks (Ikr400) in the area but only has a small supply – it may be better to buy the booklet from the Egilsstaðir tourist office.

Sights & Activities

The touristy rock shop **Álfasteinn** (Elf Stone; ☎ 897 2765, 470 2000; www.alfasteinn.is; 🕙 noon-8pm Jun-Aug, 10am-noon & 1-5pm Mon-Fri Sep-May) does a booming business collecting semiprecious stones, polishing them up, then turning them into kitsch candle holders, cheese slicers and the like. Out the front is a 2250kg piece of raw jasper, the biggest found in Iceland.

Jóhannes Sveinsson Kjarval (1885–1972), Iceland's best-known artist, was brought up on the nearby farm Geitavík and took much of his inspiration from Borgarfjörður Eystri. **Kjarvalsstofa** (☎ 472 9950; adult/child Ikr500/free; 🕙 10am-6pm mid-Jun–Aug), inside the Fjarðarborg community centre, is the village's tribute to him; we hate to say it, but it's underwhelming – a single room containing copies of his famous sketches of local people.

Better to see the touching and unusual altarpiece in the small church **Bakkagerðiskirkja**, painted by Kjarval in 1914. It depicts the Sermon on the Mount and is directly aimed at his village of fishermen and farmers – Jesus is preaching from Álfaborg, with the mountain Dyrfjöll in the background.

From the town's monument to the painter it's a signposted half-hour walk to **Smalakofi Kjarvals**, the ruins of a stone shepherd's hut that Kjarval built as a child.

You can't miss the village's hairiest house! Bright red **Lindarbakki** (1899) is completely cocooned by whiskery green grass, with only a few windows and a giant pair of antlers sticking out. It's a private home and not open to the public, but an interesting information board outside tells you more about its history. We particularly liked the estate agent's comments from 1979…

Álfaborg (Elf Rock) the small mound and nature reserve near the camp site, is the 'borg' that gave Borgarfjörður Eystri its name. From the view disc on top there's a fabulous vista of the surrounding fields, which turn white in summer with blooming arctic cotton. Some locals believe that the queen of Icelandic elves lives here. Borgarfjörður Eystri's main festival, **Elf Dance**, held on the weekend nearest 6 January, involves a bonfire and candle-lit procession led by the elf king and queen.

There's a large **puffin colony** of 10,000 pairs on the islet **Hafnarhólmi** (connected to the mainland by a causeway), about 5km northeast of Borgarfjörður Eystri at the end of the road. The viewing platform is open from 10am to 10pm daily in June and July (free) and at all times in August.

Back in the village there's a small hide for **bird-watching** behind the general store.

Tours

Skúli Sveinsson at **Borg Travel Services** (☎ 472 9870, 854 4470; gisting-borg@vlslr.is) runs 4WD tours and transports hikers and luggage to trail heads for around Ikr2500 per person, depending on where you go.

Sleeping & Eating

Camp site (☎ 472 9999; magnus@eldhorn.is; sites per person Ikr750, 3rd night free) Beside the church, this quiet green site has a kitchen and free showers.

Borgarfjörður Eystri HI Hostel (☎ 472 9962; borgarfjordur@hostel.is; sb Ikr2000; 🕙 May–mid-Sep) This small hostel offers sleeping-bag accommodation for up to 17 people. There's a guest kitchen and a washing machine.

Gistiheimilið Borg (☎ 472 9870, 894 4470; gisting -borg@visir.is; sb/s/d Ikr2100/3500/6000) Borg is a good bet for a bed, since the owner has three houses in the village. Rooms are OK if old fashioned, with cooking and lounge facilities. Breakfast (Ikr900) is available in summer.

Réttarholt (☎ 472 9913; helgima@mi.is; sb Ikr2200, s/d Ikr4500/6800) This year-round guesthouse has just three simple, brightly quilted rooms and is the nicest place to stay in the village. There's a homey guest kitchen and the house is set in the most lovely garden, full of odd sculptures and pieces of lichen-covered wood. The owner, Helgi, leads guided walks during the summer and is a good person to ask about hiking in the area.

Fjarðarborg community centre (☎ 472 9920; berg runj@mi.is; sb Ikr2000; 🕙 11am-8pm mid-Jun–Aug) In summer, there's basic sleeping-bag accommodation here, and a bit of food – mainly burgers, pancakes and ice cream.

Álfasteinn (☎ 897 2765, 470 2000; www.alfasteinn.is; ☺ noon-8pm Jun-Aug, 10am-noon & 1-5pm Mon-Fri Sep-May) The rock shop has a pleasant summer-only café serving the best coffee in town, plus traditional light nibbles such as fish soup, flatbread with lamb sausage or smoked trout, and Icelandic doughnuts.

The tiny **KHB general store** (☎ 472 9940; ☺ 12.30-5.30pm Mon-Fri) by the pier sells groceries.

Getting There & Away

The only public transport to Borgarfjörður Eystri is the **postal van** (☎ 472 9805, 894 8305) from Egilsstaðir at noon on weekdays (Ikr1500/750 per adult/child under 12). It returns at 8am, departing from Álfasteinn and stopping at the Fjarðarborg community centre too.

The village is 70km from Egilsstaðir along Rte 94, about half of which is sealed. It winds steeply up over the Vatnsskarð mountains before dropping down to the coast. There's a card-operated petrol pump by the KHB general store.

AROUND BORGARFJÖRÐUR EYSTRI

There are loads of trails crisscrossing the northeast – everything from easy two-hour strolls to serious mountain hiking for people with a head for heights! Watch your footing in nonvegetated areas – loose material makes for an experience akin to walking on thousands of tiny ball bearings.

The colourful rhyolite peak **Staðarfjall** (543m) rises 8km southeast of Borgarfjörður Eystri and makes a nice day walk. The best access is up the ridge from Desjamýri farm, across the estuary from Borgarfjörður Eystri.

Dyrfjöll

One of Iceland's most dramatic ranges, the Dyrfjöll mountains rise precipitously to an altitude of 1136m between the Lagarfljót valley and Borgarfjörður Eystri. The name Dyrfjöll means 'Door Mountain' and is due to the large and conspicuous notch in the highest peak – an Icelandic counterpart to Sweden's famous Lapporten. There are two walking tracks crossing the range, which allow for day hikes or longer routes from Borgarfjörður Eystri.

Stórurð, on the western flank of Dyrfjöll, is an extraordinary place scattered with huge rocks and small glacial ponds. It can be reached in 2½ hours from just west of the pass on the road to Egilsstaðir (Rte 94).

Njarðvíkurskriður

A habitual site of accidents in ancient times, Njarðvíkurskriður is a dangerous scree slope on Rte 94 near Njarðvík. All the tragedies were blamed on a nuisance creature (half man, half beast), Naddi, who dwelt in a sea-level cave beneath the slope.

In the early 1300s Naddi was exorcised by the proper religious authorities, and in 1306 a cross was erected on the site bearing the inscription '*Effigiem Christi qui transis pronus honora, Anno MCCCVI*' – 'You who are hurrying past, honour the image of Christ – AD 1306'. The idea was that travellers would repeat a prayer when passing the danger zone and therefore be protected from malevolent powers. The cross has been replaced several times since, but the current one still bears the original inscription.

LOÐMUNDARFJARÐARLEIÐ

In high summer, the relatively little-known mountain route between Borgarfjörður Eystri and Loðmundarfjörður is an obscure but very attractive hike. It follows a 4WD track up over the pass and opens up lots of opportunities to explore the pristine surroundings. The required topo sheet is *Dyrfjöll* 1:100,000 (1986). For 4WD transport to the trail heads or huts, contact Skúli Sveinsson at Borg Travel Services (see p261).

The route begins at the farm Hvannstöð, 7km south of Borgarfjörður Eystri, and continues for 20km over Húsavíkurheiði (477m). You can either descend along the side track to the small bay of Húsavík or continue south to the deserted fjord Loðmundarfjörður. From there the route follows the historic 20km bridle path up Hjálmárdalur and across Hjalmardalsheiði to Seyðisfjörður.

A more direct route leads due south from Hvannstöð, across the mountains to Loðmundarfjörður, via the strange **Álfakirkjan**, a huge, house-shaped rock.

The shallow bay **Breiðavík** has a deep valley and a basic Ferðafélag Íslands **hut** (N 65°27.830′, W 13°40.286′; per person Ikr2000) reached by 4WD track from the head of Borgarfjörður or a hiking trail from Húsavíkurheiði. The valley isn't on the direct Loðmundarfjarðarleið route, but it makes a fine side trip.

At the **Nesháls pass**, between Víkurá and Loðmundarfjörður, the track reaches an altitude of 435m. Just west is the peak **Skælingur** (832m), sometimes called the 'Chinese temple'.

Loðmundarfjörður

This short but beautiful fjord was once well settled, and at least six farms occupied the upper basin. However, after the coastal supply boats stopped running, construction of all-season roads into such sparsely populated outposts became uneconomical and the region was finally abandoned in 1973. Unfortunately, there is no longer any accommodation in the area. Walkers will have to wild camp and postpone the hot shower till another day!

From Loðmundarfjarðarleið it's a six- to eight-hour walk south to Seyðisfjörður, where there are plenty of facilities and buses back to Egilsstaðir.

SEYÐISFJÖRÐUR

pop 740

If you visit only one town in the Eastfjords, this picturesque place should be it. Made up of multicoloured wooden houses, and surrounded by snow-capped mountains and cascading waterfalls, Seyðisfjörður (www .sfk.is) is the most historically and architecturally interesting town in east Iceland. It's also a friendly place with a gregarious and

bohemian community of artists, musicians and craftspeople.

Summer is the liveliest time to visit, particularly when the Smyril Line's ferry *Norröna* sails majestically up the 17km-long fjord to the town – a perfect way to arrive in Iceland.

The substance and soul of the village has traditionally been focused on the fishing industry. For a glimpse of what life here was like 40 years ago, we recommend the moving film *Kaldaljós* (*Cold Light;* 2004), partly filmed in Seyðisfjörður.

If the weather's good, the scenic road from Egilsstaðir is a delight, climbing to a high pass then following the waterfall-filled river Fjarðará down. If it's bad weather you probably won't see much more than the tail-lights of the car in front!

History

Seyðistjörður started as a trading centre in 1848, but its later wealth came from the 'silver of the sea' – herring. Its long, sheltering fjord gave it an advantage over other fishing villages, and it grew into the largest and most prosperous town in east Iceland. Most of the beautiful

EAST ICELAND

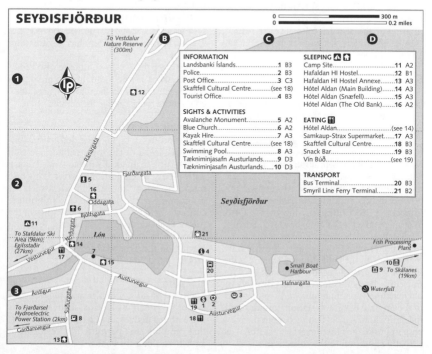

SEYÐISFJÖRÐUR

0 — 300 m
0 — 0.2 miles

INFORMATION	
Landsbanki Íslands.....................1	B3
Police...2	B3
Post Office...................................3	C3
Skaftfell Cultural Centre..........(see 18)	
Tourist Office..............................4	B3

SIGHTS & ACTIVITIES	
Avalanche Monument................5	A2
Blue Church.................................6	A2
Kayak Hire...................................7	A3
Skaftfell Cultural Centre..........(see 18)	
Swimming Pool...........................8	A3
Tækniminjasafn Austurlands......9	D3
Tækniminjasafn Austurlands......10	D3

SLEEPING	
Camp Site..................................11	A2
Hafaldan HI Hostel....................12	B1
Hafaldan HI Hostel Annexe.......13	A3
Hótel Aldan (Main Building).......14	A3
Hótel Aldan (Snæfell)...............15	A3
Hótel Aldan (The Old Bank).......16	A2

EATING	
Hótel Aldan................................(see 14)	
Samkaup-Strax Supermarket.....17	A3
Skaftfell Cultural Centre...........18	B3
Snack Bar..................................19	B3
Vín Búð....................................(see 19)	

TRANSPORT	
Bus Terminal.............................20	B3
Smyril Line Ferry Terminal........21	B2

and unique wooden buildings here were built by Norwegian merchants, attracted by the rich pickings of the herring industry.

During WWII Seyðisfjörður was a base for British and American forces. The only attack was on an oil tanker that was bombed by three German warplanes. The bombs missed their target, but one exploded so near that the ship sank to the bottom, where it remains today.

Seyðisfjörður's steep-sided valley has made it prone to avalanches. In 1885 an avalanche from Bjólfur killed 24 people and pushed several houses straight into the fjord. A more recent avalanche in 1996 flattened a local factory, but no lives were lost. The avalanche monument near the church is made from twisted girders from the factory, painted white and erected as they were found.

Information

The **tourist office** (☎ 472 1551; ☽ 10am-noon & 1-5pm Mon, Tue, Thu & Fri winter, 10am-noon & 1-8pm Wed summer, 1-5pm Wed & Thu rest of yr), in the modern ferry terminal building, sells bus passes and books onward accommodation.

There's a **Landsbanki Íslands bank** (☎ 470 3040; Hafnargata 2), which can get crowded when the ferry arrives. In summer you can access the internet at the **Skaftfell Cultural Centre** (☎ 472 1632; skaftfell@skaftfell.is; Austurvegur 42; ☐) for Ikr200 per 30 minutes.

Sights

Seyðisfjörður is stuffed with 19th-century **timber buildings**, brought in kit form from Norway: read all about them in the brochure *Historic Seyðisfjörður*, available at the tourist office.

For insight into the town's fishing and telecommunications history, there's a worthwhile museum, **Tækniminjasafn Austurlands** (☎ 472 1596; Hafnargata 44; adult/under 18yr Ikr500/free; ☽ 11am-5pm daily Jun–mid-Sep, 1-4pm Mon-Fri mid-Sep–May). It's housed in two buildings on Hafnargata: the impressive 1894 home of ship owner Otto Wathne, and a workshop from 1907. Seyðisfjörður was at the cutting edge of Icelandic technology in the 19th century – the first submarine telephone cable linking Iceland with Europe was brought ashore here in 1906. The museum charts this history with displays of old machinery, photographs, and a re-creation of the original telegraph station, foundry and machine shop. An old fishing boat in the harbour opposite the museum is being restored as a floating addition to the collection.

The **Skaftfell Cultural Centre** (☎ 472 1632; Austurvegur 42) is the place to hang out in Seyðisfjörður. It's a meeting place for local artists and musicians with a very bohemian vibe. Upstairs is a spacious gallery of changing exhibitions, and occasional concerts and poetry readings are held here.

The first high-voltage electricity in Iceland came from the **Fjarðarsel hydroelectric power station** (☎ 472 1122; www.fjardarsel.is), which opened in 1913. The power station, a 15-minute walk upriver from town, is still in operation; its small electricity museum opens on request.

Activities

For an unearthly experience, try a guided night **kayaking trip** (☎ 865 3741; www.iceland-tour .com; ☽ Jun-Aug) around the tranquil lagoon (one hour, Ikr1500) with Hlynur Oddssen. More experienced paddlers can go on a six-hour paddle (Ikr6000) to Austdalur or a two-day trip (Ikr17,000) to Skálanes – a fabulous way of getting close to the bird life and maybe seals.

Hlynur also does **mountain-bike tours** (Ikr2000 for a two-hour trip), or you can hire bikes and take off on your own (Ikr1500/2000 per half/ full day).

Seyðisfjörður's indoor **swimming pool** (☎ 472 1414; Suðurgata 5; adult/child Ikr300/150; ☽ 7-9am & 5-9pm Mon-Fri, noon-4pm Sat & Sun) has a sauna and hot pots.

In winter there's downhill and also cross-country **skiing** at the Stafdalur ski area, 9km from Seyðisfjörður on the road to Egilsstaðir – contact the tourist office for details.

Festivals & Events

Seyðisfjörður is a highly regarded artistic centre in east Iceland. The town's cultural festival **Á Seyði** runs from mid-June to mid-August, with plenty of exhibitions, workshops and music. An important part of the festival is the programme of classical-, jazz and folk-music concerts, held on Wednesday evenings in the pretty **Blue Church** (Ránargata; admission Ikr1000) at 8.30pm from late June to mid-August. If you're leaving on the Thursday ferry, this is a great way to spend your final night in Iceland.

Sleeping

Camp site (☎ 861 3097; ferdamenning@sfk.is; Ránargata; sites Ikr600) This is a pleasant, sheltered grassy site with big hedges and picnic benches. Note that camping isn't permitted in Vestdalur or anywhere along the roads.

SEYÐISFJÖRÐUR–VESTDALUR HIKE

Hafaldan HI Hostel (☎ 4/2 1410; thorag@simnet.is; Ránargata 9; sb dm Ikr1650, sb d Ikr4800, d Ikr6000; ☐) Seyðisfjörður's cheerful arty hostel is split over two sites (facilities are shared). The original building has harbour views, a sunny lounge, a newly fitted kitchen, a laundry, internet access…and even a snug Mongolian yurt (available July and August) in the garden. The central new building used to be the old hospital, but you'd never guess – Indian hangings and funky old furniture make it homey.

ourpick **Hótel Aldan** (☎ 472 1277; www.hotelaldan.com; Norðurgata 2) The hotel is shared across three old wooden buildings. Reception and the bar-restaurant (where breakfast is served) are at this location. The Snæfell location (at Austurvegur 3) is a creaky, characterful three-storey place with cheaper rooms (Ikr10,800/14,800/16,800 for singles/doubles/triples in summer, and Ikr6500/8800/10,800 for singles/doubles/

triples in winter), fresh white paintwork, draped muslin curtains and Indian bedspreads to add a splash of colour. The Old Bank location (at Oddagata 6) houses a truly gorgeous boutique guesthouse with all mod-cons. Its luxury rooms (Ikr12,800/16,800/19,800 for singles/doubles/triples in summer, and Ikr7800/11,800/14,800 for singles/doubles/triples in winter) are bright, spacious and furnished with antiques, and beds are snuggled under hand-embroidered bedspreads. The triple rooms have wicked little alcoves.

Eating & Drinking

Skaftfell Cultural Centre (☎ 472 1632; Austurvegur 42; snacks Ikr450-1100, mains Ikr2000-3500; ☺ 11am-10pm summer, cultural events only winter; ☐) This welcoming, arty bistro-bar and internet café is a great place to linger over coffee and a good book. Snacks include omelettes, waffles and toast with caviar, and the freshly caught seafood is fab.

Hótel Aldan (☎ 472 1277; Norðurgata 2; mains Ikr2600-3500; ☺ 7am-9.30pm mid-May–mid-Sep) Coffee and light meals are served all day. In the evening, damask tablecloths, crystal wine glasses and flickering candles prettify the tables, and the menu features traditional Icelandic ingredients (lamb, lobster, reindeer, fish) served with contemporary salads and sauces. The bar fairly buzzes when the boat comes in.

Snack bar (☎ 472 1700; Hafnargata 2; ☺ noon-9pm) This place at the Shell petrol station does hot dogs and sandwiches, as well as cooked lunch/dinner mains – usually something filling and Icelandic, such as fish soup or meatballs.

The **Samkaup-Strax supermarket** (☎ 472 1201; Vesturvegur 1; ☺ closed Sun) is opposite the petrol station, and there's also a **Vín Búð** (☎ 472 1191; Hafnargata 2a; ☺ 5-6pm Mon-Thu, 4-6pm Fri) alcohol shop.

EAST ICELAND

SEYÐISFJÖRÐUR–VESTDALUR HIKE

A wonderful introduction to hiking in Iceland will take you up through the Vestdalur Nature Reserve and around Bjólfur down to the Seyðisfjörður–Egilsstaðir road.

Start by walking up the road past the HI hostel to where a rough 4WD track takes off up the glacial valley to your left. The track peters out after a few hundred metres, but keep walking uphill, along the left side of the Vestdalsá river. After a couple of hours and several tiers of glorious waterfalls, you'll arrive at a small lake, Vestdalsvatn, which remains frozen most of the year. Here you'll see Bjólfur to your left.

From the lake, bear left and make your way southwards over the tundra, through the snowfields and past a small ski hut to the highway. From there, you'll have to hitch to either Seyðisfjörður or Egilsstaðir, or arrange a pick-up. The trip can also be done in the opposite direction – and more easily because most of it is downhill.

Getting There & Away
BUS
In summer there's at least one bus to/from Egilsstaðir daily – see p252 for details.

BOAT
The **Smyril Line car ferry** (www.smyril-line.com) *Norröna* sails year-round to Seyðisfjörður from Hanstholm (Denmark), Tórshavn (the Faeroes) and Bergen (Norway). From mid-May to the end of September the ferry also brings passengers from Scotland (currently from Lerwick in the Shetlands, but it's possible that the ferry will eventually depart direct from Aberdeen). From mid-May to August it sails into town at 9am on Thursday, departing for Scandinavia/Scotland at 1pm the same afternoon; check-in is at least one hour before departure. The (complicated) timetable changes at other times of the year – for more information, see p328, or check the website.

AROUND SEYÐISFJÖRÐUR
Skálanes
The remote farm **Skálanes** (☎ 690 6966; www.skalanes .com; sites per tent/sb Ikr600/2000; ☷ May-Aug), about 19km east of Seyðisfjörður, has recently been dubbed a **nature and heritage field centre**. Its isolation, plus stunning sea cliffs full of diverse and abundant bird life, will do wonders for your inner hermit/naturalist. You can stay in very simple accommodation (sleeping-bag bunks, kitchen, running water), or the centre does a neat package – Ikr7500 per day will get you a night's sleeping-bag accommodation, three light meals and an hour-long guided walk.

Getting there is an adventure in itself. You could walk the 19km; you could get there on a mountain bike or in a canoe hired from Hlynur Oddssen (see p264); in a normal car you can drive 13km along the 4WD track until you get to the river, then walk; in a Jeep you can drive the whole way there; or it may be possible for the centre to pick you up from Seyðisfjörður in a boat – contact them to ask.

MJÓIFJÖRÐUR
pop 35
The next fjord south of Seyðisfjörður is Mjóifjörður, flanked by spectacular **cliffs**, and well off the worn tourist circuit. The several abandoned **turf farmsteads** (hard to find), the site of the early-20th-century **Norwegian whaling station** at Asknes and the 19th-century **wooden church** at Brekkuþorp are worth visit-ing, but the best-known attraction is the ruin of the **Dalatangi light**, Iceland's first lighthouse. The new lighthouse and the nearby vegetable and flower gardens are also of interest.

At Brekkuþorp, **Sólbrekka** (☎ 476 0020; mjoi@ simnet.is; sb Ikr1000, cottages per person Ikr2500 to a maximum of Ikr8000; ☷ closed Dec & Jan) is the one and only place to stay around here and it's a welcome sight for hikers. There are two four-person cottages, sleeping-bag accommodation on mattresses in a classroom, and a camp site out the back. There's also a little café open from July to mid-August.

REYÐARFJÖRÐUR
pop 2120
Reyðarfjörður is currently a place of notoriety: it's the site for the controversial Alcoa aluminium smelter. This enormous industrial building is 2km long from end to end and completely dominates the end of the east coast's largest fjord. At the time of writing it wasn't operational – but it will be by 2007. It's already had an unbalancing effect on the town, whose population shot up from 700 people in early 2005 to over 2000 people at the end of 2006.

Reyðarfjörður was never the prettiest of the fjord towns – it's a relatively new settlement, which only came into existence (as a trading port) in the 20th century. The main reason to stop is for its interesting museum. Get here on sealed Rte 92 from Egilsstaðir (34km).

Sights & Activities
During WWII around 3000 Allied soldiers – about 10 times the local population – were based in Reyðarfjörður. At the end of Heiðarvegur you'll find the **Iceland Wartime Museum** (☎ 470 9063; www.fjardabyggd.is; Spítalakampur; adult/under 15yr Ikr400/ free; ☷ 1-6pm Jun-Aug), which records this strange occupation. The building is surrounded by mines, Jeeps and aeroplane propellers, and holds other war relics. Photographs and tableaux provide a good background to Iceland's wartime involvement. The museum is tucked behind a rusting set of army barracks, built as part of a hospital camp in 1943 but never used for that purpose.

Above the fjord, 2km east of Reyðarfjörður, there is a **view disc** that is accompanied by a commanding vista. Those travellers who are very energetic can make the 985m climb up **Hólmatindur**, which rises east of the village and separates it from Eskifjörður.

Sleeping & Eating

Campers can head to the free camp site on the main road into town. The adjoining pond is popular with salmon anglers; permits cost Ikr500 per fish and are available from the Veiðiflugan sports shop in the Molinn shopping centre.

The only hotel in Reyðarfjörður, **Hótel Reyðarfjörður** (☎ 474 1600; fax 474 1601; Búðareyri 6; s/d Ikr12,100/15,900; 🖵) is open year-round. It's a comfortable enough place with spacious rooms (some with facilities for the disabled) and a restaurant.

There are burgers, pizzas and snacks at the Shell or Olís petrol stations, and there's a **Krónan supermarket** (☽ 9am-6pm Mon-Sat) inside the Molinn shopping centre.

Getting There & Away

For bus information, see p253.

ESKIFJÖRÐUR

pop 1010

This friendly little town is stretched out along a dimple in the main fjord Reyðarfjörður. Its setting is superb: it looks directly onto the mighty mountain Hólmatindur (985m), rising sheer from the shining blue water.

The surrounding hills are beautiful places for walking, particularly in autumn when their green sides are splattered with bright fungi and huge bog bilberries. Eskifjörður is one of the least expensive places to fish for salmon in Iceland – it's free on the river Eskifjarðará (although most fish are trout).

Eskifjörður followed the same herring-town/trading-centre route to prosperity as Seyðisfjörður. Fishing is still important, though the nearby aluminium smelter will soon be providing a new source of wealth.

Information

For tourist information, visit the souvenir shop **Verkstæði Kötu** (☎ 894 9306; Strandgata 29; ☽ 2-6pm Mon-Fri, 11am-4pm Sat), just off the main street. Buy walking maps before you come here from the tourist office at Egilsstaðir (p253). The **Landsbanki Íslands bank** (☎ 410 4166; Strandgata 47) has an ATM.

Sights & Activities

The **East Iceland Maritime Museum** (Sjóminjasafn Austurlands; ☎ 476 1179, 476 1605; www.fjardabyggd.is; Strandgata 39b; adult/under 16yr Ikr400/free; ☽ 1-5pm Jun-Aug), in the black timber warehouse named

'Gamla Buð', which dates from 1816, illustrates two centuries of the east coast's historic herring and shark fisheries and whaling industry. The museum contains a jumble of fishing boats, nets, tools and other paraphernalia central to Iceland's maritime history. There is also a model of Eskifjörður as it was in the 1920s and a re-creation of a general store.

Take a look inside the freezing plant (almost opposite the museum), whose walls are graced with **murals** by the Spanish-Icelandic artist Baltasar.

The remains of the world's largest Iceland spar quarry, **Helgustaðanáma**, can be found east of Eskifjörður. Iceland spar (*silfurberg* in Icelandic) is a type of calcite crystal that is totally transparent and can split light into two parallel beams. It was a vital component in early microscopes, and quantities of the stuff were exported to some of Europe's top scientists starting from the 17th century through until 1924, which is when the quarry closed. The largest specimen taken from Helgustaðir weighed 230kg and is displayed in the British Museum. Science aside, you can still see calcite sparkling in rocks around the quarry – very pretty. The area is a national preserve, though, so you can't poke out pieces of crystal or take them away. Follow the rough dirt road 9km along the coastline until you get to an information panel; the quarry is then a 500m walk uphill.

HIKING

The southern shore of the **Hólmanes peninsula**, below the peak Hólmatindur, is a nature reserve. Hiking in the area offers superb maritime views – look out for pods of dolphins – and the chance to observe the protected vegetation and bird life.

There are also plenty of longer hiking routes: Oddsskarð, Helgustaðarsveit, Hellisfjörður, Vindháls and the mountain areas around the end of the peninsula, where you may even see reindeer. The main routes are marked on the map *Gönguleiðir á Austurlandi II* (Ikr750; available from Egilsstaðir tourist office).

Although it's a beautiful mountain, Hólmatindur, looming over the southwest of the fjord, also cuts out all sunlight to the village from September to April. Four rivers topple down its steep slopes, posing landslide threats.

EAST ICELAND

SKIING

From January through until May, skiing is possible on slopes near Oddsskarð, which is the pass leading over to Neskaupstaður (5pm to 9pm weekdays, 10am to 5pm weekends). The longest run is 327m and is floodlit. There's also a basic ski hut, **Skíðaskáli** (☎ 476 1465; skidam@itn.is), where you can buy ski passes (Ikr1000/500 per day for adults/children under 16) and hire equipment (Ikr1000/800 adult/child per day).

Sleeping & Eating

The free camp site is at the western end of town.

Ferðaþjónustan Mjóeyri (☎ 477 1247; www.mjoeyri .is; Strandgata 120; sb/s/d Ikr2400/4000/7000) Right at the eastern edge of town, this cosy 111-year-old wooden house has unparalleled fjord views. Sleeping-bag space is in a spick-and-span nine-person dorm with its own kitchen; the five bright guesthouse rooms all have patchwork bedspreads, TV and CD radio; or there are brand-new cabins, sleeping up to six people. Breakfast (Ikr900) and dinner (Ikr1500) can be requested; or you can hire a boat, catch your own fish, and then barbecue it in the sheltered back yard!

That's all the accommodation in town; eating options are limited, too. On Strandgata, there's a pizza place, **Valhöll** (☎ 540 0400), near the bank; a Shell petrol station with a grill and snack bar; and a **Samkaup-Strax supermarket** (☎ 476 1580).

Getting There & Away

For bus information, see p252.

NESKAUPSTAÐUR (NORÐFJÖRÐUR)

pop 1410

Just getting to Neskaupstaður feels like a real odyssey. You travel via the highest highway pass (632m) in Iceland, through an alarming single-lane 630m-long tunnel, then drop from the skies like a falcon into town; attempt to drive further east, and you simply run out of road. Although it's one of the largest of the fjord towns, this dramatic end-of-the-line location makes it feel very small and far away from the rest of the world.

Splendid isolation and beautiful scenery are the main reasons to visit. There are also a few museums, a small nature reserve and a fascinating working harbour that teems with life when the boats come in.

As with most towns in the Eastfjords, Neskaupstaður began life as a 19th-century trading centre and prospered during the herring boom in the early 20th century. Its future was assured by the building of the biggest fish-processing and freezing plant in Iceland, Síldarvinnslan (SNV), at the head of the fjord. Backed by ridiculously steep slopes, Neskaupstaður is prone to avalanches: in 1974 a large one tumbled down and killed 12 residents.

Information

There's a stand of tourist brochures at Verslun Nesbær (see opposite). There's internet access at the **library** (☎ 477 1521; Skólavegur 9), based inside the distinctive blocky blue school. Opening hours are variable, but it usually only opens on weekdays in the afternoons.

Sights & Activities

MUSEUMS

Neskaupstaður has three small **museums** (per museum adult/under 16yr Ikr400/free; ☉ 1-5pm Jun-Aug), all clustered in a warehouse by the harbour at Egilsbraut 2. Perhaps most interesting is the art gallery **Tryggvasafn** (☎ 470 9063), showcasing a collection of paintings by prominent modern artist Tryggvi Ólafsson (1940–), who was born in Neskaupstaður. His colourful abstracts, some of which hang in national galleries in Reykjavík, Sweden and Denmark, depict Icelandic scenes and are visually quite striking.

The **natural history museum** (Náttúrugripasafnið í Neskaupstað; ☎ 477 1454) has a big collection of local stones (including zeolites, spar from the Helgustaðir mine and crystal quartz), plus an array of stuffed animals, birds, fish and pinned insects; and the **Jósafat Hinriksson museum** (☎ 470 9063), one man's collection of artefacts relating to the sea.

WALKING & HIKING

At the eastern end of town where the road runs out is the **nature reserve** Folksvangur Neskaupstaðar – perfect for short strolls. Various paths

---

FJARÐABYGGÐ

If you're trying find the town of Fjarðabyggð on your map, it could take a while. This is the joint name given to the three fjord towns Reyðarfjörður, Eskifjörður and Neskaupstaður, all part of the same administrative district.

run through long grass, over tiny wooden bridges, and past boulders, peat pits, cliffs and the rushing sea. There are plenty of puffins to watch, as well as gulls and ravens.

For serious hikers, a rewarding route will take you up **Goðaborg** (1132m) from the farm Kirkjuból, 8km west of town. From the summit you can also descend into Mjóifjörður, the next fjord to the north; allow two days and, due to late snows at higher altitudes, attempt it only at the height of summer.

A more difficult walk is from **Oddsskarð** along the ridges eastward to the deserted fjords Hellisfjörður and Viðfjörður. The dramatic Gerpir cliffs, Iceland's easternmost point, can be reached with difficulty, but the only way to visit this beautiful place is on foot. For route finding, use the Landmælingar Íslands *Gerpir* 1:100,000 (1986) topo sheet or the map *Gönguleiðir á Austurlandi II*.

BOAT TRIPS
Between mid-June and mid-August the company **Fjarðaferðir** (☎ 477 1710; aust@austfjardaleid.is) runs a two-hour **boat trip** (per person Ikr3900; ☙ 11am) from the harbour opposite Egilsbúð. It sails into Hellisfjörður, hugging the coastline to give passengers the best views of caves and nesting sea birds.

KAYAKING
There's no better way to explore the fjords than in a kayak. **Kayakklúbburinn Kaj** (☎ 863 9939; www.123.is/kaj) offers guided two-hour trips (Ikr3500 per person) around Norðfjörður, exploring sea caves and resident bird life. Trips are on request; in midsummer, midnight kayaking is possible.

Sleeping
Camp site (☎ 470 9000) This excellent free site, with laundry and hot showers, is at the end of the main road on the eastern edge of town, 2km from the harbour.

Guesthouse (☎ 477 1580; www.tonspil.is; sb Ikr1800, made-up bed Ikr3800) Like an extra in the film *High Fidelity*, you need to ask the dude in the music shop Tónlistaverslun Austurlands about the rooms above! Which are very, very simple (cork floor, white ply wardrobe, bed); but there's a TV room-kitchen area with microwave and hotplates, and it's pretty peaceful.

Hotel Edda Nes (☎ 444 4000; Nesgata 40; s/d Ikr9000/11,300; ☙ 9 Jun-19 Aug) On the waterfront at the eastern end of town, the Nes summer hotel

has a nice restaurant, but there's no sleeping-bag accommodation and the overpriced rooms (all with bathroom) are predictably staid.

Hótel Capitanó (☎ 477 1800; island@islandia.is; Hafnarbraut 50; sb/s/d summer Ikr3000/7900/11,900, winter Ikr2500/6600/8900) This is a real bargain. The bright-blue corrugated iron building doesn't look like much, but all rooms have attached bathrooms and some of the doubles are spacious and well appointed. Modern art by celebrated local artist Tryggvi Ólafsson adorns the walls.

Eating
Bakarí Neskaupstaður (☎ 477 1306; Hafnarbraut 2; ☙ 7am-5pm Mon-Fri) For breakfast, cakes or pastries, the local bakery is the place. There are a few tables and chairs inside.

Verslun Nesbær (☎ 477 1115; Egilsbraut; ☙ 9am-6pm Mon-Fri, 10am-6pm Sat) This café–bakery–knick-knack shop is a great spot for fancier lattes, cake, sandwiches and soup.

Hótel Capitanó (☎ 477 1800; Hafnarbraut 50; mains Ikr1700-2900; ☙ noon-2pm & 5-9pm Thu-Sun) Four days per week the hotel serves genuine Thai food in its pleasant, informal restaurant. It makes a change from ubiquitous pizza places, and there's also an inviting small bar and lounge.

Egilsbúð/Pizza 67 (☎ 477 1321; www.egilsbud.is; Hafnarbraut; mains Ikr1800-2300; ☙ 11am-midnight Mon-Thu, to 3am Fri & Sat) This place doubles as the town bar, with two pool tables downstairs and a large-screen TV on the balcony. There's a spacious restaurant area upstairs. It has a slight community-centre feel, but there's a long menu of meat and fish dishes, pizzas, pitta sandwiches and burgers, and live music at weekends.

For fast-food grills and hot dogs, there's the **Ólís petrol station** (☎ 477 1476; Hafnarbraut). The **Samkaup-Úrval supermarket** (☎ 477 1301; Hafnarbraut 13; ☙ 9am-7pm Mon-Fri, noon-6pm Sat & Sun) opens daily.

Getting There & Away
For bus information, see p252.

FÁSKRÚÐSFJÖRÐUR
pop 620
The village of Fáskrúðsfjörður, sometimes known as Búðir, was originally settled by French seamen who came to fish the Icelandic coast between the late 1800s and 1914. In a gesture to the French heritage, street signs are in both Icelandic and French.

The population was steadily declining, but the village is near enough for people to commute to the aluminium smelter through the huge new road tunnel nearby. Although more people are moving here, it's still something of an unappealing ghost town with little on offer for visitors.

Sights & Activities

The full story about the French seamen in Fáskrúðsfjörður can be found at **Fransmenn á Íslandi** (☎ 475 1525; www.fransmenn.net; Búðavegur 8; admission Ikr400; ☼ 10am-5pm Jun-Aug), in the blue building on the main road near the harbour. The museum features pictures and historical displays.

Down on the shore on the western approach to the village is a small **cemetery** and **monument** commemorating the French seamen who died here.

At the mouth of the fjord, the island **Skrúður** contains lots of bird life, as well as the world's biggest 'puffin cave', formerly believed to have been a giant's cave. Another little islet, **Andey** (Duck Island), has a large colony of eider ducks.

If Fáskrúðsfjörður leaves you less than overwhelmed, Hótel Bjarg (see below) may be able to offer an injection of excitement with **Jet Ski hire** and **quad-bike trips**.

For **hiking**, head up to Dalir, above the head of the fjord, where you can walk the old route up over Stuðlaheiði to Reyðarfjörður.

Geologists may get a buzz from the laccolithic mountain **Sandfell** (743m), above the southern shore of Fáskrúðsfjörður, formed by molten rhyolite bursting through older lava layers. It's one of the world's finest examples of this sort of igneous intrusion (although Rio's Sugar Loaf Mountain is perhaps a mite more impressive). It's a two- to three-hour walk to the top.

Sleeping & Eating

Camp site (☎ 475 0550) This free site is on the slope just west of the village.

Hótel Bjarg (☎ 475 1466; hotelbjarg@simnet.is; Skólavegur 49; sb Ikr5000, d Ikr9000-12,000; ☼ check with hotel) New owners with big plans have bought this place, in the upper part of the village overlooking the fjord. It will be completely renovated in 2007 to become a 'health hotel', with natural stone floors, cool cream décor, adjustable orthopacdic beds, and a spa. Unusually, a stream runs through the basement of the

building (just look out of the window in the reception area), the vibrations of which are said to promote a great night's sleep! There are plans to run boat/fishing trips and quad-bike excursions into the highlands, and possibly hire out Jet Skis. The restaurant here is your best chance of a decent sit-down meal, with a menu focused on fresh, local Icelandic meat and fish dishes, with plenty of healthy vegetarian options, too.

Café Sumarlina (☎ 475 1575; www.123.is/sumarlina; ☼ 11am-11pm Sun-Thu, to 3am Fri & Sat) This brandnew café-bar down by the fjord is a great little place, in a creaking old wooden house decorated with odd ornaments. It mainly serves coffee, cakes and crêpes, with extra dishes on festive occasion.

For hamburgers and hot dogs, there's a grill at the Esso petrol station.

Getting There & Away

For bus information, see p253.

STÖÐVARFJÖRÐUR

pop 240

This tiny fishing village (sometimes called Kirkjuból) is a pretty somnolent little place. However, Petra's eye-popping rock collection makes it an unmissable stop!

Sights & Activities

Even if geology usually makes you pass out from boredom, don't miss **Steinasafn Petru** (☎ 475 8834; Fjarðarbraut 21; adult/under 14yr Ikr400/free; ☼ 9am-6pm May-Sep, phone first rest of year). This exceptional collection is octogenarian Petra Sveinsdóttir's lifelong labour of love. Inside the house, stones and minerals are piled from floor to ceiling – 70% of them are from the local area. They include unbelievably beautiful cubes of jasper, polished agate, purple amethyst, glowing-cream 'ghost stone', glittering quartz crystals…it's like a treasure chest. The garden is a wonderfully peaceful place, awash with more rocks, garden gnomes, and beachcombed flotsam and jetsam. Some of the rocks are for sale, either in raw form, polished up or mounted onto ornaments – it's hard to resist buying a memento! Petra is now in a nursing home, but she sometimes comes back to visit, and her children and grandchildren are keeping her collection going.

The owners of Kirkjubær (see opposite) organise **boat/fishing trips** from the harbour in an old six-tonne fishing boat or a Zodiac.

Hiring the boat costs Ikr5000 for two hours, and you can go at any time of year, although the fishing is best in summer.

Sleeping & Eating

The free camp site is just east of the village.

Kirkjubær (☎ 892 3319, 846 0032; sb Ikr2000) One of the most unusual places to stay in the Eastfjords is this tiny old church on the hill above Fjarðarbraut. The church dates from 1925 but is now in private hands and has been renovated into a cute one-room hostel. The pulpit and altar are still there, and some of the pews are now part of the furniture. There's a full kitchen and bathroom, and the beds (mostly just mattresses) are on the upper mezzanine level. It supposedly sleeps 10, but that would be pretty cosy! The owners live in the yellow house just below the church at Skólúbraut 1.

Brekkan (☎ 475 8939; cnr Fjarðabraut & Bankastræti; snacks Ikr400-800; ☺ 11am-7pm Sun-Thu, 10am-10pm Fri & Sat) This bare-bones room, full of fishermen warming themselves up with hot coffee, is the only sit-down place to eat in town. It sells burgers and sandwiches, or there's a grocery area in the back.

Getting There & Away

For bus information, see p253.

BREIÐDALSVÍK

pop 160

The fishing village of Breiðdalsvík is beautifully situated at the end of Iceland's broadest valley, Breiðdalur (see right). It's a very quiet place – more a base for walking in the nearby hills and fishing the rivers and lakes than an attraction in itself. The biggest excitement of the year is the **Austfjarðatröllið** strong-man competition in mid-August.

Sleeping & Eating

The free camp site is behind Hótel Bláfell.

Café Margret (☎ 475 6625; s/d Jun–mid-Sep Ikr5900/8900, mid-Sep–May Ikr4900/7500) This beautiful boutique guesthouse is built from Finnish pine. Its four spacious rooms are full of antique German furniture and Persian rugs; breakfast costs Ikr1100 extra. The attached café (open 8am to 11pm June to mid-September, 10am to 8pm mid-September to May) provides a welcome respite from hot dogs and hamburgers. The menu (mains Ikr1400 to Ikr2900) includes German specialities such as pork schnitzel (Ikr1600) and a cold-cut platter (Ikr1950), as

well as open sandwiches and Icelandic meat and fish dishes. The only downside is that the family who runs the place is quite rude. Café Margret is outside Breiðdalsvík, on Rte 96 heading towards Stöðvarfjörður.

Hótel Bláfell (☎ 475 6770; blafell@centrum.is; Sólvellir 14; s/d Ikr7900/10,800 Jun–mid-Sep, discounts mid-Sep–May) This cosy timber hotel by the harbour is popular with visiting anglers – there are three excellent salmon rivers in Breiðdalur. The pleasant, woody-smelling rooms contain patchwork-covered beds, TVs, telephones and private bathrooms. The lounge, with open fire and leather couches, is a great place to unwind, and there's a sauna, a solarium and a year-round restaurant. Breakfast costs Ikr950.

Getting There & Away

The Egilsstaðir–Breiðdalsvík bus runs Monday to Friday only. It leaves Egilsstaðir at 9.20am, stopping at Fáskrúðsfjörður (45 minutes), Stöðvarfjörður (1¼ hours), and Breiðdalsvík (1½ hours). Returning from Breiðdalsvík, it departs at 7.30am (7.20am in winter).

If you're driving, Breiðdalsvík is just off where the Ring Rd joins Rte 96.

AROUND BREIÐDALSVÍK

Breiðdalur & Norðurdalur

As the Ring Rd returns to the coast it passes through the lovely Breiðdalur valley, nestled beneath colourful rhyolite peaks. Near the head of the valley you may see reindeer. At the abandoned farm Jórvík a forestry reserve harbours native birch and aspen.

SLEEPING & EATING

Hótel Staðarborg (☎ 475 6760; www.stadarborg.is; sb/s/d/tr Jun-Aug Ikr1700/7500/10,400/13,400) Once a school, this hotel (contact it for winter opening details and prices) has neat, modern rooms with proper shutters to keep out that midnight sun! Breakfast is included with made-up beds, and dinner is available on request. You can hire horses here to explore Breiðdalur, or fish in the neighbouring lake. Staðarborg is 6km west of Breiðdalsvík on the Ring Rd, near the turn-off to Rte 964.

Berunes & Berufjörður

South of Breiðdalur along the Ring Rd is Berufjörður, a longish, steep-sided fjord flanked by rhyolite peaks. The southwestern shore is dominated by the obtrusive, pyramid-shaped mountain **Búlandstindur**, which rises

1068m above the water. The westernmost ridge is known as Goðaborg or 'God's rock'. When Iceland officially converted to Christianity in 1000, locals supposedly carried their pagan images to the top of this mountain and threw them over the cliff.

Around Berufjörður are several historical walking routes through the steeply rugged terrain. The best-known of these climbs is from Berufjörður, the farm at the head of the fjord, and crosses the 700m Berufjarðarskarð into Breiðdalur.

SLEEPING & EATING

Eyjólfsstaðir (☎ 478 8137; sites per tent Ikr500, sb Ikr1750) About halfway between Breiðdalsvík and Djúpivogur, this farm is tucked 2km off the Ring Rd in the beautifully secluded Fossá valley. The accommodation building has kitchen facilities, a bathroom, a lounge and basic rooms, and is brightened throughout by the kind of crazy 1970s nail-and-thread pictures and tapestries you sadly don't see any more!

our pick Berunes HI Hostel (☎ 478 8988; www .simnet.is/berunes; sites per person Ikr700, sb Ikr1900, s/d Ikr4500/6900, cottages Ikr8000-9500; ⊙ May-Oct; ⌨) Located on an old farm (built in 1907) with 'a good spirit', this hostel/guesthouse is one of our all-time favourites. There is space for campers; there are delightful little rooms, a kitchen and a lounge with books in the old farmhouse; plus Berunes boasts two self-contained family apartments and a separate cottage. There's also a bright dining room where you can join the owners for breakfast (Ikr950), which includes delicious homemade pancakes, and dinner if prebooked (Ikr1700 to Ikr1950). Musicians are welcome to play the organ in the neighbouring 19th-century church. The hostel is 25km along the Ring Rd south of Breiðdalsvík.

Hamraborg (☎ 476 1348; mains Ikr900-2500; ⊙ 10am-10pm Jun-Aug) About 1km past Berunes, this is a unique café-restaurant specialising in local game and small 'gourmet' courses. Special dishes include locally caught fish, puffin, reindeer and wild goose. Many of the dishes are served cold and entrée sized, such as graved reindeer with blueberry sauce, where the reindeer is marinated in herbs rather than cooked. If your tastes aren't quite so exotic, there are salads, home-baked bread, omelettes, coffee and cakes, and a well-stocked bar. Worth a stop.

DJÚPIVOGUR

pop 360

This friendly little fishing village, at the mouth of Berufjörður, gives summer visitors a flowery welcome. Its neat historic buildings, museum, and small, colourful harbour are worth a look, and it has a couple of nice eating places; but the main reason to visit is to catch the boat to Papey island (opposite).

Djúpivogur is actually the oldest port in the Eastfjords – it's been around since the 16th century, when German merchants brought goods to trade. The last major excitement was in 1627, when pirates from North Africa rowed ashore, plundering the village and nearby farms and carrying away dozens of slaves.

Information

The **tourist office** (☎ 478 8220; langabud@langabud.is; ⊙ 10am-6pm Jun-early Sep) is in the historic rust-coloured building, Langabúð, alongside the harbour. The village also has a bank (there's an ATM in Við Voginn café), a post office and a swimming pool.

Sights & Activities

Some of the town's lovely wooden **buildings** date from the late 19th century. The oldest building, **Langabúð**, is a harbourside log warehouse dating from 1790, which now houses the tourist office, a coffee shop and an unusual local **museum** (⊙ 10am-6pm Jun-early Sep; adult/child Ikr400/200). Downstairs is a collection of works by renowned woodcarver Rikarður Jónsson (1888–1977). They range from lifelike busts of worthy Icelanders to mermaid-decorated mirrors and reliefs depicting saga characters. Rikarður also championed the Icelandic woodcarving typeface, whose letters are possibly descended from runes – look out for this strangely illegible alphabet in his work. Upstairs, in the dusty, tarry-smelling attic, is a collection of local-history artefacts.

Another old harbourside building houses a small **collection** of stones, minerals and stuffed birds. Admission is Ikr300, or you can buy a joint ticket for both museums for Ikr500 (from Langabúð).

The Djúpivogur peninsula is compact and ideal for short hikes from town. A particularly nice walk is to **Álfkirkja** on the rock formation Rakkaberg, north of town. The indoor **swimming pool** (☎ 478 8999; Varða 4; adult/child Ikr300/150; ⊙ 7am-8pm Mon-Fri, 11am-3pm Sat), up behind Hótel Framtíð, is a good place to unwind after hiking.

Sleeping & Eating

Camp site (☎ 478 8887; sites per person Ikr700) Just behind the Við Voginn shop, with showers and cooking facilities, the site is run by Hótel Framtíð, so cough up your pennies at the reception there.

Hótel Framtíð (☎ 478 8887; framtid@simnet.is; Vogaland 4; s/d sb Ikr2850/5250, with bathroom Ikr10,500/13,125, without bathroom Ikr6500/8200) This friendly hotel by the harbour is impressive for a village of this size. Although it's been around for a while (the building was brought in pieces from Copenhagen in 1905), a new wing of modern rooms gives it a nice mix of history and freshness.

Langabúð coffee shop (⏰ 10am-6pm Jun-early Sep) A good option for lunch, this café has a suitably old-world atmosphere, and serves cakes, soup and homemade bread with a view over the harbour. It can get very crowded with coach parties, so order while you have a chance!

Við Voginn (☎ 478 8860; Vogaland 2; mains Ikr700-1900; ⏰ 9am-11pm) This is a lively meeting place for locals and serves a big range of fast food, such as hamburgers and pizzas, along with fish dishes.

our pick **Hótel Framtíð restaurant** (mains Ikr1700-3500) This wonderfully romantic à la carte restaurant specialises in local fish and has harbour views. Its small but select menu includes a good-value dish of the day (Ikr1890, including soup), delicious lobster tails and a veggie option.

On the main road into town is a **Samkaup-Strax supermarket** (Búland 2; ⏰ 11am-6pm Mon-Fri, to 2pm Sat) with a Vin Búð alcohol shop attached.

AROUND DJÚPIVOGUR
Papey

The name of the lovely offshore island of Papey (Friars' Island) suggests it was once a hermitage for the Irish monks who may have briefly inhabited Iceland before the arrival of the Norse. It's thought that they fled in the face of Nordic settlement. This small and tranquil island was once a farm, but it's presently inhabited only by seals and nesting sea birds. In early summer the dramatic, 45m-high cliffs are crowded with nests. Other highlights include the **Hellisbjarg lighthouse**, which dates from 1922; Iceland's oldest and smallest **wooden church**, built in 1805; and the remains of an **apartment house** from the early 20th century. There's no formal accommodation on Papey, but camping is allowed by prior arrangement.

Getting to Papey is easy enough in summer. From June to August **Papeyjarferðir** (☎ 478 8119; adult/8-13yr Ikr3500/1750; ⏰ Jun-Aug) runs four-hour tours to the island. Weather and numbers permitting, they leave from Djúpivogur harbour at 1pm daily. In fine weather this is a truly magical tour. Make sure you bring good footwear, as a visit will involve some hiking.

EAST ICELAND

Southeast Iceland

Iceland's southeast is a kingdom made for trolls and ice giants, rather than creatures of warm flesh and blood. Mighty Vatnajökull, the largest icecap outside the poles, dominates the region. Even casual visitors travelling along the Ring Rd will be awestruck by its huge rivers of frozen ice pouring down steep-sided valleys towards the sea. The glacial lagoon Jökulsárlón, at the feet of the icecap, is a photographer's paradise – wind and water sculpt its chilly-blue icebergs into fantastical shapes.

On the southern side of the Ring Rd a terrible desert of dark glacial sand unrolls. The damage is caused by the volcanoes Grímsvötn and Öræfi, trapped beneath Vatnajökull. When they blow, huge areas of the icecap melt, sending powerful rock-filled rivers smashing onto the coast. The most recent *jökulhlaup* (glacial flood) was just 11 years ago.

Further inland is the epicentre of Iceland's worst eruption. In the late 18th century the Lakagígar fissure erupted in a 30km-long sheet of flame and ash, blotting out the sun and causing famine across the northern hemisphere. Today such apocalyptic fire and darkness seem far away; the fragile lava craters are covered in soft green moss and the only sound is the wind. With desolation all around, it's not surprising the Skaftafell National Park is a popular spot. This sheltered enclave between the glaciers and the dead grey sands throbs with life and colour.

Although part of the interior, we've included Fjallabak Nature Reserve and Landmannalaugar in this section. An area with mesmerising landscape and superb hiking, this 'back road' between the southeast and southwest shouldn't be missed.

TOP FIVE

- Admire the ever-changing ice sculptures at **Jökulsárlón** (p291), a bewitching glacial lagoon
- Bathe in steaming thermal pools at **Landmannalaugar** (p277), or rise to the challenge of the **Landmannalaugar to Þórsmörk Trek** (p280) – one of the world's great walks
- Visit Iceland's favourite national park, **Skaftafell** (p285), an area of green and lovely life amid the vast dead *sandar* (sand deltas)
- Stride up **Laki** (p284) for views of three glaciers…and unbelievable volcanic devastation
- Feel like a mountaineer on an easy but exhilarating **glacier walk** (p289); make it real by scaling Iceland's highest peak, **Hvannadalshnúkur** (p289); or roar across **Vatnajökull icecap** (p294) on a snowmobile.

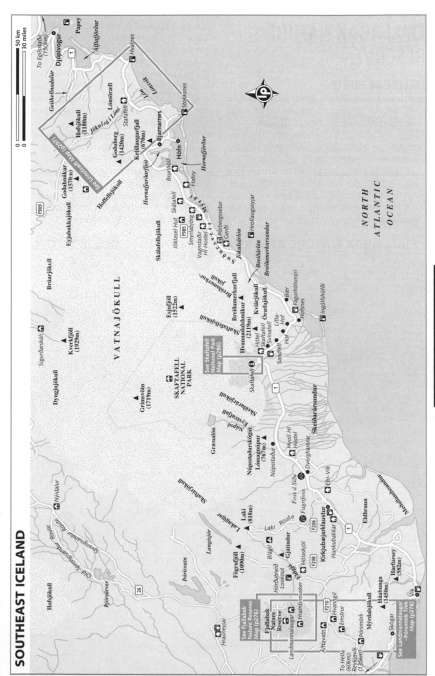

SOUTHEAST ICELAND

SOUTHEAST ICELAND

FJALLABAK NATURE RESERVE

FJALLABAK ROUTE

In summer the Fjallabak Route (F208) makes a spectacular alternative to the coast road between Hella, in southwest Iceland, and Kirkjubæjarklaustur. Its name translates as 'Behind the Mountains', and that's exactly where it goes.

First, head north from Hella on Rte 26. The F208 begins near the Sigölduvirkjun power plant on the Tungnaá river and passes through the scenic Fjallabak Nature Reserve to Landmannalaugar. From there, it continues east past the Kirkjufell marshes and enters Jökuldalur, then travels along a riverbed for 10km before climbing to the Hörðubreið lookout and descending to Eldgjá.

For the next 40km the road is fairly good, but there are a couple of river fords, so conventional vehicles going to Eldgjá from the east may have difficulties during high water. At Búland the route joins Rte 208 and emerges at the Ring Rd southwest of Kirkjubæjarklaustur.

A non-4WD vehicle wouldn't have a hope of completing the through route. In summer, if the rivers are low, a conventional vehicle can reach Landmannalaugar from the west (F208 only) and possibly Eldgjá from the east, but the route between the two would be impass-

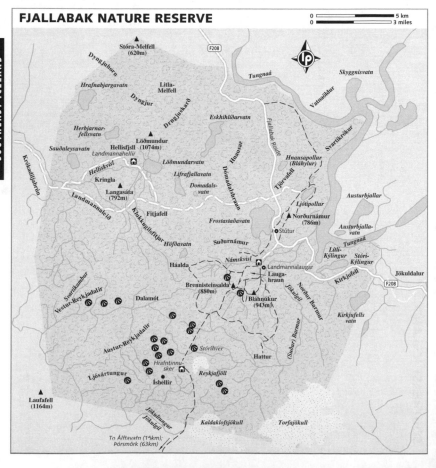

able under any conditions. Note that hire-car companies prohibit taking 2WD vehicles on any of these routes, so if something should go wrong your insurance would be void.

Since much of the Fjallabak Route is along rivers (or rather, in rivers!), it's not ideally suited to mountain bikes either. Lots of people do attempt it, but it's not casual cycling by any stretch.

Getting There & Away

If you don't have a 4WD vehicle, between mid-June and early September there's a scheduled **Austurleið-Kynnisferðir** (☎ 562 1011; www .austurleid.is) bus. It runs daily between Reykjavík and Skaftafell (via Selfoss, Hella, Landmannalaugar, Eldgjá, and Kirkjubæjarklaustur), departing at 8.30am from either end. The 11-hour journey costs Ikr8600 each way – unquestionably worth it.

The bus stops for two hours at lovely Landmannalaugar, but that's not really long enough to explore. Most travellers make a proper break here, continuing the journey to Skaftafell at a later date. The stretch from Reykjavík to Landmannalaugar (5½ hours) costs Ikr4800 each way.

LANDMANNALAUGAR

Multicoloured mountains, soothing hot springs, rambling lava flows and clear blue lakes make Landmannalaugar unique. It's a favourite with Icelanders and visitors alike…as long as the weather cooperates! If you're thinking of popping up there for a few hours, you'll kick yourself for not allowing several days.

Landmannalaugar (600m above sea level) includes the largest geothermal field in Iceland outside the Grímsvötn caldera in Vatnajökull. Its weird peaks are made of rhyolite – a mineral-filled lava that cooled unusually slowly, causing those amazing colours.

Although Landmannalaugar gets quite chilly, the weather is generally more stable than in coastal areas, and when it does rain it's more of a wind-driven horizontal mist than a drenching downpour.

Information

The Landmannalaugar hut wardens can help with specific questions, including directions and advice on hiking routes. There are also two green buses, which hold a tiny **information centre and shop** (☺ 11.30am-8pm late Jun–Aug) selling coffee, buns and plasters! It also sells a good

self-published map (Ikr700) of walks in the immediate Landmannalaugar area.

There's no petrol at Landmannalaugar. The nearest petrol pumps are 40km north at Hrauneyjar (close to the beginning of the F208), and 90km southeast at Kirkjubæjark-laustur, but to be on the safe side you should put in enough fuel to get you all the way back to Hella.

Hot Springs

Just 200m from the Landmannalaugar hut, both hot and cold water flow out from beneath Laugahraun and combine in a natural pool to form the most ideal hot bath imaginable. Unfortunately, since 2003 there have been itchy parasites (spread by ducklings) in the pool; they seem to be clearing up, but if you're worried, find out what the current situation is before bathing.

Hiking

Laugahraun, the convoluted lava field behind Landmannalaugar hut, offers vast scope for exploration. Across it, the slopes of Iceland's most colourful mountain, rainbow-streaked **Brennisteinsalda**, are punctuated by steaming vents and sulphur deposits. Climb to the summit for a good view across the rugged and variegated landscape (7km round trip from Landmannalaugar).

From Brennisteinsalda it's another 90 minutes along the Þórsmörk route to the impressive **Stórihver** geothermal field.

The blue lake **Frostastaðavatn** lies behind the rhyolite ridge immediately north of the Landmannalaugar hut. Walk over the ridge and you'll be rewarded with far-ranging views as well as close-ups of the interesting rock formations and moss-covered lava flows flanking the lake. If you walk at least one way on the road and spend some time exploring around the lake, the return trip takes two to three hours.

A fine day hike from Landmannalaugar is to the ironically named **Ljótipollur** (Ugly Puddle), an incredible red crater filled with bright-blue water. Oddly enough, although it was formed by a volcanic explosion its lake is rich in trout. That intense fiery red comes from iron-ore deposits. You can see all kinds of scenery on the way to the Puddle, from tephra desert and lava flow to marsh and braided glacial valley. To get there you can climb over the 786m-high peak **Norðurnámur**

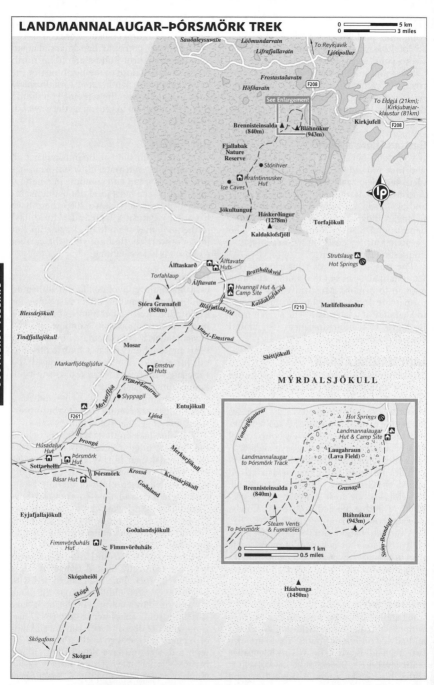

LANDMANNALAUGAR–ÞÓRSMÖRK TREK

(well worthwhile) or just traverse its western base to emerge on the Ljótipollur road (10km to 12km return trip, depending on the route). A number of routes ascend to the crater rim, but the most interesting is probably the footpath that climbs its southernmost slope. If you walk all the way around the crater rim, it's an 18km hike that takes the better part of a day.

Another good day walk from Landmannalaugar is around the peak **Tjörvafell** and the crater lake **Hnausapollur** (also known as Bláhylur).

Sleeping

Because the whole Fjallabak area is a protected nature reserve, wild camping is not allowed.

Ferðafélag Íslands' **Landmannalaugar hut** (☎ Jul-Sep 854 1192; sb Ikr2200) accommodates 78 people on a first come, first served basis, and it books up quickly with tour groups and club members. Otherwise there's a **camp site** (sites per person Ikr800) with toilet and shower facilities.

For information about other mountain huts on the Landmannalaugar–Þórsmörk route, see the boxed text, p280.

LANDMANNALAUGAR TO ELDGJÁ

East of Landmannalaugar the F208 leaves Fjallabak Reserve and skirts the river Tungnaá as it flows past the Norðurnámshraun lava field.

After dropping into Jökuldalur the road deteriorates into a valley route along a riverbed and effectively becomes a 10km-long ford interspersed with jaunts across the odd sandbar or late snowfield. When it climbs out of the valley it ascends the tuff mountain **Herðubreið**, from where there are superb views across the lowlands to the south.

Just west of the Herðubreið lookout, a rough 4WD road heads 25km northeast to the blue lake **Langisjór**. On the far side of the lake lie the astonishing green mountains of **Fögrufjöll** (1090m), and beyond them is the black-sand outwash plain of the glacial river Skaftá.

ELDGJÁ

Eldgjá (Fire Gorge) is a volcanic rift stretching 40km from Mýrdalsjökull to the peak Gjátindur. At its northeastern end Eldgjá is 200m deep and 600m across, with odd, reddish walls that recall the fire after which it's named. Although it's not as outwardly spectacular as you may expect, Eldgjá is quite intriguing and the name alone conjures up images of a malevolently mysterious and powerful place.

In the green and fertile **Hánípufit** area, 8km south of the Eldgjá turn-off, the river Skaftá widens into an entanglement of cascades and waterfalls measuring 500m across in places. It's unusual and quite beautiful.

At Lambaskarðshólar, west of the F208 road near Syðrifærá, 5km south of the Eldgjá turn-off, there are three mountain huts at **Hólaskjól** (☎ 487 4840, 894 9977; sb Ikr2000) with hot showers and a camp site. It's a great place to hole up for a couple of days.

SOUTHERN VATNAJÖKULL

Vatnajökull is earth's largest icecap outside the poles. It's three times the size of Luxembourg (8300 sq km), reaches a thickness of almost 1km, and, if you could find a pair of scales big enough, you'd find it weighed an awesome 3000 billion tonnes! This mighty mass of ice holds Iceland's highest and lowest points – the 2119m mountain Hvannadalshnúkur, and a nameless trough underneath the icecap, 300m below sea level.

Huge glaciers, pleated with crevasses, flow down from the centre of Vatnajökull. The best known is probably Skaftafellsjökull, a relatively small glacier that ends within 1.5km of the camp site at Skaftafell National Park. Another famous beauty is Breiðamerkurjökull, which crumbles into icebergs at the breathtaking Jökulsárlón lagoon.

The drive from Kirkjubæjarklaustur to Höfn is truly mind-blowing. Rte 1 takes you across vast deltas of grey glacial sand, past lost-looking farms, around the toes of craggy mountains, and by glacier tongues and ice-filled lagoons. The only thing you won't pass is a town.

KIRKJUBÆJARKLAUSTUR
pop 140

Many a foreign tongue has been tied in knots by trying to say Kirkjubæjarklaustur. It might help if you break it into bits: *Kirkju* (church), *bæjar* (farm) and *klaustur* (convent). Otherwise, do as the locals do and call it 'Klaustur' (pronounced more or less like 'cloister').

Klaustur is tiny, even by Icelandic standards – a few houses and farms scattered on a backdrop of brilliant green. It's a major crossroads to several dramatic spots in the interior – Fjallabak, Landmannalaugar and

SOUTHEAST ICELAND

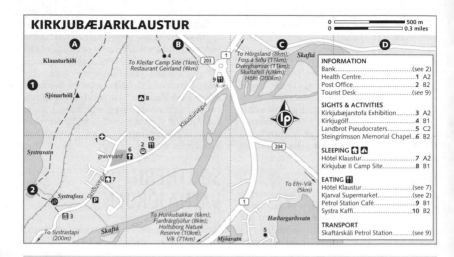

LANDMANNALAUGAR TO ÞÓRSMÖRK TREK

The trek from Landmannalaugar to Þórsmörk – known as the Laugavegurinn (Hot Spring Rd) – seems destined to be recognised one day as one of the great walks of the world. The best map of the route is Landmælingar Íslands' *Þórsmörk–Landmannalaugar* 1:100,000 (Ikr980). In addition, there's a good booklet called *The Laugavegur Hiking Trail* by Leifur Þorsteinsson (Ikr1500), which describes sights and side trips.

In high season the trek can be completed in three or four days by anyone in reasonable physical condition. Many people do it independently, but Útivist and Ferðafélag Íslands both offer organised trips (see p333).

The track is usually passable for casual trekkers from mid-July through to mid-September. Early in the season (early to mid-July) you may need an ice axe for assistance on the steeper slopes. It positively bustles in July and August, so consider walking it in early September, when you should have crisp weather and possibly a glimpse of the Northern Lights from near-empty huts. At that time in the year, however, some snow bridges across ravines may have collapsed, necessitating detours.

At any time of year the Landmannalaugar to Þórsmörk trek is not to be undertaken lightly. It requires river crossings, all-weather gear, sturdy boots, and sufficient food and water. Most trekkers walk from north to south to take advantage of the net altitude loss and the facilities at Þórsmörk. You can also continue along the Þórsmörk to Skógar track (see p137) and make a five- or six-day trip of it.

Mountain Huts

Several huts along the route are owned and maintained by **Ferðafélag Íslands** (☎ 568 2533; www .fi.is). All have camp sites (per person Ikr800). Book and pay for hut space well in advance; otherwise bring a tent and camp near the huts. The following huts are listed from north to south:

Landmannalaugar (☎ Jul-Sep 854 1192; N 63°59.600', W 19°03.660'; per person Ikr2200) Holds 78 people; has kitchen, shower, and warden July to September.

Hrafntinnusker (Höskuldsskáli; N 63°56.014', W 19°10.109'; per person Ikr2000) Holds 36 people; has kitchen, and warden July and August.

Álftavatn (N 63°51.470', W 19°13.640'; per person Ikr2000) Two huts holding 52 people; have kitchen and shower, and warden June to August. Used as an alternative to the less welcoming Hrafntinnusker hut.

Hvanngil (N 64°50.026', W 19°12.507'; per person Ikr2000) Two huts on alternative path, 5km south of Álftavatn. Holds 70 people; has kitchen and shower.

Laki. Klaustur is also the only real service town between Vík and Höfn: there's a petrol station and a good café.

History

According to the *Landnámabók*, this tranquil village between the cliffs and the river Skaftá was first settled by Irish monks *(papar)* before the Vikings arrived. Originally, it was known as Kirkjubær; the 'klaustur' bit was added in 1186 when a convent of Benedictine nuns was founded (near the modern-day church).

During the devastating Laki eruptions of the late 18th century, this area suffered greatly and, west of Kirkjubæjarklaustur, you can see ruins of farms abandoned or destroyed by the lava stream. The lava field, Eldhraun, averages 12m thick. It contains over 12 cu km of lava and covers an area of 565 sq km, making it the largest recorded lava flow from a single eruption.

Information

There's a tourist desk inside the Skaftárskáli petrol station. Further down the road is a small block of buildings containing the bank, the post office and the supermarket.

Sights & Activities

Kirkjugólf's regular basalt columns, smoothed down and cemented with moss, were once mistaken for an old church floor rather than a work of nature, and it's easy to see why. The 80-sq-metre honeycomb lies in a field about 400m northwest of the petrol station (a path leads to it from by the information board, or drive down Rte 203, where there's another gate).

Emstrur (N 63°45.980′, W 19°22.450′; per person Ikr2000) Two huts holding 40 people; has kitchen and shower, and warden June to August.

Þórsmörk (Skagfjörðsskáli; ☎ mid-May–mid-Sep 854 1191, 893 1191; N 63°40.960′, W 19°30.890′; per person Ikr2000) Holds 75 people; has kitchen, shower and shop, and warden mid-May to mid-September.

Highlights

Day 1: Landmannalaugar to Hrafntinnusker (12km, four to five hours)

Stórihver This sinister round hole, in an active geothermal zone, roars with riotously boiling water.
Hrafntinnusker Fields of black obsidian glint in the sunlight.

Day 2: Hrafntinnusker to Álftavatn (12km, four to five hours)

Ice caves (side trip) Set aside up to a day to visit the ice caves 1.5km west of Hrafntinnusker hut (but beware – falling ice is a real danger).
Háskerðingur (side trip) Across the northern spur of the Kaldaklofsfjöll icecap, the view from this 1278m summit is indescribable.
Álftavatn As you drop into the valley there are glorious views of Tindfjallajökull, Eyjafjallajökull and Mýrdalsjökull as well as many volcanic formations.
Torfahlaup (side trip) A 5km hike to where the mighty Markarfijót is constricted and forced through a 15m-wide canyon. Looming above is the velvety peak of Stóra Grænafell.

Day 3: Álftavatn to Emstrur (16km, six to seven hours)

Hvanngil Take a well-earned rest in this pleasant green oasis.
Markarfljótsgljúfor (side trip) About 2km southwest of the Emstrur huts, this gaping green canyon will take your breath away.
Fording ice-cold streams Well, maybe not so much a highlight; more a memorable experience.

Day 4: Emstrur to Þórsmörk (15km, six to seven hours)

Ljósá The view from a footbridge down to the 'River of Light', as it squeezes through a 2m-wide fissure, is mesmerising.
Þórsmörk After barren mountains, it's a delight to walk among the twisting birch trees of this grassy green woodland.

HELLFIRE & BRIMSTONE

The 18th-century eruptions of the volcano Laki brought death and devastation to much of southeastern Iceland, especially nearby Kirkjubæjarklaustur. On 20 July 1783 a particularly fast-moving river of molten lava threatened to engulf the town.

The pastor Jón Steingrímsson, convinced it was due to the wickedness of his flock, gathered the terrified parishioners into the church. There he delivered a passionate hellfire and brimstone sermon while the appropriate special effects steamed and smoked outside. By the time the oratory ended, the flow had stopped at a rock promontory – now called Eldmessutangi (Fire Sermon Point) – just short of the town. The grateful residents credited their good reverend with some particularly effective string-pulling on their behalf.

Religious connections are particularly strong in this area. The prominent rock pillar **Systrastapi** (Sisters' Pillar), near the line of cliffs west of town, marks the spot where two nuns were reputedly executed and buried for sleeping with the devil and such other no-nos.

At the western end of the village a lovely double-raced waterfall, **Systrafoss**, tumbles down the cliffs via the Bæjargil ravine. The lake **Systravatn**, a short and pleasant saunter up the cliffs above the falls, was once a bathing place for nuns.

Steingrímsson Memorial Chapel, the triangular, distinctly atypical wood-and-stone chapel on Klausturvegur, was consecrated in 1974. It commemorates Jón Steingrímsson's Eldmessa (Fire Sermon), which 'saved' the town from lava on 20 July 1783 (see the boxed text, above).

Ongoing archaeological digs have unearthed 14th- and 15th-century convent houses (at the northeast corner of the old churchyard). If you want to know more, visit the small **Kirkjubæjarstofa exhibition** (☎ 487 4645; Klausturvegur 2; ☷ 9-11am & 2-6pm Tue-Fri, 2-6pm Sat & Sun Jun-Aug).

South of the Ring Rd is a vast pseudocrater field known as **Landbrot**. They were formed during the Laki eruptions of 1783, when lava poured over marshland and fast-evaporating steam exploded through to make these barrowlike mounds.

Tours

Based at Hörgsland (see opposite), the **Jeppaferðir Ehf** (☎ 487 6655; www.horgsland.is; Hörgsland 1) company does tailor-made Jeep tours to surrounding areas, including Lakagígar. Contact it for prices.

Sleeping & Eating

Kirkjubæ II camp site (☎ /fax 487 4612; sites per person Ikr600; ☷ Jun-Sep) This neat green site with sheltering hedges is right in town. It has pretty good facilities, including a kitchen, hot showers (Ikr150 per five minutes) and a laundry (Ikr750 minimum).

Kleifar camp site (☎ 487 4675; sites per person Ikr500) There's a second, more simple, camp site 1.5km along Rte 203 (signposted towards Geirland).

Hótel Klaustur (☎ 487 4900; www.icehotels.is; Klausturvegur 6; s/d from Ikr13,000/16,200) One of the Icelandair chain, the 57-room Klaustur looks like a Soviet-bloc hotel but contains a three-star interior with the usual businesslike rooms and a spa/sauna. The restaurant (mains Ikr1900 to Ikr3900) has an à la carte menu with typical Icelandic mains and some unusual starters – snails, anyone?

ourpick Systra Kaffi (☎ 487 4848; Klausturvegur 13; light meals Ikr850-1500, mains Ikr1800-3000; ☷ 11am-11.30pm daily mid-May–Aug, 6-10pm daily Sep, weekends only Apr & Oct, closed Nov–mid-May) The most atmospheric place for a meal is this characterful little café-bar. It has a varied menu, which offers everything from sandwiches and burgers to big tilting bowls of salad, local trout and smoked-lamb mains using produce from nearby farms.

For freshly made fast-food snacks, there's the Skaftárskáli **petrol station café** (☎ 487 4628). Self-caterers have the **Kjarval supermarket** (☎ 487 4616; Klausturvegur; ☷ 9am-8pm daily Jun-Aug, shorter hr Sep-May).

Getting There & Away

The Reykjavík–Höfn bus service runs daily from 1 June to 15 September, and on Tuesday, Thursday, Friday and Saturday the rest of the year.

Summer buses depart from either end of the route at 8.30am (winter buses set off from Reykjavík/Höfn later in the day), and stop at Hótel Klaustur or the petrol station in Kirkjubæjarklaustur. Eastbound from Reykjavík, the bus passes Kirkjubæjarklaustur at 1.30pm (Ikr4400), continuing to Skaftafell and Jökulsárlón. Westbound from Höfn, it passes

Kirkjubæjarklaustur at 12.40pm (Ikr3300), continuing on to Reykjavík.

The Fjallabak bus between Reykjavík and Skaftafell passes at around 6.30pm eastbound and at 9am westbound daily from 20 June to 2 September. The entire route costs Ikr8100.

AROUND KIRKJUBÆJARKLAUSTUR
Fjarðrárgljúfur

This peculiar and darkly picturesque canyon, carved out by the river Fjarðrá, is a humbling two million years old. A walking track follows its southern edge for a couple of kilometres, and there are plenty of places to gaze down into its rocky, writhing depths. The canyon is 3.5km north of the Ring Rd; you can walk there across lava fields or drive along the Laki road (Rte 206; you'll reach the canyon before it becomes an F road).

Around the nearby Holt farm is the small **Holtsborg Nature Reserve**. This is the only place in Iceland where wild roses grow naturally.

Foss á Síðu & Dverghamrar

Foss á Síðu, 11km east of Kirkjubæjarklaustur, is an attractive **waterfall** that normally tumbles down from the cliffs. During especially strong sea winds, however, it actually goes straight up! Opposite the falls is the outcrop Dverghamrar, which contains some classic **basalt columns**.

Sleeping & Eating

There's quite a bit of farmhouse accommodation in the area immediately around Kirkjubæjarklaustur.

our pick **Hörgsland** (☎ 487 6655; www.horgsland .is; sb Ikr2300, made-up beds Ikr3000, cottages from Ikr6900) This place, a readers' favourite on the Ring Rd about 8km northeast of Kirkjubæjarklaustur, is like a minivillage of very spacious and comfortable self-contained cottages. The two-bedroom timber cabins sleep at least six and have kitchen, lounge and veranda. There are a couple of outdoor hot pots here, as well as a shop, a café and a petrol station, and you can arrange fishing permits.

Efri-Vík (☎ 487 4694; www.efrivik.is; sites per person Ikr700, sb Ikr2900, s/d Ikr5900/8900) A good choice is this farm, 5km south of Kirkjubæjarklaustur on Rte 204. As well as beds in comfortable cottages, it has a nine-hole golf course, boat rental, a sauna, a hot tub and lake fishing.

Hunkubakkar (☎ 487 4681; hunka@mmedia.is; s/d from Ikr5900/7900; ✗) This farmhouse, 7km west of Klaustur along Rtes 1 and 206, has simple parquet-floored rooms in the main building and cottages to rent in the grounds. Other facilities include a restaurant and horse hire. Between October and May you'll have to book in advance.

Restaurant Geirland (☎ 487 4677; geirland@centrum .is; Geirland; mains Ikr1500-2700; ☯ 7-11pm Jun-Aug) This new restaurant is part of the farmhouse accommodation at Geirland, about 4km along Rte 203. Mains make use of fresh local produce – sea trout, lamb steak – plus there's always a veggie course.

LAKAGÍGAR

It's almost impossible to comprehend the immensity of the Laki eruptions, one of the most catastrophic volcanic events in human history.

In the spring of 1783 a vast set of fissures opened, forming around 135 craters that took it in turns to fountain molten rock up to 1km into the air. These Skaftáreldar lasted for eight months, spewing out more than 30 billion tonnes of lava, which covered an area of 500 sq km in a layer up to 19km thick. Fifty farms in the region were wiped out.

Far more devastating were the hundreds of millions of tonnes of ash and sulphuric acid that poured from the fissures. The sun was blotted out, the grass died off, and around two-thirds of Iceland's livestock died from starvation and poisoning. Some 9000 people – a fifth of the country – were killed and the remainder faced the Móðuharðindi (Haze Famine) that followed.

The damage wasn't limited to purely to Iceland, either. All across the northern hemisphere clouds of ash in the atmosphere blocked out the sun. Temperatures dropped and acid rain fell from the sky, causing devastating crop failures in Japan, Alaska and Europe (possibly even helping to spark the French Revolution).

The whole Lakagígar area was included within the new 2004 boundaries of Skaftafell National Park. Wardens will occasionally pop out of the wilderness with brochure-maps of the area for sale. You should stick to paths in this ecologically sensitive region, and camping is forbidden. If you want a proper topographical map, the Landmælingar Íslands' 1:50,000 map *DMA 1913 II Lakagígar* shows the area, as does the Atlas Maps 1:100,000 *Langisjó* map.

A JEEP TOUR ON VATNAJÖKULL

Visitor: If there's a volcanic eruption while we're on the glacier, will we get our money back?
Jeep Driver: No, we'll charge you double!

Laki

Although Laki (818m) is extinct, it has loaned its name to the still-volatile, 25km-long Lakagígar crater row, which stretches southwestward from its base. Laki can be climbed in about 40 minutes from the parking area, and we highly recommend it. There are boundless 360-degree views from the top, of the active fissure, vast lava fields and glinting ice-white glaciers in the distance.

Lakagígar Crater Row

The Lakagígar crater row is fascinating to explore. The entire area is riddled with black sand dunes and lava tubes, many of which contain tiny stalactites. Down at Laki's feet, marked walking paths lead you in and out of the two nearest craters, including an interesting lava tunnel – bring a torch. Another cave, two hours' walk south of the Laki parking area, shelters a mysterious lake.

Nowadays the lava field belies the apocalypse that spawned it just over 220 years ago. Its black, twisted lava formations are now overgrown with soft green moss.

Fagrifoss & Hell's Back Door

Fagrifoss (Beautiful Falls) is certainly not a misnomer: this must be one of Iceland's most bewitching **waterfalls**, with rivulets of water pouring over a massive black rock. You'll come to the turnoff on the way to Laki, about 22km along the F206.

Not far from Fagrifoss is a very deep **hole** in a small slump crater, about 200m east of the Laki road. It doesn't seem to have a particular name, but locals will jokingly tell you it's the back door to hell (Hekla is the front). The hidden entrance is just 35cm across, so it's unlikely you'll find it without a guide.

Sleeping

Camping is forbidden within the Laki reserve; despite its death-dealing fissures, the area is ecologically very delicate. The nearest camp site, with toilet and fresh water, is at Blágil, about 11km from Laki.

Getting There & Away

If you want to drive, Rte F206 (just west of Kirkjubæjarklaustur) is generally passable from July to early September. It's a long 50km to the Lakagígar crater row. The road is unsuitable for 2WD cars, as there are several rivers to ford. Even low-clearance 4WD vehicles may not be enough in the spring thaw or after rain, when the rivers tend to run deep.

From 1 July to 31 August you can get to the Lakagígar area on the worthwhile **Austurleið-Kynnisferðir bus** (☎ 562 1011; www.austurleid.is). The 10-hour tour (with a jumpy CD guide!) allows around three hours' walking in the crater area. It departs daily, at 8am from Skaftafell (Ikr7300) and at 9am from Kirkjubæjarklaustur (Ikr5300). If you're staying at the camp site or one of the farmhouses, ring in advance for a pick-up.

THE SANDAR

Another area of devastation are the sandar, soul-destroyingly flat and empty regions sprawling along Iceland's southeastern coast. High in the mountains, glaciers scrape up silt, sand and gravel that is then carried by glacial rivers or (more dramatically) by glacial bursts down to the coast and dumped in huge desertlike plains. The sandar here are so impressively huge and awful that the Icelandic word is used internationally to describe this topographic phenomenon.

Skeiðarársandur is the most visible and dramatic, stretching some 40km between icecap and coast from Núpsstaður to Öræfi. Here you'll encounter a flat expanse of grey-black sands, fierce scouring winds (a cyclist's nightmare) and fast-flowing grey-brown glacial rivers.

Meðallandssandur

This region spreads across the Meðalland district south of Eldhraun and east of the river Kúðafljót. The sandy desert is so flat and featureless that a number of ships have run aground on its coast, apparently unaware they were nearing land. Shipwrecked sailors have died in quicksand while trying to get ashore. There are now several small lighthouses along the coast.

Skeiðarársandur

Skeiðarársandur, the largest sandar in the world, covers a 1000-sq-km area and was formed by the mighty Skeiðarárjökull. Since the Settlement Era Skeiðarársandur has swallowed a considerable amount of farmland and it continues to grow. The area was relatively well populated (for Iceland, anyway), but in 1362 the volcano Öræfi beneath Öræfajökull erupted and the subsequent *jökulhlaup* laid waste the entire district.

The section of Rte 1 that passes across Skeiðarársandur was the last bit of the national highway to be constructed – as recently as 1974 (until then, Höfnites had to drive to Reykjavík via Akureyri!). Long gravel dykes have been strategically positioned to channel flood waters away from this highly susceptible artery. They did little good, however, when in late 1996 three Ring Rd bridges were washed away like matchsticks by the massive *jökulhlaup* released by the Grímsvötn (or Gjálp) eruption (see the boxed text, p287). There's a memorial of twisted bridge girders and an information board along the Ring Rd just west of Skaftafell National Park.

The sands are a major breeding area for great skuas (see the boxed text, p291) – particularly appropriate birds for such a harsh and desolate region.

Núpsstaður & Núpsstaðarskógar

Bizarrely eroded cliffs and pinnacles tower over the old **turf-roofed farm** and church at Núpsstaður. The farm buildings date back as far as the early 19th century, and the church, which is dedicated to St Nicholas, was mentioned as early as 1200. It was renovated in 1957 by Einar Jónsson and is one of the last turf churches in Iceland.

Inland is Núpsstaðarskógar, a beautiful **woodland area** on the slopes of the mountain Eystrafjall. Since it's no longer possible to cross the Núpsá river by raft, this area is best explored on a tour run by the Icelandic Mountain Guides (see right).

Grænalón

From the southern end of Núpsstaðarskógar a good two-day hike will take you over the ridges and valleys west of immense Skeiðarárjökull to Grænalón. This ice-dammed **lake** has the ability to drain like a bathtub. The 'plug' is the western edge of Skeiðarárjökull and, when the water pressure builds to breaking point, the glacier is lifted and the lake lets go. It has been known to release up to 2.7 million cubic metres of water at 5000 cubic metres per second in a single burst.

To get there you'll have to join the Núpsstaðarskógar tour (see below), as it's impossible to cross the Núpsá and Súlaá rivers on foot (the Icelandic Mountain Guides have special equipment, including a big 4x4!). The topo sheet to use is *Lómagnúpur* 1:100,000 (1986).

Tours

In July and August, the **Icelandic Mountain Guides** (☎ 587 9999; www.mountainguide.is) run a guided four-day (60km) hike through Núpsstaðarskógar, over to Grænalón lagoon, across the glacier Skeiðarárjökull and then into Morsárdalur in Skaftafell National Park. The trip costs Ikr48,900 with food, camping gear, glacier equipment and transport from Skaftafell included. There's a supplement to pay if the walking group has fewer than five people – phone to check numbers.

Sleeping

Hvoll HI Hostel (☎ 487 4785; www.simnet.is/nupsstadarskogur; dm Ikr1800, s/d Ikr2800/4600; ❧ Mar-Oct) Iceland's third-largest hostel is on the edge of Skeiðarársandur (3km south off the Ring Rd via a gravel road) and feels very remote despite its size. It's very much like the Reykjavík hostel in its clean new design and busy atmosphere; facilities include several kitchens, a TV room, laundry, bookshelves full of Mickey Spillane, and a payphone. It makes an excellent base for exploring Skaftafell, Núpsstaðarskógar and the surrounding sandar.

SKAFTAFELL NATIONAL PARK

Europe's largest national park encompasses a breathtaking collection of peaks and glaciers. It's the country's favourite wilderness: 160,000 visitors per year come to marvel at thundering waterfalls, twisted birch woods, the tangled web of rivers threading across the sandar, and brilliant blue-white Vatnajökull with its lurching tongues of ice.

Skaftafell deserves its reputation, and few Icelanders – even those who usually shun the great outdoors – can resist it. On long summer weekends all of Reykjavík (including the city's raucous all-night parties) may seem to descend. It can be lots of fun but may prove disappointing if you've come to commune with nature rather than stereo systems. However, if you're prepared to get out on the more remote trails and take advantage of the fabulous hiking on the heath and beyond, you'll leave the crowds far behind.

SOUTHEAST ICELAND

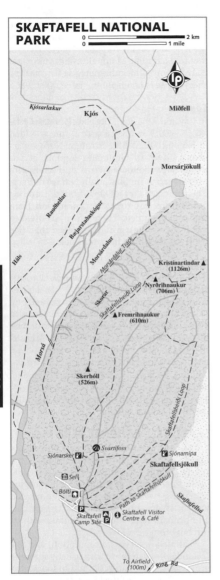

SKAFTAFELL NATIONAL PARK

site. Shifting glacial sands slowly buried the fields and forced the farm to a more suitable site, on the heath 100m above the sandar. The district came to be known as Hérað Milli Sandur (Land Between the Sands), but after all the farms were annihilated by the 1362 eruptions the district became the 'land under the sands' and was renamed Öræfi (Wasteland). Once the vegetation returned, however, the Skaftafell farm was rebuilt in its former location.

The modern park was founded in 1967 by the Icelandic government and the World Wildlife Fund (now the WWF), and was originally 500 sq km. It has been enlarged twice (in June 1984 and in October 2004), and now also includes over half of Vatnajökull and the Laki craters (see p283) to the west. Further expansion plans are under way – eventually, the Skaftafell and Jökulsárgljúfur (p242) national parks will join to form one 15,000-sq-km megapark – 40% of the entire country.

Information

The helpful **visitor centre** (☎ 478 1627; www.ust.is; ☯ 8am-9pm Jun-Aug, 10am-3pm May & Sep) has an information desk with free brochures and maps for sale, good informative displays on the Öræfi area, and a cool film about the 1996 Grímsvötn *jökulhlaup*, shown in peak season only.

All flora, fauna and natural features of the park are protected, open fires are prohibited, and rubbish must be carried out. In the busy area around Skaftafellsheiði, stick to the tracks to avoiding damaging delicate plant life.

Don't get too close to glaciers or climb on them without the proper equipment and training – the average ice block calving off Skaftafellsjökull would crush anyone within a few metres of the face.

Landmælingar Íslands (☎ 430 9000; www.lmi.is) publishes a thematic map of Skaftafell National Park showing the nonglacial area of the park at 1:25,000 and the Öræfi district at 1:100,000 (2002). It's available at the visitor centre (Ikr790) and in bookshops and tourist offices elsewhere in Iceland. You can also use the *Öræfajökull* 1:100,000 (1986) topo sheet.

Sel

This traditional **turf-roofed farmhouse** (admission free), built in Burstir style in 1912, is worth a glance. There's not much inside, but it's always open and the hill just above offers a good photo opportunity of the farmhouse and the grey sandar stretching out to the coast.

There's very little accommodation close to the park, so you'll need either a tent or a firm hotel booking plus private transport if you want to explore the park properly.

History

The historical Skaftafell was a large farm at the foot of the hills west of the present camp

Grímsvötn

The volcano Grímsvötn, mumbling away underneath the Vatnajökull ice, has been known to blow its top and release apocalyptic *jökulhlaups*. Some of its creations include the Ásbyrgi canyon (see p244), gouged out by a cataclysmic flood over just a few days. In 1934 another Grímsvötn eruption released a *jökulhlaup* of 40,000 cu metres per second, which swelled the river Skeiðará to 9km in width and laid waste large areas of farmland. Its next epic tantrum in 1996 poured 45,000 cu metres of water and icebergs the size of houses down onto the south coast, cutting off the Ring Rd – see the boxed text, below.

Grímsvötn erupted again in December 1998, and most recently in November 2004, when a five-day eruption threw steam and ash 12km into the atmosphere, disrupting air traffic. There was no *jökulhlaup* on either occasion.

Hiking

Skaftafell is ideal for day hikes and also offers longer treks through its wilderness regions. Most of Skaftafell's visitors keep to the popular routes on Skaftafellsheiði. Hiking in other accessible areas, such as upper Morsárdalur and Kjós, requires more time, motivation and effort.

Wild camping is not allowed in the park. Compulsory camping permits (Ikr600) for Kjós are available from the information centre. Also inquire about river crossings along your intended route.

SVARTIFOSS

Star of a hundred postcards, Svartifoss is a gloomy **waterfall** flanked by black basalt columns. It's reached by an easy track leading up from the camp site (about 1½ hours for the return trip). However, due to immense pressure in this area of the park, rangers are encouraging visitors to explore elsewhere. If you do go to Svartifoss, it's worth continuing west up the short track to **Sjónarsker**, where there's a view disc and an unforgettable view across Skeiðarársandur.

SKAFTAFELLSJÖKULL

Another popular and less sensitive trail is the easy one-hour return walk to Skaftafellsjökull. The (wheelchair-accessible) sealed track begins at the visitor centre and leads to the **glacier**

JÖKULHLAUP!

You might think that a volcano buried under thousands of tonnes of ice would somehow be less troublesome than the normal kind. You'd be wrong. In late 1996 the devastating Grímsvötn eruption – Iceland's fourth largest of the 20th century, after Katla in 1918, Hekla in 1947 and Surtsey in 1963 – shook southeast Iceland and caused an awesome *jökulhlaup* across Skeiðarársandur. The events leading up to it are a sobering reminder of the power of Iceland's volatile fire-and-ice combination.

On the morning of 29 September 1996 a magnitude 5.0 earthquake shook the Vatnajökull icecap. Magma from a new volcano, in the Grímsvötn region beneath Vatnajökull, had made its way through the earth's crust and into the ice, causing the eruption of a 4km-long subsurface fissure known as Gjálp. The following day the eruption burst through the surface, ejecting a column of steam that rose 10km into the sky and inspiring impressive aerial photography that was televised worldwide.

Scientists became concerned as the subglacial lake in the Grímsvötn caldera began to fill with water from ice melted by the eruption. Initial predictions on 3 October were that the ice would lift and the lake would give way within 48 hours and spill out across Skeiðarársandur, threatening the Ring Rd and its bridges, which serve as vital links between eastern and western Iceland. In the hope of diverting floodwaters away from the bridges, massive dyke-building projects were organised on Skeiðarársandur.

On 5 November, over a month after the eruption started, the ice *did* lift and the Grímsvötn reservoir drained in a massive *jökulhlaup*, releasing up to 3000 billion cubic litres of water within a few hours. The floodwaters – dragging along icebergs the size of three-storey buildings – destroyed the 375m-long Gígjukvísl Bridge and the 900m-long Skeiðará Bridge, both on the Skeiðarársandur. See video footage of the eruption and enormous multitonne blocks of ice being hurled across Skeiðarársandur at the Skaftafell visitor centre.

face, where you can witness the bumps and groans of the ice – although the glacier is pretty grey and gritty here. The glacier has been receding in recent years and over the past 50 years has lost nearly 1km of its length.

SKAFTAFELLSHEIÐI LOOP

On a fine day, the five- to six-hour walk around Skaftafellsheiði is a hiker's dream. It begins by climbing from the camp site past Svartifoss and Sjónarsker, continuing across the moor to 610m-high **Fremrihnaukur**. From there it follows the edge of the plateau to the next rise, **Nyrðrihnaukur** (706m), which affords a superb view of Morsárdalur, Morsárjökull and the iceberg-choked lagoon at its base. At this point the track turns southeast to an outlook point on the cliff above Skaftafell-sjökull (Gláma).

For the best view of Skaftafellsjökull, Morsárdalur and the Skeiðarársandur, it's worth scaling the summit of **Kristínartindar** (1126m). The easiest way follows a well-marked route up the prominent valley southeast of the Nyrðrihnaukur lookout.

MORSÁRDALUR & BÆJARSTAÐARSKÓGUR

The seven-hour hike from the camp site to the glacial lake in Morsárdalur is fairly ordinary but enjoyable. There's a footbridge across the lake outlet, and from there you can continue to **Kjós**. Alternatively, cross the Morsá on the footbridge near the point where the Kamb-gil ravine comes down from Skaftafellsheiði and make your way across the gravel riverbed to the birch woods at **Bæjarstaðarskógur**. The trees here reach a whopping (for Iceland) 12m, and 80°C springs flow into the tiny but heavenly Heitulækir to the west in Vestragil. The return walk to Bæjarstaðarskógur takes about six hours; add on an extra hour to visit Heitulækir.

OTHER HIKES

Other possibilities include the long day trip beyond Bæjarstaðarskógur into the rugged Skaftafellsfjöll. A recommended destination is the 965m-high summit of the **Jökulfell ridge**, which affords a commanding view of the vast expanses of Skeiðarárjökull. Even better is a three-day excursion into the Kjós region. When you reach Kjós, a very difficult hike leads to the base of Þumall (Thumb), then west along the glacier edge, around the valley rim and south down to your starting point.

Tours

The **Icelandic Mountain Guides** (☎ 587 9999, 894 2959; www.mountainguide.is) is the country's mountain-rescue squad, so you can feel pretty safe on the excellent organised hikes. In summer it has a base in the Skaftafell camp site where you can book places in person.

The mountain guides lead a range of walks, including glacier walks and ice-climbing (opposite and p139); guided hikes up Iceland's highest peak (opposite); and longer backpack hikes including the challenging four-day route from Núpsstaðarskógar to Skaftafell (p285), and the epic nine-day trek from Laki to Skaftafell (Ikr99,000). See the website for more suggestions.

If all this walking sounds like an effort, there are **sightseeing flights** (☎ 478 2406; www.jorvik.is) from the tiny airfield just outside the national park over Vatnajökull, Grímsvötn, the Lakagígar crater row or the glaciers. Prices start at Ikr9000 for 30 minutes.

Sleeping & Eating

Visitor-centre camp site (☎ 478 1627; sites per person Ikr600) Since Skaftafell is a national park, most people bring a tent to this large, gravelly camp site (with laundry facilities). It gets very busy and loud in summer. The only other place you're allowed to camp is at the Kjós camp site (Ikr600 per person) – buy a permit from the visitor centre before you set off.

Bölti (☎ 478 1626; fax 478 2426; Skaftafellsheiði; sb/d Ikr2200/7500; ☼ May-Sep) This farm, on the hill above the western end of the Skaftafell camp site, is in a superb location with dizzying views out over the sandur. There's sleeping-bag accommodation on bunk beds in six-person huts; tiny kitchen areas include a kettle and two electric rings. Book ahead in summer. Breakfast is a rather pricey Ikr1000.

The nearest hotel, Hótel Skaftafell, is at Frey-snes (see opposite), 5km east of the national park entrance, and there's farmhouse accommodation (sleeping-bag space and cabins) at the Hof and Lítla-Hof farms, 23km away.

Food in the park is limited. The café at the visitor centre has a woeful coffee machine, sandwiches and a tiny selection of groceries.

Getting There & Away

From 1 June to 15 September, daily buses run by **Austurleið-Kynnisferðir** (☎ 562 1011; www.austur leid.is) go between Reykjavík and Höfn, leaving at each end at 8.30am and passing Skaftafell at 2.35pm eastbound (Ikr5400) and 11.10am westbound (Ikr2300). The rest of the year the Reykjavík–Höfn bus runs on Tuesday, Thursday, Friday and Sunday, departing at 12.30pm from Reykjavík and at noon from Höfn.

From 20 June to 2 September there's another bus from Reykjavík to Skaftafell via the scenic inland route through Landmannalaugar and Eldgjá, departing daily from Reykjavík at 8.30am and arriving at Skaftafell at 7.30pm (Ikr8100). Westbound it departs from Skaftafell at 8am.

SKAFTAFELL TO HÖFN

Glittering glaciers and brooding mountains line the 130km stretch between Skaftafell and Höfn. In clear weather the unfolding landscape makes it difficult to keep your eyes on the road. The premier tourist stop is the iceberg-filled lagoon Jökulsárlón. Other attractions include exhilarating glacier walks, Jeep and snowmobile tours on the Vatnajökull icecap, puffin spotting at Ingólfshöfði and horse riding.

Freysnes, Svínafell & Svínafellsjökull

The **farm** Svínafell, 8km southeast of Skaftafell, was the home of Flosi Þórðarson, the character who burned Njál and his family to death in *Njál's Saga*. It was also the site where Flosi and Njál's family were finally reconciled, thus ending one of the bloodiest feuds in Icelandic history (see p136). There's not much to this tiny settlement now, but you can go swimming at **Flosalaug** (☎ 478 1765; ☯ 5-9pm), a complex with a shallow round pool, hot pots, showers and a camp site.

In the 17th century, the **glacier** Svínafellsjökull nearly engulfed the farm, but it has since retreated. On the northern side of the glacier (towards Skaftafell), a dirt road leads 2km to a car park, from where it's a short walk to the snout.

ICE CLIMBING & GLACIER WALKS

From mid-May to mid-September you can enjoy daily walks up Svínafellsjökull with the **Icelandic Mountain Guides** (☎ 587 9999; www

---

ON ROADKILL

(…as an arctic tern splatters against the windscreen…) 'We don't stop for birds in Iceland. Sheeps, yes! Birds, no!'
Höfn bus driver

.mountainguide.is). It's utterly liberating to strap on crampons and suddenly be able to stride up a glacier, and there's so much to see on the ice. Waterfalls, ice caves, glacial mice and different-coloured ash from ancient explosions are just some of the glacier's slightly hallucinatory joys. The 'Blue Ice Experience' (Ikr3900 per person), at 10am and 2pm, is a 2½-hour walk for beginners, but it just doesn't last long enough! We'd recommend the longer five-hour 'Glacier Adventure' (Ikr6300 per person), at 9am. There's also a three-hour ice-climbing expedition using ice walls on the glacier (Ikr5900 per person), at 4pm. The only equipment you need to bring is hiking boots.

Local company **Öræfaferðir** (☎ 894 0894; www.hofsnes.com), based at the farm Hofsnes, offers similar tours at similar prices Monday to Saturday year-round.

SLEEPING & EATING

Hótel Skaftafell (☎ 478 1945; www.hotelskaftafell.is; Freysnes; s/d May-Aug Ikr11,000/14,600, rest of yr Ikr9000/11,100; ☯ closed Dec & Jan) This is the closest hotel to Skaftafell National Park, 5km east at Freysnes. Its 63 rooms (all with bathroom and TV) are functional rather than luxurious, but staff are helpful, and even the rooms in the prefabricated buildings at the back have great glacial views. There's a good restaurant (mains Ikr2000 to Ikr3000) serving 'Sean Connery salad', fresh char, puffin, lamb and lobster, and a recommended rhubarb and cardamom mousse. A pleasant walking trail leads to Svínafellsjökull from behind the building.

Flosi (☎ 894 1765; flosihf@simnet.is; sites per person Ikr700, sb May-Sep Ikr2500, Oct-Apr Ikr2000) At the swimming pool at Svínafell, this place has a camp site and six basic cabins, each with four bunks, and a simple amenities block. If you have your own vehicle it's an alternative to the camp site at Skaftafell.

The petrol station opposite Hótel Skaftafell has a shop selling hot dogs.

Öræfajökull & Hvannadalshnúkur

Iceland's highest **mountain**, Hvannadalshnúkur (2119m), pokes out from the icecap Öræfajökull, an offshoot of Vatnajökull. This lofty peak is actually the northwestern edge of an immense 5km-wide crater – the biggest active volcano in Europe after Mt Etna. It erupted in 1362, firing out the largest amount of tephra in Iceland's recorded history: nearby glaciers are liberally spattered with bits of compressed yellow ash from the explosion. The region was utterly devastated – hence its name, Öræfi (Wasteland).

The best access for climbing Hvannadalsh-núkur is from Sandfellsheiði, above the abandoned farm Sandfell, about 12km southeast of Skaftafell. Climbers should be well versed in glacier travel, and, although most guided expeditions manage the trip in a very long and taxing day (see below), independent climbers should carry enough supplies and gear for several days.

TOURS

Local companies Öræfaferðir (☎ 894 0894; www .hofsnes.com) and the Icelandic Mountain Guides (☎ 587 9999; www.mountainguide.is) run guided 10- to 15-hour ascents of Hvannadalshnúkur. The trip costs Ikr14,900 per person (minimum of two people), including transport and use of equipment. If you're looking for a challenge, this is one of the best deals in Iceland.

Transport is provided up to the snow line, where you transfer to snowshoes for the ascent to the 1820m-high crater rim. After walking across the crater, you make the final summit ascent with crampons and ice axe. You need to bring warm clothing and your own food and water. Trips run on request between June and August. Book in advance, and allow yourself extra days in case the weather causes a cancellation.

Hof & Bær

At Hof farm is a picturesque wood-and-peat church, built on the foundations of a previous 14th-century building, and a Viking temple dedicated to Þór. It was reconstructed in 1883 and now sits pleasantly in a thicket of birch and ash with flowers growing on the grassy roof.

About 6km further east, Bær is a farm that was buried by ash in the 1362 Öræfi eruption. The walls are surprisingly intact, but visitors are asked not to trample all over them since the ruins are both protected and part of an ongoing archaeological excavation.

At the Hof farm, and beautifully situated beneath the Öræfajökull glacier, the Frost & Fire Guesthouse (☎ 478 1669; www.frostogfuni.is; s/d Ikr7800/11,400, d with bathroom Ikr12,500; ⊙ Jun–early Sep) has a variety of rooms in the main farmhouses and chalets. The majority have shared bathrooms. Prices include breakfast, and there's a brand-new sauna and hot pot. This is a good base for glacier tours to Öræfajökull. Nearby

is another farm, Lítla-Hof (☎ 478 1670), with similarly priced rooms.

The nearest shop and snack bar is at the lonely Esso petrol station at Fagurhólsmýri, 5km east along the Ring Rd.

Ingólfshöfði

The 76m-high Ingólfshöfði promontory rises from the flatlands like a strange dream. In spring and summer, this beautiful, isolated nature reserve is overrun with nesting puffins, skuas and other sea birds, and you'll often see seals and whales offshore. It's also of great historical importance – it was here that Ingólfur Arnarson, Iceland's first settler, stayed the winter on his original foray to the country in AD 871. The reserve is open to visitors, but the 9km drive across the shallow tidal lagoon isn't something you should attempt, even in a 4WD.

Luckily, you can get here by hay wagon! Farmer Sigurður Bjarnason gets out his trusty tractor between May and August and runs tours (adult/under 12yr Ikr2000/free; ⊙ noon Mon-Sat May-Aug, 9am, noon & 3pm Mon-Sat Jul) to the reserve. The half-hour ride across the sands is followed by an interesting two-hour guided walk round the headland, with the emphasis on bird-watching. You can book through Öræfaferðir (☎ 894 0894; www.hofsnes.com), or simply turn up outside the farm at Hofsnes (signposted, just off the Ring Rd) 10 minutes before the tour's due to start.

Breiðamerkursandur

The easternmost of the large sandar, Breiðamerkursandur is one of the main breeding grounds for Iceland's great skuas (see the boxed text, opposite). Thanks to rising numbers of these ground-nesting birds, there's also a growing population of arctic foxes. Historically, Breiðamerkursandur also figures in Njál's Saga, which ends with Kári Sölmundarson arriving in this idyllic spot to 'live happily ever after' – which has to be some kind of miracle in a saga.

The sandar is backed by a sweeping panorama of glacier-capped mountains, some of which are fronted by deep lagoons. Kvíárjökull glacier snakes down to the Kvíár river and is easily accessible from the Ring Rd. Leave your car in the small car park just off Rte 1 (you can't drive any further) and follow the walking path into the valley. It's quite an uncanny place: boulders line the huge western moraine like sentinels, the mossy grass is full of fairy

---

HOW TO AVOID BEING SKUA-ED

One shouldn't anthropomorphise, but great skuas *(Stercorarius skua* in Latin, *skúmur* in Icelandic) are evil. These dirty-brown birds with white-patched wings even look the part: they're large, meaty bully boys with cruel curved beaks and beady black eyes that you can't outstare. You'll often find them harassing gulls into disgorging their dinner, killing and eating puffins and other little birds, or swooping down on YOU if you get too close to their nests. They tend to build these among grassy tufts, mainly in the great *sandur* regions on Iceland's southern coast.

Thankfully (unlike feather-brained arctic terns), skuas will stop plaguing you if you run away from the area they're trying to defend. You can also avoid aerial strikes by wearing a hat or carrying a stick above your head. Occasionally ravens or groups of smaller birds will get together to mob a skua and drive it off: these aerial battles are interesting to watch.

---

rings, and a powerful glacial wind frequently surges down from the ice above.

The 742m-high **Breiðamerkurfjall** was once a nunatak enclosed by Breiðamerkurjökull and Fjallsjökull, but the glaciers have since retreated and freed it.

At the foot of the peak is the glacial lagoon **Breiðárlón**, where icebergs calve from Fjallsjökull before sailing out to sea. Although it's not as dramatic as Jökulsárlón, in some ways it's more satisfying, thanks to the lack of people. It's set back from the Ring Rd and not immediately obvious, plus the (very rough) dirt road is extremely off-putting. It's possible to get there in a car (but don't blame us if you get stuck), or else it's a 25-minute walk from Rte 1.

Jökulsárlón

A host of spectacular, luminous-blue icebergs drift through Jökulsárlón **lagoon**, right beside the Ring Rd between Höfn and Skaftafell. Even when you're expecting this surreal scene, it's still a mighty surprise – just count how many shocked drivers slam on the brakes and skid across the road, and make sure you don't do the same thing yourself. It's worth spending a couple of hours here, admiring the wondrous ice sculptures, looking for seals or taking a trip in an amphibious boat.

The icebergs calve from Breiðamerkurjökull, an offshoot of Vatnajökull, crashing down into the water and drifting inexorably towards the sea. They can spend up to five years floating in the 17-sq-km, 600m-deep lagoon, melting, refreezing and occasionally toppling over with a mighty splash, startling the birds.

Although it looks as though it's been here since the last ice age, the lagoon is only about 75 years old. Until 1932 Breiðamerkurjökull reached the Ring Rd; it's now retreating rap-

idly, and the lagoon is consequently growing at a rate of knots.

Jökulsárlón is a natural film set. It starred briefly in *Lara Croft: Tomb Raider* (2001), pretending to be Siberia – the amphibious tourist-carrying boats were even painted grey and used as Russian ships. You might also have seen it in the James Bond film *Die Another Day* (2002), for which the lagoon was specially frozen and six Aston Martins were destroyed on the ice!

BOAT TRIPS

Between late May and early September you can take a 35-minute trip on the lagoon in brilliant **amphibious boats** (☎ 478 2222; info@jokulsarlon.is; per person lkr2200), which trundle along the shore like buses before driving into the water. Guides hop on board to tell you interesting factoids about the lagoon, and you get to taste 1000-year-old ice. Trips set off around every half-hour between 10am and 5pm daily.

But if you're short of time or money, don't think that you're missing out. You can get just as close to those cool-blue masterpieces by walking along the shore, and you can taste ancient ice by hauling it out of the water.

SLEEPING & EATING

The **Jökulsárlón café** (☎ 478 2122; www.jokulsarlon .is; ☺ 9am-7pm Jun–mid-Aug, 10am-5pm late May & early Sep) beside the lagoon is a good pit stop for information and some of southeast Iceland's best seafood soup.

If you have a camper van with toilet, it's OK to stay in the car park. Otherwise camping by the lagoon isn't really condoned (particularly not on the eastern side, where there are lots of nesting birds). The nearest accommodation is at **Gerði** (☎ 478 1905, 846 0641; bjornborg@centrum.is; sites per person lkr700, sb lkr1500-3500, s/tr/q with bathroom

7000/12,500/13,500, d without bathroom Ikr7600, up to 20% off rest of yr), about 13km east along the Ring Rd. This sprawling farm has a very peaceful guesthouse with great views, and cooking and lounge facilities; meals can be preordered in summer. There's also space to pitch a tent.

Suðursveit & Mýrar

Between Jökulsárlón and Höfn the Ring Rd passes several small farms, backed by mountains and yet more glaciers.

SIGHTS & ACTIVITIES

The brand-new museum **Þórbergssetur** (☎ 867 2900; Hali í Suðursveit; admission Ikr600; ☾ 9am-9pm Jun–early Sep, to 5pm rest of yr) pays tribute to the most famous son of this sparsely populated region – writer Þórbergur Þórðarson (1888–1974), who was born at Hali in Suðursveit. The exhibition contains full-sized models of the farmhouse where he grew up and his study in Reykjavík, illustrated by quotes from his work. Þórbergur was a real maverick (with interests spanning yoga, Esperanto, astronomy, archaeology and geology), and his first book *Bréf til Láru (Letter to Laura)* caused huge controversy because of its radical socialist content. It's a shame that more of it hasn't been translated into English – you'll just have to make do with the perspicacious, humorous snippets from the accompanying museum guide.

As for glaciers, if you want to get up onto **Vatnajökull**, the daddy of them all, for a snowmobile, skiing or Jeep tour (see the boxed text, p294), then this area is where you branch vertically off into the mountains. Rte F985, which leads up to the **Jöklasel hut**, is about 35km east of Jökulsárlón.

Staying on the Ring Rd, you'll cross the lovely **Mýrar**, a region of wetlands surrounding the deltas of Hornafjarðarfljót and Kolgrímaá, home to lots of **water birds**.

The prominent and colourful mountain **Ketillaugarfjall** rises 670m above the Hornafjarðarfljót delta near Bjarnarnes. Its name derives from a legend about a woman named Ketillaug, who carried a pot of gold into the mountain and never returned. A brilliantly coloured alluvial fan at its base is visible from the road.

SLEEPING & EATING

Vagnstaðir HI Hostel (☎ 478 1048; glacierjeeps@simnet .is; sites per person Ikr650, sb dm Ikr1800; ☾ May-Sep) As the home of the Glacier Jeeps outfit (see p294), this is the obvious place to stay the night before or after a tour onto the Vatnajökull icecap. The hostel itself, by the Ring Rd 50km west of Höfn, is a simple, purpose-built house in the shadow of some imposing mountains.

Smyrlabjörg (☎ 478 1074; smyrlabjorg@eldhorn.is; s/d/tr Ikr7500/13,100/18,000, up to 30% off out of season; ☾ closed late Dec; ♿) This friendly country hotel has 45 simply furnished rooms, all with satellite TV and attached bathroom. There's a restaurant serving an Icelandic buffet for dinner in summer, and a bar. It's a great place if you're after mod-cons but still want geese in the yard, mountain views, and utter peace and quiet.

Skálafell (☎ 478 1041; skalafell@simnet.is; sb Ikr2900, d Ikr10,700-14,600) At the foot of the Skálafell glacier, this friendly working farm has a couple of rooms in the quaint family farmhouse and three two-bedroom cabins. There are no cooking facilities, but breakfast and dinner are available. The owners offer guided walking trips to Skálafellsjökull.

Flatey (☎ 478 1036; flatey1@mmedia.is; sb Ikr2800, s/d without bathroom Ikr7400/10,600, with bathroom Ikr10,700/14,600) With a pair of glacier tongues backing up to the property, Flatey has a great location and a variety of rooms in the family farmhouse or in a separate guesthouse with lounge and kitchen facilities.

Brunhóll (☎ 478 1029; brunnhol@eldhorn.is; s/d without bathroom Ikr8600/11,520, with bathroom Ikr10,700/14,600; ☾ Apr-Oct; ♿) A gorgeous farm property 30km from Höfn on the southern side of the Ring Rd, Brunhóll has a cosy guesthouse and a bright, glassed-in dining room where breakfast is served.

HÖFN

pop 1660

Although it's no bigger than many European villages, the southeast's main town feels like a sprawling metropolis after driving through the wastelands on either side. Its setting is stunning; on a clear day wander down to the waterside, find a quiet bench and just gaze at Vatnajökull and its brotherhood of glaciers.

'Höfn' simply means 'harbour', and is pronounced like an unexpected hiccup (if you're not prone to hiccups, just say 'hup' while inhaling). It's an apt name – this modern town still relies heavily on fishing and fish processing, and it's famous for its lobster and prawns (there's even an annual lobster festival). Bus travellers will have to stay overnight here, and

HÖFN

SOUTHEAST ICELAND

Sights & Activities

The **Jöklasýning Glacier Exhibition** (www.joklasyning
.is; adult/under 16yr Ikr600/free; 9am-9pm daily Jun-Aug,
1-6pm daily May & Sep, 1-4pm Mon-Fri Oct-Apr) explains
the history and geology of Vatnajökull and
southeastern Iceland in great detail. For a
break from all the reading, there are a couple
of films – an excellent 10-minute video of
the 1996 Grímsvötn eruption, plus clips
from James Bond movies made in the region.
There's also a small collection of exhibits relating to glacier exploration, some altogether-
too-strange glacial mice, a baffling plastic 'ice
cave', and a good natural-history room. You
can check that the glacier's still there from the
viewing platform on the roof.

The regional folk museum **Byggðasafnið
Gamlabúð** (478 1833; Hafnarbraut; adult/under 16yr
Ikr300/free; 1-9pm Jul, to 6pm Jun, Aug & early Sep),
near the camp site, is housed in an 1864 trade
warehouse that was moved to Höfn from Pa-
paós, further east. It has agricultural displays
as well as small natural-history and marine-
life exhibits.

Pakkhúsið (478 1540; Krosseyjarvegur; 1-6pm
Jun–early Sep), near the harbour, is really more
of a handicraft shop than a museum, but
there's a maritime display in the basement
of the building, with old fishing boats, tools

most other travellers stop to use the town's
many services, so it pays to book accommodation in summer. Höfn makes a very handy
base for trips to the glacier.

Information

The **tourist office** (478 2665; www.east.is; Hafnarbraut
30; 9am-9pm Jun-Aug, 1-6pm May & Sep, 1-4pm Mon-Fri
Oct-Apr) is also the ticket desk for the glacier
exhibition (see right). Internet access at the
library (470 8050; Litlabrú; 9am-5pm Mon-Thu, 11am-
5pm Fri), in the community centre opposite the
supermarket, costs Ikr200 per hour.

Landsbanki Íslands and Sparisjóðurinn,
both on Hafnarbraut, handle foreign exchange.
The latter has an ATM, and you'll also find an
ATM in the 11-11 supermarket.

RIDING ON THE VATNAJÖKULL ICECAP

Although the Vatnajökull icecap and its attendant glaciers look spectacular from the Ring Rd, most travellers will be seized by a wild desire to get even closer.

However, access to Vatnajökull is limited to commercial tours…unless you happen to be set up for a serious polar-style expedition. The icecap is extremely dangerous: the whole thing is riven with deep crevasses, which are made invisible by coverings of fresh snow, and there are often sudden, violent blizzards. But don't be disheartened! It's a mind-blowing experience just to get near the thing, and you can travel way up into the whiteness on organised snowmobile and Jeep tours.

The easiest route up to Vatnajökull is the F985 Jeep track (about 40km east of Jökulsárlón, 55km west of Höfn) to the broad glacial spur Skálafellsjökull. The 16km-long road is practically vertical in places, with iced-over sections in winter. Please don't even think of attempting it in a 2WD car – you'll end up with a huge rescue bill.

At the top, 840m above sea-level, is the **Jöklasel hut** (☎ 478 1703), with a café that must have the most epic views in Iceland. On a clear day you can see 10km across the icecap to towering snowcapped peaks and south towards the ocean – it's like being on top of the world.

From here, one of the most popular tour options is the one-hour **Skidoo ride** (per person Ikr8000). You're kitted out with overalls, boots and gloves, then play follow-the-leader along a fixed trail. It's great fun, and, although it only gives you the briefest introduction to glacier travel, an hour of noisy bouncing about with the stink of petrol in your nostrils is probably enough for most people! If even this sounds like too much, you can take a more sedate **super-Jeep** ride up onto the ice. It's also possible to do longer trips to Breiðamerkurjökull, Grímsvötn, Kverkfjöll, Öræfajökull and Snæfell, as well as cross-country skiing tours (Ikr16,900 per person).

If you don't have your own 4WD transport, from June to August two glacier companies can drive you up to the Jöklasel hut:

Glacier Jeeps (☎ 478 1000; www.glacierjeeps.is) At 9.30am and 2pm daily this company collects people in a super-Jeep from the little parking area at the start of the F985. You're then driven up to Jöklasel, where you can go on a Skidoo ride (Ikr9800) or Jeep tour (Ikr8800) on Vatnajökull – prices include transport from the F985.

Vatnajökull Travel (☎ 894 1616; www.vatnajokull.is) This friendly outfit does more extensive glacier 'packages'. It'll pick you up from Höfn (9.40am), or from the F985 parking area (10.30am), take you up to Jöklasel, where you can do the Skidoo or Jeep thing, and then drive you to Jökulsárlón for a lagoon boat trip. Prices vary according to what you select; for example, there's a pick-up from the F985 parking area plus Skidoo ride (Ikr9800); pick-up from Höfn with Skidoo ride and lagoon boat trip (Ikr14,800); or you can even fly from Reykjavík to indulge in Skidoo and boat trips (Ikr37,200).

Coming from Höfn or Skaftafell, scheduled buses can drop you at the F985 parking area to link up with tours. In summer, there's also a daily bus from Höfn leaving at 9am that goes up to Jöklasel and back, then on to Jökulsárlón, then straight back to Höfn.

and photographs. It's worth a look, not least because it's free.

Höfn is blessed with the most amazing glacier views. There are a couple of short **waterside paths** where you can amble and gape – one by Hótel Höfn, and another round the marshes and lagoons at the end of the promontory Ósland (about 1km beyond the harbour – head for the **seamen's monument** on the rise). The latter path is great for watching **sea birds**, though if you walk to it during nesting season you will be attacked in Hitchcock style by zillions of arctic terns on the causeway road.

The **swimming pool** (☎ 478 1157; Hafnarbraut 11; adult/child Ikr300/135; ⏱ 7am-8.30pm Mon-Fri, 9am-6pm Sat & Sun summer, 7-9am & 4-8pm Mon-Fri, 9am-3pm Sat & Sun winter) has an outdoor heated pool and hot pots.

Höfn has a nine-hole **golf course** at the end of Dalabraut at the northern end of town.

Between May and late September you can go **horse riding** from Gistihúsið Árnanes (see opposite), 6km west of Höfn.

Tours

A visit to this region wouldn't be complete without making a pilgrimage to Vatnajökull – see the boxed text, above.

Festivals & Events

Every year in early July Höfn's annual **Humarhátíð** (Lobster Festival) honours this crunchy crustacean, which is a renowned local catch. There's usually a fun fair, flea markets, dancing, music, ice-sculpture competitions, lots of alcohol and even a few lobsters.

Sleeping

Höfn camp site (☎ 478 1606; camping@simnet.is; Hafnarbraut 52; sites per person Ikr700, sb Ikr2000, 6-person cabins Ikr6500; ☺ mid-May–mid-Sep) Lots of travellers stay at the hilly camp site on the main road into town. There are also 16 good-value log cabins here, with two double and two single beds, and kitchens (but limited cooking equipment).

Nýibær HI Hostel (☎ 478 1736; hofn@hostel.is; Hafnarbraut 8; sb dm Ikr2200, sb tw Ikr5200) At the harbour end of town, Höfn's best budget option is a medium-sized place that's usually bustling with travellers in summer (it's open all year). It's in an old but cosy house with a kitchen, and a dining room that doubles as the common area (where many a glacier tour and long-distance hike has been dissected!). There are also laundry facilities.

Gistiheimilið Hvammur (☎ 478 1503; hvammur3@simnet.is; Ránarslóð 2; sb Ikr2500, s/d Ikr6500/8900; ☐) Run by the same couple that runs the hostel, Hvammur is the pick of the guesthouses for its 30 simple rooms, all with washbasins and satellite TV. Some overlook the boat-filled harbour. There's also a dining area, a guest kitchen and internet access.

Gistiheimilið Ásgarður (☎ 478 1365; asgardur@eldhorn.is; Ránarslóð 3; s/d/tr Ikr8300/10,200/12,300, up to 40% off rest of yr) Harbourside Ásgarður is more like a hotel than a guesthouse. All rooms have bathroom and a small TV, and some have good glacier views. They're a bit boxy, but the guesthouse is in a good location and the people are very friendly. Breakfast costs Ikr950.

Hótel Höfn (☎ 478 1240; www.hotelhofn.is; Vikurbraut; s/d from Ikr12,750/17,500; ☐) Höfn's business-class hotel is often busy with tour groups in summer. All rooms have bathrooms and TVs, and breakfast is included. The rooms are a bit frayed around the edges – even the deluxe ones aren't particularly flash – but perhaps you won't notice the décor if you get one with glacier views. There are a couple of decent restaurants, and discounts are available out of season.

Gistihúsið Árnanes (☎ 478 1550; www.arnanes.is; Jun–Mid-Sep sb Ikr3000, s/d without bathroom Ikr9200/11,400, with bathroom Ikr11,800/14,700, up to 30% off rest of yr)

On the Ring Rd 6km west of Höfn, this rural place is an excellent choice for its cottages and guesthouse rooms (some with balconies). Prices include breakfast. The sleeping-bag accommodation is disappointing, though – with mountain views all around, it seems a shame to be underground! There's an agreeable dining room–art gallery, with set meat and fish courses (from Ikr1800); it opens summeronly if there are enough diners – be sure to book ahead.

Eating & Drinking

Kaffi Hornið (☎ 478 2600; Hafnarbraut 42; ☺ 11am-10pm Mon-Thu, to 1am Fri, noon-1am Sat, noon-10pm Sun; light meals Ikr790-1900, mains Ikr1700-3900) This log-cabin affair is a relaxed, unpretentious bar-restaurant, decorated with old black-and-white photos of the town. The food comes in stomach-stretching portions; as well as burgers, pasta, fish and lamb mains, and a serveyourself salad bar, there are a couple of veggie options and a Höfn speciality – garlic-toasted lobster (Ikr4000).

Ósinn (☎ 478 1240; www.hotelhofn.is; Vikurbraut; mains Ikr690-3900; ☺ 9am-10pm) The family restaurant on the ground floor of Hótel Höfn has a good choice of snacky meals (burgers, pizzas etc), and some of the tastiest fish, meat and pasta mains in town…it's just a shame about the service. If you can put up with bad-tempered staff, go for local fish dishes including Höfn's famous lobster – which you can have here as an á la carte dish or on a pizza! There's a second, smarter dining room on the top floor, with great glacier views.

Víkinn (☎ 478 2300; Víkurbraut) This pizza place and pub lacks character, but it's a popular drinking hole and nightclub, open to 3am on Friday and Saturday nights.

The **11-11** (☎ 478 1205; Hafnarbraut; ☺ 9am-11pm) supermarket and bakery is in the Miðbær shopping centre near the library, while **Krónan** (☎ 478 1204; Vesturbraut; ☺ 11am-7pm) is close to the camp site.

Getting There & Away

AIR

Höfn's airport is about 4km northwest of town. **Flugfélag Íslands** (Air Iceland; ☎ 570 3030; www .airiceland.is) flies year-round between Reykjavík and Höfn (which appears on the website as 'Hornafjörður'). Flights run every day except Tuesday and Saturday, and cost around Ikr7000 one way.

BUS

Buses arrive and depart at the camp site, which is a 10-minute walk from the town centre. A daily Reykjavík–Höfn bus runs from 1 June to 15 September, leaving from either end at 8.30am and arriving at 5pm. At other times of year the bus runs on Tuesday, Thursday, Friday and Sunday only, departing at 12.30pm from Reykjavík and noon from Höfn.

From June to August a bus runs from Höfn (at 9am) up to the Jöklasel hut, on the edge of the Vatnajökull icecap. It stays up there for 2½ hours (giving you time to go snow-mobiling) before heading off to Jökulsárlón, where it stays for one hour, before returning to Höfn.

Höfn–Egilsstaðir buses run daily from 1 June to 31 August (Monday, Wednesday and Friday only in late May and early September). Buses leave from Höfn at 8.30am, calling at Stafafell, Djúpivogur and Berunes. Buses return from Egilsstaðir at 2pm.

LÓNSÖRÆFI

If you're in Iceland to escape the rat race and get in touch with your inner hermit, the nature reserve Lónsöræfi should be on your list. This protected area, east of Höfn, contains some spectacularly colourful rhyolite mountains, as well as the Stafafellsfjöll peaks and the friendly, hospitable farm and hostel Stafafell to the south. There are countless hiking opportunities, from day walks to the long-distance route taking you north to Snæfell.

It's possible to camp at sites in the reserve, and there are mountain huts along the Lónsöræfi–Snæfell hike, which begins (or ends) at the Illikambur parking area. The only road in the reserve is the rough 4WD track that ends at Illikambur. There's nowhere to eat or buy food here, so bring supplies from Höfn or Djúpivogur.

HIKING

There are many easy day hikes in the hills and valleys north of Stafafell, as well as longer hikes towards the southeast of Vatnajökull. Some of these walks require substantial river crossings, so use extreme caution, especially in warm or wet weather. For hiking in Lónsöræfi, the best maps are the *Hornafjörður* 1:100,000 (1986), *Hamarsfjörður* 1:100,000 (1987) and *Snæfell* 1:100,000 (1988) topo sheets.

The Stafafell hostel can provide information and directions for these and other hikes and routes.

Reyðarártindur

This four-hour walk begins 7km east of Stafafell. From the road, it ascends the eastern side of the Reyðará valley and circumnavigates the peak Reyðarártindur, returning to the Ring Rd via the valley **Össurárdalur**, 11km east of Stafafell. Across the Ring Rd near the start of this walk is a **view disc** that names some of the visible natural features.

Hvannagil

This is perhaps the best of the day hikes: a well-marked four- or five-hour walk from Stafafell to Hvannagil, at the end of the road on the eastern bank of the Jökulsá í Lóni. Head up this dramatic rhyolite valley and, after less than 1km, you'll see a sheep track climbing the ridge on your right. At the top of this ridge you'll have a view down Seldalur. Keep to the left side of this valley until you pass the side valley, **Raftagil**, which descends back to the Jökulsá í Lóni. You can pick your way down Raftagil or follow the ridge above the eastern side of Seldalur.

Tröllakrókur

This trip begins at the **Illikambur** parking area (about 20km north of Stafafell), accessible along 4WD Rte F980. From there, it's five or six hours to Egilssel hut at Tröllakrókur, an area of bizarre wind-eroded pinnacles. Above, you can see the tongue of **Öxárfellsjökull**, the eastern extreme of the Vatnajökull icecap. Allow two days for the return trip.

Jökulgilstindar

This two-day trip climbs up to the 1313m-high icecap Jökulgilstindar. Begin by walking from Stafafell up the 4WD track along the eastern bank of **Jökulsá í Lóni**, then continue up the valley through the Austurskógar woods toward **Hnappadalur**. You can either continue up to the headwaters of Hnappadalur or climb steeply to Jökulgilstindar from a short way up the valley. The top has a glacier, and hikers should be experienced with glacier travel before venturing onto the ice.

TOURS

Lónsöræfaferðir (☎ 864 4215) is a man with a mountain bus, who runs tours into Lónsöræfi

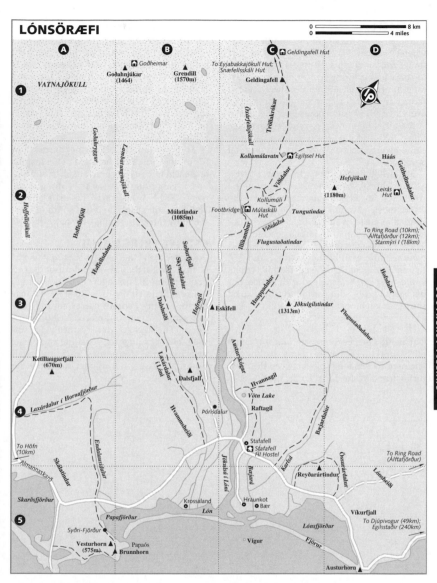

LÓNSÖRÆFI

0 ————— 8 km
0 ————— 4 miles

SOUTHEAST ICELAND

between June and August. You can phone him directly on the mobile number, or book through **Stafafell hostel** (☎ 478 1717; www.eldhorn .is/stafafell).

Visitors can join the day tour (Ikr5000 per person), departing at 9am, which includes approximately three hours at Illikambur and a 45-minute walk to the Múlaskáli hut. Any hikers who want to make their way to Illikambur, where several of the walks that are outlined above begin, can also cadge a lift with this tour (Ikr2500/5000 per person one way/return). Transfers over the Skyndidalsá river crossing cost Ikr1000 one way. Fishing permits and horse-riding tours can also be arranged.

STAFAFELL

In the absolute middle of the middle of no-where, Stafafell is a lonely farm-hostel, lost under the mountains. It makes a great hiking base for exploring Lónsöræfi; you can arrange tours and hikers' transport here, and the farmer and hostel-keeper, Bergsveinn, knows everything there is to know about the area.

Stafafell functioned as a remote parsonage until 1920, and the present church contains some lovely artefacts, including an original altarpiece.

Stafafell HI Hostel (☎ 478 1717; www.eldhorn.is /stafafell; sb Ikr2000, s/d from Ikr4500/6545) is one of the friendliest hostels in Iceland, thanks to the efforts of Bergsveinn, your good-humoured host. The hostel is full of light pine fittings and bright sunshine, and has a peaceful feel. There's also a **camp site** (per person Ikr600) and cottages for hire with kitchen, lounge and TV. In summer breakfast is available for Ikr800, and dinner can be arranged with notice, but it's best to bring your own food (the nearest shop is 25km away in Höfn).

LÓN

The name Lón (Lagoon; pronounced 'lone') fairly sums up the nature of this shallow bay enclosed by two long spits between the Austurhorn and Vesturhorn. To the northwest is the delta of **Jökulsá í Lóni**, where an enormous colony of swans nest in spring and autumn.

As with other peaks in the region, the batholithic **Austurhorn**, at the eastern end of Lón, was formed as an igneous intrusion beneath the surface and was then thrust up and revealed through erosion of the overlying material. This is the best access for strolls on the Fjörur sand spit enclosing the eastern portion of Lón.

At the western end of Lón the commanding 575m-high peak **Vesturhorn** and its companion **Brunnhorn** form a cape between Skarðsfjörður and Papafjörður. Ruins of the fishing settlement Syðri-Fjörður, which was abandoned in 1899, are still visible, and just south of it are the more intriguing ruins of Papatóttir.

GETTING THERE & AWAY

Buses between Höfn and Egilsstaðir pass Stafafell. To board the bus, flag it down at the gate or ask one of the managers to book ahead.

From Stafafell the Ring Rd starts to head north, leaving behind glacier country and following the convoluted coast of the Eastfjords. The stretch from Hvalnes peninsula to Djúpivogur hugs the coastline and passes beneath some frightening rock and shale mountain faces that appear on the verge of a landslide!

The Interior

Travelling in Iceland's interior will give you a new understanding of the word 'desolation'. You may have travelled the Ring Rd thinking that Iceland is light on towns; that sheep seem to outnumber people; that you haven't run across a McDonald's for many a mile. Well, you ain't seen nothing yet. Here there are practically no services, accommodation, hot-dog stands, bridges, mobile-phone signals or guarantees if something goes wrong. Gazing across the expanses, you could imagine yourself in Tibet or Mongolia or, as many people have noted, on the moon. And those aren't overactive imaginations at work – the *Apollo* astronauts actually trained here before their lunar landing.

This isolation, in essence, is the reason that people visit. Although some travellers are disappointed by the interior's ultrableakness, others are humbled by the sublime sight of nature in its rawest, barest form. The solitude is exhilarating, the views are vast, and it's immensely tough but equally rewarding to hike or bike these cross-country routes.

Historically, people used the trails as summer short cuts between north and south, if with heavy hearts. Myths of ghosts and fearsome outlaws spurred travellers along the tracks with all speed. Today it's probably wiser to worry about the weather. Conditions can be fickle and snow isn't uncommon, even in mid summer. Good warm clothing, and face and eye protection from gritty, wind-driven sand are particularly important. Road-opening dates given in this chapter depend on weather conditions – check www.vegagerdin.is for the latest information.

TOP FIVE

- Go swimming inside a volcano: the warm turquoise waters of **Víti crater** (p308), at the Askja caldera, make for unique holiday snaps
- Get an easy taste of the highlands on the **Kjölur Route** (p300), a scheduled bus shortcut between Reykjavík and Akureyri
- Marvel at icy sculptures in the **Kverkfjöll ice caves** (p309), carved out of the glacier by steaming hot springs
- Pity the melancholy ghosts and outlaws on Iceland's longest, loneliest north–south track, the godforsaken **Sprengisandur Route** (p302)
- Pay homage to the Queen of Mountains, **Herðubreið** (p306), before exploring the desolate volcanic wastes at **Askja** (p307)

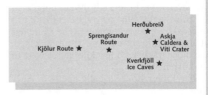

Herðubreið ★
Sprengisandur Route ★
Askja ★ Caldera & Víti Crater
Kjölur Route ★
Kverkfjöll Ice Caves ★

Driving Routes & Mountain Huts

This chapter covers the main interior driving routes and attractions (although see p280 for the popular Landmannalaugar–Þórsmörk trek; and see p276 for the Fjallabak Nature Reserve).

Most of the routes described in this chapter are strictly for high-clearance 4WD vehicles. It's recommended that vehicles travel in pairs, so if one gets bogged or breaks down the other can drag it out, fetch help or carry all passengers to shelter. Carry lots of supplies, especially if you are only taking one vehicle, rather than the recommend two. There are very few petrol stations in the highlands – you should fill up whenever you find one.

Almost all mountain huts in Iceland are operated by **Ferðafélag Íslands** (Iceland's Touring Association; ☎ 568 2533; www.fi.is; Mörkin 6, IS-108 Reykjavík). **Ferðafélag Akureyrar** (Touring Club of Akureyri; ☎ 462 2720; www.ffa.est.is; Strandgata 23, Akureyri) operates all the mountain huts and most camp sites along the Askja Way. It's wise to reserve accommodation in advance, as huts are usually booked out in summer. For more details about mountain-hut accommodation, see p314.

KJÖLUR ROUTE (KJALVEGUR)

If you want to sample Iceland's central deserts but don't like the idea of dangerous ford crossings, the 200km Kjölur Route has had all its rivers bridged. In summer there's even a scheduled bus that uses it as a shortcut between Reykjavík and Akureyri.

Rte 35 starts just past Gullfoss (p120), passing between two glaciers before emerging near Blönduós on the northwest coast. It reaches its highest point (700m) between the Langjökull and Hofsjökull icecaps, near the mountain Kjalfell.

The Kjölur Route is greener and more interesting than its counterpart, Sprengisandur. However, it was historically the less popular of the two, thanks to the general belief that it was infested by fearsome outlaws. The route has altered slightly since it was first established; the older track lies a few kilometres west of the current one.

The Kjölur Route usually opens in early June.

Hvítárvatn

The pale-blue lake Hvítárvatn, 45km northeast of Gullfoss, is the source of the glacial river Hvítá. A glacier tongue of Iceland's second-largest icecap, Langjökull, calves into the lake and creates icebergs, adding to the beauty of this spot.

In the marshy grasslands northeast of Hvítárvatn is Ferðafélag Íslands' first hut, Hvítárnes, built in 1930. The hut is believed to be haunted by the spirit of a young woman. If a female camper sleeps in one particular bed (the bunk on the west wall past the kitchen), it is said she will dream of the ghost carrying two pails of water. From the Kjölur road, where the bus will drop you, it's an 8km walk along the 4WD track to the hut.

Kerlingarfjöll

Until the 1850s Icelanders believed that this mountain range (12km southeast of Rte 35 on Rte F347) harboured the vilest sort of outlaws. It was thought they lived deep in the heart of the 150-sq-km range in an isolated Shangri-la–type valley. So strong was this belief that it was only in the mid-19th century that anyone ventured into Kerlingarfjöll, and it was only in 1941 that the range was properly explored by Ferðafélag Íslands.

It's certainly dramatic. The colourful landscape is broken up into jagged peaks and ridges, the highest of which is Snækollur (1477m), and it's scattered with hot springs. There are plans to harness the geothermal energy, although no industrial buildings scar the landscape here to date.

At **Ásgarður** (☎ 894 2132; www.kerlingarfjoll.is; sites per tent Ikr900, sb Ikr2200-2700, bed linen Ikr900; ☺ mid-Jun–Sep) in Kerlingarfjöll, there are 12 huts and houses with space for 120 people in sleeping bags. There's also a large camp site, a restaurant and hot tubs.

Hrútafell

This relatively tiny 10-sq-km icecap rises 800m above the surrounding landscape. It sits on top of Hrútafell mountain, which is a *móberg* peak – shaped like a birthday cake due to subglacial volcanic eruptions. From the Kjölur Route, as soon as Hrútafell comes into view look on the eastern side of the road for a cairn shaped exactly like a Hershey's Kiss!

Hveravellir

Hveravellir is a popular and enticing geothermal area of fumaroles and multicoloured hot springs (it's important to stay on the boardwalks to avoid damaging this sensitive area). Located 30km north of the Kerlingarfjöll

THE INTERIOR

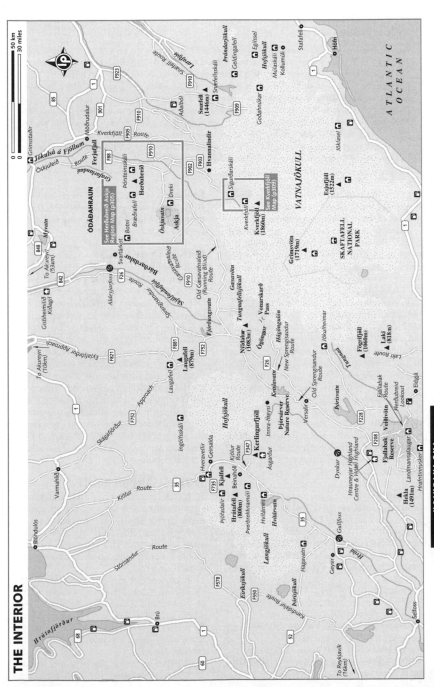

KJÖLURVEGUR TREK

A good preparation for more challenging interior trekking routes is the easy and scenic Kjölurvegur trek from Hvítárvatn to Hveravellir. The trail follows the original horseback Kjölur Route (west of the present road), via the Hvítárnes, Þverbrekknamúli and Þjófadalir mountain huts.

From the Hvítárvatn turn-off it's 8km along the 4WD track to Hvítárnes hut. From there you follow the Fúlakvísl river (14km) to Þverbrekknamúli hut. Continue between the river and Kjalhraun lava field to Þjófadalir hut (14km). A possible detour here is across the lava field to Beinahóll. The final day is a 12km walk to Hveravellir, where you can soak in hot springs. Overall, the marked route is easy to follow and huts are four to six hours apart.

The route can be done in three days at a leisurely pace. Access is by the Kjölur bus (see below), but remember to reserve a seat for the day you want to be picked up.

---

turn-off, Hveravellir is the 'hub' of the Kjölur Route and the finishing point of the Kjölurvegur Trek (see the boxed text, above).

Among its warm pools are the brilliant-blue Bláhver; Öskurhólhver, which emits a constant stream of hissing steam; and a luscious human-made bathing pool. Another hot spring, Eyvindurhver, is named after the outlaw Fjalla-Eyvindur (see the boxed text, p303). Hveravellir is reputedly one of the many hide-outs of this renegade, who spent much of his life hiding from his enemies in the highlands. On a small mound near the geothermal area are the ruins of a shelter where he's believed to have holed up with his wife, Halla, and their family during one 18th-century winter.

There are two busy huts here, owned by Hveravallafélag.

Hofsjökull

Hofsjökull, east of the Kjölur Pass, is the third-largest icecap in the country, measuring 995 sq km. A massive volcanic crater lies underneath the ice.

Sleeping

Mountain huts along or just off the Kjölur Route are maintained by Ferðafélag Íslands, except for the huts at Hveravellir, which are run by **Hveravallafélag** (☎ 894 1293; www.hveravellir .is). All have toilets and a kitchen, and most have running water. From south to north, they are:

Hagavatn (N 64°27.760', W 20°14.700'; sb Ikr1200) Small hut near the southern end of Langjökull, about 15km off the Kjölur Route by 4WD track. No running water.
Hvítárnes (N 64°37.007', W 19°45.394'; sb Ikr1800) Has a warden in July and August; hut sleeps 30.
Þverbrekknamúli (N 64°43.100', W 19°36.860'; sb Ikr1800) About 8km west of Innri-Skúti hill, or about 4km east of the mini-icecap Hrútafell. Sleeps 20.

Þjófadalir (N 64°48.900', W 19°42.510'; sb Ikr1200) Sleeps 12. About 12km southwest of Hveravellir on Rte F735.
Hveravellir (sb Ikr1980) Two huts with a total of 55 sleeping-bag spaces.

Getting There & Away

Daily from 18 June to 7 September a scheduled bus run by **SBA-Norðurleið** (☎ Akureyri 550 0700, Reykjavík 550 0770; www.sba.is) drives between Reykjavík and Akureyri (Ikr8600, nine hours). It sets off at 8am from both ends, stopping briefly at Geysir, Gullfoss and Hveravellir.

In summer 2WD vehicles may be able to travel on this route, but it's not recommended as there are rivers to ford if you venture off the route and your hire-car insurance will be invalid if anything goes wrong. Drivers with 4WD vehicles will have no problems.

Of all the interior routes, Kjölur is probably the best for cycling and hiking. For a humorous account of a bike trip on the Kjölur Route, read Tim Moore's *Frost on My Moustache* (see p21 for details).

SPRENGISANDUR ROUTE

To Icelanders, the name Sprengisandur conjures up images of outlaws, ghosts and long sheep drives across the barren wastes. The Sprengisandur Route (F26) is the longest north–south trail and crosses bleak desert moors that can induce a shudder even today in a 4WD!

Sprengisandur may be less interesting than Kjölur, but it does offer some wonderful views of Vatnajökull, Tungnafellsjökull and Hofsjökull, as well as Askja and Herðubreið from the western perspective. An older route, now abandoned, lies a few kilometres west of the current one.

The Sprengisandur Route proper begins as Rte 842 near Goðafoss in northwest Iceland.

Iceland is a harsh land and does not suffer fools. Rugged terrain and ever-changing weather have led many to their graves.

Cheery notice on a camp-site toilet block

Near where it becomes the F26 you'll find one of Iceland's most photogenic waterfalls, **Aldeyjarfoss**. It flows over a layer of intriguing basalt columns on the Skjálfandafljót in upper Bárðardalur. More basalt patterns can be seen in the shallow canyon above the falls. The route continues southwest through 240km of inhospitable territory all the way to Þjórsárdalur (meeting up with two other approaches about halfway through – see following).

Landmælingar Íslands has a 1:50,000 map of Sprengisandur (Ikr715). The route usually opens on 1 July.

EYJAFJÖRÐUR APPROACH

From the north the F821 from southern Eyjafjörður (south of Akureyri) connects to the Skagafjörður approach at Laugafell. This route is very pleasant, with few tourists, but it's a more difficult drive.

SKAGAFJÖRÐUR APPROACH

From the northwest the 81km-long F752 connects southern Skagafjörður (the nearest town is Varmahlíð on the Ring Rd) to the Sprengisandur Route. The roads join near the lake Fjórðungsvatn, 20km east of Hofsjökull.

Its main site of interest is **Laugafell**, an 879m-high mountain with some nice hot springs bubbling on its northwestern slopes. You can stay nearby at the Ferðafélag Akureyrar **hut** (N 65°01.630′, W 18°19.950′; per person Ikr2000; ⓨ Jul & Aug), with 35 beds, a kitchen and a beautiful geothermally heated pool. Some stone ruins near the springs are reputed to have housed escapees from the Black Death.

Nýidalur

Nýidalur (known as Jökuldalur), the range just south of the Tungnafellsjökull icecap, was only discovered by a lost traveller in 1845. With a camp site, two Ferðafélag Íslands **huts** (☎ summer 854 1194; N 64°44.130′, W 18°04.350′; sb Ikr2000; ⓨ 1 Jul-31 Aug) and lots of hiking possibilities, it makes a great break in a Sprengisandur journey. The huts have kitchen facilities, showers and a summer warden. Nights are particularly chilly here – something to do with the 800m elevation – so bring good warm gear.

Petrol isn't available here. There are two rivers – the one 500m from the hut may be difficult to cross (even for a 4WD). Ask locally for advice on conditions.

Although there aren't any hiking tracks per se, the hiking is great. Soft options include strolling up the relatively lush **Nýidalur valley** or wandering up the 150m-high hill east of the huts for a wide view across the desert expanses. A more challenging day hike will take you up to the colourful **Vonarskarð Pass**, a broad, 1000m-high saddle between

---

OUTLAW COUNTRY

Historically in Iceland, once a person had been convicted of outlawry they were beyond society's protection and aggrieved enemies could kill them at will. Many outlaws, or *útilegumenn*, such as the renowned Eiríkur Rauðe (Erik the Red), voluntarily took exile abroad. Others escaped revenge killing by fleeing into the mountains, valleys and broad expanses of the harsh Icelandic interior, where few dared pursue them.

Undoubtedly, anyone who could live year-round in these bitter, barren deserts must have been extraordinary. Icelandic outlaws were naturally credited with all sorts of fearsome feats, and the general populace came to fear the vast backlands, which they considered to be the haunt of superhuman evil. The *útilegumenn* thereby joined the ranks of giants and trolls, and provided the themes for popular tales, such as the fantastic *Grettir's Saga*.

One particular outlaw has become the subject of countless Icelandic folk tales. Fjalla-Eyvindur, a charming but incurable 18th-century kleptomaniac, fled into the highlands with his family, and continued to make enemies by rustling sheep to keep them all alive. Throughout the interior you'll see shelters and hideouts attributed to him and hear tales of his ability to survive in impossible conditions while always keeping one jump ahead of his pursuers. One of Iceland's best-known folk songs describes how his wife, Halla, threw their newborn child into a waterfall when food was scarce during a harsh winter.

OF BLIZZARDS & BONES

The spookily named Beinahóll (Bone Hill), 4km west of the road near Kjalfell, is the cue for a tragic tale. Although they realised it might be difficult so late in the season, in late October 1780 five farmers decided to return with their new flock of sheep to Skagafjörður along the Kjölur Route. When a blizzard set in they holed up and waited for it to pass, but the storm raged for three weeks without stopping, and all five men perished. Eerily, although the victims' bodies were discovered, when authorities arrived later to collect them two had disappeared.

Today, sheep and horse bones still lie strewn across the macabre hillock, and a memorial stone has been raised by the men's descendants. Icelanders believe that Beinahóll is haunted by the victims of this sad incident, and that to remove any of the bones or disturb the site is to invite permanent bad luck.

Vatnajökull, Tungnafellsjökull and the green Ögöngur hills. This route also passes some active geothermal fields.

Þórisvatn

Before water was diverted from Kaldakvísl into Þórisvatn from the Tungnaá hydroelectric scheme in southwest Iceland, it had a surface area of only 70 sq km. Now it's Iceland's second-largest lake at 82 sq km. It lies 11km northeast of the junction between Rte F26 and the Fjallabak Route.

Hrauneyjar

Somewhat unexpectedly, in the bleakest position imaginable (west of Þórisvatn in the Hrauneyjar region), you'll find a guesthouse and shiny new hotel – the only one in the interior! **Hrauneyjar Highland Centre & Hótel Highland** (☎ guesthouse 487 7782, hotel 487 7750; www .hrauneyjar.is; guesthouse sb from Ikr2250, s/d Ikr6500/9200, hotel s/d from Ikr12,900/16,900; ☼ Jun–mid-Sep) lies at the crossroads of the Sprengisandur Route and the F208 to Landmannalaugar, so it's very handy for lots of highland attractions. The simple guesthouse rooms have shared bathrooms. If you want luxuries – comfy rooms, a restaurant, a sauna, wireless internet…and a helicopter pad – head for the hotel.

Staff can arrange excursions to sites of interest, including the beautiful **Dynkur waterfall**, which is a worthwhile 4WD excursion about 20km north.

Petrol and diesel are available.

Veiðivötn

This beautiful area just northeast of Landmannalaugar is an entanglement of small desert lakes in a volcanic basin, a continuation of the same fissure that produced Laugahraun in the Fjallabak Nature Reserve. This is a wonderful

place for wandering, and you can spend quite a lot of time following 4WD tracks that wind across the tephra sands between the numerous lakes. On the hill to the northeast is a **view disc** pointing out the various lakes and peaks.

Veiðivötn lies 27km off the southern end of the Sprengisandur road south of Þórisvatn, via the F228 4WD road. Access from Landmannalaugar is thwarted by the substantial river Tungnaá, so you'll need private transport to get to Veiðivötn. At Tjaldvatn, below Miðmorgunsalda (650m), is a camp site with huts.

Getting There & Away

From 1 July to 24 August Austurleið buses travel the Sprengisandur Route from Landmannalaugar to Mývatn at 8.30am on Sunday, Tuesday and Thursday (Ikr7200, 10 hours). In the other direction, they depart from Mývatn at 8.30am on Monday, Wednesday and Friday. Although it's a scheduled bus, it's used as a tour, with brief stops at Hrauneyjar, Nýidalur, Aldeyjarfoss and Goðafoss. A small discount is available to Omnibus and Full-Circle Passport holders.

Drivers should note that there's no fuel along the way. The nearest petrol stations are at Akureyri if you come in on the Eyjafjörður approach; at Varmahlíð if you're driving the Skagafjörður approach; at Fosshóll, near Goðafoss, if you're coming from the north along the main route through Bárðardalur; and at Hrauneyjar if you're driving from the south.

ÖSKJULEIÐ ROUTE (ASKJA WAY)

The Öskjuleið Route runs across the interior to Herðubreið, the Icelanders' beloved 'Queen of Mountains'; and to the desert's most popular marvel, the immense Askja crater. The usual access road is Rte F88, which leaves the

Ring Rd 32km east of Mývatn, but Askja is also accessible further east from Rte F910.

For much of the way it's a flat and dull journey, following the western bank of the Jökulsá á Fjöllum, meandering across tephra wasteland and winding circuitously through rough, tyre-abusing encounters with the aptly named 5000-sq-km lava flow Ódáðahraun (Evil Deeds Lava).

Things perk up at the lovely oasis of Herðubreiðarlindir, at the foot of Herðubreið. The route then wanders westwards through dunes and lava flows past the Dreki huts and up the hill toward Askja, where you'll have to leave your car at the Öskjuop car park and walk the remaining 2.5km to the caldera.

From Askja the options are to retrace your whole journey to Rte 1; backtrack slightly onto the F910, heading east towards Egilsstaðir, or west on the Gæsavatnaleið Route (see p308) to Sprengisandur; or head east on the F910 for 22km, then south on the F902 to the Kverkfjöll ice caves (see p309).

Öskjuleið is definitely for 4WD vehicles only. Even mountain buses have been known to get bogged in treacherous sinking sands; in 2000 a tour bus was swept away; and in October 2006 a 67-year-old German woman had to walk 60km back to the Ring Rd when her engine was flooded during a river crossing! The route usually opens in mid-June.

Grafarlandaá

This tributary of the Jökulsá á Fjöllum is the first major stream to be forded on the southbound journey to Herðubreið and Askja. It's reputedly the best-tasting water in Iceland, so fill your bottles here! The banks also make a pleasant picnic spot.

Just past the second stream crossing near Ferjufjall, a short walk from the road takes you to a dramatic canyon being formed by Jökulsá á Fjöllum – a mini Jökulsárgljúfur in the making.

Herðubreiðarlindir

The green oasis Herðubreiðarlindir, a nature reserve thick with green moss, angelica and the pinky-purple flower of the arctic riverbeauty (*Epilobium latifolium*), was created by springs flowing from beneath the Ódáðahraun lava. You get a superb close-up view

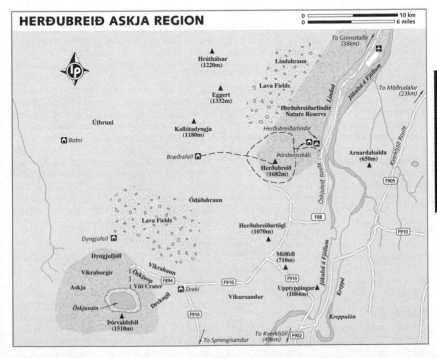

HERÐUBREIÐ ASKJA REGION

THE INTERIOR

CROSSING RIVERS

While trekking or driving in Iceland's interior you'll undoubtedly face unbridged rivers that must be crossed – a frightening prospect for the uninitiated. Don't panic – there are a few simple rules to follow.

Melting snow and ice cause water levels to rise, so the best time to cross is early in the morning before the day warms up, and preferably no sooner than 24 hours after a rainstorm. Avoid narrow stretches, which are likely to be deep – the widest ford will likely be shallowest. The swiftest, strongest current is found near the centre of straight stretches and at the outside of bends. Choose a spot with as much slack water as possible.

Never try to cross just above a waterfall and avoid crossing streams in flood (identifiable by dirty, smooth-running water carrying lots of debris and vegetation). A smooth surface suggests that the river is too deep to be crossed on foot. Anything more than thigh deep isn't crossable without experience and extra equipment.

Before attempting to cross deep or swift-running streams, be sure that you can jettison your pack in midstream if necessary. Unhitch the waist belt and loosen shoulder straps, and remove long trousers and any bulky clothing that will inhibit swimming. Lone hikers should use a hiking staff to probe the river bottom for the best route and to steady themselves in the current.

Never try to cross a stream barefoot – slicing your feet open on sharp rocks will really spoil your holiday. Consider bringing a pair of wet-suit boots or sandals if you want to keep your hiking boots dry. While crossing, face upstream and avoid looking down or you may risk getting dizzy and losing your balance. Two hikers can steady each other by resting their arms on each other's shoulders.

If you do fall while crossing, don't try to stand up. Remove your pack (but don't let go of it), roll over onto your back, and point your feet downstream, then try to work your way to a shallow eddy or to the shore.

Crossing glacial rivers can be very dangerous in a vehicle. It's best to wade across your intended route first, as described above, to check the depth. Work with the water – drive diagonally across in the direction of the current, making sure you're in a low gear. Try to drive steadily, just slightly faster than the water is flowing (too slow and you risk getting stuck, or letting water up the exhaust). If you're not travelling in convoy, consider waiting for other traffic.

of Herðubreið from here (unless, of course, you're greeted by a wall of blowing sand, as is often the case).

The mini–tourist complex has a nature-reserve information office, a **camp site** (sites per tent Ikr800) and the Ferðafélag Akureyrar 30-bed **Þorsteinsskáli hut** (N 65°11.560', W 16°13.390'; sb Ikr1800; mid-Jun–Aug), a pretty cushy lodge with showers, a kitchen and a summer warden.

Behind the hut is another Fjalla-Eyvindur shelter; this one is scarcely large enough to breathe inside. It was renovated in 1922 on the remains of the original, which had long since collapsed. Eyvindur is believed to have occupied it during the hard winter of 1774–75, when he subsisted on angelica root and raw horse meat stored on top of the hideout to retain heat inside.

Herðubreið

Iceland's most distinctive mountain (1682m) has been described as a birthday cake, a cooking pot and a lamp shade, but the tourist industry calls it (more respectfully) the 'Queen of the Desert'. It crops up time and again in the work of Icelandic poets and painters, fascinated by its unquestionable beauty.

If Herðubreið appears to have been made in a jelly mould, that's not far off base. It's another *móberg* mountain, formed by subglacial volcanic eruptions. In fact, if Vatnajökull was to suddenly be stripped of ice, Grímsvötn and Kverkfjöll would probably emerge looking more or less like Herðubreið.

HIKING

The Landmælingar Íslands topographical sheet for this region is No 84, *Herðubreið* 1:100,000 (1986).

From the Þorsteinsskáli hut a marked trail runs to Herðubreið and you can then hike all the way around it in a day. The mountain looks the same from all sides, so disorientation is a possibility, but if you remember that

Kollótadyngja is west–northwest and Herðu-breiðarlindir is east–northeast, orientation shouldn't be too difficult.

Herðubreið was once thought to be un-climbable, but it was eventually scaled in 1908. Under optimum conditions you can climb the mountain in summer over a long day. The route to the top ascends the western slope. It's a difficult climb, and snow, rock falls, land-slides or bad weather may render it impossible without mountaineering gear. From the base to the summit (route unmarked) takes three to 3½ hours each way; allow about 12 hours in total from Heiðubreiðarlindir. Note the two cairns on the rim, which are there to show you the start of the route back down. Don't go alone, prepare for the foulest weather imagi-nable, and remember to inform the attendant at Herðubreiðarlindir of your intentions.

Kollótadyngja

The peak Kollótadyngja (1180m), 10km north-west of Herðubreið, is a textbook example of a shield volcano. Its broad, shieldlike cone oozed lava gently rather than exploded violently. At its base is the Ferðafélag Akureyrar **Bræðrafell hut** (N 65°11.310′, W 16°32.290′; sb lkr1200), which ac-commodates 12 people and has a coal stove but no running water. The best access is the trail leading west from the Herðubreið circuit.

Drekagil

The name of the gorge Drekagil, 35km south-west of Herðubreið, means 'dragon ravine', after the form of a dragon in the craggy rock formations that tower over it. The canyon behind the two Ferðafélag Akureyrar **Dreki huts** (N 65°02.520′, W 16°35.720′; sb lkr2200) resembles something out of Arizona or the Sinai; bitter winds and freezing temperatures just don't suit this desert landscape!

The Dreki huts are an ideal base for a day or two of exploring the area. Not only does the dramatic Drekagil ravine offer an easy stroll up to an impressive waterfall, but you can also walk 8km up the road to Askja. The old and new huts sleep 70, and there are showers, a kitchen, an information centre and a sum-mertime warden. Camping (Ikr800 per tent) is also permitted, but the wind and cold can become oppressive.

At Dreki the Gæsavatnaleið Route (F910) turns off the Öskjuleið to cross some intimi-dating expanses and connect with the Sprengi-sandur Route at Nýidalur. See p302.

Dyngjufjöll

The stark Dyngjufjöll range, which shelters the Askja caldera and the Drekagil gorge, is what remains of a volcanic system that col-lapsed into its magma chamber. Þórvaldsfell, the highest point along its southern rim, rises to 1510m.

This inhospitable territory may be intrigu-ing, but it isn't terribly inviting to the casual hiker. If you come to explore beyond the tracks and footpaths, make careful prepara-tions and take due precautions.

You'll find overnight accommodation at the remote and basic **Dyngjufell hut** (N 65°07.480′, W 16°55.280′; sb lkr1200), also maintained by Fer-ðafélag Akureyrar, west of the caldera.

Askja

Perversely, the cold, windy and utterly desolate Askja caldera is the main destination for all tours in this part of the interior. Bleak and terrible it may be, but this immense 50-sq-km caldera shouldn't be missed. It's difficult to imagine the sorts of forces that created it – pondering the landscape will naturally produce boggling thoughts about the power of nature and the insignificance of us puny humans.

The cataclysm that formed the original Askja caldera happened relatively recently (in 1875, to be exact) when two cu km of tephra was ejected from the Askja volcano, bits of it landing in Continental Europe. Ash from the eruption poisoned quantities of cattle in northern Iceland, sparking a wave of emigra-tion to America. It's quite daunting to realise that such cataclysmic events could be replayed at any time.

After the initial eruption a magma chamber collapsed and created a craterous 11-sq-km hole, 300m below the rim of the original explo-sion crater. This new depression subsequently filled with water and became the sapphire-blue lake **Öskjuvatn**, the deepest in Iceland at 217m. It became the scene of an eerie disappearance in 1907, when German researchers Max Rud-loff and Walther von Knebel went rowing on the lake and then completely vanished; their bodies were never found. It was suggested that the lake may have hazardous quirks, possibly odd currents or whirlpools; but a rickety can-vas boat and icy water could easily explain their deaths. There's a stone **cairn** and memor-ial to the men on the rim of the caldera.

In the 1875 eruption a vent near the north-eastern corner of the lake exploded and formed the tephra crater **Víti**, which contains geothermally heated water. (This is not to be confused with the Víti near Mývatn, p236), whose water is distinctly chilly!). Swimming in this turquoise-blue pool is a real highlight – the temperature (around 25°C) is ideal for swimming. The Icelandic way is to strip off and bathe naturally; if you're shy, bring a swimsuit. The route down is slippery but not as steep as it looks.

Askja has erupted frequently over the last century, and as recently as 1961 the vents at Öskjuop, near the road entrance to the caldera, exploded and formed the Vikraborgir crater row.

Tours

Mývatn Tours runs a very popular 12-hour trip from Reykjahlíð (at Mývatn lake in northeast Iceland) between 20 July and 31 August – bring your own lunch and a towel for swimming. You can also fly over the Askja crater on an hour-long sightseeing flight from Reykjahlíð. See p231 for details on these.

Ferðafélag Akureyrar (☎ 462 2720; www.ffa.is) organises hut-based hiking tours (Ikr48,500 per person) from Þorsteinsskáli hut at Herðubreiðarlindir along the Öskjuleið Route to Svartárkot in upper Bárðardalur. The route runs via the huts at Bræðrafell, Dreki, Dyngjufell and Botni. The tour takes you over the vast Ódáðahraun lava flow and usually runs twice in July. With proper planning, this five-day trip may also be done independently.

Getting There & Away

There's no public transport along the Öskjuleið Route. Take a tour (see above), or hire a 4WD and prepare for a rocky ride.

There are no petrol stations anywhere on the route. The nearest ones are at Mývatn (100km north of Askja), Hrauneyjar (235km from Askja along the F910 west, then the Sprengisandur Route south), and Aðalból (90km from Askja on the F910 east).

GÆSAVATNALEIÐ ROUTE

The 120km-long Gæsavatnaleið Route (F910), also known as the Austurleið (it doesn't pass anywhere near its namesake Gæsavötn), connects the Sprengisandur Route and the Öskjuleið. It's not nearly as treacherous as it once was, since a new road has been built north of the old one and the largest river is now bridged. However, it's still difficult to drive

and you should attempt this route only if you have a lot of 4WD experience. There's little traffic, but the scenery is excellent. The road crosses vast lava fields and sandy stretches, and there are always high icecaps in the background.

The bits over the lava fields are naturally slow going, so plan on one day to drive them. If you report to the warden in Askja that you're going this way, the main concern will be that you don't camp along the way, as much of the route lies inside a nature reserve.

Old Gæsavatnaleið

If anyone tells you that the Gæsavatnaleið is impossible, they're speaking of the old southern route best known as the road followed by the escaping hero, Alan Stewart, in Desmond Bagley's thriller *Running Blind*. It's not really impossible, but as yet no tour company is willing to brave it and, with the opening of the new Gæsavatnaleið, the route isn't being maintained. As a result, this is one of Iceland's roughest journeys, notorious for floods and deep sand drifts. It should be tackled only with at least two hardy 4WDs if you really know what you're doing, and it's imperative that you ask for advice before venturing out.

KVERKFJÖLL ROUTE

As its name suggests, this 108km-long route creeps southwards to the amazing Kverkfjöll ice caves. It connects Möðrudalur (65km east of Mývatn, off the Ring Rd) to the Sigurðarskáli hut, 3km from the lower caves, via the F905, F910 and F902.

Along the way are several sites of interest, including the twin pyramid-shaped Upptyppingar hills near the Jökulsá á Fjöllum bridge, and the Hvannalindir oasis where there is – you guessed it – another of good ol' Fjalla-Eyvindur's winter hide-outs! He even built a rather hi-tech sheepfold at this one, so the animals could visit the stream without having to face the elements. Hvannalindir lies about 30km north of the Sigurðarskáli hut.

After visiting Askja (see p307), you can follow up with a trip to Kverkfjöll by driving south on Rte 902.

The 85-bed **Sigurðarskáli hut** (N 64°44.850′, W 16°37.890′; sb Ikr2000) and camp site can be booked through **Ferðalag Fljótsdalshéraðs** (☎ 20 Jun-15 Sep 853 6236, rest of yr 863 5813; ferdafelag@egilsstadir.is).

Kverkfjöll usually opens in mid- to late June.

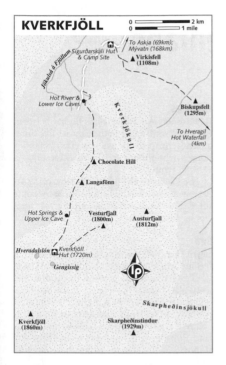

KVERKFJÖLL

the roof – don't enter the ice caves or you risk being caught in their heated combat. There's also a danger of sulphur inhalation.

Kverkfjöll

Kverkfjöll is actually a mountain spur capped by the ice of Kverkjökull, a northern tongue of Vatnajökull. Over time, it's also come to refer to the hot-spring-filled ice caves that often form beneath the eastern margin of the Dyngjujökull ice.

When hiking in this area be sure to carry plenty of water, as only silty glacial water is available higher up.

LOWER KVERKFJÖLL ICE CAVES

Besides being the source of the roiling Jökulsá á Fjöllum, central Iceland's greatest river, Kverkfjöll is also one of the world's largest geothermal areas. The lower Kverkfjöll ice caves lie 3km from the Sigurðarskáli hut, a half-hour return walk from the 4WD track's end.

Here the hot river flows beneath the cold glacier ice, clouds of steam swirl over the river and melt shimmering patterns on the ice walls, and there you have it – a spectacular tourist attraction. Perhaps this was the source of the overworked fire-and-ice cliché that pervades almost everything ever written about Iceland. Huge blocks of ice frequently crash down from

UPPER KVERKFJÖLL ICE CAVES & HUT

From the lower ice caves, the tours continue up onto the glacier itself. After an hour climbing up the glacier tongue, they stop at a nunatak called **Chocolate Hill** to stoke up energy. From there it's a stiff 1½-hour hike up **Langafönn** to the upper ice caves and geothermal area, where sulphur and rhyolite silt combine with the steam heat to create some of the gooiest mud imaginable. The caves here are larger than the lower ones – 2.5km long – but they aren't quite as impressive.

It's then a 40-minute climb to the Icelandic Glaciological Society's six-bunk **Kverkfjöll hut**, at 1720m. There's no water or heating, but it makes a viable icecap base. Nearby is the beautiful lagoon **Gengissig**, which was formed in a small volcanic eruption in 1961. Another hour beyond the hut will take you to the highest peak of western **Kverkfjöll** (1860m), with a fine view over the *kverk* (gap) through which the Kverkfjöll glacier passes.

HIKING

A one-hour marked hike from behind Sigurðarskáli hut will take you up **Virkisfell**. At the top is an amazing natural bridge and a spectacular view over Kverkfjöll and the headwaters of the Jökulsá á Fjöllum.

There's a five-hour return hike from Sigurðarskáli hut to the 30°C hot river in **Hveragil**, where you can bathe in a hot waterfall. The wardens at the hut can provide specific directions.

Tours

Without a robust 4WD vehicle the only way to visit Kverkfjöll is on a tour. The most popular and easiest to join is the three-day **Askja–Kverkfjöll–Vatnajökull tour** (www.sba.is; ☎ Akureyri 550 0700, Reykjavík 550 0770), run by SBA-Norðurleið. It leaves on Monday from 9 July to 20 August from Akureyri (Ikr21,500, 8.30am) and Mývatn (Ikr21,000, 11am).

'Tour' is slightly misleading. You really just get a bus ride and a guide for your money, and must bring your own food and organise accommodation (either book a hut or bring a tent). Hiking boots or other strong footwear, a sleeping bag and warm clothing are essential.

THE INTERIOR

Gateway to Greenland & the Faeroes

CONTENTS

For many visitors Iceland provides a stepping stone to the wild, mysterious lands of Greenland and the Faeroes. Both are easily accessible and, although the journey may seem expensive, once you've come this far it's more cost effective than planning a separate trip. Air Iceland's regular summer flights to Kulusuk, Nerlerit Inaat (Constable Point) and Narsarsuaq make it easy to tag on a trip to Greenland, while regular flights to Vágar in the Faeroes allow you to discover these little-visited islands once used as a stopping point for Viking explorers.

GETTING THERE & AWAY
Air
GREENLAND

Iceland's main domestic carrier, **Air Iceland** (Flugfélag Íslands; ☎ in Iceland 570 3030; www.airiceland .is), flies from the domestic airport in Reykjavík to Kulusuk in east Greenland (two hours, Monday to Saturday June to mid-September) and twice weekly to Nerlerit Inaat (two hours) further north and Narsarsuaq in south Greenland (three hours). In winter there are twice-weekly flights to Kulusuk and one flight per week to Nerlerit Inaat. The cheapest one-way fare on all flights to Greenland is Ikr16,500.

The isolated communities of Kulusuk and Nerlerit Inaat serve as jumping-off points for Tasiilaq and Ittoqqortoormiit respectively. **Air Greenland** (☎ 34 34 34; www.airgreenland.com) runs a helicopter service from Kulusuk to Tasiilaq (Dkr1081) and from Nerlerit Inaat to Ittoqqortoormiit (Dkr625).

Twice-weekly Air Greenland flights go from Kulusuk to Kangerlussuaq (Dkr2616 one way, 1¾ hours), where you can connect to any community on the west or south coast.

FAEROES

In summer, Air Iceland has flights between Reykjavík and Vágar in the Faeroes five times a week (cheapest one-way fare Ikr13,000, 1¼ hours), while there are flights three times a week in winter.

The Faeroese airline **Atlantic Airways** (☎ 341 000; www.atlanticairways.com) covers the same route three times weekly throughout the year for a similar fare.

Sea

Smyril Line (www.smyril-line.com) car ferries link Iceland to Denmark and Norway, and travel via Tórshavn in the Faeroes. In summer the ferry also brings passengers from Scotland (currently from Lerwick in the Shetlands but possibly direct from Aberdeen in future). If you're travelling between Iceland and mainland Europe, you'll get a two- or three-day stopover in the Faeroes either there or back. See p328 for details.

TOURS

To get the most out of a short trip to Greenland or the Faeroes you may wish to join an organised tour. Day trips to Greenland include cultural activities laid on by local Inuit villagers but are very artificial; to experience any sense of real life you need to stay overnight. Kulusuk and nearby Tasiilaq are among Greenland's most traditional communities, and they offer excellent opportunities for hiking, dogsledding, ski-trekking and kayaking. Most tours to Greenland can be expanded to take in remote Ittoqqortoormiit, from where you can access the exceptionally beautiful but little-visited Northeast Greenland National Park.

Operators in Greenland and Iceland:

Air Iceland (www.airiceland.is) Runs popular Greenland day tours (Ikr33,865 to Ikr43,745, Monday to Saturday mid-May to mid-September), and a two-night package to Tasiilaq (Ikr81,550 to Ikr97,400).

Nonni Travel (Map p213; ☎ 461 1841; www.nonni travel.is; Brekkugata 5, IS-602 Akureyri) Has a great range of adventure trips around Greenland, including dogsledding, ski-trekking, hiking and cultural tours in Scoresby Sund, Ittoqqortoormiit and Narsarsuaq. Also helps plan and prepare itineraries for independent travel in the Faeroes. Day tours to Greenland from Akureyri cost Ikr39,590 to Ikr49,210.

Red House (☎ 981650; www.east-greenland.com; PO Box 81, Naparngumut B 1025, DK-3913 Tasiilaq) Socially-responsible Greenlandic company offering a huge range of hiking, trekking, skiing, climbing, dogsledding, kayaking and hunting trips with experienced guides. Also offers daytrippers to Kulusuk a chance to cruise through the icebergs and take a dogsled tour on a glacier.

Other operators:

Arctic Adventure (☎ 33 25 32 21; www.arctic-adventure .dk; 30 Reventlowsgade, DK-1651 Copenhagen V) Danish company offering well-organised hotel-based tours around Iceland and trips across to Greenland.

Arcturus Expeditions (☎ 01432-850886; www.arcturus expeditions.co.uk; PO Box 41, Hereford, HR1 9DP) English polar specialist, with a range of dogsledding, hiking and skiing trips to Greenland as well as cruises throughout the arctic.

Discover the World (☎ 01737-218800; www.discover -the-world.co.uk; 29 Nork Way, Banstead, Surrey, SM7 1PB) Friendly and popular British tour operator to Iceland, Greenland and Scandinavia, with plenty of adventure and wildlife itineraries.

Great Canadian Travel Company (☎ 204-949 0199; www.greatcanadiantravel.com; 158 Fort St, Winnipeg, Manitoba RC3 1C9) Canadian operator with various activity-based tours to Iceland and Greenland.

Nordwind Reisen (☎ 08331 87073; www.nordwind reisen.de; Maximilianstrasse 17, D-87700 Memmingen) German company offering a huge range of tours around Iceland, Greenland and the Faeroes, with accommodation in hotels, farmhouses and hostels.

Regent Holidays (☎ 01983-864212; www.regent -holidays.co.uk; 31a High St, Shanklin, Isle of Wight, PO37 6JW) English company with an extensive range of guided and independent tours of Iceland and Greenland.

Scantours (☎ 800-223 7226; www.scantours.com; 3439 Wade St, Los Angeles, CA 90066-1533) American company running four- to eight-day trips from Iceland to the Faeroes plus many other Greenland and Iceland tours.

GREENLAND

As remote, wild and exotic as Iceland may seem to first-time visitors, it's positively pedestrian when compared to the splendours of Greenland. Nothing quite prepares you for the raw power of nature and the majestic scenery of this incredible place. Four times the size of France but with a population of just 56,500, it's a truly wild and humbling country. The sheer vastness of the icecap, the size of the icebergs, the tenacity of the wildlife and the stoical attitude of the wonderful people will stay with you for life.

Travel here requires a combination of plane and helicopter flights and ferries through ice-berg-strewn bays. Once at your destination you can choose to hike, ski, dogsled or kayak around the local area to see the towering peaks on the east coast, the gargantuan icebergs in Disko Bay or the surprisingly green fields of the south. Independent travel is easy to arrange, but there are plenty of all-inclusive packages if you'd rather let someone else do the planning.

For more information on Greenland, contact **Greenland Tourism** (☎ 32 83 38 80; www.green land-guide.gl, www.greenland.com; PO Box 1139, Strandgade 91, DK-1010, Copenhagen). Alternatively, pick up Lonely Planet's *Greenland & the Arctic*.

FAEROES

Flung out into the North Atlantic, halfway between Norway and Iceland, the Faeroes seem almost to lie on the edge of the earth. Their remote location and low media profile lend them a genuine air of mystery, and in many ways the fiercely independent residents of these 18 wind-scoured islands remain closer to their Viking roots than any of their neighbours.

Their ancestors can be traced back to the first seafaring explorers who set out from southern Norway in the 9th century and claimed Orkney, the Shetland Islands, Iceland and Greenland – and maybe even America. Today most people earn a living from farming or fishing and the laid-back atmosphere of the small and cosy villages is more reminiscent of the Scottish islands than Iceland. The landscape, too, resembles the Scottish highlands with Munro-like peaks and towering grass-topped sea cliffs, mobbed by nesting sea birds.

The capital, Tórshavn, is on the west coast of the largest island, Streymoy, while the airport is on Vágar, the next island south. Car ferries and tunnels link the various islands, providing access to remote fishing and farming villages and humbling ocean landscapes. Somehow, this is exactly how you expect the North Atlantic to look.

For more information on the Faeroes, contact the **Faroe Islands Tourist Board** (☎ 298 355 800; www .tourist.fo; undir Bryggjubakka 17; FO-110 Tórshavn, Faroe Islands), or see www.faroeislands.com.

Directory

CONTENTS

ACCOMMODATION

There's no shortage of accommodation in Iceland and a huge range of places to stay, from luxury hotels to mountain huts, camp sites, hostels, homely farmhouses, guesthouses and summer hotels set in rural schools. Iceland's best-kept secret is the sleeping-bag option (designated 'sb' in this guide) offered by numerous guesthouses and some hotels. For a fraction of the normal cost you'll get a bed without a duvet or blanket; just bring your own sleeping bag and you can keep costs down substantially.

In this guide accommodation reviews are listed according to price, with budget doubles costing up to Ikr9000, midrange doubles

Ikr9000 to Ikr18,000, and top-end doubles going for more than Ikr18,000. Many hotels and guesthouses close during the winter; where this is the case, opening times are shown in the review. If no opening times are shown, accommodation is open all year. We've given summer prices throughout; in winter most guesthouses and hotels offer discounts of between 20% and 45%. Between June and mid-August it's a good idea to book all accommodation in advance.

Camping

Tjaldsvæði (organised camp sites) are found in almost every town, at farmhouses in rural areas and along major hiking trails. The best sites have washing machines, cooking facilities and hot showers, but others just have a cold-water tap and a toilet block.

Wild camping is possible in some areas but in practice is often discouraged. In national parks and nature reserves you must camp in marked camp sites, and you need to get permission before camping on fenced land in all other places. Icelandic weather is notoriously fickle, though, and if you intend to camp it's wise to invest in a good-quality tent.

When camping the usual rules apply: leave sites as you find them, use biodegradable soaps, carry out your rubbish and bury your toilet waste away from water sources. Campfires are not allowed, so bring a stove. Butane cartridges and petroleum fuels are available in petrol stations and hardware shops, though you can often pick up partly-used canisters left behind by departing campers at the camp sites in Reykjavík and Keflavík.

Camping with a tent or campervan/caravan usually costs between Ikr600 and Ikr800 per person, with most camp sites open from June to August only. The free directory *Útilega – Tjaldsvæði Íslands* (available from tourist offices) lists many of Iceland's camp sites.

Emergency Huts

ICE-SAR (Icelandic Association for Search & Rescue; ☎ 570 5900; www.icesar.is) and **Félag Íslenskra Bifeiðaeigenda** (Icelandic Automobile Association; ☎ 562 9999; www.fib.is) maintain bright-orange survival huts on high mountain passes and along remote coastlines. The huts are stocked with food, fuel and blan-

PRACTICALITIES

- Iceland uses the metric system – distances are in kilometres and weights are in kilograms.
- The electrical current is 240V AC 50Hz (cycles); North American electrical devices will require voltage converters.
- Most electrical plugs are of the European two-pin type.
- Iceland uses the PAL video system, like Britain and Germany, and falls within DVD zone 2.
- The daily free paper *Morgunblaðið* is in Icelandic but features cinema listings in English.
- For tourist-oriented articles about Iceland in English, check out the glossy quarterly magazine **Iceland Review** (www.icelandreview.is).
- Iceland's two TV stations show Icelandic programmes during the day and American imports in the evening.
- Radio station RUV (Icelandic National Broadcasting Service, FM 92.4/93.5) has news in English at 7.30am Monday to Friday.
- Most hostels and hotels have satellite TV featuring other European channels.

kets and should only be used in an emergency. Users should sign the hut guestbook stating which items have been used, so they may be replaced for future users.

Farmhouse Accommodation

Throughout Iceland accommodation is available in rural farmhouses, many of which offer camping and sleeping-bag space as well as made-up beds and summer cabins. Most either provide meals or have a guest kitchen, some have outdoor hot pots (hot tubs) or a geothermal swimming pool, and many provide horse riding. A sign by the roadside signals which farmhouses provide accommodation and what facilities they offer. Rates are similar to guesthouses in towns with sleeping-bag accommodation costing Ikr1800 to Ikr3000 and made-up beds from Ikr3000 to Ikr5500 per person. Breakfast costs about Ikr900, while an evening meal (usually served at a set time) costs Ikr1800 to Ikr3000.

About 150 farmhouses are members of **Ferðaþjónusta Bænda** (Icelandic Farm Holidays; Map pp68-9; ☎ 570 2700; www.farmholidays.is; Síðumúli 2, IS-108 Reykjavík), which publishes an annual members' guide. Twenty-five are wheelchair accessible – see the website for details.

Guesthouses

The Icelandic term *gistiheimilið* (guesthouse) covers a wide variety of properties from family homes renting out a few rooms to custom-built minihotels. These places can vary enormously in character from stylish, contemporary options to others overwhelmed by net curtains and chintzy décor. Most include a buffet-style breakfast in the price (expect to pay about Ikr900 if not), and some also offer sleeping-bag accommodation and have guest kitchens.

As a general guide, sleeping-bag accommodation costs Ikr1800 to Ikr3500 (not including breakfast), double rooms from Ikr5000 to Ikr11,000 and self-contained units from Ikr6000 to Ikr15,000 per night.

Many Icelandic guesthouses open only from June to August; others take in students in the winter months – especially in Reykjavík.

Hotels

Every major city and town has at least one business-style hotel, usually with comfortable but innocuous rooms with private bathroom, phone, TV and sometimes minibar. The hotels also have decent restaurants serving vaguely Icelandic food. Summer prices for singles/doubles start at Ikr9000/11,000 and include a buffet breakfast. Prices can drop substantially outside peak season (June to mid-September),

BOOK ACCOMMODATION ONLINE

For more accommodation reviews and recommendations by Lonely Planet authors, check out the online booking service at www.lonelyplanet.com. You'll find the true, insider lowdown on the best places to stay. Reviews are thorough and independent. Best of all, you can book online.

and many hotels offer cheaper rates if you make your booking on the internet. Two of the largest local chains are **Fosshótels** (☎ 562 4000; www .fosshotel.is), and **Icelandair Hotels** (☎ 444 4000; www .icehotels.is), whic also runs the Edda chain (see below).

Holders of a **Skanplus card** (www.skanplus.com; €12) receive discounts of 10% to 40% on all Fosshótels.

SUMMER HOTELS

Once the school holidays begin, many schools and colleges become summer hotels offering simple accommodation in rooms or in a classroom. Summer hotels open from early June to late August and are run by local town or village councils or by **Edda Hótels** (☎ 444 4000; www.hoteledda.is). All Edda hotels have their own restaurant, and many have geothermal swimming pools. The four Edda PLUS hotels are three-star places where all rooms have private bathroom, TV and phone. Expect to pay Ikr1700 to Ikr2200 for sleeping-bag accommodation, Ikr5800/7200 for a single/double with washbasin and Ikr10,3000/12,900 for a single/double at an Edda PLUS.

Mountain Huts

Private walking clubs and touring organisations maintain *sæluhús* (mountain huts) on many of the popular hiking tracks around the country. The huts are open to anyone and offer sleeping-bag space in basic dormitories. Some also have cooking facilities, camp sites and a warden. The huts at Landmannalaugar and Þórsmörk are accessible by 4WD, and you can get to the huts in Hornstrandir by boat, but most are only accessible on foot. Even so, it's a really good idea to book with the relevant organisation as places fill up quickly.

The main organisation providing mountain huts is **Ferðafélag Íslands** (Icelandic Touring Association; Map pp68-9; ☎ 568 2533; www.fi.is; Mörkin 6, IS-108 Reykjavík), which owns 34 huts around Iceland, some maintained by local walking clubs. The best huts have showers, kitchens, wardens and potable water; they cost Ikr2200 for nonmembers. Simpler huts cost Ikr1200 for nonmembers and usually just have bed space, toilet and a basic cooking area. Camping is available at some huts for around Ikr800 per person. GPS coordinates for huts are included in the destination chapters.

The following also provide huts:

Austurleið SBS (☎ 898 0355; www.austurleid.is) At Húsadalur in Þórsmörk.
Ferðafélag Akureyrar (Touring Club of Akureyri; Map p213; ☎ 472 2720; www.ffa.is) Runs huts and most camp sites in the northeast, including the Askja Way.
Útivist (☎ 562 1000; www.utivist.is) At Básar and Fimmvörðuháls Pass in Þórsmörk.

Summer Houses

The summer house is a national institution in Iceland, with small self-catering cottages in natural beauty spots all over the country. Some Icelanders rent out their summer homes in high season for about Ikr25,000 to Ikr30,000 per three-night stay (minimum required) or Ikr44,000 to Ikr65,000 per week. Many advertise through **Viatour** (☎ 425 0300; www.viatour.is).

Youth Hostels

Iceland has 26 excellent youth hostels, administered by the **Bandalag Íslenskra Farfugla** (Icelandic Youth Hostel Association; ☎ 553 8110; www.hostel.is; Sundlaugavegur 34, IS-105 Reykjavík). All hostels offer hot showers, cooking facilities, luggage storage and sleeping-bag accommodation, and most offer private rooms. If you don't have a sleeping bag, you can hire sheets and blankets for Ikr600 per stay. Many hostels close for the winter, so check reviews in this book or online for information on opening times.

Members of **Hostelling International** (HI; www .hihostels.com) pay Ikr1600 to Ikr1900 for a dorm bed; nonmembers pay roughly Ikr300 extra per night. Single/double/triple rooms cost roughly Ikr3900/6600/8250. Children aged five to 12 years pay half price. To become a member you should apply in your home country before travelling.

ACTIVITIES

Iceland's dramatic scenery, vast tracts of wilderness and otherworldly atmosphere make it a superb playground for outdoor enthusiasts. The rugged interior and scenic coastline offer some fantastic opportunities for hiking (p52) – Þórsmörk, Landmannalaugar and Hornstrandir are particularly popular destinations – as well as horse riding (p53). Sea kayaking (p55) through dramatic fjordland scenery is also popular in many towns around the coast, and sea angling is also gaining in popularity. With Iceland's light traffic, cycling (p51) is a fantastic way to travel there. The majestic icecaps offer stunning scenery for ice trekking (p54), snowmobiling (p55) or for the more experienced – ice climbing (p54) – while the meltwater forms mighty rivers that provide plenty of whitewater rafting (p56) opportunities. During the winter months skiing (downhill and cross-country, p55) and snowboarding (p55) are popular, and a range of newer activities such as diving (p51), potholing and snowkiting (p55) are just beginning to take off. For something more leisurely, almost every town has a geothermal swimming pool and a golf course, and many coastal areas offer fantastic opportunities for bird-watching (p51) and whale watching (p56).

BUSINESS HOURS

Reviews throughout this book do not mention opening hours unless they differ from the standard opening hours below:

Banks 9.15am to 4pm Monday to Friday.

Café-bars 10am to 1am Sunday to Thursday and 10am to between 3am and 6am Friday and Saturday.

Cafés 10am to 6pm.

Off-licences (liquor stores) Variable; many outside Reykjavík only open for a couple of hours per day.

Offices 8am to 4pm Monday to Friday.

Petrol stations 9am to 10pm.

Post offices 8.30am or 9am to 4.30pm or 5pm Monday to Friday.

Restaurants 11.30am to 2.30pm and 6pm to 10pm.

Shops 9am to 6pm Monday to Friday, 10am to noon or 4pm Saturday.

Supermarkets 10am to 11pm.

CHILDREN

Iceland is a fairly easy place to travel with children, and although there aren't many activities provided especially for younger travellers, the dramatic scenery, abundance of swimming pools, and the friendliness of the locals help to keep things running smoothly. For more general advice on travelling with children, look for Lonely Planet's *Travel with Children*.

Practicalities

Children are warmly welcomed in Iceland and a range of discounts on transport and admission fees reflects this. On internal flights and tours with Air Iceland, children aged two to 11 years pay half fare and infants under two fly free, while most bus and tour companies offer a 50% reduction for children aged four to 11 years. Most tour companies and almost all museums and swimming pools offer 50% discounts for children under 12.

The changeable weather and frequent cold and rain may put you off camping as a family, but children aged two to 12 are usually charged half price for farmhouse and some other accommodation. Under twos can usually stay free. The larger hotels usually have cots and children's menus available, but you'll rarely find these in guesthouses. Many restaurants in Reykjavík and larger towns offer discounted children's meals, and most have high chairs.

Toilets at museums and other public institutions usually have dedicated nappy-changing facilities; elsewhere, you'll have to improvise. Attitudes to breast feeding in public are generally relaxed. Formula, nappies and other essentials are available everywhere, but it's hard to find child-care facilities. Best bet is to ask at the tourist office.

All the international car-hire companies offer child seats for an extra cost (these should be booked in advance), but you may want to bring your own to be safe. All cars in Iceland have front and rear seatbelts, including taxis. Buses sometimes have belts, but these are not compatible with child seats.

Sights & Activities

Once you've decided on a family holiday in Iceland one of the biggest considerations will be what to see and where to go, as distances can be long between attractions. It may be a good idea to limit yourself to one particular part of the island in order to avoid boredom-induced tantrums and frequent bouts of carsickness.

Reykjavík is the most child-friendly place in Iceland simply because it has the greatest variety of attractions and facilities. The family fun park and zoo (p79) are popular attractions, and local children can be seen feeding the birds on Tjörnin (p78) every day. The most suitable museums for older children are the open-air Árbæjarsafn (p76) and the dramatic Saga Museum (p75).

Almost every town in Iceland has a geothermal swimming pool, often with a children's play pool, water slides, and hot pots where adults can relax while the children play. Another activity ideal for children is whale watching – top spots include Reykjavík (p75), Húsavík (p241), Keflavík (p108) and Ólafsvík (p164). The short, mild-mannered Icelandic horses appear to have been specifically bred with children in mind, and horse farms all over the country offer riding by the hour from Ikr2500 – see p53.

Children will also enjoy some of the more lively geothermal areas, such as Geysir (p120), where the Strokkur geyser erupts at 10-minute intervals, and Mývatn (p227), where the abundance of odd features, lava fields and steaming vents can provide several days of entertainment for families. If you're driving long distances, the waterfalls just off Rte 1 in southwest Iceland are worthwhile detours to keep children amused, and the glaciers Sólheimajökull (p139) and Vatnajökull (p279) are also right next to the main road. Adults and children alike find the icebergs at Jökulsárlón (p291) fascinating and walks around lava fields can be spiced up with tales of elves and other little people – elf-spotting tours are available in Hafnarfjörður (p103).

CLIMATE CHARTS

Icelandic weather is unpredictable at the best of times, with bright, sunny days reverting to

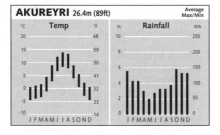

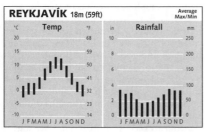

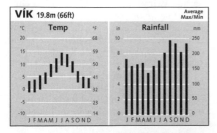

cold, wet and miserable conditions within a matter of hours. Rainfall in Iceland is fairly consistent throughout the year, but, because temperatures plummet in winter, it often falls as snow from September to May. The south and west coasts are usually the wettest parts of the country, with the north and east enjoying generally drier but colder conditions in winter. Areas with geothermal activity are often noticeably warmer than surrounding areas. Temperatures drop considerably as you go up into the mountains, particularly around the icecaps. For more information on weather in Iceland and the best time to travel, see p19.

COURSES

It is possible to study in Iceland, but most of the courses on offer are only open to exchange students in the process of studying for a relevant academic qualification at a university overseas. One summer course that is open to nonstudents is the **Snorri Program** (☎ 551 0165; www .snorri.is; Óðinnsgata 7, Reykjavík, IS-101 Reykjavík), a residential work and study programme aimed at Americans with Icelandic ancestors. The **Sigurður Nordal Institute** (☎ 562 6050; www.nordals.hi.is) offers a 70-hour summer course in Icelandic that combines classroom learning with museum visits and excursions. The University of Iceland and **Denmark's International Study Program** (www.dis.dk) offer a six-week course, including various field trips, examining the unique biology and geology of Iceland.

Most horse farms, sea-angling operators and ski fields also offer lessons in their respective fields.

CUSTOMS

Iceland has quite strict import restrictions. Duty-free allowances for travellers over 20 years of age are 1L of spirits (22% to 79% alcohol) and 1L of wine, or 6L of foreign beer (instead of wine or spirits). Alternatively, you can just bring in 2.25L of wine. People over 18 can bring in 200 cigarettes or 250g of other tobacco products. You can also import up to 3kg of food (except raw eggs, meat or dairy products), provided it doesn't cost more than Ikr13,000. This may help self-caterers to reduce costs.

To prevent contamination, recreational fishing and horse-riding clothes and equipment require a veterinarian's certificate stating that they have been disinfected. Alternatively, officials can disinfect gear when you arrive (Ikr1800 to Ikr2200).

Many people bring their cars on the ferry from Europe – special duty-waiver conditions apply for visitors staying up to one month, but vehicles cannot be sold without payment of duty.

Permits must be obtained in advance to import firearms, drugs, plants, radio transmitters and telephones (except GSM mobile phones). Contact the **Directorate of Customs** (☎ 560 0300; www.tollur.is; Tryggvagötu 19, 150 Reykjavík). Animals can only be brought in with the permission of the authorities and must be quarantined. Plants, animals (including bird eggs and eggshells) and 'natural objects' (particularly stalagmites and stalactites) may not be taken out of Iceland.

For a full list of customs regulations, see www.tollur.is.

Any purchases you make in Iceland over Ikr4000 (at a single point of sale) may be eligible for a 15% VAT refund. Shops offering VAT refunds display a special 'tax-free shopping' sign in the window. You'll need to fill out a form in the shop and present it at the airport, ferry terminal or some tourist offices before you leave to collect your rebate. Note that goods must be exported within 30 days of purchase. See www.icelandrefund.com for details of the scheme.

DANGERS & ANNOYANCES

Iceland has a very low crime rate and in general any risks you'll face while travelling here are related to the unpredictable weather and the geological conditions.

Whether travelling in summer or winter, visitors need to be prepared for inclement conditions. The weather in Iceland can change without warning, and it's essential for hikers to get a reliable weather forecast before setting off – call ☎ 902 0600 or visit www.vedur.is /english for a daily forecast in English. Extreme cold can be dangerous when walking around glaciers and throughout the country in winter, so proper clothing is essential. Even those driving in winter should carry food, water and blankets in their car. Emergency huts are provided in places where travellers run the risk of getting caught in severe weather, and car-hire companies can provide snow tyres or chains in winter.

When hiking, river crossings can be dangerous, with glacial runoff turning trickling streams into raging torrents on warm summer days. High winds can create vicious sand-storms in areas where there is loose volcanic sand. It's also worth nothing that hiking paths in coastal areas are often only accessible at low tide, so seek local advice and obtain the relevant tide tables from the **Icelandic Hydrographic Service** (☎ 545 2000; Seljavegur 32, IS-101 Reykjavík).

When visiting geothermal areas, stick to boardwalks or obviously solid ground, avoiding thin crusts of lighter-coloured soil around steaming fissures and mud pots. You also need to be careful of the water in hot springs and mud pots – it often emerges out of the ground at 100°C. Always get local advice before hiking around live volcanoes. In glacial areas beware of dangerous quicksand at the end of glaciers, and never venture out onto the ice without crampons and ice axes (even then, watch out for crevasses).

One risk most travellers must face is dangerous driving on Iceland's roads. Locals universally ignore the speed limit, cut corners and weave out of their lanes. For more information on driving in Iceland, see p333.

DISCOUNT CARDS

Students and the elderly qualify for discounts on internal flights, some bus fares, tours and museum entry fees, but you'll need to show proof of student status or age.

Seniors (67 years or older) qualify for significant discounts on internal flights and ferry fares – any proof of age should suffice.

The **International Student Identity Card** (ISIC; www.isic.org) is the most widely recognised form of student identification. Cardholders under 26 get substantial discounts (up to 50%) on internal flights, ferries, museum admissions and some bus fares. Some restaurants and bars also offer student discounts. All young people under 26 with proof of age can get special stand-by fares on internal flights.

EMBASSIES & CONSULATES

Up-to-date details of embassies and consulates within Iceland and overseas can be found (in English) on the Icelandic Ministry of Foreign Affairs website www.mfa.is.

Icelandic Embassies & Consulates

Following is a partial list of Icelandic embassies and consulates in other countries.
Australia (☎ 02-9365 7345; iceland@bigpond.net .au; 16 Birriga Rd, Bellevue Hill, Sydney 2000, New South Wales)

Canada (☎ 613-482 1944; www.iceland.org/ca; 360 Albert St, Suite 710, Ottawa ON K1R 7X7)
Denmark (☎ 33 18 10 50; www.iceland.org/dk; Strandgade 89, DK-1401 Copenhagen K)
Faeroe Islands (☎ 30 11 01; info@faroeyard.fo; JC Svabosgøta 31, Box 65, Tórshavn)
Finland (☎ 09 612 2460; www.islanti.fi; Pohjoisesplanadi 27C, Fin-00100 Helsinki)
France (☎ 01 44 17 32 85; www.iceland.org/fr; 8 Ave Kléber, F-75116 Paris)
Germany (☎ 030-5050 4000; www.iceland.org/de; Rauchstrasse 1, DE-10787 Berlin)
Greenland (☎ 98 12 93; kelly@greennet.gl; c/o Hotel Angmagssalik, Sulup Aqq B725, Postbox 117, Tasiilaq)
Ireland (☎ 01-872 9299; jgg@goregrimes.ie; Cavendish House, Smithfield, Dublin)
Japan (☎ 03-3447 1944; emb.tokyo@mfa.is; 4-18-26 Takanawa, Minato-ku, Tokyo 108 0074)
Netherlands (☎ 431 33 13; robbie@reved.nl; 2nd fl, Strawinskylaan 3037, Amsterdam)
New Zealand (☎ 09-379 4720; ebarratt@sanford.co.nz; c/o Sanford Ltd, 22 Jellicoe St, Auckland)
Norway (☎ 2323 7530; www.iceland.org/no; Stortingsgata 30, NO-0244 Oslo)
Sweden (☎ 08 442 8300; www.iceland.org/se; Kommendörsgatan 35, SE-114 58 Stockholm)
UK (☎ 020 7259 3999; www.iceland.org/uk; 2a Hans St, London SW1X 0JE)
USA (☎ 202-265 6653; www.iceland.org/us; 1156 15th St NW, Suite 1200, Washington DC 20005-1704)

Embassies & Consulates in Iceland

Although many countries have some kind of representation in Iceland, this is often merely just a trade representative working for an Icelandic company. A handful of countries do have formal embassies in Reykjavík:
Canada (Map p72; ☎ 575 6500; rkjvk@international.gc.ca; Túngata 14)
Denmark (Map p72; ☎ 575 0300; www.ambreykjavik.um.dk; Hverfisgata 29)
Finland (Map pp68-9; ☎ 510 0100; www.finland.is; Túngata 30)
France (Map p72; ☎ 551 7621; www.ambafrance.is; Túngata 22)
Germany (Map pp68-9; ☎ 530 1100; embager@internet.is; Laufásvegur 31)
Ireland (☎ 554 2355; davidsch@islandia.is; Ásbúð 106, 210 Garðabær)
Japan (Map pp68-9; ☎ 510 8600; japan@itn.is; 6th fl, Laugavegur 182)
Netherlands (Map pp68-9; ☎ 533 1002; holland@holland.is; Borgartún 33)
Norway (Map pp68-9; ☎ 520 0700; www.noregur.is; Fjólugata 17)

Sweden (Map pp68-9; ☎ 520 1230; www.sweden abroad.com; 4th fl, Lágmúli 7)
UK (Map pp68-9; ☎ 550 5100; www.britishembassy.gov.uk; Laufásvegur 31)
USA (Map p72; ☎ 562 9100; www.usa.is; Laufásvegur 21)

FESTIVALS & EVENTS

True to their Viking roots, Icelanders love to party and a host of enthusiastic celebrations is held all over the country throughout the year. The following list details the main national festivals, but there are also loads of lively regional festivals – see the individual destination chapters for further information. Reykjavík has a particularly hectic festival calendar. For upcoming festivals and events, visit www.musik.is or the 'what's on' section of www.exploreiceland.is.

January to March

Þorrablót The Viking midwinter feast (18 January to 16 February) is marked with stomach-churning treats such as *hákarl* (putrid shark meat) and *svið* (singed lamb's head).
Bolludagur (Bun Day) In preparation for Lent, on the Monday before Shrove Tuesday children are encouraged to pester adults with coloured sticks and solicit vast numbers of *bollur* (cream buns).
Sprengidagur (Shrove Tuesday) 'Bursting Day' is another pre-Lenten celebration, an excuse for a traditional feast of salted mutton and pea soup.
Öskudagur (Ash Wednesday) Another excuse for children to menace adults, this time by collecting money for goodies and tying small sacks of ash on their backs.
Beer Day A celebration of the legalisation of beer in 1989 takes place on 1 March – with buckets of the stuff on tap.
Festival of Light Reykjavík hosts a celebration of light and darkness in late February or early March, with concerts, ghost stories, parades and fireworks.

April

Sumardagurinn Fyrsti (First Day of Summer) Icelanders celebrate this welcome day on the first Thursday after April 18, with carnival-type celebrations and street parades, particularly in Reykjavík.
Easter The usual Easter-egg hunts, followed by smoked lamb for dinner. Last Sunday in April.

May

Rite of Spring An alternative festival of world music takes place in Reykjavík in May, featuring everything from jazz to folk and blues.
Reykjavík Art Festival (www.artfest.is) Iceland's premier cultural festival is in late May, with two weeks of local and international theatre performances, film, dance, music and visual art.

June

Sjómannadagurinn (Sailors' Day) The biggest party of the year in fishing villages is on the first Sunday in June, with drinking, rowing and swimming contests, tugs-of-war and mock-ups of sea rescues.

Independence Day The country's largest festival is on 17 June, celebrating the granting of independence from Denmark in 1944. Expect lots of drinking, dancing, music and parades.

Midsummer The longest day of the year (24 June or thereabouts) is celebrated with lots of partying. Some superstitious souls even roll naked in the midsummer dew for its 'magical' healing powers.

August

Verslunarmannahelgi (August Bank Holiday, first weekend in August) A long weekend where Icelanders flock to rural festivals, family barbecues, massive rock concerts and wild camp-site parties. Vestmannaeyjar residents use this weekend for the massive Þjóðhátíð, which began as Vestmannaeyjar's celebration of the making of Iceland's constitution in 1874 (local residents missed it due to bad weather).

Culture Night Midmonth, Reykjavík turns out in full for a night of art, music, dance and fireworks.

Reykjavík Marathon (www.marathon.is) This race takes place on the same day as Culture Night, with full and half-marathons and fun runs for the fabulously fit.

Gay Pride (www.gaypride.is) Merriment and wild costumes as thousands parade carnival-style through the streets of Reykjavík to an open-air stage show featuring live music and entertainment. It's on the third weekend of the month.

September

Réttir The annual farmers' roundup of sheep, accompanied by festivals in the highlands.

Reykjavík Jazz Festival (www.jazz.is) On the last weekend of the month, this festival attracts international names as well as Iceland's leading jazz musicians.

Reykjavík International Film Festival (www.filmfest.is) In late September or early October, this 10-day event features the hottest new international films as well as seminars and workshops.

October

Fyrsti Vetrardagur (First Day of Winter) On the third Saturday of the month families get together to mourn the passing of summer. It's generally a low-key affair.

Iceland Airwaves (www.icelandairwaves.com) Reykjavík is home to this cutting-edge music festival at the end of the month. It features four days of top DJs, international live music and hard-core partying.

November & December

Unglist (Young Art Festival) In the first week of November in Reykjavík, this festival features theatre, music,

visual art, photography and fashion from the city's younger artists.

New Year's Eve Dinner, bonfires, fireworks, parties and clubbing on 31 December till the early hours to celebrate the arrival of the new year.

FOOD

Eating is going to be one of the main expenses of any trip to Iceland. If you choose to eat out, your evening meal could easily cost as much as your bed for the night. For the purposes of this book, restaurants with average main courses costing under Ikr1000 are classified as budget, those from Ikr1000 to Ikr3000 are midrange and those with main courses above Ikr3000 are top end.

The best way to keep costs down is to cook for yourself. Most places offering hostel beds or sleeping-bag space have guest kitchens, and supermarket prices are reasonable. For campers it's worth noting that most supermarkets also have a microwave where you can heat up purchases, and some also serve free coffee. The next cheapest option is to eat at the fast-food grills and snack bars found in most villages (usually at the petrol station), where you can pick up a burger, chips and a drink for about Ikr500, but the food is unhealthy and quickly becomes tedious. At formal restaurants, expect to pay Ikr1800 to Ikr4000 for main courses. Pizza restaurants are a cheaper bet, with main courses around Ikr1500. Otherwise, opt for the good-value lunch buffets and eat a smaller meal in the evening. Even in the best restaurants, tipping the staff is not expected; service is always included in the bill.

You'll find more information on food and special dishes on p57.

GAY & LESBIAN TRAVELLERS

Icelanders have a fairly open attitude towards gays and lesbians, though the gay scene is quite low-key, even in Reykjavík (see p67). Aggression against gays and lesbians is rare. The main gay and lesbian organisation is **Samtökin '78** (Map p72; ☎ 552 7878; office@samtokin78.is; 4th fl, Laugavegur 3, IS-101 Reykjavík), which doubles as an informal gay community centre with a drop-in café (open 8pm to 11pm Monday and Thursday). Other useful sources of information on news, events and entertainment venues include the websites http://gay.mis.is and www.gayice.is. Several companies offer tours to Iceland with a gay focus – try an Internet search using the terms 'gay tours iceland'.

HOLIDAYS

Icelandic public holidays are usually an excuse for a family gathering or, when they occur at weekends, a reason to rush to the country-side and go camping. If you're planning to travel during holiday periods, particularly the August holiday, you should book camping areas, mountain huts and transport well in advance, particularly in popular areas such as Þórsmörk. Icelandic hotels and guesthouses generally shut down from Christmas Eve to New Year's Day.

Public Holidays

National public holidays in Iceland:

New Year's Day 1 January
Easter March or April (Maundy Thursday and Good Friday to Easter Monday; changes annually)
First Day of Summer First Thursday after April 18
Labour Day 1 May
Ascension Day May or June (changes annually)
Whit Sunday and Whit Monday May or June (changes annually)
Independence Day 17 June
Shop & Office Workers' Holiday First Monday in August
Christmas 24 December to 26 December
New Year's Eve 31 December

School Holidays

The main school summer holiday runs from June to August, which is when most of the Edda and summer hotels open up. There are big student parties when school breaks up and when school restarts, so popular camping areas may be packed out. Þórsmörk is the venue for a huge student bash in July, which is either a reason to come or a reason to stay away. The winter school holiday is a two- to three-week break over the Christmas period (December to January).

INSURANCE

Although Iceland is a very safe place to travel, theft does occasionally happen and of course illness and accidents are always a possibility. A travel-insurance policy to cover theft, loss and medical problems is strongly recommended. Always check the small print to see if the pol-icy covers any potentially dangerous sporting activities, such as trekking, rock climbing, horse riding, skiing or snowmobiling. For more information on the health aspects of travel in Iceland, including insurance, see p335. For information on motor insurance, see p331.

> **ARE YOU OLD ENOUGH?**
>
> Iceland has legal minimum ages for many activities:
> **Voting** 18 years.
> **Drinking** 20 years.
> **Driving** 18 years (20 to 25 years for car hire, depending on the company).

INTERNET ACCESS

You'll find public internet access available in most Icelandic libraries, even in small towns. These are by far the best and cheapest places to check your mail, with most offering internet access for about Ikr100 to Ikr200 per hour – a fraction of the cost of hotels or net cafés. Reykjavík and some larger towns have private internet cafés, and most top-end hotels, youth hostels and tourist offices have internet termi-nals with fast and reliable connections.

Wi-fi access is becoming more common in Iceland and with a wireless-enabled laptop you'll be up and running in seconds. Some ho-tels do still have wired access however, and to use your own laptop you'll need either a dial-up account with global access numbers or an account with a local internet service provider (ISP) – the main provider in Iceland is **Síminn** (www.siminn.is). Most hotels have telephones in the bedrooms, but you should bring an adapter with the correct type of telephone jack – Iceland uses RJ11 jacks like the USA.

For information on useful websites about Iceland, see p22.

LEGAL MATTERS

Icelandic police are generally low-key and there's very little reason for you to end up in their hands. It's worth knowing, however, that drink-driving laws are very strict – one drink can put you over the legal limit of 0.05% blood-alcohol content. The penalty is loss of your licence plus a large fine. If you are involved in any other traffic offences – speeding, driving without due care and attention etc – you may be asked to go to the station to pay the fines immediately.

Drunk and disorderly behaviour may land you in a police cell for a night, but you will usually be released the following morning. Take note, however, that the penalties for pos-session, use or trafficking of illegal drugs are strict; these activities usually incur long prison sentences and heavy fines.

If you are arrested by the police, they can notify your embassy or consulate, or anyone else you specify, on your behalf. Lawyers are not provided by the state in Iceland, but the police can arrange a lawyer for you at your own expense. You can generally be held for 24 hours without being charged, and you can only be searched if you give consent, unless they have reason to be suspicious.

MAPS

The best maps of Iceland are produced by **Landmælingar Íslands** (National Land Survey of Iceland; ☎ 430 9000; www.lmi.is; Stillholt 16-18, IS-300 Akranes), and they cover the entire nation in fine detail. You can order any of these maps online or by mail, or pick them up at bookshops and tourist offices around the country.

The best map for driving around Iceland, the 1:500,000 *Ferðakort Touring Map* (Ikr787) includes all the larger villages and roads, and many small farms and B&Bs. The more in-depth 1:200,000 *Road Atlas* (Ikr2614) has full mapping plus details of accommodation, museums, swimming pools and golf courses.

More detailed maps include the 1:250,000 maps of Westfjords and north Iceland, west and south Iceland, and northeast and east Iceland (Ikr1084); a 1:25,000 map of Skaftafell (Ikr787); and 1:100,000 hikers' maps for Hornstrandir, Húsavík/Lake Mývatn, and Þórsmörk/Landmannalaugar (Ikr787).

The tourist offices of the various regions produce useful maps showing sites of tourist interest and they stock the free tourist booklet *Around Iceland*, which has bags of information and town plans.

MONEY

Iceland is an almost cashless society where the credit card is king. Icelanders use plastic for even small purchases and as long as you're carrying a valid card you'll have little need for travellers cheques and will only need to take out a limited amount of cash.

For information on costs, see p20.

ATMs

Almost every town in Iceland has a bank with an ATM where you can withdraw cash using MasterCard, Visa, Maestro or Cirrus cards. Íslandsbanki ATMs also allow withdrawals with a Diners Club card. You'll also find ATMs at larger petrol stations and in shopping centres.

Cash

The Icelandic unit of currency is the generally stable króna (Ikr). Coins come in denominations of one, five, 10, 50 and 100 krónur. Notes come in 500-, 1000-, 2000- and 5000-króna denominations. For exchange rates, see inside the front cover.

Credit & Debit Cards

Icelanders use credit and debit cards for nearly all purchases, and major cards such as Visa, MasterCard, Maestro and Cirrus – and to a lesser extent American Express, Diners Club and JCB – are accepted in most shops, restaurants and hotels. You can also pay for the Flybus from the international airport to Reykjavík using plastic – handy if you've just arrived in the country. If you intend to stay in rural farmhouse accommodation or visit isolated villages it's a good idea to carry enough cash to tide you over.

Moneychangers

The Icelandic love of plastic makes changing foreign currency almost unnecessary. However, if you prefer more traditional methods of carrying cash then foreign-denomination travellers cheques and banknotes can be exchanged for Icelandic currency at all major banks. Most banks charge a small commission fee for the transaction, but Landsbanki Íslands offers the service free of charge. Out of normal banking hours, you will have to rely on the poor rates and high charges of commercial exchange offices, or hope that your hotel or guesthouse can help you out.

Tipping

As service and VAT are always included in prices, tipping isn't required in Iceland.

Travellers Cheques

Travellers cheques in major currencies such as euros, US dollars, UK pounds and Danish krone are accepted by all banks and by the commission-hungry private exchange offices.

POST

The **Icelandic postal service** (Pósturinn; www.postur.is) is reliable and efficient, and rates are comparable to those in other Western European countries. An airmail letter or postcard to Europe costs economy/priority Ikr65/75; to places outside Europe it costs Ikr70/95. You'll find a full list of postal rates for letters and parcels online.

The best place to receive poste restante is the central post office in Reykjavík – tell potential correspondents to capitalise your surname and address mail to Poste Restante, Central Post Office, Pósthússtræti 5, IS-101 Reykjavík, Iceland.

SHOPPING

Typical Icelandic souvenirs include traditional woollen sweaters, dried fish and trolls of all descriptions. You'll also find a good selection of T-shirts and silver jewellery inspired by Icelandic runes. Products such as candle holders made from volcanic rock are becoming popular and CDs of Icelandic music can be good buys. For less traditional souvenirs such as high-quality ceramics, try the boutiques and galleries on Skólavörðustígur in Reykjavík.

If you're making any purchases over Ikr4000 it's worth claiming back the permitted 15% VAT refund. For more details of the scheme, see p317.

Normal opening hours for shops are listed on p315.

SOLO TRAVELLERS

There's no difficulty in travelling alone in Iceland, but if you fancy hooking up with other travellers the Reykjavík City Hostel is an excellent place to start. The noticeboard here usually has lots of messages from other travellers, and, as with all hostels, the communal kitchens can be the starting point for many shared trips and interesting friendships.

Another place you may be able to find travel companions is Lonely Planet's **Thorn Tree** (http://thorntree.lonelyplanet.com) – post a message on the forum's Scandinavia branch and see if any other travellers are going to be in Iceland when you are. Failing all that, you may want to join an organised adventure tour – see p333 for listings of tour companies operating in Iceland.

TELEPHONE & FAX

Iceland Telecom **Síminn** (www.siminn.is) provides all phone, mobile phone and internet services in the country. Public payphones can usually be found at post offices and public places such as bus or petrol stations, and most now accept credit cards as well as coins. Public fax services are provided at most post offices.

> **EMERGENCY NUMBERS**
>
> For police, ambulance and fire services in Iceland, dial ☎ 112.

The telephone directory and *Yellow Pages* are in Icelandic, but directory-inquiries operators usually speak English. Telephone directories are alphabetised by first name, so Guðrun Halldórsdóttir would be listed before Jón Einarsson. There's an online version of the phone book at www.simaskra.is.

Service numbers:
Directory inquiries (local) ☎ 118.
Directory inquiries (international) ☎ 1811.
Operator assistance ☎ 115.
Reverse-charge (collect) calls ☎ 533 5019 for assistance.

Mobile Phones

Iceland has the highest per-capita mobile phone use in the world and uses the GSM network in populated areas. The NMT network covers the interior and other remote regions; to have coverage in these areas you'll need to hire an NMT phone locally. Visitors with GSM or multiband phones will be able to make roaming calls, providing the service has been activated – contact your local phone company for more information.

If you're going to be in Iceland for a while it may be worth buying a local prepaid SIM card (Ikr2500 including Ikr2000 of free call credit) that will allow you to make calls at local rates. You can get additional prepaid cards at shops and petrol stations. You'll need an unlocked phone for this to work. Alternatively, you can rent a mobile phone (GSM or NMT) from **Síminn** (☎ 550 6000; www.siminn.is; Ármúli 27, Reykjavík) for around Ikr400 per day plus deposit.

Phone Codes

There are no area codes in Iceland, so you can dial the seven-digit number from anywhere in the country for the same price. For international calling, first dial the international access code ☎ 00, then the country code (listed in telephone directories), the area or city code, and the telephone number. International call rates are the same around the clock. To phone Iceland from abroad, dial the local international access code, the country code (☎ 354) and the seven-digit phone number. Toll-free numbers in Iceland begin with ☎ 800, and most seven-digit mobile phone numbers start with an eight.

Phonecards

The smallest-denomination phonecard (for use in public telephone boxes) costs Ikr500, and can be bought from post offices and Síminn telephone offices. Low-cost international phone cards are also available in many shops and youth hostels.

TIME

Iceland's time zone is the same as GMT/UTC (London), but there is no daylight-saving time. So from late October to late March Iceland is on the same time as London, five hours ahead of New York and 11 hours behind Sydney. In the northern hemisphere summer, it's one hour behind London, four hours ahead of New York and 10 hours behind Sydney.

TOURIST INFORMATION

Icelandic tourist-information offices are helpful, friendly and well informed and can be invaluable in assisting you to find accommodation, book tours or see the best an area has to offer. Employees usually speak several European languages including English.

Most tourist offices provide the useful booklets *Around Iceland* (a general tourist guide), *Iceland On Your Own* (a public-transport guide) and *Áning* (a guide to accommodation). All are free and published annually. If you plan to stay in farmhouse B&Bs, pick up a copy of *The Ideal Holiday*, a guide to farmhouse accommodation.

The **Icelandic Tourist Board** (Map p213; ☎ 535 5500; www.icetourist.is; Lækjargata 3, IS-101 Reykjavík) is the umbrella organisation in charge of tourism. There are tourist offices at **Keflavík International Airport** (☎ 425 0330; www.reykjanes.is) and in Reykjavík at the **Main Tourist Office** (Upplýsingamiðstöð Ferðamanna; Map p213; ☎ 590 1500; www.visitreykjavik.is; Aðalstræti 2). Reykjavík also has several private tourist-information offices, and there are council-run information offices in towns and villages around the country.

The main regional tourist offices:

East Iceland (☎ 471 2320; www.east.is; Kaupvangur 10, IS-700 Egilsstaðir)
North Iceland (Map p213; ☎ 462 7733; www .eyjafjordur.is, www.northiceland.is; Hafnarstræti 82, IS-600 Akureyri)
Southeast Iceland (☎ 478 1500; www.east.is; Hafnarbraut 30, IS-780 Höfn)

Southwest Iceland (☎ 483 4601; www.southiceland .is; Sunnumörk 2-4, IS-810 Hveragerði)
Westfjords (☎ 456 5121; www.westfjords.is, www .vestfirdir.is; Aðalstræti 7, IS-400 Ísafjörður)
West Iceland (☎ 437 2214; www.west.is; Hyrnan Complex, IS-310 Borgarnes)

Icelandic Tourist Board offices overseas:
Denmark (☎ 32 833 741; www.visiticeland.com; Islands Turistråd, Strandgade 91 opgang C, 2 loft, 1401 København K)
Germany (☎ 6102 254 388; www.icetourist.de; Isländisches Fremdenverkehrsamt, City Center, Frankfurter Strasse 181, D-63263 Neu-Isenburg)
USA (☎ 212-885 9700; www.goiceland.org; 655 Third Ave, New York, NY 10017)

If you arrive in a town after the tourist office has closed, the local petrol station is generally a good bet for information on the area.

TRAVELLERS WITH DISABILITIES

Iceland is on a par with most of northern Europe when it comes to access for travellers with disabilities. International and internal flights can accommodate most disabilities, but some flights use small aircraft that may be unsuitable for the mobility impaired. The car ferries *Baldur* and *Herjólfur* have facilities for wheelchairs, but public buses generally don't have lifts or ramps, with the exception of Reykjavík city buses. Many hotels, restaurants and large shops have facilities for people with disabilities, and there are reduced admission fees for most museums, galleries and tourist attractions. Air Iceland and Smyril Line offer discounts for disabled travellers on flights and ferries.

For more details of facilities for disabled people – including wheelchair-accessible hotels and tours – contact the tourist office in Reykjavík or get in touch with **Sjálfsbjörg** (☎ 550 0300; www.sjalfsbjorg.is; Hátún 12, IS-105 Reykjavík).

The Icelandic company **Hopferdathjonusta Reykjavikur** (☎ 587 8030; hrtravel@simnet.is; Brunastadir 3, IS-112 Reykjavík) specialises in tours for the disabled and may be able to help or advise on planning a trip around the country.

The UK-based website **Door-to-Door** (www .dptac.gov.uk/door-to-door) is a good starting point when planning overseas travel, and has a helpful section on air travel and getting to and from UK airports. In the USA you'll get similar, valuable information from the **Society for Accessible Travel & Hospitality** (☎ 212-447 7284;

www.sath.org; 347 5th Ave, Suite 610, New York, NY 10016)
or **Accessible Journeys** (☎ 610-521 0339; www.disa
bilitytravel.com; 35 West Sellers Ave, Ridley Park, PA 19078).
Access Able Travel (www.access-able.com) has a worldwide travel forum where you can post questions about disabled travel.

VISAS

Citizens of Schengen nations (Austria, Belgium,
Denmark, Finland, France, Germany, Greece,
Italy, Luxembourg, the Netherlands, Norway,
Portugal, Spain and Sweden) can enter Iceland
as tourists for up to three months with a valid
identity card. Citizens of the European Economic Area (EEA), including Ireland and Britain, do not require visas for stays up to three
months. To stay longer you must apply for a
residence permit, which is only available from
Icelandic embassies or consulates overseas.

Citizens from America, Australia, New Zealand, Japan and Canada can travel without a
visa for up to three months within any six-
month period; this period is deemed to begin
on the first entry to any Schengen nation.
Other nationalities need a visa from an Icelandic consulate before arriving – see p317 for
details of Icelandic embassies and consulates
around the world. The fee varies depending
on nationality, and the visa typically allows a
three-month stay. Officials will usually request
proof that you have sufficient funds for your
visit and an onward plane or boat ticket.

VOLUNTEERING

A volunteering holiday is a good (and relatively cheap) way of getting intimately involved with Iceland's people and landscape.
One of the most popular programmes is run
in conjunction with **Umhverfisstofnun** (UST, Environment & Food Agency; http://english.ust.is/of-interest/
ConservationVolunteers), recruiting up to 100 volunteers each summer for work on practical
conservation projects around the country.

For an overview of other possibilities and
projects, try **Volunteer Abroad** (www.volunteerabroad
.com) or **Working Abroad** (www.workingabroad.com),
both of which list projects from a variety of
sources.

Alternatively, you can try the following
organisations:
British Trust for Conservation Volunteers (www.btcv
.org) Short-term conservation work in Skaftafell and Jökulsárgljúfur National Parks, as well as Mývatn and Fjallabak
Nature Reserves in association with the Icelandic Ministry
of Environment. Volunteers pay BTCV a fee (roughly

UK£300 to UK£500 for 10 to 14 days) for accommodation
and food costs and must pay for their own transport to a
designated pick-up point.
Earthwatch (www.earthwatch.org) Scientific expeditions where volunteers pay full costs (roughly UK£1000
for eight days) to participate. Recent Iceland expeditions
included geological fieldwork on the glaciers of Skaftafell
National Park.
Service Civil International (www.sciint.org) Network
of voluntary organisations facilitating participation in
short-term volunteering projects working with local
community groups; projects include conservation, tree
planting, trail building, eco-villages, and archaeological
and festival work. Volunteers pay a membership and
administration fee (UK£145) to their local branch and make
their own way to a project, but once they're there all food
and accommodation is provided free of charge.
United Planet (www.unitedplanet.org) Long-term
(six- to 12-month) projects including humanitarian service,
language and intercultural training, cultural learning
activities, and exploration. Costs (US$5000 to US$7000)
cover housing, insurance and a language course.

WOMEN TRAVELLERS

Women travelling alone in Iceland should
encounter few problems, though common-
sense precautions apply – walking around city
streets alone after dark and hitching alone are
not really recommended. When out on the
town in Reykjavík be prepared for the advances of Icelandic men – if you think they're
being too forward, just make this clear and
they will leave you be. In rural areas pubs and
restaurants are often combined and attract
mainly couples during the week, so single
women should have few problems.

In Reykjavík, rape-crisis advice is available
from the women's organisation **Stígamót** (☎ 562
6868; www.stigamot.is).

WORK

Citizens of EEA countries do not require a
work permit to apply for jobs in Iceland; all
other citizens must secure a job offer and
work permit before arriving. Work permits
are generally only granted to fill seasonal job
shortages or for highly skilled professions that
are underrepresented in Iceland. For information on residence permits, visit the **Icelandic
Directorate of Immigration** (www.utl.is).

Although unemployment is low in Iceland
(about 3.1%), it can be difficult to find work,
especially if you are looking for anything better than cleaning, waiting tables or seasonal
farm work. For all other work, companies may

be reluctant to hire foreigners who cannot speak Icelandic.

The website of **Vinnumalastofnun** (Directorate of Labour; ☎ 515 4800; www.vinnumalastofnun.is) is a good source of information on living and working in Iceland and has links to the Eures job-search facility (http://europa.eu.int /eures), which lists public-employment jobs online. EU-flagged vacancies are those where Icelandic language skills are not essential. If you're interested in doing farm work, **Nínukot** (☎ 487 8576; www.ninukot.is; Skeggjastaðir, 861-Hvólsvöllur) is an employment agency specialising in farm placements.

See opposite if you wish to do voluntary work in Iceland.

Transport

> **THINGS CHANGE...**
> The information in this chapter is particularly vulnerable to change. Check directly with the airline or a travel agent to make sure you understand how a fare (and any ticket you may buy) works and be aware of the security requirements for international travel. Shop carefully. The details given in this chapter should be regarded as pointers and are not a substitute for your own careful, up-to-date research.

GETTING THERE & AWAY

Iceland has become far more accessible in recent years with a greater variety of flights and destinations available. Ferry transport is also possible and makes a good alternative for European travellers wishing to take their own car to the country.

You can book your fights, tours and rail tickets online at www.lonelyplanet.com/travel_services.

ENTERING THE COUNTRY

As long as you are in possession of the right documentation, immigration control should be a quick formality at the air or ferry port where you arrive. Citizens of Schengen nations, the European Economic Area (EEA), the US, Australia, New Zealand, Japan and Canada can travel in Iceland without a visa for up to three months. Other nationalities require a visa; for more information, see p324.

AIR
Airports & Airlines

Iceland's main international airport is **Keflavík International Airport** (KEF; ☎ 425 0600; www.keflavik airport.com), 48km west of Reykjavík. Internal flights and those to Greenland and the Faeroe Islands use the small **Reykjavík Domestic Airport** (REK) in central Reykjavík. A couple of international flights per week land at tiny **Akureyri Airport** (AEY), in Iceland's 'second city' in the north.

AIRLINES FLYING TO & FROM ICELAND

Only a handful of airlines fly to Iceland and all have great safety records.

Air Iceland (NY; ☎ 570 3030; www.airiceland.is)
Atlantic Airways (RC; ☎ Faeroes 341 010; www.atlantic airways.com)
British Airways (BA; ☎ 421 7374; www.britishairways.com)
Iceland Express (HW; ☎ 550 0600; www.icelandexpress.com)
Icelandair (FI; ☎ 505 0700; www.icelandair.net)
SAS (SK; ☎ 505 0300; www.scandinavian.net)

Tickets

The best ticket deals to Iceland are available online, but don't assume that budget airlines are always offering the best rates. With increasing competition on these routes it's well worth checking all possible options before booking.

Australia & New Zealand

To get to Iceland from Australia or New Zealand, you will need to connect through Europe or the USA. Travel agents can book you all the way through to Keflavík, or you can buy a discount ticket to London, Copenhagen or New York and then arrange your onward ticket to Iceland online or through an airline (see p327).

Continental Europe

Icelandair has regular flights between Keflavík and Copenhagen (from Dkr1737), Oslo (from Nkr2934), Stockholm (from Skr2085), Paris (from €308), Frankfurt (from €388) and Amsterdam (from €340). The flight time is roughly 3½ hours.

Icelandair also has seasonal flights between Keflavík and Barcelona, Berlin, Helsinki, Madrid, Milan, Munich and Zürich, taking between six and nine hours.

Iceland Express flies year-round 14 times weekly between Keflavík and Copenhagen (from Dkr2120, three hours). In summer, there are also between two and four flights weekly between Keflavík and Alicante (Spain; from €370, four hours), Berlin, Frankfurt, Friedrichshafen (all from €300, 3½ hours), Gothenburg and Stockholm (both Skr3000, three hours); and twice-weekly flights from Copenhagen to Akureyri (Dkr3300, three hours).

SAS operates direct flights from Keflavík to Oslo (Nkr3000, 2¾ hours) three times a week.

UK & Ireland

Icelandair (☎ 0870 7874020; www.icelandair.net) has flights to Keflavík from London Heathrow (from £163, three hours) at least twice daily. Between April and October there are flights from Glasgow (from £161, two hours) four or five times per week, and two flights per week from Manchester (from £172, 2½ hours).

Iceland Express (☎ 0870 2405600; www.icelandexpress.com) flies twice daily (less frequently in winter) from London Stansted to Keflavík (from £139, three hours), and twice weekly to Akureyri (from £177, three hours).

British Airways (☎ 0870 8509850; www.britishairways.com) has also begun a London to Keflavík route, flying up to five times a week from Gatwick (from £142, three hours).

From Ireland, the cheapest way is to fly with **Ryanair** (www.ryanair.com) from Dublin to London Stansted, where you can catch the Iceland Express flight to Keflavík. **Wallace Travel Group** (☎ 01 8347888) offers three- and four-night packages direct from Dublin.

USA & Canada

Icelandair flies daily between Keflavík and Boston and most days between Keflavík and Baltimore, Minneapolis, New York, Orlando and Washington DC. A summer service departs from San Francisco four times weekly. You can also include Iceland as a free stopover on the way to Britain or continental Europe. Online return fares from New York to Reykjavík start at US$650. From Canada, you need to connect through the USA, Copenhagen or London.

TRANSPORT

CLIMATE CHANGE & TRAVEL

Climate change is a serious threat to the ecosystems that humans rely upon, and air travel is the fastest-growing contributor to the problem. Lonely Planet regards travel, overall, as a global benefit, but believes we all have a responsibility to limit our personal impact on global warming.

Flying & Climate Change

Pretty much every form of motorized travel generates CO_2 (the main cause of human-induced climate change) but planes are far and away the worst offenders, not just because of the sheer distances they allow us to travel, but because they release greenhouse gases high into the atmosphere. The statistics are frightening: two people taking a return flight between Europe and the US will contribute as much to climate change as an average household's gas and electricity consumption over a whole year.

Carbon Offset Schemes

Climatecare.org and other websites use 'carbon calculators' that allow travellers to offset the level of greenhouse gases they are responsible for with financial contributions to sustainable travel schemes that reduce global warming – including projects in India, Honduras, Kazakhstan and Uganda.

Lonely Planet, together with Rough Guides and other concerned partners in the travel industry, support the carbon offset scheme run by climatecare.org. Lonely Planet offsets all of its staff and author travel.

For more information check out our website: www.lonelyplanet.com.

TRANSPORT

SEA
Ferry
Smyril Line (in Seyðisfjörður ☎ 472 1111; www.smyril-line
.com) has a car ferry from Bergen (Norway) or
Hanstholm (Denmark) to Seyðisfjörður in east
Iceland, stopping on the way at Tórshavn in
the Faeroes. When travelling from Hanstholm
to Seyðisfjörður there is a two-night stopover
in the Faeroes on the outbound journey, and
when travelling from Bergen there is a three-
night stopover on the return journey. The
service also calls at Lerwick (Shetland Islands)
from May to September and Scrabster (Scotland) from mid-June to August. The Lerwick
and Scrabster schedule may change after summer 2007, however, so check the website for
up-to-date information.

Passengers have a choice of couchettes
(bed-seats) or one- to four-berth cabins. From
Hanstholm to Seyðisfjörður, the one-way cou-
chette fare for a car and two passengers is €535/
400/240 in high/mid/low season, from Bergen
the fare is €440/325/200. Passengers travelling
with a motorbike or bicycle from Hanstholm
pay €1815/1380/856, while foot passengers
on the same route pay €1560/1195/755. High
season runs from mid-June to mid-August,
midseason from mid-May to mid-June and
mid-August to mid-September. Low-season
fares apply from mid-September to mid-May.
Children, seniors and students qualify for reduced rates year-round.

The company also offers a variety of packages including accommodation in the Faeroes
and Iceland.

Cargo Ship
The Icelandic cargo carrier **Eimskip** (☎ 525
7000; www.eimskip.com), accepts passengers on
its vessels *Detifoss* and *Godafoss* from mid-
April to mid-October. Because the shipping
route loops around, the shortest journey from
Europe to Reykjavík is from Gothenburg or
Fredrikstad (four days). See the website for a
full schedule. The trip from Rotterdam costs
€1124 per person (€806 for the return journey) and €488 for a car.

GETTING AROUND

AIR
Iceland has an extensive network of domestic
flights, which locals use almost like buses.
In winter a flight can be the only way to get

> **DEPARTURE TAX**
>
> A tax of Ikr930 applies for each one-way leg,
> paid when you buy your ticket for domestic
> flights or those to the Faeroes or Greenland.
> Taxes are included in the price for all inter-
> national flights.

between destinations, but weather at this time
of year can play havoc with schedules.

See the Iceland Airline & Ferry Routes map
(opposite) for the current routes operating
in Iceland.

Air Iceland (☎ 570 3030; www.airiceland.is) operates flights between Reykjavík and Akureyri
(Ikr10,565, 45 minutes, around seven flights
daily), Egilsstaðir (Ikr11,975, one hour, three
or four daily) and Ísafjörður (Ikr10,565, 40
minutes, two to four daily). From Akureyri
there are regular flights to Grímsey (Ikr8090,
25 minutes), Vopnafjörður (Ikr10,190, 45 minutes) and Þórshöfn (Ikr10,190, 1¼ hours).

Landsflug (City Star) operates flights to
smaller airstrips, including Vestmannæyjar,
Sauðárkrókur, Höfn, Bildudalur and Gjögur.
All bookings should be made through Air
Iceland.

Air Passes
Air Iceland offers a couple of air passes,
which must be purchased either outside
Iceland or in Icelandic travel agencies ca-
tering for foreign visitors. The Air Iceland
Pass is available with four/five/six sectors for
Ikr30,300/34,400/39,500. There's an extra tax
of Ikr930 for each departure and the maximum validity is one month. Fly As You Please
gives 12 consecutive days of unlimited flights
in Iceland for Ikr47,000, excluding airport
taxes. Children under 12 pay half rates.

Air Charters & Air Sightseeing
Flugfélag Vestmannaeyjar (☎ 481 3255; www.eyjaflug
is) runs charter flights over to Vestmannæyjar
from tiny Bakki airport, about 20km south
of Hvolsvöllur. Other charter airlines include
Ernir Air (☎ 562 4200; www.ernir.is), at Reykjavík
airport, and **Mýflug** (☎ 464 4400; www.myflug.is),
at Mývatn.

BICYCLE
Cycling through Iceland's dramatic landscape
is a fantastic way to see the country, but you
should be prepared for some harsh conditions

along the way. Gale-force winds, driving rain, sandstorms, sleet and sudden flurries of snow are all possible at any time of year.

It's essential to know how to do your own basic repairs and to bring several puncture-repair kits and spares, as supplies are hard to come by outside the city. Reykjavík has several well-stocked bike shops. Two of the best include **Örninn** (☎ 588 9890; Skeifan 11d, IS-108 Reykjavík) and **Markið** (☎ 553 5320; Ármúli 40, IS-108 Reykjavík).

If you want to tackle the interior, the Kjölur route has bridges over all major rivers, making it fairly accessible to cyclists. A less challenging route is the F249 to Þórsmörk. The Westfjords also offers some wonderful cycling terrain, though the winding roads and steep passes can make for slow progress.

Transporting Bicycles

Most airlines will carry your bike in the hold if you pack it correctly. You should remove the pedals, lower the saddle, turn the handlebars parallel to the frame and deflate the tyres. Domestic airlines charge Ikr3200 per bicycle; buses charge between Ikr600 and Ikr1000, but space may be a problem.

If you've brought your own bicycle along you can store your bike box at the camp site in Keflavík for free for the duration of your visit.

Hire

Various places around Iceland rent out mountain bikes, but these are generally intended for local use only and aren't up to long-haul travel. If you intend to go touring, bring your bike from home.

BOAT

Several ferries operate in Iceland. The car ferry *Herjólfur* sails between Þorlákshöfn and Vestmannaeyjar, and the *Baldur* sails between Stykkishólmur, Flatey and Brjánslækur – both run year-round. Passenger ferries include the *Sævar* between Arskógssandur and Hrísey, the *Sæfari* between Dalvík and Hrísey or Grímsey, and the *Anný* between Neskaupstaður and Mjóifjörður. Small summer-only ferries run from Reykjavík's Sundahöfn harbour to the island of Viðey, and from Ísafjörður and Drangsnes to stops at Hornstrandir in the Westfjords.

ICELAND AIRLINE & FERRY ROUTES

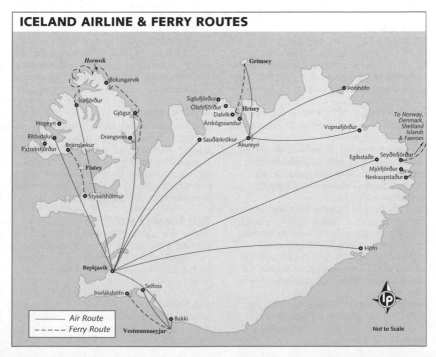

TRANSPORT

BUS

Iceland has an extensive network of bus routes with services operated by a number of bus companies. All are members of the consortium **BSÍ** (Bifreiðastöð Íslands; ☎ 562 1011; www.bsi.is), based in the BSÍ bus terminal on Vatnsmýrarvegur in Reykjavík. The booking desk sells tickets and distributes the free *Ísland á Eigin Vegum* (Iceland on Your Own) brochure, which contains timetables. From June to August there are regular buses to most places on the Ring Rd, and to larger towns in the Westfjords and on the Reykjanes and Snæfellsnes peninsulas. During the rest of the year services are limited or nonexistent. In small towns and villages buses usually stop at the main petrol station.

Main bus companies:

Austurleið-Kynnisferðir (☎ 545 1717; www.austurleid .is) South and east Iceland.

Flybus (☎ 562 1011; www.flybus.is) Reykjavík to Keflavík airport.

SBK Travel (☎ 420 6000; www.sbk.is) Keflavík and Reykjanes.

Stjörnubílar (☎ 456 5518; www.stjornubilar.is) Westfjords.

Trex-Hópferðamiðstöðin (☎ 587 6000; www.trex.is) West and north Iceland.

Bus Passes

BSÍ offers several bus passes that can save you money on longer journeys. However, passes bought late in the summer season can be next to useless once buses switch to their very irregular winter service (usually on 1 September).

Some options:

Full-Circle Passport (Ikr21,300) Buses run June to August. Valid for one circuit of the Ring Rd in one direction, stopping wherever you like.

Full-Circle Passport Extended (Ikr25,500) Buses run mid-June to August. As above, but allowing travel from Reykjavík to Akureyri through the interior (via the Kjölur route), and between Kirkjubæjarklaustur and Hella via Landmannalaugar.

Full-Circle Passport Including Westfjords (Ikr31,400) Buses run June to August. Same as the Full-Circle Pass but taking in a wider western route to include the Westfjords, reached via the ferry *Baldur* (from Stykkishólmur).

Highland Passport (3/5/7/9/11 days Ikr13,000/20,50 0/26,900/32,800/37,900) Buses run mid-June to August. Valid on bus routes in the southern highlands and through the interior.

Omnibus Passport (7/14/21 days Ikr23,100/37,000/ 45,000) Buses run mid-May to mid-September. Unrestricted travel on most scheduled buses (excluding highland and interior routes).

CAR & MOTORCYCLE

Driving in Iceland gives you unparalleled freedom to discover the country and, thanks to good roads and light traffic, it's all fairly straightforward. One major route, mostly paved, circles the country and beyond it fingers of pavement or gravel stretch out to most communities. Outside the Ring Rd (Rte 1) you are likely to pass no more than a handful of cars each day, even in high season.

In coastal areas driving can be spectacularly scenic and incredibly slow as you weave up and down over unpaved mountain passes and in and out of long fjords. Even so, a 2WD vehicle will get you almost everywhere in summer.

In winter heavy snow can cause many roads to close and mountain roads generally remain closed until the end of June. For up-to-date information on road and weather conditions, visit www.vegagerdin.is.

Bring Your Own Vehicle

Car hire in Iceland is expensive, and taking your own vehicle to the country may not be as daft as it sounds. Drivers must carry the vehicle's registration documents, proof of valid insurance (a 'green card') and a driving licence. Import duty is initially waived for one month, so you must either re-export the vehicle within this period or apply for an extension, which is valid for an additional two months. For more information, contact the **Directorate of Customs** (☎ 560 0300; www.tollur.is; Tryggvagötu 19, 150 Reykjavík).

Driving Licence

You can drive in Iceland with a driving licence from the US, Canada, Australia, New Zealand and most European countries. If you have a licence from anywhere else you may need to get an international driving licence, which is normally issued by the local automobile association in your home country.

Fuel & Spare Parts

There are regularly spaced petrol stations around Iceland, but in more remote areas you should check fuel levels and the distance to the next station before setting off on a long journey. Unleaded petrol costs about Ikr134 per litre, diesel about Ikr128 per litre. Leaded petrol isn't available. Most smaller petrol stations are unstaffed, you simply swipe your credit card in the machine, enter the maximum amount you wish to spend and

FOUR-WHEEL FOLLY

Four-wheel drive vehicles, especially the souped-up versions available in Iceland, can cause enormous damage to the already fragile environment and for the most part are completely unnecessary. Only the Jeep tracks and mountain roads (designated with an 'F') are 4WD only. Off-road driving is prohibited by law everywhere in Iceland, as tyre tracks can scar the landscape for years. These vehicles also guzzle petrol and have high carbon emissions, further adding to their environmental impact. Consider hiring a conventional vehicle instead and joining a Jeep tour for any mountain trips.

fill up. You will only be charged for the cost of fuel put into your vehicle. It's a good idea to check that your card will work at a staffed station while it is open, just in case you have any problems.

Icelandic roads can be pretty lonely, so carry a jack, a spare tyre and jump leads just in case. Although the Icelandic motoring association **Félag Íslenskra Bifreiðaeiganda** (FIB; ☎ 414 9999; www .fib.is; Borgartún 33, Reykjavík) is only open to residents of Iceland, if you have breakdown cover with an automobile association affiliated with ARC Europe you may be covered by the FÍB – check with your home association.

Hire

Hiring a car is the only way to get to many parts of Iceland, and, although rates are expensive by international standards, they compare favourably against bus or internal air travel. The cheapest cars on offer, usually a Toyota Yaris or similar, cost from Ikr6900 per day. The cheapest 4WD vehicles cost from Ikr12,900 per day. Rates include unlimited mileage and VAT.

To rent a car you must be 20 years old (25 years for a 4WD) and you will need to show a valid licence. When deciding check the small print, as additional costs such as extra insurance, airport pick-up charges and one-way rental fees can really rack up. You can also check sites such as www.holidayautos.co.uk and www.travelsupermarket.com for a comparison of rates between rental agencies.

Note that most hire companies, regardless of whether they have an airport office, pick you up with the car at the airport and collect

the car from there or from your hotel. Some car-rental agencies in Iceland:

ALP/Budget (Map pp68-9; ☎ 562 6060; www.budget .is, www.alp.is; Reykjavík Domestic Airport, Keflavík International Airport)

Arctic (Map pp68-9; ☎ 421 2220; www.arctic.is; Idjustig 1, IS-230 Keflavík)

Átak (☎ 554 6040; www.atak.is; Smiðjuvegur 1, IS-200 Kópavogur)

Avis (Map pp68-9; ☎ 591 4000; www.avis.is; Reykjavík Domestic Airport, Keflavík International Airport)

Bílaleiga Akureyrar/National (Map pp68-9; ☎ 568 6915, www.eurorent.is; Reykjavík Domestic Airport, Keflavík International Airport)

Europcar (Map pp68-9; ☎ 565 3800; www.europcar.is; Reykjavík Domestic Airport, Keflavík International Airport)

Geysir (Map p107; ☎ 893 4455; www.geysir.is; Holtsgata 56, IS-260 Njarðvík)

Hasso (☎ 555 3330; www.hasso.is; Smiðiuvegur 34, IS-200 Kópavogur)

Hertz (Map pp68-9; ☎ 505 0600; www.hertz.is; Reykjavík Domestic Airport, Keflavík International Airport)

Rás (☎ 426 7100; www.ras.is; Keflavík International Airport)

Saga (☎ 421 3737; www.sagacarrental.is; Keflavík)

Sixt (☎ 540 2222; www.sixt.is; Reykjavík)

Insurance

If you are bringing your own vehicle into Iceland you'll need a so-called 'green card', which proves that you are insured to drive while in Iceland. Green cards are issued by insurance companies in your home country. Contact your existing insurer for details.

When hiring a car check the small print carefully; as most vehicles come with third-party insurance only you'll need to take out additional Collision Damage Waiver (CDW) to cover you for damage to the hire car. Also check the excess (the initial amount you will be liable to pay in the event of an accident) as this can be surprisingly high.

Hire vehicles are generally not covered for damage to the tyres, headlights and windscreen, or damage caused to the underside of the vehicle by driving on dirt roads, through water or in sandstorms. Some policies also prohibit 'off-road driving'. This usually only refers to mountain roads (F roads) and Jeep tracks, but check with the car-hire company to be sure. Car-hire agreements do not cover damage to the hire car caused by collisions with animals, and if you do hit an animal you may be required to compensate the owner.

TRANSPORT

ROAD DISTANCES (KM)

	Akureyri	Borgarnes	Egilsstaðir	Höfn	Ísafjörður	Reykjavík	Selfoss	Seyðisfjörður	Stykkishólmur	Vík
Akureyri	---									
Borgarnes	315	---								
Egilsstaðir	265	580	---							
Höfn	512	519	247	---						
Ísafjörður	567	384	832	902	---					
Reykjavík	389	74	698	459	457	---				
Selfoss	432	117	640	402	500	57	---			
Seyðisfjörður	292	607	27	274	859	680	667	---		
Stykkishólmur	364	99	629	618	391	173	216	656	---	
Vík	561	246	511	273	630	187	129	538	345	---

Parking

Other than in central Reykjavík parking in Iceland is easy to find and free of charge. For information on parking in the capital, see p99.

Road Conditions & Hazards

Good road surfaces and light traffic make driving in Iceland relatively easy, but there are some specific roads hazards that drivers will encounter. Not all roads are sealed, and the transition from sealed to gravel roads is marked with the warning sign *Malbik Endar* – slow down to avoid skidding when you hit the gravel. In most cases roads have two lanes with steeply cambered sides and no hard shoulder; be prepared for oncoming traffic in the centre of the road, and slow down and stay to the right when approaching blind rises, marked as *Blindhæð* on road signs. You'll also need to be prepared to give way when approaching single-lane bridges, *Einbreið Brú*.

Most accidents involving foreign drivers in Iceland are caused by the use of excessive speed on unsurfaced roads. If your car does begin to skid take your foot off the accelerator and gently turn the car in the direction you want the front wheels to go. Do not brake. In other areas severe sandstorms can strip paint off cars and even overturn them; areas at risk are marked with orange warning signs.

In winter make sure your hire car is fitted with snow tyres or chains, carry blankets, food and water, and take extra care when driving on compacted snow. Always brake gently to avoid skidding, and check road conditions on www.vedur.is/english before setting out.

Roads suitable for 4WD vehicles only are F-numbered. Always travel in tandem on these roads and carry emergency supplies and a full tool and repair kit. Always let someone know where you are going and when you expect to be back. River crossings can be extremely dangerous, as few interior roads are bridged. Fords are marked on maps with a 'V', but you'll need to check the depth and speed of the river by wading into it – do not attempt this without a life jacket and lifeline. To cross the river use a low gear in 4WD mode and cross slowly and steadily without stopping or changing gear.

You'll find useful information and a video on driving in Iceland at www.umferdarstofa.is/id/2693.

TRANSPORT

ROAD RULES

- Drive on the right
- Front and rear seat belts are compulsory
- Dipped headlights must be on at all times
- Blood alcohol limit is 0.05%
- Mobile-phone use is prohibited except with a hands-free kit
- Children under six must use a car seat

Speed limits

- Built-up areas 50km/h
- Unsealed roads 80km/h
- Sealed roads 90km/h

HITCHING

Although Iceland is generally a very safe place to travel, hitching is never entirely without risk, and we don't recommend it. If you choose to hitch, travel in pairs and let someone know where you are going. Hitching is really only possible in Iceland during the summer months, but even so traffic is light and you can be in for some long waits. If you can plan ahead, check **Samferda** (www.samferda .net), a new travel site connecting willing drivers and would-be passengers on Icelandic journeys.

LOCAL TRANSPORT
Bicycle

You can hire bicycles for local riding from some tourist offices, hotels, hostels and guesthouses. The standard daily charge is about Ikr1700 per day, plus a deposit (a credit-card imprint will usually suffice). Helmets are a legal requirement for all children aged under 15.

Bus

Reykjavík has an extensive network of local buses running out to all the suburbs, including Kópavogur and Hafnarfjörður. There are also local bus networks in Keflavík, Akureyri and Ísafjörður.

Taxi

Most large towns have some kind of taxi service, but expect to pay at least Ikr1000 for a short journey of around 3km.

TOURS

Although joining a bunch of other travellers on an organised tour may not be your idea of an independent holiday, Iceland's rugged terrain and high costs can make it an appealing option. Tours can save you time and money and can get you into some stunning but isolated locations where your hire car will never go. Many tours are by bus, others by 4WD or super-Jeep, and some by snowmobile or light aircraft. Most tours give you the option of tacking on adventure activities such as whitewater rafting, kayaking, snowmobiling, horse riding and ice trekking.

There are usually substantial discounts for children and for making bookings online, so shop around before making any decisions. The following is a list of some of the best companies around; you'll find other specific tours and tour operators covered in the destination chapters.

Activity Group (☎ 580 9900; www.activity.is) This group of adventure-tour companies offers activities all over Iceland, including snowmobile tours, whitewater rafting, dogsledding and ATV rides. It has a base at the Húsafell recreation centre in west Iceland.

Air Iceland (☎ 570 3030; www.airiceland.is; Reykjavík Domestic Airport, IS-101 Reykjavík) Iceland's largest domestic airline runs a wide range of combination air, bus, hiking, rafting, horse riding, whale watching and glacier day tours around Iceland from Reykjavík and Akureyri. It also runs day tours to Greenland and the Faeroes from Reykjavík.

Dick Phillips (☎ 01434-381440; www.icelandic-travel .com; Whitehall House, Nenthead, Alston, Cumbria, CA9 3PS) British-based Dick Phillips runs a specialist Icelandic travel service, and has decades of experience leading wild hiking, cycling and skiing trips.

Explore Adventures (☎ 562 7000; Laugavegur 11, IS-101 Reykjavík) Adventure-tour company offering glacial hiking, snorkelling, kayaking, caving, canyoning, ice climbing, climbing, hiking and cycling day tours from Reykjavík.

Ferðafélag Íslands (Icelandic Touring Association; Map pp68-9; ☎ 568 2533; www.fi.is; Mörkin 6, IS-108 Reykjavík) Leads summer treks in Hornstrandir, Landmannalaugar and Þórsmörk, and also has some bus tours and cross-country skiing trips.

Guðmundur Jónasson Travel (Map pp68-9; ☎ 511 1515; www.gjtravel.is; Borgartún 34, IS-105 Reykjavík) This ever-popular company offers multiday bus tours with light hiking each day. It's an excellent option for active people who'd rather not make their own arrangements.

Highlanders (Map pp68-9; ☎ 568 3030; www.hl.is; Suðurlandsbraut 10, IS-108 Reykjavík) This super-Jeep operator offers tours up to Landmannalaugar, Hekla,

Langjökull and along the south coast. It also offers rafting on the Þjórsá river in southwest Iceland.

Iceland Excursions (Allrahanda; Map pp68-9; ☎ 540 1313; www.icelandexcursions.is; Höfðatún 12) Offers a comprehensive and inexpensive range of day trips around the Golden Circle, south coast, Snæfellsnes and Landmannalaugar, plus Northern Lights tours, horse riding, fissure diving, snorkelling and super-Jeep trips.

Iceland Rovers (☎ 567 1720; www.icelandrovers.is; PO Box 8950 Reykjavík) Runs a range of adventure day tours to Hekla and Landmannalaugar, Northern Lights tours, and history and geology tours.

Ísafold Travel (☎ 544 8866; www.isafoldtravel.is; Suðurhraun 2b, IS-210 Garðabær) Tailor-made tours for small groups and individuals, including angling, geology, hiking, photography, wellness, and women-only tours.

Mountain Guides (☎ 587 9999; www.mountainguide .is; Vagnhöfði 7, IS-110 Reykjavík) This adventurous company offers a wide range of hiking and climbing tours, including day trips to Heiðmörk (near Reykjavík), Hengill and Sólheimajökull, and a series of ice-climbing and trekking tours around Skaftafell. It also provides equipment rental and private guiding for more serious climbers.

Mountain Taxi (☎ 544 5252; www.mountain-taxi.com) This company runs all-year 4WD tours covering popular tourist sites such as the Golden Circle, Landmannalaugar, Hekla volcano, Mýrdalsjökull and Fjallabak as well as multiday and winter Jeep tours.

Mountaineers of Iceland (☎ 581 3800; www .mountaineers.is; Krókhála 5a, IS-110 Reykjavík) Specialises in adventure tours, including day trips to the Golden Circle and Hengill, multiday super-Jeep expeditions, snowmobile and photographic tours, snowmobiling, glacier tours, river rafting, kayaking, canyoning and horse riding.

Nonni Travel (Map p213; ☎ 461 1841; www.nonnitravel .is; Brekkugata 5, IS-602 Akureyri) The main tour agent in Akureyri, Nonni Travel offers rafting, horse riding, whale-watching, super-Jeep and Arctic Circle tours as well as excursions to Greenland.

Reykjavík Excursions (Kynnisferðir; Map pp68-9; ☎ 562 1011; www.re.is; BSÍ bus terminal, Vatnsmýrarvegur 10, Reykjavík) Reykjavík's most popular day-tour agency, with a comprehensive range of year-round tours.

Touris (☎ 897 6196; www.tour.is; Frostaskjól 105, IS-107 Reykjavík) This super-Jeep operator offers Golden Circle tours with an off-road highland drive, and 4WD tours to Langjökull, Þórsmörk and Landmannalaugar.

Útivist (Map pp68-9; ☎ 562 1000; www.utivist.is; Laugavegur 178, IS-105 Reykjavík) This recommended organisation runs friendly informal trekking trips and covers just about every corner of Iceland. It also runs one of the mountain huts at Þórsmörk.

Vestfjarðaleið (☎ 562 9950; www.vesttravel.is; Hestháls 10, IS-110 Reykjavík) This friendly company runs day trips to Þórsmörk, Landmannalaugar, Snæfellsnes and the Golden Circle, as well as a five-day hiking trip from Landmannalaugar and Þórsmörk and four-day hikes from Hengill to Þingvellir.

Vesturferðir (☎ 456 5111; www.vesturferdir.is; Aðalstræti 7, IS-400 Ísafjörður) The main tour company in the Westfjords, Vesturferðir offers a huge range of tours in the surrounding area, including various day trips and multiday hikes to Hornstrandir.

Youth Hostel Travel Service (Map pp68-9; ☎ 553 8110; www.hostel.is; Sundlaugavegur 34, IS-105 Reykjavík) In conjunction with other companies, the hostel association organises a wide range of tours, including sightseeing, horse riding, glacier trips, rafting, trekking and whale watching.

Health

CONTENTS

Travel health depends on your predeparture preparations, your daily health care while travelling and how you handle any medical problem that does develop. If you do fall ill while in Iceland you will be very well looked after, as health care is excellent.

BEFORE YOU GO

Prevention is the key to staying healthy while abroad. A little planning before departure, particularly for pre-existing illnesses, will save trouble later – see your dentist before a long trip, carry a spare pair of contact lenses and glasses, and take your optical prescription with you. Bring medications in their original, clearly labelled containers. A signed and dated letter from your physician describing your medical conditions and medications, including generic names, is also a good idea. If carrying syringes or needles, be sure to have a physician's letter documenting their medical necessity.

INSURANCE

If you're a citizen of the EU, a European Health Insurance Card (EHIC) entitles you to reduced-cost emergency medical treatment in Iceland. It doesn't cover nonemergency medical treatment, dental treatment, ambulance

---

CHECK BEFORE YOU GO

It's usually a good idea to consult your government's travel-health website (if available) before departure:
Australia www.smartraveller.gov.au
Canada www.travelhealth.gc.ca
UK www.dh.gov.uk/PolicyAndGuidance /HealthAdviceForTravellers
USA www.cdc.gov/travel

---

travel or emergency repatriation home. The EHIC has replaced the old E111 form, which ceased to be valid in January 2006. The easiest way to apply for an EHIC is online – check your country's Department of Health website for details; in the UK, you can also pick up a postal application form from post offices.

Citizens from other countries should find out if there is a reciprocal arrangement for free medical care between their country and Iceland. If you do need health insurance, strongly consider a policy that covers you for the worst possible scenario, such as an accident requiring an emergency flight home. Find out in advance if your insurance plan will make payments directly to providers or reimburse you later for overseas health expenditures. The former option is generally preferable, as it doesn't require you to pay out of pocket in a foreign country.

RECOMMENDED VACCINATIONS

The World Health Organization (WHO) recommends that all travellers should be covered for diphtheria, tetanus, measles, mumps, rubella and polio, regardless of their destination. Since most vaccines don't produce immunity until at least two weeks after they're given, visit a physician at least six weeks before departure.

INTERNET RESOURCES

The WHO's publication *International Travel and Health* is revised annually and is available online at www.who.int/ith. Other useful websites include www.mdtravelhealth.com (travel-health recommendations for every country, updated daily), www.fitfortravel.scot.nhs.uk

HEALTH

(general travel advice), www.ageconcern.org
.uk (advice on travel for the elderly) and www
.mariestopes.org.uk (information on women's
health and contraception).

FURTHER READING

Health Advice for Travellers (currently called
the 'T7.1' leaflet) is an annually updated leaflet by the Department of Health in the UK,
and is available free of charge in post offices,
or on page 460 of Ceefax (BBC2). It contains general health information, details of
legally required and recommended vaccines
for different countries, details of reciprocal
health agreements and information about
the EHIC.

Lonely Planet's *Travel with Children* includes advice on travel health for younger
children. Another recommended reference
is *The Traveller's Good Health Guide*, by Ted
Lankester (Sheldon Press).

IN TRANSIT

DEEP VEIN THROMBOSIS (DVT)

Blood clots may form in the legs during plane
flights, chiefly because of prolonged immobil-
ity – the longer the flight, the greater the risk
of developing a clot. The chief symptom of
DVT is swelling or pain of the foot, ankle
or calf, usually but not always on just one
side. When a blood clot travels to the lungs,
it may cause chest pain and breathing difficulties. Travellers experiencing any of these
symptoms should immediately seek medical
attention.

To prevent DVT on long flights you should
walk about the cabin, contract leg muscles
and wiggle your ankles and toes while sitting,
drink plenty of fluids, and avoid alcohol and
tobacco.

JET LAG & MOTION SICKNESS

To avoid jet lag (common when crossing more
than five time zones) try drinking plenty of
nonalcoholic fluids and eating light meals.
Upon arrival, get exposure to natural sunlight
and readjust your schedule (for meals, sleep
and so on) as soon as possible.

Antihistamines such as dimenhydrinate
(Dramamine) and meclizine (Antivert, Bon-
ine) are usually the first choice for treating
motion sickness. A herbal alternative is
ginger.

IN ICELAND

AVAILABILITY & COST OF HEALTH CARE

High-quality health care is readily available,
and for minor, self-limiting illnesses, phar-
macists can dispense valuable advice and
over-the-counter medication. They can also
advise when more specialised help is required.
Doctor's appointments cost Ikr700, with a 25%
reduction for children under the age of 16.

The standard of dental care is usually good;
however, it's sensible to have a dental checkup
before a long trip.

TRAVELLER'S DIARRHOEA

It's very unlikely that you will suffer diarrhoea
in Iceland. The tap water is absolutely safe to
drink and is probably less contaminated than
bottled water, since it generally flows straight
from the nearest glacier.

If you are susceptible to upset stomachs,
do what you would do at home: avoid dairy
products that contain unpasteurised milk,
make sure your food is served piping hot
throughout, and avoid buffet-style meals.

If you are unlucky enough to develop diarrhoea, be sure to drink plenty of fluids, preferably an oral rehydration solution (eg dioralyte).
If diarrhoea is bloody, persists for more than
72 hours or is accompanied by fever, shaking,
chills or severe abdominal pain, you should
seek medical attention.

ENVIRONMENTAL HAZARDS
Giardia

Giardia is an intestinal parasite that lives
in the faeces of humans and animals and is
normally contracted through drinking water.
Problems can start several weeks after you've
been exposed to the parasite, and symptoms
may sometimes remit for a few days and then
return; this can go on for several weeks or
even longer. The first signs are a swelling of the
stomach, followed by pale faeces, diarrhoea,
frequent gas and possibly headache, nausea
and depression. If you exhibit these symptoms
you should visit a doctor for treatment.

Although most unpopulated areas in Iceland serve as sheep pastures, there seems to
be very little giardia; however, while most
people have no problems drinking untreated
water from streams and rivers, there's still a
possibility of contracting it. If you are unsure,
purify your drinking water by boiling it for

10 minutes or use a chemical treatment such as iodine.

Hypothermia & Frostbite

Proper preparation will reduce the risks of getting hypothermia. Even on a hot day in the mountains, the weather can change rapidly – carry waterproof garments and warm layers, and inform others of your route.

Acute hypothermia follows a sudden drop of temperature over a short time. Chronic hypothermia is caused by a gradual loss of temperature over hours.

Hypothermia starts with shivering, loss of judgment and clumsiness. Unless rewarming occurs, the sufferer deteriorates into apathy, confusion and coma. Prevent further heat loss by seeking shelter, wearing warm, dry clothing, drinking hot, sweet drinks, and sharing body warmth.

Frostbite is caused by freezing and the subsequent damage to bodily extremities. It is dependent on wind-chill, temperature and the length of exposure. Frostbite starts as frostnip (white, numb areas of skin), from which complete recovery is expected with rewarming. As frostbite develops, however, the skin blisters and becomes black. Loss of damaged tissue eventually occurs. You should wear adequate clothing, stay dry, keep well hydrated and ensure you have adequate calorie intake to prevent frostbite. Treatment involves rapid rewarming. Avoid refreezing and rubbing the affected areas.

Insect Bites & Stings

Mosquitoes are found even in Iceland – they're not as ferocious as their southern cousins and may not carry malaria, but they can cause irritation and infected bites. Use a DEET-based insect repellent.

Bees and wasps cause real problems only to those with a severe allergy (anaphylaxis). If you have such an allergy, carry EpiPen or similar adrenaline injections.

Seasickness

The sea around Iceland is an unpredictable beast. Things can sometimes get rough aboard whale-watching trips, or on the little ferries that run to islands off the coast of Iceland (eg to the Vestmannaeyjar or to Grímsey).

If you're feeling queasy, fresh air and watching the horizon may help, as this balances the sensations in the inner ear and the visual information received by the eyes. If possible, move to the centre of the boat where the rocking is least pronounced, and try lying down and closing your eyes or sucking on crystallised ginger. If you are vomiting a lot, be sure to rehydrate with liquids.

It's usual to take seasickness medication half an hour before you sail. Bring your preferred brand from home, or buy over-the-counter medications such as Dramamine from a pharmacist before your journey. Seasickness medication is not available on board any of the Icelandic boat services.

TRAVELLING WITH CHILDREN

All travellers with children should know how to treat minor ailments and when to seek medical treatment. Make sure the children are up to date with routine vaccinations well before departure, and discuss any possible travel vaccines are not suitable for children under a year.

Remember to avoid contaminated food and water. If your child is vomiting or has diarrhoea, lost fluid and salts must be replaced. It may be helpful to take rehydration powders for reconstituting with boiled water.

Children should be encouraged to avoid and mistrust any dogs or other mammals, because of the risk of diseases. Any bite, scratch or lick from a warm-blooded, furry animal should immediately be thoroughly cleaned.

SEXUAL HEALTH

Condoms are widely available, and can be found most easily at *apótek* (pharmacies) and supermarkets. When buying condoms, look for a European CE mark, which means they have been rigorously tested, and then keep them in a cool, dry place or they may crack and perish.

Emergency contraception is most effective if taken within 24 hours after unprotected sex. It's available from the national hospital in Reykjavík, and at other hospitals around Iceland.

HEALTH

Language

CONTENTS

Icelandic is a Germanic language, one of the family that includes German, English, Dutch and all the Scandinavian languages except Finnish. It's the nearest thing in existence to Old Norse, the language spoken by the Vikings. In fact, modern Icelandic has changed so little since the Settlement that even children can read the language of the 12th- and 13th-century sagas without difficulty. Interestingly, Icelandic still retains the ancient letters 'eth' (ð) and 'thorn' (þ) that existed in Old English but have disappeared from modern English.

Icelanders are proud of their literary heritage, and they are particularly conservative when it comes to the written word. To avoid having to adopt foreign words for new concepts, neologisms (new words) are created. Neologisms, such as *útvarp*, 'radio', *sjónvarp*, 'television', *tölva*, 'computer', and *þota*, 'jet', are just a few that have become part of the Icelandic vocabulary in the last 50 years.

Icelanders are a rather informal people. A person is very rarely addressed by title and/or surname. Icelanders use the ancient patronymic system, where *son*, 'son' or *dóttir*, 'daughter' is attached to the genitive form of the father's or, less commonly, the mother's, first name. The telephone book entries are listed according to first names.

Most Icelanders speak English, and often as many as three or four other languages, so you'll have no problems if you can't muster any Icelandic. While any attempts you do make to speak the lingo will certainly be much appreciated, Icelanders are so unused to hearing their language spoken with a foreign accent that you might be greeted by a blank look and a shout of 'Ha?'. If you'd like a more in depth guide to Icelandic, pick up a copy of Lonely Planet's *Scandinavian Phrasebook*.

You should be aware that the complex grammar of Icelandic can lead to confusion, especially when you're trying to read bus timetables and find names of towns, which can be spelled several different ways. For example, the sign that welcomes visitors to the town of Höfn in the southeast reads *Velkomin til Hafnar*. In grammatical terms, Hafnar is the dative form of of Höfn.

PRONUNCIATION & ALPHABET

Most letters are pronounced as they are in English. The trickier ones are listed below. Stress generally falls on the first syllable.

If you're searching for words in an Icelandic dictionary, index or telephone book, be aware that ð, þ, æ and ö have their own separate places in the alphabet. Ð usually comes between d and e, and the other three letters usually appear at the very end of the alphabet.

Vowels

á	as the 'ow' in 'cow'
é	as the 'ye' in 'yet'
i, y	as the 'i' in 'hit'
í, ý	as the 'i' in 'marine'
ó	as in 'note'
ö	as the 'er' in 'fern', without the 'r' sound
ú	as the 'oo' in 'cool'
æ	as th 'y' in 'cry'
au	as the word 'furry' without 'f or 'rr'

Consonants

Ð ð	as the 'th' in 'lather'
Þ þ	as the 'th' in 'thin'
dj	as the 'j' in 'juice'
f	as in 'farm'; as the 'v' in 'van' between vowels or at the end of a word; as the 'b' in 'big' before l or n
hv	as 'kv'
j	as the 'y' in 'yes'
ll	as the 'ddl' in 'fiddle'

p   as in 'pit'; before **s** or **t**, it's as the 'f'
       in 'fit'
r   always trilled

ACCOMMODATION

Do you have any rooms available?	*Eru herbergi laus?*
May I see it?	*Má ég sjá það?*
I'd like (a) ...	*Gæti ég fengið ...*
single room	*einstklingsherbergi*
double room	*tveggjamannherbergi*
a bed	*rúm*
camping ground	*tjaldstæði*
guesthouse	*gistiheimili*
hotel	*hótel*
motel	*gistihús*
youth hostel	*farfuglaheimili*
Where is a ... hotel?	*Hvar er ... hótel?*
cheap	*ódýrt*
nearby	*nálægt*
clean	*hreint*
Could you write the address, please?	*Gætir þú skrifað niður heimilisfangið?*
Do you have any rooms available?	*Eru herbergi laus?*
I'd like ...	*Gæti ég fengið ...*
a single room	*einstaklingsherbergi*
a double room	*tveggjamannaherbergi*

CONVERSATION & ESSENTIALS

Hello.	*Halló.*
Good morning/ afternoon.	*Góðan daginn.*
Good evening.	*Gott kvöld.*
Good night.	*Góða nótt.*
Goodbye.	*Bless.*
Excuse me.	*Afsakið.*
Sorry.	*Mér þykir það leitt.*
Thank you.	*Takk fyrir.*
You're welcome.	*Ekkert að þakka.*
Yes.	*Jái.*
No.	*Nei.*
How are you?	*Hvernig hefur þú það?*
Well, thanks.	*Gott, takk.*
Cheers!	*Skál!*
What's your name?	*Hvað heitir þú?*
My name is ...	*Ég heiti ...*
Where are you from?	*Hvaðan ert þú?*
I'm from ...	*Ég er frá ...*

Do you speak English?	*Talar þú ensku?*
I (don't) understand.	*Ég skil (ekki).*
What does ... mean?	*Hvað þýðir ...?*

HEALTH & EMERGENCIES

Help!	*Hjálp!*
I'm lost	*Ég er villt/villtur.* (f/m)
I'm sick	*Ég er veikur*
Go away!	*Farðu!*
antibiotics	*fúkalyf*
condoms	*smokkar*
contraceptive	*getnaðarvörn*
tampons	*vatttappar/tampónar*
Call ...!	*Náið í ...!*
a doctor	*lækni*
the police	*lögregluna*
an ambulance	*sjúkrabíl*
Where is a ...?	*Hvar er ...?*
chemist	*apótek*
dentist	*tannlæknir*
doctor	*læknir*
hospital	*sjúkrahús*

NUMBERS

0	*núll*
1	*einn*
2	*tveir*
3	*þrír*
4	*fjórir*
5	*fimm*
6	*sex*
7	*sjö*
8	*átta*
9	*níu*
10	*tíu*
11	*ellefu*
12	*tólf*
13	*þrettán*
14	*fjórtán*
15	*fimmtán*
16	*sextán*
17	*sautján*
18	*átján*
19	*nítján*
20	*tuttugu*
21	*tuttugu og einn*
30	*þrjátíu*
40	*fjörutíu*
50	*fimmtíu*
60	*sextíu*
70	*sjötíu*
80	*áttatíu*

LANGUAGE

90	*níutíu*
100	*eitt hundrað*
1000	*eitt þúsund*

SHOPPING & SERVICES

I'm looking for (a/the) ...	*Ég er að leita að ...*
bank	*banka*
city centre	*miðbænum*
market	*markaðum*
police	*lögreglunni*
post office	*pósthúsinu*
public toilet	*almenningssalerni*
telephone centre	*símstöðinni*
tourist office	*upplýsingaþjónustu fyrir ferðafólk*

What time does it open/close?	*Hvenær er opnað/lokað?*
I'd like to buy ...	*Mig langar að kaupa ...*
How much is it?	*Hvað kostar þetta?*
Where is the toilet?	*Hvar er snyrtingin/klósettið?*
Where can I get Internet access?	*Hvar get ég fengið að nota internetið?*
I'd like to send an email.	*Mig langar til að senda tölvupóst.*

TIME & DATES

Monday	*mánudagur*
Tuesday	*þriðjudagur*
Wednesday	*miðvikudagur*
Thursday	*fimmtudagur*
Friday	*föstudagur*
Saturday	*laugardagur*
Sunday	*sunnudagur*

What time is it?	*Hvað er klukkan?*
today	*í dag*
tomorrow	*á morgun*

TRANSPORT & DIRECTIONS

Where is a/the ...?	*Hvar er ...?*
Could you write the address, please?	*Gætir þú skrifað niður heimilisfangið?*
How do I get to ...?	*Hvernig kemst ég til ...?*
Is it far from here?	*Er það langt héðan?*
near	*nálægt*
far	*langt í burtu*
Go straight ahead.	*Farðu beint áfram.*
Turn left.	*Beygðu til vinstri.*
Turn right.	*Beygðu til hægri.*
Can you show me (on the map)?	*Getur þú sýnt mér (á kortinu)?*

bus stop	*strætisvagnabiðstöð*
ferry	*ferja*
ticket office	*miðasala*
first	*fyrst*
next	*næst*
last	*síðast*

What time does the ... leave/arrive?	*Hvenær fer/kemur ...?*
boat	*báturinn*
bus	*vagninn*
plane	*flugvélin*
tram	*sporvagninn*

Glossary

See p57 in the Food & Drink chapter for useful words and phrases dealing with food and dining. See the Language chapter (p338) for other useful words and phrases.

á – river (as in Laxá, or Salmon River)
álfar – elves
álfhóll – 'elf hillock'; small wooden house for elves, often seen in Icelandic gardens
Alþingi – Icelandic parliament

bær – farm
basalt – hard volcanic rock that often solidifies into hexagonal columns
bíó – cinema
bolla – cream bun
brennivín – local schnapps

caldera – crater created by the collapse of a volcanic cone

dalur – valley

eddas – ancient Norse books
ey – island

fjörður – fjord
foss – waterfall
franskar – chips
fumarole – vents in the earth releasing volcanic gas

gata – street
geyser – spouting hot spring
gistiheimilið – guesthouse
gjá – fissure, rift
glíma – Icelandic wrestling
goðar – chieftan

hákarl – putrid shark meat
harðfiskur – dried fish
hestur – horse
huldufólk – hidden people
höfn – harbour
hot pot – Jacuzzi-like spa pool, found at swimming baths and some accommodation
hraun – lava field
hver – hot spring

icecap – permanently frozen glacier or mountain top
Íslands – Iceland

jökull – glacier, icecap
jökulhlaup – glacial flooding caused by volcano erupting beneath an icecap

kirkja – church

Landnámabók – comprehensive historical text recording the Norse settlement of Iceland
laug – hot spring
lava tube – underground tunnel created by liquid lava flowing under a solid crust
lón – lagoon

mörk – woods or forest
mudpot – bubbling pool of superheated mud

nes – headland
nunatak – hill or mountain completely surrounded by a glacier

puffling – baby puffin
pylsa – hot dog

Ragnarök – in Norse mythology, the end of the world as the gods are destroyed in a battle with evil, following which a new order will emerge
reykur – smoke, as in Reykjavík (literally 'Smoky Bay')
runtur – 'round tour', Icelandic pub crawl or aimless driving around town

sagas – Icelandic legends
samloka – sandwich
sandur – glacial sand plain
scoria – glassy volcanic lava
shield volcano – gently sloped volcano built up by fluid lava flows
skáli – hut; snack bar
skyr – Icelandic yogurt
sundlaug – heated swimming pool

tephra – rock/material blasted out from a volcano
tjörn – pond, lake
torg – town square

vatn – lake (as in Mývatn, or Midge Lake)
vegur – road
vents – natural clefts where hot steam emerges from the ground
vík – bay
vogur – cove, bay

Behind the Scenes

THIS BOOK

This 6th edition of *Iceland* was researched and written by Fran Parnell and Etail O'Carrol. The 1st edition was written by Deanna Swaney, who also updated the 2nd edition. The 3rd edition was updated by Graeme Cornwalls and Deanna Swaney, and Graeme updated the 4th edition on his own. We sent Paul Harding and Joe Bindloss on the road to update the 5th edition.

This guidebook was commissioned in Lonely Planet's London office, and produced in the Melbourne office by the following:

Commissioning Editor Ella O'Donnell
Coordinating Editors Sarah Bailey, Evan Jones
Coordinating Cartographer Ross Butler
Coordinating Layout Designer Steven Cann
Managing Cartographers Mark Griffiths, Julie Sheridan
Assisting Editors Susan Patterson, Laura Gibb, Rosie Nicholson, Justin Flynn
Assisting Layout Designers Pablo Gastar, Jacqui Saunders
Cover Designer Jane Hart
Colour Designer Steven Cann
Indexer Laura Gibb
Project Manager Craig Kilburn
Language Content Coordinator Quentin Frayne

Thanks to Katie Lynch, Stephanie Pearson, Trent Paton, Sally Darmody, Celia Wood, Avril Robertson, David Burnett, Mark Germanchis, Geoff Howard, Wayne Murphy, James Hardy, Carol Jackson

THANKS
FRAN PARNELL

A big thank you to everyone who helped during the research and writing of *Iceland*. This includes all the tourist-office staff, particularly Oddný at Vík; Sibba at Egilsstaðir; Heiða María at Hveragerði; and Jórunn Eggertsdóttir at the South Iceland tourist board; and to Anna Soffia Oskarsdóttir at Útivist for her great patience! It was especially wonderful to listen to Hlíf Gylfadóttir at the Vestmannaeyjar folk museum; Ragnar Kristjánsson, ranger at Skaftafell National Park; and Skotta at Skriðuklaustur; and the people who agreed to be interviewed – Villi Knudsen (Volcano Show); Jónas Þorsteinsson (Original Reykjavík Haunted Walk); Óttar Ottósson (Ásatrúarfelagið); Barbara J Kristvinsson (A-Hús Intercultural Centre); and Hrefna (Sjávarkjallarin). It's always fun catching up on Reykjavík gossip with Jón Trausti Sigurðarson at *Grapevine*. Thanks to all the readers who helped with comments and tips, in particular Dick and Margaret Hasselman, who provided some brilliant information, advice and anecdotes. Thank you too to the Lonely Planet crew: Mark Griffiths, Emma Gilmour and especially Etain O'Carroll – it was fun working with you! – and Ella O'Donnell for fine ideas, patience and conscientiousness. At home, thanks to Stuart for everything – and sorry I drove you to despair/a caravan.

ETAIN O'CARROLL

Huge thanks to the patient and knowledgeable staff at all the tourist offices around the country,

---

THE LONELY PLANET STORY

The story begins with a classic travel adventure: Tony and Maureen Wheeler's 1972 journey across Europe and Asia to Australia. There was no useful information about the overland trail then, so Tony and Maureen published the first Lonely Planet guidebook to meet a growing need.

From a kitchen table, Lonely Planet has grown to become the largest independent travel publisher in the world, with offices in Melbourne (Australia), Oakland (USA) and London (UK). Today Lonely Planet guidebooks cover the globe. There is an ever-growing list of books and information in a variety of media. Some things haven't changed. The main aim is still to make it possible for adventurous travellers to get out there – to explore and better understand the world.

At Lonely Planet we believe travellers can make a positive contribution to the countries they visit – if they respect their host communities and spend their money wisely. Every year 5% of company profit is donated to charities around the world.

with special thanks to the staff in Borgarnes and Akranes, the Seatours staff in Stykkishólmur, the tourist office and Vesturferðir staff in Ísafjörður for all their time and help, and to Hornstrandir park ranger Jorn Bjornsson for his assistance in keeping our facts straight. Sincere thanks also to the team at Snorrstofa in Reykholt for a fascinating insight into Snorri's world and to Doddi and all the librarians in Akureyri for the lowdown on the films to watch and books to read for an authentic look at Icelandic culture. Also in Akureyri, thanks to Ragnheiður 'Agga' Kristjánsd Ogata for her generous hospitality, help and insights into Iceland and her native city. Thanks also to Mo Docherty in Aberdeen and Clare Langan in Dublin for pre-departure tips, travel information and insights, to Ella and Fran for advice and guidance throughout the project, and to Mark for company on the last part of the journey and putting up with the sea of papers all over the floor on return.

OUR READERS

Many thanks to the travellers who used the last edition and wrote to us with helpful hints, useful advice and interesting anecdotes:

A Abigail Aiken, Amy Azzarito **B** Antje Becker, Debbie Board **C** Josh Calder, Steve Carter, Stephen Chipp, Aaron Contreras, Richard Crampton, Gergo Cseh **D** Edwin Damhuis, Joseph de Luca, Sarah Delaney, Mark Dolan **E** Jórunn Eggertsdóttir, Beth Erkhart F Michael Fuller **G** Klaus Gerasch, Nanette Girolamo, Maria Goeth, Johanna Goetze **H** Philip Haggerty, Helgi Hard, Graham Harman, Sven Hoexter, Martin Hölzl, Manu Humppi, Torben Huss **K** Jann Kjærbæk, Hilmar Kjartansson, Mark Klein **L** Stephen Leong **M** Neil Maccallum, Paul Maenhout, Mark Magielsen, Brigitte Meneveau, Martina Miertsch, Benjamin Monreal, David Morton, Alison Mummery **O** Anders Olsen, Vicki Olson **P** Jon Pallon,

Daniel Pankratz, Elliot Podwill, Chris Prechel, B Pritchard, Tom Pritchard **R** Eric Ralph, Kirsten Rauwerda, Stephanie Rowatt **S** Emmanuel Saint-Christophe, Alex Sanmark, Kevin Schmidt, Sören Sonntag, Verena Sonntag **T** Thorir Tryggvason, Satoru Tsushima, Paula Tyroler **U** Gabriela Ulke **V** Martijn van der Krogt, Floris van Moppes, Ian Vandewalke, Michel Veldhorst, Elke Vermeulen, Laura Verzeri, Sarah Vilece, Holmfridur Vilhjalmsdóttir **W** Jonas Wallander, Xuess Wee, Deborah Willott, Sharon Woodward, Zoe Wyatt

SEND US YOUR FEEDBACK

We love to hear from travellers – your comments keep us on our toes and help make our books better. Our well-travelled team reads every word on what you loved or loathed about this book. Although we cannot reply individually to postal submissions, we always guarantee that your feedback goes straight to the appropriate authors, in time for the next edition. Each person who sends us information is thanked in the next edition – and the most useful submissions are rewarded with a free book.

To send us your updates – and find out about Lonely Planet events, newsletters and travel news – visit our award-winning website: **www.lonelyplanet.com/contact.**

Note: we may edit, reproduce and incorporate your comments in Lonely Planet products such as guidebooks, websites and digital products, so let us know if you don't want your comments reproduced or your name acknowledged. For a copy of our privacy policy visit www.lonelyplanet.com/privacy.

Index

000 Map pages
000 Photograph pages

MAP LEGEND

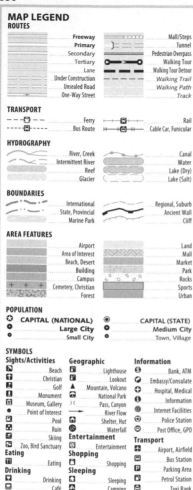

LONELY PLANET OFFICES

Australia
Head Office
Locked Bag 1, Footscray, Victoria 3011
☎ 03-8379 8000, fax 03-8379 8111
talk2us@lonelyplanet.com.au

USA
150 Linden St, Oakland, CA 94607
☎ 510-893 8555, toll free 800 275 8555
fax 510-893 8572
info@lonelyplanet.com

UK
72–82 Rosebery Ave,
Clerkenwell, London EC1R 4RW
☎ 020-7841 9000, fax 020-7841 9001
go@lonelyplanet.co.uk

Published by Lonely Planet Publications Pty Ltd
ABN 36 005 607 983

© Lonely Planet Publications Pty Ltd 2007

© photographers as indicated 2007

Cover photograph: Young Men at the Blue Lagoon, Reykjanes Peninsula, Stuart Westmorland/Getty Images. Internal photographs: p4, p7 (bottom), p11 (bottom), p12, p181, p182 Mark Williams; p6, p186 Frans Lemmens/Lonely Planet Images; p7 (top) Paul Harding/Lonely Planet Images; p9 (top), p184 Graeme Cornwallis/Lonely Planet Images; p8, p9 (bottom), p10 Jonathan Smith/Lonely Planet Images; p11 (top) Wade Eakle/Lonely Planet Images; p183, p185 Grant Dixon/Lonely Planet Images; p186, p187 Anders Blomqvist/Lonely Planet Images.

Many of the images in this guide are available for licensing from Lonely Planet Images: www.lonelyplanetimages.com.